SOCIAL
DEVIANCE

TIM DELANEY

State University of New York at Oswego

ROWMAN & LITTLEFIELD

Lanham • Boulder • New York • London

Executive Editor: Nancy Roberts
Editorial Assistant: Megan Manzano
Senior Marketing Manager: Deborah Hudson
Interior Designer: Ilze Lemesis
Cover Designer: Sally Rinehart

Published by Rowman & Littlefield

A wholly owned subsidary of The Rowman & Littlefield Publishing Group, Inc.

4501 Forbes Boulevard, Suite 200, Lanham, Maryland 20706

www.rowman.com

Unit A, Whitacre Mews, 26–34 Stannary Street, London SE11 4AB, United Kingdom

British Library Cataloguing in Publication Information Available

Library of Congress Cataloging-in-Publication Data
Names: Delaney, Tim, author.
Title: Social deviance / Tim Delaney, State University of New York at Oswego.
Description: Lanham: Rowman & Littlefield, [2017] | Includes bibliographical references and index.
Identifiers: LCCN 2016049701 (print) | LCCN 2016050524 (ebook) | ISBN
    9781442252523 (cloth: alk. paper) | ISBN 9781442252530 (pbk.: alk.
    paper) | ISBN 9781442252547 (electronic)
Subjects: LCSH: Deviant behavior.
Classification: LCC HM811.D45 2017 (print) | LCC HM811 (ebook) |
    DDC 302.5/42—dc23

LC record available at https://lccn.loc.gov/2016049701

∞™ The paper used in this publication meets the minimum requirements of American National Standard for Information Sciences—Permanence of Paper for Printed Library Materials, ANSI/NISO Z39.48–1992.

Printed in the United States of America

Dedication

While the content may change over time, and vary by setting and context, social deviance will always exist.

Brief Contents

Contents

Preface

The topic of social deviance is inherently intriguing. People in general and college students in particular seem to find the topic of deviant behavior fascinating, and a great number of sociologists seem willing and eager to teach the subject matter. This can be explained, at least in part, by a combination of the subject matter itself, our own past deviant behaviors, and our willingness and desire to evaluate and comment on the behaviors of others. While the topic of deviant behavior seems straightforward at the surface, the study of social deviance reveals how complicated it really is.

While *Social Deviance* utilizes a textbook-style approach in its coverage of deviant behavior, this comprehensive, straightforward, and student-friendly book design will maintain the interest of students because of the author's writing style and use of real-life phenomena and current examples. Each chapter includes chapter objectives, an introductory story, a glossary of key terms, discussion questions, and boxed material. The boxed materials include an "A Closer Look" box that zooms in on topics that warrant deeper explanation and a "Connecting Social Deviance and Popular Culture" box that shows how contemporary forms of popular culture illustrate deviant behavior.

Each chapter in *Social Deviance* focuses on a specific subject area. The first chapter explores the very concept of "deviance" by highlighting the difficulty in setting clear-cut parameters around which behaviors are considered deviant and which are not. As a result, five perspectives on deviance will be presented. These five perspectives on deviance will be applied in subsequent chapters. The opening chapter also articulates the idea that describing certain behaviors as deviant involves the judgment and evaluation of the behaviors of others, incorporates interpretations of morality, and acknowledges that definitions of deviance change over time and vary from culture to culture.

The second chapter of *Social Deviance* is unique among deviance texts as a link is drawn between social problems and social deviance. Among the specific examples of social problems discussed are unemployment, social stratification and poverty, and obesity and the associated health concerns associated with obesity. In chapter 3, a wide variety of theoretical explanations of social deviance are reviewed, including a number of sociological, psychological, biological, and demonic possession perspectives.

Chapters 4 and 5 discuss a large number of deviant behaviors that violate formal social norms and, thus, are considered criminal. Chapter 4 focuses on white collar, political, and organized crime while chapter 5 examines the two major subcategories of street crime (violent offenses and property offenses). The major forms of violence found in society warrant their own chapter and, thus, chapter 6 focuses on such topics as self-directed violence (self-harm, suicide, and suicide by cop); interpersonal violence (bullying, hazing, "bum fights," and intimate interpersonal violence); and collective violence (riots and war).

Chapters 7 and 8 focus on two longtime standard topics under the social deviance umbrella: alcohol and other drugs. Topics discussed in chapter 7 include alcohol and its effects, including a brief history of alcohol use; alcohol abuse and alcoholism, including the causes of alcoholism and alcohol use disorder (AUD) in the United States; behaviors associated with problem drinking (binge drinking, health problems associated with problem drinking, alcohol use and crime, and drunk driving); a number of deviant behaviors committed by persons who abuse alcohol but justify their behaviors by brushing aside their actions as excusable (public intoxication, public nuisance, indecent exposure, relationship issues, and acting impulsively); and my original research on drunk shamings. In chapter 8, we will explore explanations as to why people use drugs, factors that influence drug effects and the categorization of drugs (stimulants, depressants, hallucinogens, narcotics, inhalants, cannabis, performance-enhancing drugs, prescription drug abuse), and the role of Big Pharma.

With the advent of technology that affects nearly all spheres of life comes a corresponding dramatic increase in the number of cyber-related variations of social deviance, and this topic is reviewed in chapter 9. Topics discussed include catfishing, cyberbullying, cyberstalking, swatting, identity theft and fraud, and cyberscams. Mental illness is the topic of chapter 10, and we contrast the idea of good mental health with poor mental health and also discuss various types of mental illness and disorders (e.g., depression, bipolar disorder, schizophrenia and other psychoses, dementia, dissociative disorders, posttraumatic stress disorder, and developmental disorders).

Sexual social deviance is discussed in chapter 11. The topics range from serious issues that may involve criminal activities (e.g., sexual harassment, prostitution, and pornography) to sexual fetishisms (including some of the most popular sexual fetishes and some of the strangest). Chapter 12 provides a review of a type of social deviance often ignored in other deviance texts—environmental social deviance. Among the topics discussed are the realization that the earth has a limited carrying capacity, mass extinctions, the application of the environmental imagination, and the many forms of human behavior that compromise the earth's ability to sustain itself as inhabitable for future generations of humans.

The important topic of social control was saved until chapter 13 so that students have the opportunity to acquaint themselves with some of the many forms of deviance. The role of socialization and the two broad types of social control—formal and informal—are presented along with the role of shaming as a method to try and encourage or force people to comply with societal expectations. Chapter 14 helps to sum up the reality that social deviance is so commonplace that it is omnipresent in society.

Instructor and Student Resources

Instructor's Manual and Test Bank. For each chapter in the text, the Instructor's Manual provides student learning objectives, key terms with definitions, discussion questions, and web resources. The Test Bank includes a variety of multiple-choice, true/false, and short-answer questions and is available in either Word or Respondus formats. In either format, the Test Bank can be fully edited and customized to best meet your needs. The Instructor's Manual and Test Bank are available to adopters for download on the text's catalog page at www.rowman.com.

PowerPoint Slides. The PowerPoint® slides provide the tables and figures from the text. The PowerPoint® presentation is available to adopters for download on the text's catalog page at www.rowman.com.

Companion Website. Accompanying the text is an open-access Companion Website designed to reinforce the main topics. Our Companion Website to *Social Deviance* will help students to master key vocabulary and concepts through flashcards and self-graded quizzes. Students can access the Companion Website from their computer or mobile device on the text's catalog page at http://textbooks.rowman.com/delaney.

Acknowledgments

Professor Delaney would like to thank the reviewers of this text for their valuable comments, suggestions, and support: Brenda Chaney, The Ohio State University; Jackie Eller, Middle Tennessee State University; Philip Kavanaugh, Pennsylvania State University at Harrisburg; Justin A. Martin, University of Tennessee at Martin; Linda McAllister, Berkeley City College; Megan Schlegel, San Jose State University; Steven Stack, Wayne State University; Lisa Lamb Weber, Texas State University; Egbert Zavala, The University of Texas at El Paso.

Special thanks to Nancy Roberts, Molly White, Alden Perkins, and Kathy Dvorsky and the rest of the editorial staff, the marketing staff, and to the rest of the fine folks at Rowman & Littlefield who helped to put this book together.

Tim would like to acknowledge all the social deviants who have crossed his path—and there are far too many to mention individually—who helped to shape his lifelong pursuit of the study of social deviance.

As always, a special thanks to Christina.

About the Author

Tim Delaney is a professor and department chair of sociology at the State University of New York at Oswego. He earned his B.S. in sociology from SUNY Brockport; an M.A. degree in sociology from California State University, Dominguez Hills; and a Ph.D. in sociology from the University of Nevada, Las Vegas. Delaney has published 17 books (to date); numerous book chapters, journal, and encyclopedia articles; and has been published on five continents. Among his book publications are *Sportsmanship: Essays from a Multidisciplinary Perspective* (editor and contributing author, 2016); *Lessons Learned from Popular Culture* (coauthored, 2016); *The Sociology of Sport: An Introduction* (coauthored, 2015); *Beyond Sustainability: A Thriving Environment* (coauthored, 2014); *Classical and Contemporary Social Theory: Investigation and Application* (2014); *American Street Gangs*, Second Edition (2014); *Connecting Sociology to Our Lives: An Introduction to Sociology* (2012); *Shameful Behaviors* (2008); and *Social Diseases: Mafia, Terrorism and Totalitarianism* (coeditor, 2004).

CHAPTER 1

What Is Social Deviance?

CHAPTER OBJECTIVES

After reading this chapter students should be able to:

- Provide five different variations of the definition of deviance
- Explain the role of morality on social deviance
- Explain how deviance is often a matter of context
- Describe how definitions of deviance change over time
- Explain how deviance varies from culture to culture and from subculture to subculture

"Dude . . . Stop the Spread, Please." If you haven't heard that expression in the context that it is meant here, you might think the slogan refers to something sexual, perhaps a postmodern anti-rape campaign. However, if you live in New York City, or nearly any city that is highly dependent on mass transit, you know that the "Dude . . . Stop the Spread, Please" campaign is directed to bring shame on subway passengers (generally men) who sit with their legs wide open and take up more than the designated, or expected, amount of space. News reports generally cite actress Kelley Rae O'Donnell as the person who started the anti-man-spreading campaign. In 2014, O'Donnell started taking photos of man spreaders and tweeted them in hopes of shaming man spreaders while also finding others who share her disdain for them. O'Donnell was quoted in the *New York Times* saying, "It drives me crazy. I find myself glaring at them because it just seems so inconsiderate in this really crowded city" (Fitzsimmons 2014). O'Donnell gained such a following both in the traditional media and the social media that the New York Metropolitan Transportation Authority (MTA) decided to start a poster campaign to encourage men not to spread their legs while sitting. According to *The Week* (2015), the MTA spent $76,707 on the advertising campaign aimed to encourage male subway riders to keep their legs together while sitting. In essence, O'Donnell and the MTA were attempting to label "man spreading" as a deviant behavior.

Predictably, there are many men who refuse to be labeled "deviant" just because they sit with their legs spread open. Men sitting with their legs spread apart is anything but new and dates back at least to the era (19th and early 20th centuries) when women generally wore dresses and were taught to keep their legs closed tight and men correspondingly felt that they had the right to take up that extra space for comfort. A 2014 subway rider echoed this tradition by telling the *New York Times*, "I'm not going to cross my legs like ladies do. I'm going to sit how I want to sit" (Fitzsimmons 2014). There was also an anti-man-spreading campaign in

A female passenger appears frustrated by two men sitting next to her with their legs spread wide apart.

Toronto at the same time as the MTA was addressing the issue in New York City. One male subway rider tried to explain to *CTV News Toronto* (2014) that men biologically need more space then women: "It's basic anatomy. Men have some extra bits between their legs that make sitting with their legs far apart more comfortable." The Canadian Association for Equality (2014) is against the ban on man spreading for a number of reasons, including the idea that the term "man spreading" is sexist (implying women too may sit and take up too much space) and that "there are a lot more things taking up seats on busses than men opening their legs, such as purses, strollers, back packs and the like."

Is "man spreading" a form of deviant behavior? What do you think?

Defining Social Deviance

The introductory story on "man spreading" helps to illustrate some of the many complicated issues (gray areas) involved when attempting to label certain behaviors as acceptable, others as deviant, and still others as criminal. Who decides which behaviors are deviant and which ones are not? Is it a public transit authority or an actress who sends out tweets? Or is it the participants themselves (the man spreaders)? Are all "deviant" behaviors actually deviant in every situation or do context and the "era of the times" play a role? Surely a man can sit with his legs spread wide apart in his own home, so why not in a public area? And if we are to be outraged by someone who takes up too much space on a bus, train, or plane, should we also be equally upset by a person who parks a car in such a manner as to take up two or three spaces?

Few topics in academic discourse contain more shades of gray than does "social deviance." The sociological study of social deviance reveals that a number of conditions influence how some behaviors come to be defined as deviant, while others are defined as acceptable. We must also realize that no behavior is inherently deviant; therefore, in order for any act to be "deviant" it must be defined, or labeled, as deviant in order to *be* deviant. But who decides which behaviors are defined or labeled as deviant? And what if one person thinks that it is okay to take up three seats on a subway train with a baby stroller while another person thinks that such behavior is improper? Is marrying a dead person, animal, or object deviant? Is deviant behavior the same thing as criminal behavior; that is to say, are all deviant behaviors criminal and are all criminal behaviors deviant? These are among the questions concerning the issue of defining deviance that will be addressed here. For the purposes of this text, **deviance** is defined as any behavior that is labeled by some members of society, especially those in a position of authority or power, or specific subcultural groups, as an unacceptable violation of social norms and codes of morality that may elicit negative reactions from others. **Norms** are socially defined rules and expectations regarding human behavior. **Social deviance** implies that the study of deviant behavior is directed toward human behavior. When people violate social norms and cultural codes of morality, they are considered **deviants**.

Varying Definitions of Deviance

When defining deviance, sociologists nearly always employ some variation of a clause that incorporates the idea that certain behaviors represent a violation of a social norm. This perspective is derived from the realization that all families, groups, organizations, and societies establish social norms that lead to rules of expected behavior that participants are supposed to abide by. Rules, although they may change, have existed throughout time. Rule-breaking behavior is consequently deemed as deviant behavior. As a result, people who abide by the rules are less likely to be labeled as "deviant" than those who violate the rules. Definitions of deviance (such as the one provided above) that incorporate the idea that deviance is a violation of a social norm may be referred to as normative. Thus, when it comes to wedding ceremonies, it is the norm that the participants involved are both alive and real human beings. Marrying an animal or an object would go against the norm and thus be labeled as deviant. Normative ideals of marriage are used as an example here because later in this chapter we will examine a number of variations of marriages that lend themselves applicable to a discussion on social deviance.

The normative perspective of social deviance is not the only viewpoint of what constitutes social deviance. A number of people who study deviant behavior include a statistical component in their definition of deviance. From the statistical point of view, deviance is that which is unusual, rare, or uncommon. Getting the measles (rubeola) in the United States is statistically very rare, especially considering that the disease, "a childhood infection caused by a virus," has been nearly completely eradicated since 2000 because it can be prevented by administering a vaccine (Mayo Clinic 2015a). The United States has averaged just about 60 total cases per year in the 2000s, and most of them originated outside the country where vaccines are not usually available. Thus, we can say that getting the measles in the United States is statistically very rare. However, does that mean that a person with the measles is deviant? The statistical definition of deviance would lead us in that direction. Further linking measles to deviancy is the realization that a growing number of American parents have opted not to give their children the vaccination.

The deviant parents (from the statistical definition) who refuse to give their children the vaccination are not only putting their own offspring in danger of catching the virus but also everyone else the infected child comes into contact with. In 2014 and 2015 there was a mini outbreak in measles cases. The Centers for Disease Control and Prevention (CDC) (2015a) reported, "From January 1 to January 16, 2015, more than 50 people from six states were reported to have measles. Most of these cases are part of a large, ongoing outbreak linked to an amusement park [Disneyland] in California. The United States experienced a record number of measles cases in 2014, with 644 cases from 27 states reported to the CDC's National Center for Immunization and Respiratory Diseases (NCIRD). This is the greatest number of cases since measles elimination was documented in the U.S. in 2000." In nearly all cases, the people who got the measles were unvaccinated, and in most of those cases it was because parents did not immunize their children. That a parent would refuse to have their children receive the vaccine is statistically rare, and from the statistical perspective, deviant.

Among the social scientists that utilize the statistical component in their definition of deviance is Frank Schmalleger. Schmalleger (2004) defines deviance as "human activity that violates social norms or is statistically different from the average" (p. 9). Henry Vandenburgh (2004) combines a customary definition of deviance with a statistical characteristic: "In one sense, *deviance* is behavior that goes against norms, that is, behavior patterns that we expect others (and ourselves) to engage in. In another sense, deviance has a statistical definition. It's unusual behavior—behavior we seldom see others engage in" (p. 4). Vandenburgh and others do, however, recognize the inherent problem with equating deviance merely to the statistical rare occurrence. Consider, for example, the 18-year-old basketball player who skips playing college hoops and is drafted directly into the National Basketball Association (NBA) following his completion of high school. Contemporary college stars Kobe Bryant and LeBron James are among the small number of people who made this rare transition from high school to professional basketball, but this variable alone does not make them deviant. Many students drop out of college following their sophomore year, but few go on to create a social-network phenomenon worth billions of dollars as Mark Zuckerberg did when he left Harvard and went on to become CEO of Facebook. And yet we are unlikely to label Zuckerberg a deviant because he is one of the very rare people to accomplish this achievement. Then again, if Zuckerberg suddenly decided he had enough of the social world and opted to give away his fame and fortune and live the life of a hermit hidden away somewhere in the Rocky Mountains without human contact, we would likely refer to him as a deviant. Thus, we can say that deviance may overlap with that which is statistically rare, but rarity is not a sole criterion when deciding which behaviors should be defined as deviant and which ones are acceptable.

Another perspective on deviance involves the absolutist definition. Absolutist definitions of deviance argue that certain behaviors *are* inherently deviant (and others are inherently "right") regardless of context, times, and the diversity of the members of a society. (Some variations of the absolutist perspective go so far as to suggest that notions of what constitutes deviant behavior transcend all societies.) The absolutist perspective is often connected with notions of morality that have been established by religious, social, scientific, or international edict. An example of deviance from the absolutist perspective would be a belief that abortion *is* murder and is never an acceptable alternative to giving birth under any condition (e.g., the mother was raped or the mother's life would be put at risk via a full-term pregnancy). The absolutist position puts forth the notion that there is no ambiguity, no gray area, about deviance and the need for people to follow rules— rules are assumed to have widespread appeal and to be agreed upon by nearly, if not all, members of society.

Classical social theorist Emile Durkheim's term of the **collective conscience** represents one of the earliest sociological connections between issues of morality and deviance from the absolutist perspective. As Adler and Adler (2016) explain, Durkheim's absolutist perspective is reflected by his view that the laws of any given society are objective facts. "According to this position, there is a general agreement among citizens that there is something obvious within each deviant act, belief, or condition that makes it different from the conventional norms" (Adler and Adler 2016:2). Durkheim had proposed that instead of worshipping a religion or God, people should worship society; in turn, this devotion to society would result in a collective conscience and a common morality (to be discussed shortly). Durkheim defines the collective conscience as "The totality of beliefs and sentiments common to average citizens of the same society forms a determinate system which has its own life; one may call the *collective* or *common conscience*" (Durkheim 1938:79). In Durkheim's era, French society was not nearly as diverse as it is today, and as a result we might wonder if the notion of collective conscience is still relevant today. That is to say, are there any examples of beliefs and sentiments common to average citizens of the same society in the contemporary era? It is put forth here that the answer is yes. Consider for example the ideals that most of us, especially in Western societies, cherish, including the dignity of persons; freedom from oppression, prejudice, and discrimination; protecting children from predators; and the right to strive for self-actualization.

There are two other variations of defining social deviance worth mentioning here, the relativist and reactivist. The relativist position on social deviance examines the manner in which social norms are created and the people who create them. This perspective addresses the part of the definition of deviance provided in this text that references "those in a position of authority or power." In this regard, the relativist viewpoint takes on a Marxist/conflict outlook that those in power can dictate to others what is right and what is wrong (see chapter 3 for a further explanation of the Marxist/conflict theory). The relativist perspective also acknowledges that definitions of deviance vary from culture to culture and within subcultures, thus making deviance relevant to specific circumstances, conditions, and social environments.

The reactivist definition of social deviance takes into consideration deviant behavior that could be considered as positive (Heckert and Heckert 2002). We will examine positive deviance later in this chapter, but suffice it to say that reactivist deviance generally occurs in reaction against some norm, rule, or law that people find unjust. The 1965 Selma-to-Montgomery March for voting rights serves as an example of reactivist deviance. Those who marched for voting rights were met with heavy resistance culminating on Bloody Sunday, March 7, 1965, when "some 600 civil rights marchers headed east out of Selma on U.S. Route 80 [but] only got as far as the Edmund Pettus Bridge six blocks away, where state and local lawmen attacked them with billy clubs and tear gas and drove them back to Selma. Two days later on March 9, Martin Luther King, Jr., led a 'symbolic' march to the bridge" (National Park Service 2015). MLK Jr. and other civil rights leaders then "sought court protection for a third, full-scale march from Selma to the state capital in Montgomery" (National Park Service 2015). Less than five months after these marches, President Lyndon Johnson signed the Voting Rights Act of 1965, which directly addressed the grievances posed by the civil rights marchers.

In the following chapters, it will become clear that the definition of deviance provided by the author, as well as the approach of the text, attempts to blend aspects of these varying perspectives on deviance. The normative approach allows for both the discussion of the role of social norms as a primary factor in labeling certain behaviors as acceptable or deviant and the discussion on the social control efforts that attempt to encourage conformity. The statistical component is slightly less relevant but will become applicable from time to time. The absolutist perspective is relevant when the majority of people express a belief that certain behaviors are simply right and others are just as simply wrong, and therefore anyone who would challenge certain societal norms must be deviant. The relativist perspective allows for the realization that notions of deviance are subject to change and vary among diverse peoples and cultures, and yet those in power will try to impose their will on all people. The reactivist position allows for the discussion of positive deviance. And with the reactivist perspective in mind, let's take a close look at positive deviance.

Positive Deviance

When discussing deviance, the focus (as it will be in this text) is nearly always on its "negative" connotations. However, as the *reactivist* definition of social deviance indicates, there are times when people violate the norms of society in what could be construed as doing so in a positive manner. **Positive deviance** refers to behavior in which a rule violation generates a positive reaction from others and may or may not bring about positive consequences. The individuals or groups that commit positive deviance have developed techniques and strategies that enable them to utilize strategies different from others as they attempt to solve social problems (Positive Deviance Initiative 2014). Many acts of civil disobedience fall under the category of positive deviance. "Rosa Parks's refusal to give up her bus seat on December 1, 1955, in Montgomery, Alabama, which set the tone for the civil rights movement, and Harriet Tubman's attempts to free slaves through the Underground Railroad prior to the Civil War, are considered examples of positive deviance" (Delaney 2012a:186). People such as Parks and Tubman may have violated the established norms and laws of the land that were established at that time, but they are generally acknowledged as having "fought the good fight" necessary for social and moral reform.

As described in a 2013 *New York Times* Opinion Page article written by Tina Rosenberg, Jerry and Monique Sternin and their son are examples of positive deviants because of their early-1990s work to help the estimated two-thirds of Vietnamese children who were malnourished. While Western government programs such as Save the Children helped to provide a temporary solution to the hunger epidemic, countless villages fell back into hunger when the program funding dried up. In their previous work, the Sternins had documented "how big programs run by outsiders created dependency" (Rosenberg 2013). The Sternins and their volunteers found that the poorer the family, the more likely the children would be malnourished—certainly not a new discovery, but one that led them to seek out very poor families that did not have malnourished children. The key was then to find out what these families were doing differently than the other poor families who had malnourished children. A small number of such families were discovered, and for the sake of research the parents of these families were labeled as "deviant parents"—in the tradition of the statistical and normative definitions of deviance. The deviant parents, it was discovered, went against such village norms as "Don't feed a child who has diarrhea," "Don't feed a child more than once a day," and "Don't worry about washing the hands of children before they eat." The deviant parents went against all these norms and as a result, their children did not suffer from malnourishment and related diseases. "Five and a half months after the Sternins had arrived in Vietnam, authorities weighed the children in the district who had participated in the program. More than 40 percent were now well nourished, and another 20 percent had moved from severe to moderate malnutrition. The Sternins got their visa extended. Vietnam eventually replicated the program in 250 communities" (Rosenberg 2013).

The positive deviance approach utilized by the Sternins involved asking community members themselves who were having success in fighting malnourishment and then sharing these deviant behavioral ideas with other community members. The focus of such an approach highlights the strengths of the community rather than focusing on the weaknesses. Local people, and not program people, would help to design and facilitate the changes necessary to fight the social problem of malnourishment in their own communities. Community members, and not just community leaders, had an equal say in decision-making matters. Since this positive deviance approach was utilized in Vietnam it has been replicated in dozens of countries to attack a wide variety of programs (Rosenberg 2013). Still, because such an approach means going against the established norms of a community or society, positive deviance methods are often met with resistance by local and national politicians and policy makers, as they may feel as though their authority is being challenged or threatened. The people in the position of power like being looked at as the experts, and they may resent those who challenge their authority. Consequently, while program approaches such as the one developed by the Sternins may have positively helped children in Vietnam, there are those in a position of power and authority who view such behaviors nonetheless as deviant. Thus, the term "positive deviance."

Positive deviance can occur in less grandiose situations than fighting for civil rights and combating social problems. The world of music, for example, provides us with examples of positive deviance. Seemingly, musicians perform in a wide variety of public places, including subway stations, bus stops, and outside sports stadiums. Some musicians are quite talented and others quite amateurish. Typically they play for tips, but in nearly all cases they simply want to perform and be heard. Chances are, we have all walked briskly past these public musicians because we don't want to be guilted into feeling as though we have to pay them money. From time to time, however, we come across a performer that sounds so good we have to stop and listen; after all, what if they become famous some day and we can say, "I knew him when . . ." But what if the performer is already famous and decides to play for free? Is that deviant? And what if this performance was unannounced and was a part of a breaching experiment conducted by a newspaper writer to see whether or not busy commuters would stop to listen to a Grammy Award–winning violinist? Does anything in this scenario sound like a possible positive deviance story? What do you think?

In 2007, Gene Weingarten, a *Washington Post* writer, asked Joshua Bell, a world-renowned classical violinist, to take his $3 million violin underground at the

Washington, D.C., Metro station and perform as a random street performer as part of a story on art and context. No one knew Bell was going to perform. "So, instead of fans arriving two hours early to get a good view, more than 1,000 commuters in L'Enfant Plaza rushed by Bell without stopping to hear the music" (Contrera 2014). Seven people did stop and listen to Bell perform, but it was not reported whether or not these commuters knew Bell's identity. The resulting article ("Pearls Before Breakfast") by Weingarten earned him a Pulitzer Prize for his observations on art and life in context. Bell was disappointed that people did not stop to listen to him. In 2014, Bell made a scheduled return to the D.C. Metro and performed in front of a packed grand station crowd. "Bell noted more than once how excited he was to see kids there. When he played incognito in 2007, it was the children who most often stopped to listen before their parents rushed them away" (Contrera 2014). When he took to the makeshift stage and stood in front of a thunderous crowd, most of whom knew of the story of his last appearance at the Metro in 2007, Bell said, "Wow! This is more like it!" His 2014 performance was scheduled and hugely satisfying to all in attendance, including Bell; but his 2007 unannounced performance and attempted positive deviance (playing for free when he has played in front of sold-out crowds across the world) had not gone off as planned. This raises the question, if someone conducts an act of positive deviance but no one is aware such a behavior occurred, is it positive deviance? What do you think? (For another example of positive deviance from the world of music see box 1.1.)

CONNECTING SOCIAL DEVIANCE AND POPULAR CULTURE

Box 1.1 Maroon 5 Crashed My Wedding Reception!

In this chapter, a number of deviant marriages will be discussed. Maybe you have participated in, or witnessed, an unusual wedding. Following most marriages is a wedding reception, a big party for friends, family, and invited guests to honor the married couple. There have been occasions when people "crash" a wedding reception, and perhaps some of you are aware of such hijinks. Or maybe you have watched the movie *Wedding Crashers* (2005), starring Owen Wilson and Vince Vaughn as "a pair of committed womanizers who sneak into weddings to take advantage of the romantic tinge in the air" and free food and drink (IMDb 2015).

Wedding crashers, as uninvited guests, are automatically deviants. Some wedding crashers may have crashed the wedding with the intent to disturb the bride or groom directly because of a lost love or some sort of vendetta. In some extreme deviant cases, the wedding crashers may have criminal intent in mind (e.g., to rob the guests, steal the gifts, or kidnap or murder someone at the party). In other cases, wedding crashers are simply out to

have some fun and may be taking advantage of a situation that presents itself, such as when a hotel guest notices a big party in a reserved room and decides to sneak in.

Depending on the type of reception breach, the wedding couple, wedding organizers, and guests may act with anger, disgust, confusion, laughter, or with no concern at all. The wedding crashers may even go completely undetected. Sometimes you hear about a famous person who happens to be near a wedding reception popping in to take a peek and, depending on their level of popularity, much to the delight of the wedding couple and invited guests. In January 2015, a music video filmed by Maroon 5, with frontman Adam Levine—who is also a judge on *The Voice* and was once voted *People* magazine's "sexiest man alive," thus adding to his popularity—went viral in the world of social media. The video begins with Levine explaining, "We're gonna drive across LA and hit every wedding we possibly can" (Meyers 2015). The band teamed up with *Wedding Crashers* director David Dobkin to crash real weddings on December 6, 2014.

The band drove in black convertible cars throughout Los Angeles and snuck into reception halls. Dobkin's crew preceded Maroon 5 and quickly assembled framing so that they could hang a large white sheet for the band to hide behind until the big reveal at each wedding. Camera crews filmed the reactions of confused brides and grooms and guests. After the band successfully hid behind the sheet the bride and groom were led in front of it, not knowing what was on the other side. Understandably, some of the wedding couples were reluctant but played along. When the sheet was dropped, the band started to play their new song "Sugar." Not everyone knew who Maroon 5 were, but certainly anyone who follows music or has a fundamental knowledge of popular culture quickly realized it was Adam Levine. The reactions of the faces of the guests were priceless. These wedding crashers were more than welcomed!

Levine said of the day, "It was an out-of-body experience. I had no idea I would be affected by the overwhelming reactions we received from the couples and guests. Being able to create an unforgettable experience for several people was the highlight of it all" (Meyers 2015). Adding to the layers of deviance, cynics quickly pointed out that many of the guests and some of the brides and grooms were stage actors. A representative for Maroon 5 later admitted that the grooms knew about the performance but were unaware if the brides and guests knew about it. Maroon 5 insists that at least one of the weddings was really crashed and no one knew about it (Meyers 2015).

The Maroon 5 wedding-crashing video is good entertainment (available online, of course) and serves as a good example of positive deviance, especially for those who truly did not know that the band was going to perform.

Judging and Evaluating the Behavior of Others

Judging and evaluating the behavior of others is a feature common with nearly all humans, and it eventually leads to certain behaviors being labeled "acceptable" and other behaviors as "deviant." There exist an infinite number of social expectations, rules, and laws that each of us are expected to abide by. Most of us conform to nearly all of these social expectations rather routinely, and we generally expect others to do so as well. This sentiment is reflected in some variation of the adage "If I have to wait in line for my turn, so should you." In some instances, especially when dealing with minor social expectations, we may choose to ignore the offender's deviant behavior. Thus, while many people may find "man spreading" or any type of behavior that results in someone taking up too much space on a subway train or bus as an irritant, they choose to ignore this breach of etiquette.

Still, nearly all of us evaluate the behaviors of others and place judgment. If it's not man spreading, it's someone who cuts into traffic at the last minute because they would not merge in an orderly fashion like everyone else. Or perhaps you have viewed someone with multiple tattoos and face piercings as being a bit odd without realizing they have viewed your conventional lifestyle as peculiar. Students often look around the classroom and form judgments of their classmates as well as their professors. Professors, in turn, observe the behavior of students in the classroom and their class work. We judge the service of bartenders, waiters, and waitresses when attempting to determine how much of a tip to leave. We judge our friends' behaviors as well as our own. Having conducted survey research and laboratory sessions, German researchers Leising, Gallrein, and Dufner (2014) have found that self- and peer judgments of people's behavior in specific situations are affected by what the perceivers thought of the targets (of judgment) *before* observing their behavior. Specifically, if we already like a person whose behavior is being judged, we tend to be more positive in our evaluations than are unacquainted observers.

As put forth here, everyone will eventually do something that others, friends, family, or the unacquainted disapprove of. These breaches may be mild, such as smacking loudly while eating, or more serious acts, such as committing an assault or homicide. Either way, whenever someone violates the norms of a group, organization, or society, they risk having their behaviors labeled as deviant, which, in turn, bestows the deviant label on the perpetrator. In the following pages a few examples of unusual weddings and love of animated objects will be discussed. As you read these stories, make note of how you evaluate and judge the behaviors of those involved.

Deviant Weddings

Most people have attended, or will attend, at least one wedding in their lifetime, especially when we realize that 80 percent of Americans ages 25 and older have themselves been married at least once in their lifetime (Wang and Parker 2014). As evaluative creatures, we seemingly cannot help but judge the circumstances of a wedding. Some people are known to attend weddings and evaluate whether or not they think the marriage will last, or how long it will last based on the compatibility of the couple (e.g., "they look great together" or "what was she thinking?") or the circumstances of the wedding ("I hear they *had* to get married because she is pregnant"). We hear of celebrities getting married and often utter, "That will never last." In addition to the weddings we have witnessed firsthand are the unusual wedding stories we have heard about from others or have watched on television or YouTube videos. Take a moment to contemplate the oddest wedding you have ever attended or heard about; were any of these weddings what you would describe as "deviant"? What do you think?

Marriage is defined as "a relatively enduring, socially approved sexual and socio-economic relationship between at least two persons for the purpose of creating and maintaining a family" (Delaney 2012a:327). Monogamy involves one person married to one other person at any give time, while polygamy involves the marriage of one person to more than one other person at any given time. The Western ideal of marriage involves the idea that romantic love (a deep physical and emotional attraction) should come before the wedding. But the reality is, people get married for a variety of reasons. The stories below will describe some of the more unusual weddings, and as we shall see, people marry for many reasons other than romantic love. Evaluate for yourself whether or not you think these wedding ceremonies are deviant.

From the definition of marriage provided above, a marriage involves "at least two persons," it is implied that both of the people involved would be alive at the time of the wedding ceremony. This absolutist assumption that marriage must involve (at least) two (living) people is challenged in the following deviant wedding ceremony stories designed to illustrate examples of what most people would consider instances of social deviance. Our first story takes place in August 1996, when Patricia Montenez, of France, married Claude Darcy in a ceremony attended by 100 guests and presided over by then-Mayor Guy Hermier. Montenez, then 36 years old, said following the ceremony, "Every minute I think of Claudie—he never leaves my side" (*The Post-Standard* 9/1/96). Nothing so unusual about this story—so far, anyway. The deviant issue here comes with the revelation that Darcy, a police officer in Marseille, was not by her side during the ceremony because he had been slain two and a half years before the ceremony took place. Darcy's parents petitioned the courts in an attempt to stop the unusual wedding dreams of Montenez, who had a child from him. Following a decree issued by then-French president Jacques Chirac, the wedding was allowed to take place and Darcy's presence was symbolically represented by an empty chair.

In a 2012 wedding ceremony in Thailand, Chadil Deffy placed a ring on the finger of Sarinya Kamsook, his girlfriend of 10 years, during a joint funeral and wedding ceremony in Thailand (Llorens 2012). Kamsook had always wanted to marry her longtime boyfriend, but he kept putting it off. But Kamsook died in a road accident, and the wedding was Deffy's attempt to right a wrong (Llorens 2012). While most people at the ceremony thought the service was strange, others expressed their sympathies to the grieving groom. Both the Montenez and Deffy weddings would be considered deviant by most people's standards because their spouses were deceased at the time of the ceremony.

A number of examples of unusual weddings do not involve the love of a dead spouse, and yet they still involve the notion of love. Case in point, it is often said that some people, perhaps men more than women (but let's not be sexist and assume one gender is more prone to this type of love than the other), love their cars. In 1999, Buster Mitchell of Knoxville, Tennessee, wanted to make his love affair with his car official. "Jilted by his girlfriend, a bereft Mitchell decided he wanted to marry his true love—his 1996 Mustang GT. 'I've been broken hearted and hung out to dry, so I am going to the courthouse and try to marry my car,' Mitchell said before attempting to get a marriage license." On the marriage license, the 28-year-old Mitchell listed his fiancée's birthplace as "Detroit," her father as "Henry Ford," and her blood type as "10-W-40" (*Buffalo News* 3/6/99:A5). The clerk at the courthouse would not accept Mitchell's application because (at the time) Tennessee only allowed marriages between a man and a woman.

It is safe to say that many people love their pets and consider them to be a part of the family. However, there are very few people who have considered marrying their pet for love, or any other reason for that matter. Nonetheless, "A man in southern India married a female dog in a traditional Hindu ceremony as an attempt to atone for stoning two other dogs to death, an act he believes cursed him" (*The Post-Standard* 11/14/07:A-2). P. Selvakumar married a sari-draped former stray dog named Selvi, who was chosen by Selvakumar's family members and then bathed and clothed for the ceremony at a Hindu temple in the southern state of Tamil Nadu. Selvakumar told the press that he had been suffering ever since he stoned two dogs to death and hung their bodies from a tree 15 years prior to the wedding ceremony. Selvakumar stated that his legs and hands were paralyzed and that he lost hearing in one ear since stoning the two dogs to death. He was told by an astrologer that the only way he could cure his woes was by marrying a dog. "Deeply superstitious people in rural India sometimes organize weddings to dogs and other animals, believing it can ward off certain curses. After the wedding, the groom and his family had a feast. The dog got a bun" (*The Post-Standard* 11/14/07:A-2). No details were provided about the honeymoon or whether or not the marriage cured Selvakumar of his maladies. In most societies, a human marrying an animal would be considered deviant, but as we have learned here, such a belief is not an absolute.

For the Love of Animated Characters and Inanimate Objects

Have you ever found an animated character such as Marge Simpson (*The Simpsons*), Lois Griffin (*The Family Guy*), John Smith of *Pocahontas*, or Gambit of *X-Men* fame attractive? Would it be deviant to have a crush on an animated character?

Many people still consider Jessica Rabbit from the *Who Framed Roger Rabbit* (1988) film as among the most attractive female animated characters. In one scene, Jessica Rabbit makes an account for her good looks and the impact it has on others.

Jessica Rabbit: You don't know how hard it is being a woman looking the way I do.

Eddie Valiant: You don't know how hard it is being a man looking at a woman looking the way you do.

Jessica Rabbit: I'm not bad. I'm just drawn that way.

Some men have admitted to having a crush on Jessica Rabbit, and interestingly at least one woman has had enough plastic surgery done to look like her. Annette Edwards, a 57-year-old grandmother, underwent surgical procedures in London to make herself look like Jessica Rabbit (Murano 2010). Like her fictional cartoon idol, Edwards reportedly loves rabbits.

If you think Edwards is a bit bizarre for wanting to look like a fictional cartoon character, what do you think about humans being allowed to marry their favorite fictitious characters? Just such a campaign has been launched in Japan. "In a reflection of the nation's growing obsession with escaping reality, more than 1,000 people have signed an online petition to present to the government to establish a law permitting marriage to comic characters. Comic books known as 'manga,' animated 'anime' films and online virtual reality games have become increasingly popular in Japan, with fictitious characters frequently elevated to celebrity status." The "mastermind" behind the online campaign for cartoon marriages is Taichi Takashita, who claimed that he was motivated to pursue the odd change in law because he felt more at ease in the "two dimensional world" than reality (Demetriou 2008). A supporter of the "single sex" marriage campaign stated that he had trouble falling in love with three-dimensional people and hoped to find love with an animated character: "Even if she is fictional, it is still loving someone. I would like to have legal approval for this system at any cost" (Demetriou 2008).

The story above introduced the concept of a single sex marriage. Typically, when we hear of single sex marriages we think of gay and lesbian couples, but in the previous instance single sex marriage referred to the variation of marriage that involves just one human. In this final story of deviant wedding ceremonies the concept of **objectum sexuality** is presented. An objectum sexual is a person who has an orientation to love objects, including inanimate objects. An example of objectum sexuality was introduced to the American public during a January 2015 edition of the TLC Network's *My Strange Addiction*. A Florida woman named Linda professed her love for her soul mate, Bruce. Bruce is a 70-foot-tall SkyDiver carnival ride located outside of Tampa. Linda states that she has been married to Bruce for three years (she admits it's not a legally state-sanctioned marriage). She also said that her first relationship was with an airplane and her longest relationship was with a locomotive, but that didn't work out. Then she met Bruce and fell in love. Bruce needs repairs, so the carnival ride actually resides on Linda's property while she sinks tens of thousands of dollars into Bruce's repairs. As with most objectum-sexual relationships, sexuality is not the moving force in her relationship; it's the feeling in her heart that matters to her. She simply enjoys having quality time with Bruce and reports being very happy (AOL News 2015).

Deviance and Morality

As previously stated, morality often plays a role in determining whether certain behaviors are defined as deviant or not. Identifying certain behaviors as moral and others as immoral is often as complicated as claiming specific behaviors as deviant and others as acceptable because it often involves subjective interpretations. Before we examine the role of morality in deviance we should first attempt to establish what is meant by the term "morality." Most dictionaries use such descriptive parameters as "goodness," "proper manners," "good character," "ethical behaviors," "virtue," and "a system of guiding principles" in their attempt to define morality. Bernard Gert (2011) defines morality descriptively in terms of codes of conduct put forth by a society or some other group, such as a religious group, or as a code of conduct that individuals put forward for themselves, as in "a personal code of conduct." With these thoughts in mind, **morality** can be defined as a code of conduct that includes ideals of proper and ethical behavior used to guide human behavior and to develop or maintain good character.

Morality, like deviance, boils down to describing certain behaviors as "good" or acceptable and others as "bad" or unacceptable. Some moral principles (e.g., older, bigger, and stronger kids from high school should not physically assault younger, smaller, and weaker children in first grade) are adhered to by most people within a given society, organization, or group, while other moral principles (e.g., the rights of women to choose whether or not to abort a late-term pregnancy) are quite debatable. If ideals of morality originated with logic and sound reasoning, there would be far fewer gray areas about its true meaning. This is not the case; instead, as Jonathan Haidt describes, moral judgments arise from gut feelings and not from reason. That moral judgments originate from one's personal feelings about social matters helps to explain why conservatives and liberals often disagree on matters of morality (Haidt 2013). Neurophilosophy pioneer Patricia Churchland (2012) takes a different perspective than Haidt's "gut feelings" approach about the origin of morality. She believes that morality has evolved as humanity has evolved, arguing that morality is part of a process of bonding evolutionary pressures with cultural values, all of which takes place in the biology of the brain. This bonding process in turn leads to different styles of human moral behavior.

Sociologists also examine the origins of morality and contemplate whether or not we are born with the need for morality. Is it a matter of gut feelings, or did it evolve over time as humans evolved? According to Wilhelm Wundt, a 19th-century scientist and philosopher, morality developed to make individuals feel as though they are not a whole, but part of a whole; thus, individuals are insignificant without reference to the plurality of contexts that surround them. To make a meaningful contribution to the greater whole, individuals are to act morally, or properly, in order to help stabilize the whole into a cohesive unit. Morality is, therefore, a collection of precepts, of rules of conduct. Any violation of these rules of morality will lead to consequences. Like Wundt, Durkheim believed that notions of morality evolved as humanity evolved (Kenny 2010). Durkheim, the first full professor of sociology, argued that morality, like all social phenomena, can best be examined sociologically. Durkheim, in his *Moral Education* (first published in 1925 and likely taken from his lecture notes first developed at the Sorbonne), states that art originates from the domain of the unreal, of the imaginary, while morality, in contrast, is of the domain of human action and can only be understood in relation to real phenomena (Giddens 1972; Durkheim 1973 [1925]; Delaney 2014a).

In the following pages, we will look at a few examples of the relationship between deviance and morality.

Ethics and Cheating

An aspect of morality involves ethical behavior. The issue of ethics overlaps with morality and deviance because, once again, important aspects of its parameters involve the ideals of proper behavior, honesty, fairness, equality, dignity, and basic decency. Ethics provides people with a sense of a moral compass; that is, ethical behavior is driven by the desire to do the right thing, to make the right choices in the face of optional courses of actions (Thiroux and Krasemann 2011). Consequently, **ethics** can be defined as having the ability to distinguish between right and wrong courses of actions and the ability to understand the difference between the virtuous and the nonvirtuous aspects of human behavior.

There appears to be an abundance of unethical behavior in society involving politicians and business leaders (see chapter 5), athletes and professional sports organizations, in nearly every profession, and among individuals and groups during the course of their everyday life activities. It is impossible to provide adequate coverage of the prevalence of unethical cheating that occurs in society in the space allocated here, but the following two examples give us a glimpse of the problem. The first story involves U.S. military officers at a nuclear missile program. In 2014, nine Air Force commanders were fired from "their jobs in the wake of a cheating scandal involving systemic cheating on tests by officers in the U.S. nuclear missile program. . . . The fired officers were in 'leadership positions' at Malmstrom Air Force Base in Montana, Air Force Secretary Deborah Lee James said." Another 100 lower-level officers were, at one point during the investigation, implicated in cheating on monthly proficiency exams. Some of these officers were cleared, while others could face punishments ranging from forced counseling to court-martial. The cheating scandal was discovered essentially by mistake as military investigators were looking into alleged drug activity involving airmen at the Montana base. The public should be concerned because these officers oversee the readiness of nuclear weapons systems at Malmstrom. Lieutenant General Stephen Wilson, the commander of the Air Force Global Strike Command, said, "Our nation demands and deserves the higher standards of accountability from the force entrusted with the most powerful weapon on the planet. We are committed to living up to those standards" (Botelho 2014).

If we cannot trust our current leaders to act ethically, perhaps we have to turn to our future leaders for signs of morality. Unfortunately, there are countless examples of cheating on college campuses as well. That some college students cheat is not a new revelation, but is it too much to ask for students in an *ethics class* not to cheat? During the fall 2014 semester, up to 64 Dartmouth College students faced suspension or other disciplinary action for cheating in an ethics class. "Dartmouth officials said students implicated in the cheating scandal misrepresented their attendance and participation in the undergraduate course, 'Sports, Ethics & Religion' . . . Some of the students have been found in violation of the school's honor code and have been told they will be suspended for one term, a college official with knowledge of the proceedings said" (Rocheleau 2015).

Right to Die

Is it immoral or unethical to want to take one's own life? Is it unethical for someone else to tell another they do not have a right to die even when they face extreme pain and discomfort before they will eventually die from an inoperable/incurable health issue? These are among the questions related to the "right-to-die" issue. Death with dignity, assisted suicide, and euthanasia are similar aspects, all of which are connected to the right-to-die issue. Proponents of the right-to-die decision among terminally ill people refer to such a decision-making choice as a human rights matter.

The right-to-die issue gained a great deal of attention and stimulated significant social discourse in 2014 because of Brittany Maynard's highly publicized decision to end her own life under her own conditions. Maynard was diagnosed with inoperable brain cancer, and she and her husband, Dan Diaz, moved "from California to Oregon, where she was born, because Oregon was one of just five states in the national that allowed Maynard to obtain medication to end her own life." Oregon passed its Death with Dignity Act in 1997. The Death with Dignity National Center (2015) states that "years of data show the law is safe and utilized the way it's intended with no evidence of a slippery slope for vulnerable Oregonians." "For years, the so-called right-to-die movement was most associated with Jack Kevorkian, the Michigan physician known as Dr. Death for participating in dozens of physician-assisted suicides, one of which led to a conviction of second-degree murder" (Sanburn 2015). Washington (2008) and Vermont (2013) followed the template created by Oregon and passed legislation that allows assisted suicide while New Mexico and Montana have effectively legalized it by saying there is nothing barring doctors from prescribing life-ending medication (Death with Dignity National Center 2015).

Maynard, a 29-year-old newlywed, "offered a far more sympathetic face" for the right-to-die movement than did "Dr. Death." During the summer of 2014 Maynard approached the advocacy group Compassion & Choices,, who helped to make her case go public, because she hoped to raise enough awareness to convince voters in California and other states to pass legislation in favor of death with dignity, or right to die. In the first two months following Maynard's death in November (2014), four states, including California, had introduced right-to-die legislation. California Senator Lois Wolk, who along with Senator Bill Monning, both Democrats, coauthored a bill giving terminally ill patients with six months or less to live the ability to obtain life-ending medication. Wolk said, "The fact that Brittany Maynard was a Californian suffering from an incurable, irreversible illness who then had to leave the state to ease her suffering was simply appalling, simply unacceptable" (Sanburn 2015).

A number of religious and social conservative groups (e.g., the American Life League) are against the right-to-die movement. "Days after Maynard's Nov. 1 [2014] death at age 29, the Vatican's top bioethics official called her choice 'reprehensible' and said physician-assisted suicide should be condemned" (CBS News 2015a). Maynard's mother, Debbie Ziegler, made a statement through the Compassion & Choices advocacy group, saying that the comments from the Vatican were "more than a slap in the face" (CBS News 2015a). Pope Francis, who has made more than a few relatively shockingly liberal statements during his tenure, made it clear where he stands on euthanasia. Pope Francis stated, "Euthanasia is a sin against

God and creation. Thinking of euthanasia as an act of dignity provides a 'false sense of compassion'" (CBS News 2015a). Judie Brown, president of the American Life League, a Catholic advocacy group, said (in response to the attention given to Maynard), "Suicide is never a good solution, regardless of the situation that one is confronting" (*The Citizen* 11/14/14). Maynard and her supporters feel that it is immoral to make someone stay alive simply so that they can extend their period of pain and suffering before dying.

Cannibalism

Chances are, most people are against cheating, and yet many of those who profess to be against it will, in fact, cheat at something (e.g., cheat on their spouse, a test, or their taxes) sometime in their lifetime. On the other hand, there's more ambiguity about the right-to-die issue. So is there anything that most people would find immoral or unethical? How about the cannibalism? More than likely, most people would see cannibalism as immoral and unethical, and they certainly are not too likely to participate in it. **Cannibalism** is the act of one individual of a species consuming all or part of another member of the same species. Nearly every species engages in cannibalistic acts, including birds, bees, cats, and so on. According to *The Most* (2014), the 10 most cannibalistic animals are (starting at 10th place) cats, lobsters, octopuses, bullfrogs, sand tiger sharks, polar bears, king cobras, orangutans, fish, and praying mantis. **Human cannibalism** refers to the eating of human flesh by another human. Cannibalism is perhaps the ultimate symbol of savagery and degradation (Avramescu 2011). The very idea of cannibalism seems to conjure images of depravity, evil, and immorality. Nonetheless, human cannibalism dates back to prehistoric times and has occurred all over the globe at one point or another (Stern 2008).

In his *A History of Cannibalism* (2009), Peter Constantine describes how the rather straightforward topic of cannibalism itself has gray areas. Chewing on a human liver would seem to be a clear example of cannibalistic behavior, and yet when people chew off chunks of their fingernails, that is rarely considered as cannibalistic. Constantine therefore puts forth the idea that there are degrees of cannibalism. At one extreme is the mild form of cannibalism (e.g., chewing fingernails) and at the other extreme are the "murder, mutilation and the roasting of flesh" (p. 8). In between the two extremes are any number of possibilities. Addressing the issue of morality and ethics, Constantine states, "In ethical terms it clearly makes a huge difference whether the source of meat is alive or dead. If the former, it obviously matters whether the donor was willing or not; in the latter, whether the would-be consumer was also the cause of death" (p. 8). Constantine states that there are three essential reasons for cannibalism: duty, desperation, and desire. Duty cannibalism refers to a cultural expectation of a given society (mostly from the past) that its members partake in eating human flesh because of traditional obligations, norms, and values. Desperation cannibalism refers to situations (e.g., widespread famine, plane crash in a remote area) wherein one's very survival is dependent upon the consumption of any ready food supply, including human flesh. Desire cannibalism seems to be the most unethical version of cannibalism, as it involves someone's craving to eat human flesh. Desire cannibalism is somewhat hard to understand, but it is related to "abusive fathers, overbearing mothers, animal torture, [and] extreme sexual dysfunction" (Constantine 2009:10).

In the modern era, desire cannibalism is mostly restricted to individual cases. One such case involves Armin Meiwes. A Rotenburg, Germany, resident, Meiwes placed an online advertisement seeking a "long pig" for slaughter and consumption. The term "long pig" has roots with some cannibal tribes that used the expression to describe a human being roasted over an open fire (Schofield 2013). Reports indicate that between 200 and 400 people responded to Meiwes's advertisement and volunteered to fulfill his fantasy to "slaughter and consume a human." Meiwes, a computer technician, chose Bernd-Jurgen Brandes (then 43 years old), a successful software engineer from Berlin. While on trial in December 2003, Meiwes informed the court that he and his victim chatted for several weeks online. When they finally decided to meet, Brandes undressed and reportedly said, "Now you can see my body. I hope you'll find me tasty," Meiwes is quoted as saying (*The Post-Standard* 12/4/03:A-4). Meiwes admitted to having fantasies since childhood about killing and eating another human being. His chilling court testimony included a description of his fantasy to find someone to become "a part of him." Meiwes said that he stabbed his victim the morning after their first meeting. He videotaped himself chopping up the body and freezing some of the dismembered body parts to be eaten over the course of several months. Other parts were buried in the garden. Police searched his home and found human flesh and bones. After eating Brandes, Meiwes claimed that he acquired his victim's ability to speak English. Meiwes also described the experience "as a merging of souls" (Schofield 2013).

Despite the seemingly deviant and depraved manner of his behavior, court-appointed psychiatrists found Meiwes fit to stand trial. He also ostensibly met one of the key criteria of Constantine's attributes of a desire cannibal, as prosecutors claimed that the killing was sexually motivated. His original 2003 trial would lead to a 2004 court decision to sentence Meiwes to eight and a half years in prison for manslaughter; however, later, under new charges of murder, he was sentenced to life in prison with a minimum sentence of at least 15 years (Schofield 2013).

In 2013, another case of a German desire cannibal emerged involving the killer known only as Detlef G., a 55-year-old chief inspector with the Saxon Germany state police, who freely admitted to killing his human "long pig" after the victim, identified as Wojciech S., responded to a cannibalism website that hooks up those who want to dine on human flesh with those hoping to be eaten (Schofield 2013).

A seemingly ultimate example of social deviance is the number of Internet sites attempting to "hook up" would-be cannibals with people looking to be consumed. There are other sites that seek humans to serve as bait for hunts. A quick online search led to a number of such sites, including Human-Bait.com, which advertises a variety of cannibalistic endeavors that will not be described here.

Deviance Is a Matter of Context

The topic of cannibalism, especially the concept of desperation cannibalism, introduces another variable when defining deviance—the realization that deviance is often a matter of context. Constantine (2009) describes a situation when people isolated from civilization and facing certain death because of a lack of food may begin to look at one another as a source of nourishment. Recently deceased persons may be the first to become consumed. While such a scenario may be rare, it may indeed become necessary for people to consume other people. From an ethical standpoint, we are likely to give a pass to those who engage in desperation cannibalism, as such an act was actually a horrible necessity. (See box 1.2 for a specific case of desperation cannibalism.)

A CLOSER LOOK

Box 1.2 Desperation Cannibalism: Uruguayan Air Force Flight 571

On October 13, 1972, the chartered Uruguayan Air Force Flight 571, carrying 45 people, including a Uruguayan rugby union team, their friends, families, and other invited guests, crashed into the Andes mountains between Chile and Argentina, killing 12 men on impact, another 5 within hours, and 1 more a week later (*Daily Mail* 2012). On the 17th day following the crash, an avalanche killed 8 more passengers. The survivors had to deal with no source of heat in the harsh conditions of 11,800-foot altitude, and what little food was on the plane at the time of the crash did not last long. The survivors were occasionally able to pick up radio reports and learned that the search for them had been abandoned. Two brave survivors, Nando Parrado and Roberto Canessa, trekked the mountains for 20 days in search of help; 72 days after the crash, the remaining 14 men (16 in total, counting the 2 who went for help) were rescued (*Daily Mail* 2012). The survivors had been forced to consume the meat of their deceased follow passengers who had been preserved in the cold snow. Such a decision was difficult for the all–Roman Catholic passengers, but the decision had to be rationalized or face the consequences of death by starvation. Canessa, retelling the story 40 years after his ordeal, told the *Daily Mail* (2012), "It was repugnant. Through the eyes of our civilized society it was a disgusting decision. My dignity was on the floor having to grab a piece of my dead friend and eat it in order to survive." The story of the 1972 Andes plane crash was told in the 1993 film *Alive*.

Cannibalism represents an extreme example of deviance as a matter of context. Let's consider a few additional illustrations. In situation A, one person is beating up another person. In situation B, one person is beating up another person. So far, both scenarios are equal, so let's put the behavior in context of the different situations. In situation A, the beating is taking place in front of an ATM outside of a convenience store and the person beating up the other is committing assault during an attempted robbery. In situation B, the person beating up the other is doing so at Caesar's Palace in Las Vegas during a boxing match. Situation A would be labeled deviant and B would not (unless you find boxing an example of deviance). In another scenario, we have situation C wherein one person shoots and kills another, and we have situation D wherein one person shoots and kills another. The same behavior in both situations, yet which one is deviant and which one is not? What do you think? Did you come up with a variation in the two situations similar to the following elaboration? Situation C involves a drive-by shooting as a part of street gang initiation that requires a recruit to shoot the first random person spotted on the street as they cruise the streets. This behavior is deviant. What sort of contexts will make situation D not likely to be labeled deviant? There are at least two situations. One, an intruder enters one's home in an attempt to cause bodily harm or to burglarize the home and the homeowner defends herself. Two, a police officer shoots a criminal during the commission of a crime (all police shootings result in an investigation to determine if the shooting was justified under police policy).

Dressing up as a superhero at Halloween is socially acceptable and not likely to be described as deviant. Dressing up as a superhero or cartoon character in everyday life while in public is likely to be considered deviant. Then again, a number of people dress up as superheroes and cartoon characters in public in Hollywood, California (and recently, in Times Square, New York), and they do so to entertain tourists. For decades, these costumed characters gathered outside Grauman's Chinese Theatre on Hollywood Boulevard in Hollywood, where tourists would ask to have their picture taken with the character, and then they might offer a token payment. (Note: This author, as a former resident of Los Angeles, often went to Grauman's Chinese Theatre in the 1980s and 1990s and recalls that most tourists were oblivious to the idea of tipping these characters after having their photo taken with them.) Times Square is now the home of costumed characters. Costumed characters entertaining tourists in Times Square is virtually inconceivable for anyone old enough to remember going to this part of New York City decades ago. From the 1960s through the 1980s, Times Square was one of the most dangerous areas of New York City. (Note: The 1969 film *Midnight Cowboy* provides a good depiction of Times Square in this time period.) By the 2000s, Times Square was all cleaned up and a destination spot for tourists. Like the scene in Hollywood, costumed characters started to pop up throughout the area. Many of these characters have become notorious for shaking down tourists (demanding as much as $10 to $20) who take photos of them, and they certainly demand to be paid to have their photo taken with the tourists (Velez and Fasick 2014). In 2014, a panhandler dressed as Spider-Man repeatedly punched a police officer in the face during a violent confrontation in Times Square. The officer was responding to tourists who complained that this particular Spider-Man was overly aggressive in demanding money from tourists who walked by him (Velez and Fasick 2014). This antagonistic costumed character is likely to be viewed as deviant regardless of how one defines deviance.

The appeal of costumed superheroes is especially evident at the box office. It seems people of all ages have a romanticized view of what it must be like to be a superhero. Superheroes like Superman, Spider-Man, Batman, Wolverine, Wonder Woman, and Buffy the Vampire Slayer don't actually exist; they are make-believe. And yet there are those, like "Geist," who roam the streets as a superhero with the goal of helping others. If you have not heard of Geist (German for ghost), he is part of a group of "flamboyant do-gooders who call themselves real life superheroes (RLSH), a phenomenon that springs from the intersection of real life and comic books" (Strickler 2013:A-19). Tea Krulos has been studying RLSH for years and estimates that there are anywhere between 200 and 500 of them across the country. They are ordinary people who often take extraordinary risks and are motivated by a deep need to make the world safer (Krulos 2013).

Definitions of Deviance Change over Time

Susan B. Anthony was arrested, indicted, tried, and convicted for voting illegally (she cast a ballot) in the presidential election of 1872 in her hometown of Rochester, New York. Why? Was it because she was trying to vote for incumbent President Ulysses S. Grant? No, of course not, it was because she was a woman, and women did not have the right to vote in 1872. At Anthony's "two-day trial in June 1873, which she later described as 'the greatest judicial outrage history has ever recorded,' she was convicted and sentenced to pay a fine of $100 and court costs" (National Archives 2015a). It would be nearly 50 years later before women would be granted the right to vote via the Nineteenth Amendment to the U.S. Constitution (passed by Congress in 1919 and ratified in 1920). From that point on, it was no longer deviant for women to vote.

In the past, wearing torn jeans was the sign of being poor or being someone who performs hard physical labor. Today it can be an in-vogue fashion statement.

The Anthony case serves as an exemplary illustration of how definitions of deviance can change over time. There are a plethora of examples of behaviors defined as deviant changing over time, including some with serious subject matter (e.g., women's right to vote) and some far less serious, such as the concept of torn jeans as an in-vogue fashion statement. Not so long ago, a person wearing torn jeans might be **stigmatized** (defined as being characterized or branded as disgraceful or ignominious) as being poor, or at the very least too poor to afford new jeans; or it would be assumed that such a person performed hard physical labor, and worn-out clothes were a by-product of blue-collar labor. Many leading clothing stores now sell torn or ripped jeans as a fashionable look for chic consumers. As Hannah Lyons Powell (2014) explains in *Glamour*, "Be it skinny, mom, boyfriend or cropped, ripped jeans are the hot new denim trend *du jour*." Interestingly (or is it deviantly?), torn or ripped jeans may cost more than jeans without holes.

Throughout the remaining chapters many instances of serious subject matters that have changed in definition from being deviant in the past but not today, or things that are deviant today, but not in the past, will be discussed, including the banning of slavery; the granting of civil rights to women and minorities; the changing view of gay marriage and the general and legal acceptance of marriages between whites and blacks; the movement to legalize marijuana for medical and recreational purposes; the realization that the earth is not a dumping ground for human-made toxic materials; viewing a number of corporate leaders and corporations as white collar criminals; and so on.

Deviance Varies from Culture to Culture and from Subculture to Subculture

There is one additional topic related to defining deviance, and that involves the realization that diverse cultures and subcultures will have their own standards of which behaviors are acceptable and which ones are considered deviant. This topic is relevant to many of the perspectives on deviance but especially the normative and relativist.

Deviance Varies from Culture to Culture

One of the most important subject matters examined by sociologists is culture and its impact on human behavior. Sociologists point out that while every society has a culture, each culture is unique. So what is culture? **Culture** may be defined as "the shared knowledge, values, norms and behavioral patterns of a given society that are passed on from one generation to the next, forming a way of life for its members" (Delaney 2012a:108). Because the concept of "culture" places a strong emphasis on a society's "shared knowledge, values, norms and behavioral patterns," those who use the normative perspective on the study of deviance rely heavily on cultural determinations of what is "proper" and what is "improper" behavior. Deviance researchers who utilize the normative perspective need to be mindful that aspects of culture may change over time and, thus, one's interpretation of acceptable or unacceptable behavior must also be modified. Consider, for example, the advancements in communications that have transformed telephone usage from landlines to mobile, cellular devices. Landline usage of phones was conducted mostly in private settings such as a person's home or place of business, and as a result phone conversations seldom disturbed others. Today, people use cell phones nearly everywhere, including public places where such conversations are often bothersome to others. Interestingly, cell phone usage is not restricted to actual verbal conversations with others; rather it involves sending texts and photos and streaming videos. Many cell phone users are oblivious, or simply don't care, if their need to use their smartphone agitates other people or not. Professors have to contend with rude students who use their cell phones in class, movie patrons have to put up with the bright glare of the phone screen in darkened movie theaters, friends and dating partners have to deal with their dining partners who use smartphones to communicate with others at the expense of the people sitting at the same table, and the examples go on and on. The introduction of the ubiquitous cell phone has led to gray areas of determining social deviance. The definition one uses to define deviance and the context and situation at hand dictate whether or not using cell phones is deviant. What do you think? Is there a time and place when using cell phones would be considered deviant?

Culture has both material and nonmaterial components. The **material** aspects of culture refer to the physical, tangible products and creations of a society. Some societies, especially those in the West (e.g., the United States of America), are quite materialistic and value the creation and consumption of consumer products. It was the embracement of industrialization centuries ago that allowed certain societies to produce mass amounts of products, provided an abundance of free time for the masses, and increased the purchasing power for most members of industrialized societies. The nonmaterial aspects of culture consist of beliefs and ideologies, norms, values, and accepted behavioral patterns. Beliefs are mental acts that involve opinions, convictions, faith, creed, and placing trust or confidence in others or a cause or condition. A collection of a number of similar beliefs leads to the creation of an **ideology**. Norms, as described earlier, are socially defined rules and expectations regarding human behavior. They are standards of expected behavior that people are supposed to adhere to. Sociologists identify three different categories of norms:

1. **Folkways**—The conventional rules of everyday life that people follow almost automatically, such as holding a door open for the person behind you
2. **Mores**—Norms that constitute the basic moral judgments of a society, such as the taboos against incest, pedophilia, and cannibalism
3. **Laws**—Formalized norms, as determined by a political authority.

Values refer to standards of societal expectations that are deeply rooted principles cherished by the people of a given society, such as the American values of the right to pursue success and happiness, equality, loyalty, and the idea that hard work should be rewarded. Accepted **behavioral patterns** may include mundane acts such as the way strangers, friends, or loved ones greet one another, to more serious concerns such as the ideal that Americans are supposed to stand and show reverence during the playing of the national anthem.

While nations may be divided into such categories as developed or underdeveloped, Western or non-Western, there are no two societies in the world that share all of the same ideals of beliefs and ideologies, norms, values, and accepted behavioral patterns. In fact, cultures around the world are quite unique in several ways, and this diversity is the result of such variables as a society's adaptation to its specific natural environment (e.g., climate and geography) and its traditional customs, habits, values, norms, beliefs, and ideologies that developed over time, forming a way of life for its people. The diversity of cultures across the world leads to different interpretations as to what constitutes proper or deviant behavior.

One example of a behavior that is generally viewed differently based on Western or non-Western ideals is the concept of "honor killings." **Honor killings** involve the homicide of a female member of a family by her male family members because she has "dishonored" or shamed the family because of her behavior (e.g., she refused to take part in an arranged marriage; she was involved in an unauthorized relationship; she had sex outside of her marriage; she was raped; she dressed in an inappropriate manner; or she engaged in lesbian sex). Honor killings result in the murder of thousands of females every year because they violated (or allegedly violated) patriarchal social codes (Pope 2011). Honor killings generally involve painful and public torture, including stoning and being buried alive. As an example of an honor killing, Pakistani fashion model, social media celebrity, and feminist Qandeel Baloch (real name, Fauzia Azeem), was strangled to death by one of her six brothers as she slept in the family home in Multan. Baloch offended many conservatives by posting pictures of herself with Mufti Qavi, a prominent cleric. She wrote in her post that she enjoyed soft drinks and cigarettes together during the daylight hours in the holy month of Ramadan when practicing Muslims fast from dawn to dusk (BBC News 2016).

While some people may be surprised to learn that honor killings still exist today, it becomes a little more understandable when we realize that violence may be perceived as a normal and acceptable way to resolve conflict in many parts of the world (UNICEF 2014). "Understanding the norms that govern a society can provide clues to the underlying causes of [violence against children and women] and how it can be prevented. Different social norms can help explain the widespread use of violence against children. . . . Data on attitudes towards wife-beating offer clues on how girls and women are perceived within a given society" (UNICEF 2014). The data from female respondents is especially enlightening, and perhaps disturbing from a Western perspective, as close to half of all girls aged 15 to 19 worldwide (the highest percentages are found in Eastern and Southern Africa; the Middle East and North Africa; West and Central Africa; and South Asia) think a husband is sometimes justified in hitting or beating his wife (UNICEF 2014).

Cultures vary in a great number of ways, and all these differences lead to different interpretations of acceptable behavior. Some of these differences include whether or not the consumption of alcohol is acceptable, or tolerated; number of hours worked per year; and vanity. The highest adult per capita consumption of alcohol is "found in the developed world, mostly the Northern Hemisphere, but also in Argentina, Australia and New Zealand. Medium consumption levels can be found in southern Africa, with Namibia and South Africa having the highest levels, and in North and South America. Low consumption levels can be found in the countries of North Africa and sub-Saharan Africa, the Eastern Mediterranean region, and southern Asia and the Indian Ocean. These regions represent large populations of the Islamic faith, which have very high rates of abstention" (World Health Organization 2011:3). As this data would indicate, drinking alcohol in Islamic cultures is more likely viewed as deviant than in Australia.

According to 2013 data compiled by the Organization for Economic Cooperation and Development (OECD), the Dutch (Netherlands) work the fewest hours each year (1,380 hours per worker on average), while Mexicans (Mexico) work the most (2,237 hours per worker on average). Only two other nations among the 34 countries studied had workers that averaged more than 2,000 hours per worker on average (Chile 2,015 and Greece 2,037). Americans averaged 1,777 hours per worker in 2013 (OECD 2015). In a nation such as Mexico, people who do not work are more likely to be viewed as deviant than in the Netherlands.

If plastic surgery procedures (nips, tucks, and Botox injections) are used as a means to measure vanity, the United States qualifies as a vanity nation. There were 3.1 million procedures performed in 2011, accounting for 21 percent of the world's total. According to the International Society of Aesthetic Plastic Surgery, however, when it comes to the top plastic surgery nations (by percentage of population) in the world, the vanity award goes to South Korea (Conley 2012). South Korea is followed by Greece, Italy, Brazil, Columbia, the United States, and Taiwan (Conley 2012). It is less likely that people in these top seven plastic surgery nations are going to be viewed negatively than in cultures where such acts of vanity would be looked down upon.

Deviance Varies from Subculture to Subculture

Just as there is a great difference between cultures around the world, so too is there a great variety of subcultures. A **subculture** is "a culture within a culture consisting of a category of people who share a distinctive set of cultural beliefs and behaviors that distinguish them from the larger society" (Delaney 2012a:129). Members of a subculture are not trying to overthrow the existing society (like a countercultural group), as they agree with most of the aspects of the greater society; instead, they have a distinctive aspect that sets them apart from the mainstream. Subcultures consist of groups of people who share a like-minded philosophy on life or enjoy participating in a specific behavior to the exclusion of most other activities. Recreational pot smokers prefer hanging out with friends who also like to smoke pot. Snowboarders like to hang out with other thrill seekers who like to spend time in nature snowboarding.

Joining a subcultural group is fairly common for most people, young and old. Sociologist Charles Cooley points out that people often feel the most at ease when they are with their primary group associates. Cooley (1909) described a primary group as those "characterized by intimate face-to-face association and cooperation. . . . The result of intimate association, psychologically, is a certain fusion of individualities in a common whole, so that one's very self, for many purposes at least, is the common life and purpose of the group" (p. 23). The initial primary group is one's family. As the child ages, he or she seeks out peers with common interests, resulting in a new, subcultural primary group. The primary group is relatively small and informal, involves close personal relationships, and has an important role in shaping one's sense of self and self-esteem (Delaney 2004a).

There are many examples of subcultural groups, including recreational drug users, athletes, gang members, college students, fraternities and sororities, Goths, runway models, and surfers. Among the characteristics that distinguish members of a subculture from mainstream society may be a style of clothing (especially important to athletes, gang members, Goths, and runway models); mannerisms (e.g., surfers act "chill," Goths act disenchanted, athletes act pumped); and language (all subcultures have a unique variation of the mainstream language with slang being especially important). Considerations of deviancy involve the conflict between the subcultural norms and values and those of the mainstream society. Thus, within the subcultural context participants may be engaging in behavior that mainstream society considers deviant (e.g., smoking marijuana in states where it is illegal), but within the subculture, the behavior is deemed acceptable.

Summary

Few topics in academic discourse contain more ambiguity than does "social deviance." The sociological study of social deviance reveals that a number of conditions influence how some behaviors come to be defined as deviant, while others are defined as acceptable. We must also realize that no behavior is inherently deviant; therefore, in order for any act to be "deviant" it must be defined, or labeled, as deviant in order to *be* deviant. For the purposes of this text, deviance is defined as any behavior that is labeled by some members of society, especially those in a position of authority or power, or specific subcultural groups, as an unacceptable violation of social norms and codes of morality that may elicit negative reactions from others. Social deviance implies that the study of deviant behavior is directed toward human behavior. When people violate social norms and cultural codes of morality, they are considered deviants.

Five variations of defining deviance were described in this chapter, including the normative, statistical, absolutist, relativist, and reactivist. In many scenarios, elements of one or more perspectives on defining deviance may come into play. The reactivist definition of deviance leads us to the concept of positive deviance, a behavior in which a rule violation generates a positive reaction from others.

Judging and evaluating the behavior of others is a feature common with nearly all humans, and it eventually leads to certain behaviors being labeled "acceptable" and other behaviors as "deviant." Most of us conform to nearly all of the infinite number of social expectations, rules, and laws of society, and this tendency leads us to judge and evaluate those who do not. Still, there are plenty of people who like to express their individuality and engage in behaviors that deviate from the norm.

Many factors influence whether or not a behavior will likely be considered deviant, including issues of morality and ethics; the idea that deviance is a matter of social context, that is to say, the exact same behavior in one context may be acceptable but deviant in another context; definitions of deviance change over time, so behaviors once considered deviant may later become acceptable and conversely, behaviors considered acceptable in the past may later be deemed deviant; and the realization that deviance varies from culture to culture and from subculture to subculture.

Key Terms

absolutist deviance, 4

cannibalism, 16

collective conscience, 5

culture, 20

deviance, 3

deviant, 3

ethics, 14

folkways, 21

honor killings, 22

human cannibalism, 16

ideology, 21

laws, 21

morality, 13

mores, 21

normative deviance, 7

norms, 3

objectum sexuality, 12

positive deviance, 6

reactivist deviance, 5

relativist deviance, 5

social deviance, 3

statistical deviance, 3

stigmatized, 20

subculture, 23

Discussion Questions

1. Think of the deviant wedding ceremonies discussed in this chapter and identify at least two of the examples that seemed the oddest to you. Explain your answer. Have you ever considered marrying anything other than a living human being?

2. Was the Maroon 5 video recording of their hit song "Sugar" deviant? Explain your answer. Would you like Maroon 5 to crash your party? If you could have any musical artist crash your party, wedding or otherwise, who would you choose?

3. Cheating in any class is considered unethical, but it seems worse when it occurs in a class on ethics. What do you think?

4. Is the "right-to-die" movement moral or immoral? Is it ethical or unethical?

5. Is it morally reprehensible for people to desire cannibalism? Is it morally wrong to desire to be a victim of cannibalism?

6. Are people who dress up and act like superheroes deviant?

7. Using the five variations of defining deviance provided in this chapter (normative, statistical, absolutist, relativist, and reactivist), describe whether or not the following behavior is deviant or not: A motorist enters an interstate with a posted 55-miles-per-hour speed limit. The flow of the traffic is speeding along at an average speed of 65 miles per hour, so this motorist also drives 65 miles per hour.

CHAPTER 2

Social Problems and Social Deviance

CHAPTER OBJECTIVES

After reading this chapter students should be able to:

- Explain the concept of "social problems"
- Describe in detail specific examples of social problems
- Analyze the subjective and objective nature of social problems
- Identify a number of reactions to social problems held by people
- Explain the seriousness of unemployment
- Describe how poverty can be viewed as an example of a social problem
- Analyze whether or not obesity is a social problem

During the course of the life cycle individuals go through many different stages, and with each stage come certain social expectations and norms of behavior. Infants and toddlers are given a great deal of leeway in terms of their behaviors, but over time they are expected to develop a number of skills, including learning to behave and obey authority figures, developing language skills (learning how to read and write), learning to cope with others while building friendships, and so on. Once children reach the age of 4 or 5 they go to school, where it is essentially their job to learn a great deal of information and further develop their social skills. Around age 17 or 18, the aging teenager is expected to graduate from high school and begin adulthood. Some of these young adults will join the military, go to college, or start working. After graduating from college, graduates are expected to join the work-force. Thus, by the time most people reach their early 20s, it is the societal norm to work. Working is important both at the micro and macro levels. At the micro level, individuals are expected to work so that they can support themselves (and perhaps their own family of procreation) and not be a drain on society. At the macro level, it takes a viable workforce to keep society running. All adults, then, are expected to work; it is the norm, it is a statistical reality. Sociologist Thorstein Veblen (1964) suggests that working is not just an obligation, it is a human instinct—an "instinct of workmanship." Veblen (1964) describes the instinct of workmanship as a natural desire and willingness to work. He claims that the very survival of the human species has been contingent on workmanship and, furthermore, workmanship is what provides humans with a sense of purpose in life; it allows us to feel as though we have contributed to society in some positive manner.

Interior designers hard at work.

Whether it is an instinct, a societal norm, a means of maintaining self-esteem, or an individual necessity, able-bodied persons (both mentally and physically speaking) are expected to work throughout their adulthood until retirement, and even then, many retired folks will give back to society in one form or another. To not work throughout adulthood, from this perspective, would be considered deviant. But what if we have a scenario wherein two young adults in their 30s are sitting home playing video games in the middle of a workday because they were recently laid off from their jobs; are they deviant? Utilizing the "sociological imagination" will reveal that one person is far more deviant than the other. Let's find out how this is the case.

Explaining Social Problems

In chapter 1, we learned that many variables must be considered before we can define particular acts and behaviors as deviant. The exploration of those variables led to a primary focus on micro forms of deviance. In this chapter, we shall explore how social forces contribute to social problems in a given society for a large number of people, thus leading to a macro orientation in the study of social deviance. By incorporating the study of social problems and its relationship to social deviance we enter the domain of the "sociological imagination."

The **sociological imagination** is a concept created by sociologist C. Wright Mills during his study of human behavior. According to Mills (1959), the sociological imagination reveals how our private lives are influenced by the social environment and the existing societal forces. To highlight the importance of this point, Mills (1959) made distinctions between "the personal troubles of milieu" and "the public issues of social structure" (p. 8). Mills (1959) described troubles and issues as follows:

1. **Personal troubles** occur within the character of the individual and within the range of her or his immediate relations with others. They have to do with the self and with those limited areas of social life of which the person is directly and personally aware.
2. **Public issues** transcend these local environments of the individual and the range of her or his inner life. They have to do with the organization of many milieus into the institutions of a historical society as a whole and from the larger structure of social and historical life (p. 8).

Through this type of reasoning, the sociologist acknowledges that social forces, which are generally completely out of the control of the individual, affect the individual's life for both the good and the bad. If we return to the introductory story of two young adults who were recently laid off from work, we can see the sociological imagination in play. Let's say that person A was laid off from work because she was lazy, showed up for work consistently late, tried to sneak out of work early, and often used her cell phone for personal calls during work hours. Fed up with A's work habits, the employer fires her from her job. Her personal troubles (poor work habits) caused her to lose her job. She is doubly deviant, as she has poor personal character and is unemployed because of it. Person B, however, was laid off because the CEO of the corporation had been embezzling money from the company for years, and after a financial investigation it became apparent that the corporation was no longer viable; they declared bankruptcy and dismissed their entire workforce. While person B is without work, like person A, her discharge was out of her control. She was a hard worker and through no fault of her own, she is a victim of a public issue. In this scenario, person A is far more deviant than person B.

Defining Social Problems

Unemployment is one of many specific topics will we explore as a social problem in this chapter. In order to gain a fuller understanding of what is meant by a "social problem" we should explore definitions and parameters of the concept by experts in the field who have studied social problems. Definitions of the term "social problem" have nearly always included some sort of reference to a social issue found in society that at least some people view as undesirable and/or harmful. Henslin (1994) defined a social problem as "an aspect of society about which people are concerned and one that they would like changed" (pp. 4–5). Sullivan and Thompson (1994) agree with Henslin's notion of a social problem being connected to an issue that negatively affects a segment of the population, but they also put forth the idea that a social problem is a matter of an influential group declaring a particular issue as such. "A social problem exists when an influential group defines a social condition as threatening its values; when the condition affects a large number of people; and when the condition can be remedied by collective action" (Sullivan and Thompson 1994:6). As we can see from this definition, Sullivan and Thompson also place an emphasis on the values of society being compromised as a criterion for designating a particular situation as a social problem. They note, however, that "because values are necessarily ranked in terms of priority in any group or society, there is a disagreement over which conditions will be viewed as social problems (Sullivan and Thompson 1994:6). Some Americans, Sullivan and Thompson (1994) suggest, value hard work and industriousness, and because of this they will come to view those who receive welfare as a social problem and, therefore, deviant. Other Americans may possess strong humanitarian values and argue that poverty, not the poor, is the real social problem.

Heiner (2002) explains that a social problem is both undesirable and harmful to a segment of the population and that it requires collective action in order to eradicate the situation. "Sociologically, a social problem is a phenomenon regarded as bad or undesirable by a significant number of people, or a number of significant people who mobilize to eliminate it" (Heiner 2002:3). Causing harm and mobilization of collective action is important for Diana Kendall as well. "A social problem is a social condition (such as poverty) or pattern of behavior (such as substance abuse) that harms some individuals or all people and that a sufficient number of people believe warrants public concern and collective action to bring about change" (Kendall 2013:2–3).

Building upon the previously established themes of a social problem as a cause of harm to a segment of society and the need for mobilization, John Macionis (2010) defines a social problem as "a condition that undermines the well-being of some or all members of a society and is usually a matter of public controversy" (p. 3). The "condition" that Macionis speaks of refers to any situation (social issue) that at least some people within the community find bothersome or problematic, such as unemployment, living in fear of crime, **homelessness**, poverty, or victimization due to prejudice and discrimination. The "undermines the well-being" of people refers to the realization that people are actually physically or mentally harmed by the given social issue. For example, folks who live in a community where gang activity is prominent are mentally tormented via the gang's intimidation tactics and at risk of being physically harmed, or murdered. The inclusion of "usually a matter of public controversy" that Macionis adds to his definition of social problems is not a universal aspect of all definitions of the term. For Macionis, the idea of a "public controversy" refers to problems that disturb a significant number of people (e.g., lack of proper health care) and yet leads to a disagreement among members of society as how to best address the public issue. Thus, while all Americans understand that there are countless millions of fellow citizens without proper health care, they do not all agree on the best method to solve the situation (e.g., the Affordable Care Act), or whether it is even up to the government to solve the problem. Thus, the public issue of affordable health care is a public controversy.

With all these ideas in mind, we can define **social problems** as social situations found in society that at least some people view as undesirable and/or harmful. Social problems are generally macro forms of deviance and are often created as a result of social institutions that are designed to help those in power maintain their advantageous position in society. The overlap between social problems and social deviance is quite evident as both involve attitudes (generally involving achieved statuses based upon beliefs or convictions), behaviors, and social conditions (generally involving ascribed statuses that are assigned at birth)—what Adler and Adler (2016) describe as the "ABCs of Deviance"—that are deemed undesirable, troublesome, and unwanted.

Claims Making

In cases where there is a lack of public controversy or discourse concerning a particular social issue, government officials, experts in a specific field, or a particular segment of the population may make claims that such a social issue *should* be perceived as a social problem. As Macionis (2010) explains, **claims making** "is the process of convincing the public and important public officials that a particular issue or situation should be defined as a social problem" (p. 5). Theoretically, anyone can make a claim about a particular social issue and assert that it should be treated as a social problem. Macionis cites as an example when, in 1980, women who had lost children in auto accidents caused by drunk drivers joined together to form Mothers Against Drunk Driving (MADD), an organization that (successfully) campaigned for tougher laws against drunk driving. Before this time period, many people regularly drove drunk, but it was not considered a social problem. Currently, there are a handful of people worried about the growing presence of drones in nearly all aspects of life (military, consumer, and personal use) who think that the continued escalation of drone use will cause significant problems in future society and therefore the use of drones should be considered a social problem.

Mobile MADD displays of crashed automobiles are used to demonstrate the potential fatal consequences of drinking and driving.

Macionis (2010) states that the transition from "claims making" to "social problem" involves a process wherein the efforts of the "claims makers" evolve into a social movement. "A social movement is an organized effort at claims making that tries to shape the way people think about an issue in order to encourage or discourage social change" (Macionis 2010:6). Macionis indicates that there are four stages in social movements:

1. Emergence—The initial formation of claims makers describing a particular situation as a public issue that has a negative effect on a number of people.
2. Coalescence—The uniting of people into one body or mass via rallies and demonstrations, political lobbying, creation of online sites, and spreading the word via traditional and social media.

3. Formalization—Social movements begin with volunteers, concerned citizens, and those affected by the situations. The formalization process generally involves hiring trained and salaried staff that have experience in the political arena. The formal organization will attempt to streamline main ideas and concerns in an attempt to gain some sort of official recognition of their social issue.
4. Decline—Inevitably, most social movements come to an end, and they do so for any number of reasons, including meeting their goals; losing momentum and/or running out of money; or takeover by an opposing organization.

At the conclusion of the social movement the claims makers were either successful in reaching enough people to help change the public's view of a situation or it was unsuccessful, leaving those initially affected by the situation searching for new ways to address their claims.

Subjective and Objective Forms of Social Problems

Social problems have subjective and objective components. The **objective** nature of social problems underscores the reality that a particular issue has been acknowledged to exist (e.g., poverty, homelessness, and gang warfare) and that it does cause physical or psychological harm for certain segments of the population. People do not debate the existence of objective social problems. They may not agree on how to best address the situation, but they do agree that it is a social problem. The **subjective** reality of a social problem underscores the idea that "A social condition does not have to be personally experienced by every individual to be considered a social problem" (Leon-Guerrero 2013:9). Subjective social problems come about based on the assertion among certain members of society that a particular social issue (e.g., police brutality directed toward minority males) is indeed a real problem and that it should be treated as such.

The idea that social problems have a subjective aspect originates from the Berger and Luckmann (1966) concept of the "social construction of reality." The **social construction of reality** "refers to how our world is a social creation, originating and evolving through our everyday thoughts and actions. Most of the time, we assume and act as though the world is a given, objectively predetermined outside of our existence. However, according to Berger and Luckmann, we also apply subjective meanings to our existence and experience" (Leon-Guerrero 2013:9). From this perspective, social problems are not simply objective realities; they may be rather unique to a select number of people.

A number of variables surround the labeling of subjective and objective social problems. Subjective social problems may be shrugged off by the mainstream society and deemed inconsequential when compared to objective social problems. Thus, when claims makers make a case for a situation as a social problem, we might witness a backlash against such a claim from the general public. Public opinion and sentiment cannot be a sole criterion to define a situation as a social problem. After all, just because the majority of people of a society may not view a certain situation as a social problem does not mean it is not a problem for those experiencing the situation.

There are also variables involved with the designation of certain situations as objectively problematic. For instance, we need to realize that "objective" social problems may come to be labeled as such because people in power, who may have a hidden agenda, may deem a certain situation as a real problem for their own gain (political, economic, or otherwise). Using a critical constructionist point of view, Heiner also warns of the role of power in determining which public issues are labeled as social problems and which ones are not. Heiner (2002) argues that the public's view of social problems is often "distorted by the power relations involved in the construction of social problems" (p. 11). Consider, for example, during the early 1830s, when the U.S. government deemed Native Americans as a real "social problem" and forcibly relocated them to reservations. "Nearly 125,000 Native Americans lived on millions of acres of land in Georgia, Tennessee, Alabama, North Carolina and Florida—land their ancestors had occupied and cultivated for genera- tions. . . . The federal government forced them to leave their homelands and walk thousands of miles to specially designated 'Indian territory' across the Mississippi River" (History.com 2015). During this march, U.S. soldiers provided blankets infected with smallpox in an attempt to eradicate as many native people as possible along the relocation route. This deadly journey is known as the Trail of Tears. The government decided that the native people were an objective threat to the growth of the United States because a number of white settlers living on the western frontier feared them. Governments and large, powerful corporations around the world often attempt to brainwash the public into believing that their "objective" presentation of events leads to the undeniable conclusion that a certain situation is a social problem or a serious public issue that must be addressed in a specific manner. (See chapter 5 for a discussion on corporate, organized, political, and white collar crime for exam- ples of the role of powerful entities and social deviance.)

Attitudes toward Social Problems

Individual reactions to "claims making" regarding what is, and what is not, a social problem are influenced by personal attitudes and values (Macionis 2010). Among the more common attitudes toward social problems are:

1. The "whatever" attitude—Many people act with indifference toward the many social problems facing society unless the situation directly threatens them. The "whatever" attitude is fueled by the reality that most people have their own personal troubles, duties, responsibilities, and desires; or they simply don't care about the plight of strangers affected by a social problem with no relevance to their own personal lives.
2. Fatalism—Some social problems (e.g., the violent crime associated with liv- ing in a gang-infested neighborhood) seem so overwhelming that people sim- ply accept the negative aspects of a situation as an inescapable fate they must endure. From the fatalistic perspective, poverty is the result of the simple fact that everyone cannot be wealthy.
3. Cynicism—Some people apply a cynical attitude to social problems, arguing that victims have no one else to blame but themselves. From this perspec- tive, the poor are blamed for their misfortune and not the conditions that lead to poverty. Cynics also question the motives of reformers (those who attempt to mobilize others into collective action), believing that they suffer from self-delusion and/or that the reformer's professed sympathy is a façade or an attempt to gain notoriety from the press or general public. For example, in 2014, many people participated in the Ice Bucket Challenge to raise money for ALS (amyotrophic lateral sclerosis) research; more than $115 million was pledged. Critics of the Ice Bucket Challenge claimed that much of the money raised via the trendy phenomenon was spent on ALS Association adminis- tration costs rather than on research. Data provided by the ALS Association

reveals that 28 percent is spent on research with the rest going toward public and professional education (32 percent), patient and community services (19 percent), fund-raising (14 percent), and administration (7 percent) (Richter 2014; ALS Association 2014).

4. Slacktivism—An offshoot of the cynical attitude toward social problems is *slacktivism*— "where people click and post online for social causes with little actual impact on the cause" (Steel 2014). From this perspective, it is argued that a number of people who participated in the Ice Bucket Challenge never actually contributed to ALS Association, and thus their behavior was "basically narcissism masked as altruism" (Steel 2014). Thus, instead of pouring a bucket of ice water over one's own head (a potentially dangerous health concern for some folks, by the way), a truly giving person would quietly donate money to ALS Association (or some other charity) rather than attempting to draw attention to themselves via social media outlets.

5. Religious retribution—The attitude of religious retribution views certain social problems as a sign that God has punished humans for their sins. When the HIV/AIDS epidemic first broke out, some people claimed that God was punishing homosexual activity. Aside from the fact that they had no proof to support such a contention is the simple fact that all people, including heterosexuals, can be infected with HIV/AIDS. The religious retribution attitude would not support possible solutions to such social problems as HIV/AIDS via social policy or institutional change, but instead, would argue for infected persons to pray to God for forgiveness.

A woman pours a bucket of freezing water over a friend as part of the Ice Bucket Challenge to raise money for ALS (amyotrophic lateral sclerosis) research.

6. Violation of common morality—Similar to the religious retribution perspective but not limited to religious ideals is the idea that certain social problems are the result of a violation of common morality. Thus, if an economically poor couple decides to have children but does not have the financial means to support the children, it is the fault of the parents for bringing children into the world and not the responsibility of society to take care of them. Teen mothers would be blamed for violating the codes of morality that suggest they wait until they are married adults before having children. A number of people cite morality issues as their justification against a number of social problems, including abortion, suicide, and unemployment.

7. Rationalistic and scientific—This attitude promotes the idea that social problems can be evaluated in an objective, empirical, honest, and intellectual manner and promotes the notion that social problems can be solved through the use of rational and scientific means. This approach would also mean neutralizing political, religious, and other often irrational approaches toward solving major social problems such as the deteriorating environment.

There are many examples of social problems; in fact, there are far too many to review them all here. However, in the following pages we will examine a number of social problems confronting American society. Many of these same social problems are found in societies across the globe. As we explore these social problems, consider how they are linked to social deviance. The first social problem we will examine is unemployment.

Unemployment

The idea of finding a job and remaining employed throughout one's adult life in order to become a functioning member of society was highlighted in this chapter's introductory story. Employment is necessary so that people can support themselves and their loved ones. Veblen went so far as to suggest that humans have an instinct to work because it gives people a purpose in life. To not work and sustain oneself is nearly always considered deviant. However, if we apply the sociological imagination to the idea of employment, we realize that there are instances when people become unemployed, or underemployed, through no fault of their own but rather because of public issues beyond the control of individuals.

Because of the value placed on being gainfully employed, it should come as no surprise that unemployment has consistently been a major concern among Americans as a leading serious social problem. A 1935 survey of U.S. adults conducted by Gallup revealed that "unemployment and a poor economy" was the number one serious social problem in American society (Macionis 2010). In 2008, a Gallup survey found that "the economy" was the number one concern and "unemployment" was number two (Macionis 2010). The great concern over unemployment and a poor economy in the mid-1930s is understandable, as the United States was then in the midst of the Great Depression.

Unemployment Statistics

Although the U.S. government did not systematically collect statistics on joblessness until 1940, the Bureau of Labor Statistics later estimated that over 12.8 million persons were out of work in 1933, about one-fourth of the civilian labor force of over 51 million (U.S. Department of Labor 2015). Unemployment reached its highest level ever in the United States in March 1933, with about 15.5 million people without work. (The United States reached its all-time low rate of 1.2 percent unemployment in 1944 with nearly all able-bodied persons working in some capacity to help support the World War II effort.) The massive unemployment rate of the mid-1930s contributed to many other social problems and spearheaded a population shift among millions of Americans to leave their farms in search of work. Many farmers lost their livelihoods during the "dust bowl" era in the Great Plains because they were unable to make payments on mortgages. As is generally the case whenever the United States experiences high rates of unemployment, the federal government attempted to stimulate the economy by creating government jobs programs. For example, in 1933, President Franklin D. Roosevelt signed the Federal Emergency Relief Act (FERA), which provided financial assistance to the poor; the National Recovery Administration established codes of "fair competition," a minimum wage, and maximum hours of employment; and the Public Works Administration was established to stimulate major capital improvements programs (U.S. Department of Labor 2015).

Through the decades that followed the Great Depression and the corresponding record-high percentage of unemployment, the United States has experienced numerous recessions and resultant fluctuations in the unemployment rate. One of the most serious setbacks in American employment sectors since 1933 occurred in late 2007 through mid-2009 with the Great Recession. In 2009, the Great Recession of the United States was prolonged because of the ensuing global recession in 2009. The major contributing force behind America's Great Recession was the crash of the overly inflated housing market, which, in turn, brought down large mortgage-backed securities and derivatives, causing a negative rippling effect in the economy. A crippling economy contributes to higher rates of unemployment, and in October 2009 unemployment reached the double digits at 10.0 percent (U.S. Department of Labor, Bureau of Labor Statistics 2015a). The unemployment rate was consistently over 9 percent from April 2009 through September 2011. However, from October 2011 through January 2015 the unemployment rate continued to go down; it was at 5.7 percent in January 2015 (U.S. Department of Labor, Bureau of Labor Statistics 2015a).

Defining Unemployment

Although the concept **unemployment** is quite clear, defined by the U.S. Department of Labor, Bureau of Labor Statistics (2015b), as "people who are jobless, looking for a job, and available for work," the measurement of unemployment is not so straightforward. The Bureau of Labor Statistics (BLS) does not, of course, track every single person in the United States. Rather it takes a sample of about 60,000 households on a monthly basis; this translates into approximately 110,000 individuals each month. The sample is considered representative of the entire U.S. population (U.S. Department of Labor, Bureau of Labor Statistics 2015b). When calculating the unemployment rate, the BLS considers the following people as unemployed:

- All those who did not have a job at all during the survey reference week, made at least one specific active effort to find a job during the prior 4 weeks, and were available for work (unless temporarily ill).
- All those who were not working and were waiting to be called back to a job from which they had been laid off. (They need not be looking for work to be classified as unemployed.) (U.S. Department of Labor, Bureau of Labor Statistics 2015b).

It is important to also recognize that the national unemployment rate (as described above) is determined by calculating the number of people in the labor force who are not working. The **labor force** is a "measure of the sum of the employed and unemployed. In other words, the labor force level is the number of people who are either working or actively seeking work" (U.S. Department of Labor, Bureau of Labor Statistics 2015b). People who are not considered part of the labor force include college students and retired persons. Family responsibilities keep a number of people (e.g., parents who do not work so that they can raise their children and adults who care for family members on a full-time basis) out of the labor force. "Since the mid-1990s, typically fewer than 1 in 10 people not in the labor force reported that they want a job" (U.S. Department of Labor, Bureau of Labor Statistics 2015b).

The monthly employment reports and Economic News Releases (i.e., "The Employment Situation") generated by the Bureau of Labor Statistics are among the most-watched indicators of the U.S. economy. The unemployment rate in particular is one of the most important indicators of the strength of the American economy. Unofficially, it has become a measure of overall satisfaction with the government and political leaders, as the employment/unemployment data reveals a great deal about the direction of the nation's economy. BLS data reports describe the labor situation based on a number of variables, including gender, race, and age categories (teenagers or adults), and concentrates on the civilian labor force. The data provides a great deal of information about employment trends as well. For example, the January 2015 Employment Situation report indicated that the civilian labor force rose by 703,000 in January 2015 (U.S. Department of Labor, Bureau of Labor Statistics 2015c). This figure equates to an increase of 0.2 percent of the labor force, raising the total participation rate of the labor force in the United States up 62.9 percent (January 2015). The Employment Situation report also provides data on "discouraged workers." **Discouraged workers** are "persons not currently looking for work because they believe no jobs are available for them" (U.S. Department of Labor, Bureau of Labor Statistics 2015c).

Causes of Unemployment

The statistical data provided by the Bureau of Labor Statistics described above clearly reveals that there are millions of people unemployed at all times. We already learned that students, retired persons, and those with family responsibilities are not considered part of the labor force and therefore are not counted as "unemployed." So let's next turn our attention to those who are in the labor force and yet remain unemployed and identify some of the causes of their unemployment. A number of personal troubles and public issues might cause a person to be unemployed. Among the personal troubles that contribute to unemployment is the realization that a number of people are too lazy or unwilling to work. Such people may have acquired poor work habits (e.g., showed up late for work, left work early, took extended breaks, never performed assigned job duties, and spent work time checking electronic devices for personal reasons) while they did work and now find it hard to find a job. In some cases, people simply do not look for work because they don't want to work, and they are likely to turn to the government, friends, or families for support. Some people, especially high-school dropouts, may lack the necessary job skills to find gainful employment in the ever-expanding technologically driven economy. There are also a number of people suffering from alcoholism (see chapter 7) and other drug addictions (see chapter 8) that hamper their employment prospects. These are just three possible examples of people with personal troubles who may find themselves unemployed.

Sociologists and economists often discuss the concept of frictional unemployment as a factor in joblessness. **Frictional unemployment** is one of the most recurring causes of unemployment and stems from the temporary transitions that people take when graduating from college and looking for employment or when workers leave one job in search of a better one. Frictional unemployment isn't so much a "trouble," but it does represent a personal decision and cannot be blamed on public issues. (See box 2.1 for a further look at possible public issues explanations for unemployment.)

A CLOSER LOOK

Box 2.1 Public Issues Explanations for Unemployment

There are a number of possible public issues explanations for unemployment, including the sampling listed below:

1. **Outsourcing** may cause a number of people to become unemployed. Outsourcing occurs when a company moves its operations away from one market to another, generally to another country where labor and/or raw materials are cheaper. In this scenario, as with all public issues, the worker was acting in good faith but lost his or her job because of a situation outside their control.

2. A number of companies move overseas because they claim the United States has some of the highest business taxes in the world.

3. The scarcity of job openings in many socio-economic sectors means fewer people finding employment. Such a scenario is especially prevalent during a recession.

4. Government sector jobs often face elimination as state and local governments continually attempt to cut costs.

5. Employers that downsize the number of full-time workers and increase the number of part-time workers in an attempt to eliminate paying health benefits to employees. Colleges and universities are contributing to this downsizing trend by hiring part-time instructors instead of tenure-track positions.

6. **Structural unemployment**, the mismatch of skills in the labor force to the composition of the local industry, may lead to unskilled local people being unemployable or skilled local people without the proper industry to find employment.

7. **Cyclical unemployment** occurs when there is not enough demand for goods and services in the market to provide enough employment opportunities for all who want to work.

8. Mismanagement, corruption, and illegal activities (to be discussed in further detail in chapter 4) on the part of ownership/management may cause a company to go bankrupt or be shut down by the government, leading to layoffs of innocent workers.

Long-term unemployment is not only potentially financially destructive, it can be physiologically (unemployed people often lack health insurance), emotionally, and psychologically (e.g., poor self-esteem and a poor sense of worth) disparaging. Long-term unemployment can contribute to numerous social problems, such as physical and/or mental illness, marital and familial conflict, sleeplessness, low self-esteem, depression, poverty, and in some cases, suicide.

Unemployment and Social Deviance

Undoubtedly, unemployment is a social problem. At the macro level, an entire society may suffer if large numbers of people are unemployed. At the micro level, individuals who are unemployed and looking for work, and need to work to support themselves and others (e.g., spouse and children), may suffer financially, emotionally, and physically. However, we still have to address the issue at hand in this chapter, is this social problem connected to social deviance in any manner? Ideally, as suggested (for this social problem and all remaining social problems to be discussed), you have been thinking about the link between unemployment and

A significant number of people in society resort to begging for work opportunities in order to raise enough money for food to eat.

social deviance. So what do you think? How does unemployment relate to social deviance?

If we begin at the macro level, functionalists would tell us that unemployment puts a strain on the entire social system and such disequilibrium would be considered deviant for the well-being of society. Conflict theorists would inform us that workers are always disadvantaged by those who control the means of production and thus the entire employment sector is deviant. They would also point out that those in power always seem to remain financially viable even if it's at the expense of the labor force. Critical theorists would point out that unemployment contributes to an imbalance in society that benefits the privileged at the expense of the masses. Utilizing a Marxist perspective, critical theorists would argue that labor is never rewarded as equally as ownership and that capitalism is alienating because it is not harmonious with the social world (Held 1980).

At the micro level, we have learned that some people are unemployed by choice, while others are unemployed due to circumstances beyond their control. Generally, we would not consider a person who is suddenly unemployed because of outsourcing or corporate mismanagement, fraud, or illegal activities as being a deviant, as such a person had worked in good faith only to have their job eliminated. There are those who are unemployed by choice, and yet their circumstances may be quite different. College students, caregivers, and retired persons would rarely be considered deviant because they were unemployed. On the other hand, people who are too lazy to work and take care of themselves are likely to be viewed as deviant.

Social Stratification and Poverty

Every society has some degree of social stratification. Stratification can be viewed as a ranking system; that is to say, society is stratified into layers based on a number of criteria, including socioeconomic status (SES). A critical aspect of stratification is the realization that these different strata have a corresponding value component that characterizes some people as having higher social status than others. **Social stratification** can be defined as "a system for ranking members of a social system into levels with different or unequal evaluations" (Delaney 2012a:221). Being wealthy, of course, is more valuable than being poor. It is interesting that in a land that promotes equality between all, the United States maintains a laissez-faire economic policy. As a result, the disparity in wealth in the United States is among the highest in the world. The gap in wealth disparity has been rising for the past four decades. In 2013, the U.S. wealth disparity reached the highest level since the Great Depression. "The wealthiest 160,000 families own as much wealth as the poorest 145 million families" (Matthews 2014). Put another way, the top 0.1 percent of households (the 160,000 families with total net assets of more than $20 million in 2012) controlled 22 percent of the total wealth in 2012; in 1970 the top 0.1 percent of families owned just 7 percent of the total wealth. "For the bottom 90 percent of families, a combination of rising debt, the collapse of the value of their assets during the financial crisis [the Great Recession], and stagnant real wages have led to the erosion of wealth" (Monaghan 2014). Although not as extreme as the disparity in wealth, there is also a significant income disparity in the United States. "The share of total income earned by the top 1 percent of families was less than 10 percent in the late 1970s but now exceeds 20 percent as of the end of 2012" (Matthews 2014). When it comes to social problems, it is poverty that is generally labeled the "problem" and not the disparity in wealth and income. Certainly it is the poor who suffer the most as a result of wealth and income disparity.

Defining Poverty

Nearly all of us can conjure an image of poverty conditions, or of poor people. This image may even coincide with our previous discussion on homelessness. Poverty itself refers to a social condition, while being poor describes people. "At its core, poverty restricts people's ability to live a decent life because it imposes restrictions on what they can buy or do, and hence be. Those who are poor must devote all of their resources to meeting their basic needs, with nothing left over with which to exercise the freedom to consume and participate" (Saunders 2005:59). With this in mind, we can define **poverty** as the lack of basic necessities, goods, or financial means of support.

Poverty has existed throughout most of history and across the globe, and for the most part, it was simply a fact of life for the masses. During its history, the United States has also played witness to poverty. An attempt to end poverty began in 1964 when President Lyndon B. Johnson declared a "War on Poverty" during his first State of the Union address. Acknowledging poverty as a social problem of national concern, Johnson set into motion a series of bills and acts that created a number of social programs designed to combat poverty. Many of these programs still exist today, including Medicare, Medicaid, Head Start, food stamps, and work-study. In order to determine whether or not the war on poverty was being won, specific standards, or thresholds, were established in order to measure poverty.

A key variable in the measurement of poverty was the cost of food. A researcher for the Social Security Administration, Mollie Orshansky (1963, 1965), determined that food represented about one-third of after-tax income for the typical family. In 1969, the U.S. Bureau of Budget, now the Office of Management and Budget, used Orshansky's variable of food representing one-third of the after-tax income of families and established a number of poverty thresholds with a multiplier of three based on different family size, number of children, age and sex of the head of the family, and farm or nonfarm residence. Since 1969, the government computes a low-cost food budget and multiplies by three, yielding a determination that those whose incomes are less than this amount should be considered poor and those earning above this figure as not poor. As an example, the poverty threshold for a family of four living in the 48 continuous states (there are different thresholds for Alaska and Hawaii) was $24,250 in 2015 (U.S. Department of Health and Human Services 2015a). The poverty threshold for a single person was set at $11,770.

The Demographics of Poverty

It has been more than 50 years since President Lyndon Johnson used his first State of the Union address to declare war on poverty. We have not won the war. According to data compiled by the U.S. Census Bureau nearly 50 million (48.8 million) people, or 15.8 percent of the U.S. population, had income below the poverty level threshold (Bishaw and Fontenot 2014). The CDC also measures the poorest of the poor: "In 2013, the percentage of people in the United States with income below 125 percent of their poverty threshold was 20.6 percent. The proportion of people with an income-to-poverty ratio less than 50 percent was 7.0 percent" (Bishaw and Fontenot 2014).

Citing U.S. Census data, the Pew Research Center has complied a great deal of information on the demographics of poverty:

- Most poor Americans are in their prime working years—In 2012, 57 percent of poor Americans were ages 18 to 64 (DeSilver 2014).
- The percentage of elderly living in poverty has decreased—In 1966, 28.5 percent of Americans ages 64 and over were poor; in 2012, the percentage dropped to 9.1 percent (DeSilver 2014).
- The feminization of poverty—In 1973, more than half (51.4 percent) of poor families were headed by a married couple, and 45.4 percent were headed by women; in 2012, slightly more than half (50.3 percent) of poor families were female-headed, and 38.9 percent were headed by married couples (DeSilver 2014).
- Poverty is heaviest in the South—While poverty is more evenly distributed throughout regions of the United States today than in the past, the South region has a much higher percent of people living below the poverty line. "In 2012, the South was home to 37.3% of all Americans and 41.1% of the nation's poor people; though the South's poverty rate, 16.5%, was the highest among the four Census-designated regions [West, Midwest, Northeast, and South], it was only 3.2 percentage points above the lowest (the Midwest)" (DeSilver 2014).
- The poverty rate has fallen for African Americans—In 1966, 41.8 percent of blacks were poor compared to 27.2 percent in 2012. Still, this figure is more than twice the rate of poverty for whites (12.7 percent) (DeSilver 2014).
- The poverty rate has risen for Hispanics—In 1972 (the first year such data was collected), 22.8 percent of Hispanics lived below the poverty threshold; in 2012, however, the rate increased to 25.6 percent. It should also be noted that during this same time period the U.S. Hispanic population has quintupled (DeSilver 2014).

A significant number of people work full- or part-time and yet still live in poverty. These people are referred to as the "working poor." The **working poor** are those persons who spent at least 27 weeks in the labor force, working or looking for work, but whose incomes still fall below the official poverty thresholds (U.S. Department of Labor, Bureau of Labor Statistics 2013). The Department of Labor's Bureau of Labor Statistics reports that 10.4 million individuals were considered as "working poor" in 2011. This figure translates to a "working-poor rate"—the ratio of the working poor to all individuals in the labor force for at least 27 weeks—of

7 percent (U.S. Department of Labor, Bureau of Labor Statistics 2013). As one might expect, full-time workers were less likely to be among the working poor than part-time workers. "Among persons in the labor force for 27 weeks or more, 4.2 percent of those usually employed full time were classified as working poor, compared with 14.4 percent of part-time workers" (U.S. Department of Labor, Bureau of Labor Statistics 2013). The working poor are more likely to be women than men, and blacks and Hispanics are more likely to be working poor than Asians and whites. The working poor are more likely to be poorly educated: just 2.4 percent of those in the labor force for at least 27 weeks were college graduates compared with 20.1 percent of those with less than a high school diploma. The working poor are concentrated in nonprofessional or service-oriented occupations such as sales clerks and restaurant workers (especially dishwashers and waitresses) (U.S. Department of Labor, Bureau of Labor Statistics 2013).

Child Poverty

According to the Pew Research Center, the percentage of children (those below 18 years old) living in poverty in 2012 was nearly 22 percent (21.8 percent) (DeSilver 2014). While any type of poverty is a social problem, child poverty is especially problematic in that children rarely control their situation. Furthermore, because children are still developing, lacking basic necessities can cause a child to have emotional, behavioral, or physiological problems throughout their lives. Living in poverty may also hinder a child's ability to learn and compromise their level of educational attainment. As explained by Dearing and Wade (2006), there are four major negative effects of poverty on child development:

1. Poverty affects child functioning in most areas of development, although effects are greater for cognitive and language achievement than for physical and mental health.
2. Poverty experiences during early childhood have greater negative effects compared with impoverishment during later life stages.
3. Effects become increasingly negative the longer children live in poverty.
4. Effects are transmitted through family investments and family stress (Dearing and Wade 2006:1015).

The physical health risks associated with childhood poverty include elevated blood lead levels, chronic illness, and growth retardation, which, in turn, become risk factors for later developmental problems such as lowered intelligence, school failure, and obesity (Dearing and Wade 2006). The mental health problems confronting poor children include a greater likelihood of depression (internalizing the problem of poverty) and aggressive behavioral problems (externalizing the problem of poverty). Poverty is also a risk factor to children's cognitive and language development, and these issues are likely to cause problems in school, which may result in a greater likelihood of repeating grades, being placed in special education classes, and dropping out of school (Dearing and Wade 2006). Children who experience poverty are also more likely to fall into the "cycle of poverty." The cycle of poverty refers to the phenomenon wherein poor families become trapped in poverty for multiple generations because they never attained the necessary resources, such as education and financial stability, to raise themselves above poverty thresholds.

Poverty and Social Deviance

Previously, the term *poverty* was defined as "the lack of basic necessities, goods, or financial means of support." This definition does not lend itself toward an implication of the poor as social deviants. However, if the definition of poverty was modified a bit, like the one provided by *Merriam-Webster Dictionary* (2015)—"The state of one who lacks a usual or socially acceptable amount of money or material possession"—being poor (lacking a "socially acceptable" amount of money or material possession) might qualify as a form of social deviance if we equate "socially acceptable" with "normative." As with many social problems, especially those discussed here, personal troubles account for a portion of those living in poverty, but it is public issues that contribute to the fate of most poor people. One could argue, however, that poor people who violate the laws of the land in order to attain their basic necessities are being deviant.

Presumably, we would excuse children raised in poverty from the category of social deviance, as their fate was out of their control. It is the responsibility of parents to take care of their children and provide for them the necessities of life. Children are merely expected to attend school and learn the necessary skills to become productive members of society. If they cause trouble in school or drop out of school, we might look at them as deviant. However, as we learned, childhood poverty is associated with a number of developmental problems, problems that may not have surfaced if they were raised in a nonpoor environment.

While it is poverty that is considered a social problem, perhaps those who have, or control, a disproportionate amount of resources are the real deviants. How is it socially acceptable for one individual or family to possess enough resources that, if distributed to others, could benefit a dozen, or dozens, or hundreds of other families?

A man works on his car in a poor neighborhood of South Bronx, New York.

In Western societies like the United States, the accumulation of wealth is generally praised, while the lack of wealth is frowned upon. Andrew Abbott (2014) is among those who attempt to draw a connection between many of our social problems and the culture of accepting excess as the norm. "Budget constraints, tradeoffs, impoverishment: these are concepts of scarcity. Confronted with excess, we nevertheless make scarcity the center of our attention" (Abbott 2014:1). If we use the statistical perspective on deviance, having an excessive amount of wealth is more deviant than being poor. And yet the normative perspective of deviance indicates that being poor is deviant because it goes against the expectations society has placed on individuals.

When discussing "excess," we are more likely to associate the expanding social problem of obesity as deviant than we are the great accumulation of wealth. With that in mind, we shift our attention to the social problem of obesity.

Obesity

Obesity and being overweight is a growing national social problem in the United States, as well as in many nations across the world. Obesity has a negative impact on individuals and society in general. For obese individuals, there is the obvious concern over their physical and psychological health as well as the negative economic impact on their personal lives. Obesity also places a considerable strain on society through increased health care costs and disability payments, especially those that are pooled through group health insurance and public programs.

Defining Obesity

Although the "eye test" (visual verification) often helps us to categorize individuals as overweight or obese, such a measurement is hardly scientific. As a result, a more clinical explanation of "overweight" and "obesity" is provided by the CDC. The CDC uses two variables—weight and height—to determine the categorization of overweight and obesity. For adults, the most common method used to measure being overweight and obese is the body mass index, commonly known as the BMI. "BMI is used because, for most people, it correlates with their amount of body fat" (CDC 2012). Body fat, more accurately described as adipose tissue, stores energy and cushions and insulates the body; however, an excessive amount of fat can cause a great deal of harm to the human body. Body fat is located primarily beneath the skin, but it can also be found around internal organs. The BMI, while correlating with body fat, does not measure the amount of fat in an individual's body.

While calculators are available on multiple online sites to determine one's BMI, the formula works like this: take one's weight (in pounds) and multiply by 703, then divide this number by one's height (in inches) squared. The CDC (2012) has established parameters for BMI results: a BMI score below 18.5 is considered underweight; BMI score between 18.5 to 24.9 is healthy weight; 25.0 to 29.9 is considered overweight; and a BMI score 30 or higher is considered obese. There is also a category of morbid obesity (BMI above 40). Utilizing the CDC's approach, **obesity** is defined as having a BMI score between 30 and 40. While a number of people who calculate their own BMI may be surprised to learn that they are overweight or obese, the measurement is quite effective except for people who have an excessive amount of muscle weight. The BMI does not factor in muscle weight, and since muscles weigh more than fat, a very fit and athletic person with a great deal of muscle weight may mistakenly be labeled as obese. Thus, the BMI is not a good measuring device of obesity if one is very muscular. Conversely, unless the individual is pumping iron regularly, the BMI measurement is quite accurate.

In cases where the BMI may not be the best method to measure obesity, assessing one's risk of developing overweight- or obesity-related diseases can, according to the National Heart, Lung, and Blood Institute, be measured by looking at two other predictors: "The individual's waist circumference (because abdominal fat is a predictor of risk for obesity-related diseases). [And] other risk factors the individual has for diseases and conditions associated with obesity (for example, high blood pressure or physical inactivity)" (CDC 2012).

The Demographics of Obesity

According to the CDC (2014c), more than 1 in 3 (35.1 percent) of American adults age 20 years and over are obese, and a nearly equal number of people are overweight, equating to 69 percent of American adults age 20 and over as overweight. Six percent of American adults are considered morbidly obese (Begley 2012). Adults are not the only Americans who are obese. The CDC (2014c) reports that 12.1 percent of children age 2 to 5 are obese; 18 percent of children age 6 to 11 are obese; and 18.4 percent of adolescents age 12 to 19 are obese. When examining the racial/ethnic demographics of obese American adults, it is revealed that "Non-Hispanic blacks have the highest age-adjusted rates of obesity (47.8 percent) followed by Hispanics (42.5 percent), non-Hispanic whites (32.6 percent), and non-Hispanic Asians (10.8 percent)" (2014d). Obesity is highest for middle-aged (40 to 59 years old) adults (39.5 percent), followed closely by older (60 or above) adults (39.4 percent), and lowest with younger (age 20 to 39) adults (35.4 percent) (CDC 2014d). When examining obesity and socioeconomic status, the CDC (2014d) reports that "Among non-Hispanic black and Mexican-American men, those with higher incomes are more likely to have obesity than those with low income. Higher income women are less likely to have obesity than low-income women. There is no significant relationship between obesity and education among men. Among women, however, there is a trend—those with college degrees are less likely to have obesity compared with less educated women."

Obesity is an escalating social problem around the world. According to the World Health Organization (2015a), "Worldwide obesity has more than doubled since 1980. In 2014, more than 1.9 billion adults, 18 years and older, were overweight. Of these over 600 million were obese." It is interesting to note that in a world where millions of people, especially young children, die each year because of being underweight, "most of the world's population live in countries where overweight and obesity kills more people than underweight" (WHO 2015a).

The World Health Organization (2015a) reminds us that "obesity is preventable." It is preventable because, for most people, being overweight or obese is a simple matter of taking in more calories than the body burns off. Thus, proper diet and exercise will keep nearly everyone in the "healthy weight" BMI category. From this regard, being overweight and obese is a matter of social conditions and individual lifestyle choices. For some people, however, biology plays a role in obesity. Below, we will take a quick look at some of the biological and social causes of obesity.

Causes of Obesity

Many people struggle with reaching and maintaining their ideal weight. It seems that regardless of the diet and exercise program they implement, losing weight is a difficult challenge and most likely one that continues throughout the life course. This perception of the difficulty of fighting off obesity is reinforced by research that indicates "About 90% of people who lose weight dieting gain every pound back regardless of their weight-loss method" (Health Central 2015). There are a number of biological and social explanations as to why people have such a hard time reaching a healthy weight.

From a biological perspective, we can look at how the process of an appetite works; after all, if losing weight is as theoretically simple as burning off more calories than one consumes, we simply need to limit our consumption of unhealthy foods. "Appetite is determined by processes that occur both in the brain and gastrointestinal tract. Eating patterns are controlled by areas of the hypothalamus and pituitary glands (in the brain)" (Health Central 2015). Appetite is triggered by a number of molecules in the body, including leptin. Leptin is a hormone that fat cells release in order to help regulate energy balance by reducing appetite. When someone has low levels of leptin, they feel hungry and an appetite develops. Some people genetically have low levels of leptin, which tricks the brain into thinking it is always hungry, often resulting in overeating and weight gain (Health Central 2015). Rogers (1999), on the other hand, argues that appetite is tied to an unevenness of food supply across time (a social factor). "Consequently, when food is abundant, the diet is energy dense and energy expenditure is low, there is a strong tendency to become obese. . . . Under such conditions the most common method of avoiding obesity is through the cognitive control of eating" (p. 59). Conversely, when food is scarce, a greater amount of energy is exerted to secure food and a lower amount of food is consumed, thus making obesity less likely to occur.

Some people retain high levels of body fat because of their insulin regulation within the body. Insulin, a hormone created in the pancreas, helps to direct the storage and usage of energy in the body by turning the food we eat into glucose, or sugar, for our bodies to use for energy. As Wilborn and associates (2005) explain, improper regulation of insulin can result in excess energy storage, commonly in the form of body fat. People with diabetes have a particularly hard time with insulin, as the body either doesn't make enough of it or cannot use its own insulin as well as it should, leading sugar to build up in the blood. Diabetes can cause a number of health complications, including heart disease, blindness, kidney failure, and lower-extremity amputations. "Diabetes is the seventh leading cause of death in the United States" (CDC 2014e).

Those with thyroid problems or low metabolism may also have a biological inclination in their difficulty in fighting off body fat. "Long before the definition of the metabolic syndrome, alterations in thyroid function were reported in obese patients. Body composition and thyroid hormones appear to be closely related since the latter is known to be involved in the regulation of basal metabolism and thermogenesis, playing an important role in lipid and glucose metabolism, food intake and fat oxidation" (Longhi and Radetti 2013:41). If the thyroid gland, which is located in the neck, does not produce enough thyroid hormone, our metabolism slows down, and a slower metabolism can contribute to weight gain.

There are many social factors to be considered as well when attempting to find plausible causes of obesity. The social learning theory perspective would claim that children model the behaviors of their parents. Thus, if the parents are eating a proper diet and provide a nutritious diet to their children, the children are less likely to become overweight or obese. In addition to providing healthy nutrition standards to stave off obesity in their children, adults need to teach portion control and the value of moderation in food consumption as well as instill the value of physical activity.

There are occasions when children may not want to try healthy foods introduced to them by their parents. Such a fear is known as **food neophobia**—the fear of trying new foods. Neophobia is believed to be a trait that was originally meant to prevent humans from ingesting harmful or toxic materials by inducing the fear of trying something new (Cooke, Haworth, and Wardle 2007). Food neophobia in the contemporary era is generally an unnecessary trait, as most food is safe for consumption; nonetheless, it may serve as a barrier when parents try to get their children to eat their vegetables. Sweet and sugary foods are more desirable to the palates of children and, understandably, it is more likely that the child will choose a sugary treat over a vegetable (Cooke et al. 2007). Cooke and associates (2007) claim that because food neophobia is a genetic trait, "parents can be assured that their child's reluctance to try new foods is not simply the result of poor parental feeding practices, but it is partly in the genes" (p. 432). Still, new foods can be introduced to children through repeated presentation and role modeling, as children viewing their parents eating nutritious foods such as vegetables will learn that such foods are not harmful.

Changes in the socioeconomic employment sector have also contributed to the expanding waistlines of people. Many people find themselves sitting at a desk all day long while at work. They drive a car or take a train to work and nearly everywhere they need to go (rather than walking or riding a bicycle, which equates to exercise). People expect most businesses (e.g., banks, coffee shops, and fast-food restaurants) to have a drive-thru window so that they can stay in their car to avoid the minimal amount of effort it takes to park the car and walk inside a place of business. Many folks spend much of their nonwork time sitting and watching television, playing video games, or using electronic devices as a means of recreation. Physical activity is now something that most people have to schedule into their daily routines, often blowing it off because they "don't have enough time." All of this physical inactivity equates to a sedentary lifestyle.

It was once considered deviant to be so inactive, but today it is the norm for many people. According to America's Health Rankings (2014), slightly more than 1 in 4 (25.3 percent) adult Americans report doing no physical activity or exercise (such as running, calisthenics, golf, gardening, or walking) other than their regular job in the last 30 days. Mississippi (38.1 percent) is home to the highest percentage of physically inactive people, while Colorado (17.9 percent) has the lowest percentage of physically inactive people (America's Health Rankings 2014). The sedentary lifestyle adopted by so many people in contemporary society is certainly a contributing factor to obesity. The coexistence of obesity and sedentary behavior is a leading factor associated with cardiovascular disease (CVD) (Barnes and Coulter 2012).

Technology has added to the sedentary lifestyle of many people. Advancements in so many spheres of life, including home maintenance requirements, have freed people from a great deal of physical labor. Microwaves and partially made store-bought food allow meals to be prepared quicker than ever before; dishwashers, vacuum cleaners, washing machines, and other appliances have alleviated a great deal of time once needed to do housework; and gas and electric, propane, or other heating systems have freed people from the chore of cutting and splitting wood or shoveling coal into a furnace. These are just a few examples of devices that freed most people from labor in their daily lives. It's actually ironic that people claim not to have time to work out or exercise when so many people have so far fewer manual labor responsibilities today when compared to the past.

Decades ago (1950s–1970s) it was common for families to enjoy home-cooked meals, but many parents—primarily because of economic demands (the need for both parents to work or a single parent to work more than one job)—are too busy working a job to prepare healthy meals and opt to stop at the fast-food drive-thru on the way home from work instead. If it's not fast food being served at home, many people are eating processed foods, which are generally unhealthy because of the sodium and preservatives. Highly caffeinated energy drinks and sugary sodas are also common food-choice items among adults and children. Nearly all food commercials targeted at youth are for products with high sugar, fat, and sodium contents. In 2009, the food industry spent $1.8 billion in U.S. marketing targeted to young people (Powell, Harris, and Fox 2013). The marketers do a good job in promoting their unhealthy foods, and when combined with the reality that most people like sugary treats, there is little wonder that an increasing number of people are becoming overweight and obese.

Health Concerns Associated with Obesity

As one would expect, there is a long list of health concerns associated with obesity, including some of the leading causes of preventable death: coronary heart disease, high blood pressure, stroke, type 2 diabetes, abnormal blood fats, metabolic syndrome, a variety of cancers (e.g., endometrial, breast, and colon), osteoarthritis, sleep apnea, obesity hypoventilation syndrome, reproductive problems (e.g., menstrual issues and infertility in women), and gallstones (National Heart, Lung and Blood Institute 2012; CDC 2014d; WHO 2015a).

The risk for coronary heart disease (CHD) increases as one's body mass index rises. "CHD is a condition in which a waxy substance called plaque (plak) builds up inside the coronary arteries. These arteries supply oxygen-rich blood to your heart. Plaque can narrow or block the coronary arteries and reduce blood flow to the heart muscle" (NHLBI 2012). Coronary arteries blockage can result in angina (chest pain or discomfort) or heart failure. The heart receives the necessary blood via blood pressure—the force of blood pushing against the walls of the arteries as the heart pumps blood. If this pressure stays high over a period of time, it can damage the body in a variety of ways (NHLBI 2012). Overweight, and especially obese people, run a high risk for high blood pressure. The aforementioned plaque buildup in one's arteries may cause a blood clot to form, and if this clot is close to the brain, "it can block the flow of blood and oxygen to your brain and cause a stroke" (NHLBI 2012). There is a positive correlation between the rise in one's BMI and the likelihood of suffering a stroke.

Diabetes was previously described, but it is worth repeating that obese people run a higher risk of become a type 2 diabetic. "Diabetes is a leading cause of early death, CHD, stroke, kidney disease, and blindness. Most people who have type 2 diabetes are overweight" (NHLBI 2012). Diabetics generally have their blood tested for sugar levels and have blood work done to measure their levels of triglycerides, LDL ("bad") cholesterol, and HDL ("good") cholesterol. When the measures are abnormal, the diabetic runs a greater risk for CHD. Levels of triglycerides, LDL, and HDL along with a large waistline and high blood pressure are all risk factors under the metabolic syndrome umbrella, and all these risk factors raise one's risk for heart disease and other health problems (NHLBI 2012). As for cancer, "being overweight or obese raises your risk for colon, breast, endometrial, and gallbladder cancers" (NHLBI 2012).

Osteoarthritis is a highly disabling degenerative disease to the joints (WHO 2015a). The more one weighs, the greater the pressure placed on joints. As the joints wear down, this will cause pain.

Overweight and obese persons run the risk of breathing disorders such as sleep apnea (one or more pauses in breathing or shallow breaths while you sleep) and obesity hypoventilation syndrome (OHS) (too much carbon dioxide—hypoventilation—or too little oxygen in the blood—hypoxemia). OHS can lead to a number of serious health problems, including death, and sleep apnea is likely caused by fat stored around the neck (NHLBI 2012).

People who are overweight or obese also run the risk of suffering from gall-stones, hard pieces of stone-like material formed in the gallbladder made mostly of cholesterol. Gallstones can cause stomach or back pain (NHLBI 2012).

Obesity as Deviant Behavior

Is it deviant to be overweight or obese? To best answer that question we should apply the five different perspectives of defining deviance (see chapter 1). The normative perspective of deviance would point out that people should strive for a "healthy weight" as determined by such measures as waistline size, signs of risk factors (e.g., high blood pressure or physical inactivity), and the calculations utilized by the BMI. From the normative perspective, the review of health problems associated with being overweight and obese should be enough of a stimulus to motivate people to strive for a healthy weight. Because of this, the normative perspective of deviance would view obesity as deviant, if for no other reason than all of the negative health concerns associated with being overweight and obese.

From the statistical perspective, deviance is that which is unusual, rare, or uncommon. The data provided here revealed that 35.1 percent of American adults are obese and 69 percent of American adults are overweight; and, worldwide, more than 1.9 billion adults are overweight and 600 million of those are obese. Statistically speaking, it would be more uncommon to be of healthy weight than overweight. Thus, from the statistical perspective of deviance, obese people are not deviants.

The absolutist definition of deviance argues that certain behaviors are inherently deviant regardless of context, times, and the diversity of the members of a society. While there are some people in society who find obesity morally wrong, there isn't a prevailing sentiment in society that obesity is absolutely deviant based on a religious, social, scientific, or international morality edict.

The relativist perspective on social deviance deserves special attention when discussing obesity, especially when talking about the costs of obesity to society. Various subcultures, such as those who are not overweight, employers, insurance providers, and health officials, are more likely to view obesity as a form of social deviance, as relativists examine deviance in terms of its relevance to specific circumstances, conditions, and social environments. The estimated medical spending cost attributed to obesity was $147 billion in 2008 (Finkelstein, Trogdon, Cohen, and Dietz 2009). As the cost of medical services increases and the number of obese people increases, it is not surprising to learn that medical spending costs attributed to obesity climbed to $190 billion (20.6 percent of U.S. health care expenditures) in 2011 (Begley 2012). The costs attributed to treating the obese are often borne by the non-obese. Begley (2012) compares this realization to secondhand smoke. "Only when scientists discovered that nonsmokers were developing lung cancer and other diseases from breathing smoke-filled air did policymakers get serious about fighting the habit, in particular by establishing nonsmoking zones. The costs that smoking added to Medicaid also spurred action. Now, as economists put a price tag on sky-high **body mass indexes (BMIs)**, policymakers as well as the private sector are mobilizing to find solutions to the obesity epidemic" (Begley 2012). The non-obese are also paying as much as 105 percent higher costs for their own prescriptions in order to offset the costs of prescriptions for the obese and are paying 39 percent higher primary-care costs because of the obese (Hammond and Levine 2010).

Because obesity is associated with a number of medical conditions, it is a contributing factor to lost productivity, another social cost to society. "Due to relative ease of measurement, studies estimating the absenteeism costs of overweight and obesity make up the largest category of productivity costs studies to date" (Hammond and Levine 2010:288). Absenteeism is indeed easy to measure. Begley (2012) states, "The most obese men take 5.9 days more sick days a year; the most obese women, 9.4 days more. Obesity-related absenteeism costs employers as much as $6.4 billion a year." Aside from absenteeism is the concept of "presenteeism." Presenteeism refers to those people who are less productive than others while present at work (Hammond and Levine 2010). Begley (2012) explains, "Even when poor health doesn't keep obese workers home, it can cut into productivity, as they grapple with pain or shortness of breath or other obstacles to working all-out." Absenteeism and presenteeism are both considered deviant behaviors in nearly any context. Relativists would certainly consider it deviant when obese people have higher rates of absenteeism and presenteeism than non-obese people. "In addition to absenteeism and presenteeism, obesity may lead to an increase in disability payments and insurance premiums. Such an increase could reflect a loss in productivity beyond what is captured in absenteeism data if recipients are unable to hold a job altogether" (Hammond and Levine 2010:289). Premature mortality (another form of productivity loss) has also been associated with obesity

Some of the many health-related issues connected to being overweight and obesity have already been discussed. But a number of other, seemingly mundane, or often forgotten, costs are also associated with obesity. U.S. hospitals are replacing wall-mounted toilets with more expensive floor models to better support obese patients. Wheelchairs have also been redesigned hold wider and heavier people. Emergency medical technicians (EMTs) are experiencing back injuries while performing their duties that include lifting obese patients onto stretchers. Ten years ago, the National Association for Emergency Medical Technicians (NAEMT) reported that 47 percent of its technicians suffered from back injuries while performing their duties (McCutcheon 2006). In 2012, the NAEMT reported that it had become common for patients to weigh 300 or 400 pounds. As a result, certain ambulances have specially equipped Stryker Power-LOAD stretcher lift systems costing more $32,000 each but with the availability to lift patients who weigh up to 750 pounds (Leavenworth 2012). It is interesting to note that many EMT workers are themselves obese and the new recruits are increasingly overweight (44 percent) or were obese (33 percent), according to a study conducted in Boston (Smith 2012a). Greater amounts of fuel are being consumed to transport obese people in cars and planes. "Increases in body weight among Americans mean more fuel, and potentially, larger vehicles are needed to transport the same number of commuters and travelers each year" (Hammond and Levine 2010:291). U.S. airlines alone are consuming an extra 350 million gallons of fuel per year due to overweight passengers (*Aircraft Interiors International* 2015).

There are countless other examples of the social costs of obesity that could be cited to further support the relativist perspective that obesity is an example of social deviance.

We are left with the reactivist perspective on social deviance, a view that takes into consideration the idea that deviance can take on a positive form. Although most reactivists are unlikely to consider embracing being overweight or obese as their exemplar for positive deviance, a number of people *have* embraced the idea of being fat. Maria Southard Ospina, for example, wrote a blog for the *Huffington Post* titled "My name is Marie, and I love my fat" (Ospina 2013). Folks like Marie find beauty in excessive adipose tissue. She is a part of various trends that are attempting to normalize, and perhaps even nurture, obesity. The clothing industry, for example, has profited from obesity by creating a "plus-size" clothing line. One online clothing line, Woman Within, claims on its website that it "is dedicated to comfort, fit and value for plus size women in sizes 12W to 44W, S to 6X" and claims that "Unlike other apparel brands that sell plus sizes, we custom design for each size on a unique mannequin, so that each style will look and feel just right on you" (Woman Within 2015). Other plus-size sites encourage women to "love their curves" and "embrace being full-figured." Applying such favorable terms as "curvy" and "full-figured" is a way for obese women to feel proud of being obese; or at the very least, to feel comfortable with who they are and not what others might want them to be. As a further example of the expanding trend toward embracing terms such as "curvy" for obese women is the "fatkini"—bikinis designed for overweight women who view wearing the two-piece swimwear as "inspiring" and "empowering" (McNally 2014).

Obese men have not been ignored in the clothing world. Obese men often shop in the "Big and Tall" sections of clothing stores. One men's clothing line refers to obese men as "real men" and offer "real style" clothing. Other clothing lines embrace the label "fat" and offer "fat guy–friendly" clothes, both formal and informal. Furthermore, in the "embrace being obese" developing trend, obese men are increasingly being described as "big men," a concept that seems designed to pump up the ego and self-esteem of obese men. (See box 2.2 for a further discussion of people embracing the idea of being overweight and obese.)

Sociology teaches us to embrace diversity and generally is not critical of those who express their uniqueness, including those who find beauty in varying body shapes and sizes. Health officials, employers, and many others in society are not so willing to accept the fat is beautiful concept. And yet a number of obese people are embracing idealistic terms and slogans such as "curves are beautiful" and "being big is better" in an attempt to shift the attention away from the health concerns connected with being overweight, obese, and morbidly obese.

CONNECTING SOCIAL DEVIANCE AND POPULAR CULTURE

Box 2.2 Fat Studies: We're Here, We're Fat, Get Used to It

There is a growing trend among obese people to embrace their largeness as a type of badge of honor. In some instances, these folks have become self-righteous in their defense of their right to be fat. For example, the Popular Culture Association/American Culture Association for the past few years has regularly held sessions dedicated to "Fat Studies" at their annual national meeting and a number of regional meetings. The Fat Studies academics have taken the parallel route of the LGBTQ community and their Queer Studies approach wherein they commonly hold sessions at many academic (especially in sociology) conferences. The Q of LGBTQ stands for "queer," a term that was used by homophobes in the past as an offensive insult. Alyssa Howe (2004) explains that the term "queer" became popularized in the early 1990s because it was meant to be an inclusive expression that included lesbians, gay men, bisexuals, transgendered persons, and other "sexual radicals (those who practice sadomasochism, bondage and discipline, etc.)" (p. 251). The "queer" title, then, serves to rally gay people under an umbrella "identity" (Howe 2004). Sociologist Maayan-Rahel Simon (2005), for example, claims that she has chosen "to identify as queer because where *lesbian* suggests only that my orientation is sexually related, *queer* associates me with a movement to reclaim myself and come out from under my oppression. . . . To embrace the term *queer* with 'gay and lesbian culture' is to finally put an accurate name to all the feelings of awkwardness and insecurity in being comfortable with our desires and affections as nonheterosexual individuals in a heterosexist society" (p. 14). The queer movement embraced a slogan so popular—"I'm here, I'm queer, get used to it"—that its usage has passed into popular culture.

Much like the large number of LGBTQ people who have attempted to neutralize the offensive intent behind the usage of the term "queer," obese people have come to embrace the term "fat" in order to neutralize the offensive intent behind that word. At the 43rd annual PCA/ACA conference, held March 27–30, 2013, in Washington, D.C., there were 14 workshops, roundtables, and panel sessions under the Fat Studies umbrella. The description of one such workshop (Fat Studies: Workshop 1), states, "One of the perpetual challenges in the fat acceptance movement is how to take on the task of responding to acts of hate speech and fat oppression. Often in the moment we are so overcome with our own emotions that we are left speechless, voiceless and powerless. Part of the work of the fat acceptance movement is to find ways of overcoming this speechlessness and to regain strength in our most vulnerable moments of oppression" (PCA/ACA National Conference Program 2013:35).

The Fat Studies promotion of accepting obese people as regular people who contribute to society represents a social movement that attempts to neutralize the negative implication of being labeled "fat." Health officials describe obesity as a growing epidemic and a very real and objective social problem. By describing obesity as an objective social problem, a number of social movements aimed at curtailing the expanding waistlines of the majority of Americans have been designed to promote a healthier lifestyle, including diet and exercise. Many school districts have eliminated fatty "junk foods" from their cafeterias and vending machines. Some schools promote the idea that their students should exercise, and still other schools and colleges have targeted specific students who they believe are in need of making healthier life decisions. Bryn Mawr, a small, suburban, all-female liberal arts college in Philadelphia, for example, sent out e-mails to students in January 2015 who were identified as having an "elevated" body mass index, offering them a specialized program designed to help them lose weight. The program would provide the students counseling, nutrition advice, and a fitness plan. The college had twice previously made students aware of this program without any negative backlash (*USA Today* 2/1/15). The January 2015 e-mail correspondence, however, caused a huge controversy with many targeted students claiming the e-mail was a type of "fat shaming," unethical, and an invasion of privacy. Bryn Mawr officials later sent out an apology to the entire student body stating that they had not intended to upset or offend anyone (Calderone 2015).

A number of students at Bryn Mawr were upset because their college was trying to help them lower their BMI score and therefore live a longer and healthier life. Some researchers also question the "objective" reality of health risks associated with obesity. Kwan and Graves (2013), for example, question the motives of claims makers and popular sentiments about "the fat body" as "fodder to be used in constructing a version of reality" (p. 2). Kwan and Graves (2013) point out, for example, that there have been times throughout history when being fat was a sign of good health (being fat was better than being skinny as a result of starvation) and wealth (fat people had enough money to purchase food).

Preceding the Fat Studies movement was the National Association to Advance Fat Acceptance (NAAFA) organization, a nonprofit civil rights organization "dedicated to ending size discrimination in all of its forms" (NAAFA 2015). The NAAFA (2015) organization has as its goal "to help build a society in which people of every size are accepted with dignity and equality in all aspects of life. NAAFA will pursue this goal through advocacy, public education and support."

From the perspective of NAAFA and Fat Studies proponents, being obese is fine and making fun of the overweight is a form of intolerance and discrimination.

Summary

In this chapter we took a closer look at three specific social problems in order to evaluate whether or not these social problems are deviant. Sociologists employ a "sociological imagination" in their study of social problems, and this method allows for an examination of personal troubles and public issues. This chapter demonstrates the relationship between social problems and issues of social deviance. It was shown that describing a social problem as deviant depends on, among other things, the definition of deviance that one chooses to use and who the claims makers are.

Definitions of the term "social problem" have nearly always included some sort of reference to a social issue or social condition found in society that at least some people view as undesirable and/or harmful. Claims making is often an important consideration when deciding whether or not a certain situation should be considered a social problem. Social movements often arise to combat certain social problems. Social problems have subjective (based on the assertion among certain segments of society) and objective (generally acknowledged as real and measurable) components.

The specific categories of social problems discussed in this chapter are unemployment, poverty, and obesity. Finding, maintaining, and securing gainful employment has been a consistent concern among Americans since (at least) the time of the Great Depression. As illustrated by the sociological imagination, unemployment can be the result of personal troubles or public issues.

Unemployment may lead to another serious social problem, poverty. Poverty is defined as the lack of basic necessities, goods, or financial means of support. Living in poverty restricts people's ability to live a decent life. Poverty has existed throughout most of history and across the globe and, for the most part, it was simply a fact of life for the masses. Nearly 50 million Americans live below the poverty threshold. Millions of people work full- or part-time and yet still live in poverty; they are referred to as the working poor.

Obesity and being overweight is a growing national social problem in the United States, as well as in many nations across the world. Obesity has a negative impact on individuals and society in general. For obese individuals, there is the obvious concern over their physical and psychological health as well as the negative economic impact on their personal lives. Obesity also places a considerable strain on society through increased health care costs and disability payments, especially those that are pooled through group health insurance and public programs. Despite the seemingly undeniable perspective of obesity as an objective social problem, there is a trend in American society spearheaded by "Fat Studies" academics and the National Association to Advance Fat Acceptance to consider obesity as an acceptable way of life.

Key Terms

body mass index (BMI), 49
claims making, 29
cyclical unemployment, 37
discouraged workers, 36
food neophobia, 46
frictional unemployment, 36
homelessness, 29
labor force, 35
obesity, 43
objective social problems, 31

outsourcing, 37
poverty, 39
social construction of reality, 31
social problems, 29
social stratification, 38
sociological imagination, 27
structural unemployment, 37
subjective social problems, 31
unemployment, 35
working poor, 40

Discussion Questions

1. Define the concept "social problems." Explain what the term "social problems" means to you. What are the top five social problems facing the United States?
2. What would you consider to be the top five social problems facing the world?
3. Provide an example of an objective social problem and explain why you believe it to be an objective social problem. Provide an example of a subjective social problem and explain why you believe it to be a subjective social problem.
4. Is it deviant to be unemployed? Explain your answer by using the five different perspectives (definitions) of deviance.

5. Is it possible for a family of four to survive on $24,251, a figure one dollar over the 2015 poverty guideline threshold? Is it possible for a single person to survive on $11,771, one dollar over the 2015 poverty guideline threshold? Be sure to consider all costs, including rent/mortgage, food, and so on.
6. Is obesity a subjective or objective social problem? Explain your answer.
7. What are the pros and cons of embracing being overweight and obese? Be sure to reference box 2.2 with your answer.

CHAPTER 3

Explaining Social Deviance

CHAPTER OBJECTIVES

After reading this chapter students should be able to:

- Explain what is meant by "demonic possession" and how it applies to explain deviancy

- Compare and contrast the biological theories of the classical school and the positivist school and their perspective on social deviance

- Analyze psychological theories—intelligence-based theories, personality trait theories, and social

learning—on the study of social deviance

- Explain and apply the sociological theories—social disorganization (the Chicago school), anomie/strain, subculture/cultural deviance, control/social bond, social learning/differential association, labeling, Marxist/conflict/radical, and feminist—on the study of social deviance

One of the most extreme examples of social deviance is murder. On May 21, 2014, Carol Coronado allegedly stabbed her three young daughters (Sophia, 2 1/2; Yazmine, 16 months; and Xenia, 2 months) to death in their home in an unincorporated area near Carson, California, while her husband, Rudy, the girls' father, was outside working on his pickup truck parked across the street from their home (Altman 2014a). Carol Coronado then stabbed herself and attempted to kill her mother when she arrived at the family's home to find the bloody scene (Mazza 2014). Rudy Coronado and other family members and friends, along with the general community, were in shock. All of them, along with law enforcement, were hard-pressed to try to explain such an act of deviance. Rudy Coronado told a reporter that "his wife must have been possessed by a demon to commit such an act" (Altman 2014a). Sandra Coronado, Rudy's sister and Carol's sister-in-law, countered her brother's theory, claiming she "never saw any demons inside her sister-in-law, but thought she [Carol] lacked a 'mother's instinct'" (Altman 2014a). Carol Coronado initially explained, simply, that she was "tired and exhausted" (Altman 2014a). Months later (September 2014), Carol Coronado offered another possible theory when she entered two pleas of not guilty and not guilty by reason of insanity to three counts of murder and one count of attempted murder (Mazza 2014). Her lawyer believes that Coronado was suffering "some sort of psychosis" when she allegedly killed her daughters, lined their bodies up on her bed, and stabbed herself in the chest before lunging at her own mother, who arrived later (Mazza 2014). In October 2014, Carol Coronado was indicted on three counts of capital murder; with the special-circumstance allegation she committed multiple murders, she is facing possible life in prison with no chance of release, or the possibility of the death penalty if prosecutors decide to pursue that path (Altman 2014b).

Three very young, innocent girls lost their lives at the hands of their mother that fateful day in May 2014. In an attempt to cope with their loss, loved ones were left trying to explain how such a tragedy could occur. Rudy Coronado, his sister Sandra, lawyers, prosecutors, and Carol herself tried to explain what happened. Each offered up different theories based on their respective perspectives. The Coronado case provides us with a unique glimpse into the world of trying to explain why deviance occurs.

Explaining Social Deviance via Social Theory

In general, a wide variety of theories attempt to explain social deviance. A **theory** proposes to explain or relate observed phenomena or a set of concepts via a collection of interrelated statements and/or arguments that seek to describe and explain cause-effect relationships. Theoretical approaches utilized by researchers generally reflect contemporary social currents and knowledge available at the time. To the layperson, a theory may seem to *merely* imply notions of speculation, abstraction, or hypothetical ideals and not a statement of "truth." In this regard, a theory would seem to be in contrast with "facts" or "truths." However, researchers grounded in the scientific tradition realize that a theory is much more than mere speculation, as it may already be established as true, or factually based. Furthermore, scientifically driven theories are designed in such a manner as to make themselves available for empirical verification via systematic observation and data collection (research). A theory supported by research offers a causal account of phenomena; it provides explanations as to why something occurs. Thus, while evolution is commonly expressed as the "theory of evolution," scientists realize that evolution is more accurately described as "the laws of evolution."

In this chapter, we will look at an ample variety of theoretical explanations of social deviance, including demonic possession, biological, psychological, and sociological theories.

Demonic Possession, Biological, and Psychological Theories

The first theory we will learn about lacks in scientific reasoning, but it reflects one of the earliest attempts to explain social deviance. This theory is demonic possession.

Demonic Possession

In this chapter's introductory story, Rudy Coronado believed that his wife must have been possessed by a demon in order to commit such a heinous crime as murdering their three children. He could not imagine a scenario wherein anyone in their right mind could possibly act in such a manner unless she was indeed possessed by some sort of evil spirit. Although he could not offer any proof of his theory, he believed it to be true regardless. The circumstances of his daughters' deaths were anything but normal, so why should the explanation of their deaths be otherwise?

Coronado is hardly the first person to express the notion that a demon or evil spirit is responsible for acts of deviancy. Throughout most of human history there have been those who believed that evil spirits, including the devil, influenced behavior. Most of these "possessed" people would today likely be labeled as "mentally ill," but such scientific knowledge and diagnosis has only recently existed. A belief in demonic possession reflects the absolutist perspective of deviance in that one must believe that certain behaviors are inherently deviant, or evil. **Demonic possession** refers to being under the power or influence of a demon or evil spirit to the point where one cannot control their mind or actions. To rid the person of demonic possession an exorcism may be performed. An exorcism, from the Greek **exorkizein**, literally means "to out an oath" (Kiely and McKenna 2007:xxiv). "To exorcise, then, is to place a demon on oath, and to command it by the power of God to depart and not trouble the afflicted again" (Kiely and McKenna 2007:xxiv).

The belief in demonic possession dates back at least to 5000 BCE, as evidenced by archaeological discoveries of trephines (surgical instruments with a cylindrical blade) and skulls found with drill holes in them (Porter 2002). It is believed that humans drilled holes in the skulls of individuals who engaged in odd and bizarre behaviors because they were believed to be possessed by demons or sorcery. The holes were drilled so that the evil forces could escape the afflicted (Porter 2002). Naturally, drilling holes in people's skulls led to their premature deaths. The procedure of trephining (also known as trepanning) first occurred during Neolithic times and continued through the ancient Mesopotamian period and throughout biblical times (Butcher, Mineka, and Hooley 2007). In ancient Mesopotamia, priest-doctors treated the possessed with pseudoreligious ritualistic procedures such as exorcisms, incantations, prayer, atonement, and other unusual mystical means in an attempt to drive out evil spirits from the afflicted person (Alexander and Selesnick 1966). The ancient Hebrews also believed that demons could possess humans and the afflicted were being punished by God because they had committed sin (Alexander and Selesnick 1966). All of the people described here are likely to simply have suffered from mental illness and certainly were not possessed.

As explained by Cheryl Pero (2013), "Demonic possession has been equated with evil, and exorcism has signified the triumph of good over evil. The canonical Gospel of Mark presents contemporary Christian audiences with narratives describing demonic possession and exorcism in ancient Syro-Palestine" (p. 1). Pero (2013) adds, "The most vivid picture of Jesus' ministry recorded in the Gospel of Mark is one of exorcism. In the biblical world, Jesus' exorcisms were holistic and powerful events. Jesus not only restored to wholeness and community those who were broken and marginalized, but also, in the process, attempted to restore the broken community itself to wholeness, urging those whom he had exorcized to return home" (p. 1).

The idea that people could be possessed by demons existed in many parts of the world and throughout history beyond those described above, including the ancient Greeks and Romans, through the Middle Ages, Renaissance Europe, and the witch hunts in Salem, Massachusetts. (Note: The Salem witch hunts had as much, if not more, to do with the power elites of the community trying to quiet women who spoke their minds and spoke out against societal inequalities.) By the mid-1700s, the idea of demonic possession and the use of exorcisms nearly completely died out. Interestingly, or perhaps oddly, exorcisms and a belief in demonic possession have made a minor comeback in the postmodern era. To learn more about this, see box 3.1.

Box 3.1 Exorcising the Devil

It seems hard to believe that in the 21st century there has been a slight resurgence in reports of demonic possession, leading others to think that an exorcism is necessary in order to save that person. Consider, for example, Latoya Ammons, a mother of three young children in Gary, Indiana, who claims that all three of her children have shown signs of being possessed, including " 'evil' smiles and strangely deep voices" (Howerton 2014). According to Ammons, her 9-year-old son walked backward up a wall and ceiling and her 12-year-old daughter has levitated in their home. Gary police Captain Charles Austin reports that he is a "believer" after making several visits to the home and interviewing witnesses that include a child services case worker and a nurse (Howerton 2014). Sanctioned by the Diocese of Gary, a Catholic priest, in a number of ceremonies, has exorcised the Ammons's home in an attempt to rid the dwelling of evil forces. The family moved to the home in November 2011 and the children, reportedly, did not exhibit any characteristics of being possessed prior to moving to the home. In addition to turning to the Catholic Church, the family contacted a number of other churches and clairvoyants for help. "The clairvoyants allegedly told the family their house was haunted by more than 200 demons" (Howerton 2014). A psychiatrist reportedly evaluated Ammons and claims that she is not mentally ill (Howerton 2014).

Exorcism experts have told Pope Francis that the number of claims of demonic possessions have surged around the world (Day 2014). Valter Cascioli, a psychiatrist and the spokesperson for the International Association of Exorcists (IAE), states, "The practice of the occult, Satanism and abnormal things is opening the gateway to an extraordinary amount of demonic activity" (Day 2014). Cascioli believes that there exists a true danger from the Devil. He places the blame on the "proliferation of media messages, books, television programs and films that encourage younger people to look at, and even practice, Satanism" (Day 2014). In October 2014 Pope Francis expressed his concern over demonic possession as a real and present danger and gave his approval to the IAE, a group that

consists of more than 300 demon-busting exorcist-priests spread across 30 countries, when they met at the Vatican (Lewis 2014). Pope Francis formally recognized the IAE, founded in 1990 by Father Gabriele Amorth, an exorcist for the diocese of Rome, in June 2014 (Lewis 2014).

Exorcisms, generally relegated to the realm of make-believe television and movie screens, have long been recognized by the Catholic Church and several other religions and, according to Pope Francis, priests who pursue the ministry of exorcism "manifest the Church's love and acceptance of those who suffer because of the devil's works" (Lewis 2014). According to the Catholic Church, signs that a person may be possessed may include a great aversion to anything to do with the church, such as holy water or crucifixes; preternatural strength or knowledge; alien voices; and levitation or other paranormal phenomena (Lewis 2014). The IAE will first look for natural explanations, such as mental illness or addiction problems, before assuming someone is possessed, but it believes it is doing the work of the church since the time of Jesus—casting out demons—when it performs exorcisms against the possessed (Lewis 2014). The world of science, meanwhile, denies the existence of demonic possession.

While exorcisms performed by the church may not be quite as dramatic as those depicted by Hollywood, there are some similarities. The most obvious example of Hollywood's version of an exorcism comes from the 1973 movie *The Exorcist*. Directed by William Friedkin and adapted from William Peter Blatty's 1971 novel of the same name, *The Exorcist* is a film about a 12-year-old girl named Regan (Linda Blair) who is possessed by a mysterious entity and the two priests solicited by the girl's mother who are called upon to cast the evil spirits from her. At the time of its release, *The Exorcist* was one of the best true horror films ever made. *The Exorcist* was preceded by other worthy horror ("scary") movies such as *Rosemary's Baby* and followed by other scary movies such as the 1976 classic *The Omen*. The subject matter of *The Exorcist* was a bit disturbing for many moviegoers, and the special effects, such as they were in the early 1970s, were quite good, as audiences had rarely been treated to a horror movie made so professionally. *The Exorcist* was nominated for 10 Academy Awards (losing Best Picture to *The Sting*) and became one of the highest-grossing horror films of all time. *The Exorcist* garnered more than $232 million, or more than $686 million in adjusted gross domestic box office receipts, ranking it second only behind (the not-so-scary by today's standards) *Jaws* (Hollywood.com 2015).

Most viewers were truly scared, or at the very least, uneasy while watching the film. Furthermore, when the film was first made available for home viewing, people were warned not to watch it alone. Among other things, Regan's demonic possession caused her to use vulgar language and gave her abnormal strength. When the priests came to implement the exorcism, Regan's bed would shake violently and rise to the air. Spoiler alert: the exorcism would cause the evil spirit to leave Regan's body and enter the priest's body. The priest then jumped out the window (as a type of self-sacrifice), causing a fatal head injury, killing both himself and, supposedly, the evil spirit. Regan was, therefore, saved.

As presented by the concept of demonic possession, a perspective most commonly associated with the preindustrial era, there was little scientific research conducted to test the validity of any theory of crime and deviancy prior to the late 19th century.

Biological: The Classical School and The Positivist School

Early biological theories attempted to link crime and delinquency to genetics and specific physical attributes of individuals. The idea that genetics may cause social deviance led to such notions as a **"born criminal"** and "natural criminal." Some of these early biological theories utilized the practice of examining body types as a means of determining a person's character, leading to the implication that some individuals "look like criminals." **Physiognomy,** for example, involved the study of faces and skulls and other physical features in order to reveal an individual's natural disposition (to commit crime and deviant acts). This pre- and early-industrial-era "reasoning" followed centuries of ancient Greek and Roman beliefs that a person's character could be determined based on a physical examination (Curran and Renzetti 1994). During medieval times there existed a law that specified that if two people were suspected of having committed a crime, the uglier person should be considered the more likely guilty party (Curran and Renzetti 1994). Two schools of thought represent the earliest of the biological attempts to explain social deviance: the classical school and positive school.

1. The Classical School

The classical school emerged in the 18th century and consisted mostly of writers and philosophers who were focused primarily on lawmaking and legal processing (Williams and McShane 1994). The name "classical school" is derived from the social movements of the 18th-century era, highlighted by a challenge to faith and tradition, the rise of early industrialization, and the idealism of democracy that was blooming in the Western world. Two social thinkers, Cesare Beccaria and Jeremy Bentham, stood out as the leading figureheads of the classical school of thought.

Beccaria (1738–1794) was an Italian nobleman born into an aristocratic family in Milan, Italy, who gained prominence with his publication *On Crimes and*

Punishment (1764). The essay was written to support his friends in the "academy of fists"—a society that was against "economic disorder, bureaucratic petty tyranny, religious narrow-mindedness, and intellectual pedantry" (Constitution Society 2015; Beccaria 1963). Beccaria proclaimed that people had "free will" and thus were free to choose whether to follow the rules or be deviant. The formerly unknown Beccaria gained public praise from many world leaders and leading thinkers, including Thomas Jefferson and John Adams. His essay would impact the U.S. Constitution, the Bill of Rights, and the American judicial system. Beccaria never published again, leaving the chore of expanding on his idea of free will to others.

Jeremy Bentham (1748–1832), an English philosopher, was an instrumental leader of the classical school approach who promoted the idea of **hedonism**—the idea that humans seek pleasure and try to avoid pain in their activities. He also believed in **utilitarianism**—the idea of doing what is best for the greatest number of people. Bentham's utilitarian and hedonistic beliefs are sometimes referred to as "hedonic calculus" (Clear, Reisig, and Cole 2012). "Bentham claimed that one could categorize all human actions and, either through pleasurable (hedonic) incentives or through punishment, direct individuals to desirable activities. Underlining this idea was his concept of utilitarianism, the doctrine that the aim of all action should be 'the greatest happiness of the greatest number'" (Clear et al. 2012:37). Bentham believed that criminals were unable to control their hedonistic desires and that their pursuit of happiness would lead to criminal or deviant acts. "In Bentham's view, criminals were somewhat childlike or unbalanced, lacking the self-discipline to control their passions by reason. Behavior was not preordained, but rather was an exercise of free will. Thus, crime was not sinful, but the result of improper calculation. Accordingly, the criminal law should be organized so that the offender would derive more pain than pleasure from a wrongful act" (Clear et al. 2012:37).

The combined ideas of Beccaria and Bentham form the foundation of the classical school. Williams and McShane (1994) sum up the basic tenets of the classical school below:

1. An emphasis on free will choices and the human rationale
2. A view of behavior as hedonistic
3. A focus on morality and responsibility
4. A concern with political structure and the way in which government deals with its citizens
5. A concern for the basic rights of all people (p. 21)

As the classical school tenets indicate, those who engage in deviant behavior do so because they are free to do so and find enjoyment in pleasurable deviant acts. However, if everyone engages in deviant acts, civil society is not possible, and therefore the severity of punishments (pain) must exceed any pleasure gained. The idea of a moral, collective good leads to collective sentiments (a Durkheimian notion) and the labeling of certain behaviors as "wrong," "evil," or "deviant" that are subject to punishment (Champion 2004). Punishments must fit the crime, with those found guilty of committing particularly heinous deviant acts punished the most severely.

The classical school of thought regarding deviance and punishment represents an improvement over the days of rule by monarchies and religion where punishment was often arbitrarily administered based on who committed the crime. And while the idea of creating a rationally based criminal justice system represents an improvement over faith (e.g., demonic possession) and tradition (justice administered by those in power), the belief that all people act rationally all the time and that legitimate extenuating circumstances do not exist are just a couple of examples of the flaws in the classical school approach to social deviance.

2. The Positive School, or Positivist School

The positivists had a different perspective on social deviance than the theorists of the classical school. Instead of viewing people as having the ability to make rational choices based on free will, theorists from the positive school saw behavior as determined by an individual's biological traits. From the perspective of the positive school, people who engaged in crime and deviance did so because they had a pathology; in other words, they were "sick." The belief that deviants are "sick" implies that one needs to find the "cause" of social pathologies among individuals.

While the true roots of the positive school approach to the study of social deviance are difficult to determine precisely (given the fact that the attribution of criminality and deviance to biological causes dates to prebiblical times), it is the work of Italian physician and criminologist Cesare Lombroso (1835–1909) that generally receives credit for spearheading its origins (Champion 2004). Lombroso was a trained psychiatrist who devised a theory of criminality and social deviance determined by physiological traits, and although his theory is now scoffed at, he was once renowned as the "father of modern criminology." His background in psychology and psychiatry, combined with his studies of the physiology and anatomy of the brain while he was in charge of the insane at hospitals in Pavia, Pesaro, and Reggio Emilia (1863–1872) led Lombroso to develop an anthropometric analysis of criminals and the concept of the "born criminal." As the concept implies, the born criminal refers to people who are born to deviate from the norm and who inevitably commit crime. Lombroso believed that the less-developed (evolutionarily speaking) individuals were those most likely to be born criminals because they were less capable of abiding (or less willing to abide) by the laws and norms set by conventional society. Lombroso drew his conclusions from empirical data and clinical case studies conducted on criminals, a common practice among positivists of his era. His publication *Criminal Man* (1876, first edition) articulates his anthropometric approach.

As a young military doctor, Lombroso first studied Italian soldiers during the wars of Italian unification. "Lombroso quickly developed his signature approach of measuring and observing the bodies of his patients, in this case soldiers. He later applied this method, supplemented with psychological interviews, to mental patients and, finally, criminals. Holding posts in both mental asylums and prisons, Lombroso examined thousands of individuals during his lifetime, carrying out his own famous prescription to "study the criminal rather than the crime" (Lombroso 2006:7). Lombroso's biological approach reflected the infancy of the field of biology and its lack of scientific prestige. He drew upon the popularity of Charles Darwin's theory of evolution in an attempt to convince readers of *Criminal Man* of the scientific validity of his theory of criminal atavism (Lombroso 2006).

In the first edition of *Criminal Man*, Lombroso labeled criminals on the basis of physical characteristics (e.g., thickness of the bones in the skull, pigmentation of the skin, hair type). Lombroso proposed that criminals were the product of heredity; that is, behavioral predispositions toward criminal conduct or antisocial proclivities were passed down through successive generations of bloodlines. Lombroso went so far as to claim that criminals possess a certain type of physical appearance, and because of this, one could determine a criminal or deviant simply based on their looks. In the second edition of *Criminal Man*, Lombroso began a rudimentary system of classification by establishing the "criminal of passion"—people with otherwise good reputations before committing a crime but with the good sense to repent immediately following their deviant act, and driven by motives that were "generous and often sublime" (Lombroso 2006:10). Today, we use the term "crimes of passion" to describe a situation wherein otherwise "good" people commit a crime but were driven to acts of crime or deviance because of situational arousal (e.g., a spouse who catches his/her significant other with another while they engage in sexual activity, which triggers an act of crime on the part of the victim of the cheating spouse). In the third edition, Lombroso adopts Ferri's term of "born criminal," a term that gained international recognition but also "drew instant criticism, as opponents ridiculed the inability of Italian criminal anthropologists to identify a single anomaly that disfigured all born criminals" (Lombroso 2006:10). In the fourth edition of *Criminal Man*, "Lombroso adds epilepsy to atavism and moral insanity as causes of born criminality" (Lombroso 2006:11). In his fifth and final edition of *Criminal Man*, Lombroso added a number of other deviant types beyond the born criminal. "This proliferation of categories across the five volumes of *Criminal Man* increases the weight of sociological factors in Lombroso's explanation of the causes of crime. However, because of the notoriety of the concept of the born criminal, Lombroso has rarely been credited with recognizing environmental factors as significant to the etiology of deviance" (Lombroso 2006:12).

Lombroso considered women inferior to men, describing them as weak and easily impressionable, believing that only their maternal instinct saved normal women from criminality (Lombroso 2006). Race was an important variable in Lombroso's theory of atavism (evolutionary throwbacks, primitive people). He believed that white men were responsible for civilization and thus equated with civilization while black, brown, and yellow men were equated with "primitive" or "savage" societies." He believed that the "problem" with southern Italians (those from Sicily and Sardinia) was their direct connection to the black race. "Having been conquered over centuries by a number of foreign peoples—including North African Arabs—the south was inhabited by a racially mixed people, who, in Lombroso's view, shared a propensity for murder with their nonwhite ancestors" (Lombroso 2006:18). Lombroso also regarded tattoos as a sure sign of inferiority. "One of the most singular characteristics of primitive men and those who still live in a state of nature is the frequency with which they undergo tattooing. . . . It occurs only among the lower classes—peasants, sailors, workers, shepherds, soldiers, and even more frequently among criminals" (Lombroso 2006:58). It is the positive school's outlook on tattoos that led to the expression of "tattoos as the art of the poor."

Another proponent of the positive school of deviance is William H. Sheldon (1898–1977). Sheldon employed the use of somatotypes. A somatotype refers to the overall shape of the body with particular attention paid to relative development of the various parts of the body compared to each other. Practitioners who used this approach believed that deviance could be explained in terms of body shape and structure of individuals (Shoemaker 2000). Sheldon provided three categories of body types:

1. The mesomorph—Strong, athletic, aggressive, and extroverted individuals
2. The ectomorph—Thin, frail, and introverted individuals
3. The endomorph—Fat, jovial, and extroverted individuals

Sheldon studied a number of juveniles and observed them as they aged in an effort to draw a correlation between body type and criminality and social deviance. He studied hundreds of boys assigned to the Charles Hayden Goodwill Inn, a division of Morgan Memorial Goodwill Industries, a facility that offered a variety of services, including residential care, education, vocational training, and rehabilitation counseling (Hartl, Monnelly, and Elderkin 1982). The youthful population grew up during the middle 1930s and early 1940s and represented a segment of Americans that came of age during the Great Depression. Their early adulthood coincided with World War II. Most of the boys at this facility, and under the study of Sheldon, were those who were already "in trouble" in their home communities, homes, and foster homes (Hartl et al. 1982). In 1981, a few years after Sheldon's death, a follow-up study was conducted on the remaining living "boys" from the Goodwill institute (Hartl et al. 1982).

Sheldon came to conclude that the mesomorphs were the most likely to commit crime. Although it is true that that some criminals fall into the mesomorph category, deviants also include the ectomorph and endomorph. Furthermore, research has never been able to substantiate a correlation between body types and criminality and social deviance. Nonetheless, in the mid-1900s a number of colleges and universities found it valuable to examine the postures of incoming students (see box 3.2).

A CLOSER LOOK

Box 3.2 Posture Photos

It is interesting to note that the idea of body types being correlated with deviance and criminality was relatively common in the early 20th century, and it was also fairly common for frontal and profile nude photos (known as "posture photos") to be taken of generations of elite college students from the 1940s through the 1960s (Rosenbaum 1995). All freshmen at some colleges, including Yale, Princeton, Mount Holyoke, Vassar, and Smith, among many others, were required to pose in the nude. Metal pins were attached (via an adhesive, not any sort of piercing) to each student's spine, who were then positioned against a wall with a floodlight illuminating the profile and a camera to capture the image. The idea was to measure body types and curvature of the students' spines. "Those whose pins described a too violent or erratic postural curve were required to attend remedial posture classes" (Rosenbaum 1995). Among the students who were subjected to the posture photos are former President George H. W. Bush, Hillary Rodham Clinton, Diane Sawyer, and George Pataki. For quite a while these photos were available at the Smithsonian Institution, where the public had access to them—they have since been destroyed or made unavailable (*Billings Gazette* 1995:1A).

Today, biology still attempts to explain social deviance by linking specific physical characteristics of individuals to their behaviors, but instead of using such primitive procedures as measuring skull sizes and examining body types, contemporary biologists attempt to link genes and chromosomes to the study of crime and deviancy. Many students have benefited from the discovery of "learning disabilities" as a means to explain why they have a more difficult time than others learning. In the past, students who did poorly in school might have been labeled as slow, feebleminded, dumb, or uninterested in school work. Studies involving the XYY syndrome have attempted to show that the presence of an extra Y chromosome (the Y chromosome secretes the testosterone hormone) may result in increased aggressiveness, and by implication, criminality and social deviance.

Psychological: Intelligence-Based Theories, Personality Trait Theories, and Social Learning

Psychological theories of social deviance represent an improvement over biological theories. Psychological theories of deviance are grounded on the idea that differences in individuals' intelligence and personality predict delinquency.

1. Intelligence-Based Theories

At their most fundamental level, intelligence-based theories on social deviance are centered on the idea that individuals who commit crime and deviance make poor decisions because they are mentally deficient, possess some hereditary degeneration, are feebleminded, or are just too plain dumb to understand the consequences or meanings of their delinquent behaviors. "Decision making is perhaps the most fundamental intellectual enterprise. Indeed, the word *intelligent* comes from the Latin roots *inter* (between) + *legere* (to choose). The study of motives and methods regarding how decisions might and should be made has long captured the interest of philosophers and social scientists" (Stirling 2014:1). The development of the concept of "insanity," especially moral insanity, represents one of the earliest psychological triumphs in linking behavior to some sort of mental deficiency and using it as a rationale (or defense) for individual criminal or deviant behavior (Fink 1938). "It was typically suggested that criminals and delinquents were deficient in basic moral sentiments and that, furthermore, this condition was an inherited trait and contributed to the fusion of biological and psychological properties in the explanation of criminality" (Shoemaker 2000:47). With the introduction of intelligence tests in the 20th century, there were attempts to link intelligence with crime and delinquency. These intelligence tests, however, were based on the assumption that intelligence was somehow an inherited trait, and consequently, these psychological-based theories were compromised by biological predispositions of intelligence-based explanation.

Intelligence-based theories grounded in hereditary explanations of criminality traditionally default to the idea that deviance is a form of mental deficiency. "At the heart of the early hereditary studies was the belief that intellectual inferiority or low intelligence was a basic cause of crime. With the development of Alfred Binet and Theodore Simon's *Scale of Intelligence* in 1905, numerous studies conducted on prison inmates tested the hypothesized relationship between low intelligence, especially feeblemindedness, and crime" (Thornton and Voight 1992:143). Goddard's research on feeblemindedness (see Goddard's *Feeblemindedness: Its Causes and Consequences*, 1914) as a causation of deviance and crime were inconclusive (Vold 1958). In his *The English Convict* (1913), Charles Goring found no evidence to support Lombroso's theory of atavism, but he did claim that low intelligence was an indication of hereditary inferiority (Curran and Renzetti 1994). Such a claim represents quite a leap in causation as, even if convicts are, as a whole, less intelligent than the general population, how does that prove heredity had anything to do with it?

2. Personality Trait Theories

Psychologists do not agree on a universal definition of personality; some look at unconscious mechanisms, others look at learning histories, and still others focus on the way people organize their thoughts. Burger (2014) defines personality as "consistent patterns and interpersonal processes originating within the individual" (p. 4). Among the more popular psychologically based theories of personality is Freud's psychoanalytical theory. Freud himself did not study delinquency, but others who have used his perspective explain deviance and criminality as a matter of an underdeveloped superego.

Personality-based theories on deviant behavior have led to the development of such concepts as **neurosis** (a relatively mild personality disorder typified by excessive anxiety and social maladjustment) and **psychosis** (a symptom of mental illness) and their application to social deviance. People dominated by an overdeveloped id tend to be psychotics, and their behavior may be characterized by bizarre and inappropriate behaviors. The field of psychology has convinced nearly everyone of the validity of the idea that individuals can possess multiple personalities (**dissociative identity disorder**) and that such a disorder can, among other things, contribute to deviant behavior (Haddock 2001). Erik Erikson speculated that individuals who suffer from an *identity crisis* may commit acts of delinquency.

The label of "sociopath" (a person with a psychopathic personality whose behavior is antisocial, often criminal or deviant, and who lacks a moral compass) and "psychopath" (a person with a genetic predisposition and underdeveloped components of the brain that result in a lack of impulse control) has successfully been used in courtrooms to excuse improper social behavior. "The sociopath is thought to be a dangerous, aggressive person who shows little remorse for his or her action, who is not deterred by punishments, and who does not learn from past mistakes. Sociopaths often appear as someone with a pleasant personality and with an above-average level of intelligence. They are, however, marked by an inability to form enduring relationships" (Lyman and Potter 2000:70).

3. Psychological-Social Learning Theories

Of all the biological and psychological theories that attempt to explain social deviance, the psychological version of social learning theory represents the best approach. Similar to many sociological approaches to the study of deviance, psychological-social learning theories are based on the idea that delinquency, as with nearly all behaviors, is socially learned. "Traumatic early childhood experiences may be important determinants of subsequent adult personality characteristics, but the primary factors influencing whether one conforms to or deviates from societal rules are those experiences youths have while learning from others such as their parents. Adults in any institutional context (e.g., schools, churches, homes) provide role models for children to follow" (Champion 2004:94). Thus, children learn how to become deviants based on interaction with deviant others.

Social learning, according to the psychological perspective, takes place through two primary methods: reinforcement and modeling. **Reinforcement**, a term used in operant conditioning, refers to the manner in which behaviors are rewarded or punished with its consequence of strengthening or weakening a behavior in the future. For example, when aggression is rewarded instead of punished, future aggressive behavior is likely to continue and increase (Bandura and Walters 1963; Thornton and Voight 1992). Reinforcement is most likely to occur when a behavior is continuously and consistently rewarded or punished and most effective with significant others (e.g., parents, peers, and the media). As it pertains to deviance, when the developing child associates with other delinquents and he or she becomes identified with a particular deviant peer group, his or her likelihood of engaging in deviant behavior increases when it is positively reinforced.

Another important aspect of the psychological version of social learning theory involves the **modeling** of behavior. Most research on the value of modeling has been applied to children, but adults may also benefit from modeling successful others. Modeling occurs by watching and listening to significant others and then copying their behaviors and attitudes. While most people model their behaviors after those who are in close proximity (e.g., parents, teachers, coaches, and older athletes), it is important to note that the model does not need to come in contact with the person who is emulating their behavior. Research conducted by Delaney and Madigan (2015) on sports heroes reveals that whether or not a particular athlete wants to serve as a hero, youth may still admire the athlete and, thus, they become a hero who serves as a role model. In the gang world, many youngsters grow up as "wan-nabes"—meaning they want to be a gang member when they grow older, so they emulate the behaviors of existing gang members. The psychological-social learning theory involving the impact of modeling on gang participation has a high degree of validity, although certainly not as a cause of gang participation but as a partial explanation as to why youth grow up wanting to be gang members. "When young children growing up in poverty see gangsters with new clothes, shiny jewelry, and cash, they see a 'role model'" (Delaney 2014b:82).

Sociological Theories

Sociological theories incorporate a varied, multicausal framework in their attempt to explain social deviance. Sociological theories focus on environmental and social factors that influence behavior, and they are grounded in the scientific tradition of data collection and analysis. The first, and oldest, of the sociological theories is the **social disorganization** approach utilized by the Chicago school in studying deviance and crime.

Social Disorganization Theory (The Chicago School)

The idea that social deviance is caused by environmental factors dates back to the 19th century with urban studies in Europe that regularly demonstrated correlations between delinquency and crime and such factors as population density, age and sex composition, poverty, and education (Shoemaker 2009). "A distinguishing feature of the earlier, European environmental analyses of criminality, particularly those conducted by A.M. Guerry and Adolphe Quetelet, was the use of maps and charts to demonstrate the quantitative distribution of crime and delinquency" (Shoemaker 2009:99). Sutherland and Cressey (1978) referred to the use of such a research methodology as the "Cartographic School."

The use of maps and charts as a means to quantify and illustrate crime locations in specific urban neighborhoods was a regular component of ecological studies of deviancy utilized by sociologists at the University of Chicago during the 1920s and 1930s. The "Chicago school" approach (as it is known in the United States) of ecological research became the trademark of the social disorganization theory. Established in 1892, the University of Chicago became the first college in the United States to have a sociology department. The city of Chicago was growing rapidly during the early years of the sociology department, and the sociologists of this era took advantage of this "living laboratory" ripe with social problems that regularly accompany high-density urban life by regularly conducting ethnographic research. The vastly expanding industrial city of Chicago drew waves of immigrants, many of whom had great difficulty coping with the social problems that urban life presents. The researchers at Chicago attempted to explain why certain neighborhoods produced high rates of crime and delinquency while others did not.

Robert Park, Ernst Burgess, Louis Werth, and others from the Chicago school drew maps and identified areas of the city that expanded outward in a pattern of concentric circles. Each of the concentric zones was numbered; Zones 4 and 5, for example, were populated predominantly by white, middle- and upper-class homeowners who had lived in their communities for many years and were well integrated into the dominant culture of society. The researchers found little crime in these areas. Zone 1 was the inner core of the city, which contained the downtown area occupied by businesses and government offices. In Zone 2 were the poor, the recent immigrants, and transients who faced poor housing conditions. This is the zone where ghettos were found. Zone 3 consisted mostly of neighborhoods occupied by second- and third-generation immigrants; they were the working class. "The Chicago sociologists observed that not all urban zones were plagued equally by alcoholism, high rates of mental illness, and other similar problems. Indeed, the further one moved away from the city center, the lower the incidence of social problems" (Curran and Renzetti 1994:136). According to the Chicago school sociologists, the social problems found in Zones 2 and 3 were the result of social disarray, or social disorganization. Social disorganization most directly affected those who lived in poor living conditions, which resulted in feelings of hopelessness and further triggered deviant manifestations. No zone was found to be free from delinquency, but the highest rates were found in Zone 2. Furthermore, the farther away neighborhoods were from Zone 2, the fewer the social problems confronting their inhabitants. The use of the concentric zone model stimulated subsequent research to analyze delinquency, deviance, and crime rates by incorporating fundamental environmental factors such as neighborhood location.

Sociologists from the Chicago school put forth the notion that social disorganization was caused by social change that was too rapid for the smooth operation of the social system. Socially disorganized areas were characterized by the contrasting values and norms of the established residents and the new values and norms of immigrants; the breakdown of social cohesion; high rates of unemployment; and a disregard for established social control agents (e.g., existing community leaders and law enforcement). The elements of social disorganization sowed the seeds for social deviance.

According to Sampson and Groves (1989) there are four elements that constitute social disorganization:

1. Low economic status
2. A mixture of different ethnic groups
3. Highly mobile residents moving in and out of the area
4. Disrupted families and broken homes

Social disorganization, which still characterizes many contemporary American cities, stimulates the creation of subcultures that are in opposition to the dominant cultural norms and values, which in turn stimulates further deviance. (Note: We will examine subculture/cultural deviance theory later in this chapter.) Proponents of the social disorganization theory point out that crime patterns might be different in

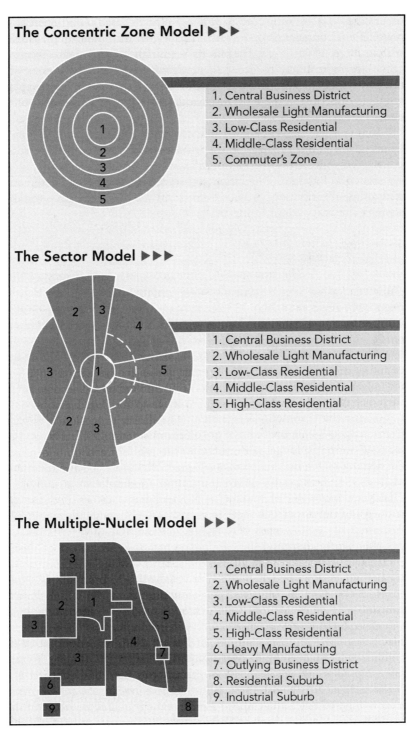

The Concentric Zone Model ▶▶▶

1. Central Business District
2. Wholesale Light Manufacturing
3. Low-Class Residential
4. Middle-Class Residential
5. Commuter's Zone

The Sector Model ▶▶▶

1. Central Business District
2. Wholesale Light Manufacturing
3. Low-Class Residential
4. Middle-Class Residential
5. High-Class Residential

The Multiple-Nuclei Model ▶▶▶

1. Central Business District
2. Wholesale Light Manufacturing
3. Low-Class Residential
4. Middle-Class Residential
5. High-Class Residential
6. Heavy Manufacturing
7. Outlying Business District
8. Residential Suburb
9. Industrial Suburb

FIG. 3.1 The concentric zone model approach to studying delinquency, deviance, and crime can be traced to sociologists at the University of Chicago.

other cities and are subject to how a city is built based on differences in geography/ physical environment. Proponents of this theory also indicate that the theory works best in large urban areas. Despite its seemingly valid premise—that deviance and crime are more likely to occur in neighborhoods with high rates of other social problems—the social disorganization theory cannot adequately explain why large numbers of people in the most disorganized neighborhoods do not turn to deviancy and criminal activities.

Schmalleger (2004) believes that the most significant and lasting contribution from the social disorganization theorists of the Chicago school was its "formalized use of two sources of information: (1) official crime and population statistics and (2) ethnographic data. Population statistics, or demographic data, when combined with crime information, provided empirical material that gave scientific weight to ecological investigations" (p. 209).

Anomie/Strain Theory

In his 1893 book *The Division of Labor in Society*, Emile Durkheim used the word "anomie" (which comes from the Greek *anomia*, meaning "without law") to refer to a condition of deregulation occurring in society. This deregulation led to a sense of "normlessness" among people because they were confused about societal expectations. Feelings of normlessness, Durkheim believed, served to encouraged deviant behavior because a common morality of society was disappearing. In his 1897 publication *Suicide*, Durkheim used the term *anomie* to describe a general sate of moral deregulation, which had left people with an inadequate moral compass to direct their behavior in a proper fashion. Ever since Durkheim introduced the concept, sociologists have come to define *anomie* as the absence of norms, or normlessness, characterized by the breakdown of social norms and rules and a condition in which existing norms no longer control the activity of individuals.

Decades later, Robert Merton adopted Durkheim's notion of anomie as a means of explaining how people adapt to the *strain* of chaotic social conditions. "Whereas Durkheim conceived of anomie as a problematic social condition resulting from sudden and rapid social change, Merton saw it as an endemic feature of the everyday operation of certain types of society" (Curran and Renzetti 1994:149). Merton's anomie theory (first published as "Social Structure and Anomie" in 1938) is based on the idea that society encourages all persons to attain culturally desirable goals— what Merton described as the "cultural structure"—but the opportunities to reach these goals—the "social structure"—are not equal for all members of society. Merton believed that a functional society was one that found the balance between cultural structure and social structure; conversely, a dysfunctional society is one that places a greater emphasis on one of the societal components over the other. The United States, according to Merton, is a dysfunctional society because it places a great emphasis on cultural goals—primarily economic and material success—but is characterized by a social structure that does not provide everyone with an equal opportunity to reach the cultural goals. Minorities and members of the lower class, according to Merton, often encounter obstacles in their pursuit of culturally desired goals that the wealthy and privileged members of society do not. Confronted by the strain of being unable to attain culturally defined goals by legitimate means, some people will pursue unconventional, illegal, or deviant means. Thus, Merton's anomie theory argues that deviance is the result of the social strain people experience and that it is a symptom of a social structure that has not provided an equal opportunity for all members to attain culturally desired goals.

Merton claimed that when individuals are faced with the strain caused by anomic conditions they have a choice between five **modes of adaptation** within the culture-bearing society, or group. The modes of adaptation are schematically presented in table 3.1, where (+) signifies "acceptance," (–) signifies "elimination," and (+/–) signifies "rejection and substitution of new goals and standards" (Merton 1938).

TABLE 3.1	Merton's Modes of Adaptation	
Method	**Culture Goals**	**Institutional Means**
Conformity+	+	+
Innovation	+	–
Ritualism	–	+
Retreatism	–	–
Rebellion	+/–	+/–

Source: Merton 1938

Conformity (to both cultural goals and the means to attain them) is the most common and widely diffused adaptation and involves the general acceptance of things as they exist in society. Merton points out that if conformity was not the most common response to the strain experienced in society, the very stability and continuity of society could not be maintained. While conformity is the most common adaptation, retreatism (adaptation #4), a deviant adaptation, is the least common. Merton (1938) states, "Persons who 'adjust' (or maladjust) in this fashion are, strictly speaking *in* society but not *of* it. Sociologically, these constitute the true 'aliens'" (p. 677). Retreatists (e.g., hermits, drug addicts, street people, and bag ladies) have rejected both society's goals and the means of attaining them, and as a result, they choose to cut themselves off from the world. This mode of adaptation seems to be more common today than in Merton's era.

Innovation is deemed a deviant adaptation because the course of action involves illegitimate pursuits of cultural goals. Innovation is the most common form of deviant adaptation and includes such behaviors as bank robbery and selling drugs and stolen merchandise. Rebellion, the fifth category of adaptation, is a deviant course of action pursued by those persons (e.g., anarchists, militant groups) who are so strained by society that they wish to replace both the goals and the means of attaining them. Ritualism is a type of behavior deemed as deviant by many contemporary social scientists because its practitioners have given up on attaining culturally desired goals and instead put their focus on making sure everyone else strictly follows the rules. "In this mode the means can become the aspirations of the individual, as when one may attempt to treat a job (means) as a form of security instead of using the job as a means of achieving success. In this example, keeping the job has become a goal by itself, resolving the frustration of unsuccessfully chasing the original goal" (Williams and McShane 1994:92). Clerks and petty bureaucrats are a common example of ritualists.

Another variation of strain theory comes from the work of Cloward and Ohlin from their publication *Delinquency and Opportunity* (1960). These researchers believed that social problems block the pursuits of people who try to attain culturally desired goals. The result is frustration and poor self-concepts, which in turn may lead to social deviance. Culturally frustrated persons are more likely to be found in the lower socioeconomic classes. Cloward and Ohlin used the concept of "differential opportunity structure" to describe the reality that there is an uneven distribution of legitimate and illegitimate means of achieving society's success goal. This differential opportunity theory stresses the importance of the social environment in determining which opportunities individuals choose. Youths from wealthy families have more legitimate opportunities to choose from than youths from lower-SES families.

Subculture/Cultural Deviance Theory

By the 1950s and early 1960s, sociologists were studying social deviance in the context of the new sociological term "subcultures." A **subculture** refers to a category of people found within the greater society who share a distinctive set of cultural beliefs and behaviors that distinguish them from the larger society. Members of a subculture generally agree with most of the cultural aspects of the prevailing, conventional society but share a key characteristic that provides them with a sense of identity. There are many examples of subcultures, including gang members, recreational drug users, college students, rodeo clowns, runway models, Goths, and surfers.

Because subcultural groups develop their own cultural norms and values, some of their behaviors may be deemed deviant by conventional society standards.

College students are an example of a subcultural group.

Subcultural theorists believe that deviance is committed by members of a particular subculture who identify more closely with the values and norms of their subculture than of those of the larger society. New members to a deviant subculture will also feel the pressure to conform to deviant norms and values. Goldstein (1991) argues that delinquent youth are especially likely to feel this pressure. "Subcultural deviance theory holds that delinquent behavior grows from conformity to the prevailing social norms experienced by youths in their particular subculture groups" (p. 12).

The influence of the Chicago school tradition (looking for the relationship between community and social deviance), especially the social disorganization theory (previously discussed), is quite evident within the subculture/cultural deviance perspective. "Cultural deviance theory proposes that delinquency is a result of a desire to conform to cultural values that are to some extent in conflict with those of conventional society. In part, this perspective is a direct offshoot of social disorganization theory because part of that theory . . . suggests that criminal values and traditions emerge within communities most affected by social disorganization" (Shelden, Tracy, and Brown 2001:172). In essence, the deviant individual has adopted the norms and traditions that emerged within neighborhoods (rather than those of the greater society) most affected by social disorganization. Lilly, Cullen, and Ball (2015) concur that deviance is often a matter of cultural context: "This perspective maintains that 'antisocial attitudes' (as they are sometimes called) or criminal beliefs exist that define criminal actions as permissible or, even more positively, as required. For example, if an inner-city youth is 'disrespected,' the use of retaliatory violence would be seen as normative. . . . In this framework, the *context of culture matters*" (p. 53).

In addition to the concept of "subculture," sociologists introduced the term "reference groups" during the 1950s. Reference groups are quite similar to subcultural groups, as there must be some reference for individuals to point toward that serves as a primary identifier of the subculture group. Reference points are the common goals and traits that unite members into a subculture. "The concept of reference group can . . . greatly facilitate research on the manner in which each actor's orientation toward his world is structured" (Shibutani 1955:562). Members of a subculture group share specific reference points of importance, and thus a strong sense of loyalty to one's fellows develops. In addition, subculture members aspire to gain or maintain acceptance from the group and, as a result, group norms take on a higher value than society's.

Among the significant founders of the subculture/cultural deviance theory are Albert Cohen, Richard Cloward and Lloyd Ohlin, and Walter B. Miller. Cohen's *Delinquent Boys: The Culture of the Gang* (1955) is one of the first versions of cultural deviance theory that explains how deviant subcultures form. "Delinquent subcultures exist, according to Cohen, within the greater societal culture. But these subcultures contain value systems and modes of achievement and gaining status and recognition apart from mainstream culture" (Champion 2004:100). Cohen believed that lower-SES youth lacked the material and symbolic advantages of middle- and upper-class youth, and therefore any competition against those youth would likely be a losing proposition; consequently, lower-SES youth compete against one another. It is from this competition among lower-SES youth that a subculture of delinquency was likely to emerge. Cohen's (1955) subcultural theory has the following assumptions:

1. A high proportion of lower-class youths (especially males) do poorly in school.
2. Poor school performance relates to delinquency.

3. Poor school performance stems from a conflict between dominant middle-class values of the school system and values of lower-class youths.
4. Most lower-class male delinquency is committed in a gang context, partly as a means of meeting some basic human needs, such as self-esteem and belonging (Shelden, Tracy, and Brown 2001:173).

Working with these assumptions, Cohen (1955) identified five central characteristics of lower-class delinquent gangs, which, when combined, comprise the delinquent subculture:

1. Nonutilitarianism—The acts of delinquency committed by delinquents are not always done for specific purpose (utilitarianism). Instead, profound satisfaction from committing crimes, such as theft, may come from the act itself—being delinquent.
2. Maliciousness—A great deal of delinquency is committed simply for the purpose of being mean and the corresponding rush and thrill of committing deviant acts. Vandalism is a primary example of malicious behavior.
3. Negativism—The delinquent subculture is not only at odds with the greater society, it attempts to take its norms and turn them upside down.
4. Short-term hedonism—There is little planning in regard to long-term goals; instead, gang members [and other delinquents] live for the moment and immediate gratification.
5. Group autonomy—Delinquents, and especially gang members, do not recognize any authority figure (e.g., parents, teachers, agents of social control) other than those in charge of the gang (Curran and Renzetti 1994:153–54).

Cloward and Ohlin's contribution to subculture/cultural deviance theory resides with their concept of degree of integration The idea of this concept is rather self-evident; the stronger the degree of integration to the subcultural norms and values the greater the pull of the subculture on individuals. In their review of anomie theory, Cloward and Ohlin (1960) described the concept of "differential opportunity structure." Their related concept of "illegitimate opportunity structure" is relevant to subcultural theory in that, much like Cohen's focus on lower-SES youth, Cloward and Ohlin argued that "whereas legitimate opportunities are generally available to individuals born into middle class culture, participants in lower-class subcultures are often denied access to them. As a consequence, illegitimate opportunities for success are often seen as quite acceptable by participants in so-called illegitimate subcultures" (Schmalleger 2004:218).

Walter Miller also focused on lower-SES cultures. Miller (1958) identified six basic features or aspects of a subculture that require constant monitoring, attention, and care. Miller referred to these six features as focal concerns. The six focal concerns identified by Miller are trouble, toughness, smartness (street smarts), excitement, fate, and autonomy. Also like Cohen, Miller believed that lower-SES subcultures are primarily concerned with instant gratification, a concern in contrast to the middle-class ideology of valuing delayed gratification (e.g., go to college now in the hope and belief of greater riches in the future).

While subculture/cultural deviance theories had a great impact on liberal political policies of the 1960s (e.g., the War on Poverty and the creation of the Peace Corps), there is a flaw to the application of this perspective as it has historically maintained a focus on lower-SES subcultures. There are numerous middle- and upper-class subcultural groups, including those who are not young delinquents, and yet who engage in behavior outside of the norm. For example, a number of people who have the financial means enjoy "high-altitude" (elevations more than two miles above sea level) skiing and snowboarding that requires a helicopter ride to reach the summit to begin their descent. Members of high-altitude skiing adhere to a number of subcultural norms including proper preparation for high altitude (e.g., wearing proper clothing and taking precautions for altitude sickness); protecting against the sun (at 9,600 feet, the sun is 40 percent stronger than at sea level); taking high-altitude ski and snowboard lessons, and learning how to pack clothing, food, and water. The subculture of skiers and snowboarders (high altitude or not) seemingly has little, or nothing, to do with lower-SES values. Then again, high-altitude skiers and snowboarders do possess many of the same focal concerns described by Miller (but applied just to lower-SES youth) in that they may enjoy getting in trouble (they sometimes ski or snowboard in forbidden areas); envision themselves as tough; possess smartness (nature smarts rather than street smarts); and value the excitement that comes from the rush of pursuing their thrills in areas that may be prone to avalanches. Thus, subculture/cultural deviance theory is poten-

This snowboarder was dropped off atop a mountain in South Tyrol, Italy, via a helicopter.

tially relevant to all subcultural groups, but research is mostly limited to delinquent, lower-SES groups.

Control/Social Bond Theory

One of the most unique theories of social deviance and delinquency is the "control/ social bond" theory. Its uniqueness stems from its basic question of concern that is, essentially, the opposite of all theories that ask, "Why is someone a deviant?" The social bond/control theory perspective asks, "Why doesn't *everyone* commit acts of social deviance and delinquency?" Control theorists argue that deviance is inherently attractive and exciting. As explained by Curran and Renzetti (1994), control theorists have adopted a Hobbesian view of human nature—that everyone in society is capable of committing deviancy, crime, and acts of violence. Thus, while most of us can easily conceive of the notion of street gang members as violent criminals committing all sorts of antisocial behaviors, we must also acknowledge that a mother of small children in danger is also capable of violence (in order to protect her children). Similarly, there are enough news reports of seemingly conventional persons who go on a violence or killing spree much to the surprise of neighbors, friends, and family members who tell news reporters and law enforcement officers how surprised they are to hear that their neighbor or someone they thought they knew closely could commit heinous crimes because they "seemed so nice." Such was the case involving Darren Deon Vann, who was arrested in October 2014 for the murder of at least seven women in Gary and

Hammond, Indiana. Vann's ex-wife told a local news station, "This is all unbelievable to me. A total shocker. I never knew him to be violent, never" (Walsh 2014).

The sociological roots of control theory can be traced back to Durkheim and his analysis of anomie and its connection to the existence, or lack thereof, of proper social control. Durkheim believed that social control was necessary in order for society to exist and for people to understand the boundaries of acceptable behavior. "When relationships and norms begin to break down, the controls they create begin to deteriorate. Durkheim noted that a breakdown of those controls leads to crime and suicide. . . . Whenever anomie exists in society, controls begin to disappear" (Williams and McShane 1994:184). Furthermore, Durkheim's work on "collective conscience" demonstrated his belief that deviant behavior can be controlled when people share societal values and norms.

While control theory has roots with Durkheimian theory, this perspective developed in earnest in the 1950s and 1960s with the ideas of Albert Reiss, Gresham Sykes and David Matza, Walter Reckless, and especially, Travis Hirschi. Social control theories of deviance, delinquency, and crime examine many of the standard variables studied by contemporary sociologists, including the role of family, education, peer groups, SES, and so on. Control theorists argue that individuals who remain unattached to society's norms are free to engage in a variety of deviant activities. Deviants, then, lack self-control. Consequently, to curtail deviancy, individuals must somehow be controlled by society, or they must learn to control their own behaviors.

One of the earliest versions of control theory was articulated by Albert Reiss Jr. (1951), who combined the concepts of personality and socialization within the Chicago school framework. Reiss's version of social control theory has three components:

1. A lack of proper internal controls developed during childhood
2. A breakdown of those internal controls
3. An absence of, or conflict in, social rules provided by important social groups (the family, close others, the school) (Reiss 1951:196)

These three elements have remained a constant in nearly every version of control theory since Reiss first presented them. Reiss believed that delinquency was behavior that represents a failure of personal and social controls to produce behavior in conformity with the norms of society. Since individuals learn core values in early childhood via the family and school, deviance is the result of poor socialization.

A decade after Reiss presented his version of control theory Walter Reckless (1961) introduced his "containment theory." By describing deviancy as a combination of a character disorder and a social pursuit, Reckless provides us with a sociopsychological synthesis. Reckless believed delinquency can be explained in terms of two forms of control, or his term, containment—outer and inner containment. Reckless believed that **inner containments** are self-controls (e.g., self-concept, ego strength, tolerance of frustration, goal directedness, and identification with lawfulness) that develop during the socialization process. **Outer containment** refers to the social control agents found in society (e.g., law enforcement, the judicial systems, and others in a position of authority). According to Reckless, the key to avoiding a deviant lifestyle involves avoiding the lure of deviant subcultures, internalizing the rules of society, and developing a positive sense of self and a sense of direction in life. In 2014 and 2015, the many young Westerners drawn to the Islamic extremist rebel group Islamic State of Iraq and Syria (ISIS) possessed the characteristics described by Reckless, and because they lacked inner and outer containment, felt that they could find a sense of belonging with a rebel group.

The most popular version of social control theory is the one provided by Travis Hirschi. In his book *Causes of Delinquency* (1969), Hirschi presents his survey findings from data collected on 4,000 high school students in California. He concluded that deviant acts were the result of an individual's weakened or broken bond to society. As a result of this conclusion, Hirschi (1969) specified four elements of the social bond with society necessary to help minimize social deviance: attachment, commitment, involvement, and belief. They are described below:

1. Attachment—A strong connection to significant others (especially parents and peers) and to the school represents the best mechanism on constraining deviant behaviors. As Siegel and Welsh (2014) explain, "The acceptance of social norms and the development of a social conscience depend on attachment to and caring for other human beings. Attachment to parents is the most important" (p. 161). Ultimately, developing a strong sense of attachment to others in childhood will lead to a strong connection with society in adulthood.
2. Commitment—Involves the amount of time that individuals spend with conventional behavior and their dedication to long-term goals (delayed gratification) and the simple reasoning that the more time individuals spend with conventional activities, the less time they have to pursue deviant activities.
3. Involvement—A continuation of the commitment element with the premise that individuals need to maintain heavy involvement in conventional activities. A bond with society can be formed when youth fill their time by doing their homework and chores, playing sports, or participating in other after-school activities and when adults become involved in charity work or community service and maintain regular employment.
4. Belief—People who live in a societal setting must learn to foster a belief in the law and the common morality shared by other members of society. Durkheim referred to this as the *collective conscience*.

Hirschi believed that all four of these elements of the social bond were interconnected. He also believed, in the control theory tradition, that social deviancy can be reduced when people form a strong bond with society.

If we revisit the basic question asked by social control theorists—"Why doesn't *everyone* commit acts of social deviance and delinquency?"—we will discover that one other element from this theoretical perspective must be addressed, and that is, that deviance is inherently attractive and exciting. If this is true, many people will ignore forming a bond with society because they prefer engaging in deviant behaviors. To that end, it is important to mention the work of Sykes and Matza.

Sykes and Matza (1957) noted that deviants generally find a way to justify their behavior. Their famous concept of **"techniques of neutralization"** (a term familiar to sociologists and criminologists) illustrates how norm violators attempt to rationalize their deviant behaviors, thus freeing them from their commitment to societal values and norms. In their 1957 article, "Techniques of Neutralization: A Theory of Delinquency," and in Matza's book *Delinquency and Drift* (1964), Sykes and Matza claim that delinquency cannot be explained simply as an absence of social controls;

instead it must also involve a will to commit deviant acts. The five techniques of neutralization that individuals use to justify their delinquent behavior described by Sykes and Matza are as follows:

1. **The denial of responsibility**—The first line of defense in attempting to neutralize accusations of wrongdoing is to simply say, "I didn't do it." Denying responsibility for some act of deviance implies an attempt to shift blame to someone else. "It is not the validity of this orientation that concerns us here, but its function of deflecting blame attached to violations of social norms and its relative independence of a particular personality structure" (Sykes and Matza 1957:667). This technique has also come to be referenced in court cases when an individual attempts to escape responsibility by means of "insanity" (temporary or otherwise).

2. **The denial of injury**—This technique is used when the deviant attempts to neutralize the severity of a deviant act by saying something like, "As long as no one was hurt, what's the big deal?" This technique may also be used by the deviant in attempting to alleviate any guilty feelings he or she may have.

3. **The denial of the victim**—This technique is used when the deviant attempts to deny the "victim status" of the person harmed. Sykes and Matza (1957) state, "The moral indignation of self and others may be neutralized by an insistence that the injury is not wrong in light of the circumstances. The injury, it may be claimed, is not really an injury; rather, it is a form of rightful retaliation or punishment" (p. 668).

4. **The condemnation of the condemners**—Another basic line of defense involves counterblaming the accusers. "The delinquent shifts the focus of attention from his own deviant acts to the motives and behavior of those who disapprove of his violations. His condemners, he may claim, are hypocrites, deviants in disguise, or impelled by personal spite" (Sykes and Matza 1957:668).

5. **The appeal to higher loyalties**—Within this technique of neutralization the deviant justifies violating a social norm by claiming his or her actions were conducted on behalf of a more important entity (e.g., a social movement or religion). Sykes and Matza (1957) explain, "Internal and external social controls may be neutralized by sacrificing the demands of the larger society for the demands of the smaller social groups to which the delinquent belongs such as the sibling pair, the gang, or the friendship clique" (p. 669).

When deviants use a technique of neutralization, they are in a state of limbo or drift that makes deviant acts permissible, but such a state may cause feelings of guilt. "Techniques of neutralization may not be powerful enough to fully shield the individual from the force of his own internalized values and the reactions of conforming others, for as we have pointed out, juvenile delinquents often appear to suffer from feelings of guilt and shame when called into account for their deviant behavior" (Sykes and Matza 1957:669). In his later work, Matza (1964) used the term "bond to the moral order" to describe the connection that exists between individuals and the dominant values of society.

This concludes our discussion of control/social bond theory. We turn our attention back to a number of theories, beginning with social learning/differential association theory, that attempt to answer the more typical question—Why does someone commit social deviance?

Social Learning/Differential Association Theory

Earlier in this chapter we learned about the psychological perspective of social learning theory and the emphasis placed on reinforcement and modeling. The sociological perspective of social learning theory implies that deviance is learned, but the process of learning is different from the psychological standpoint. The sociological perspective of social learning theory can trace its origins to the work of Gabriel de Tarde in his *The Laws of Imitation* (1903), where he linked crime with imitation. "One of the first theorists to associate the origins of crime with a learning process was Gabriel Tarde. . . . Tarde argued that crime results from one person's imitating the actions of another. Although he also took into account biological and psychological factors, he believed that crime is essentially a social product" (Kratcoski and Kratcoski 1996:56).

Social learning theorists believe that the process of imitation is not possible without interaction with others and further argue that individuals learn behavior through interaction with others. As a result, individuals may learn and imitate the behavior of conventional or deviant individuals depending upon whom they associate with. Direct association with deviant others, especially over a period of time, is the most likely manner in which individuals will learn to become deviants. From the social learning theory perspective, learning takes place through three related processes: acquisition, instigation, and maintenance.

As it pertains to social deviance, acquisition refers to the individual's initial introduction to a deviant form of behavior. This introduction to a deviant behavior allows for reinforcement through modeling. Thus, when an individual is introduced to a group of friends who smoke marijuana and finds the behavior positively reinforced by the group members, he/she is more likely to imitate the behavior and come to view pot smoking in a positive manner. Instigation is the second step in the social learning process, and it involves the individual actually participating in some form of deviant behavior (the person smokes pots with her friends). Maintenance refers to continued participation over an extended period of time (the person regularly smokes pot with her friends). From the social learning perspective, maintenance is the only way deviant behavior will continue. "There needs to be consistent reinforcement or maintenance. Social learning theory suggests four specific kinds of reinforcement: (1) direct reinforcement, (2) vicarious reinforcement, (3) self-reinforcement, and (4) neutralization of self-punishment" (Shelden et al. 2001:178).

Perhaps the most prominent of all social learning theorists is Edwin Sutherland, who developed a theory of **differential association**, which he first introduced in the third edition of his textbook *Principles of Criminology* (1939). The final version of his theory appeared in 1947, and when he died in 1950, Donald Cressey, his longtime associate, continued Sutherland's work (Siegel and Welsh 2014). Sutherland employed a solid sociological approach to his differential association theory and was highly critical of biological and psychiatric theories of deviance and crime. "Sutherland expressly incorporated the notion that all behavior is learned and, unlike other theorists of the time, moved away from referring to the varied cultural perspectives as 'social disorganization' and used the term 'differential social disorganization' or 'differential group organization.' This allowed him more clearly to apply the learning process to a broader range of American society" (Williams and McShane 1994:75–76).

Sutherland put together nine basic and formal theoretical propositions that, when taken together, constitute his differential association theory, which is reminiscent of Tarde's imitation theory (Thornton and Voight 1992). The final version of Sutherland's differential association theory is as follows (Thornton and Voight 1992:165–66):

1. Criminal behavior is learned.
2. Criminal behavior is learned in interaction with other persons in a process of communication.
3. The principal part of the learning of criminal behavior occurs within the intimate personal groups.
4. When criminal behavior is learned, the learning includes (a) techniques of committing the crime; (b) the specific direction of motives, drives, rationalizations, and attitudes.
5. The specific direction of motives and drives is learned from definitions of the legal codes as favorable or unfavorable.
6. A person becomes delinquent because of an excess of definitions favorable to violation of law over definitions unfavorable to violation of law.
7. Differential associations may vary in frequency, duration, priority, and intensity.
8. The process of learning criminal behavior by association with criminal and anticriminal patterns involves all the mechanisms that are involved in any other learning.
9. While criminal behavior is an expression of general needs and values, it is not explained by those general needs and values, since noncriminal behavior is an expression of the same needs and values (Sutherland and Cressey 1978:80-82).

Although Sutherland spoke most often and specifically about crime, his differential association theory is applicable to all forms of social deviance. The basic idea of this theory boils down to, if the greater number of (or the more important) associations one has are with deviant others, one is more likely to adopt that deviant lifestyle; conversely, if the greatest number of (or the most important) associations one has are with positive, conventional aspects of society, one is less likely to become deviant.

Sutherland and Cressey (1978) acknowledged the primary criticism of their theory as the vagueness of the term "association" and admitted that their differential association theory was not precise enough to undergo rigorous empirical testing. However, differential association theory remains one of the most popular theories of deviant and criminal behavior. The basic premise of differential association theory has long reached the everyday thinking as reflected by the familiar instruction of parents to their children, "I don't want you associating with that person, or group of people, because they are a bad influence on you."

Labeling Theory

In chapter 1, deviance was defined as "any behavior that is labeled by some members of society, especially those in a position of authority or power, or specific subcultural groups, as an unacceptable violation of social norms and codes of morality that may elicit negative reactions from others." The idea that a behavior must be *labeled* as deviant in order to be considered deviant comes primarily from the labeling theory perspective. Who and what is labeled as deviant is the utmost concern for labeling theorists. Thus, labeling theory does not examine how or why or why not people become deviants; rather it concentrates on the effect that *being* labeled a deviant has on a person and the processes that lead to who gets to decide what behaviors are deviant or criminal and which ones are not.

Howard S. Becker ([1963] 2010) believed that deviance was a concept created by society and specifically stated that "social groups create deviance by making rules whose infraction constitutes deviance, and by applying those rules to particular people and labeling them as outsiders. From this point of view, deviance is not a quality of the act of the person commits, but rather a consequence of the application by others of rules and sanctions to an 'offender'" (Becker 2010:39). Thus, a particular act is only deviant because it has been labeled as deviant, and a person becomes labeled a deviant after violating the rules that others have created. Rule-breaking behavior comes to be viewed as deviant, but again, as Becker points out, only because someone else labeled it as deviant. Marijuana smokers, for example, do not feel as though they are deviant because they smoke pot, and they certainly don't consider themselves as criminal just because they choose to smoke marijuana. And yet others in society have labeled marijuana smoking as deviant and criminal and insist on imposing their rules onto others (marijuana will be discussed in further detail in chapter 8). There are U.S. states that have recently labeled marijuana smoking as legal, and yet people in nearby states cannot legally smoke it, and all of this is the result of certain people labeling a behavior as acceptable or not acceptable and having the authority to impose such rules onto others.

Once someone is labeled a deviant or a criminal, it often becomes a primary identifier of the person. Consider, a person need only commit one criminal act (e.g., burglary) while having committed hundreds of thousands of other acts over the course of a lifetime, and yet that one criminal act now becomes a primary identifier—the person is a "criminal." The criminal label carries such a negative connotation that it becomes generalized to future situations—"he's a criminal, he broke into one home, he's likely to break into another, so we better keep an eye on him" (a police and community viewpoint). Labeled a criminal, the onetime burglar may now be seen as having the potential to commit any type of crime. Becker (2010) states, "Treating a person as though he were generally rather than specifically deviant produces a self-fulfilling prophecy. It sets in motion several mechanisms which conspire to shape the person in the image people have of him" (p. 41). From the labeling perspective, when an individual continually receives negative feedback from significant others and then begins to accept the negative label, a self-fulfilling prophecy has been created. People, especially children who take to heart the labels (e.g., "You're worthless," "You'll never amount to anything," or "You're a bum") bestowed upon them by family and teachers come to see themselves as others have labeled them.

No one wants to acquire a label that he or she considers an inaccurate assessment of his/her character, and as a result each of us attempts to *negotiate* his/her role identity. Individuals, of course, want a say in the outcome of the role identity allocation process (Spencer 1987). However, the assignment of labels is often determined by external social control agents, and there are times when these attached, unwanted labels come to consume the identity of individuals. In an attempt to restore and maintain preferred identities, individuals will often engage in the use of disclaimers as a means of fighting off unwanted identities and labels (Hewitt and Stokes 1975). In fact, people utilize any number of techniques of neutralizing negative labels, including making **accounts**, a linguistic device employed whenever an action is subjected to valuative inquiry that may compromise the identity of individuals (Scott and Lyman 1968). There are two general types of accounts: excuses and justifications. Excuses are used when mitigating circumstances are involved with the behavior in question. Justifications are accounts in which an individual admits to some undesired behavior but denies the pejorative quality associated with the act in question (Delaney 2014b). Disclaimers and accounts are means of attempting to neutralize a negative label that compromises one's role identity. As Fontana (1973) explains, "Labeling places the actor in circumstances which make it harder for him to continue the normal routines of everyday life and thus provoke him to 'abnormal' actions" (p. 179). The type of infraction and the previous role of the labeled individual in the community may impact how quickly one's role identity is compromised.

Becker found that those who are in positions of power in society are the ones who also control the labeling process. He also believed that rules were created by those in power so that they could increase their own personal wealth, social position, and status. Ideas such as these serve as a perfect transition to the Marxist/conflict/radical perspective.

Marxist/Conflict/Radical Theory

Marxist, conflict, and radical theories are each unique but are linked by a general belief that those who control the means of production control the labeling of certain behaviors as acceptable and others as unacceptable. This theoretical perspective is especially concerned with the parts of the definition of deviance that state "those in a position of authority or power" dictate what constitutes "an unacceptable violation of social norms" and address the "negative reactions from others"—especially the manner in which the judicial system appears to favor those in power at the expense of those without sociopolitical power.

The Marxist perspective of social deviance is derived from the ideas of a social thinker who never specifically addressed law or crime as primary topics in his theories. Marx blamed the capitalistic system for nearly all the "evils" of society in his era. He was especially interested in the role of production and theorized that power was related to one's position in the economic structure. Marx believed that those who controlled the means of production (e.g., industry and property) could exercise their will and power over those who did not control the means of production and therefore had no significant input on the creation and maintenance of rules and laws. Marx believed that the control over the means of production created a two-class socioeconomic system with the rich and powerful elites (bourgeoisie) controlling the major aspects of societal decision making designed to keep the masses (proletariat) powerless. Marx argued that the bourgeoisie maintained their power positions by creating political and economic systems that helped them to create laws designed to maintain their advantageous position. The gap between the richest and poorest Americans has dramatically increased since the days of Marx, leading many contemporary Marxists to argue that the capitalistic system is designed to make sure that the rich get richer and the poor get poorer. Rules and laws are established to give the rich financial benefits not afforded the poor, while at the same time, rules and laws are established to keep the poor in their place—ghettos and correctional facilities.

Conflict theorists, like the Marxists, also believe that the creation of laws is not an expression of a broad consensus to protect members of society, but rather the law is a means of forcing the masses into conforming to the way of life of the power group. Conflict theorists emphasize the role of power and the inequality found systematically throughout society. The conflict perspective also believes that society's values, norms, and laws are really those of the dominant group that have been forced upon the masses. "Because power can be equated with resources, then it seems evident that those who are higher up in the social class structure will be more powerful members of society. Their influence in the making of social decisions, and their ability to impose values, will also be greater than those of the lower social class" (Williams and McShane 1994:158). The law, consequently, represents one of the most valuable resources that the powerful possess because they can use the law to manipulate further control and maintain the status quo.

Conflict theorists argue that there is a constant struggle for scarce resources and that this competition throws off the equilibrium of society until a dominant group gains control and reinstitutes stability by the means of power. A stable society, from the conflict perspective, is one with a stable system of power. An unstable society is a sign that there is a battle over power. For conflict theorists, power is the core of all social relationships. It is the most precious of the scarce resources. The designations of certain behaviors as deviant and others as acceptable are the result, then, of those in power making such designations because such a label will somehow help them maintain their power.

Radical theorists also blame capitalism as the root cause of much criminal behavior in society, especially the crimes committed by the economically poor. Two of the more prominent radical theorists are William Chambliss and Robert Seidman. Chambliss (1964) focused on the importance of labor, resources, and social control methods as the key ingredients used by capitalists to maintain their advantageous power position. In their 1971 publication, *Law, Order and Power*, Chambliss and Seidman argue that the ruling class maintains its power by exercising control in two ways: through the creation of laws that are focused on controlling the behaviors of the poor and by creating a "myth" that the law serves the interests of the public.

Donald Shoemaker (2000) described the basic assumptions of the radical approach to deviance as follows:

1. Most behavior is the product of a struggle among the classes within a society, particularly between those who own the tools of production (the bourgeoisie) and those who do not (the proletariat).
2. The economic system of capitalism is primarily responsible for the class divisions within society.
3. The bourgeoisie, either directly or through its agents, such as the State, controls the proletariat, economically, institutionally, or legally.
4. Most official crime and delinquency is committed by the lower and the working classes as a form of accommodations to the restraints placed on them by the bourgeoisie (pp. 215–16).

For Marxist, conflict, and radical theorists, social deviance is the result of those in power (those who control the means of production) creating laws and rules designed to keep them in power while keeping the proletariat powerless. These three theoretical perspectives all blame capitalism for the great disparity between the social classes. While there is validity to the substantial financial gap between the rich and poor in capitalistic societies, there are rich and poor, and examples of the masses being exploited, in nearly all socioeconomic-political systems.

Feminist Theory

Throughout much of human history women have not enjoyed the same rights as men. Many brave women have served as pioneers in the fight for gender equity for the past few centuries. These women are known as "feminists." Feminists point out that the patriarchal design of most societies left women in a secondary power role to men. The roots of this secondary power role are connected to biological realities—women give birth to babies and provide their initial nourishment. Men, because of their (on average) larger biological size, became responsible for protecting their families and hunting for food. Over time, these biological differences became transformed into gendered roles with a specific set of gender expectations; that is to say, men are supposed to be the providers and women are supposed to be the primary caregivers. In *The German Ideology*, Marx and Engels (1970) traced the origin of the modern division of labor to the early family structure, describing the wife and children as the "slaves" of the husband. The mindset of societal rulers that women should be subservient to men continued until around the time of industrialization, when Western societies promoted ideals of equality and democracy. Even the idealistic founders of American society were guilty of sexism, as women were not allowed to vote until 1920 with the passage of the Nineteenth Amendment to the U.S. Constitution.

The "first wave" of feminism (beginning in the 1830s with the abolitionist movement and continuing through the early 20th century), which was highlighted by the Women's Rights Convention, held in Seneca Falls, New York, in 1848, spearheaded the start of the American feminist movement. The first-wave feminists had a strong commitment to gaining rights for women in many social spheres, including the family, politics, and education. The "second wave" of feminism, which began in the 1960s and led to such landmark legislation as the Equal Pay Act of 1963, the Civil Rights Act of 1964, and Title IX of the Education Amendments of 1972, was designed to address the many inequalities found in society that women sought to end. The second-wave feminists sought to achieve, among other things, "gender equity," "equal pay for equal work," and to change the mindset of "the woman's role is in the household." The accomplishments achieved by the first two waves of feminism and feminist theory helped to benefit many women around the world and led to the "third wave" of feminism, which began at the start of the 21st century. Third-wave feminists are concerned about civil rights, gay and lesbian issues, homelessness, AIDS activism, environmental concerns, and human rights in general (Delaney 2014a).

This brief background of the three waves of feminism helps to illustrate that feminism is as much a social movement designed to empower women worldwide as it is a theory. As a theoretical perspective, feminist theory attempts to demonstrate the importance of women, to reveal the historical reality that women have been subordinate to men due to cultural constructs and not biological mandates, and to bring about gender equity. **Feminism**, then, can be defined as a social theory and a social movement designed to empower women in an attempt to reach gender equity—especially with regard to sharing scarce resources (e.g., power, prestige, and status).

By now, most students have come to realize that feminism is very similar to conflict theory. Both theories seek to find equality for all persons and highlight the struggles confronting so many people as they attempt to gain equality. While conflict theory argues that the scarce resources of society are controlled by the bourgeoisie (those who control the means of production), feminist theory argues that scarce resources are controlled by men in general (not just the power elites). The feminist perspective on social deviance also argues that agencies of social control (e.g., police and the judicial system in general) reinforce women's place in male society (Chesney-Lind [1989] 2012).

A number of theoretical perspectives (e.g., social disorganization, subculture/cultural, social learning, and labeling) have demonstrated that boys and girls are socialized differently, especially in regard to a cultural expectation that boys are supposed to be rough, tough, and aggressive (focal concerns) and unemotional. All of these characteristics assist the individual to create a mindset that supports acts of deviance. Joining a street gang, for example, an ultimate sign of toughness and a willingness to commit acts of deviance and crime, is far more common with males than it is with females (it is generally estimated that 90 percent of all street gang members are males). The third wave of feminism has taken on the issue of domestic violence as a cause of concern, and for good reason, as women are far more likely to be a victim (see chapter 6).

Summary

One of the fundamental concerns in the study of social deviance centers on answering the question, "Why do people commit deviant acts?" In an attempt to answer that question, a number of theoretical perspectives, including biological, psychological, and sociological theories, were reviewed.

Perhaps the oldest explanation of social deviance is demonic possession; that is to say, people who commit deviant acts are possessed by some evil entity such as the "devil." Most of these "possessed" people would today be labeled as "mentally ill," but such scientific knowledge and diagnosis is a recent phenomenon. Despite scientific knowledge that disproves the notion of demonic possession as a plausible explanation of social deviance, there has been a modest resurgence in this far-fetched theoretical perspective.

Biological explanations of social deviance attempt to link genetics and physical attributes of individuals as the cause of socially defined violations of social norms. The classical school perspective states that humans have free will and choose to commit acts of social deviance because they find it pleasurable. In order to discourage individuals from engaging in hedonistic behaviors, the classical school suggests making punishments more severe than the pleasure derived from deviancy. The positive school approach promotes the concept of the "born criminal" and examines body shapes to look for correlations between crime and physical attributes of individuals.

Psychological theories of deviance are grounded on the idea that differences in individuals' intelligence and personality predict delinquency. Intelligence-based theories on social deviance are centered on the idea that individuals who commit crime and deviance make poor decisions because they are mentally deficient, possess some sort of hereditary degeneration, are feebleminded, or are just too plain dumb to understand the consequences and meanings of their deviant behaviors. Personality-based theories on deviant behavior have led to the development of such concepts as "neurosis" and "psychosis" and their application to social deviance. Erik Erikson speculated that individuals who suffer from an "identity crisis" may commit acts of delinquency. Psychological-social learning theory is built on the idea that people learn (including learning to become deviants) through two primary methods—reinforcements and modeling.

A wide range and number of sociological theories on social deviance were presented in this chapter. Sociological theories focus on environmental and social factors that influence behavior, and they are grounded in the scientific tradition of data collection and analysis. The sociological theories reviewed were social disorganization theory (the oldest of the sociological theories); anomie/strain theory; subculture/cultural deviance theory; control/social bond theory (the theory that asks the question, "Why doesn't everyone commit deviant acts?"); social learning/differential association theory; labeling theory; Marxist/conflict/radical theory; and feminist theory.

Key Terms

born criminal, 58

demonic possession, 56

differential association, 77

dissociative identity disorder, 64

hedonism, 59

inner containments, 74

modeling, 65

modes of adaptation, 69

neurosis, 64

outer containments, 74

physiognomy, 58

psychosis, 64

reinforcement, 64

social disorganization, 65

subculture, 70

techniques of neutralization, 75

theory, 55

utilitarianism, 59

Discussion Questions

1. What is an exorcism? Do you believe in the validity of "demonic possession" as a plausible explanation of deviant behavior? Explain your answer.

2. Explain what is meant by the concept "born killer." Do you think there is such a thing as a "born criminal"? Which theoretical perspective utilizes this concept?

3. Explain the primary similarities and differences of social learning theory from the psychological perspective and from the sociological perspective.

4. Explain how the social disorganization theoretical perspective explains social deviance.

5. Name and explain Merton's five modes of adaptation. Be sure to identify whether or not the mode of adaptation signifies acceptance, elimination, or the rejection and substitution of new goals and standards.

6. Identify at least three subcultural groups you belong to and describe the norms, values, and expectations of your behavior in each of these groups. Would you describe any subcultural groups you belong to as "deviant"? Explain.

7. Describe the similarities and differences between feminist theory and the conflict perspective.

CHAPTER 4

White Collar, Political, and Organized Crime

CHAPTER OBJECTIVES

After reading this chapter students should be able to:

- Explain the origin of the term "white collar crime"
- Describe what is meant by the "power structure" of society
- Explain the role of the power elites and white collar crime

- Provide a contemporary definition of white collar crime
- Comprehend and give examples of political crime
- Explain organized crime and give examples of different crime syndicates

As the judge levied a punishment of 150 years in prison against the defendant, the people in the courtroom erupted in cheers. While making his decision, U.S. District Judge Denny Chin had described the defendant's crimes as "extraordinarily evil." Prior to the sentencing, the defendant sat inertly as his victims called him a "beast," an "animal," and a "lowlife" (McCool and Graybow 2009). Who was this extraordinarily evil lowlife, you ask? He must be a mass murderer or a serial rapist; or perhaps a vicious pedophile, right? As you might've guessed, he was not a street criminal, as this is a chapter on white collar crime. At the time of this trial, this "animal" of a criminal was 71-year-old Bernard (Bernie) Madoff, the onetime NASDAQ chairman who was found guilty of operating a classic Ponzi scheme—paying off early investors with funds from subsequent clients and sending out fraudulent investment statements to keep the illusion of profit alive (Zambito and Smith 2008). In March 2009, Madoff pleaded guilty to 11 federal crimes, including securities fraud, investment advisor fraud, wire fraud, mail fraud, international money laundering to promote specified unlawful activity, money laundering, making false statements, perjury, theft from an employee benefit plan, and making false filings with the SEC (FBI 2009). In addition to the 150-year sentence, U.S. District Judge Chin ordered Madoff to pay $170 billion—symbolic of the amount of money that flowed through Madoff Investment Securities.

U.S. District Court judge Chin appointed Irving Picard as the Securities Investor Protection Act (SIPA) trustee tasked with the challenge of recovering the investors' money from Madoff's estate. In 2014, on the five-year anniversary of his sentencing, only a few of Madoff's victims had regained all of their losses (Yang 2014). The rest of his victims are still trying to pick up the pieces of their shattered lives. In January 2015, Madoff sent an e-mail to NBC News (2015) saying that the damage he inflicted on thousands of investors was "nothing" compared to the pain he feels from the loss of his two sons since he has been incarcerated. Madoff's son Mark committed suicide in 2010 at age 46 on the second anniversary of his father's arrest and son Andrew died in September 2014 after a long battle with cancer. In his e-mail to NBC News (2015), Madoff acknowledged that his sons never forgave him for betraying their love and trust.

This introductory story represents a mere sampling of the types of crimes that have come to be known as white collar crimes. Although most people are surprised when they hear this, far more damage, both in terms of loss of life and total dollars, is caused by white collar crime than by street crime. In this chapter we will learn much more about white collar crime, which includes corporate crime, and we will explore the worlds of organized and political crime.

Edwin Sutherland Creates a Category of Crime

The term "white collar crime" was coined by sociologist Edwin Sutherland (see chapter 3 for a discussion on Sutherland) in his 1939 presidential address to the American Sociological Association. The concept of **white collar crime** has since become recognized throughout the world, although its meaning has been modified from Sutherland's ([1949] 1983) original definition of "crime committed by a person of respectable and high status in the course of his occupation" (p. 7). There was great significance in Sutherland's labeling certain types of crime as "white collar" because it helped to change the perception of criminality from one where only street thugs committed crime (e.g., assault, robbery, and murder) to one where people in any profession (e.g., business owners, managers, bankers, lawyers, and doctors) could be perceived as criminals. The timeliness of Sutherland's usage of "white collar" crime beckons to an era when professional officer workers wore white shirts with ties. The significance of "color-coding" crime also made it easy for the public to comprehend the difference between professional categories of crime via the white collar image of the criminal with the nonprofessional worker (street criminals) characterized by a blue working shirt.

While Sutherland's white collar crime concept has stood the test of time, his definition has not. "White collar crime" does still refer to almost any nonstreet crime—such as tax evasion, receiving illegal Social Security payments, identity theft, insider trading, embezzlement, and financial fraud—and is generally committed by professionals during the course of their occupation. Similarly, as described by the Cornell University Law School (2015), white collar crime generally refers to nonviolent crimes usually committed in commercial situations for financial gain. Today, however, we would not use the sex-specific term of "his" (as in "his occupation"), as women are found in all professional occupations and are equally capable of committing white collar crime. Additionally, one does not have to be a professional to commit many white collar crimes. For example, anyone, regardless of their SES, can commit tax fraud, computer and Internet fraud, credit card fraud, phone and telemarketing fraud, health insurance fraud, and so on. Geis (2002) acknowledges that many white collar crimes can be committed by nonprofessionals as well as by professionals and states, "While antitrust conspiracies are not likely to be carried out by lower-echelon employees (though they could in theory involve executives' secretaries), bribery transactions often include lower-level go-betweens, and fraud against medical insurance programs is perpetrated by pharmacy employees and ambulance drivers as well as medical doctors" (pp. 7–8).

While it is true that many nonprofessionals commit white collar crimes, it remains equally true that professionals of high standing (e.g., Bernard Madoff) are the ones involved in high-stakes financial fraud. High-ranking professional white collar criminals have many advantages over street criminals. For one, they typically hold positions of high status, making it difficult for others to accuse them of criminal activity. This is especially true if their family name holds weight in the community or if their businesses employ a substantial number of people from the community. Secondly, because of their high-status positions, professional white collar criminals are in a position to prevent effective investigation when wrongdoing is suspected. They are also in a position to cover their tracks and to set up underlings to take the fall (creating scapegoats). Third, even when a suspected white collar criminal is arrested, prosecution is more difficult than it is for a street criminal, as the high-ranking professional has the financial means to hire top lawyers and cause havoc during the judicial process. Fourth, judges and juries are sometimes biased in favor of a professional accused of a white collar crime if he or she is a pillar of the community or has donated to the campaign fund of judges. Fifth, if a professional is found guilty of committing a white collar crime, he or she generally receives a far more lenient sentence than a street criminal and is more likely to be sent to a low-level-security correctional facility. With all these advantages typically afforded to a professional of high standing, we gain further insight to the seriousness of the crimes committed by Bernard Madoff.

The Power Structure and the Power Elites

It takes a certain type of socioeconomic system in order for white collar crime to flourish, and societies of the West provide an environment for professionals to prosper in a deviant/criminal manner. In the United States, for example, a power structure—a network of organizations and roles within a city or society that is responsible for maintaining the general social structure and shaping new policy initiatives—exists that has given rise to **power elites**. Domhoff and Dye (1987) describe the *power elite* as "the set of people who are the individual actors within the power structure" (p. 9). "Because the social order maintained by the power structure is a stratified one, with great inequalities of wealth and income, a power structure is also a system of organized domination, and the power elite often will use intimidation and coercion on its critics and opponents if necessary" (Domhoff and Dye 1987:9).

Domhoff and Dye believe that the power elites have a disproportionate amount of influence over public policy in the United States, and they are certainly not the first academics to call attention to this concern. C. Wright Mills (discussed in chapter 2), a conflict theorist, coined the term "power elites" in his 1956 book *The Power Elite*. For Mills, the power elites were the people at the top of major corporations and influential government persons. Mills believed that the power elites also control the military. Thus, for Mills the power structure of the United States consisted of three interconnected powers: business, government, and military. Mills described such collaboration as the "triangle of power" or the "tripartite elite" and warned that this triangle of power was an increasing threat to American democracy. Mills believed that the triangle of power worked together to dictate policy that best benefited their common goals. Mills claimed that it was easy for these entities to work together because the power elite among them were of similar social type, including their origin, level of education, style of life, and the fact that they are sociable, especially with "like-minded" others. In this manner, the power elite constitute a close-knit category of people who do not have to work behind closed doors in a covert manner; rather, because of their positions as captains of industry, they operate in open view through legitimate means afforded to those with great wealth and power-making decision positions within the government (politics), military, and industrial/private sectors (Mills 1956).

Building on the ideas of Mills and Domhoff and Dye, Mizruchi (1987) also discussed the power structure and the role of power elites: "One of the most crucial issues in the study of elites is the degree of elite cohesion" (p. 204). Mizruchi (1987) argues that it is in the best interests of the leading power structure corporations to stick together in their decision making because it affords them the best option to maximize their profits. Cohesion between the power structure entities is accomplished in numerous ways, including (1) *kinship*, especially important in traditional societies but still relevant in capitalist societies as power (and class interest) is often handed down from generation to generation; (2) *similar backgrounds*; as discussed by Mills (1956) and Domhoff (1970), similar backgrounds lead to social and corporate cohesion; (3) *special club membership* (reinforces a certain worldview), such as belonging to private country club that excludes all non-elites; (4) *policy-making organizations* (power elites from corporations serve as heads, or board members, of other decision-making organizations); (5) *financial institutions* (Mizruchi was on the cusp of revealing something very big here as he foresaw, to a limited degree, the role and power of banks in decision making); (6) *inner group* (those power elites that keep a focus on long-term interests of business as a whole while other businesses fight among themselves for individual goals); and (7) *the state* (politicians must be included among the power elites as businesses cannot directly dictate political policy) (Mizruchi 1987).

In their 1999 book *White-Collar Deviance* Simon and Hagan described the power structure and warned readers about the increasing power and control elite corporations held over the U.S. financial system. "Today, just five gigantic corporations (Exxon, Ford, General Motors, IBM and General Electric) possess 28 percent of the nation's industrial assets. The largest 100 corporate firms own nearly 75 percent of all industrial assets and account for 72 percent of all manufacturing jobs, and three-fourths of all U.S. Department of Defense contracts. Eleven banks own one-third of all banking assets, and the top 50 (out of nearly 15,000) own nearly two-thirds of all banking assets" (p. 9). The trend identified by Simon and Hagan nearly 20 years ago has dramatically increased, continuing through the present time. In other words, the largest corporations are controlling a larger percentage of the total U.S. assets. Upon reading the previous statement, most people are likely to think that oil and gas companies control the largest percentage of U.S. assets. However, it's really the banks that control the largest percentage of wealth in the nation.

According to the National Information Center (2015), a repository of financial data and institution characteristics collected by the Federal Reserve System, there were 104 U.S. holding corporations with assets greater than $10 billion as of December 31, 2014. The top 29 companies held at least $100 billion in assets, but just the top 4 held assets over $1 trillion: JPMorgan Chase & Co ($2.57 trillion); Bank of America Corp. ($2.10 trillion); CitiGroup Inc. ($1.84 trillion); and Wells Fargo & Company ($1.68 trillion) (National Information Center 2015). The significance of the money in the hands of banks is amplified by the realization that at the end of the fourth quarter of 2010, six bank companies (the four previously listed and Goldman Sachs Group Inc. and Morgan Stanley) had assets valued at just over 63 percent of the U.S. GDP (Jacobson 2011). As a matter of perspective, Exxon Mobil Corp., the largest oil/energy company (based in Texas), had total assets valued at over $346 billion in 2014 (Platts 2015).

From a power elite perspective the corporate-dominant power structure of the United States has increasingly fallen under the control of select elite entities, and right now, it is the banks and lending companies that are dominating the direction of social policy. Let's hope they *are* too big to fail . . . oh yeah, we already faced that scare (the 2007–2010 global financial crisis), so we clearly know deviance is occurring in the banking industry. But who will assure we do not face another financial crisis, the power elite?

Traders working on the floor of the New York Stock Exchange.

Corporate Crime

The study of corporate crime, a subcategory of white collar crime, reveals the answer to the above question: "No, we cannot rely on the power elite to assure we do not face another global financial crisis." Simon and Hagan (1999) state, "Another frightening consequence of concentrated corporate ownership and corporate-held political power is that corporate practices are unregulated by either government or effective political opposition by consumers and workers. This lack of control over corporations has contributed to the drastic economic changes of the United States over the last quarter-century, and to numerous other social harms" (p. 27). The result of such a power structure is an atmosphere that breeds corporate deviance. **Corporate deviance** refers to "acts of immense physical, financial, and moral harm committed by wealthy and powerful corporations no longer being constrained by government in their relentless pursuit of profits" (Simon and

Hagan 1999). According to Simon and Hagan (1999), the harms of corporate deviance involve:

1. "The frequent breaking of antitrust and other corporate laws
2. Physical harm inflicted on consumers (from dangerous products) and workers (from dangerous working conditions), and pollution of the environment
3. Financial harm stemming from monopolistic pricing practices (price-fixing)" (p. 28)

When it comes to corporate crime, corporate fraud continues to be one of the FBI's highest criminal priorities. The FBI (2015b) states, "As the lead agency investigating corporate fraud, we focus our efforts on cases that involve accounting schemes, self-dealing by corporate executives, and obstruction of justice." Corporate fraud came to light as a top concern of the FBI in 2002 in the wake of corporate scandals such as those perpetrated by Enron and WorldCom. Then-President George H. Bush created a corporate fraud task force to investigate and prosecute such crimes. In a speech delivered to a business group just blocks from the New York Stock Exchange, Bush said in support of the task force, "With strict enforcement and higher ethical standards, we must usher in a new era of integrity in Corporate America" (Gongloff 2002).

The FBI (2015b) investigates a variety of corporate fraud cases, many of them involving accounting schemes designed to deceive investors, auditors, and analysts about the true financial condition of a corporation or business entity. FBI (2015a) corporate fraud investigators concentrate primarily on the following activities:

1. Falsification of financial information of public and private corporations, including false accounting; entries and/or misrepresentations of financial condition; fraudulent trades designed to inflate profits and hide losses; and illicit transactions designed to evade regulatory oversight
2. Self-dealing by corporate insiders, including insider trading; kickbacks; misuse of corporate property for personal gain; and individual tax violations related to self-dealing
3. Obstruction of justice designed to conceal any of the above-noted types of criminal conduct, particularly when the obstruction impedes the inquiries of the SEC, other regulatory agencies, and/or law enforcement agencies

The FBI (2015b) underscores the importance of their attempt to curtail corporate fraud by stating that "in addition to significant financial losses to investors, corporate fraud has the potential to cause immeasurable damage to the U.S. economy and investor confidence."

White Collar Crime

The FBI's concern with corporate fraud's costs to investors specifically, and the costs to the U.S. economy in general, become magnified in urgency when the costs of all forms of white collar crime are calculated. Trying to estimate the cost of all white collar crimes is nearly impossible, as the sheer number of examples of white collar crime is overwhelming, and when we add to that the realization that a great deal of white collar crime goes unreported or is undetected, the costs easily exceed $1 trillion annually. Unlike street crime, the number of incidences of white collar crime, in nearly every category, has continually increased over the past several years.

Earlier in this chapter the original definition of white collar crime from Edwin Sutherland was provided; however, as we have learned, there are elements of that definition that needed to be modified. As a result, an updated definition is provided here. White collar crimes are typically nonviolent, nonstreet crimes committed by someone, generally a professional of high status, in commercial situations for financial gain. A wide variety of specific categories of crime fall under the white collar crime umbrella. In the following pages a number of specific examples will be discussed (but due to space constraints a number of other examples have been omitted). We begin our review with securities fraud.

Securities Fraud

Securities fraud is a type of serious white collar crime, such as a Ponzi scheme, in which a person or persons or a company misrepresents information that investors use to make decisions. In this chapter's introductory story we learned about Bernie Madoff and his Ponzi scheme that led to his conviction for 11 different, but related, federal crimes. A Ponzi scheme is an investment opportunity that lures investors by guaranteeing unusually high returns. The expression "Ponzi scheme" is named after Charles Ponzi, who promised 50 percent returns on investments in only 90 days (Yang 2014). Ponzi schemes are run by a central operator who uses money from new investors to pay off early investors, thus giving the illusion to early investors that they are involved in a legitimate investment opportunity. In order to keep the pyramid scheme operating the Ponzi operator has to convince early investors to stay on board longer to make even more money. Naturally, it's only a matter of time before the money to pay off investors is nonexistent. The Ponzi operator generally can either leave the country with as much as possible or attempt to cover his tracks by claiming unforeseen difficulties. "In Madoff's case, things began to deteriorate after clients requested a total of $7 billion back in returns. Unfortunately for Madoff, he only had $200 million to $300 million left to give" (Yang 2014). Madoff was able to run his scheme so successfully for so long because he was a part of the financial world's power structure (e.g., he sat on the board of the National Association of Securities Dealers and advised the Securities and Exchange Commission on trading securities) (Yang 2014).

Madoff's Ponzi operation was an example of securities fraud. The FBI (2015c) places a high priority on securities fraud cases because "the nation's economy is increasingly dependent on the success and integrity of the securities and commodities markets." The term "securities fraud" includes a wide range of illegal activities, all of which involve the deception of investors or the manipulations of financial markets: high-yield investment fraud; Ponzi schemes; pyramid schemes; advanced fee schemes; foreign currency fraud; broker embezzlement; hedge fund–related fraud; and late-day trading (FBI 2015c). The number of securities fraud cases increased from 1,139 in 2005 to 1,510 in 2009 (FBI 2015c).

Identity Fraud and Identity Theft

Among the growing issues of concern for nearly everyone living in the 21st century is the threat of identity theft and becoming a victim of identity fraud. Identity theft has been around in one form or another (e.g., fake IDs) for some time now; however, because of cybertechnology, the threat is more pervasive and the scams more sophisticated than ever before. Among the items identity thieves hope to attain from their victims are Social Security numbers, driver's license numbers, banking account numbers, and credit cards. This information, when stolen, not only allows thieves an opportunity to create false credentials wherein they can run up a sizable debt, but it also provides thieves a false identification to present to police, thus creating a criminal record or leaving outstanding arrest warrants for the victim whose identity has been stolen.

So what are identity fraud and identity theft? According to the U.S. Department of Justice (DOJ), "Identity theft and identity fraud are terms used to refer to all types of crime in which someone wrongfully obtains and uses another person's personal data in some way that involves fraud or deception, typically for economic gain." The DOJ (2015a) points out that while everyone's fingerprints are unique, our personal data, especially our Social Security numbers, bank account and credit card numbers, telephone calling card numbers, and other valuable identifying data can be used, if they fall into the wrong hands, by criminals who hope to profit at our expense. Americans and people around the world have fallen victim to identity fraud when unauthorized others have taken funds out of their bank or financial accounts, or, in the worst-case scenarios, have taken over their identities altogether, running up vast debts and committing other crimes while using the victim's identity (DOJ 2015a).

To highlight the reality that people around the world have fallen victim to identity theft and fraud consider that nearly 4 of 5 (78.2 percent) Chinese netizens (a term used to describe a "citizen of the net," or a regular user of the Internet, especially a habitual or avid one) have had their personal details—names, addresses, or identity numbers, including their "hukou" (also known as a household registration certificate)—disclosed without authorization, according to a report by the Internet Society of China (*China Daily* 2016).

The FBI (2015d) states, **identity theft** "occurs when someone assumes your identity to perform a fraud or other criminal act," and they warn that criminals can get the information they need to perform identity theft and fraud from a variety of sources, including by "stealing your wallet, rifling through your trash, or by compromising your credit or bank information." **Identity fraud** refers to crime in which a criminal uses a victim's personal data through fraud or deception for economic gain or other deceitful purposes. Identity fraud does not have to include identity theft as the thief has, for example, obtained a victim's credit card, uses it, but does not assume the victim's identity. Another example of identity fraud involves an individual who falsifies their own identity by changing their birth date to appear either older than they are (e.g., to purchase alcohol when underage) or to appear younger than they are (e.g., to maintain athletic eligibility in a league that has age limits).

Among other reasons, identity theft has become increasingly common because people share so much information online. People make banking transactions and file their taxes online, and all of these folks are increasingly likely to become victims of identity theft. In 2015, for example, many people learned that when they tried to file their tax return, it was rejected because someone else claiming to be that person had already filed a return. In addition to stealing the identity of working adults, white collar criminals will also use the Social Security numbers of young children to file tax returns in their names. A number of tax preparers are now offering identity protection services. H&R Block, for example, offers their clients a "Tax Identity Shield" to help protect taxpayer identity. Clients who sign up for the shield protection must create a password, and once that step has been taken, no one can prepare a tax return on that person's identity without the password. The H&R Block shield product also runs a scan of the enrollee's identity in January in preparation for that year's tax season. An evaluation is conducted on the enrollee and a "tax identity threat rating" score is provided.

The FBI warns us that the sources of information about each of us are so numerous that it is essentially impossible to prevent the theft of your identity, especially if criminals have specifically targeted a person(s). To try and minimize the chances of being victimized by identity theft and identity fraud, the DOJ (2015a) recommends, essentially, to consider every unsolicited form of electronic communication as a scam. (See box 4.1 to learn of ways to minimize the risk of identity theft.)

A CLOSER LOOK

Box 4.1 Ways to Minimize the Risk of Identity Theft

While the FBI (2015j) warns that it is nearly impossible to prevent the theft of your identity, it does provide a number of ways to help minimize the risk of having your identity stolen:

- Never throw away ATM receipts, credit statements, credit cards, or bank statements in a usable form. [Note: The author of this text has a strict policy of shredding every bit of written information where his name and any financial information about him appear in writing.]

- Never give your credit card over the telephone unless you make the call.

- Reconcile your bank account monthly, and notify your bank of discrepancies immediately. [Note: If your bank statement and your personal records—such as a checkbook—do not balance to the penny, you are not doing your best to minimize the threat from identity fraud.]

- Report unauthorized financial transactions to your bank, credit card company, and the police as soon as you detect them.

- Review a copy of your credit report at least once each year.

- If your identity has been assumed, ask the credit bureau to print a statement to that effect in your credit report.

The DOJ uses the acronym SCAM as a series of basic steps that individuals should take (the letter *C* is oddly not spelled out) in an effort to minimize the risk of being scammed by identity thieves:

S—Be *stingy* about giving out your personal information to others unless you have a reason to trust them. Be especially wary of anyone who offers you a chance to receive a major credit card, prize, or some other valuable item when they ask for personal data such as your SSN, credit card number or expiration date, or mother's maiden name.

A—*Ask* periodically for a copy of your credit report. Suspicious activities, such as new banking accounts in your name, should be investigated immediately.

M—*Maintain* careful records of your banking and financial accounts. Banking institutions are required to maintain copies of your checks, debit transactions, and so on for five years, but you should retain your monthly statements and checks for at least one year, if not more. You should balance all of your checking and debit accounts and minimize your online banking transactions; after all, the more often you use cybertechnology for financial purposes, the more often you are vulnerable to attack.

If you think, or know, that you've become a victim of identity theft or fraud, act immediately and contact appropriate government agencies, including the Federal Trade Commission (call 1-877-ID THEFT), Social Security Administration, Internal Revenue Service, or mail the Consumer Response Center. Identity theft is a real concern, and everyone should heed the warning to protect themselves the best they can from being a victim.

Credit and Debit Card Fraud

Credit card fraud is one form of identity theft and "involves the unauthorized taking of another's credit card information for the purpose of charging purchases to the account or removing funds from it" (Cornell University Law School 2015). Credit card fraud occurs in two primary forms: application fraud and account takeover. **Application fraud** occurs when an unauthorized person opens up a credit card account in another person's name. If the unauthorized person has enough information on another person, he or she can open an account in the identity theft victim's name. As with many forms of identity theft, the victim of a credit card application fraud scheme may not know the crime is being committed until it's too late (if the victim ever learns of it). An *account takeover* involves an unauthorized person taking over an existing credit card account either by gaining enough personal information of the credit card holder to change the account's billing address, subsequently reporting the card lost or stolen in order to obtain a new card, and then making fraudulent purchases with it (Cornell University Law School 2015). Account takeover can also occur via "skimming"—when businesses' employees illicitly access customers' credit card information—and then either sell the information to identity thieves or use the victim's credit card themselves.

Debit card fraud has certain similarities with credit card fraud but also has a primary distinction. Debit cards became popular following the Great Recession as many Americans needed to curtail and rethink their spending habits. Some people feared they could not control themselves enough to use a credit card, which allowed cardholders to spend more money than they had, so they opted for debit cards, which are capped based on how much money the cardholder has in their account. Millennials are especially more likely to have a debit card than a credit card (Schulz 2014). Like credit cardholders, debit cardholders have to worry about their cards being used by unauthorized persons who gained access to their personal identity information. Unfortunately for debit cardholders, when their card is used illegally, the costs of the unauthorized purchases come directly out of the victim's personal account, which is *not* the case with fraudulent credit card purchases. To make matters worse, it is much more difficult to recoup money lost from fraudulent debit card usage than it is for fraudulent credit card purchases. Federal law states that people are only liable for $50 in fraudulent charges, but only if you tell your bank within 2 business days of learning about them, while waiting more than 2 days but fewer than 60 days after receiving a statement the victim can be liable for up to $500, and after 60 days there are no limits on liability (Schulz 2014). (Check your bank's debit card liability policy to find how fraud may affect you if your card is lost or stolen.) When it comes to fraud protection, credit cards are much safer than debit cards (Schulz 2014).

Would-be credit or debit card thieves should heed the warning of the consequences for the unauthorized use of debit and credit cards. While such a crime may seem to pale in comparison to other, seemingly more serious crimes (e.g., attacking a police officer inside police headquarters), a person caught using another's card without permission may face a number of felonies. Consider, for example, the case of a 34-year-old man who was charged with stealing his friend's debit card and using the card to make multiple purchases. The thief was charged with two counts of first-degree identity theft, two counts of second-degree forgery, and two counts of fourth-degree criminal possession of stolen property, all felonies (House 2015). While the alleged debit card thief was being arrested, he physically resisted police and attempted to flee from the detective bureau, and for that, he was charged with one count of resisting arrest, a misdemeanor.

Health Care Fraud and Health Insurance Fraud

The Department of Justice estimates that health care fraud alone costs the United States upwards of $100 billion per year (DOJ 2015b). With national health care expenditures estimated to exceed $3 trillion in 2014, the potential for fraud costs to far exceed $100 billion annually seems a certainty. Health care fraud schemes are complex and serious, and law enforcement will have a difficult time exposing, arresting, successfully prosecuting, and recouping financial losses from these criminals.

One variation of health care fraud is practitioner fraud. Among the fraudulent practitioner schemes are:

- Obtaining subsidized or fully covered prescription pills that are actually unneeded by patients and then selling them on the black market
- Billing practitioners for care they never rendered
- Filling duplicate claims for the same services rendered
- Altering the dates, description of services, or identities of members or providers
- Intentional incorrect reporting of diagnoses or procedures to maximize payment
- Accepting or giving kickbacks for member referrals (Cornell University Law Center 2015)

Practitioners certainly qualify as professionals and meet the white collar crime definition criterion of "professional of high status"; however, the definition used for our purposes in this chapter (and modified from Sutherland's original definition) actually states "generally a professional of high status" to allow for the fact that people other than professionals in a given field may commit white collar crime. In the case of health care fraud, patients, or insurance members, may also commit fraud by "providing false information when applying for programs or services, forging or selling prescription drugs, using transportation benefits for non-medical related purposes, and loaning or using another's insurance card" (Cornell University Law Center 2015). Whenever, or however, health care fraud is committed, the health care provider passes the costs along to its customers, meaning that honest people will have to pay for the crimes of criminals. "Because of the pervasiveness of health care fraud, statistics now show that 10 cents of every dollar spent on health care goes toward paying for fraudulent health care claims" (Cornell University Law Center 2015). These health care fraud costs could, and should, be factored into the total costs of white collar crime to society.

Health care fraud and health insurance fraud often go hand in hand. The FBI (2015d) describes four examples of insurance fraud directly connected to health care fraud:

1. Medical equipment fraud—Equipment manufacturers offer "free" products to individuals and insurers and are then charged for products that were not needed and/or may not have been delivered.
2. "Rolling lab" schemes—Unnecessary and sometimes fake tests are given to individuals at health clubs, retirement homes, or shopping malls and billed to insurance companies or Medicare.
3. Services not performed—Customers or providers bill insurers for services never rendered by changing bills or submitting fake ones.

4. Medicare fraud—Medicare fraud can take the form of the health insurance frauds described above. Senior citizens are frequent targets of Medicare schemes, especially by medical equipment manufacturers who offer seniors free medical products in exchange for their Medicare numbers. Although medical doctors must sign off on such products, fraud scheme operators fake signatures or bribe corrupt doctors to sign the forms. Once the signature is in place, the manufacturers bill Medicare for merchandise or service that was not needed or not ordered.

The DOJ reports that its Medicare Fraud Strike Force team investigates hundreds of cases. In 2013, the Medicare Fraud Strike Force team issued 137 indictments "involving charges filed against 345 defendants alleged to have collectively billed the Medicare program more than $1.1 billion" (DOJ 2015b).

As with our discussion on every topic of white collar crime presented in this chapter, the examples of health care fraud and health insurance fraud provided here represent a mere sampling.

Extortion

Extortion involves the criminal behavior of trying to get money, property, or some sort of other favors from a person, entity, or institutions through coercive means. On the streets, extortion is sometimes referred to as a "shakedown." It may also be presented to business owners as a type of "protection service." Of course, the business owner only needs the protection service because the people committing the shakedown are the ones that legitimate business owners need to be protected from. Because extortion often involves physical threats, or acts of violence, this criminal activity is often discussed as a street crime. However, extortion is also a tool utilized by white collar criminals, including political entities and organized crime syndicates. Extortion has occurred once the threat has been made; the targeted victim need not actually have paid the money or property in order to qualify as an example of extortion. Extortion works via scare tactics. The targeted victim is told that bad things will happen unless payment is made. In this regard, extortion is different from the street crime of robbery (see chapter 5), wherein the criminals take what they want at the time of the confrontation with the victim. The use of blackmail—threatening to reveal some sort of information about the victim or their loved ones—is a common feature with extortion. The use of blackmail is what often qualifies extortion as a white collar crime, especially in the world of politics.

The FBI (2014a) reports that "virtual kidnapping" is a type of extortion, and its incidence is on the rise. "These schemes typically involve an individual or criminal organization who contacts a victim via telephone and demands payment for the return of a 'kidnapped' family member or friend. While no actual kidnapping has taken place, the callers often use co-conspirators to convince their victims of the legitimacy of the threat. For example, a caller might attempt to convince a victim that his daughter was kidnapped by having a young female scream for help in the background during the call" (FBI 2014a).

Forgery

Forgery is another example of white collar theft and consists of making false legal documents or altering existing documents. A common form of forgery involves signing someone else's name to a document such as a check, money order, credit card, mortgage, deeds, and stocks and bonds. The FBI (2015d) defines **forgery** as "The altering, copying, or imitating of something, without authority or right, with the intent to deceived or defraud by passing the copy or thing altered or imitated as that which is original or genuine; or the selling, buying, or possession of an altered, copied, or imitated thing with the intent to deceive or defraud." Forgery can be accomplished via handwriting, printing, engraving, typewriting, and via the use of someone's electronic signature. Passing bad checks, counterfeiting money, and running confidence (con) games are included as types of forgeries.

Insider Trading

Insider trading refers to the "trading of securities or stocks by 'insiders' with material, non-public information pertaining to significant, often market-moving developments to benefit themselves or others financially" (FBI 2012). The parameters of people with access to this nonpublic information is expanding and includes "securities professionals (traders and brokers); corporate executives and employees, along with employees of banking and brokerage firms and even contractors; lawyers working with companies on mergers and acquisitions; government employees who misuse their legitimate need-to-know position; and even friends, family members, and business associates who are tipped off about the information" (FBI 2012). All of these individuals are obligated to keep this information in the strictest confidence so as to maintain the public trust in the socioeconomic system.

Nearly everyone involved with investing has heard of the term "insider trading" and generally associates it with illegal conduct. However, according to the U.S. Securities and Exchange Commission (SEC), insider trading includes both legal and illegal conduct. Legal insider trading occurs when corporate insiders—officers, directors, and employees—buy and sell stock in their own companies. When corporate insiders trade their own securities, they are required to report their trades to the SEC (SEC 2015). **Illegal insider trading** generally refers to "buying or selling a security, in breach of a fiduciary duty or other relationship of trust and confidence, while in possession of material, nonpublic information about the security" (SEC 2015). "Tipping" someone off about confidential information is considered the misappropriation of such information and is a criminal offense for both the person who tipped the information and the one who received the tip. "Because insider trading undermines investor confidence in the fairness and integrity of the securities markets, the SEC has treated the detection and prosecution of insider trading violations as one of its enforcement priorities" (SEC 2015). Whenever insider trading occurs, it comes at a cost to society.

Occupational Crime

White collar crimes involve instances of crime committed in commercial situations for financial gain. Many, but not all, white collar crimes take place during the course of one's occupation. For example, we have already found that identity thieves need not work at the same occupation as their victims, and credit and debit card fraud, health care fraud, and forgery can all be accomplished by people who do not have jobs. This reality justifies the white collar crime subcategory of occupational crime. Occupational crime can be committed by higher-status and rank-and-file status employees given that an opportunity presents itself, or an opportunity is created. With this in mind we can define **occupational crime** as deviant or criminal behavior committed during the course of one's occupation for the purpose of seeking ill-gotten personal gain. Examples of occupational crime include money laundering, racketeering, stocks and securities violations, and corruption of government officials. To best illustrate occupational crime we will take a look at government bailouts as a result of lax regulation and the case of Enron.

When it comes to huge government bailouts, most younger people are likely to think of the Troubled Asset Relief Program (TARP) that bailed out Wall Street and the U.S. auto industry at the end of the first decade of the 21st century. "Although Congress initially authorized $700 billion for TARP in October 2008, that authority was reduced to $475 billion by the Dodd-Frank Wall Street Reform and Consumer Protection Act (Dodd-Frank Act)" (U.S. Department of the Treasury 2015). Decades earlier, it was the savings and loan (S&L) financial institutions that were bailed out at a cost of nearly a half trillion dollars, with about one-third coming from taxpayers (Stevenson 1996). "The money went to clean up the financial mess from the failure of more than 700 savings institutions in the 1980s and the early 1990s as a result of mismanagement, fraud and an economic downturn in states in states like Texas and California" (Stevenson 1996).

The S&L crisis began in 1982 under President Ronald Reagan with the congressional passage of the Garn-St. Germain Depository Institutions Act of 1982—which freed S&Ls to make risky loans, eliminate deposit caps, and hold less capital. Reagan was a big fan of deregulation and the "S&Ls used their new freedom to pay higher rates to depositors and invested those new deposits in commercial and real estate and junk bonds" (Cohan 2010). The S&Ls earned high up-front fees, but that was followed by "an implosion of reckless investments" leading to the collapse of the thrift financial industry (McFadden 2014). Many investors, duped by bankers, lost their homes and life savings. Reagan's successor, George H. W. Bush, had to oversee what was then the biggest bailout in U.S. history (Cohan 2010).

The common thread between these two financial crises is the lax regulation in multiple related occupational settings with risky behavior put into action by professionals during the course of their occupation. "Clever manipulation of the banking system allowed financial firms to reap huge profits while shifting the risks, and ultimately the costs, onto taxpayers. Deregulation allowed the S&Ls to deviate dramatically from their fiscally conservative missions and that deviation led them to create all sorts of investments that purported to generate higher returns but were really just bad deals" (Cohan 2010).

The case of Enron serves as a warning for all occupational workers. Enron was a solid company throughout the 1990s and was universally hailed as one of the nation's most innovative companies that shunned the traditional commitment to hard assets in favor of e-commerce. "The company continued to build power plants and operate gas lines, but it became better known for its unique trading businesses. Besides buying and selling gas and electricity futures, it created whole new markets for such oddball 'commodities' as broadcast time for advertisers, weather futures, and Internet bandwidth" (NPR 2015). With its roots in the utility business, a seemingly safe and stable industry, Enron invested strongly in e-commerce, much to the delight of Wall Street investors, who invested heavily in Enron, sending its stock values skyrocketing. At its peak, Enron was worth nearly $70 billion and its shares traded for about $90 each (NPR 2015).

Eventually, it was revealed that Enron had inflated, by billions of dollars, its equity, and in an attempt to cover it up, the company hid huge sums of debts in its trading businesses. At best, Enron's executives and financial officers were neglectful, and at worst, they were "complicit in perpetrating one of the biggest frauds in corporate history" (NPR 2015). In late 2001, Enron's collapse led to bankruptcy. The day before filing, Enron fired 4,000 workers, one-quarter of its 21,000 employees. The company followed up these layoffs with additional ones. Suddenly, thousands of Enron employees had lost their jobs, health care, and life savings through no fault of their own. Mortgages could not be paid, and current and pending retirements became uncertain (Bragg 2002). The employees, understandably, felt betrayed. Blame their troubles on the public issue of occupational white collar crime.

In addition to the thousands of Enron employees who lost their occupations was the ripple effect to Enron's affiliate associations. The aftermath of the Enron collapse has led to this case being known as one of the America's greatest business debacles and failures. "In the immediate aftermath of Enron, there were at least a half dozen other big corporate blowups: WorldCom turned out to be cooking its books, and CEO Bernie Ebbers went to jail. Tyco became embroiled in scandal, and its chief, Dennis Kozlowski, also went to prison. But none of these disasters have resonated like Enron" (McLean and Elkind 2013).

Enron represents the epitome of an occupational white collar crime. Furthermore, "Enron remains the defining scandal of the 21st century. . . . This is partly because no other modern-day company, prior to the financial crisis of 2008, had Enron's vaunted reputation. But it is also because almost everything we later found out about how Enron operated was a harbinger of scandals yet to come" (McLean and Elkind 2013).

Unsafe Products

As mentioned earlier in this chapter, white collar crime has associated costs (as measured in terms of total dollars and loss of life) that far exceed street crime. We have learned quite a bit about the *economic costs* of white collar crime with some references to loss of life; it is our discussion on unsafe products that best shines the light on the *associated deaths* caused by white collar crime (and bear in mind, we have yet to discuss organized and political crime—which are variations of white collar crime and also result in the loss of many lives).

Unsafe products are those that cause undue or unexpected harm, including death, to those who use them. These products generally fail to meet industrial, state, or federal regulatory standards, or they are not regulated by any governing body at all. In many cases, unsafe products contain design flaws and are later taken off the market—but not until people have been injured or died—and are subject to consumer lawsuits. The U.S. Consumer Product Safety Commission (CPSC) is tasked to, among other things, prevent unsafe products from reaching the hands of consumers. In the last quarter of 2011 alone the CPSC (2012a) prevented more than a half million violative and hazardous imported products from reaching the hands of U.S. consumers. "Working with U.S. Customs and Border Protection (CBP) agents, CPSC port investigators successfully identified consumer products that were in violation of U.S. safety rules or found to be unsafe. CPSC and CBP teamed up to screen more than 2,900 imported shipments at ports of entry into the United States. . . . Their efforts prevented more than 647,000 units of about 240 different noncomplying products from reaching consumers, between October 1, 2011 and December 31, 2011" (CPSC 2012a). During the fiscal year 2011, the CPSC inspected more than 9,900 product shipments at ports nationwide and stopped almost 4.5 million units of violative or hazardous consumer products from entering stores and homes of U.S. consumers (CPSC 2012a). The most common products stopped were children's products, most of which contained lead or presented a choking hazard for children younger than 3 years old, and toys and children's clothing that contained banned phthalates. The most common nonchildren's products found in violation of U.S. safety codes were holiday lights, hair dryers, lighters, and luminaries (CPSC 2012a).

The CPSC cannot stop all unsafe products from reaching consumer outlets and eventually consumer homes. Manufacturers may choose to ignore safety guidelines altogether, thus putting consumers at risk for injury or death. In some instances, manufacturing industries are self-regulating (which generally equates to little or no regulation). The toy industry, for example, was once a self-regulating industry and was not forced to comply with federal safety standards until 2008 with the congressional passage of the Consumer Product Safety Improvement Act of 2008 (CPSC 2013). It seems very deviant that children's toys were only recently regulated and required to meet federal safety requirements. (See box 4.2 for a satirical look at the toy industry as it once was, before federal regulation and oversight.)

CONNECTING SOCIAL DEVIANCE AND POPULAR CULTURE

Box 4.2 What's So Dangerous about a Bag o' Glass?

Before the passage of the Consumer Product Safety Improvement Act of 2008, the toy industry was essentially a self-regulating industry. Harmless and harmful new toys alike were shipped to retail outlets; consumers purchased them and in the case of harmful products, children would get injured. Whenever a child was injured, complaints would be filed, and eventually the toy was removed from shelves (although not in all cases). Many of us have wondered for decades, how do certain, seemingly obviously harmful toys make it to the shelves in the first place? Didn't toy manufacturers care about children's safety?

A classic, 1976 *Saturday Night Live* skit (season 2, episode 10) provided a great satire and social commentary about the lack of safety regulation in the toy industry during that era. In this skit, Candice Bergen (guest star) played a consumer reporter and host of a show called *Consumer Probe* and Dan Aykroyd (cast member) played Irwin Mainway, president of Mainway Toys. The consumer reporter was reviewing a number of toys (e.g., "Johnny Switchblade, press his head and two sharp knives spring from his arms") on her "Holiday Edition" of the *Consumer Probe* show

and had as her guest Irwin Mainway. She was a hard-hitting reporter who wanted answers as to why Mainway Toys seemed to manufacture so many dangerous toys for children. Mainway would retort with callous comments to all her questions. Often disgusted with Mainway's answers, the consumer reporter would reluctantly accept the toy maker's responses and move on to the next product until she finally came to the toy she viewed as the most unsafe.

> Consumer reporter: Alright. Fine. Fine. Well, we'd like to show you another one of Mr. Mainway's products. It retails for $1.98, and it's called Bag o' Glass. [She holds up the bag of glass for the camera.] Mr. Mainway, this is simply a bag of jagged, dangerous, glass bits.

> Mainway: Yeah, right, it's you know, it's glass, it's broken glass, you know? It sells very well, as a matter of fact, you know? It's just broken glass, you know?

> Consumer reporter: [Laughs] I don't understand. I mean, children could seriously cut themselves on any one of these pieces!

Mainway: Yeah, well, look—you know, the average kid, he picks up, you know, broken glass anywhere, you know? The beach, the street, garbage cans, parking lots, all over the place in any big city. . . . If you hold this up, you know, you see colors, every color of the rainbow! I mean, it teaches him about light refraction, you know? Prisms, and that stuff!

Consumer reporter: So you don't feel this product is dangerous?

Mainway: No! Look, we put a label on every bag that says, "Kid! Be careful—broken glass!"

Irwin Mainway was an exaggerated character representing a fictitious toy manufacturer. Nonetheless, his attitude of "profits-come-first" capitalism underscored the devious nature of an industry without proper regulations. The consumer reporter summed up the thoughts of most parents of small children: "Well, I just don't understand why you can't make harmless toys."

Recognizing that the CPSC is stretched too thin to guard against all unsafe product dangers, a number of consumer groups have sprung into action in an attempt to protect people from unsafe products, such as toys. The Take Justice Back (2012) consumer group is especially interested in unsafe children's toys, and they compiled a list of the "10 Most Dangerous Toys of All Time." The top five items from the Take Justice Back (2012) list are provided below:

1. *CSI* Fingerprint Examination Kit—Based on the popular CBS TV show, this kit contained a special powder and brushes so that children could look for fingerprints. The powder in question contained up to 5 percent asbestos.
2. Magnetix (building sets)—Contained many plastic pieces that could break open and be easily swallowed. While many toys contain small pieces that young children may swallow, and then pass through their digestive system, Magnetix toys included magnets that do not pass through the digestive system and instead connect to each other, leading to such problems as forming large masses that cut off blood supply to vital organs. Painful deaths could occur in a matter of a few hours.
3. Inflatable Baby Boat—The boat's leg straps were prone to tear, causing the baby or toddler in question to slip through and possibly lead to drowning. In 2009, 4 million of these boats were recalled. The manufacturer, Aqua-Leisure, knew about this problem for at least 6 years and was fined $650,000 by the CPSC.
4. Hannah Montana Pop Star Card Game—Contained nearly two times the legally allowed amount of lead in a product, and lead is the second-most-deadly household toxin in existence, trailing only arsenic.
5. Aqua Dots—One of the most popular toys of 2007, Aqua Dots were small, colorful beads that could be arranged into different designs and then permanently set with a small amount of water. Reports of problems came to light immediately as children would swallow the beads and vomit. It was then discovered that the glue contained chemicals that metabolized into gamma-hydroxybutyrate, otherwise known as GHB—the date rape drug.

Once a product has been deemed unsafe, the most common course of action is a product recall. A **product recall** may be defined as the process of retrieving defective products from consumers and providing those consumers with compensation (e.g., monetary compensation or product replacement). "Virtually any product sold can be subject to a recall. These can include food, drugs, toys, appliances, cribs, cosmetics, clothing, boats and automobiles. There are six government agencies that do testing for safety concerns of products on the market. Last year [2014] was a record year for auto recalls, as well as medicine recalls. But other, less headline-grabbing product recalls are taking place constantly" (*The Topeka Capital-Journal* 2015). Recalls are so common these days that many people tend to ignore them. The Better Business Bureau (BBB), however, urges consumers to pay attention to recall notices, because complacency can have deadly consequences (*The Topeka Capital-Journal* 2015). Manufacturers and retailers generally notify the public if they have a recall product. News agencies and a number of government websites (e.g., Recalls.gov) also provide recall information. Providing any sort of list of recall products would be an exercise in futility here; suffice it to say, consumers should heed the warning of the BBB and keep their eyes and ears open to recall notices. This is especially true for anyone who owns an automobile or takes prescription drugs.

Recall notices of unsafe products are designed to try and save people from injury or death. Despite the large number of recalls, millions of people are injured and tens of thousands are killed annually due to unsafe products. In their 2012 report, the CPSC estimated that in 2010 more than 38.5 million people sought medical attention for an injury related to, but not necessarily caused by, a consumer product, an increase of 5.6 percent from the 2009 estimate (CPSC 2012a). The CPSC (2012b) also estimated that nearly 36,000 deaths were related to, but not necessarily caused by, a consumer product in 2008, an increase of 4.1 percent from the 2007 estimate. The 2008 rate marks the eighth consecutive year that the number of deaths increased from the previous year. The CPSC (2012b) reports that the rates of injury and death are not constant among all age groups; instead, the very young and the elderly have much higher rates of death than the population in the middle. As the baby boomers continue to age, the number of deaths related to unsafe products is expected to continue to increase for the foreseeable future.

Among the more common items to face a recall are unsafe automobile devices. Consider, for example, the Chrysler recall of its Jeeps; specifically, the 1993–2004 Jeep Grand Cherokee and 2002–2007 Jeep Liberty models. According a March 2015 *CBS This Morning* report, more than 50 people have died due to deadly fires as a result of crashes into the rear end of the defective Jeeps (Pegues 2015). On April 15, 2015, CBS reported that 75 people had died as a result of postcrash fires. Safety advocates say that the death count figure is much higher and that the number of fatalities rivals the GM faulty ignition switch recall models, which, as of January 22, 2016, resulted in 1,385 death and injury cases and the recall of more than 30 million vehicles (GM paid nearly $600 million to settle 399 claims made to a fund it established; those claims covered 124 deaths), mostly Chevrolet Cobalts and Saturn Ions, from the 2003 through 2007 model years (Gardner 2015; Associated Press 2016a). The location of the Jeep fuel tanks is not safe because it is lower than the rear bumper. Making matters worse, the gas tanks are made of plastic. If another vehicle crashes into the back of the defective Jeeps, the fuel tank can rupture, causing a deadly fire. In 2010, the National Highway Traffic Safety Administration (NHTSA) started investigating consumer complaints of the troublesome Jeeps. Chrysler, for 3 years, argued that the vehicles were not defective. In June 2013, NHTSA told Chrysler to recall the vehicles, saying that the defect caused an unreasonable risk of burning to death in rear-end collisions (NHTSA 2013). Chrysler knew the Jeeps were defective but did not want to incur the costs to recall the 1.5 million vehicles involved. Instead, Chrysler put out a voluntary recall notice. On November 19, 2014, NHTSA ordered a recall because only 3 percent of the defective vehicles were brought in for service. Some local dealers told the Jeep owners that the problem was "not real" or that "they did not have the part" needed as ordered by the recall (Pegues 2015). In March 2015 Chrysler dealers were still telling customers that the Jeeps were safe (Pegues 2015). By mid-April, just 4 percent of the Jeeps and 27 percent of Libertys covered by the recall had actually been serviced (CBS 2015).

An automobile on fire on the shoulder of a road.

Jeeps with defective gas tanks that can explode upon a rear-end collision and the automaker's refusal to want to incur the costs to make their product safe for customers is reminiscent of the Ford Pinto scandal in the 1970s in which many people died by burning. Ford utilized a practice, which was legal at the time, known as the "cost-benefits analysis" to determine whether or not to go ahead with the recall. If Ford could show that the costs to them (the cost of a replacement part, that cost $11, times the number of vehicles) were higher than the benefits (saving lives) gained, they did not have to go through with the recall. In order to calculate the benefits, a value had to be placed on human life, and that value was set at $200,000 (a serious burn injury was worth about $67,000) (Dowie 1977). Ford determined that it was not cost-effective for them to go through with an unsafe product recall and for years successfully fought the recall. Eventually a recall was ordered, and the automaker was forced to pay millions of dollars to settle damage suits (out of court) following the 1978 recall of over 1.5 million 1971–1976 Pinto sedans and Runabouts, plus similar 1975–1976 Mercury Bobcats.

The auto industry has recalled millions of vehicles to replace faulty air bags as well. By June 1, 2016, eight automakers recalled more than 12 million vehicles in the United States to replace potentially dangerous Takata air bag inflators. This recall was a part of a massive expansion of Takata air-bag recalls announced in May 2016, which included 17 automakers and 35 million to 40 million inflators. The faulty inflators are responsible for 11 deaths and more than 100 injuries worldwide (Krisher 2016).

Summing up the seriousness of unsafe products, the CPSC (2012a) reports that "deaths, injuries, and property damage from consumer product incidents cost the nation more than $1 trillion annually." When we add up the costs from all the other categories of white collar crime, we begin to understand just how serious a problem this type of deviant behavior truly is.

Political Crime

Imagine corrupt government officials and their associates stealing a billion dollars from an economic development fund designed to promote economic development, and then imagine a large portion of that money being spent to finance a major Hollywood film centered on the topic of corruption. Such is the case alleged against Malaysian officials and their associates from 1Malaysia Development Berhad, also known as 1MDB, who reportedly stole a total of $1 billion in assets. According to the U.S. Attorney General's Office, more than $100 million of the stolen loot allegedly went to produce *The Wolf of Wall Street*, a 2013 film that has earned nearly $400 million in ticket sales worldwide (making this the highest-grossing film of its director, Martin Scorsese). *The Wolf of Wall Street* is based on the true story of Jordan Belfort (played by Leonardo DiCaprio), from his rise to a wealthy stockbroker living the high life to his fall from his loft because of corruption. *Wolf* spent 6 years in development due to its salacious, R-rated subject matter before it was finally green-lighted by a virtually unknown production company, Red Granite Pictures, which footed almost all of the costs, according to a *Wall Street Journal* report. The suit says that Red Granite bankrolled *Wolf* with 1MDB funds funneled into a Swiss bank account held in the name of Good Star Limited. Cash was then transferred into various accounts at City National Bank in Los Angeles and paid out to cover the film's production costs (Gould and Golding 2016). This story reflects a mere sampling of political crimes and their overlap with so many other aspects of social life.

Political crime refers to acts perpetrated by, or against, a government or state. There are many types of political crime, ranging from violations of the law (e.g., political corruption, bribery, espionage, treason, illegal lobbyist activities, and political torture) committed by individuals and groups, to those committed by government or their agencies as they attempt to prevent or control dissent within their borders or as they attempt to manipulate the political system of foreign nations. In the following pages, we will explore a few examples of political crime.

Political Corruption

Politics is generally viewed as the guiding influence of governmental policy. The political system operates on behalf of the government. The *government* is the political unit that exercises authority via laws and customs. While the government may appear to be a faceless political unit, it actually consists of a group of people who control and make decisions for a country, state, or local municipality. The individuals who are active in government, either as seekers or holders of public office, are known as politicians. Politicians, like everyone else, are capable of making mistakes in judgment; unfortunately for citizens, the mistakes made by politicians can have deadly consequences. Sometimes politicians make honest mistakes based on information available to them at the time of the decision, or vote, and in cases such as these, constituents are likely to go with the adage "to err is human." However, there are many instances when politicians are more concerned about winning favor or retaining power than they are about maintaining integrity and ethical principles. In this regard, many politicians may be guilty of fraudulent behavior.

Fraudulent behavior in the political arena is known as political corruption. Corruption may be defined as dishonest or illegal actions committed by powerful people or people in authority (e.g., government officials or police officers) that destroy the people's trust in the person or the group. According to the United Nations Office on Drugs and Crime (UNODC), "Corruption is a complex social, political and economic phenomenon that affects all countries. Corruption undermines democratic institutions, slows economic development and contributes to governmental instability. Corruption attacks the foundation of democratic institutions by distorting electoral processes, perverting the rule of law and creating bureaucratic quagmires whose only reason for existing is the soliciting of bribes" (UNODC 2015).

Public corruption is an aspect of political corruption. Public corruption involves a breach of public trust and/or the abuse of power by political officials and their private sector accomplices. Public corruption occurs when an elected, appointed, or hired government official asks, demands, solicits, accepts, or agrees to receive anything of value in return for being influenced in the performance of their official duties (FBI 2010; Cornell University Law School 2015). The FBI considers public corruption a very serious white collar crime. "Public corruption poses a fundamental threat to our national security and way of life. It impacts everything from how well our borders are secured and our neighborhoods protected . . . to verdicts handed down in courts . . . to the quality of our roads, schools, and other government services. And it takes a significant toll on our pocketbooks, wasting billions in tax dollars every year" (FBI 2015e). The FBI (2010) states that while most government officials are honest and work hard to improve the lives of the American people, a small number of federal, state, and local officials make decisions for the wrong reasons—usually for financial gain for themselves, or their friends and family.

Many types of crime fall under the public corruption category of political crime, including extortion, embezzlement, racketeering, kickbacks, and money laundering, as well as wire, mail, bank, and tax fraud. The most common example of public corruption is bribery (FBI 2010).

Bribery

Bribery involves the offering of money or gifts to a person in power, especially a public official in the discharge of his or her legal duties, in an effort to entice that public official to do something on behalf of the briber. The person offering the bribe to someone to betray their responsibility and the public trust is known as seeking undue influence over that official's actions. If a public official seeks payment in exchange for certain deeds, that person is said to be peddling influence. Regardless of who initiates the exchange of money or gifts for political favors, bribery is considered a serious offense.

Echoing the concerns of the FBI with regard to the serious nature of public corruption, President Barack Obama has described the fight against corruption as "one of the great struggles of our time" (U.S. Mission to the Organization for Economic Cooperation and Development 2015). The OECD (2015) states that the costs of political corruption are immeasurable but include injustice, misallocation of resources and lives, and erosion of the faith of citizens in their governments and in the rule of the law. So serious is political corruption that the United States views "corruption as a growing threat to the national security of our country and allies around the world" (OECD 2015). Among the great threats from political corruption is international bribery. The United States has led the fight against international bribery and took its first significant action with the passage of the Foreign Corrupt Practices Act (1977), "domestic legislation which prohibits Americans and other persons and businesses that fall under the jurisdiction of the law from bribing foreign officials in order to obtain or retain business" (OECD 2015). The United States has been working for the past few decades to encourage other nations to criminalize bribery.

In 2014, the White House under President Obama issued a press release outlining the U.S. effort in fighting bribery and corruption. Part of the press release reads:

> Preventing corruption preserves funds for public revenue and thereby helps drive development and economic growth. By contrast, pervasive corruption siphons revenue away from the public budget and undermines the rule of law and the confidence of citizens in their governments, facilitates human rights abuses and organized crime, empowers authoritarian rulers, and can threaten the stability of entire regions. The United States views corruption as a growing threat to the national security of our country and allies around the world. (The White House 2014)

The ways the Obama administration attempted to stem worldwide corruption include:

- Pursuing corrupt actors and the proceeds of corruption
- Working with U.S. businesses
- Improving transparency in the extractives industry (the extraction of raw materials, such as oil, natural gas, coal, diamonds, and other minerals from the earth to be used by consumers)
- Working with other countries to promote anticorruption, transparency, and open government
- Galvanizing global efforts to promote open government principles in the Open Government Partnership (OGP) (The White House 2014)

The World Bank (2015) shares a particular concern with improving transparency in the extractives industry because of the 3.5 billion people who live in countries rich in oil, gas, or minerals. "With good governance and transparent management, the revenues from extractive industries can have a transformed impact on reducing poverty and boosting shared prosperity, while respecting community needs and the environment" (The World Bank 2015).

In sum, the White House, U.S. government, governments around the world, and worldwide organizations such as the World Bank all consider political corruption and bribery as a very serious problem and a source of a great number of costs, both economic and otherwise (e.g., a threat to the stability of the U.S. economy and economies worldwide).

Espionage

Another threat to the U.S. political system is espionage. **Espionage** refers to the act of spying or of using spies to obtain, deliver, or transmit secret or confidential information, especially regarding a government or business, without the target's permission or knowledge. Nations around the world have long worried about being victimized by espionage. A century ago, the United States passed the Espionage Act of 1917 as a result of its declaration of war with Germany and the concern that some of the millions of American men and women of German ancestry might have loyalties to Germany, and thus serve as German spies. The Espionage Act of 1917 defines espionage during wartime and has as its focus the issue of national loyalty. Among the features of the act was the legal authority given to postal officials to ban the mailing of newspapers and magazines that contained an anti-American message. A year later, Congress passed the Sedition Act of 1918, which made it a federal offense to use "disloyal, profane, scurrilous or abusive language" about the Constitution, the government, the American uniform, or the flag (Digital History 2014).

The U.S. government has prosecuted over 2,100 people under the Espionage and Sedition acts. In 2014, for example, Stephen Kim, a former contractor for the U.S. State Department, was prosecuted for violating the Espionage Act of 1917 and for making false statements. Kim disclosed privileged information to Fox News reporter James Rosen in 2009 regarding a possible nuclear test being planned by North Korea in retaliation to sanctions from the West. A grand jury found that Kim "knowingly and willfully" shared information "about the military capabilities and preparedness of a particular foreign nation" (RT America 2014). The most famous person to have a criminal complaint filed against him for violating the Espionage Act is Edward Snowden. In 2013, Snowden was charged with three felonies, two of which come under the Espionage Act. The complaint shows that Snowden was charged with "unauthorized communication of national defense information"—an Espionage Act violation—and "willful communication of classified communications intelligence information to an unauthorized person," a violation of U.S. Code 987 that prohibits the disclosure of classified information (Gosztola 2013). At the time, Snowden was the eighth person (Stephen Kim's arrest came after Snowden's) to be charged under the Espionage Act under Obama (Gosztola 2013). Snowden fled U.S. jurisdiction and, as of this writing (March 2015), he was still living in exile in Russia.

The FBI (2015f) warns about the seriousness of foreign intelligence operations and espionage and states, "Today, more foreign spies—not just traditional adversaries but also allies, hackers, and terrorists—are trying to steal more U.S. secrets from more places than ever before. They are after our country's most significant classified information—from military plans to national security vulnerabilities to our own intelligence activities. They also want our nation's trade secrets, innovations that give us a leg up in the global marketplace and technologies that could be used to develop or improve weapons of mass destruction."

While the FBI and other government officials worry about keeping their secrets, whistle-blowers and some news reporters feel that it is their duty to keep the public informed about certain secrets, especially those that could harm the public.

Consider, for example, in March 2015, Amy Goodman, award-winning journalist and host of a daily international TV/radio show, warned about President Obama working in secret to pass the Trans-Pacific Partnership (TPP), "one of the most far-reaching trade agreements in history. TPP will set rules governing more than 40 percent of the world's economy" (Goodman 2015b:A4). The TPP is praised by Republicans and despised by progressive Democrats. Obama was in such a hurry to try and pass the TPP that he tried to also pass the Trade Promotion Authority (TPA), a type of "fast-track" giving "the president authority to negotiate a trade deal, and to then present it to Congress for a yes-or-no vote, with no amendments allowed" (Goodman 2015b:A4). In a statement that sounds like a reference to the Espionage Act, Goodman (2015b) describes the seriousness of Obama's secret work on the TPP: "Members of Congress also have been given limited access to briefings on the negotiations, but under strict secrecy rules that, in at least one instance recently, include the threat of imprisonment if details are leaked" (p. A4). (Note: In January 2017, President Donald Trump took executive action to assure that the United States would pull out of the TPP.) People, like Goodman, only know what little they know because WikiLeaks, the document disclosure and whistle-blower website, released several chapters more than a year ago. Leaking information may be viewed as espionage in some cases, but in other instances it may be a necessary tool to keep the public informed, and an informed public is a fundamental principle of a democracy. Perhaps leaking information that affects and ultimately informs the public can be viewed as an example of positive deviance. What do you think?

Treason

"One of the oldest political crimes is treason" (Ross 2012:36). Treason involves an attempt to overthrow the government of the society of which one is a member (Ross 2012). **Treason** is defined as the offense of the betrayal of one's own country by waging war against it or by consciously or purposely acting to aid its enemies. Treason is the only crime specifically defined in the Constitution, and it carries the possibility of a death sentence. Treason is punishable under U.S. law Title 18 U.S. Code 2381: "Whoever, owing allegiance to the United States, levies war against them or adheres to their enemies, giving them aid and comfort within the United States or elsewhere, is guilty of treason and shall suffer death, or shall be imprisoned not less than five years and fined under this title but not less than $10,000; and shall be incapable of holding any office under the United States." Proving treason involves either the accused admitting to it in open court or the testimony of two eyewitnesses. Very few Americans have actually been convicted of treason.

Political Torture

Torture is the act of causing excruciating pain as a form of punishment or revenge or as a means of forcing someone to give up information or a confession. Torture causes anguish of body or mind via the infliction of intense pain such as burning the victim, crushing bones, tearing ligaments, or any other manner of delivering agony. Jean Kellaway, the author of *The History of Torture and Execution* (2000), states, "The progress of mankind has been shadowed by the grisly history of torture and execution. For every shining triumph of human endeavor there has been a dark example of state-sanctioned depravity" (p. 6). Kellaway (2000) states, "From the earliest known legal code, drawn up by the Babylonian king Hammurabi in the

18th century BC, capital punishment has been used both for retribution and as a deterrent. . . . In the Bible the death penalty is applied to more than 30 different offenses; the ancient Greeks went further still, demanding death for most misdemeanors. The callous disregard for human life was not universal. In England King Canute and William the Conqueror were reluctant to employ the death penalty, although torture was applied" (p. 6).

Among the variations of torture used over the millennia are:

- Early civilization: Stoning; crucifixion; and sawing a person in half
- The first millennium: The use of gallows; bastino (caning); chaining by the neck; and condemning the accused to mud bogs
- The Middle Ages: Chopping off heads (e.g., ax and block technique); using a sword to cut off someone's head (ISIS uses this ancient form of execution today); hanging; the gibbet (placing the condemned in a metal cage to die while birds and vermin strip away the flesh); burning; water torture, various forms including boiling to death (the CIA uses this form of torture on suspected terrorists today via waterboarding); amputation; branding; and decapitation by guillotine (in 2015 the state of Utah proposed using this form of barbaric execution and also considered death by firing squad)
- Post–Middle Ages to the present: Asylums; solitary confinement in prison; hangings; electric chair executions; gas chambers; and lethal injections. It is worth noting that many of these forms of torture are still used today. Interestingly, in April 2015, Oklahoma Governor Mary Fallin signed a bill that would allow the state to perform executions with nitrogen gas (she was preparing for a constitutional ban on lethal injection, a decision under consideration by the U.S. Supreme Court at this same time). A strong proponent of the death penalty, Fallin stated, "I believe capital punishment must be performed effectively and without cruelty. The bill I signed today gives the state of Oklahoma another death penalty option that meets that standard" (Ellis 2015).

As the brief review of the history of torture provided above reveals, this form of punishment has a long history throughout "civilization." Sadistic individuals and groups, certain cults, terrorist groups, and governments themselves are all potential sources of executors of torture.

When governments are the source of torture, we have political torture. "Universally condemned and everywhere considered illegal, torture goes on and on in liberal Western democracies as well as in dictatorships" (Clarke 2012:1). The international condemnation of torture has led to a widely accepted international definition of torture as set out by Article 1 of the United Nations Convention against Torture and other Cruel, Inhuman or Degrading Treatment or Punishment (UNCAT):

> Torture means any act in which severe pain or suffering, whether physical or mental, is intentionally inflicted on a person for such purposes as obtaining from him or a third person information or a confession, punishing him for an act he or a third person has committed or is suspected of having committed, or intimidating or coercing him or a third person, or for any reason based on discrimination of any kind, when such pain or suffering is inflicted by or at the instigation of or with the consent of acquiescence of a public official or other person acting in an official capacity. It does not include pain or suffering arising only from, inherent in, or incidental to lawful sanctions. (International Rehabilitation Council for Torture Victims 2013)

This definition provides political torture parameters by clearly stating that torture of this sort comes from the consent of a public official or other person acting in an official capacity.

Undoubtedly, most readers noticed the repeated pronoun of "him" leaving a sexist undertone. This is important because of the many atrocities against women, especially in developing nations, that go on without international condemnation. A number of agencies, such as UNICEF, have described female genital mutilation/cutting (FGM/C) as a type of torture performed by African and Middle Eastern nations against the will of girls and women. FGM/C refers to "all procedures involving partial or total removal of the female external genitalia or other injury to the female genital organs for non-medical reasons" UNICEF (2015). More than 130 million girls and women alive today have been cut in the 29 countries in Africa and the Middle East where FGM/C is concentrated. If current trends continue, as many as 30 million girls are at risk of being cut against their will before their 15th birthday (UNICEF 2015a).

When discussing political torture, most people think of torture against prisoners of war (POWs). Americans and citizens of the West like to think that political torture is restricted to dictatorship nations, and yet while many repressive governments have a history of torturing their own citizens, let alone POWs, political torture is a feature of some democratic nations, including the United States. We have known for years now that the U.S. government sanctioned torture and cruel and inhuman and degrading treatment of prisoners suspected to be terrorists following the attacks of 9/11. "Democratic U.S. allies not only became complicit with renditions to torture but also found their own creative ways to transfer prisoners into the hands of some of the worst human rights violators. In short, as America embraced ever-harsher interrogation techniques, both it and its allies subcontracted the nastiest and most brutal torture" (Clarke 2012:1). The fear of violent attack by terrorists and the need to gain quick intelligence fueled the U.S. government's approval of torture, and cruel, inhumane, and degrading treatment of prisoners at Guantanamo Bay (Clarke 2012; Center for Constitutional Rights 2015).

It was the CIA that developed, refined, and established a torture culture in response to the "war on terrorism." "The Department of Justice's Office of Legal Counsel (OLC) approved so-called harsh or alternative interrogation techniques, and these came to be accepted practices in the treatment of detainees. Some of the approved techniques included repeatedly drowning people on 'waterboards' scientifically designed to maximize suffocation and with personnel trained to intensify distress. This was combined with other abuses, such as stress positions, dietary manipulation, sleep deprivation, wall shaming, and other techniques to accentuate and prolong the misery" (Clarke 2012:3–4). In an attempt to downplay their extreme level of torture, the CIA referred to their techniques as "torture lite" (Clarke 2012). When the CIA released its official report in December 2014, admitting to torturing prisoners at Guantanamo Bay, it caused political ripples overseas (Kurlantzick 2014). At home in the United States, citizens were divided on the subject. Liberals were more likely to condemn the very idea that the U.S. government would resort to torture; conservatives, on the other hand, were more likely to use the Sykes and Matza technique of neutralization of "the denial of the victim," arguing that the detainees were not real victims, they were terrorists.

Regardless of where one stands ideologically, the U.S. government has indeed committed political torture, just like many of its allies and enemies overseas.

Organized Crime

Organized crime, sometimes called syndicate crime, involves criminal activity committed by members of formal organizations that exist to operate profitable illicit enterprises (e.g., insurance fraud, counterfeiting, tax evasion, and money laundering). Schneider (2002) describes organized crime as broadly defined as "two or more persons conspiring together on a continuing and secretive basis, with the aim of committing one or more serious crimes to obtain, directly or indirectly, a financial or other material benefit" (p. 1112). Wherever there is a demand for prohibited goods and services (e.g., prostitution, drugs, firearms, pornography, gambling, or smuggling), there is an opportunity for organized crime to become a major supplier (Best and Luckenbill 1994).

Kenney and Finckenauer (1995) describe a number of characteristics of organized crime groups:

- They are nonideological,
- have an organized hierarchy,
- have continuity over time,
- use force or the threat of force,
- restrict membership,
- obtain profit through illegal enterprises,
- provide illegal goods and services desired by the general populace,
- use corruption to neutralize public officials and politicians,
- seek a monopoly position to obtain exclusive control over specific goods and services,
- have job specialization within the group,
- have a code of secrecy, and
- plan extensively to achieve long-term goals (Kenney and Finckenauer 1995:3).

None of the attributes described above alone constitute an organized crime syndicate, but when taken together they produce clear parameters of organized crime.

Some variations of organized crime, such as smuggling, necessitate crossing national borders and yet, prior to the 1980s, most organized crime groups were confined to and controlled specific local territories, seldom seeking to expand their operations outside their spheres of influence. However, since the 1980s, organized crime has increasingly become international in character: "The unprecedented frequency with which criminal groups and activities now cross national boundaries, combined with the global structure and reach of some crime groups, has led to the emerging spectre of what is now commonly referred to as transnational organized crime (TOC)" (Schneider 2002:1112). There are a number of transnational organized crime syndicates, including transnational street gangs. "A transnational street gang is a gang that acts as a criminal enterprise in multiple countries and whose members reside, and/or operate, in multiple nations wherein primary criminal activities take place in public areas (the streets)" (Delaney 2014b:218). Organized crime syndicates other than street gangs also operate in public areas in order to provide public access to goods and services that have been declared illegal and yet are desired by a large segment of the population.

Organized crime syndicates are generally characterized as possessing structured control over their marketplaces via violence and corruption. The corruption of political and community leaders helps organized crime syndicates to continually operate free from legal threats while the use of violence and intimidation is used to maintain control over the marketplace. Extortion (the collection of payments from people) represents an important means of maintaining control over the marketplace while also serving as a valuable tool for generating necessary operating funds. Extortionists may also demand that their victims conduct exclusive business relationships with other businesses already under the control of the crime syndicate. For example, organized criminals may demand that construction companies must hire crews that include those on the syndicate's payroll and demand that they purchase materials (e.g., lumber or electrical and plumbing supplies) from businesses operated by the syndicate. Maintaining control over interlinking businesses helps the crime syndicate maintain a monopoly.

Some variation of organized crime has existed throughout a great deal of human history. Crime syndicates in the United States have their roots in such organizations as Boss Tweed and Tammany Hall in New York City in the mid-1800s, and the traditional Asian organized crime syndicates such as the Chinese triads and tongs and the Japanese yakuza. These developed through the years to include other organized crime syndicates such as the Italian Mafia and the Russian Mafia. Discussion here will be limited to the Italian Mafia and the Russian Mafia. Once again, it is important to point out that there are other organized crime syndicates operating in the United States.

Italian Mafia

As the Italians began to migrate in large numbers to the United States in the early 1900s, so too did members of factions of organized criminal societies known collectively as the "Mafia." The Mafia is one of the world's oldest (these criminal enterprises date back 3,000 years) and most well-known international crime groupings. The Mafia originated in Sicily. Over the millennia, Sicilians had become clannish and relied on familial ties for safety, protection, justice, and survival (FBI 2015h). There are a number of Mafia organizations currently active in the United States, including the Sicilian Mafia (based in Sicily); the Camorra or Neapolitan Mafia (based in Naples); the 'Ndrangheta or Calabrian Mafia (based in Calabria); and the Sacra Corona Unita or United Sacred Crown (based in the Puglia region) (FBI 2015h). The FBI (2015h) estimates that these four organizations alone consist of approximately 25,000 members. La Cosa Nostra (literally translated into English as "this thing of ours") is the foremost organized criminal threat to American society. The LCN consists of different "families" or groups that are generally arranged geographically and participate in significant organized racketeering activity. Named after legendary boss Vito Genovese, the Genovese Crime Family was once considered the most powerful organized crime family in the United States.

The Italian Mafia operates primarily in major cities across the United States but have their most significant presence in New York City, southern New Jersey, and Philadelphia. Most commonly known as the criminal enterprise that traffics in heroin, the Mafia is involved in nearly all the criminal activities associated with organized crime, including drug trafficking; money laundering; prostitution; extortion; loan sharking; weapons and diamond smuggling; illegal disposal of radioactive waste; skimming public and private works contracts; labor racketeering; the infiltration of legitimate businesses; illegal gambling; political corruption, kidnapping; fraud; counterfeiting; murder, including murder for contract; and bombings (FBI 2015h; Schneider 2002).

The Mafia has served as the focal point in many films and television shows; among the best-regarded ones are the *Godfather* trilogy, *The French Connection*, and *The Sopranos*. Many Italian Americans condemn the depiction of the Italians as Mafia members, believing that it leads to the creation and perpetuation of a negative stereotype.

A still photo from the highly popular TV show *The Sopranos* with Steve Van Zandt, James Gandolfini, and Tony Sirico.

Russian Mafia

The Russian Mafia (also known as *mafiya* and/or *maffya*) does not have a huge impact on American business or politics, but it does play a significant role in certain geographical areas, such as New York City and Los Angeles. In the former Soviet Union the term "Mafia" was used to refer not to broad criminal conspiracies but to occupationally specific corruption. "There was a fishing mafia and a fruit and vegetable mafia, both of which diverted goods away from state outlets onto the lucrative black market" (Naylor 2002:38). There was a hotel mafia, which extorted hotels to collect additional room booking charges and then kick the payments back to them; likewise, there was a transportation mafia that did the same with airlines and trains (Naylor 2002).

The Russian Mafia is a crime syndicate that formed to meet the "black market" or "underground market" needs of Russian citizens. "Corruption and corrupt bureaucrats in Russia date back to the time of the czars; and so, too, does the blasé attitude toward legality that accepted stealing from the state as normal behavior" (Finckenauer 2002:1428). Evidence of the Russian Mafia dates back at least to the 18th century. Nicholas II, Russia's last czar, could not control the Mafia, in part, because the people were frustrated with Nicholas's inability to provide the goods and services they desired. Vladimir Lenin admired the organizational, hierarchical structure of the Mafia. Under the strict rule of Joseph Stalin, who led the Soviet Union until 1953, the Mafia flourished. Stalin's socialist regime refused to publicly acknowledge the existence of such an illegal enterprise as the Russian Mafia (Vaksberg 1991).

As the primary destination of most Russian emigrants, Brighton Beach, Brooklyn, New York, is home to one of the largest Russian communities outside Russia's borders. Brighton Beach is referred to as "Little Russia" or "Little Odessa" because many of its residents came from Odessa, a Black Sea port in Ukraine. "Odessa has long had a thriving black market. And not unlike many other seaports, it also has a well-developed criminal subculture dating back to the times of the pirates. The Odessukya Vory, or Odessa Thieves, according to Russian sources, were in fact the most notorious of all the thieves in Russia" (Kenney and Finckenauer 1995:275). Members of Russian Mafia crime syndicates joined regular Russians as they emigrated to Brighton Beach and soon formed their own organizations in the Brooklyn and greater New York and New Jersey area. The Russian Mafia has since fanned out to such U.S. cities as Philadelphia, Los Angeles, Baltimore, Chicago, Cleveland, Dallas, Phoenix, and to Toronto, Canada.

The Russian Mafia came to the United States with the desire to make illegal money, and their long history of skillfully manipulating Russian "red tape" became a valuable asset in the bureaucracy-laden United States. The Russian Mafia is particularly violent in their dealings with associates and those who cross them. They have little regard for U.S. law enforcement. Among the crimes committed by the Russian Mafia in the United States are forgery; the trafficking, distribution, and sale of illegal drugs; counterfeiting; insurance fraud; tax evasion (e.g., the "Daisy Chain Fuel" tax scam); prostitution and human trafficking; money laundering; extortion (including the extortion of Russian NHL players); kidnapping (including family members of NHL players for extortion); corruption (including fixing judging events during the 2002 Salt Lake City Winter Olympics); and violent crimes (Delaney 2004b). More recently, Russian crime syndicates have engaged in a wide variety of cybercrimes including "ransomware" (see chapter 9 for a discussion on ransomware). In brief, Russian ransomware may be launched from such places as Crimea, Russia, as a virus that encrypts files stored on business or personal computers of people in such places as the United States. The files stay restricted until a ransom is paid for the key to unlock the files, thus the name ransomware (Doran 2016).

Typically, multiple white collar crimes are committed simultaneously when organized crime syndicates are involved. And, as we have learned in this chapter, there are a wide variety of white collar crimes, and they are being committed by a wide variety of individuals, groups, and organizations of white collar criminals.

Summary

The term "white collar crime" was coined by sociologist Edwin Sutherland in an effort to draw attention to crime committed by professional people. Over the years, Sutherland's parameters of white collar crime have been adjusted, but the focus remains primarily on professional people and corporations. Conflict sociologists such as C. Wright Mills argue that the power elites (the interconnected tripartite elite consisting of the captains of industry, military heads, and corrupt politicians) of society are the ones committing the most serious acts of white collar and political crime. The FBI is especially concerned with corporate fraud, a subcategory of white collar crime, claiming that in addition to significant financial losses to investors, corporate fraud has the potential to cause immeasurable damage to the U.S. economy and investor confidence.

Both in terms of total dollars and loss of life, white collar crime costs society a great deal. White collar crime was defined as crimes that are typically nonviolent, nonstreet crimes committed by someone, generally a professional of high status, in commercial situations for financial gain. There are a wide variety of specific categories of crime that fall under the white collar crime umbrella. The white collar crimes discussed in this chapter were securities fraud; identity fraud and identity theft; credit and debit card fraud; health care and health insurance fraud; extortion; forgery; insider trading; occupational crime; and unsafe products.

Political crime refers to acts perpetrated by, or against, a government or state. There are many types of political crime (e.g., political corruption, bribery, espionage, treason, and political torture) that may be committed by individuals and groups or by governments or their affiliated agencies as they attempt to prevent or control dissent within their borders or as they attempt to manipulate the political system of foreign nations.

Organized crime, sometimes called syndicate crime, involves criminal activity committed by members of criminal enterprises that exist to operate profitable illicit enterprises (e.g., insurance fraud, counterfeiting, tax evasion, and money laundering). Wherever there is a demand for prohibited goods and services (e.g., prostitution, drugs, firearms, pornography, gambling, or smuggling), there is an opportunity for organized crime to become a major supplier and for criminal enterprises to flourish. Two specific examples of organized crime syndicates—the Italian Mafia and the Russian Mafia—operating in the United States were discussed.

Key Terms

application fraud, 94
bribery, 105
corporate deviance, 89
credit card fraud, 94
espionage, 107
extortion, 96
forgery, 97
identity fraud, 92
identity theft, 92
illegal insider trading, 97
insider trading, 97

occupational crime, 97
organized crime, 111
political crime, 104
power elites, 87
product recall, 101
securities fraud, 91
torture, 108
treason, 108
unsafe products, 99
white collar crimes, 86

Discussion Questions

1. Why did Edwin Sutherland create the concept of "white collar crime"? How did he define white collar crime? How do we define it today?

2. What is corporate fraud? Why does the FBI consider this among the most serious of all crimes?

3. Explain how identity fraud and identity theft occur. What are you doing that puts you at risk of being a victim of identity fraud or theft? What are you doing to decrease the odds of being victimized by identity fraud or theft?

4. Explain what is meant by unsafe products. Why are unsafe products so costly to American society?

5. Define the terms "politics" and "government." Why would the government dupe its own citizens?

6. Explain the terms "bribery," "undue influence," and "peddling influence."

7. At present, the United States utilizes many of the same forms of torture as during the Middle Ages and post–Middle Ages. Explain how this is possible in a "civil" society. Why do other nations utilize torture? Should the U.S. government participate in the torture of political prisoners? Why or why not?

CHAPTER 5

Street Crime: Violent Offenses and Property Offenses

CHAPTER OBJECTIVES

After reading this chapter students should be able to:

- Define the term "street crime"
- Explain the trend of decreased street crime rates
- Describe a variety of violent offenses
- Analyze a variety of property offenses
- Compare and contrast violent offenses and property offenses victimization statistics

It's a hot, steamy summer afternoon, and Eddie and his friends are bored and restless. Like many young preteens, Eddie and his friends decide to try and find some fun and excitement. They walk a few blocks until they reach the seldom-used railroad tracks that lead through the once-bustling industrial area of town. As they walk down the tracks, the buddies joke with one another. They pick up rocks and throw them down the tracks to see who can throw the farthest. They give praise to the winner and jokingly mock Scott, who had the weakest throw. As they reach a long-abandoned factory site, one of the boys, Vince, throws a rock toward the old packaging building. He manages to throw the rock through a windowpane. The crashing sound of the shattered glass elicits gasps of joy and laughter from the group. Eddie and then Billy take their turn and also throw rocks at the building, hoping to break any of the few glass windows still intact. These boys are clearly not the first to cause property damage to this unoccupied building.

As far as the boys are concerned, throwing rocks through windows of a vacated building is no big deal. They are simply having fun and certainly have no intention of hurting anyone. The boys are surprised when a truck containing two security guards approaches them. The security guards have been hired by the new property owners to keep delinquents, homeless folks, and drug addicts out of the area, as they plan to revitalize the once-thriving industrial park. One of the guards yells from her window, "Hey! You delinquents stop throwing rocks and get over here." Scott and Billy run away, but Eddie and Vince abide by the security guard's command. The security guards yell at the two boys for being little criminals. They also demand the names of the two boys who ran away. Eddie and Vince do not give up their friends' names. As a result, the security team calls the local police.

When the police arrive, one officer takes a rather cavalier approach to the situation and states, "The boys are just being boys; at worst they are deviants." When one of the security guards complains that the new property owners have taken a "zero tolerance" approach to vandalism, the other officer decides to arrest Eddie and Vince and demands to know the names of their friends who ran away. The first police officer, however, convinces his partner to deliver the boys to their respective families and let their parents dictate the punishment.

Street Crime

The story described above introduces a number of elements to the study of street crime and raises quite a few questions. First, we must realize that often it is a thin line between describing particular acts as delinquent or deviant or labeling those acts as criminal. Second, we have already learned (see chapter 1) that violating a social norm is generally the key parameter in determining whether a behavior is deviant or not. Third, when a norm has been written down by a political authority it becomes formalized, and violating formal norms is the criterion for determining criminal activity. Fourth, when social control agents (e.g., law enforcement or private security firms) become involved in a given situation, such as kids throwing rocks through windows of an abandoned building, behaviors that participants deem harmless and fun may be redefined. The boys believed they were engaged in harmless fun. The new property owners of the abandoned building are concerned about liability issues if someone was injured on the property. Issues of liability lead to such questions as, "What if one of the boys was injured by falling glass?" and "What if someone was inside the building and got injured?" When buildings are being vandalized we have property crime; however, if someone was injured because of the purposive behavior of the juveniles throwing rocks, we have the potentiality of charges of assault. In this chapter, we will explore the issue of street crime and behaviors that transcend deviance and enter the realm of criminality.

Crime

Crime can be defined as any deviant behavior or omission of behavior that violates a law of the land. **Crimes of omission** refer to the failure to act when called upon to do so either by law or by law enforcement representatives; such acts constitute an *actus reus* (Latin for "guilty act"). Child neglect, negligence, and the failure to disclose terrorist acts are examples of crimes of omission. Crimes of omission occur when an individual(s) fails to do what is required by law and someone else is harmed as a result. (See box 5.1 for an example of a crime of omission from the TV show *Seinfeld*.)

Crime contains two aspects: an *act* (or, again, the failure to act when the law requires it) and **criminal intent** (in legal terminology, *mens rea*, or "guilty mind"). Criminal intent varies by degree, ranging from willful conduct (the perpetrator had full intention to commit the crime, such as robbery, aggravated assault, and murder) at one extreme to negligence (meaning that the criminal act was not deliberate) at the other end. Prosecutors consider the degree of intent in determining whether, for example, to charge someone with first-degree murder, second-degree murder, negligent manslaughter, or justifiable homicide (e.g., self-defense).

Box 5.1 Crimes of Omission: *Seinfeld* and the Good Samaritan Law

The two-part series finale of the hugely popular TV show *Seinfeld* (1998a, 1998b) centered on a crime of omission. In this two-part finale, Jerry Seinfeld and George Costanza have just accepted a contract with NBC to create a show based on Seinfeld's stand-up comedy act (mirroring the reality that *Seinfeld* itself was a show about Jerry Seinfeld's stand-up comedy). Seinfeld and Costanza will have to leave New York City and move to Hollywood. The four friends, Jerry, George, Elaine, and Kramer (the main characters of the show) are worried that they might never hang out together again like they once had. As a result, they decide to accept NBC's generous offer to provide them a private jet and fly them anywhere they want to go for a vacation prior to starting the production of the show. The group of friends decide to go to Paris.

Shortly after takeoff, the private jet develops mechanical troubles and is forced to land in Latham, Massachusetts. The pilot assures them that the plane will be repaired in a timely manner and that they will soon be safely on their way to Paris. The friends decide to pass the time by taking a walk around Latham. All of a sudden, a carjacking takes place in front of them. The armed carjacker forces an overweight motorist out of his car and robs him of his wallet. Kramer, who was filming their stroll through Latham, captures the carjacking incident. Instead of showing empathy toward the carjacking victim, the four friends mock him by saying things like he could afford to lose a few meals because of his weight. Interestingly, a police officer is nearby and does nothing about the carjacking. Instead, he approaches the four friends and arrests them for violating Article 223–7 of the Latham County Penal Code. The four friends are shocked by this development and question the legitimacy of the law. The police officer informs them that the law is new and that it is referred to as the "Good Samaritan law." (Note: This law is derived from the biblical "Parable of the Good Samaritan"—Luke 10:25–37.) The Latham law was modeled after the French law that was passed after Princess Diana was killed in a car accident and dozens of photographers on the scene stood around taking photos instead of assisting in the rescue effort. Thus, by omission (failure to act) the four friends were being charged with violating the Good Samaritan law.

The four friends, having never heard of such a law, assume that they can simply pay a fine and move on with their vacation plans. However, upon learning of the seriousness of their violation, they contact their lawyer, Jackie Chiles, a character that has made other hilarious appearances on the show. (Note: The fictional Jackie Chiles character was a parody of famed attorney Johnnie Cochran, known at the time of this episode primarily for his defense of O.J. Simpson in the murder trial of his wife, Nicole Brown.) Over the phone, Jerry explains to Chiles their situation.

Jackie Chiles replies: "Uh-huh. Good Samaritan law? I never heard of it. You don't have to help anybody. That's what this country's all about. That's deplorable, unfathomable, improbable. Hold on. Suzie [his secretary], cancel my appointment with Dr. Bison and pack a bag for me. I want to get to Latham, Massachusetts, right away."

When the Latham prosecutor learns that high-profile lawyer Jackie Chiles is taking the case, he realizes that the whole town will be swarmed with media. But that also means full hotels and lots of business for the local community. The prosecutor attempts to discredit the character of the four friends by introducing a number of folks (who had appeared on *Seinfeld* over its nine-year run) who testify on the shallowness of the four friends. Kramer's video of the carjacking is also introduced during the trial. The video is damning in that it shows that the group of friends not only omitted helping the carjacking victim, they also mocked him.

While *Seinfeld* fans, including this author (Delaney 2006), have pointed out the flaws of this trial (e.g., the four friends could not safely assist the victim and the police officer himself did nothing to help the victim), the primary point has been made; that is, certain acts of omission can be considered criminal. As for the four friends, they were found guilty and sentenced to one year of incarceration.

Defining Street Crime

Street crime is an umbrella term used by sociologists, criminologists, and law enforcement agencies to describe criminal acts committed in public outdoor places, including the streets, playgrounds, shopping areas, business districts, and residential neighborhoods, including private homes, and encompasses violent offenses and property offenses. The definition of street crime concludes with "and encompasses violent offenses and property offenses" because the FBI classifies the wide variety of street crimes in that manner. **Violent offenses** include such crimes as homicide, robbery, assault and battery, and rape/sexual assault. **Property offenses** include burglary, larceny-theft, motor vehicle theft, arson, and vandalism.

Street crime is very common in the United States. In 2010, a violent crime occurred every 25.3 seconds and a property crime occurred every 3.5 seconds (U.S. Department of Justice 2011). The statistics in table 5.1 provide us with a quick glance of the prevalence in frequency of select violent and property crimes committed in the United States in 2010 (see table 5.1). The data in table 5.1 come from the Uniform Crime Report (UCR) issued by the U.S. Department of Justice. The Department of Justice notes that the statistics are the result of total crimes committed in 2010 and that crime is not fixed to time intervals.

Bureau of Justice Statistics statisticians Jennifer L. Truman and Michael Planty (2012) underscore the prevalence of street crime in a report for the U.S. Department of Justice by stating, "In 2011, U.S. residents age 12 or older experienced an estimated 5.8 million violent victimizations and 17.1 million property victimizations."

TABLE 5.1	Frequency of Select Violent and Property Crimes Committed in the United States (in 2010)
Type of Crime	**Frequency**
Violent Offenses	
Murder	One every 35.6 minutes
Forcible rape	One every 6.2 minutes
Robbery	One every 1.4 minutes
Aggravated assault	One every 40.5 seconds
Property Offenses	
Burglary	One every 14.6 seconds
Larceny-theft	One every 5.1 seconds
Motor vehicle theft	One every 42.8 seconds

Source: U.S. Department of Justice 2011

Violent Offenses

Violent offenses include homicide, robbery, assault and battery, forcible rape, extortion, and witness intimidation. In chapter 4, we learned about the prevalence of white collar crime and the likelihood that we all run the risk of being victimized by a white collar crime; and yet most people are far more concerned about being a victim of street crime—especially violent street crime. The increased fear of being victimized by a street crime, especially a violent offense, compared to a white collar crime is fueled by the concern of the physicality component of victimization that is more commonly associated with street crimes. After all, no one wants to be murdered, raped, robbed, or physically assaulted. Furthermore, violent offenses seem far more intimidating than fraud, embezzlement, or some other form of white collar crime (including unsafe products).

Research indicates that between 2010 and 2011, the overall victimization rate for violent crime increased 17 percent, from 19.3 to 22.5 victimizations per 1,000 persons age 12 or older; however, the increase in aggravated and simple assault during this time frame accounted for all the increase in total violent offenses (Truman and Planty 2012). Whites, Hispanics, younger persons, and males account for the majority of the increase in violent victimizations of violent crime. It is important to note that the violent crime rate, overall, has actually been steadily decreasing since 1993. "Since 1993, the rate of violent crime has declined by 73% from 79.8 to 22.5 per 1,000 persons age 12 or older" (Truman and Planty 2012). It is important to define the U.S. Department of Justice's (DOJ) term "victimization," as this term will appear throughout this chapter and may lead to confusion when data from other sources, such as the FBI's Uniform Crime Report (UCR), are incorporated in specific street crime discussions. Victimization is the basic unit of analysis used by the DOJ that affects an individual person or household; the number of victimizations is equal to the number of victims present during a criminal incident. Thus, one incident of robbery could have more than one victim depending on how many people were victimized during the robbery.

The U.S Department of Justice's Bureau of Justice Statistics has established a subcategory of violent offenses known as "serious violence," which includes rape or sexual assault, robbery, aggravated assault, and murder. Between 2010 and 2011, no statistically significant difference was detected in the rate of serious violence. "In 2011, the rate of serious violent victimizations was 7.2 per 1,000 persons age 12 or older. Since 1993, the rate of violent crime had declined by 75% from 29.1 to 7.2 per 1,000 persons age 12 or older" (Truman and Planty 2012). In 2011, residents in urban areas were the most likely to experience victimization of serious violent offenses (27.4 per 1,000) followed by those in the suburbs (20.2 per 1,000) and rural areas (20.1 per 1,000). Also in 2011, residents in the West were the most likely to be victimized by violent offenses (27.1 per 1,000) followed by the Midwest (26.3 per 1,000), Northeast (20.3 per 1,000), and the South (18.3 per 1,000) (Truman and Planty 2012).

In the following pages we will examine specific examples of violent offenses and then switch our attention to property offenses.

Homicide

Homicide is the killing of one human being by another. Homicides can be criminal or noncriminal. According to the U.S. Department of Justice (2010), *criminal homicides* include murder and nonnegligent manslaughter, both of which involve the willful (nonnegligent) killing of one human being by another. There are variations of murder, including premeditated murder, "lying in wait," and felony murder. Premeditated murder, also known as first-degree murder ("murder 1" in police jargon), involves the planned killing of an individual(s) and includes such criteria as "malice aforethought," "lying in wait," or deliberate and premeditated deliberation. Malice aforethought generally includes an evil disposition or purpose and an indifference to human life. Each U.S. state may have different interpretations of malice aforethought. Lying in wait murder involves the intentional infliction of violence upon the victim in which a wanton disregard for human life was demonstrated.

When attempting to convict someone of a "lying in wait" homicide, the prosecution must prove that the accused harbored malice aforethought. Each state may establish specific criteria (e.g., concealment of purpose; a substantial period of watching and waiting for the opportune time to act; and/or a surprise attack on an unsuspecting victim from a position of advantage). **Felony murder** refers to the killing of an individual(s) during the commission of a felony such as rape or robbery. Felony murder generally involves a number of other crimes, in addition to another felony, being committed during the commission of a homicide.

In the world of street gangs, the drive-by shooting (known generally as a "drive-by") has become a popular method of homicide, or attempted homicide. Drive-bys are very popular with Southern California street gangs, as the automobile is an important aspect of street gang life. The **drive-by** combines the use of firearms and automobiles in a mobile attempt by assailants to kill targeted victims. There are variations of the drive-by, including the scenario of gang members driving to a specific location, finding the target, jumping out of the car, and chasing the victim down to shoot him and then making their escape via a fleeing automobile. Beyond the obvious act of killing an enemy, the drive-by shooting serves as a very powerful act of intimidation to promote fear. Often, when drive-bys are conducted, innocent bystanders—nongang youths and older people—are victimized. Without fair warning targets and innocents have no chance of defending themselves.

Nonnegligent manslaughter, sometimes called voluntary manslaughter, involves the killing of a human being in which the offender had no prior intent or forethought of committing the homicide. An example of nonnegligent manslaughter could include two people getting into a fistfight with one punching the other, causing the other to fall and hit his head on a concrete sidewalk, inflicting severe head trauma leading to his death some time later, or a maintenance person who spills a slippery cleaning chemical on the top of a staircase but forgets to put up a warning sign or fails to clean the substance only to have a person slip on the surface and fall down the stairs, leading to her death. "Heat of passion" crimes often fall under the nonnegligent manslaughter label as well. A heat of passion crime occurs when the offender was angered by a circumstance, such as coming home early and finding his/her spouse in bed and sexually involved with someone else, and becomes so enraged that he/she reacts violently by killing the spouse and/or lover. In this regard, the courts often view such circumstances as "adequate" or "reasonable" provocation to cause a person to act in a manner that was not planned. Nonetheless, a homicide has occurred. Closely related to "heat of passion" crimes are "crimes of passion." One of the more deviant examples of a crime of passion occurred in 1993 when Lorena Bobbitt attacked her husband, John Wayne Bobbitt, and cut off approximately 2.5 centimeters of his penis after he allegedly raped her. Lorena left the house and threw his severed penis along the side of a highway; only later did she realize the seriousness of her crime and call 911. Surgeons were able to reattach John's penis. The jury found Lorena not guilty due to her husband's sexual abuse that triggered her crime of passion. Adding to this tale of deviancy, John Wayne Bobbitt later starred in a porn film called *John Wayne Bobbitt Uncut* (Siemaszko 2013).

According to Statista.com (2013), there were 14,827 reported murder and nonnegligent manslaughter cases in the United States in 2012; this equates to a homicide rate of 4.7 per 100,000, a figure much lower than 1990 (9.4 per 100,000) but still much higher than any other Western nation. Germany, for example, has a national homicide rate of 0.8 per 100,000 (Statista.com 2013). The CDC (2015b) reports a higher U.S. homicide rate of 5.1 per 100,000 and a total of 16,121 homicides in

2013. Firearms account for the highest number of homicides with 11,208 firearm homicides with a 3.5 death rate per 100,000 (CDC 2015b).

In cities with a population of 50,000 or more, street gangs are likely to be responsible for more than half of all homicides (Delaney 2014b). Coming up with reliable gang-related homicide totals is often difficult, as many gang homicides go undetected or unreported; some law enforcement agencies choose not to respond to surveys on gang homicide; some agencies report a gang homicide only if it is committed in relation to a gang function (e.g., a street battle or drug-related incidents); and some agencies choose not to identify certain crimes as gang related for a variety of reasons. While we are not surprised to learn that street gangs are responsible for a large percentage of homicides in cities such as Los Angeles and Chicago (because of their huge street gang presence), research conducted by Delaney (2014b) on the New York State cities of Syracuse, Rochester, and Buffalo reveals that street gangs are responsible for the majority of homicides. These upstate New York cities have homicide rates that are typically 3 to 5 times the national average—rates (15 to 25 per 100,000) that are much higher than New York City. (See box 5.2 for a discussion on the murder capital of the United States.)

A CLOSER LOOK

Box 5.2 Murder Capital, USA

When attempting to determine the "murder capital" of the United States, the variable of *population size* plays an important role. For example, when calculating the homicide *rates* for all cities, we have this listing of the top 10 "murder capital" cities for 2013: East St. Louis, IL (population just under 27,000); Camden, NJ (population just under 77,000); Gary, IN (population just over 78,000); Chester, PA (just over 34,000); Saginaw, MI (just over 50,000); Flint, MI (just under 100,000); Detroit, MI (nearly 690,000); Trenton, NJ (just over 84,000); New Orleans, LA (nearly 380,000); and Newark, NJ (nearly 280,000) (*Neighborhood Scout* 2015). However, when considering just larger cities (population size over 200,000), we have a different top 10

listing of cities for the "murder capital" of the United States: Detroit (45 homicides per 100,000; approximately nine times the national average); New Orleans (41 per 100,000); Newark (40 per 100,000); St. Louis, MI (38 per 100,000); Baltimore, MD (37 per 100,000); Birmingham, AL (30 per 100,000); Cincinnati, OH (24 per 100,000); Oakland, CA (22 per 100,000); Baton Rouge, LA (21 per 100,000); and Kansas City, MO (21 per 100,000) (Abbey-Lambertz 2014). With a population size of just over 145,000, Syracuse does not qualify as a large city, but Rochester (210,000+) and Buffalo (292,000+) do, and in many recent years have had homicides rates that would easily put them in the listing of the top 10 "murder capital" cities.

Noncriminal homicides include excusable and justifiable homicide wherein the death of another person was not the result of wanton disregard, malice aforethought, premeditation, or during the commission of a felony. Each state has its own criteria as to what types of homicides might be classified as noncriminal homicides, but there are examples that generally fall under this label. Excusable homicides are accidents or misfortunes where neither negligence nor unlawful intent is involved. "A homicide is excusable when it is committed by accident in the course of doing any lawful act by lawful means or by accident in the heat of passion, upon any sudden and sufficient provocation or upon a sudden combat without any dangerous weapon being used and not being done in a cruel or unusual manner" (ABC News 2005). In a 2005 case involving a fight between Martin Robless-Taylor and Anthony Makowski in a McDonald's parking lot, Robless-Taylor killed aggressor Makowski by choking him to death (ABC News 2005). Prosecutors said that videotape showed that Makowski charged Robless-Taylor, then battered and body-slammed him. The 21-year-old Makowski, 6-foot-4, 271 pounds, jumped on top of Robless-Taylor, an Army-trained 25-year-old who put Makowski into a choke hold and held on for 2 to 3 minutes. By the time police and paramedics arrived Makowski was unresponsive and stopped breathing when paramedics began CPR. Florida prosecutors said that they had no legal basis to charge Robless-Taylor with homicide (ABC News 2005).

Hunting accidents may qualify as an excusable homicide. For example, a hunting party is in the woods, and one of the hunters mistakenly shoots and kills another member of the group. A childhood friend of the author of this text, for example, shot and killed his own brother by mistake while hunting. He did not face jail time but has lived a lifetime with the guilt of accidentally killing his own brother.

Justifiable homicides are killings that result from necessity or lawful duty to protect oneself or loved ones. Examples would include a police officer who kills a suspect within the line-of-duty guidelines set forth by that specific law enforcement agency; and self-defense cases, such as when an intruder enters someone's home and attacks the occupant.

Robbery

As defined by the U.S. Department of Justice, **robbery** is the taking or attempting to take anything of value from the care, custody, or control of a person or persons by force or threat of force or violence and/or by putting the victim in fear. The Bureau of Justice Statistics (BJS) (2013) defines robbery as the completed or attempted theft, directly from a person, of property or cash by force or threat of force, with or without a weapon, and with or without injury. The BJS (2013) expands on each aspect of their definition of robbery:

- Completed/property taken—The successful taking of property from a person by force or threat of force, with or without a weapon, and with or without injury
- Completed with injury—The successful taking of property from a person, accompanied by an attack, either with or without a weapon, resulting in injury
- Completed without injury—The successful taking of property from a person by force or threat of force, either with or without a weapon, but not resulting in injury
- Attempted to take property—The attempt to take property from a person by force or threat of force without success, with or without a weapon, and with or without injury
- Attempted without injury—The attempt to take property from a person by force or the threat of force without success, either with or without a weapon, but not resulting in injury
- Attempted with injury—The attempt to take property from a person without success, accompanied by an attack, either with our without a weapon, resulting in injury

Most robberies occur on the streets as opposed to inside the home. Siegel (1995) created a typology of robberies to help illustrate this point:

1. Robbery of persons, who, as part of their employment, are in charge of money or goods. Convenience stores and banks represent relatively easy targets for quick cash.

2. Robbery in an open area. These robberies include street offenses, muggings, purse snatchings, and other attacks. In urban areas, this type of robbery constitutes about 60 percent of reported totals. Street robbery is most commonly known as "muggings."

3. Robbery on private premises. This type of robbery involves robbing people after breaking into their homes. The FBI reports that this type of robbery accounts for about 10 percent of all robbery offenses.

4. Robbery after preliminary association of short duration. This type of robbery comes in the aftermath of chance meeting—in a bar, at a party after a sexual encounter, or at an ATM.

5. Robbery after previous association or some duration between victim and offender (p. 317).

Robbery is a serious crime and a crime of violence because it puts the victim's life in jeopardy. There were over one-half million (556,760) robberies in the United States in 2011, an 11 percent drop from 2002, when there were 624,390 robberies (see table 5.2). In addition, 2.2 of every 1,000 Americans were victims of robbery in 2011, a decrease from 2.7 (per 1,000) Americans that were victimized by a robbery in 2002 (see table 5.3).

TABLE 5.2 **Total Number of Violent Victimizations and Percent Change, by Select Type of Violent Crimes, in 2002 and 2011**

| | Number of Victimizations | | Percent Change |
Type of Violent Crime	2002	2011	(From 2002 to 2011)
Robbery	624,390	556,760	−11
Assault	6,450,350	5,004,860	−22
Aggravated assault	1,332,520	1,052,080	−21
Simple assault	5,117,840	3,952,780	−23
Rape/sexual assault	349,810	243,800	−30

Source: Truman and Planty 2012/U.S. Department of Justice, Bureau of Justice Statistics 2012

TABLE 5.3 **Rate of Violent Victimizations and Percent Change, by Select Type of Violent Crimes in 2002 and 2011**

| | Number of Victimizations | | Percent Change |
Type of Violent Crime	2002	2011	(From 2002 to 2011)
Robbery	2.7	2.2	−20
Assault	27.9	19.4	−30
Aggravated assault	5.8	4.1	−29
Simple assault	22.1	15.3	−31
Rape/sexual assault	1.5	0.9	−37

Source: Truman and Planty 2012/U.S. Department of Justice, Bureau of Justice Statistics 2012

All crimes, including robberies, are examples of deviant behavior. The potentiality of serious injury and death generally dictates a more somber examination of street crimes. However, there are plenty of examples of bizarre robberies, or attempted robberies, that remind us of the deviant nature of such crimes. In light of the man who allegedly attempted to hijack a plane with a Toblerone Swiss chocolate bar, the British national daily tabloid newspaper, the *Mirror*, put together a top five listing of the most bizarre items used in armed robberies:

5. A banana—A Philadelphia man stuffed a rotten banana in his trousers to make it look like he had a gun while robbing a bank. It was easy to catch this bank robber, as he " left his wallet at the scene, containing two ID cards and a social security card" (Smith 2014).

4. Apple pies—A man was arrested after trying to hold up a Sacramento bank, claiming a bag containing two apple pies was a bomb (Smith 2014).

3. A vibrator—Nicki Jex used his girlfriend's "rampant rabbit" sex toy to rob a Ladbrokes shop in Leicester. The robber was arrested shortly after the robbery at a nearby pub, where he used the cash attained from the robbery to buy bar patrons rounds of drinks (Smith 2014).

2. An eight-inch sausage—A California man allegedly broke into a home, stealing $900 and assaulting the homeowner with an eight-inch sausage. Police reports describing the apprehension of the home invader mentioned that the "weapon" was not recovered (Smith 2014).

1. Permanent marker disguise—A pair of would-be burglars were arrested while trying to rob houses wearing masks scrawled on their faces in permanent marker. The two drunk men were easily apprehended, and Carroll, Iowa, police described the markings on their face as "the worst disguise ever" (Smith 2014).

Other examples of deviant and laughable robbery incidents involve the following:

•   A Russian robber broke into the salon of a hairdresser trained in martial arts who then held the robber captive for two days as her personal sex slave (Murano 2010).

•   In Columbus, Ohio, a trio of robbers held a couple in their home, but one of the men came back two hours later to ask the female victim out on a date. A relative called the police while the wayward lothario was still in the home (Murano 2010).

•   A robber holding a gun on a bank cashier apologized to the woman but went ahead with his robbery even after praying with the victim (Murano 2010).

•   A hidden robber was discovered after a couple returned to their home, the husband made a joke to his wife, and the couple heard a laugh upstairs (Murano 2010).

•   Perhaps one of the most deviant attempts of being a robber involves the case of Aaron Evans, who was filmed breaking into a Peugeot. Evans not only failed to see the covert camera filming his every move but he forgot to cover up his name and birth date tattooed on his neck (Murano 2010).

The case of Aaron Evans reminds all would-be robbers, if you are going to attempt robbery, make sure you do not have visible tattoos, as you are just making the job of law enforcement that much easier to accomplish.

Assault and Battery

The terms "assault" and "battery" are often used interchangeably, but in reality most law enforcement jurisdictions make a specific distinction between the two forms of violent offenses. This primary distinction between the two offenses is the existence or nonexistence of touch or contact, with contact as an essential aspect of battery and the absence of contact for assault. Thus, the threat of doing bodily harm may constitute an assault, while battery involves the actual infliction of unwanted touching. Directing insults or provocative words without threat, regardless of how repulsive, does not constitute an assault. In addition, just as we learned with our discussion on homicide—that there are instances when otherwise unlawful behaviors may be labeled as "excusable" and "justifiable"—there are occasions when threats and unwanted touching are not considered criminal battery and assault. These exceptions include police officers during the course of their duty; parents who discipline their children (within certain parameters); those who are defending their property; those who are defending their loved ones; and athletes during the course of athletic competition. With regard to athletic competition, sport participants realize there is always a chance of injury when playing sports. This notion is based on

Hard tackles in football are just one example of sport violence.

the English common law notions of *volenti fit injuria*, or voluntary assumptions of risk (Delaney and Madigan 2015). Assumption of risk assumes that both management/ownership and labor understand the medical hazards inherent within sport. Athletes realize that broken bones, torn ligaments, missing teeth, fistfights, scars, concussions, and occasional deaths are among the risks confronting athletes when they play sports. A hockey player, for example, is not going to press battery charges when he is violently, and unwantedly, pushed into the boards. Athletes who threaten violence against their opponents are not subject to battery charges.

Some jurisdictions do not make such a distinction and thus consider assault and battery as one and the same and a singular act of a violent offense. With this background information in mind, we can define **assault** as an act of violence that creates an apprehension in another of an imminent harmful, unwanted, or offensive contact. Thus, assaults do not require actual physical contact. Furthermore, a verbal attack (e.g., berating or verbally threatening another person) could be considered an assault. **Battery** refers to the harmful or offensive touching of another. Examples of battery offenses include slapping, hitting, or punching a victim.

Generally, assault and battery offenses are treated as felonies, especially when the perpetrator uses a weapon or if they occur during the commission of a felony (e.g., assaulting a victim during a robbery). Assault and battery offenses fall under the jurisdiction of both criminal and *tort law* (a body of rights, obligations, and remedies that is applied by courts in civil proceedings—noncriminal—to provide compensation for persons who have endured harm from the wrongful acts of others) and can, therefore, lead to criminal or civil liability. In civil tort cases compensation for personal injuries generally centers on the issue of intention; that is to say, was the act done with the *intention* of bringing about a harmful or offensive contact? Proving intent to harm is generally satisfactory in a civil proceeding. Interestingly, in *Garratt v. Dailey* (1955) Brian Dailey, a five-year-old child, was found liable for his case of battery. His offense? He pulled a chair out from under Ruth Garratt just as she was about to sit, causing her to fall and break her hip. Garratt brought suit for personal injuries and alleged that Dailey had acted deliberately. Since the five-year-old pulled the chair out from under Garratt as she attempted to sit, the court ruled Dailey had committed an intentional tort with force. Garratt was awarded $11,000 in damages and court fees. This case is often used in law schools to help students understand the definition and understanding of intent.

When government agencies collect data on assaults, they generally combine battery charges within the total number; in this manner, assault comes to be defined as the intentional infliction of bodily injury on another person, or the attempt to inflict such injury (Bartol and Bartol 2005). When assault is defined within this parameter, it is common to separate assaults into two subcategories: aggravated assault and simple assault. **Aggravated assault** occurs when there is an intention to inflict serious bodily harm. The U.S. Department of Justice (2010) defines aggravated assault as an unlawful attack by one person upon another for the purpose of inflicting severe or aggravated bodily injury. This type of assault usually is accompanied by the use of a weapon or by means likely to produce death or great bodily harm. **Simple assault** is applied to acts of violence against a person that inflict less than serious bodily harm without a deadly weapon (e.g., punching someone during an argument).

In recent years, a very disturbing form of aggravated assault has emerged on the streets—the "knockout game." The knockout game involves someone trying to knock out an unsuspecting, usually defenseless, victim with just one punch. Typically, the victim is an elderly person or someone who is distracted with another task at hand (e.g., walking down a sidewalk talking on a cell phone or someone carrying groceries in both hands), while the perpetrator is a young, strong male in the company of other young males. A case study example of the knockout game occurred in Syracuse, New York, on September 21, 2013. Jim Gifford, a 70-year-old man, exited his local 7-Eleven store like he had done so many times before. Seemingly out of nowhere, Romeo Williams, 18, jumped out of a car, lunged at Gifford, and struck him in the face, leaving him unconscious on the ground. Syracuse Police Chief Frank Fowler told reporters that Williams had the audacity to go inside the store to let everyone know how good he felt. "He was actually celebrating after he struck Mr. Gifford," Fowler said (*The Post-Standard* 9/24/13:A-3). A minute or two after celebrating, Fowler said, the teenager left the store, "returned to where Gifford lay and began kicking him in the face, causing critical injuries. Williams stopped only when four of his friends pulled him off the victim and drove him away" (*The Post-Standard* 9/24/13:A-3). Over a year later (October 2014), Williams received a 25-year sentence for manslaughter for killing Gifford (Dowty 2014).

Presently, some street gangs are using the knockout game as a form of gang initiation; however, it remains a form of aggravated assault by nongang members as well, who somehow feel that being able to knock out a defenseless victim with one punch is worth celebrating as an accomplishment. The so-called (many people are upset with this label because being victimized by a street tough is not a game) knockout game would certainly seem to qualify as a form of social deviance.

Assaults, whether simple or aggravated, represent the most common violent offense in the United States. There were over 5 million total assaults in 2011, a decrease of 22 percent from 2002 (see table 5.2). Of these 2011 assaults, over 1 million (1,052,080) were aggravated assaults, a decrease of 21 percent from 2002; and nearly 4 million (3,952,780) were categorized as simple assaults, a decrease of 23 percent from the 2002 total (See table 5.2). In 2011, the rate of assault victimization was 19.4 per 1,000, a decrease of 30 percent from 2002 (see table 5.3). Correspondingly, the number of both aggravated and simple assault victims decreased in 2011 from 2002 (see table 5.3).

Rape/Sexual Assault

One of the most heinous crimes is rape/sexual assault. Acts that are today described as "rape" and/or "sexual assault" have existed throughout the recorded history of humans and are likely to have occurred since the dawn of humanity. As Estelle Freedman (2013) explains, "At its core, *rape* is a legal term than encompasses a malleable and culturally determined perception of an act. Different societies define which nonconsensual sexual acts to criminalize, which to condone, and how forcefully to prosecute the former. . . . The meaning of rape is thus fluid, rather than transhistorical or static" (p. 3). In early civilization, rape was a common occurrence, only it was never labeled as "rape" because the concept of rape did not exist. Instead, rape was often a matter of men claiming ownership of women by forcibly abducting them and having their way with them. Such behavior assisted males' solidification of power and their historical domination of women (Siegel 1995). Siegel (1995) explains that during the Middle Ages, for example, it was a common practice for ambitious men to abduct and rape wealthy women in an attempt to force them into marriage.

> The practice of "heiress stealing" illustrated how feudal law gave little thought or protection to women and equated them with property. It was only in the late fifteenth century that forcible sex was outlawed and then only if the victim was of the nobility; peasant women and married women were not considered rape victims

until well into the fifteenth century. . . . Throughout recorded history, rape has also been associated with warfare. Soldiers of conquering armies have considered sexual possession of their enemies' women one of the spoils of war. . . . [This has been true] from the Crusades to the war in Vietnam. (Siegel 1995:298)

Siegel is correct to say that rape is associated with war, but it did not end with Vietnam; it has continued with every war since he discussed this topic more than two decades ago.

Today, Western societies associate rape with intimidation and fear. Rape is a means of one (or more than one) person dominating another against the other's will. Even in prison, alpha males demonstrate their power within the correctional system by "claiming" physically weaker men for their own by raping them to show dominance. Such perpetrators of sexual assault do not view themselves as being gay, but as being dominant.

Over the years, the parameters of rape have changed quite a bit. Freedman (2013) explains that the effort to redefine rape has come about following generations of women's rights and racial justice advocates' attempts to draw attention to the brutality of sexual assault. "In the early nineteenth century, white women sought legal remedies to make it easier to prosecute coercive but nonviolent sexual relations with acquaintances. After emancipation, African American activists insisted that black women could be victims of rape and that white men should be held accountable for assault [when they were the perpetrators]. Suffragists claimed that women required equal political rights to ensure their public safety and fair rape trials. In the late twentieth century, feminists renamed nonconsensual sex with acquaintances and husbands as rape" (Freedman 2013:1–2). Late 20th-century feminists claim white men have their political power because they have historically enjoyed the freedom to be sexually violent or coercive toward women (Freedman 2013).

The parameters of rape have continued to change during the second decade of the 21st century. Consider that as recently as 2012, the FBI's UCR definition of rape was "the carnal knowledge of a female forcibly and against her will" (FBI 2014b). Such a definition was interpreted by many law enforcement agencies as excluding a long list of sex offenses including oral or anal penetration, penetration with objects, and rapes of males. Effective January 1, 2013, the FBI's UCR defines rape as "penetration, no matter how slight, of the vagina or anus with any body part or object, or oral penetration by a sex organ of another person, without the consent of the victim" (FBI 2014b). Individual law enforcement agencies (LEA) must now use this definition when they report rape statistics to the FBI's UCR or if they report to the FBI directly. Agencies in Indiana, Mississippi, New Mexico, and Ohio report their data directly to the FBI and not to the UCR (FBI 2014b). In light of the FBI's UCR updated interpretation of the term, **rape** is defined as the unlawful compelling of a person, or persons, through the use of physical force, or the threat of physical force, or duress to have unwanted vaginal, anal, and/or oral sex, without the consent of the victim.

The FBI's UCR also distinguishes between categories of rape: (1) rape completed, (2) attempts to commit rape, and (3) statutory rape (U.S. Department of Justice 2013). Rape completed refers to "penetration, no matter how slight, of the vagina or anus with any body part or object, or oral penetration by a sex organ of another person, without the consent of the victim. This definition includes any gender of victim or perpetrator" (U.S. Department of Justice 2013). Rape completed cases also include an instance in which the victim is incapable of giving consent because of temporary or permanent mental or physical incapacity (including due to the influence of drugs or alcohol), and physical resistance is not required on the part of the victim to demonstrate lack of consent. Attempted rape involves any sexual assault with the intent of committing rape even though the actual rape act was not completed. **Statutory rape** involves any sexual contact with an underage person.

As with every category of crime, the true number of "rape/sexual assault" victimizations is unknown. It is, however, generally understood that rape/sexual assault is one of the most underreported crimes. The Rape Crisis Center of Medina and Summit Counties (Ohio) (2015) estimates that just 39 percent of all rapes are reported to the police each year. The closer the relationship between the female victim and the offender, the greater the likelihood that the incident will not be reported; for example, when the offender was a current or former husband or boy-friend, about 75 percent of all victimizations were not reported to the police, and when the offender was a friend or acquaintance, an average of 71 percent were not reported (Rape Crisis Center of Medina and Summit Counties [RCCMS] 2015). The drastic underreporting of rape/sexual assault is correlated with the relationship between victim and perpetrator because most victims know their assailants (White House Council on Women and Girls 2014).

Despite the dramatic underreporting of rape/sexual assault, a great deal of data exist on this violent crime. The U.S. Department of Justice reports that there were 243,800 reported rape/sexual assaults in 2011, a decrease of 30 percent from the nearly 350,000 reported rape/sexual assaults in 2002 (see table 5.2). In 2011, the rate of rape/sexual assault victimization was 0.9 per 1,000, a decrease of 37 percent from 2002 (see table 5.3). Because rape/sexual assault is an underreported violent crime, statistics from various reporting agencies often do not align with each other. For example, RCCMS (2015) reports that 1 out of every 6 American women has been the victim of an attempted or completed rape in her lifetime, while the White House Council on Women and Girls (WHCWG) (2014) reports that nearly 1 in 5 women—or nearly 22 million—have been raped in their lifetimes. The RCCMS reports that 1 out of nearly 33 American men has been a victim of an attempted or completed rape in his lifetime, while the WHCWG reports that 1 in 71 men—or almost 1.6 million—have been raped during their lives. When it comes to the race of the victims, the RCCMS reports that 34.1 percent of American Indian/Alaskan Native women will be victims of rape, fol-lowed by mixed-race women (24.4 percent), African American women (18.8 percent), white women (17.7 percent), Hispanic women (14.6 percent), and Asian/Pacific Islander women (6.8 percent). The WHCWG reports multiracial women have the highest per-centage (35.5) of victimizations of rape/sexual assault followed by American Indian and Alaska Native women (27 percent), black women (22 percent), white women (19 per-cent), and Hispanic women (15 percent). The RCCMS and WHCWG both report that young people are especially at risk, as nearly half of female victims were raped before they were 18, while, as reported by WHCWG, over 25 percent of male victims were raped/sexually assaulted before they were 10 years old.

Demographic Characteristics of Violent Crime Victims

The U.S. Department of Justice has compiled demographic data on violent crime vic-tims (Truman and Planty 2012) (see table 5.4). The data presented in table 5.4 clearly indicate that overall 2011 violent crime victimization (22.5 per 1,000) has decreased significantly since 2002 (32.1 per 1,000). The data also reveal that males are more likely to be victims of violent crimes than females; American Indian and Alaska natives have the highest rate of victimization, and Asian/Native Hawaiian/other Pacific Islanders are

TABLE 5.4	Rate (per 1,000) and Percent Change of Violent Victimization, by Demographic Characteristics of Victim in 2002 and 2011		

| Demographic Characteristic of Victim | Rates | | Percent Change |
	2002	2011	2002–2011
Total	32.1	22.5	–30
Sex			
Male	33.5	25.4	–24
Female	30.7	19.8	–36
Race/Ethnicity			
White	32.6	21.5	–34
Black	36.1	26.4	–27
Hispanic	29.9	23.8	–20
American Indian/Alaska Native	62.9	45.4	–28
Asian/Native Hawaiian/ other Pacific Islander	11.7	11.2	–4
Age			
12–17	62.7	37.7	–40
18–24	68.5	49.0	–28
25–34	39.9	26.5	–34
35–49	26.7	21.9	–18
50–64	14.6	13.0	–11
65 or older	3.8	4.4	+17
Marital Status			
Never married	56.3	35.5	–37
Married	16.0	11.0	–31
Widowed	7.1	3.8	–46
Divorced	44.5	37.8	–15
Separated	76.0	72.9	–4

Source: Truman and Planty 2012/U.S. Department of Justice, Bureau of Justice Statistics 2012

the least likely to be victimized by violent crimes; people 24 and under are the most likely to be victimized; and, when it comes to marital status, separated people have the highest rate of victimization, while widowed persons have the lowest.

While there are other examples of street crimes that fall under the violent offenses category (e.g., witness intimidation and crimes associated with extortion), we have limited our discussion to the most vicious examples. We turn our attention now to property offenses.

Property Offenses

While the crime rate continues to decline in the United States, the review of violent offenses presented in this chapter underscores the general concern that most Americans have about being victimized by a violent crime; after all, no one wants to be murdered, raped, assaulted, or robbed. It should be noted, however, that we are far more likely to be victimized by a **property offense** than we are a violent offense. According to the U.S. Department of Justice, there were over 17 million property victimizations of household burglary, motor vehicle theft, and larceny-theft alone in 2011 (Truman and Planty 2012) (see table 5.5). Property crime occurs when something of value is destroyed or taken from its owner by another. Property offenses do not include force or threat of force against the victims, as once threat or threat of force is involved, we have a violent offense. Thus, breaking into someone's home with the intent to steal property (e.g., cash and electronic equipment) but no intent to harm residents would constitute a burglary; however, a "home invasion" (when criminals force their way into an occupied home, apartment, hotel room, etc.) would be classified as a robbery. Most burglars prefer to break into and enter a structure when no one is home in an effort to avoid confrontation and the risk of being charged with a violent offense such as robbery.

The primary examples of property offenses are burglary, larceny-theft, motor vehicle theft, arson, and vandalism.

Burglary

Burglary accounted for nearly one out of four (23.8 percent) of the estimated number of property crimes committed in 2010 (FBI 2011a). **Burglary** (breaking or entering) is defined as the unlawful entry of a structure to commit a felony or a theft (U.S. Department of Justice 2010). The UCR definition for "structure" includes an apartment, barn, house, trailer or houseboat when used as a permanent dwelling, office, railroad car (but not automobile), stable, or vessel (e.g., ship). The use of force to gain entry need not have occurred in order to be classified as a burglary. Thus, if an intruder enters someone's home via an open door or window, the crime of burglary has occurred. The UCR Program has three subdivisions for burglary: forcible entry, unlawful entry where no force is used, and attempted forcible entry (FBI 2011a). The FBI (2011a) provided a general overview of burglary in 2010:

- In 2010, there were an estimated 2,159,878 burglaries.
- In 2010, 60.5 percent of all burglaries involved forcible entry, 33.2 percent were unlawful entries (without force), and the remainder (6.3 percent) were forcible entry attempts.
- Victims of burglary offenses suffered an estimated $4.6 billion in lost property in 2010; overall, the average dollar loss per burglary offense was $2,119.
- Burglaries of residential properties accounted for 73.9 percent of all burglary offenses.

According to the U.S. Department of Justice, there were over 3.6 million household burglary victimizations in 2011, a figure that represents an increase of 11 percent when compared to the number (3,251,810) of burglary victimizations in 2002 (Truman and Planty 2012) (see table 5.5). (Note: As described earlier in this chapter, the number of victimizations includes the total number of victims involved during any criminal offense; this explains how there were less than 2.2 million burglaries, but more than 3.2 million victimizations.) As shown in table 5.6, the rate of burglary victimization in 2011 was nearly equal to 2002, and as a result there was no statistically significant percent change in burglary victimization.

From time to time, we hear of would-be burglars conducting less than mastermind status attempts of burglaries. In Thousand Oaks, California, for example, a woman named Genoveva Nunez-Figueroa managed to get stuck in the chimney of a home she attempted to burglarize. In an October 2014 incident, it took a glob of

| TABLE 5.5 | Number of Property Victimizations and Percent Change, by Select Type of Violent Crimes in 2002 and 2011 |

Type of property crime	Number of Victimizations		Percent Change 2002–2011
	2002	**2011**	
Total	18,554,320	17,066,780	−8
Household burglary	3,251,810	3,613,190	+11
Motor vehicle theft	1,018,690	628,070	−38
Larceny-theft	14,283,820	12,825,510	−10

Source: Truman and Planty 2012/U.S. Department of Justice, Bureau of Justice Statistics 2012

| TABLE 5.6 | Rate of Property Victimization (per 1,000) and Percent Change, by Select Type of Violent Crimes in 2002 and 2011 |

Type of property crime	Victimization Rates		Percent Change 2002–2011
	2002	**2011**	
Total	168.2	138.7	−18
Household burglary	29.5	29.4	---
Motor vehicle theft	9.2	5.1	−45
Larceny-theft	129.5	104.2	−19

Source: Truman and Planty 2012/U.S. Department of Justice, Bureau of Justice Statistics 2012

dish soap squeezed by California firefighters to lubricate Nunez-Figueroa free from the chimney of her ex-boyfriend. This was the second time the woman attempted to break into and enter the man's home after he ended their brief relationship, according to KABC-TV (Hensley 2014). While Nunez-Figueroa has a chance to go on with her life, a serial burglar in Derby, England, was not so lucky. Police found the body of Kevin Gough, a man with a history of breaking and entering, stuck in a chimney of a Grade II–listed building in Derby, but only after he had been stuck there for weeks. (Note: A Grade II–listed building means it has officially been recognized as having special historical or architectural interest and is therefore protected from demolition or alteration.) The smell of his decomposing body was the only thing that drew attention to the fact that he was stuck in the chimney (Hough, Duffin, and Dixon 2013).

Larceny-Theft

With an estimated number of larceny-thefts at just over 6.1 million in 2010, this offense represents 68.1 percent of all property crimes nationwide (FBI 2011b). The U.S Department of Justice defines **larceny-theft** as the unlawful taking, carrying, leading, or riding away of property from the possession or constructive possession of another. Examples of larceny-theft include the thefts of bicycles or motor vehicle parts and accessories, shoplifting, pocket-picking, or the stealing of any property or article that is not taken by force and violence or by fraud (FBI 2011b). Attempted larcenies are considered larcenies. Various forms of white collar crime thefts (e.g., embezzlement, forgery, check fraud) and other forms of fraud that lead to theft (e.g., confidence games) are not included as larcenies. The FBI (2011b) provided a general overview of larceny-theft in 2010:

- In 2010, there were an estimated 6,185,867 larceny-thefts in the United States.
- The rate of larceny-thefts in 2010 was 2,003.5 per 100,000 residents.
- The average value of property taken during larceny-thefts was $988 per offense. Applying this average value to the estimated number of larceny-thefts reveals that the total loss to victims nationally was over $6.1 billion.
- Over one-quarter (26.4 percent) of larceny-thefts were thefts from motor vehicles; 17.2 percent from shoplifting; 11.3 percent from buildings; 8.9 percent from motor vehicle accessories; 3.3 percent from bicycles; a little more than 1.2 percent from purse snatching, theft from coin-operated machines, and pocket-picking; and 31.8 percent from all others.

According to the U.S. Department of Justice, there were over 12.8 million theft victimizations in 2011, a figure that represents a decrease of 10 percent when compared to the number (14,283,820) of theft victimizations in 2002 (Truman and Planty 2012) (see table 5.5). As shown in table 5.6, the rate of theft victimization in 2011 (104.2 per 1,000) was down 19 percent compared to 2002 (129.5 per 1,000) (Truman and Planty 2012).

A woman places jeans into her bag with the intent of stealing them.

We will learn shortly that motor vehicle theft itself has decreased tremendously over the past decade or so, in part because it is much harder to steal cars today than it used to be; and yet, as stated above, thefts *from* motor vehicles account for over 26 percent of larceny-thefts. Ironically, a contributing reason for the popularity of stealing from cars is the development of simple devices and gadgets that allow criminals to easily and quickly break into parked cars. Chances are you, or someone you know, has had their car broken into via some sort of wireless device, including mysterious-looking black boxes. In April 2015, a *New York Times* blogger, Nick

Bilton, posted that he watched two youths walk up to his locked car, press a button on a small black device that unlocked the car, and then broke in and stole whatever items were inside the vehicle. Bilton wrote, "So much for our keyless future" (Orlove 2015; Lavrinc 2015). The device used on Bilton's 2013 Prius was a cheap power amplifier that can be purchased online on sites like eBay, Amazon, and Craigslist and many retail stores that sell electronics. "There are two kinds of keyless entry systems: The ones where you have to press a button on a key fob to unlock the door and the proximity-based systems that broadcast a low frequency signal to recognize when the key is in your pocket, and then unlock the doors when you're close by or touch the door handle" (Lavrinc 2015). Bilton's car had the latter, and that system is easily susceptible for break-in via the power amplifier, as thieves hold up the box near the car and, if the owner is nearby, the amplifier picks up the signal and opens the car door. Car owners are advised to keep their keys stored in something that will not allow the amplifier to boost the signal and detect the key.

As early as 2012, ABC News had reported on a different trick used by thieves—the use of key decoding systems that essentially work like keys to the car. The thieves simply place a decoding system box near the external security panel on a vehicle and the gadget runs a system through a series of possible combinations. Suddenly, usually within 10 to 15 seconds, the door unlocks. The coding system basically mimics the real signal and tricks the system into unlocking the vehicle. The code-grabbing technology is most effective in vehicles made before 2010 and especially those that have the external security panel, although such panels are not necessary.

Motor Vehicle Theft

Motor vehicle theft is a common type of larceny offense, but because of its frequency and seriousness, it has its own separate category in the UCR. **Motor vehicle theft** is the theft or attempted theft of a motor vehicle; a motor vehicle is defined as a self-propelled vehicle that runs on land surfaces and not on rails (U.S. Department of Justice 2010). Examples of motor vehicles include sport utility vehicles, automobiles, trucks, buses, motorcycles, motor scooters, all-terrain vehicles, and snowmobiles. Motorboats, construction equipment, airplanes, and farming equipment are specifically excluded from this category. The FBI (2011c) provided a general overview of motor vehicle theft in 2010:

- Nationwide in 2010, there were an estimated 737,142 thefts of motor vehicles. The estimated rate of motor vehicle thefts was 238.8 per 100,000 inhabitants.
- More than $5.4 billion was lost nationwide to motor vehicle thefts in 2010. The average dollar loss per stolen vehicle was $6,152.
- Nearly 73 percent (72.9) of all motor vehicles reported stolen in 2010 were automobiles.

According to the U.S. Department of Justice, there were 628,070 motor vehicle theft victimizations in 2011, a figure that represents a 38 percent decrease from the number (1,018,690) of motor vehicle theft victimizations in 2002 (Truman and Planty 2012) (see table 5.5). The 628,070 motor vehicle theft victimizations reported by the U.S. Department of Justice do not statistically mesh well with the FBI's reporting of 737,142 thefts of motor vehicles in 2010. We would expect a higher number of motor vehicle thefts in 2010 than in 2011, but a 100,000-plus differential does not bode well. As shown in table 5.6, the rate of motor vehicle theft victimization in 2011 (5.1 per 1,000) was down 45 percent compared to 2002 (9.2 per 1,000) (Truman and Planty 2012). Once again, we have a significant statistical difference in reporting, as the FBI

(2011c) reports that the rate of motor vehicle thefts was 238.8 per 100,000 in 2010, but the U.S. Department of Justice reports 5.1 per 1,000 victims of motor vehicle thefts in 2011. Both the FBI and U.S. Department of Justice agree, however, that the number and rate of motor vehicle victimizations has been decreasing throughout the 2000s.

Motor vehicle theft, especially auto theft, has been around for as long as there have been motor vehicles. In some cases, such as "carjacking," auto thieves confront the motor vehicle owner directly and demand the vehicle. Carjacking is the criminal taking of a motor vehicle from its driver by force, violence, or intimidation. Such an act is recognized as "a completed or attempted robbery of motor vehicle by a stranger to a victim" (Bureau of Justice Statistics 2004). A carjacking is different from most motor vehicle thefts because the victim is present and the offender uses or threatens to use violence (Bureau of Justice Statistics 2004). In a number of cases, the driver of the automobile makes the mistake of reacting too slowly and is injured or murdered.

Most motor vehicle thefts, or attempted thefts, are conducted without direct confrontation between the thief and the owner/driver of the motor vehicle. Some people are very skilled at stealing cars. "Hot-wiring" (opening up the steering column, unbundling the wires, and connecting the on/off wire to the battery wire) and other techniques of stealing cars have been popularized in so many television shows and movies that it makes most of us wonder how all motor vehicles are *not* stolen on a more regular basis. The 2000 film *Gone in Sixty Seconds* (starring Nicolas Cage and Angelina Jolie), for example, set the standard for auto theft, as the premise of the movie centers on the idea that *any* car can be stolen in less than 60 seconds. This film pointed out that exotic cars were especially likely to be targeted because rich clients overseas were willing to pay any price for a car not available in their home countries. Still today, U.S. Customs and Border Protection recover dozens of autos that thieves try to smuggle out of the Ports of Los Angeles and Long Beach in shipping containers (Barro 2014). As we shall learn shortly, however, the most popular-selling automobiles, as well as older-model vehicles, are the most likely target for auto thieves.

Advanced automobile design has made it challenging for thieves to steal automobiles. Hot-wiring, for example, is much more difficult with cars newer than mid-1990s models because newer models have outfitted the steering column with safety measures to prevent hot-wiring. Newer-model vehicles have a host of locking mechanisms and, of course, alarms. Additional technological advancements such as engine immobilizer systems, adopted by manufacturers in the late 1990s and early 2000s, make it nearly impossible for the average thief to start a car without the ignition key—which contains a microchip uniquely programmed by the dealer to match the car (Barro 2014). Many newer cars come equipped with GPS tracking devices that allow stolen cars to be more easily found. Thus, while thieves have found a way to break into automobiles to steal contents left behind, they have a harder time stealing the car itself. In addition to the increased difficulty in stealing cars is the realization that automobile theft is a felony offense in most states and may be punished by imprisonment and/or a financial penalty of a fine, often between $500 and $1,000.

With the increased technology in safeguarding and possible felony imprisonment for committing automobile theft it is understandable that motor vehicle theft has decreased so dramatically since the early 2000s (see tables 5.5 and 5.6). As reported by Josh Barro (2014) of the *New York Times*, there were 147,000 reported auto thefts in New York City in 1990, one for every 50 residents; in 2013, there were just 7,400, or one per 1,000 residents. That equates to a 96 percent drop in the rate of car theft.

The most popular stolen vehicle in the United States is the Honda Accord. In 2012, the 1996 Honda Accord was the most stolen vehicle model in the United

States; it replaced the 1994 Honda Accord, which had been the most popular stolen vehicle throughout the first decade of the 21st century (DMV.org 2013). In 2013, nearly 54,000 (53,995) Accords were stolen, and 84 percent of them were from model years 1997 or earlier (Barro 2014; Gorzelany 2014). "Not coincidentally, Accords started to be sold with immobilizers in the 1998 model year. The Honda Civic, America's second-most stolen car, shows a similar pattern before and after it got immobilizer technology for model year 2001" (Barro 2014). Data compiled by the National Insurance Crime Bureau (NCIB) reveals the top 10 most stolen cars from all models taken during 2013 (see table 5.7).

TABLE 5.7   **Top 10 Most Stolen Vehicles from All Model Years Taken during 2013**

Make/Model	Total Number Stolen
1. Honda Accord	53,995
2. Honda Civic	45,001
3. Chevrolet Silverado	27,809
4. Ford F-150	26,494
5. Toyota Camry	14,420
6. Dodge/Ram Pickup	11,347
7. Dodge Caravan	10,991
8. Jeep Cherokee/Grand Cherokee	9,272
9. Toyota Corolla	9,010
10. Nissan Altima	8,892

Source: Gorzelany 2014

Based on data compiled by the NCIB, the two most popular new-model (2013) vehicles stolen in 2013 were the Nissan Altima and the Ford Fusion. See table 5.8 for the top 10 listing of most stolen new vehicles (from 2013 model year).

TABLE 5.8   **Top 10 Most Stolen New Vehicles (From the 2013 Model Year)**

Make/Model	Total Number Stolen
1. Nissan Altima	810
2. Ford Fusion	793
3. Ford F-150	775
4. Toyota Corolla	669
5. Chevrolet Impala	654
6. Hyundai Elantra	541
7. Dodge Charger	536
8. Chevrolet Malibu	529
9. Chevrolet Cruze	499
10. Ford Focus	483

Source: Gorzelany 2014

Older-model vehicles are targeted for theft for a few primary reasons, including the fact that they are easier to steal than newer-model vehicles; there are a lot of them still on the road; they are stolen for parts; and they can be sold to salvage yards as scrap. In New York State, for example, it is easy to sell a car to be scrapped because the law allows for any vehicle more than eight years old and worth less than $1,250 to be sold for scrap without the title of the vehicle (Barro 2014).

In some cases, auto theft takes on the pretense of legal activity, such as using tow trucks to steal motor vehicles. In Topeka, Kansas, for example, police began noticing a trend in auto thefts involving the use of tow trucks. An automobile theft ring that set up in Topeka utilized its own tow trucks to hook up to a vehicle on the street, usually in a residential neighborhood and very early in the morning, then tow the vehicle to another location to strip its parts (Jones and Anderson 2012). The Topeka police were not sure how many vehicles were stolen via this auto theft ring, but it was enough to issue a public notification for residents to be on the lookout for unmarked tow trucks. The police did arrest at least one tow truck driver.

It is also interesting to point out that some motor vehicle thefts are actually fraudulent scams run by the auto owners themselves. Vehicle owners that suffer financial setbacks might resort to motor vehicle theft fraud as a means of earning money. A 2008 report on auto theft prevention from the National Conference of State Legislatures estimated that at least 10 percent of all reported auto thefts are fraudulent (Jay 2015). Vehicle owners who decide to "steal" their own automobiles for the purpose of committing auto theft fraud take several approaches, including the following:

- Owner give-ups—This approach is one of the most common forms of auto theft fraud and involves the vehicle owner simply driving the vehicle to a remote location and abandoning it. The vehicle owner may also pay another person to take the vehicle away and abandon it.
- Export scams—Some owners will arrange with thieves to steal their vehicle with the purpose of exporting it to a foreign buyer.
- Use of a stolen title or vehicle identification number (VIN)—The perpetrator of this type of auto theft fraud will use a stolen VIN or title from a different car, create the pretense of owning a vehicle ("paper car"), insure it, then claim it was stolen and file an insurance claim.
- Purchasing multiple auto insurance policies on the same car—The owner of the vehicle will claim that the car was stolen or that made-up items were inside the car and stolen, and file multiple claims with different insurance companies hoping to collect on all of them.

With all the different types of auto theft and auto theft fraud discussed above, it's no wonder that the UCR has created a special category of crime for auto theft.

Arson

Arson is defined as "any willful or malicious burning or attempting to burn, with or without intent to defraud, a dwelling house, public building, motor vehicle or aircraft, personal property of another, etc." (FBI 2011d). As a UCR crime, the FBI collects statistics on arson, but its data is limited to "only the fires that investigation determined to have been willfully set"; fires labeled as suspicious or of unknown origin are excluded from FBI data (FBI 2011d). With these limitations in mind, the FBI (2011d) reports that:

- In 2011, 15,640 law enforcement agencies provided 1 to 12 months of arson data and reported 52,333 arsons. Of the participating agencies, 14,887 provided expanded offense data regarding 43,412 arsons.
- Nearly 46 percent (45.9) of all arson offenses involved structures (e.g., residential, storage, public, etc.). Mobile property was involved in 23.9 percent of arsons, and other types of property (such as crops, timber, fences, etc.) accounted for 30.2 percent of the reported arsons.
- The average dollar loss per arson was $13,196.
- Arsons of industrial/manufacturing structures resulted in the highest average dollar losses (an average of $68,349 per arson).
- Arson offenses decreased 4.7 percent in 2011 when compared with 2010 arson data.
- Nationwide, there were 18.2 arson offenses for every 100,000 inhabitants.

Any type of structure fire is likely to lead to an investigation by an arson investigator. "An arson investigator is part detective, part fire scientist. After fires are reported and suppressed, arson investigators help determine the cause of the blaze and, if appropriate, whether criminal activity is involved" (*Fire Science* 2015). Richard J. Keyworth (2010), a fire investigator for nearly 40 years, states that fire investigation is 80 percent perspiration and 20 percent inspiration; the implication being that fire investigation involves detective work and creative thinking.

Building fires are investigated in order to determine whether the fire was an accident or arson.

The key to any initial fire investigation is preserving physical evidence. "Preserving evidence is a major problem because much of the evidence is very fragile. [The investigator should] use disposable cellulose sponges to sop up accelerants for transfer to a container. Use hypodermic or cooking syringes to suck up accelerants between boards and cervices. Sift ashes to detect small objects such as the timing device from an igniter. Incendiary evidence at the point of origin can be part of a candle, an empty flammable liquid container, excessive amounts of unburned newspaper folded together or a number of unburned matches" (Orthmann and Hess 2013:494). Some arson investigators use K-9 dogs to sniff out accelerants such as small quantities of highly diluted flammable and combustible liquids, including paint remover and thinner, lacquer thinner, charcoal lighter fluid, kerosene, naphtha, acetone, dry gas, heptone, gasoline, diesel fuel, octane, and Jet-A-Fuel (Orthmann and Hess 2013). It is important to search for all manner of accelerants because professional arsonists use a variety of methods to ignite fires, including:

- Connecting magnesium rods to timed detonators and placing them in a building's electrical system. The rods burn with extreme intensity and cause a fire that looks as though it was caused by faulty wiring.
- Connecting a timed explosive on one or more barrels of gasoline or other highly flammable liquid. This method is often used when large areas such as warehouses are to be burned.
- Pouring acid on key support points in a steel-structured building to make the building wall collapse during the fire (Orthmann and Hess 2013:494).

In addition to their examination of the physical traces of the fire, arson investigators will interview the owner(s) of the structure, surviving victims, and witnesses and coordinate their efforts with fire departments, law enforcement agencies, the courts, and the criminal justice system (Orthmann and Hess 2013; *Fire Science* 2015). Many law enforcement agencies have trained fire investigators who belong to such organizations as the International Association of Arson Investigators (IAAI). "The IAAI is an international professional association of more than 8,000 fire investigation professionals, united by a strong commitment to suppress the crime of arson through professional fire investigation" (IAAI 2015). Although professional arson investigators are trained to make critical decisions regarding the nature of the fire, that is to say, whether it was deliberately set, an accident, or the result of nature (e.g., a lightning strike), they are not infallible. The Truth in Justice organization claims that there are 500,000 total structure fires overall per year and that 75,000 of them are labeled "suspicious." Of these suspicious fires, Truth in Justice (2015) estimates that as many as 15,000 mistaken investigations occur each year, leading to thousands of wrongful convictions of arson.

According to the National Fire Protection Association (2014), during 2007–2011, an estimated 282,600 intentional fires were reported to U.S. fire departments each year, with associated annual losses of 420 citizen deaths, 1,360 civilian injuries, and $1.3 billion in direct property damage. Structure fires accounted for 92 percent of civilian deaths, 84 percent of civilian injuries, and 86 percent of direct property damage caused by intentional fires (National Fire Protection Association 2014). Nearly two-thirds (64 percent) of intentional structure fires occurred in structures that were occupied and operating, and these fires account for most of the associated losses. A little more than half (51 percent) of intentionally set home structure fires occurred between 3:00 p.m. and midnight. Lighters (27 percent) and matches (23 percent) were the most common heat source in intentional home fires. The most common area of origin in intentional home structure fires was the bedroom (National Fire Protection Association 2014). According to the FBI, one in five (19 percent) arson cases were cleared by arrest or exceptional means, and two out of five of the individuals arrested for arson were under 18 years of age (National Fire Protection Association 2014).

Vandalism

The term "vandalism" can be traced back to the Vandals, a Germanic people associated with senseless destruction as a result of their sacks of Carthage in 439 CE and Rome in 455 CE under their most famous king Geiseric (Merrills and Miles 2014). History shows that the Vandals prospered for a century following the collapse of Rome (Merrills and Miles 2014). **Vandalism** involves the willful or malicious destruction, damaging, or defacing of public or private property. Vandalism includes such behaviors as breaking windows, slashing tires, keying (or scratching) paint off someone's automobile, egging someone's home, spray-painting a wall with graffiti, knocking down road signs, salting lawns, poisoning trees, placing glue into locks, clogging a sink and leaving the water running, painting graffiti, and destroying a computer system via the use of a computer virus.

Vandalism is a criminal offense governed by state statutes, which vary from state to state. (Consequently, data is not collected by the FBI's UCR, as was the case with the previously discussed property offenses.) The state of Arizona, for example, distinguishes between two types of vandalism: criminal damage and aggravated criminal damage (ARS 13–1602 and ARS 13–1604). Criminal damage is the most common property damage crime in the state of Arizona and involves recklessly doing any one of the following:

A. Damaging or defacing the property of another,
B. Tampering with someone else's property to impair its function or reduce its value,
C. Tampering with utility property (gas, water, telephone, etc.),
D. Parking your vehicle to block livestock from getting access to water, or
E. Graffiti on a public or private building.

Criminal damage charges in Arizona are based on the dollar value of the damage with the following range: Class 2 misdemeanor (less than $250 damage; up to 4 months in jail and $750 in fines); Class 6 felony ($250 to $2,000; 6 to 18 months in prison); Class 5 felony ($2,000 to $10,000; 8 months to 2 years in prison); and Class 4 felony ($10,000 or more; 1.5 to 3 years in prison) (ARS 13–1602).

Aggravated criminal damage, the more serious vandalism offense in Arizona, involves more intent in the actions of the perpetrator and carries much harsher penalties. An aggravated criminal damage offense has occurred when any of the following activities has been committed either intentionally or recklessly:

A. Defacing, damaging, or changing the appearance of any building, structure, personal property, or church,
B. Defacing or damaging any place used as a school, or
C. Defacing, damaging, or tampering with any cemetery, mortuary, or the property of one.

Aggravated criminal damage charges are based on the dollar amount with the following range: Class 6 felony (Less than $500; 6 to 18 months in prison); Class 5 felony ($500 to $10,000; 8 months to 2 years in prison); and Class 4 felony ($10,000 or more; 1.5 years to 3 years in prison) (ARS 13–1604).

The state of Ohio has three categories of vandalism: criminal damage, criminal mischief, and vandalism. Criminal damage occurs when one creates a substantial risk of harm to any property without the owner's consent; criminal offense is labeled a second-degree misdemeanor punishable by up to 90 days in jail and $750 in fines (ORC 2909.06). Criminal mischief offense occurs under such conditions as knowingly defacing, damaging, destroying, or tampering with the property of another; deploying a stink bomb, gas device, or smoke generator; tampering with boundary markers or survey markers; tampering with, defacing, or destroying a safety device; and impairing the functioning or security of a computer network system. Criminal mischief is punishable as high as first-degree misdemeanor, up to 6 months in jail, and a fine of $1,000 (ORC 2909.07). Vandalism penalties are the most serious category of vandalism offenses in Ohio because many of the same acts described previously are coupled with a serious injury or knowingly aware that a substantial risk to the victims (including people, parks, preserves, forest, or similar lands) could occur. All Ohio vandalism penalties of this category are felony offenses with punishment associated with the dollar value of the damage (e.g., damage of greater than $100,000 is a third-degree felony and can lead to 1 to 5 years in prison and up to $10,000 in fines [ORC 2909.05]).

One of the most common forms of vandalism is graffiti. Graffiti refers to drawings, inscriptions, markings, scratching, or painting of property including, but not limited to, buildings, vehicles, cemeteries, parks, informational signs, and freeway overpasses. Because it is such an eyesore and a blight on a community, graffiti represents an attack on property, citizens, and on society as a whole. A great deal of graffiti is caused by street gangs; consequently, any neighborhood overrun by graffiti is usually a clear indication of gang activity and gang presence. Through a variety of methods, such as the use of certain symbols, numbers and letters, specific colors, and elaborate drawings, street gang graffiti is one of the most prevalent ways a gang identifies itself within the neighborhood. Among other functions, graffiti is used to mark turf, make certain pronouncements, commemorate the dead, and issue challenges. For gang members (and those who can read the symbolism—certain members of law enforcement, gang researchers such as myself, and street-smart residents), graffiti is like a social network site filled with information ("posts") on gang activity. A form of graffiti is scratchiti. **Scratchiti** involves using a sharp object like a knife to scratch painted surfaces, wood, and glass windows. Scratchiti is very common on buses, subway trains, and bathroom stalls.

Not all graffiti vandals are members of street gangs. The most common non-gang subculture to utilize graffiti are taggers. A tagger does not (necessarily) belong to a gang; instead, he/she enjoys defacing the property of others by "tagging" his/her "name" (an alias is commonly used) on numerous forms of property. Tagger crews also exist. Tagger crews typically lack the formal organization of street gangs, but some carry weapons for protection against other tagger crews or gangs (Delaney 2014b). Graffiti and tagging should not be confused with **street artists** who are commissioned by the property owners themselves to create street art via paintings and drawings on private buildings.

The economic costs of graffiti are enormous. Schools, businesses, local governments, public works, and property owners spend millions of dollars each year to clean graffiti, repair buildings, or replace vandalized equipment. Local governments pass the costs on to taxpayers, and businesses pass the costs of graffiti vandalism on to customers via higher retail prices. Graffiti cleanup takes a big chunk of money out of certain municipal budgets. According to GraffitiHurts.com (2015), Phoenix, Arizona, spends more than $6 million annually on graffiti cleanup; San Jose, California, spent about $2 million in 2006; Las Vegas spends about $3 million annually; and Chicago budgeted $6.5 million in 2006. California Department of Transportation (Caltrans) and Metro in Los Angeles County spent about $28 million in 2006 to remove more than 16,000 square feet of graffiti (California Department of Transportation 2015; Delaney 2014b).

This concludes our look at street crime. Among the many lessons learned in this chapter, as well in chapter 4 (White Collar, Political, and Organized Crime), is the realization of the overwhelming total costs of crime, both in terms of loss of life and total dollars. The costs are staggering. We believe that the wide number of criminal activities involved in street crime and white collar crime warranted a separate chapter for each topic.

Summary

In this chapter, some of the many forms of street crime were discussed. *Street crime* is an umbrella term used by sociologists, criminologists, and law enforcement agencies to describe criminal acts committed in public outdoor places, including the streets, playgrounds, shopping areas, business districts, residential neighborhoods, and private homes, and encompasses violent offenses and property offenses.

Violent offenses involve criminal offenses committed against other persons and include such crimes as homicide, robbery, assault and battery, and, rape/sexual assault. Research indicates that between 2010 and 2011, the overall victimization rate for violent crime increased 17 percent, from 19.3 to 22.5 victimizations per 1,000 persons age 12 or older; however, the increase in aggravated and simple assault during this time frame accounted for all the increase in total violent offenses. Homicide is the killing of one human being by another. Homicides can be criminal or noncriminal. According to the U.S. Department of Justice (2010), criminal homicides include murder and nonnegligent manslaughter, both of which involve the willful (nonnegligent) killing of one human being by another. Noncriminal homicides include excusable and justifiable homicide wherein the death of another person was not the result of wanton disregard, malice aforethought, premeditation, or during the commission of a felony. As defined by the U.S. Department of Justice, robbery is the taking or attempting to take anything of value from the care, custody, or control of a person or persons by forces or threat of force or violence and/or by putting the victim in fear. The terms "assault" and "battery" are often used interchangeably but, in reality, most law enforcement jurisdictions make a specific distinction between the two forms of violent offenses. This primary distinction between the two offenses is the existence or nonexistence of touch or contact, with contact as an essential aspect of battery and the absence of contact for assault. As with every category of crime, the true number of "rape/sexual assault" victimizations is unknown. It is, however, generally understood that rape/sexual assault is one of the most underreported crimes.

Property crime occurs when something of value is destroyed or taken from its owner by another. Property offenses do not include force or threat of force against the victims, as once threat or threat of force is involved, we have a violent offense. The primary examples of property offenses are burglary, larceny-theft, motor vehicle theft, arson, and vandalism. Burglary (breaking or entering) is defined as the unlawful entry of a structure to commit a felony or a theft. The U.S. Department of Justice defines **larceny-theft** as the unlawful taking, carrying, leading, or riding away of property from the possession or constructive possession of another. Motor vehicle theft is the theft or attempted theft of a motor vehicle; a motor vehicle is defined as a self-propelled vehicle that runs on land surfaces and not on rails. Arson is defined as any willful or malicious burning or attempting to burn, with or without intent to defraud, a dwelling house, public building, motor vehicle or aircraft, personal property of another, etc. Vandalism involves the willful or malicious destruction, damaging, or defacing of public or private property.

Key Terms

aggravated assault, 128

arson, 139

assault, 128

battery, 128

burglary (breaking or entering), 133

crime, 118

crimes of omission, 118

criminal intent, 118

drive-by shootings, 122

felony murder, 122

homicide, 121

larceny-theft, 134

motor vehicle theft, 136

noncriminal homicides, 123

property offenses, 120

rape, 129

robbery, 124

scratchiti, 143

simple assault, 128

statutory rape, 131

street crime, 120

vandalism, 142

violent offenses, 120

Discussion Questions

1. Define the term "crime." What is a crime of omission? Explain the circumstances that led to the four main characters in the TV show *Seinfeld* being found guilty of a crime of omission. Do you think they should have been tried for this?

2. Define the term "homicide." Name and briefly describe the two major subcategories of homicide and their subcategories. Give an example of each.

3. Do you think children as young as five years old should be held liable for acts of assault and battery? What do you think of the *Garratt v. Dailey* case?

4. Explain in detail how and why the parameters and definition of rape/sexual assault have changed over the years. What do you think the punishment for rape should be?

5. What is meant by the term "property offenses"? Identify, describe, and give an example of each of the primary examples of property offenses described in this chapter.

6. What criminal acts fall under property offense of "motor vehicle theft"? Have the number of motor vehicle thefts gone up in recent years, or gone down? Explain why this is the case. What are the most commonly stolen automobiles? What makes certain autos more susceptible to being stolen than others?

7. With the high frequency of crime in the United States, is criminal behavior deviant? As you think about the answer to this question, utilize the five definitions of social deviance provided in chapter 1 and decide for yourself.

CHAPTER 6

Violence and Social Deviance

CHAPTER OBJECTIVES

After reading this chapter students should be able to:

- Explain why violence is so prevalent in contemporary society
- Better understand self-directed violence
- Describe interpersonal violence and give specific examples
- Provide a history of riots in the United States
- Provide a review of the many explanations of riots
- Describe collective violence using war as an example

In an attempt to appease Slender Man, two 12-year-old girls in Wisconsin plotted for months to kill their friend at a sleepover. The two naïve young girls not only believed that the web comics fictional character Slender Man was real, they also believed that if they killed a friend of theirs as a type of offering, he would take them to live with him in a mansion in a national forest. Slender Man (also known as "Slenderman") appears on the Internet site Something Awful as a paranormal being who lurks near forests and who absorbs, kills, or carries off victims. This tall, fictional, faceless character is often depicted as sprouting tentacles. He is essentially a boogeyman-type character that in various connotations has appeared in nearly every culture throughout time.

According to prosecutors, in May 2014, Anissa Weier and Morgan Geyser, of Waukesha, Wisconsin, plotted to kill their Horning Middle School classmate Payton Leutner during a birthday celebration for Geyser at her home. Weier told police that it was Geyser's idea to kill their friend to please Slender Man and prove that he was real and that she was excited about the prospect of proving skeptics wrong (News Service Reports 2014). While playing hide-and-seek in the wooded park near the Geyser home, the two girls tackled the victim and started stabbing her. The victim screamed as she was stabbed a total of 19 times. Thinking they had killed Leutner, the two girls left her behind. Instead, the victim managed to crawl out of the woods, where a bicyclist found her and called 911. The victim was taken to the hospital, where she underwent surgery for her wounds.

In March 2015, the two girls were officially charged with one count each of being party to attempted first-degree intentional homicide, which automatically places them in adult court under Wisconsin law. They each could face up to 65 years in the state prison system if convicted (Associated Press 2015a). While the court listened to expert testimony as to whether or not the brain of a 12-year-old is developed enough to control their impulses and should be held legally responsible as an adult for their actions, the judge was expected to issue his decision in August 2015 (Sanchick 2015). On August 19, 2015, Judge Michael Bohren ruled that the case would stay in adult court.

While the actions of the two girls are considered criminal offenses, it is their willingness and eagerness to engage in violent behavior, especially at such a young age, that draws our attention to their story. One might wonder, are these two girls the exception to the contention held by some members of society that human beings are, by their nature, creatures capable of extreme acts of care, love, and affection, or do these girls serve as a case study in support of the notion that the human species is violence-prone?

Explaining Violence

In the introductory story described above we learned about two girls who were, at the very least, disenchanted with their lives to the point where they came to believe that a mythical creature who lurks near forests and who absorbs, kills, or carries off victims to his hideaway mansion offered them the potentiality of a more appealing way of life. They believed that if they violently killed a friend of theirs, Slender Man would be pleased and take them home with him. Seemingly rational people, including preteens, would realize that premeditated murder against a friend is morally and ethically deviant. Perhaps these girls were not mentally sound? Their attorneys argued that very point. "Anthony Cotton, an attorney for one of the girls, called his client a schizophrenic in court" (Associated Press 2015a:A5). The defense attorneys also claimed that the girls actually believed that Slender Man was going to kill their family members unless they made a sacrificial offering to him (Associated Press 2015a). Waukesha County Circuit Judge Michael Bohren did not accept the defense attorneys' claims. Judge Bohren noted that "the girls also thought killing Leutner would make them Slender Man's servants, earn them the right to live in his mansion, and prove to others the creature was real. Those motivations outweigh self-defense [assertions]" (Associated Press 2015a:A5). News reports revealed aspects of the girls' level of premeditation. On the evening of the sleepover, the three girls returned to the Geyser home around 9:30 p.m. from their skating outing at the skating rink in Waukesha. Geyser and Weier had planned on killing the victim at 2:00 a.m. Saturday in her sleep. They had planned on using duct tape to shut the victim's mouth so that she could not scream, stab her in the neck, cover her body with bed covers, and then run into the woods. But their plans changed and they decided to kill her in the bathroom at a nearby park the next morning because Weier knew there was a drain in the floor for the blood to go down, she told police (News Service Reports 2014). Weier had also packed a backpack with clothes, granola bars, water bottles, and a picture of her mother, father, and siblings in preparation for her trip with Geyser and Slender Man to the mansion in the forest (News Service Reports 2014).

To fully understand the motivations behind the Wisconsin girls who attempted to murder their friend in order to gain favor from Slender Man would take full access to their families, friends, those involved in their judicial case, and, of course, the girls themselves. Even then, we might not ever truly discover the motives behind their violent behavior. Still, scholars and laypeople alike have long pondered what makes a person(s) tick; that is, why do people do the things they do? To this end, a number of theories of human development and theories of violence itself have been proposed as viable explanations. In fact, entire volumes have been written on the topics of "human development" and "violent human behaviors," which, inevitably, have never led to a consensus of opinion as to the absolute and definitive explanation as to why people do the things they do. However, the diversity in theoretical explanations of human behavior is a worthwhile venture in that certain explanations are plausible in certain instances. Let's take a brief look at some of the prevailing theories of human development and violent behavior.

Theories of Human Development and Their Application to Violent Tendencies

A number of significant theories have been put forth in an attempt to explain how human development occurs. Some of these theories lean toward a genetic/biological explanation (nature), while other theories, including sociological explanations, favor accounts that include the role of learning, socialization, past experiences, modeling, and environmental factors (nurture). We can take these theories of human development and apply them to the violent tendencies of humans.

As discussed in chapter 3, there are some people who believe in the concept of "demonic possession." Demonic possession presumes that there is such a thing as a "Devil" or "evil spirits" that roam the earthly, or some other, realm and are capable of taking over the mind and body of humans. Once possessed, the person will engage in all manner of behaviors, including violence. People described as "possessed" are actually "mentally ill," but still there is a small segment of the world's population that believes in demonic possession as an explanation for violent behavior. The lawyers of the two Wisconsin girls in the Slender Man case did not use demonic possession as a form of defense, but if they had, they would have attempted to explain their violent behavior as a result of evil spirits. This defense strategy would have been in line with the whole notion of the existence of a "Slender Man."

Sigmund Freud (1856–1939) and his psychoanalysis perspective provide us with a classic example of utilizing a biological approach to the study of human behavior. During Freud's era, and for some time after, it was common for the fields of biology and psychology to attribute human behavior to biologically driven internal forces commonly known as instincts. In recent decades, psychologists have come to replace instincts as the cause of violent and deviant behavior in humans with the notion of mental disorders. Freud believed that humans developed via a dynamic unconscious that gives rise to drives, instincts, and urges that are nearly uncontrollable. He believed that the individual personality is composed of three structures: the id, the ego, and the superego. The id (Latin for "it") is totally unconscious of, or unconnected to, reality and is consumed with satisfying basic human drives, or instincts. (The "superego" represents society's rules and expectations, and the "ego" seeks the balance between one's id and superego.) An instinct may be defined as an innate impulse, or tendency to act, that is common to a given species (Delaney 2012a). Freud believed that humans were especially controlled by two basic instincts: the need for sexual gratification and aggressive tendencies. From a psychoanalytical perspective, both of these instincts could drive humans to act in a violent manner. Thus, humans are always capable of violence because it is in our nature to be aggressive, especially if it is related to the pursuit of sexual gratification.

The biological notion of "born criminals" and "natural criminals" (see chapter 3) implies that at least some humans are born with the capacity to commit violent acts. Cesare Lombroso, who developed the concept of "born criminal," argued that less-developed (evolutionarily speaking) individuals are those most likely to be born criminals, and yet violence occurs among all persons of all socioeconomic classes and in societies that consider themselves evolutionarily advanced. Lombroso (2006) also argued that women were not born criminals because they possessed a "maternal instinct," and yet once again, we know that women are capable of acts of violence, including murder and terrorist attacks.

Social disorganization theory, one of the earliest sociological theories designed to explain social deviance, examined environmental factors (social problems) as a cause of delinquency, deviance, and crime. The use of violence becomes a common by-product of social disorganization. Robert Merton's (1938) anomie theory describes how people become frustrated when their attempts to reach culturally desired goals are blocked. Violence is often a consequence of this type of frustration and cultural strain. Cloward and Ohlin's (1960) concept of differential opportunity structure stresses the importance of the social environment in determining which opportunities individuals have to choose from, with wealthy families having more legitimate opportunities to choose from than youths from lower-SES families. Once again, faced with strain and frustration, many people turn to violence as a means of attaining desired goals, goods, and services.

Subcultural and cultural deviance theories discuss the importance of the influence of peer groups. Members of particular subcultures (e.g., street gangs) are more likely to accept violence as a normal way of reacting to certain issues in life. When acts of violence are normalized in certain subcultures, members of those subcultures are far more likely to view violence in a positive light.

Proponents of control/social bond theory argue that everyone is capable of deviant, criminal, and violent acts and behaviors and put forth the notion that only because of socialization do we have any semblance of law and order and social stability. Control/social bond theorists argue that only when individuals become attached to society's norms and form a bond with society are they likely to curtail their deviant and violent behaviors. Thus, it is important to present positive role models to children at an early age so that they learn to accept society's norms and expectations.

Social learning and differential association theories place an emphasis on reinforcement and modeling. Proponents of the social learning theory elaborate on the process of learning itself. They propose that learning is a three-step procedure that entails three critical aspects: acquisition (an individual's initial introduction to a particular behavior); instigation (an individual actually participates in some form of behavior); and maintenance (an individual consistently repeats some form of behavior). An individual learns a behavior either through direct interaction with others, wherein such behavior is reinforced, or indirectly through observation (via a role model, such as a highly publicized entertainer). If the behavior in question is a violent behavior, the individual has learned to value violence. Differential association comes into play because it is proposed that the greater the number of (or the more important) associations one has with deviant others, including violent others, the more likely one is to adopt that deviant or violent lifestyle; conversely, if the greatest number of (or the most important) associations one has are with positive, conventional aspects of society, they are less likely to become deviant.

Conflict Theory and Violence

The theory, sociological or otherwise, that specifically utilizes the concept of "violence" the best is conflict theory. The conflict perspective views society as a system of social structures and relationships that are shaped primarily by economic forces.

These economic forces are controlled by the wealthy, especially the power elites, in a manner that best maintains the interests of the rich at the expense of the poor, thus creating social classes via economic conditions. Because of their economically advantageous position, the wealthy are able to use their power to coerce and manipulate others to accept their view of their society—and the world. In addition, since there is a clear power differential among individuals and social classes, resentment and hostility are constant elements of society. The obvious implication of this social reality is that conflict and violence are inevitable.

One of the leading proponents of conflict theory is Lewis Coser (1913–2003). Coser believed that conflict and violence are often linked. Furthermore, Coser (1967) argued that violence serves three specific purposes:

1. Violence as achievement—Causing violence is an achievement for some people, and the more violence they cause, the more they achieve in their own minds. As a result, some people, such as protestors, deviate from the normal expectations of behavior and commit acts of deviance, including violence, as a means of achieving success (Coser 1967).
2. Violence as a danger signal—When there is a great deal of violence in society, it should serve as an alarm to society, especially to political leaders, that there are underlying societal problems that need to be addressed. In recent years, a number of people have reacted to cases of police shootings against unarmed citizens in a violent manner. That protestors have deemed it necessary to resort to violence is, from Coser's perspective, indicative of the perception of many people that the police are not doing their jobs properly. It is also a signal that more acts of violence are likely to occur until the problem is corrected.
3. Violence as a catalyst—Acts of violence, especially when conducted simultaneously by large numbers of people, can start the process of correcting a social problem, or it can cause an increased level of violence. "Whether given forms of conflict will lead to changes in the social system or to the breakdown and to formation of a new system will depend on the rigidity and resistance to change, or inversely on the elasticity of the control mechanisms of the system" (Coser 1967:29). Violence draws the attention of the public, including those not directly involved with a particular social problem, and informs it that something needs to be done about specific social issues. When society unites to solve the problem, the catalyst has completed its job. Then again, violence can act as a catalyst to cause more problems and attract others to join in the violence.

Coser (1967) believed that violence has both positive and negative functions in society and viewed it as a necessary and important aspect of society.

Randall Collins (1941–), considered among the most prestigious sociological thinkers of this era, incorporates the role of violence in his social theories, especially his conflict perspective of social reality. Collins examines violence from both the macro and micro perspectives. From the macro perspective, Collins examines the "state" via Weber's definition of the state as the monopolization of legitimate force (Collins 1999). When describing the sociopolitical state in relation to violence, Collins (2009) writes, "The state consists of those people who have the guns or other weapons and are prepared to use them; in the version of political organization found in the modern world, they claim monopoly" (p. 170). A state may use violence in order to exercise power, gain or defend resources, or as a defense from attacking states. Collins's view of the role of the state and his take on those with guns and weapons will be especially applicable to our look at war, terrorism, suicide bombers, snipers, and school shootings.

Collins also examined violence at the micro level. As we know, **interpersonal violence** is a very common occurrence in the contemporary era; in fact, like violence at the macro level, micro-level forms of violence have been a common feature of humans throughout history. As Coser also believed, Collins holds that violence may serve some pragmatic purpose, as it may serve as a means to an end for individuals. Violence may also be directed toward another person as an act of aggression, or it may be a defense mechanism. Collins (2009) is quick to point out, however, that violence at the micro level is never effective against the state, as individuals or small groups of people do not possess enough power to coerce the larger state or the power elites.

Defining and Categorizing Violence

The term "violence" has been used a number of times already in this chapter, but it has yet to be defined. According to the Violence Prevention Alliance (VPA), **violence** is "the intentional use of physical force or power, threatened or actual, against oneself, another person, or against a group or community, that either results in or has a high likelihood of resulting in injury, death, psychological harm, maldevelopment, or deprivation" (WHO 2015b). The VPA is an organization that was officially formed in January 2004 by the World Health Organization (WHO) to unite groups (governmental, nongovernmental, and private) around a shared vision and approach to violence prevention that works to both address the root causes of violence and to improve services for victims (WHO 2015c).

The VPA divides its general definition of violence into a typology of three distinct categories:

1. Self-directed violence—Refers to violence (e.g., self-abuse such as cutting; and suicide) in which the perpetrator and the victim are the same individual
2. Interpersonal violence—Refers to violence between individuals. This category of violence includes violence between individuals and groups; violence against intimate partners; and community violence.
3. Collective violence—Refers to violence committed by larger groups of individuals and political states (WHO 2015b)

The three categories of violence used by the VPA/WHO (2015b) are a useful way of examining social deviance and violence and represent an improvement from Collins's simple micro/macro distinction. Consequently, in the remainder of this chapter, we will examine a wide variety of forms of violence using the VPA typology. By the end of this chapter it should become clear why the topic of violence warrants its own chapter discussion here even though violent offenses were discussed in chapter 5. For now, suffice it to say, most of the examples of violence to be discussed in this chapter would not have neatly fit into the criminal violence offense categories utilized in chapter 5.

Self-Directed Violence

With all the violence in the world, one might wonder why people would purposively injure, harm, or mutilate themselves. And if someone wanted to direct violence toward self, what means are available? In addition, who are the people most likely to engage in self-abuse? These questions, related issues, and more will be addressed below.

Self-Harm

Deliberate **self-harm** (also known as self-injury and/or self-mutilation) occurs when a person purposively inflicts physical harm to self via such methods as self-cutting, head banging, self-biting, and self-scratching (CDC 2015c). Self-harm does not include suicide or attempted suicide, as that has its own category of self-directed violence (CDC 2015c). The absence of the goal of trying to kill oneself is an important aspect of defining self-harm as revealed by the definition of self-harm provided by Gratz and Chapman (2009): "Deliberate self-harm is when one intentionally damages one's one bodily tissue without intending to die" (p. 2). Self-harm becomes a way in which people, especially young people, cope with strong emotions. While some people may cry, drink, use drugs, or talk with friends when faced with stressful situations, others resort to self-harm. Natasha Tracy (2015) describes specific criteria for the variations of self-harm:

1. Self-harm—Often occurs when people are seeking attention; however, once accustomed to the pain, they may inflict greater levels of self-harm so that they can achieve the same previous level of relief.
2. Self-injury—Generally starts as a spur-of-the-moment outlet for anger and frustration (such as punching a wall) but then develops into a method of coping with stress that, because it remains hidden, generates more stress.
3. Self-mutilation—Can be a hidden problem that goes on for years (e.g., self-cutting; self-burning or "branding"; picking at skin or reopening wounds; hair-pulling; and bone breaking).

Tracy (2015) expands upon the concept of self-mutilation to include behaviors that people engage in that are harmful to themselves, such as smoking or drinking to excess, as an unfortunate side effect of participating in an act that is viewed as self-pleasurable even though its ultimate consequence results in self-harm.

People who self-harm often feel completely alone a lot of the time. They may feel as though they are "the only one who struggles with such intense urges, emotional turmoil, or feelings of being out of control" (Gratz and Chapman 2009:1). Self-harmers may become frustrated with themselves because it is so hard to stop and their sense of self is compromised, as they know how society views people who harm themselves; consequently, they isolate themselves with their personal struggles (Gratz and Chapman 2009). Self-harmers are not alone, however. Research indicates that there are as many as 12 million people in the United States alone who self-harm (Gratz and Chapman 2009). In fact, if we examine the three primary categories of self-harm described above, we quickly realize that many of us have engaged in this behavior. Combing multiple sources (Gratz and Chapman 2009; *WebMD* 2015; ReachOut.com 2015), the people most likely to sustain self-harm are:

- Adolescent females
- People who have a history of physical, emotional, or sexual abuse
- People who have coexisting problems of substance abuse, obsessive-compulsive disorder, or eating disorders
- Individuals who were raised in families that discouraged expression of anger
- Individuals who lack skills to express their emotions and lack a good social support network

- Individuals who are/have been bullied or discriminated against
- Individuals who lost someone close to them, such as a parent, sibling, or friend
- Someone who has broken up with a boyfriend or girlfriend
- Someone who has a serious illness or disability that affects their sense of self
- Someone with a borderline personality disorder (BPD)

There are a number of reasons why someone might self-harm. As previously mentioned, some people self-harm because it becomes a means of dealing with stressful situations. Self-harm may also occur as an act of rebellion, as a rejection of parents' values, and as a means of individualizing oneself (*WebMD* 2015). Self-harm may also be viewed as a mechanism utilized by those who have a difficult time expressing their feelings that they need love and support; as a means of proving to oneself that they are not invisible; and as a means of feeling as though they are in control. The idea that self-harm conveys an expression of difficult or hidden feelings and/or that deliberate self-harm may provide the individual with a temporary sense of feeling again, let alone a way to express anger, sadness, grief or emotional pain (ReachOut.com 2015), is brilliantly displayed in the Nine Inch Nails song lyrics to "Hurt" written by Trent Reznor (see box 6.1).

CONNECTING SOCIAL DEVIANCE AND POPULAR CULTURE

Box 6.1 "I Hurt Myself Today, to See If I Still Feel"

Nine Inch Nails is an alternative (sometimes referred to as "industrial") rock band founded by Trent Reznor in Cleveland, Ohio, in 1988. Reznor remains as the guiding force of NIN (the second *N* is stylized in backward fashion) and has often changed the members of the band over the years. While many NIN songs became radio hits and album sales exceed 20 million worldwide, it is the haunting song "Hurt" from the 1994 *The Downward Spiral* album that has garnered the most attention.

The *Downward Spiral* album was written in a Hollywood Hills (California) house at 10050 Cielo Drive that Reznor had rented. Little did Reznor realize at the time that this was the infamous house where Charles Manson's minions killed Sharon Tate and four others in 1969 (Bozza 1999). The front door of the house had the word "Pig" written on it by the murderers, and although it had been painted over numerous times, you could faintly see the outline of the word on the door. Reznor apparently never noticed the word until after he was told whose mansion it was. After Reznor finished *The Downward Spiral*, he moved out of the house and the owner had the mansion demolished. Reznor, however, kept the front door handle "to remind him of what happened and the events that took place inside" (*Song Facts* 2015).

According to Reznor, the song "Hurt" is about realizing consequence and regret. It is meant to send a powerful message that we should all proceed through life wisely, because nothing is worse than wishing we had done things differently, especially things that lead to being stuck with pain, sickness, or death (*Song Facts* 2015). The self-loathing nature of the songs on the *Downward Spiral* album, especially "Hurt," reflects Reznor's state of mind at the time. Reznor had told *USA Today* that "I'm not proud to say I hate myself and don't like what I am, but maybe there is real human communication that ends up positive even though everything said is negative" (*Song Facts* 2015). The lyrics to "Hurt" begin with:

I hurt myself today

To see if I still feel

I focus on the pain

The only thing that's real

The needle tears a hole

The old familiar sting

Try to kill it all away

But I remember everything

The second stanza begins with the question, "What have I become? My sweetest friend." Reznor was not only going through a period of pain, he was engaging in self-harm via a heroin addiction. "The needle tears a hole" is a literal reference, in addition to metaphoric, once one realizes he has a heroin addiction at this time. Reznor's words speak loudly to many who self-harm, as he states that he hurts himself to feel the pain, to feel something, to feel anything. Feeling pain, due to self-harm, means that at least he feels something. In such a scenario, the self-harmer experiences an immediate sense of relief—because they feel something—but even they know it is just a temporary solution.

The song "Hurt" has served as background music in many movies and TV shows, including an episode of *Homicide: Life on the Street* and in the film *The Hangover Part III*. Interestingly, Johnny Cash covered the song in his *American IV: The Man Comes Around* album. Cash changed Reznor's line "I wear this crown of sh★t" to "crown of thorns" as a means of removing profanity and keeping his focus on his devout Christianity. Cash made a video of himself singing "Hurt." At the time of the video, Cash was 71 years old, and he appears very fragile as he sings the song from his home in Hendersonville, Tennessee. Cash wore no makeup, and there were no attempts to make him look more vibrant. The video was interspersed with footage of his younger days and came across as an obituary, as he was in failing health after a life filled with drug abuse (self-harm) (*Song Facts* 2015). The "Hurt" video seemed a bit odd for country star Johnny Cash to perform, but it was well received by the public and the media, and Reznor himself was very impressed and moved by the video (*Song Facts* 2015).

Trent Reznor performing at a sold-out show in Las Vegas.

Beyond the social factors that contribute to self-harm already discussed, sociologists Patricia and Peter Adler (2011), who have studied self-injury for nearly two decades, conclude that self-injury is a sociological occurrence utilized as a coping mechanism, a form of teenage angst, an expression of group memberships, rebellion, and as a means to convert emotional pain into manageable physical pain (Depression Connect 2011). The Adlers titled their book *The Tender Cut* to counter the common usage of terms such as "mutilation" in an attempt to show a different side to self-harm. Based on their research, the Adlers found that many of their test subjects used the term "self-therapy" to describe why they harmed themselves physically. They also found that the individuals under study regarded their behavior as a coping strategy, perhaps one they wished they did not need (and might someday be able to quit), but one that functioned to fill needs for them nevertheless (Adler and Adler 2011).

In addition to the sociological factors that may contribute to self-harming, Gratz and Chapman (2009) suggest there may be biological considerations, as the areas of the brain that seem to be involved in self-harm are the same areas that are directly related to pain and emotional distress. Working with the premise that self-harm involves tissue damage that, at the very least, results in pain, it is argued that the chemical messengers in one's brain (called neurotransmitters) are directly connected to one's natural pain-relieving system (the opioid system) and emotional system (the serotonin system) (Gratz and Chapman 2009). "Serotonin is a neurotransmitter that regulates mood, hunger, temperature, sexual activity, sleep, and aggression, among other things. Low levels of serotonin are related to depression, emotional distress, and aggression. Some research on serotonin has suggested that people who self-harm might actually have less serotonin activity in their brains' synapses that people who don't self-harm" (Gratz and Chapman 2009:39). That biological forces are involved in the manner in which the brain interprets pleasure in pain is certainly plausible; nonetheless, the source of pleasure and pain comes from social forces such as the factors previously discussed (e.g., physical or sexual abuse; loss of a loved one; and problems at school, work, or home).

There are a number of strategies to stop or cope with self-harm, including support from a friend, family member, or health professional. Removing sharp objects from the immediate environment is also advisable. ReachOut.com (2015) provides a list of other strategies a self-harmer might want to try in order to avoid self-injury:

- Choose to put off self-harming until you've spoken with someone who might be able to help you; or, at the very least, wait 15 minutes to see if the desire to self-harm still exists.
- Write in a journal.
- Go to a support group meeting.
- Draw or write in a marker over your body.
- Exercise as a means of releasing pent-up frustration or excess energy.
- Play video games as a means of distraction.
- Yell or sing at the top of your lungs to your own favorite music.
- Use relaxation techniques.
- Cry.
- Use a punching bag or pillow to release your frustrations or excess energy.
- Take a cold shower.
- Eat something really spicy.

As the list above implies, there are plenty of options to consider before resorting to self-harming. Interestingly, Trent Reznor writes lyrics to his songs, including "Hurt," from journal entries (see box 6.1). Because writing in a journal is being used to substitute for self-harming, the entries are often intensely personal.

Suicide

Suicide, the intentional killing of oneself, represents the epitome of self-directed violence. Attempted suicide occurs when people harm themselves with the intent to end their lives, but they do not die as a result of their actions. Many more people attempt suicide than actually die from suicide, but they often have serious injuries. In some cases, attempted suicide (e.g., drug overdose) does not end in physical injury. Suicide has been a topic of interest for sociology dating back to French sociologist Emile Durkheim's seminal work on suicide in the late 1800s (see box 6.2 for a further discussion on Durkheim's study of sociology).

A CLOSER LOOK

Box 6.2 Emile Durkheim and Suicide

It was Durkheim's 1897 publication of *Le Suicide* that helped sociology first gain full legitimacy in the academic world. Durkheim chose to study suicide because it is a relatively concrete and specific phenomenon that lends itself to statistical analysis. He applied his empirical methodology outlined two years earlier in his 1895 publication *The Rules of the Sociological Method* (*Les Regles de la Methode Sociologique*) to the study of suicide (Hadden 1997). The sociological importance of Durkheim's study on suicide rests with the realization that he was able to show that this act, which is generally highly individualistic, could be understood sociologically. Durkheim's (1951/1897) *Suicide* provides an example of a sociological study that emphasizes social facts rather than individual experiences (Phillips 1993). The lasting importance of Durkheim's study on suicide resides with the reality that his primary premise—that suicide is a multicausal phenomenon—is still true today. Durkheim acknowledged that individuals can be seen as having many "reasons" for committing the act of suicide, but he wanted to establish sociological "causes" that influence suicide. As Farganis (2011) explains, "Durkheim shifts our attention away from psychological questions about the motivations of particular individuals who commit suicide, a focus he viewed as reductionist, to sociological questions, concerning larger social conditions associated with suicide rates" (p. 52).

Le Suicide not only represents a pioneering study for sociology, it is among the very first modern examples of consistent and organized use of the statistical method in social investigation in any academic discipline. In this book, Durkheim outlined four types of suicide: egoistic, altruistic, anomic, and fatalistic. He linked each of the categories of suicide to the degree of integration into, or regulation by, society.

1. **Egoistic suicide**—High rates of egoistic suicide are likely to be found in societies, collectivities, or groups in which the individual is not well integrated into the larger social unit, such as someone who is suffering from deep depression or social isolation. A person who is dumped by a spouse or significant other, for example, may feel so broken-hearted that he or she feels compelled to commit suicide.

2. **Altruistic suicide**—Occurs when social integration is too strong, and the individual is compelled by social forces into committing suicide, as happened in 1997 when 39 members of the Heaven's Gate religious cult killed themselves by ingesting poison. Many of today's terrorists are willing to kill themselves because they feel so strongly about their cause and believe that they will be rewarded in the "afterlife."

3. **Anomic suicide**—This type of suicide occurs when periods of disruption unleash currents of anomie. (Durkheim described *anomie* as a sense of "normlessness" due to the breakdown of social norms found in society, collectivity, or a significant reference group.) A crash in the stock market or some other sudden loss of financial stability may cause people to experience anomie and commit suicide. Conversely, people who have never known wealth or power and suddenly attain it, may have difficulty handling newfound prosperity. Many of today's big-dollar lottery winners have reported that their lives were ruined after their sudden economic "fortune."

4. **Fatalistic suicide**—Durkheim actually spent little time clarifying this category of suicide other than to say it occurs when regulation is too excessive, leaving the individual with little or no sense of control over his or her life. Candidates for this type of suicide would include people facing a life sentence in prison or forced into slavery or prostitution.

The topic of suicide is certainly still relevant today. The CDC (2015d) considers suicide as a serious public health problem that can have lasting harmful effects on individuals, families, and communities. Certainly friends can be added to the list of those who are negatively affected when someone chooses to commit suicide. Complete strangers may also mourn the suicidal deaths of public persons such as sports stars, celebrities, musicians, and politicians. Furthermore, society itself is negatively impacted by suicide. In 2012, suicide and self-inflicted injuries resulted in an estimated $41.2 billion in combined medical and work loss costs (CDC 2014f).

In 2013, there were 41,149 reported suicides (for a death rate of 13.0 per 100,000 population), making suicide the tenth leading cause of death in the United States (CDC 2013). More than one-half (21,175) of the 2013 suicides were caused by the use of firearms, followed by 10,062 suffocation suicides and 6,637 poisoning suicides (CDC 2013). In 2011, suicide was the second leading cause of death among persons aged 15 to 24 years, the second among persons aged 25 to 54 years, the eighth among persons 55 to 64, and the tenth leading cause of death across all ages (CDC 2014f). In the United States, there is one suicide every 15 minutes (CDC 2010). For every two homicides committed in the United States, there are three suicides (CDC 2011). It is even more commonplace for people to think about committing suicide. According to the CDC (2010), among young adults ages 15 to 24, there are approximately 100 to 200 attempts for every completed suicide. Suicide statistics also reveal that women are more likely than men to attempt suicide, but men are almost four times as likely to succeed (CDC 2010). Most experts in the study of suicide believe that women attempt suicide as a "cry for help," while men attempt suicide to actually succeed at it. This point is further illustrated by the passive methods generally used by women (e.g., taking pills) and aggressive methods used by men (e.g., the use of a firearm). When controlling by race/ethnicity, suicide rates are highest among American Indian/Alaskan Native males, with 27.61 suicides (per 100,000 population), and non-Hispanic white males, with 25.96 suicides (per 100,000 population).

Beyond age, gender, and race/ethnicity, there are a number of other social factors applicable to the study of suicide. For example, there are instances of "suicide pacts" made between couples or groups of people to commit suicide, and an increasing number of veterans commit suicide. Other social issues surrounding suicide are the debate over the legal right to kill oneself (euthanasia) or to deny oneself of medical treatment via "do not resuscitate" (DNR) orders.

Couple the above-described social issues surrounding suicide with the risk factors of previous suicide attempts, history of depression or other mental illness, alcohol or drug abuse, family history of suicide or violence, physical illness, and feeling alone, and clearly we can see that the study of suicide is consumed with sociological ramifications. More importantly (to the study of deviance), suicide is clearly a serious form of self-directed violence that affects victims and survivors alike.

Suicide by Cop

"Suicide by cop" represents a rather interesting crossover topic that does not neatly fit into self-directed violence or interpersonal violence. On the one hand, "suicide by cop" does involve a law enforcement officer(s) killing another person, thus making it an example of interpersonal violence; however, on the other hand, this phenomenon only occurs because a person wants to die but does not want to kill him- or herself. As explained by the FBI (2014c), **suicide by cop** (SBC) "is a situation where individuals deliberately place themselves or others at grave risk in a manner that compels the use of deadly force by police officers." The FBI (2014c) has identified many warning signs or risk factors that characterize those suspects who may wish to die via SBC: "Individuals who feel trapped, ashamed, hopeless, desperate, revengeful, or enraged and those who are seeking notoriety, assuring lethality, saving face, sending a message, or evading moral responsibility often attempt SBC."

The FBI (2014c) reports that the field of suicide prevention pays little attention to SBC, and yet such scenarios (of people putting themselves in the position where the police officer is forced to shoot them) are fairly common and cause great distress for police officers. SBC incidents are very dangerous to police officers because they never know if the individual who wants to die will try to kill them as well. "Some suicidal individuals will point an empty gun at the police because they know the police will shoot back in self-defense. Yet others will have a loaded gun and will want to kill as many police officers as possible before they die" (Caruso 2015). Like other people who commit suicide, SBC individuals will often leave a note explaining their reasons for taking their actions; sometimes they apologize to the officers. Regardless, most police officers who are involved in suicide by cop suffer emotional difficulties afterward, and sometimes they suffer from posttraumatic stress disorder (Caruso 2015). Nearly all those involved in SBC are males (98 percent in one 10-year study); many had a history of domestic violence; abused alcohol or other drugs; had a prior history of suicide attempts; used a weapon, real or otherwise; and were likely to suffer from an untreated mental illness such as depression (Caruso 2015).

As we shall see later in this chapter (when we discuss riots), police officers have a hard enough time maintaining public trust, so one of the last things they want to be involved in is a suicide by cop case. As Miller (2006) explains, "Due to a combination of interpersonal manipulativeness, personal identification, and lack of heroic status, most officers find SBC calls to be among the most disturbing shooting incidents when they are forced to take the subject's life" (p. 172).

Interpersonal Violence

Interpersonal violence refers to violence between individuals, individuals and groups, groups and individuals, and groups against groups. In some cases, the topics to be discussed below cross over to the domain of violent crimes, but in other situations they remain in the gray area of noncriminal violent offenses. The first example of interpersonal violence to be examined is bullying.

Bullying

Bullying is an example of interpersonal violence that takes place mostly in schools and the workplace. Bullying can be defined as "the repeated exposure of one person to physical and/or emotional aggression including teasing, name calling, mockery, threats, harassment, taunting, hazing, social exclusion or rumors" (Srabstein and Leventhal 2010). The growing body of research on bullying indicates that bullying victims are at risk of experiencing a wide range of psychosomatic symptoms, including "running away from home, alcohol and drug abuse, absenteeism and, above all, self-inflicted, accidental or perpetrated injuries" (Srabstein and Leventhal 2010).

The consequences of bullying often extend into adulthood, as there is evidence of a significant association between childhood bullying behavior and later psychiatric morbidity (Srabstein and Leventhal 2010). Approximately 160,000 teens skip school every day because they are victims of bullying (DoSomething.org 2015).

School bullying statistics indicate that about one in four kids in the United States is bullied on a regular basis; teens in grades six through ten are the most likely to be involved in bullying-related activities (Bullying Statistics 2013). DoSomething. org (2015) reports that over 3.2 million students are victims of bullying each year. Every 7 minutes, a child is bullied on school grounds (National Association of People Against Bullying 2015). Verbal bullying is the most common type with about 77 percent of all students being bullied victimized by such verbal abuse methods as having rumors spread about them, being called vulgar names or having obscenities directed toward them, or being yelled at. Regular victims at school are especially worried about being bullied in the bathroom at school. About one in five students admits to bullying others. Nearly 85 percent of school bullying cases involve no intervention or effort made by a teacher or administrator to intervene (*Bullying Statistics* 2013). Fear and anxiety often stop fellow students from intervening against bullies.

The National Association of People Against Bullying (NAPAB) (2015) offers the following tips on what to do if you are being bullied:

1. Speak up—Let parents and school authorities know about the bullying. Don't stop talking about it until someone does something about it.
2. Realize that it is not your fault—Don't self-blame; the issue is not with you, it's with the bully.
3. Don't respond with inappropriate behavior—This will be used against you.
4. Recognize the symptoms of bullying—Headaches, stomachaches, and sleeplessness are common, along with a loss of interest in friends and school.
5. Seek counseling—Bullying results in psychiatric injury (Doran 2014).

Anyone being bullied in school is not going to be pleased to learn that bullying takes place in many work environments as well. According to the Workplace Bullying Institute (WBI) (2014a), **workplace bullying** is the repeated, health-harming mistreatment of one or more persons (the targets) by one or more perpetrators in the work environment. It is a form of abusive conduct that involves threats, intimidation, humiliation, work interference (including sabotage) that prevents work from getting done, or verbal abuse. Workplace bullying occurs for a variety of reasons but is driven by the perpetrators' need to control the targeted individual(s). It escalates when the bully involves others to side with the bully, either voluntarily or through coercion. Workplace bullying undermines legitimate business interests when bullies' personal agendas take precedence over work itself (WBI 2014a). The World Health Organization (2008) concurs with the WBI's assertion that workplace bullying undermines the workplace environment but also introduces the idea that victims of workplace bullying may suffer many of the same problems as victims of school bullying. "Work-related psychosocial risks concern aspects of the design and management of work and its social and organizational contexts that have the potential for causing psychological or physical harm" (WHO 2008). Srabstein and Leventhal (2010) add, workplace bullying often involves the victims being prone to suffer from a variety of health risks, including depression and cardiovascular problems.

Workplace bullying comes in a variety of forms. Sometimes the targeted person is a coworker, and other times it may involve contact with people during the course of one's occupation. As for the later version of workplace bullying, consider the case of Congressman Michael Grimm (R-NY) who bullied NY1-TV news reporter Michael Scotto. In January 2014, Grimm and his ex-girlfriend Diana Durand were arrested by the FBI on charges of illegally contributing funds to Grimm's 2010 campaign through straw donors (people who make political contributions provided by an anonymous third party). Following the 2014 State of the Union Address (January 28, 2014), Scotto asked Grimm about the scandal. Grimm, an ex-Marine and FBI agent, who is known as a "tough guy," was not pleased by the line of questioning and while still on camera said to Scotto, "Let me be clear to you, you ever do that to me again I'll throw you off this f-----g balcony." Scotto replied, "Why? Why? It's a valid question." Grimm then stated, "No, no, you're not man enough, you're not man enough. I'll break you in half. Like a boy" (WBI 2014b). Mind you, this is a U.S. congressman speaking to a reporter in a public building while on the air. Grimm was not forced to give up his role as congressman, but he did lose in a 2015 special election.

The second type of workplace bullying—which takes place in the workplace by fellow workers—is often referred to as a workplace mobbing. A **workplace mobbing** is like "bullying on steroids," a horrifying new trend whereby a bully enlists coworkers to collude in a relentless campaign of psychological terror against a targeted coworker (Henshaw 2015). A workplace mobbing is akin to being "ganged up" on by coworkers, subordinates, or superiors, with the intent to force someone out of the workplace via such techniques as rumor, intimidation, threats, discrediting, and isolation. It is a malicious form of harassment. Targets are likely to be competent, educated, resilient, outspoken, challengers to the status quo or are more empathic or attractive (Henshaw 2015). In the academic world, for example, a workplace mobbing victim, such as an untenured professor, likely possesses a superior work ethic, produces higher quality levels of academic work, and makes his or her colleagues look bad. The most threatened member of the department may then attempt to discredit the up-and-coming star via a variety of means described above and may then elicit others (either through intimidation or lies about the target). If the workplace mobbing target gains tenure, he or she can then rise to the top, leaving the bullies in the dust. If the target does not survive the mobbing, he or she will be "let go" and may struggle throughout his or her attempted academic career.

Hazing

Many social institutions have a long-held tradition that involves the practice of hazing. **Hazing** is a means of initiating a person into a group with or without the consent of the participants. Nuwer (2004) explains, "Hazing is an encompassing term that covers silly, potentially risky, or degrading tasks required for acceptance by a group of full-fledged members" (p. xiv). Crow and Rosner (2004) incorporate the aspects of humiliation and shaming in their legal interpretation of hazing. They define hazing as "any activity expected of someone joining a group that humiliates, degrades, abuses, or endangers, regardless of the person's willingness to participate" (Crow and Rosner 2004:200). Susan Lipkins (2009) describes hazing as a process, based on tradition, that is used by groups to discipline members and to reinforce a hierarchy. Like Crow and Rosner, Lipkins incorporates the idea that hazing activities can be humiliating, demeaning, intimidating, and exhausting, all of which results in physical and/or emotional turmoil. Hazing is quite common in sports, fraternities and sororities, the military, and street gangs. Incidents of hazing date back at least as far as 387 BCE with Plato's account of the savagery of young boys' hazing behavior. Hazing was common during the age of the rise of European universities in the 1400s (Delaney and Madigan 2015). Nuwer (2004) states, "Martin Luther endured hazing at Erfurt as a student. Later, in 1539, at Wittenberg, he advocated hazing as a means of strengthening a boy to face and endure life's challenges" (p. xxv). At American universities hazing was a method first utilized by upperclassmen against freshmen to "keep them in line." Hazing in American sport can be traced back to Harvard University in the late 1700s (Smith 1988). Since the early 1800s, and until recently, hazing has endured as a relatively acceptable form of a "rite of passage."

Today, however, hazing is viewed in a negative light. American high schools and colleges and universities have taken a hard stand against hazing in sports and Greek life activities. They have taken such a stand because of the increasing number of injuries and rare number of deaths that often accompany secretive hazing ceremonies. "Hazing in sports has received a significant amount of media attention in the last several years, especially on high school and col-

Rookie professional athletes, including former Denver Broncos quarterback Tim Tebow, are often subjected to various forms of hazing, including such things as unusual haircuts.

lege campuses nationwide. More student-athletes are being prosecuted under state anti-hazing laws and more institutions are being held responsible for their care" (Crow and Rosner 2004:200).

Inside Hazing (2014) has compiled data on high school and college hazing and on hazing trends. Among their findings:

- More than 1.5 million high school students are hazed each year.
- Forty-three percent of high school students were subjected to humiliating activities and 30 percent performed potentially illegal acts as part of their initiation.
- Every kind of high school group was involved in hazing, including 24 percent of the students involved in church groups.
- Ninety-two percent of high school students will not report a hazing.
- More than 250,000 students experienced some sort of hazing to join a college athletic team; 40 percent of these students report that a coach or club advisor was aware of the hazing; and 22 percent reported that the coach or advisor was involved in the hazing.
- Ten percent of female NCAA athletes were physically hazed, including being branded, tattooed, beaten, or thrown in water, or having their head forcibly shaved.
- Sixty percent of athletes agree that it is important to tolerate psychological stress and 32 percent believe it is important to tolerate physical pain.
- Sixty-seven percent agree that a significant aspect of initiation is humiliation.
- Slightly less than half (46 percent) believe that it is important to keep the code of silence.

- Just 29 percent of Greek leaders are concerned with the overuse of alcohol during pledge activities.
- Students are more likely to be hazed if they knew an adult who was hazed.

Historically, it was understood that hazing would be a part of an indoctrination process into many clubs, especially high school and college sports teams and the Greek system in college. Consequently, in most instances, hazing was not considered a form of social deviance. Today there is less tolerance for hazing, and many people feel that such behaviors are deviant, even if certain acts are not criminal and freely engaged in by consenting participants. In addition, while students who knew an adult who was once hazed are more likely to accept being hazed, an increasing number of students, especially in college, are becoming turned off by hazing and the humiliation and violence often associated with it.

"Bum Fights"

Whenever a social phenomenon is labeled with a term that some people will certainly find offensive—such as "bum fights"—we are likely describing a form of social deviance. Bum fights are staged acts of violence wherein homeless people, usually men, are paid to fight one another for the entertainment of the viewers. In most instances, these fights are filmed; many of the videos appear on YouTube (there were over 60,000 such videos available on YouTube in May 2015) and other websites.

There is a specific film series called *Bumfights*, produced by Indecline Films, that drew the attention of the cyber-viewing public and helped to make bum fights a social phenomenon. The first video, *Bumfights: A Cause of Concern* (2002), was produced by Ryan McPherson and three of his friends, Daniel Tanner among them. After reportedly making millions of dollars (they claimed sales of about 300,000 copies at $20 each), McPherson and his friends sold the rights to *Bumfights* (to start a different film company) following the first video; three more *Bumfights* videos were subsequently released (Mancini 2014). The videos feature homeless men in metropolitan areas (mostly San Diego, San Francisco, and Las Vegas) fighting other homeless people and attempting amateur stunts in exchange for money, alcohol, and other incentives. "*Bumfights* are brutal video depictions of street life, portrayed with rapid-cut, handheld camera images. Most of the images are too brutal to describe here, but suffice it to say that the participants often endure violent attacks that may include being set on fire; some received payment to defecate on a sidewalk or pull their own teeth out with pliers, and so on" (Delaney 2012a:243). One of the homeless men involved in the *Bumfights* videos was paid to have "Bumfights" tattooed across his forehead.

A few years after the release of the first *Bumfights* video, McPherson was arrested and sentenced to 280 community service hours at a homeless shelter (Palmer 2014). McPherson and his crew were also ordered to pay an undisclosed amount of money to three of the homeless men involved in the videos as part of an out-of-court settlement. The men were attempting to sue the filmmakers for emotional and physical damages in connection with the videos (Palmer 2014). Interestingly, in 2014, McPherson and Tanner were arrested in Bangkok, accused of attempting to smuggle body parts back to the United States after three parcels they possessed were found to contain a baby's head, a sliced-up baby's foot, an adult heart with a stab wound, and a "sheet of skin" with tattoo markings (Palmer 2014; Mancini 2014; Doksone and Gecker 2014). McPherson and Tanner fled the country, according to Thai police (Palmer 2014).

Understandably, the *Bumfights* video specifically, and bum fights in general, are condemned by numerous organizations, such as the National Coalition for the

Homeless, and are banned in a number of countries, including England, Scotland, Northern Ireland, and Canada, and most mainstream retail video outlets refuse to rent or sell them (Delaney 2012a; Doksone and Gecker 2014). There are other variations of violent street fights wherein participants are paid to inflict and receive violent forms of pain, including out-and-out brawls by homeless people, gang fights, girl fights, school fights, random street fights (like the "knockout game" described in chapter 5), and so on.

With bum fights we have another example of interpersonal violent behavior that involves consenting participants who engage in borderline criminal behavior (and sometimes criminal behaviors), thus making it more relevant for a chapter on violence than street crime.

Intimate Interpersonal Violence (IIV)

Intimate interpersonal violence may be defined as acts carried out with the intention of, or perceived as having the intention of, physically or emotionally hurting one's partner (in marriage, cohabitation, or dating), child, parent, sibling, or some other intimate person (e.g., close family member such as a niece or nephew, aunt or uncle, or grandparent). As the definition of intimate interpersonal violence implies, IIV victims know the perpetrator of said violence. Abuse and violence among intimate persons takes many forms, including intimate partner violence/spousal abuse; child abuse; parental abuse; sibling abuse; and abuse of the elderly. IIV abuse and violence may be emotional or physical. With physical abuse—which is the result of violence—the scars are visible; emotional abuse, however, scars the victim on the inside (e.g., the human psyche, self-esteem). Sexual violence and abuse victimization often cross over into both the emotional and physical realms. Physical abuse includes, but is not limited to, hitting, shoving, pushing, punching, kicking, tripping, biting, twisting arms, throwing items, pulling hair, choking, and the use/threat of weapons. Emotional abuse includes, but is not limited to, verbal yelling, swearing, or directing insults toward another; pretending not to notice the other person's presence, conversation, or value; and public humiliation. Sexual abuse may involve, but is not limited to, sexual assault (e.g., rape), molestation, displaying pornography, and being subjected to unwanted sexual advances.

Intimate Partner Violence (Domestic Violence)

Intimate partner violence (IPV), or domestic violence, is a serious, preventable public health problem that affects tens of millions of Americans. The term IPV describes physical, sexual, or psychological harm caused by a current or former partner or spouse, occurs between heterosexual or same-sex couples, and does not require sexual intimacy (CDC 2015e). Domestic violence involves situations where there is an abuser and a victim. The abuser, who is generally a male, engages in intimate interpersonal violence as a means of gaining power and control in the relationship. The male abuser often engages in abusive behavior because he believes in male superiority. The male aggressor feels compelled to "correct" the perceived improper behavior of his partner and believes that it is his responsibility to maintain authority through intimidation, which is interpreted as respect from the abuser's perspective. The victim, in addition to experiencing the brunt of the abuse and violence, is made to believe that she or he must take the abuse for a variety of reasons, including a dependence on the abuser for care (especially financial), in order to keep the family together, and feelings of shame and fright (in reporting the violence). Many victims are made to believe that they actually deserve the abuse. Domestic violence often entails a cyclic style of events. Pressure builds until the abuser snaps. Afterward, there is an unconventional grieving period of silence and guilt until the event is ultimately forgotten about, or ignored. Some time later, another event of violence occurs, and the cycle continues.

An aspect of intimate partner violence that has garnered increased attention over the past decade is stalking. **Stalking** is a criminal activity that consists of the repeated following or harassing of another person via such means as waiting outside the home or workplace of the targeted person, following the target, sending flowers or notes to the target, and placing tracking devices on the target's automobile or cell phone. Breiding and associates (2014) report that an estimated 15.2 percent of American women (18.3 million) and 5.7 percent of American men (roughly 6.5 million) have experienced stalking during their lifetimes that made them feel very fearful or made them believe that they or someone close to them would be harmed or killed.

Child Abuse and Neglect

The Federal Child Abuse Prevention and Treatment Act (CAPTA), as amended by the CAPTA Reauthorization Act of 2010, defines child abuse and neglect as, at minimum, "Any recent act or failure to act on the part of a parent or caretaker which results in death, serious physical or emotional harm, sexual abuse or exploitation or an act or failure to act which presents an imminent risk of serious harm" (U.S. Department of Health and Human Services 2015b). In cases involving child abuse and neglect, the term "child" refers to a person who is younger than age 18 or who is not an emancipated minor. The abuser would be the parent or caregiver of the child. Physical, emotional, and sexual abuse are included under the child abuse umbrella as well as neglect and the failure to provide medical treatment to a sick or injured child. Effects of child abuse may include shame, self-blame, depression, anxiety, posttraumatic stress disorder, self-esteem issues, self-injury, suicidal ideation, sexual dysfunction, increased likelihood of abusing drugs, and borderline personality disorder.

According to the CDC (2015f), there were 678,932 victims of child abuse and neglect reported to the Child Protective Services (CPS) in 2013; 27 percent were under the age of three. In 2013, more than 1,500 children died from abuse and neglect in the United States. The CDC indicates that CPS reports may underestimate the true occurrence of child abuse and neglect. The Child Help organization provides statistics that may represent a clearer picture of child abuse and neglect and its consequences in the United States:

- Every year more than 3 million reports of child abuse are made in the United States involving more than 6 million children (a report can include multiple children).
- The United States has one of the worst records among industrialized nations— losing on average between 4 and 7 children every day to child abuse and neglect.
- A report of child abuse is made every 10 seconds.
- Eighty percent of 21-year-olds who reported childhood abuse met the criteria for at least one psychological disorder.
- Nearly two-thirds of people in treatment for drug abuse reported being abused or neglected as children.
- Children who experience child abuse and neglect are about 9 times more likely to become involved in criminal activity (Child Help 2015).

A fairly typical form of child punishment that sometimes crosses over to the domain of child abuse involves the punishment of children who misbehave. Among the more common methods of punishing a misbehaving child is spanking. While some parents refuse to physically punish their children via any means, including spankings, other parents find it as an effective manner of instilling conformity to expected behavioral patterns. Spanking is generally considered a mild form of physical punishment, but there are instances when physical punishments cross over to the world of corporal punishment. See box 6.3 for a discussion on corporal punishment.

A CLOSER LOOK

Box 6.3 Adrian Peterson, Spanking, and Corporal Punishment

In September 2014, Adrian Peterson, a star running back for the Minnesota Vikings, made national and international news when it was reported that he used a tree branch to hit his 4-year-old son (and a later accusation that he injured another 4-year-old son) as part of punishment for the child's misbehavior (Samakow 2014). The revelation led to the Vikings suspending Peterson (after he had played just one game in the 2014 season) and his eventual suspension from the NFL on November 18, 2014. Peterson was placed on the NFL's "exempt list," barring him from all team activities until his child-abuse case was resolved. Peterson's suspension from the NFL and his use of physical punishment against his young son sparked a national conversation on the topic of physical/corporal punishment. (Peterson was reinstated by the NFL effective April 17, 2015.)

Corporal punishment is defined as punishment of a physical nature for some violation of conduct that involves the infliction of pain on, or harm to, the body. Among the methods used via corporal punishment are spankings (paddling) to beating to caning or flogging. Corporal punishments were, historically, quite common in American schools but have fallen out of favor in recent years. As of September 2014, it was still legal in 19 states for schools to use corporal punishment (Associated Press 2014). In the judicial system, corporal punishment is also referred to as capital punishment and may involve such tactics as cutting off the hand of a thief to public floggings and to violent forms of execution.

Peterson, finding nothing wrong with his actions, defended his behavior by saying that he used the same form of punishment on his children as his father had used on him as a boy. A number of polls, including one by the *Huffington Post*

(81 percent in favor) found that most Americans believe spanking is an effective form of punishment (Samakow 2014). Americans who had been on the receiving end of corporal punishment as children were especially likely to view it in a favorable manner, using such clichéd justifications as "I was spanked when I was a child and I turned out okay." Corporal punishment as a form of child punishment is legal in every state in the United States so long as the force is "reasonable." Interpretations of "reasonable" lead to many gray areas but are generally distinguished by whether or not an injury was caused as a result of the punishment. In Texas, where Peterson was accused of administering corporal punishment, punishment is abusive if it causes injury. "While a blow that causes a red mark that fades in an hour is not likely to be judged as abusive, a blow that leaves a bruise, welt, or swelling, or requires medical attention, could be judged abusive" (Associated Press 2014). In November, 2014, Peterson pleaded no contest to a reduced charge of misdemeanor reckless assault as part of a plea deal with prosecutors to resolve his felony child abuse case. As part of the deal, Peterson avoided jail time and instead paid a fine of $4,000, court costs, and 80 hours of community service (Prisbell and Schrotenboer 2014).

As of September 2014, thirty-nine countries prohibit corporal punishment in all settings, including at home, where most abuse occurs. Worldwide, about 6 in 10 children between the ages of 2 and 14 are subjected to corporal punishment by caregivers on a regular basis, according to a UNICEF report. The report also found that people with less education and wealth are more likely to support corporal punishment (Associated Press 2014).

Parent Abuse (Abuse of Parents)

Just as parents are capable of abusing their children, older children, primarily teenagers, are capable of abusing their parents. Parent abuse may be defined as "any act of a teen/young adult that is intended to cause physical, emotional or financial damage to gain power and control over a parent and/or any behavior that is deliberately harmful to the parent" (Envision Counselling and Support Centre 2014). While occasional conflict between parents and children is commonplace, abuse of parents generally takes place when teens/young adults are attempting to separate themselves from their parents and establish their own independence. During this transition period they may resist the authority of parents and become defiant. This defiance may reveal itself via physical or emotional/psychological abuse.

Abuse of parents represents a power play wherein the teen/young adult wants to have control and power. The conflict is regular and ongoing. The teen/young adult will manipulate and attempt to intimidate parents. The abused parent is a parent who has lost the ability to parent their teen/young adult in an effective manner (Envision Counselling and Support Centre 2014). The continued trend of young adults living with their parents through their 20s has contributed to parent abuse. "A recent Canadian census showed that 44 percent of children aged 20–29 live with their parents. An adult child living with their parents can put a lot of stress on family relationships and in some cases play a role in parent abuse, especially when there are drug and/or alcohol addictions and financial problems" (Envision Counselling and Support Centre 2014). Parent abuse crosses all social lines including rich and poor, highly educated and poorly educated, and both males and females may abuse their parents, although males are generally more physically violent than females.

Verbal forms of parent abuse include yelling, arguing, challenging authority, being sarcastic or critical, laughing in the parent's face, name calling, and swearing at a parent. Emotional abuse includes playing mind games, trying to make the parent think they are going crazy, manipulative threats (such as threats of suicide), and expecting the parent to meet every need of the child. Physical abuse includes throwing things at the parent, breaking objects, punching holes in the walls, and personal physical attacks such as hitting, punching, slapping, spitting, shoving, and pushing the parent. Financial abuse includes stealing or "borrowing" the parent's belongings without permission (e.g., automobile); damaging the home or possessions; demanding things the parent cannot afford; and using a parent's credit cards to run up large bills.

Sibling Abuse

Many of us with siblings in our youth (or even in adulthood) are likely to recall some sort of incidence of sibling violence that had it occurred at the hands of a stranger would likely have violated some sort of criminal code. Consider, for example, a sibling who pushed you out of a tree, or an open window, or punched you repeatedly for your toy or just because he or she walked into the room and saw you sitting there. Because it was at the hands of a sibling, the perpetrator of the violence was likely yelled at by a parent/guardian and instructed to stop the violence, or perhaps you retaliated in kind. Now consider if a complete stranger had done some of these same things and your parent/guardian observed it. You may also recall cruel things that a sibling has said to you at some point in time in your life. Were your self-esteem and sense of identity compromised? Many of us with siblings endured quite a bit of abuse growing up with brothers and/or sisters.

Much of what was described above is normal for many siblings. They tease each other or they test each other because siblings represent a safe zone to test the parameters of social norms. But sibling abuse goes much deeper. Sibling abuse is the physical, emotional, or sexual abuse of one sibling by another that can be described as a repeated pattern of aggression with the intent to inflict harm and motivated by a need for power and control (American Association for Marriage and Family Therapy 2014). About 53 percent of children report abuse between brothers and sisters; the percentage of youths being abused by siblings increases if adults are also abusing the children (Teen Violence Statistics 2009). Parents and caregivers must be diligent in watching for signs of normal sibling rivalry that may escalate into something far more abusive. A younger sibling hurt by an older or stronger sibling has both long- and short-term consequences. The younger child may show signs of depression, anxiety, fear of the dark, school behavior problems, and, in some cases, self-harm. The sibling aggressor may also have some problems, as he or she may be bullying children at school and may experience long-term effects, like being aggressive with dating partners or spouses in adulthood (American Association for Marriage and Family Therapy 2014). A particularly deviant form of sibling abuse is sexual sibling abuse. The victim of sexual sibling abuse is likely to feel trapped, ashamed, helpless, responsible, and powerless to stop the abuse. The abuser may use physical abuse and threats to ensure that the victim will not talk about the abuse to anyone else in the family.

Collective Violence

With our look at self-directed and interpersonal violence complete, we turn our attention to collective forms of violence. With our definition of **collective violence**— violence committed by larger groups of individuals and political states—in mind, it seems most appropriate to examine two extreme forms of collective violence: riots and wars.

Riots

A **riot** is defined as a violent public disorder involving a large number of people assembled together and acting with a common intent—the wanton destruction of human life and/or property. Riots take on many characteristics but are generally characterized by rampant vandalism, looting, assault, intimidation, robbery, and homicide. In nearly all cases, the riot itself followed a series of social problems confronting a specific category(ies) of people who, generally, feel as though they are being treated unfairly and unequally. Such folks have likely voiced their complaints, but their concerns have fallen on deaf ears. Typically, a specific incident, such as a confrontation between the police and a member of the oppressed group, sparks a violent reaction that leads to open protest. Open protests in the daytime are generally relatively subdued. However, when the open protest continues into the night, the nature of the protest often becomes increasingly violent. The seeds of a riot have now not only been sowed, they have grown into fruition. As the numbers of violent protestors increase, we have a full-fledged riot. Responses from the police and city, state, and federal (when necessary) officials dictate just how violent, deadly, and costly the riot will become.

Collective violence in the form of riots has been a part of American history since its earliest inception. The American Revolution was sparked by a riot—the Boston

Tea Party. The Boston Tea Party, which occurred on December 16, 1773, involved a colonist uprising against the sociopolitical authority of England. The New England colonists, who had voiced displeasure with the existing power structure that governed them via such proclamations as "no taxation without representation" (the colonists believed that in order to be taxed by the British Parliament, they should have legislators sitting and voting in London), were especially infuriated with the Tea Act passed by Parliament on May 10, 1773. The Tea Act granted the British East India Company a monopoly on tea sales in the American colonies. This legislation would ultimately compel a group of "Sons of Liberty" members to disguise themselves as Mohawk Indians, board three ships (the *Beaver, Dartmouth,* and *Eleanor*) moored in Boston Harbor, and destroy over 92,000 pounds of tea (Boston Tea Party 2015).

The Boston Tea Party riot was not the only riot on American soil in the 1700s. The first "American" riot (post–Revolutionary War), was the 1788 "Doctors' Riot" in New York City. The Doctors' Riot began on April 16, 1788, and resulted in 20 deaths; the riot would, however, change the way medicine was carried out for decades to come (Lovejoy 2014). The medical profession was quite primitive (comparatively speaking) in the late 18th century, and New York City had just one medical school—Columbia College. Many courses were taught at New York Hospital, and an essential aspect of medicine involved anatomical dissections; however, such procedures were generally viewed by the public as sacrilegious. "In the winter of 1788, the city was abuzz with newspaper stories about medical students robbing graves to get bodies for dissection, mostly from the potter's field and the cemetery reserved for the city's blacks, known as Negroes Burial Ground" (Lovejoy 2014). Accusations of barbarity eventually led to a mob attacking the New York Hospital and the apartments of doctors and medical students. Most doctors and medical students fled for their safety, but others stayed behind to protect the "valuable collection of anatomical and pathological specimens" (Lovejoy 2014). Nearly two dozen doctors and medical students were killed, the body parts set ablaze in the streets, and other medical professionals were hunted by the mob.

In the 1800s, a number of riots occurred in American cities, including the Cincinnati riots of 1829 (primarily pitting Irish immigrants against African Americans who fought for jobs); Baltimore bank riot (as a result of the failure of the Bank of Maryland); Cincinnati riots of 1836 (race riot pitting whites versus blacks); Philadelphia Nativist riots of 1844 (an anti-Catholic and Irish American–based riot); New York City Police riot of 1857 (involving competing defunct police forces); Buffalo riot of 1862 (Irish and German workers versus dock bosses); the New York City draft riots of 1863 (started as a protest against the draft but changed to blacks being targeted by white mobs); Memphis riots of 1866 (racial tensions following the Civil War); New Orleans riot of 1866 (racial tensions following the Civil War); Pulaski (Tennessee) riot of 1867 (race riot following Civil War); Camilla (Georgia) riots of 1868 (race riots); New York City riots of 1870 and 1871 (Protestants versus Catholics); Los Angeles anti-Chinese riot of 1871 (racially motivated); and a number of other U.S. cities that had race-related riots through the remainder of the century.

The 1900s were also characterized by numerous riots on American soil, most of which were race-related. Sociologists often comment on the social significance of the 1960s. No other decade, arguably, had so much social turmoil and social protest, ranging from anti–Vietnam War protests, the women's rights movement, the antiestablishment and pro–recreational drug hippie movement, and, of course, the civil rights movements. Having been freed as slaves a century earlier, African Americans faced many forms of overt and covert racism, discrimination, and prejudice. The long-simmering tensions between blacks and the white establishment came to full blows in many U.S. cities in the 1960s, resulting in record-setting amounts of financial damage and the loss of countless lives. While many U.S. cities endured rioting in 1968 following the assassination of Dr. Martin Luther King Jr. (a beacon of hope for black Americans specifically, and pro–civil rights Americans in general), no other riot in the 1960s better illustrated the problems between blacks and the white establishment than the 1965 Watts (Los Angeles) riots.

Watts is located in an area of Los Angeles known as South-Central (although city leaders prefer to call it Southern Los Angeles today). The mostly African American residents of Watts had long complained of discrimination, prejudice, and police brutality. Like many predominantly black urban neighborhoods of the 1960s, Watts was an area with underfinanced schools, marked with high rates of unemployment and underemployment, residents victimized by racial profiling by the police, and so on. In brief, lying just slightly below the surface was an explosion ready to occur. On a hot August 11, 1965, summer's day, the spark needed to set off the explosion arrived when police attempted to arrest Marquette Frye, a young black motorist who was pulled over and arrested by Lee W. Minikus, a white California Highway Patrolman, for suspicion of driving while intoxicated. With countless residents outdoors to escape the heat of their non-air-conditioned homes, and with strained tensions between police and Watts residents, an outbreak of violence ensued very quickly. The violence escalated to a full-fledged riot centered in the commercial section of Watts. "For several days, rioters overturned and burned automobiles and looted and damaged grocery stores, liquor stores, department stores and pawnshops" (Civil Rights Digital Library 2015). Thirty-four people lost their lives, over 1,000 were injured, and more than 4,000 were arrested. While some public officials insisted that the looting and arson were caused primarily by "outside agitators," an official investigation, prompted by Governor Pat Brown, found that "the riot was a result of the Watts community's longstanding grievances and growing discontentment with high unemployment rates, substandard housing, and inadequate schools" (Civil Rights Digital Library 2015).

In an attempt to assure that no such rioting similar to the Watts riot would ever occur again in Los Angeles, a gubernatorial commission recommended a number of specific measures be taken to address the concerns of lower-SES folks, especially African Americans. Los Angeles city leaders and state officials failed to implement the measures, and to the surprise of no one (at least those who lived in Los Angeles and/or studied riots), Los Angeles would indeed face another mass riot, a riot so notorious it remains (to date) the most costly and violent riot in American history. Table 6.1 illustrates the 10 costliest riots in U.S. history and, unfortunately for Los Angeles, it has the dubious distinction of "Riot Capital of the U.S." (*The Richest* 2014).

As we can see in table 6.1, the Los Angeles riots of 1992 are the most costly in American history. The LA riots came about primarily because the same issues that led to the Watts riots of 1965 were never addressed. The riots started in South-Central, not too far from Watts. Socioeconomic conditions had not changed for most urban blacks throughout the United States, including in Los Angeles. Among the biggest complaints from South-Central residents was the manner in which police treated them. The first spark that would set the future fire of the 1992 LA riots occurred

TABLE 6.1   The 10 Costliest Riots in U.S. History

1. Los Angeles, 1992: $1.268 billion (rioting followed the acquittal of four white police officers accused of beating Rodney King; 6 days of rioting, random acts of violence, destruction, robbery, mob assault,arson, Korean stores targeted by African Americans, 58 deaths, 3,700 buildings burned, 11,000 arrests)

2. Watts (Los Angeles), 1965: $321 million (6 days of unrest following the arrest of Marquette Frye on a DUI suspicion; property damage, looting, arson, 34 deaths, streets similar to a war zone when 14,000 National Guard troops arrived)

3. Detroit, 1967: $289 million (violence followed the attempted arrest of celebrants at an unlicensed drinking club hosting a party of 82 African Americans; violent confrontations, vandalism, 5 days of rioting, 43 dead, over 7,299 arrested, President Lyndon B. Johnson declaring a state of insurrection against the government leading to over 8,000 National Guardsmen and 4,700 paratroopers being called in)

4. Miami, 1980: $181 million (following the acquittal of four officers accused of beating Arthur McDuffie, a black man arrested for traffic violations; looting, arson, thefts, and sniper fire)

5. Washington, D.C., 1968: $158 million (from mob vandalism following the assassination of MLK; violence led to over 13,600 federal troops and 1,750 National Guardsmen, 12 dead, over 1,000 injured, 6,000 arrested, looting, and arson)

6. New York City, 1977: $106 million (following a massive blackout; over 1,600 stores looted and over 1,000 arson fires)

7. Newark, 1967: $103 million (26 killed, over 1,000 injured; mob vandalism, looting, and arson)

8. Baltimore, 1968: $92 million (from mob vandalism following the assassination of MLK; looting and arson)

9. Chicago, 1968: $86 million (from mob vandalism targeting mostly white-owned stores following the assassination of MLK; looting and arson)

10. New York City, 1968: $26 million (from mob vandalism, looting, and arson)

Source: The Richest 2014

on March 3, 1991, when Rodney King and two passengers were pulled over by the California Highway Patrol (CHP). The two passengers cooperated with CHP, but King, reputedly high on PCP, repeatedly refused police orders. His resistance to arrest led to his brutal beating by multiple police officers. The year 1991 precedes the present era of the ever-present smartphone in the hands of nearly ever citizen recording nearly every event; nonetheless, the King beating was caught on film by resident George Holiday on his camcorder. This became the first case of a beating caught on film that was replayed repeatedly on the news across the nation. Outrage ensued among most civilians but especially for black folks in South-Central. Surely a police beating caught on film and shown to the American public, residents of South-Central presumed, would lead to the conviction of the four primary officers accused of using excessive force and thus would give vindication to the black community that had long complained of unfair police treatment.

The months, then weeks, then days that led to the court trial of the four officers accused of beating Rodney King were the talk of all Angelenos. Nearly everyone living in the greater Los Angeles area knew, without a doubt, that a riot would ensue if the police officers were acquitted. Unfortunately, the dysfunctional city leaders (the chief of police and mayor despised each other so much they hadn't spoken to each other for a long period of time) seemed completely unprepared for what might happen if the officers were acquitted. (Note: As a former Los Angeles resident, and as a person who witnessed the riots firsthand, I can attest to this. The overall images of the riots will never leave me. Also, as a first-year Ph.D. student at the University of Nevada, Las Vegas, my first television interview as a sociologist was as an "expert" on collective behavior and riots, and I spoke of the 1992 riots in Los Angeles and Las Vegas.)

On April 29, 1992, the four white police officers, whose trial had been moved outside of Los Angeles to the white community of Simi Valley, were found innocent. Immediately after the verdicts were announced, protestors in Los Angeles hit the streets, and violence quickly ensued. Black protestors initially targeted random white people (look up the Reginald Denny incident that occurred on the corner of Florence and Normandie) and then Korean shop owners in South-Central. Rioting ensued throughout the metropolitan area of Los Angeles and, depending on one's source, anywhere from 53 to 63 people died during the riots, fires raged throughout the city for days, all variations of violent acts were committed, and property damage exceeded a billion dollars.

As a nation, we would like to hope that riots are a thing of the past. However, the 21st century has witnessed a number of riots. In the spring of 2015 there were riots in Baltimore; Ferguson, Missouri; Cleveland; and Staten Island. And in all these cases, the spark was the manner in which police, generally white police officers, have attempted to arrest and apprehend black criminal suspects. The largest riot during this time occurred in Baltimore. The background story of Baltimore parallels many of the past riots, especially the Watts, Los Angeles, and Newark riots. The Baltimore neighborhood that played witness to the death of Freddie Gray at the hands of arresting police officers suffers from high unemployment; low high school graduation rates; over

Two men throw beer bottles at burning vehicles during riots following the funeral of Freddie Gray on April 27, 2015, in Baltimore, Maryland.

one-third of housing is empty or abandoned; and one-fourth of youths aged 10 to 17 had been arrested in a recent 4-year period. The sense of hopelessness experienced by the affected people of Baltimore seemed to boil over on April 27, 2015—the day of Gray's funeral—when relatively peaceful protests turned into a violent riot by nightfall. (It should be noted that of the 6 police officers implicated in the death of Freddie Gray, 3 were white and 3 were black.) Once again, looting and arson characterized this riot and caused property damage exceeding $9 million in the city, and residents had fewer jobs and fewer stores to shop at. Federal drug enforcement agents said that gangs targeted 32 pharmacies in the city, taking roughly 300,000 doses of opiates. The large number of opiates on the street was credited as a major variable in the continued violence that ensued in Baltimore through the summer. The number of homicides in July 2015 reached 43, the highest number for a single month since August 1972 (Associated Press 2015k). By the end of July 2016, prosecutors had dropped all charges against all 6 officers involved in the Freddie Gray case, citing that it was clear that the government could not win a conviction (Hawkins, Bui, and Hermann 2016).

As this brief review of the history of riots reveals, strained race relations are often a cause of rioting. In many instances, there are actually a number of underlying reasons why people riot. As Tipton (2002) explains, "Many times the true causes of a riot elude the public, and therefore the riot appears to have a single cause. Most riots have several variables, such as race, discrimination, and economics, that work in concert to fuel the motivation and intensity of rioters" (p. 1404). Still, with this caution in mind, Tipton (2002) believes that there are four categories of riots:

1. **Race riots**—Occur in cities where years of oppression, discrimination, lack of opportunities for minorities, and unjust treatment affect certain racial categories of people. The riots (described above) in Los Angeles, Watts, Detroit, Miami, and Newark are examples of race-based riots.
2. **Economic riots**—Impoverished communities that provide little opportunity for upward mobility may produce people who use the riot as a means to voice their concerns. Economic riots, such as the 1931 Chicago riot, occurred in the early 1900s following the Great Depression. In other countries around the world, economic conditions are especially likely to be a cause of riots.
3. **Political riots**—Occur when people are dissatisfied with government officials and government practices. In the United States, many college campuses have played witness to politically charged riots. The 1773 Boston Tea Party is an example of a political riot.
4. **Religious riots**—Occur when people from different religions confront one another in a violent manner. The 1870 and 1871 New York City riots pitted Catholics against Protestants. The emphasis in American society on the "separation of church and state" has largely eliminated religious riots.

I would add two additional categories of riots to the list provided by Tipton: opportunistic riots and sports riots:

1. **Opportunistic riots**—This category of riot occurs because certain unplanned circumstances give rise to collective violent behavior. Such behavior was not spurred by racial, economic, religious, or political concerns but rather because the opportunity to engage in collective violent behaviors presented itself. The 1977 New York City riot was caused by a blackout. The blackout was not planned, and participants of the rioting were not limited to a particular race,

religion, or political affiliation. Dating back to the mid-1980s, the annual Huntington Beach (California) surfing competition held on July 4 has often led to collective forms of violent behavior, including riots that have caused a great deal of property damage, arson, violent confrontations between primarily white beachgoers, and the police. Alcohol and youthful exuberance often spark these riots.

2. **Sports riots**—A very disturbing occurrence following sports championships or other important sporting events has led to sports fans engaging in a pattern of riotous behavior. Since the mid-1980s a number of sports-related riots have occurred in such North American cities as Detroit (following the Tigers' 1984 World Series title); Montreal (following their 1993 NHL title); Denver (following their 1999 Super Bowl title); San Francisco (following their 2014 World Series title); and Columbus (following Ohio State's 2015 national football title).

The variables of sports and race combined led to many massive riots between whites and blacks across the country following the July 4, 1910, boxing championship fight between African American boxer Jack Johnson (who won the fight) and Jim Jeffries (popularly known as the "Great White Hope"), who had not fought in six years (Delaney 2012a). In many instances over the years, sports events have been affected, or canceled, due to rioting. For example, during the 2015 Baltimore riots, the Orioles had to cancel the first two games of their home series versus the Chicago White Sox (April 27 and 28) and on April 29, Major League Baseball (MLB) took the highly unusual step of allowing Baltimore to host Chicago in a baseball game that was closed to the public. The scheduled night game was moved to an afternoon start to assure the game would be over prior to the 10:00 p.m. curfew. It is believed to be the first game in MLB history that was played when fans were not allowed to attend. The reason: fear of rioting.

As this review of riots in the United States indicates, American history, both before its official birth in 1776 and ever since then, is a history of riots. Regardless of the cause or circumstance, riots may lead to numerous deaths, countless injuries, millions of dollars of property damage, countless victims of violent assault, police officers pelted with rocks, firefighters attacked while trying to put out fires, and neighborhoods that were already in dire straits left in worse conditions than before the riot began. The reality of riots also reveals the fragile nature of human society, as it is subject to disarray and collapse at any time.

War

The history of the United States is much more than a history of riots; it is also a history of waging war. It is almost hard to believe that the United States, a nation that reluctantly joined both world wars *after* they had been started by other nations, is now known globally as the nation that seems to love to wage war. The United States not only wages war against other political states, it has waged war against social problems and concepts, including a "War on Poverty," a "War on Drugs," and a "War on Terrorism." By most accounts, our wars against poverty and drugs have failed, as poverty certainly exists and regular drug use is as prevalent a fixture of American society now as it was decades ago. Our war against terrorism is directly connected to our most recent military wars in Iraq and Afghanistan.

War, above everything else, highlights the spirit of the human species and its willingness to engage in collective violence with wild abandon and seemingly total disregard for human life, other species, and the physical environment. **War** can be defined as a state or period of collective fighting between large groups or countries via the use of armed combat. War has been waged throughout history between clans of people and entire nation-states. As sociologist C. Wright Mills (1958) states, "To reflect upon war is to reflect upon the human condition" (p. 1). What is the human condition with regard to war? War is so commonplace, so expected, that there exist "laws" of war. The laws of war reflect a global ideology that there will always be war and that rules must be abided by. Thus, rather than agreeing to adhere to a notion that a law should be in place to forbid war, the global nations have resigned to the fact that there will always be war. "The law of war is usually divided into *jus ad bellum* (the right to resort to war) and *jus in bello* (the law during war)" (Wallace 2002:1699). The first aspect of the law of war (*jus ad bellum*) states that nations have the *right* to go to war. And if the nation so desires, it can continually go to war because it has the right to do so. Because war is viewed as inevitable and nearly constant, at least somewhere across the globe, there are rules established to govern the way war is waged. There are many rules of war that must be followed, including rules of engagement and rules of treatment toward prisoners of war (POW). Consequently, the second aspect of the law of war dictates that warriors must abide by certain protocols; otherwise they risk being accused of "war crimes." War crime violations include the ill treatment of prisoners, mass murder of an indigenous population, subjecting a population to slavery, killing hostages, and wanton destruction of property not justified by military necessity (Wallace 2002). The wanton destruction of cultural landmarks and heritage by the Islamic State of Iraq and Syria (ISIS) of various places of historical, architectural, and religious importance in Iraq, Syria, and Libya in 2015 would qualify as a violation of the law of war. Thus, while the world's nations have attempted to normalize the existence of war, there are aspects of war that may be deemed deviant.

U.S. Army Rangers in action during war.

The global community also has rights of war. For example, nonwarring nations have the right to evaluate other wars to make sure they are "just" wars. The right to judge the wars of other nations gives outside nations the right to join in on one side or the other. When multiple nations join an existing war, we have the possibility of a world war. Humanity has survived two world wars, but can it survive another one? What if nuclear and chemical weapons are used by both sides in the next world war? If humanity survives the next world war, will we survive the environmental fallout? As the Sierra Club of Canada (2012) points out, "Although ecological disturbances brought on by war have been occurring for thousands of years, modern day warfare has made its impact increasingly severe. Recognizing the long-term and widespread impacts caused by such degradation, experts have coined the term ecocide, literally meaning the killing of the environment." *Ecocide* reflects humanity's willingness to violently destroy that which it is most dependent upon, while war reflects a willingness to destroy itself. War is a fixture of human history, and its consequences are collectively and violently deadly.

Summary

In this chapter we have learned that violence, whether it is an instinct or a learned behavior, is a prevalent aspect of human behavior and society. It was argued that nearly all of us are capable of violence, especially if someone threatens our life or the lives of our loved ones. Violence was defined as the intentional use of physical force or power, threatened or actual, against oneself, another person, or against a group or community, that either results in or has a high likelihood of resulting in injury, death, psychological harm, maldevelopment, or deprivation. As presented in this chapter, there are three types of violence: self-directed violence, interpersonal violence, and collective violence.

Self-directed violence refers to violence in which the perpetrator and the victim are the same person. Self-directed violence includes self-harm, also known as self-injury and/or self-mutilation, and occurs when a person purposively inflicts physical harm to him- or herself via such methods as self-cutting, head banging, self-biting, and self-scratching; suicide and attempted suicide; and suicide by cop, an action that involves a person purposively creating a situation wherein responding police officers will have to take the life of the victim.

Interpersonal violence refers to violence between individuals, individuals and groups, groups and individuals, and groups against groups. Interpersonal violence includes bullying, a behavior that takes place mostly in schools and the workplace; hazing, a means of initiating a person into a group with or without the consent of the participants; so-called bum fights, an offensive form of behavior that involves staged acts of violence wherein homeless people, usually men, are paid to fight one another for the entertainment of the viewers; and intimate interpersonal violence, acts carried out with the intention of, or perceived as having the intention of, physically or emotionally hurting one's partner (in marriage, cohabitation, or dating); child; parent; sibling; or some other intimate person (e.g., close family member such as a niece or nephew, aunt or uncle, or grandparent).

Collective violence refers to violence committed by larger groups of individuals and political states. Two primary examples were provided: riots, violent public disorder involving a large number of people assembled together and acting with a common intent—the wanton destruction of human life and/or property; and war, a state or period of collective fighting between large groups or countries via the use of armed combat.

Key Terms

collective violence, 167

hazing, 160

interpersonal violence, 151

intimate interpersonal violence, 163

riot, 167

self-directed violence, 175

self-harm, 152

suicide by cop (SBC), 158

violence, 151

war, 174

workplace bullying, 159

Discussion Questions

1. Violence appears to be an integral aspect of contemporary society. Why is this the case? Will there ever be a time, or society, free of violence?

2. Name and briefly describe the three distinct categories of violence described in this chapter.

3. Why do people commit self-harm? Have you or has someone you know closely self-harmed? Why did this behavior take place?

4. What is bullying? Why does it exist in society? Will it ever be possible to eliminate bullying from society?

5. What did you think of the discussion on "bum fights"? How does such an activity exist in "civilized" societies like the United States?

6. Provide a brief history of riots. What are some of the positive and negative consequences of riots?

7. What is the human condition with regard to war?

CHAPTER 7

Alcohol and Social Deviance

CHAPTER OBJECTIVES

After reading this chapter students should be able to:

- Explain the effects of alcohol
- Describe how people learn to act drunk via drunken comportment
- Provide a history of alcohol use in the United States
- Define alcoholism
- Provide a description of a number of harmful behaviors associated with the consumption of alcohol

How many times have you heard someone say, "It wasn't my fault; I was drunk"? The answer to this question might depend on whom you associate with, but chances are you've heard of such a disclaimer being used by someone who awkwardly attempts to justify or rationalize their behavior while under the influence of **alcohol**. Why would someone think that being drunk is a valid excuse for inappropriate behavior? The origin of using such an excuse may date back centuries, but E. Adamson Hoebel, in his *The Law of Primitive Man* (1964), chronicles the laws of the Ashanti tribe of the Gold Coast of West Africa (modern state of Ghana), which included the notion that "drunkenness was a valid defense for all crimes but homicide and cursing the king" (p. 237). Likewise, a person labeled by the Ashanti as a "madman" (mentally ill) would not be executed for committing homicide but would be chained to a tree and left to die, unless his relatives chose to feed him. Despite its brutality, the confinement of the mentally ill murderer was viewed more as social precaution than as a punishment.

Hoebel further explains, however, that during the reign of King Osai Yao the two laws described above were set aside. The king decided to run an experiment by putting a drunk and a "madman" into a house that was then set ablaze. The "madman" screamed that he was on fire and ran from the burning house while the drunk, in his stupor, was burned to death. "The conclusion was obvious to Osai Yao. A drunk does not know what is going on. Ergo, drunkenness shall remain as a mitigating plea in defense. Insanity, though it may impair, does not completely paralyze perception. Ergo, there is no validity to the old plea of insanity as a defense. The plea was abolished" (Hoebel 1964:238). While this story may also be relevant as an introduction to chapter 10 (Mental Illness and Disorders and Social Deviance), it is told here as a means to stimulate thought on matters of alcohol consumption and the deviant behaviors that sometimes accompany it.

Alcohol and Its Effects

Alcohol, or more precisely, ethyl alcohol, or ethanol, is an intoxicating ingredient found in beer, wine, and liquor. It is produced by the fermentation of yeast, sugars, and starches (CDC 2014g). Alcohol is served in liquid form as a "drink." A standard drink equals 0.6 ounces of pure ethanol, or 12 ounces of beer; 8 ounces of malt liquor; 5 ounces of wine; or 1.5 ounces (a "shot") of 80-proof distilled spirits or liquor (e.g., rum, gin, vodka, or whiskey). Alcohol is a legal drug (for those of legal drinking age) that affects the way we feel, think, and behave. Generally speaking, people are capable of consuming alcohol without any negative consequences. On the other hand, alcohol often causes or contributes to many personal and social problems. This dichotomy is explained by the realization that the effects of alcohol on human behavior are subject to great variation.

Many people are capable of drinking responsibly.

A Brief History of Alcohol Use

It is generally recognized that throughout the history of humanity, people have sought ways to alleviate pain and/or heighten pleasure. Alcohol consumption is one method utilized by people to attain this goal. Still, we are not exactly sure when people first consumed fermented and brewed beverages. "No record is to be found which tells the story of man's first use of alcoholic beverages. In all probability he began to use them in prehistoric times. Although alcohol per se was not known in antiquity, fermented and brewed beverages, wines and beers . . . have been known to practically all peoples from the dawn of history, and doubtless long before" (Patrick 1952:12). The Harvard T.H. Chan School of Public Health (2015) provides a slightly more specific time frame and estimates that humans have been drinking fermented beverages for approximately 10,000 years. Phillips (2014) states, "We can trace alcoholic beverages made by humans to about 7000 BC, nine millennia ago, but it is almost certain that prehistoric humans consumed alcohol in fruits and berries past the point of optimum ripeness and sweetness [when they started to decay and produced] alcohol by a spontaneous process of fermentation" (p. 6). Phillips explains that our primate forebears lived primarily on a diet of fruit and berries and it is entirely conceivable that they, at various times, ate fruit and berries past the point of optimal ripeness. Phillips (2014) concludes that "at least 9,000 years ago—but almost certainly much earlier—a human history of alcohol was added to the natural history of spontaneous fermentations in rotting fruits and berries" (p. 8).

The earliest evidence of the consumption of fermented drinks is traced to China and the Middle East, where natural climatic conditions would most likely assist the fermentation process. "The earliest Chinese medical and pharmaceutical works cite wine as an important drug and antiseptic and as a means of circulating medicines in the body . . . and in the Taoist period it was an ingredient in longevity elixirs" (Phillips 2014:23). Alcohol use in China was an important aspect of religion and other spheres of social life. It was used when holding a memorial ceremony, offering sacrifices to gods or ancestors, pledging resolution before going into battle, celebrating victory, before feuding and official executions, and for taking an oath of allegiance (Hanson 2013). China is also one of the first places to recognize the dark side of consuming fermented drinks, as it was argued that heavy drinking among those in the royal court helped to bring about the collapse of the Shang dynasty (1750–1100 BCE). In reaction, subsequent rulers not only warned against excessive drinking, they made it punishable by death (Phillips 2014).

The ancient Indo-Aryan tribes of India had an intoxicating drink called *soma*, which was offered as a libation to their deities. Distilled from rice, soma became an integral aspect in their ceremonies from 3000 BCE to 2000 BCE.

In ancient Babylon, the primary drink was beer, but wine was also important, and by 2700 BCE the Babylonians regularly used both beer and wine as offerings to their gods. Around 1700 BCE, the Code of Hammurabi was established in an attempt to establish fair commerce in alcohol (Hanson 2013).

Mendelson and Mello state in the introduction to Alan Lang's *The Encyclopedia of Psychoactive Drugs: Alcohol and Teenage Drinking* (1992) that alcohol use and misuse was associated with the worship of gods and demons during the ancient Greek and Roman eras. "One of the most powerful Greek gods was Dionysus, lord of fruitfulness and god of wine. The Romans adopted Dionysus but changed his name to Bacchus. Festivals and holidays associated with Bacchus celebrated the harvest and the origins of life. Time has blurred the images of the Bacchanalian festival, but the theme of drunkenness as a major part of celebration has survived the pagan gods and remains a familiar part of modern society" (p. 13).

In Greece, one of the first alcoholic beverages to gain popularity was mead, a fermented drink made from honey and water (Foundation for a Drug-Free World 2015a). Laborers building the pyramids of Giza received a daily ration of one and one-third gallons of beer. The beer provided nourishment, and the estimated 5 percent alcohol content provided much-needed calories (Hanson 2013). "The drink was believed to be a necessity of life invented by the god Osiris and was brewed daily in the typical home. At least 17 types of beer and 24 varieties of wine were produced and used for pleasure, nutrition, medicine, religious ritual, remuneration, and funeral purposes" (Hanson 2013). Wine appeared in Egypt around 4000 BCE. Early Egyptian carvings reveal that drinking excessively was quite common among pharaohs and citizens alike. "The general tolerance and even encouragement of drinking during festivities is suggested by a scene from the Egyptian tomb of Nakhet, where a girl is shown offering her parents wine and saying, 'To your health! Drink this good wine, celebrate a festive day with what your lord has given you'" (Phillips 2014:23). Egyptian carvings also reveal that public intoxication also occurred during festivals, as wall drawings depict men and women vomiting and being carried unconscious from banquet rooms. While there is no explicit suggestion of moral outrage toward public drunkenness, some writings suggest that public intoxication was more frowned upon than excessive drinking in private. Egyptian sages also described the lack of tolerance toward some drunks. "When you speak, nonsense comes out of your mouth; if you fall down and break your limb, no one will come to your assistance." Another sage advises, "Do not get drunk, lest you go mad" (Phillips 2014:23).

While the ancient Roman culture is perceived as the epitome of drunkenness, from the founding of Rome in 753 BCE until the third century BCE the Romans consumed alcohol in moderation. Wine was considered of such importance to Roman society that in 160 BCE the Roman Senate ordered the translation of a Carthaginian book on viticulture in order to promote its production (Hanson 2013). As the Roman Empire grew throughout the Mediterranean region (509–133 BCE), however, the values of temperance, frugality, and simplicity were gradually replaced by heavy drinking, ambition, degeneracy, and corruption. "Excessive drinking in the Roman Empire was exacerbated by such practices as drinking before meals on an empty stomach, inducing vomiting to permit the consumption of more food and wine, and playing drinking games. The latter promoted the rapid consumption of large amounts of alcohol" (Hanson 2013:4). The decay of the Roman Empire is often attributed to its abuse of alcohol, and this decay appears to have peaked around 50 CE.

As the Roman Empire was collapsing, the spread of Christianity and the beliefs of Christians and the Church became increasingly important. Jesus is said to have used wine (Matthew 15:11; Luke 7:33–35) and approved of its moderate consumption (Matthew 15:11). However, he was very critical of drunkenness (Luke 21:34, 12:42; Matthew 24:45–51). Paul the Apostle (d. 67 CE) considered wine to be a creation of God and therefore inherently good (1 Timothy 4:4) and recommended its use for medicinal purposes (1 Timothy 5:23), but condemned intoxication (1 Corinthians 3:16–17, 5:11, 6:10) and recommended abstinence for those who could not control their drinking. The merits of drinking fermented drinks is a subject of analysis throughout the Bible, as contradictory opinions on the matter of drinking alcohol, especially wine, abound. Paul the Apostle's First Epistle to Timothy 3 describes the qualifications of bishops: A bishop must be sober and of good behavior and his wife must be sober (*The Holy Bible: King James Version* 2000). Proverbs 20:1 states, "Wine is a mocker, strong drink is raging; and whosoever is deceived thereby is not wise." On the other hand, there are many references in the Bible that acknowledge the positive aspects of drinking: wine is praised; it rejoices God and men (Judges 9:13); it gladdens the heart of men (Psalms 104:15); it gladdens life (Exodus 10:19); it makes the heart exult (Zechariah 10:7); it cheers the spirits of the depressed (Proverbs 31:6) (McKenzie 1965). Much like the medical profession today, there are passages in the Bible that stress the moderation of alcohol consumption: "Let your moderation be known unto all men" (Philippians 4:5); Paul tells Timothy, "Drink no longer water, but use a little wine," and when he writes to the Ephesians, he states, "And be not drunk with wine, wherein is excess."

Around 400 CE the Huns invaded much of Europe and seriously disrupted the production and consumption of alcoholic beverages for a period of time. They destroyed vineyards, killed vineyard workers, and consumed all stored quantities of wine. During the period 850 to 1100 CE, alcohol was a central aspect of Viking culture, and while they preferred mead, they usually drank ale, a sweeter drink than the alcohol of the past. The development of distillation and the subsequent production of distilled spirits occurred during the Middle Ages (500–1500 CE). Initially, those who distilled spirits were more concerned with its medicinal properties than with its recreational use properties (Hanson 2013).

On the other side of the globe, many native tribes, especially the Mayans (located in present-day Mexico) were known to consume alcohol. By 1000 BCE, the Mayans were a drinking society. They fermented a drink from corn (maize), and its consumption was commonplace among the people (Hanson 2013). Several indigenous civilizations in the Americas had developed alcoholic beverages from corn, grapes, or apples, called "chicha" (Foundation for a Drug-Free World 2015a).

Vodka, long a favorite drink of Russians, can trace its history back to the mid-16th century with conflicting reports as to whether it originated in Poland or Russia. Polish King Jan Olbrecht issued a decree allowing every citizen the right to make vodka in 1546 and as a result, many families distilled their own spirits. There were 49 commercial distilleries in the town of Poznan alone in the 16th century (Food and Beverage Underground 2014). In the 1540s, Russian tsar Ivan "the Terrible" established his own network of distilling taverns and ensured that the profits went directly into the imperial treasury (Food and Beverage Underground 2014). Most vodka is 80 proof and has no color and carries only the clean aroma and character of pure spirit from the still. The 100-proof vodka (which is 50 percent alcohol) burns the mouth, but it can be fine-tuned by simply adding water. In Russian, the word "vodka" itself means "little water." Similarly, the word "whiskey" comes from the Gaelic for "water of life" (Russian Vodka 2015; Food and Beverage Underground 2014). (Note: This author took a tour of the Russian Vodka Museum located in St. Petersburg, Russia, in November 2015, and can attest to the rich history of vodka in Russia as well as the fine taste of pure Russian vodkas!)

A patron enters the Russian Vodka Museum in St. Petersburg, Russia.

Source: Tim Delaney.

Not sure what they might find in their travels, European explorers brought plenty of alcohol with them to the New World. In 1620, the Puritans brought more beer than water on the *Mayflower*, and they landed at Plymouth rather than continue their journey because their provision of beer was running low. "Subsequently, brewing beer became one of the earliest industries in colonial North America" (Hanson 2013:7). Alcohol consumption would remain popular in the colonies through the time of the establishment of the United States of America. "Taverns were central to colonial life and were often legally required to be located near schools and churches. Religious services and court sessions were often held in taverns and they also served as venues for plays, political debates, lodge meetings, and socializing" (Hanson 2013:7).

During the American revolution, General George Washington, viewing alcohol as an important means to maintain morale, issued daily rations of rum and other forms of alcohol to the Continental Army. After six years of struggle and despite frequent setbacks, Washington managed to lead the army to key victories, and Great Britain eventually surrendered in 1781. Americans overwhelming elected Washington as their first president in 1789.

Alcohol consumption would remain popular with many Americans throughout its early history, continuing through the present day. However, the legality of alcohol was put on hold in the early 1900s following a constitutional prohibition. The prohibition, established by the Eighteenth Amendment, followed the temperance movement that began in the 1800s. The temperance movement was spearheaded by the first wave of feminism in the 1830s. These feminists, led by "the Ladies of Seneca Falls" (i.e., Elizabeth Cady Stanton, Lucretia Mott, Martha Wright, Jane Hunt, and Mary Ann McClintock) argued that male domestic violence directed toward women and children was the result of their intoxication. Eliminating alcohol from family life, they argued, would help eliminate domestic violence (Delaney 2004a). The prohibition movement led by Stanton and Mott failed but spirited future antialcohol movements.

By the turn of the 20th century, temperance societies (antialcohol) were prevalent throughout the United States. These citizens were following the lead of the Ladies of Seneca Falls (so named because they were the architects of the first Women's Rights Convention, held in Seneca Falls, New York, on July 19–20, 1848) who had pledged to pass a national ban on alcoholic beverages. Assisted by factory owners (who felt workers would be more productive without alcohol in their lives) and progressive reformers (who saw ridding society of alcohol as a means of improving society in general), prohibitionists managed to change the view of alcohol in American society (National Archives 2015b). In the early 1900s, many states were imposing laws that prohibited the manufacture and sale of intoxicating beverages. In 1917, the Eighteenth Amendment to the Constitution (known as the prohibition amendment) was adopted by the required majority of both houses of Congress, and in 1919 the amendment was ratified and set to go into effect the following year. In October 1919, the Volstead Act was passed by Congress over President Wilson's veto, clarifying and broadening the base of the Eighteenth Amendment and defining the methods of enforcement. On January 16, 1920, the Eighteenth Amendment took effect, prohibiting the manufacture, sale, transportation, import, and export of intoxicating liquors for beverages purposes.

Initially, the Eighteenth Amendment was viewed as a success as liquor consumption dropped, arrests for drunkenness fell, and the price for illegal alcohol rose higher than the average worker could afford. But then something very profound occurred—bootlegging. **Bootlegging** refers to the unlawful production, sale, and transportation of alcoholic liquor without registration or payment of taxes. Organized crime syndicates sprung up across the United States but especially in larger cities to meet the underground demand for alcohol. From 1920 to 1933 the illicit alcohol trade flourished, and prohibition was deemed a failure. In 1933, with the passage of the Twenty-First Amendment, the Eighteenth Amendment was repealed; it remains as the only amendment ever repealed. A number of other laws controlling and supervising the sale, distribution, and consumption of alcohol would follow. In 1978, U.S. President Jimmy Carter signed a bill legalizing home brewing of beer for the first time since Prohibition, a move that would please home brewers and later stimulate the craft beer craze of the early 21st century.

At the present time, alcohol remains very popular (statistics on Americans' alcohol consumption will be provided later in this chapter). It is especially popular with college students. Sociologists have long used the term "culture of alcohol" to describe some of the activities and attitudes that foster a pro-alcohol environment on college campuses. Despite attempts among many college administrations, drinking is common in fraternity and sorority initiations and parties, non-Greek student parties, football tailgate parties, birthday celebrations (especially the 21st birthday), end of final exam celebrations, "bar crawls," and so on. For young college students, the culture of alcohol places pressures on them to drink or risk being ostracized by peers. Although the culture of alcohol is often overblown and less relevant on some campuses than others, the image of college students holding epic parties, such as toga parties, continues. As Lederman and Stewart (2005) explain, "The image of excessive drinking and perpetually inebriated college students is a cliché in the media and contemporary American culture" (p. 5). The film industry is filled with examples of party scenes with college students drunk and disorderly, and perhaps no other film tops *Animal House* in its classic, stereotypical portrayal of excessive drinking (see box 7.1). The culture of alcohol on college campuses is not limited to the students. The entire academic community needs to evaluate its own alcoholic behavior, as alcohol is often a regular fixture at many social events and campus gatherings that include administrators, alumni, faculty, and college guests. When alcohol is included with on-campus activities, the culture of alcohol is normalized.

CONNECTING SOCIAL DEVIANCE AND POPULAR CULTURE

Box 7.1 *Animal House*: The Stereotypical Portrayal of Excessive Drinking

There are many classic movies that portray a stereotypical view of college students who attend wild parties and drink to excess. Various websites that rank the top college-drinking movies using such monikers as the "Greatest College Movies of All Time," "25 Greatest College Party Movies Ever," and "Top 10 College Movies of All Time" seem to include some of the same movies—*Road Trip* (2000), *Back to School* (1986), *National Lampoon's Van Wilder* (2002), *Revenge of the*

Nerds (1984), *Old School* (2003)—and they all agree that the best movie of all time is *Animal House* (1978). As explained by Dillon Cheverere (2015) of Total Frat Move, *Animal House* is "the gold standard"; it is "an all-timer in every sense" as it "reveals the most accurate portrayal of fraternity culture over any same-genre movie in existence, and it's a riot."

The movie *Animal House*, among other things, forever immortalized the toga party as an accepted form of behavior for American college students. At a 1962 college, Dean Vernon Wormer is determined to expel the entire Delta Tau Chi fraternity. Among the tools at his disposal is the infamous usage of the "double secret probation," a classic line for clever folks to use still today. The cast is led by John Belushi, who plays the character John "Bluto" Blutarsky and manages to steal every scene he appears in. Kevin Bacon (Chip Diller), Karen Allen (Katy), and Tim Matheson (Eric Stratton, "Otter") are among the many future stars to get their first big breaks in *Animal House*.

The Deltas of Faber College are disreputable and will take anyone who wants to join the house. Another house, Omega Theta Tau Chi House, is filled with white, Anglo-Saxon, rich young men who want the Deltas kicked off campus. The dean of Faber College also wants the Deltas gone, so the two forces work together in an attempt to expel the Deltas. Belushi's character, of course, is a member of the Deltas. The Delta House is already on probation because of various violations and an abysmal academic standing. Various incidents, including an accidental death of a horse belonging to an Omega member and ROTC cadet commander Douglas Neidermeyer (played by Mark Metcalf), a parade with politically incorrect floats, and the classic toga party highlight the hijinks of this film. At the toga party there are the typical drunken displays of out-of-control behavior, sexual innuendo, and a scene wherein Delta frat boy Otter has sex with Dean Wormer's wife.

For those who have never seen the movie before, treat yourself; and perhaps begin by looking at the toga party scene on YouTube. It is just prior to the toga party that the dean informs the Delta House that they have been on double secret probation and that one more slip-up ends their house. Sensing the inevitability of their closure, the Deltas decide to go out in a blaze of glory via the toga party. The party attendees wear togas, drink to excess, and dance to the tunes of Otis Day and the Knights, who perform live at the party. Other scenes include the accidental horse murder, projectile vomiting, a classic food fight, and Belushi's character playing a "peeping Tom" as sorority students have a lingerie pillow fight.

Effects of Alcohol

When people drink, some become happy, others depressed; some become outgoing, others withdrawn; some vicious, others pleasant; and some become energetic, while others are more passive. Furthermore, some people can "hold their liquor" and others cannot.

A common belief about the effect of alcohol on behavior is that alcohol automatically reduces inhibitions; that is, drinkers expect alcohol to improve their sociability. Alan Lang (1992) argues that "it may be the expectation itself that gives alcohol this property" (p. 35). The Raj Koothrappali character on the highly popular TV show *The Big Bang Theory*, for example, suffers from an inability to speak with women unless he has consumed alcohol. MacAndrew and Edgerton (1969) conducted an extensive and often-cited study of alcohol and its impact on human behavior. In their book *Drunken Comportment*, MacAndrew and Edgerton report that the view of alcohol as universally acting as a "releaser of inhibitions" is false. People are not simply under the control of alcohol. Instead, people act as they have been taught to act when drunk. This concept has been illustrated on such early TV shows as *The Honeymooners*, where in one episode, Ralph Kramden and Ed Norton got "drunk" on grape juice.

MacAndrew and Edgerton argue that individuals *learn* that they should feel less inhibited when drunk and therefore *act* drunk. In other words, one's behavior while "under the influence" of alcohol does not follow a predetermined, biochemically fixed pattern—it follows a learned pattern of behavior.

Rather than viewing drunken comportment as a function of toxically disinhibited brains operating in impulse-drive bodies, we have recommended that what are fundamentally at issue are the learned relations that exist among men living together in society. More specially, we have contended that the way people comport themselves when they are drunk is determined not by alcohol's toxic assault upon the seat of moral judgment, conscience, or the like, but by what their society makes of and imparts to them concerning the state of drunkenness (MacAndrew and Edgerton 1969:165).

MacAndrew and Edgerton conclude that if we are ever to understand drunken comportment, we must concentrate research on the shared understanding of the nature of drunkenness among groups of people found in society. Having explained the concept of **drunken comportment** to my introductory sociology students one semester, a group of older students (seniors who were 21 years or older) decided to test this concept as part of the class requirement to conduct a breaching experiment. A **breaching experiment** seeks to examine people's reactions to violations of commonly accepted social rules, or norms, in order to shed light on the methods by which people construct social reality. This particular group of three students (roommates in off-campus housing) threw a keg party, but unbeknownst to their guests, the beer was nonalcoholic. Nearly everyone at the party "acted" drunk despite the fact that they had not consumed alcohol. This breaching experiment supported the premise put forth by MacAndrew and Edgerton.

Medical research indicates that the effects of alcohol on the body and brain function are quite real and not simply a matter of drunken comportment. According to the National Institute on Drug Abuse (2014a), alcohol affects every organ in the drinker's body and can damage a developing fetus. Intoxication can impair brain function and motor skills; heavy use can increase risk of certain cancers, stroke, and liver disease. Alcohol is a central nervous system depressant that is quickly absorbed from the stomach and small intestine into the bloodstream. It is then metabolized in the liver by enzymes; however, the liver can only metabolize a small amount of alcohol at a time, leaving the excess alcohol to circulate throughout the body. The intensity of the effect of alcohol on the body is directly related to the amount consumed (National Institute on Drug Abuse 2014a).

The National Institute on Alcohol Abuse and Alcoholism (NIAAA) (2015a) explains the effects of alcohol on specific parts of the body:

1. Brain function: Alcohol interferes with the brain's communication pathways and can affect the way the brain looks and works. These disruptions can change mood and behavior and make it harder to think clearly and move with coordination.
2. Heart: Drinking a lot over a long time or too much on a single occasion can damage the heart, causing problems that include cardiomyopathy (stretching and drooping of heart muscle); arrhythmias (irregular heartbeat); stroke; and high blood pressure. Research also shows that drinking moderate amounts of alcohol may protect healthy adults from developing coronary heart disease.
3. Liver: Heavy drinking takes a toll on the liver and can lead to a variety of problems and live inflammations, including steatosis, or fatty liver; alcoholic hepatitis; fibrosis; and cirrhosis.
4. Pancreas: Alcohol causes the pancreas to produce toxic substances that can eventually lead to pancreatitis, a dangerous inflammation and swelling of the blood vessels in the pancreas that prevents proper digestion.
5. Mouth, esophagus, throat, liver, and breast: Too much alcohol consumption can increase the risk of developing cancer.

6. Immune system: Drinking too much can weaken your immune system, making your body a much easier target for disease. Chronic drinkers are more liable to contract diseases like pneumonia and tuberculosis than people who do not drink excessively. Drinking a lot on a single occasion slows your body's ability to ward off infections—even up to 24 hours after getting drunk.

According to the NIDA (2014), individual reactions to alcohol vary and are influenced by many factors, including the following:

- Age
- Gender
- Race/ethnicity
- Physical condition (weight, fitness level, etc.)
- Amount of food consumed before drinking
- How quickly the alcohol was consumed
- Use of drugs or prescription medicines
- Family history of alcohol problems

Drinking alcohol can have many effects on the mind and body and may extend to alcohol abuse and alcoholism.

Alcohol Abuse and Alcoholism

Drinking is common in many cultures, including the United States. Many people drink on a regular basis. They may have a glass of wine during dinner and another glass after dinner. Some people regularly drink on a social basis with friends, family members, and associates. As a result, it's not always easy to identify people with a drinking problem. Generally, someone is said to have a **drinking problem** if their alcohol consumption causes problems for them. Problems may include feeling guilty or ashamed about your drinking, lying to others about your drinking habits, having friends who are worried about your drinking, the need to drink in order to relax or feel better, growing personal relationship problems, making up excuses to celebrate just to drink, "blacking out" or forgetting what you did while drinking, and regularly drinking more than you intended.

Alcohol Abuse

A drinking problem crosses over to the domain of "alcohol abuse" when one's alcohol use becomes self-destructive and dangerous either to one's self or others. **Alcohol abuse** is a pattern of drinking that results in harm to one's health, interpersonal relationships, or ability to work (CDC 2014g). "Unlike alcoholics, alcohol abusers have some ability to set limits on their drinking. However, their alcohol use is still self-destructive and dangerous to themselves or others" (Smith, Robinson, and Segal 2015). There are a number of manifestations of alcohol abuse, including the following:

- Failure to fulfill major responsibilities at work, school, or home
- Drinking in dangerous situations, such as drinking while driving or operating machinery
- Legal problems related to alcohol, such as being arrested for drinking while driving or for physically hurting someone while drunk

- Continued drinking despite ongoing relationship problems that are caused or worsened by drinking
- Drinking as a way to relax or de-stress (CDC 2014g)

Long-term alcohol abuse can turn into alcohol dependence, also known as alcohol addiction (and sometimes known as alcoholism). The signs and symptoms of alcohol dependence include:

- A strong craving for alcohol
- Continued use despite repeated physical, psychological, or interpersonal problems
- The inability to limit drinking

Not all alcohol abusers become alcoholics, but alcohol abuse is a significant risk factor.

Alcoholism

Alcoholism represents the most extreme form of problem drinking and involves all of the symptoms of alcohol abuse but also involves one additional and important element, physical dependence on alcohol. "If you rely on alcohol to function or feel physically compelled to drink, you're an alcoholic" (Smith, Robinson, and Segal 2015). As defined by the Mayo Clinic (2015b), **alcoholism** is a chronic and often progressive disease that includes problems controlling your drinking, being preoccupied with alcohol even when it causes problems, having to drink more to get the same effect (physical dependence), or having withdrawal symptoms when you rapidly decrease or stop drinking.

There are a number of symptoms of alcoholism. The Mayo Clinic (2015b) provides a sampling:

- Inability to limit the amount of alcohol consumed
- Feeling a strong need or compulsion to drink
- Development of a tolerance to alcohol so that the user needs more to feel the effects of alcohol
- Drinking alone, or hiding your drinking
- Experiencing physical withdrawal symptoms—such as nausea, sweating, and shaking—when you don't drink
- Experiencing blackouts (forgetting conversations or commitments)
- Ritualistic drinking built in throughout the day and becoming upset when something or someone interferes with this compulsive behavior
- Becoming irritable when alcohol is not available
- Showing multiple symptoms of problem drinking such as hiding alcohol at work, in your car, and at home; legal problems as a result of drinking; personal relationship problems; and a loss of interest in activities and hobbies that once brought pleasure

The problem drinker progresses to alcoholism through a series of stages of alcohol addiction. A number of researchers and health providers, including the National Association of Addiction Treatment Providers (NAATP) (2015), reference the Seven Stages of Alcohol Addiction (shown below):

Stage 1: Abstinence—Some individuals may exhibit alcohol addiction tendencies before they start to drink (e.g., possessing attitudes and perceptions consistent with addicts).

Stage 2: Initial use—This includes the initial experimental use of alcohol, occasional use, and the occasional binge drinking.

Stage 3: High-risk use—This stage refers to an abundance of drinking and poor choices made under the influence. The frequency in alcohol consumption has increased at this stage.

Stage 4: Problematic use—Negative consequences (e.g., health concerns, liver impairment, and/or DUI conviction) of drinking become evident.

Stage 5: Early stage of dependency—Noticeable issues occur at this stage; the user begins to miss work, picks fights with family members and friends while under the influence of alcohol. Rehab is recommended by this stage.

Stage 6: Middle stage of dependency—Negative consequences of drinking escalate; the user is considered an alcoholic.

Stage 7: Crisis stage of dependency—Everyone in the user's life, including the alcoholic, realizes that problem drinking has escalated to the point where alcohol is now in control of the user.

As demonstrated by the Seven Stages of Alcohol Addiction, the process of becoming addicted to alcohol occurs gradually, although some people have an abnormal response to alcohol from the time of their initial drink. "Over time, drinking too much may change the normal balance of chemicals and nerve tracks in your brain associated with the experience of pleasure, judgment and the ability to exercise control over your behavior. This may result in your craving alcohol to restore good feelings or remove negative ones" (Mayo Clinic 2015b).

Causes of Alcoholism

Alcoholism is influenced by genetic, psychological, social, and environmental factors. Genetics is viewed as playing an important role in causing alcoholism, as it seems to run in some families. "Multiple genes play a role in a person's risk for developing alcoholism. There are genes that increase a person's risk, as well as those that may decrease that risk, directly or indirectly" (NIAAA 2008). The NIAAA (2008) states that some people of Asian descent carry a gene variant that alters their rate of alcohol metabolism, causing them to have symptoms like flushing, nausea, and rapid heartbeat while they drink, thus causing an unpleasant drinking experience. As a result, many people who experience these effects avoid alcohol, which helps protect them from developing alcoholism.

Genetics alone does not explain why some people become alcoholics. Consider, for example, the simple realization that a number of people labeled as alcoholics come from families who do not have a history of alcoholism. The NIAAA (2008) claims that genetics is responsible for about half of the number of alcoholics. The implication of this statement means other factors are also involved. The environment, for example, plays a key role in whether an individual may become an alcoholic. The social learning theory is very applicable when it comes to examining the role of the environment on alcoholism. If a child is raised in a family environment wherein drinking is common, they are provided many opportunities to watch their role models with drinks in their hands and may feel that regular drinking is not only acceptable, it is expected. In addition to the home environment, and the home environments of the friends a child associates with, are such environmental influences as alcohol consumption acceptance by society; the availability of alcohol; advertising and marketing of alcohol; and public policies and enforcement of alcohol consumption. AlcoholPolicyMD.com (2005) elaborates on these four additional environmental factors on alcohol use and abuse:

1. Acceptance by society—The acceptance of dangerous drugs such as alcohol is encouraged through the mass media via such ways as movies, videos, music, and television shows that glorify drinking and drunken behavior and sports figures and celebrities that promote alcoholic beverages.
2. Availability—The more licensed liquor establishments in an area, the more likely individuals are to drink. Also, the lower the price of alcohol, the more likely younger and lower-SES people are to drink.
3. Advertising and marketing of alcohol—Americans are bombarded with alcohol advertising that generally makes drinking look like fun and a normal occurrence. Many advertisements utilize extremely good-looking people that imply if you drink their product, you might "get lucky," an enticement that is sure to draw the attention of especially impressionable people.
4. Public policies and enforcement—Laws and regulations around alcohol affect the community as a whole and can help change social norms, thereby affecting alcohol use. People who heed the warning about drinking and driving will drink less and lower their chances of developing a problem with drinking. However, if penalties against drinking and driving are not strictly enforced, it sends a message that public policy is not really concerned with drinking and driving. Reducing advertising and alcohol sponsorship of commercial events, such as sports, concerts, and plays, as well as restricting alcohol use or sale in parks, public places, and community events, can all help reduce alcohol consumption and ultimately problem drinking and alcoholism.

Social and psychological factors that contribute to problem drinking and alcoholism include having friends or a close partner who drinks regularly; drinking while taking certain medications that may either increase or decrease their effectiveness; having a mental health disorder such as anxiety, depression, or bipolar disorder; and steady drinking over time (Mayo Clinic 2015b). Perhaps the most commonly studied psychosocial motivation for drinking is the idea that alcohol helps to reduce anxiety, thus making it a way to cope with stress (NIAAA 2000). The NIAAA (2000) found that people who use alcohol to reduce stress will have mixed and inconsistent results. For example, while some people who are depressed and then drink may become (temporarily) happy, others will become even more deeply depressed. In addition, people who "drink to cope" with stress are more likely to come from a family with a history of alcoholism. College students, on the other hand, may drink after a particularly stressful exam and feel relieved from the stress that studying had placed on their mental state of well-being. More than a decade after the NIAAA released their findings, other researchers, including Rose and Cherpitel (2011), have also found that people often turn to alcohol in stressful situations but are also likely to have mixed and inconsistent consequences to their "drinking to cope" strategy.

Alcohol Use Disorder (AUD) Statistics in the United States

The United States is a nation that enjoys drinking alcohol. In 2013, 86.8 percent of Americans ages 18 or older reported that they drank at some point in their lifetime; 70.7 percent reported that they drank in the past year; and 56.4 percent reported that they drank in the past month. (A person who drinks a minimum of 12 drinks a year is considered a "regular" drinker.) Nearly one in four (24.6 percent) of people ages 18 or older reported that they engaged in binge drinking in the past month, and 6.8 percent reported that they engaged in heavy drinking in the past month (NIAAA 2015b).

Problem drinking that becomes severe (causes distress or harm to the drinker) is given the medical diagnosis of "alcohol use disorder" or AUD. To be diagnosed with an AUD, individuals must meet certain criteria outlined in the *Diagnostic and Statistical Manual of Mental Disorders* (DSM). Under DSM-5, anyone who met any 2 of 11 specific criteria during the same 12-month period received a diagnosis of AUD. The severity of an AUD—mild, moderate, or severe—is based on the number of criteria met (NIAAA 2015c). The NIAAA (2015b) claims that in 2013 there were 16.6 million adults ages 18 and older (7.0 percent of this age group) with an AUD. This includes 10.8 million men (9.4 percent of men in this age group) and 5.8 million women (4.7 percent of women in this age group). About 1.3 million adults received treatment for an AUD at a specialized facility in 2013 (7.8 percent of adults who needed treatment). As for youth (ages 12 to 17), an estimated 697,000 adolescents had an AUD, including 385,000 females (3.2 percent of females in this age group) and 311,000 males (2.5 percent of males in this age group). As with their adult counterparts, only a fraction (73,000 of the 697,000 with an AUD) of the adolescents received treatment for an alcohol problem in a specialized facility in 2013.

Behaviors Associated with Problem Drinking

To this point, we have examined the effects of alcohol consumption, alcohol abuse and problem drinking, and alcoholism. Abusing alcohol and problem drinking would likely be considered deviant regardless of which definition of deviance we use, although the reactivist perspective on deviance might not be nearly as applicable as the normative, absolutist, statistical, and relativist. Alcoholism, because it is generally considered a disease, is a little more difficult to describe as an example of deviant behavior (e.g., we would not label someone with cancer as a deviant) even though it certainly can be argued that it is statistically not the norm to be an alcoholic and that the concept of alcoholism is relative to the definition that one uses to define it. That being said, most people who drink alcohol do not have a drinking problem nor are they alcoholics; consequently, we would not label drinkers as deviants simply because they consume beer, wine, spirits, or liquor. In fact, there is a great deal of research, although sometimes conflicting, that suggests a moderate amount of alcohol consumption actually provides health benefits. **Moderate alcohol consumption**, according to the Dietary Guidelines for Americans (2010), is defined as up to one drink per day for women and up to two drinks per day for men.

According to the NIAAA (2015b), moderate alcohol consumption may have such health benefits as decreasing the risk for heart disease and mortality due to heart disease; decreasing the risk of ischemic stroke (in which the arteries to the brain become narrowed or blocked, resulting in reduced blood flow); and decreased risk of diabetes. "In most Western countries where chronic diseases such as coronary heart disease (CHD), cancer, stroke, and diabetes are the primary causes of death, results from large epidemiological studies consistently show that alcohol reduces mortality, especially among middle-aged and older men and women—an association which is likely due to the protective effects of moderate alcohol consumption on CHD, diabetes, and ischemic stroke" (NIAAA 2015b). The NIAAA estimates that 26,000 deaths were averted in 2005 because of reductions in ischemic heart disease, ischemic stroke, and diabetes from the benefits attributed to moderate alcohol consumption.

The Mayo Clinic (2015c), among nearly every other medical facility and association, cautions that alcohol use can be a slippery slope, as moderate drinking can offer some health benefits, but heavy drinking, and especially binge drinking, can have serious health and social consequences. According to the Dietary Guidelines for Americans (2010), *heavy or high-risk drinking* is the consumption of more than 3 drinks on any day or more than 7 per week for women and more than 4 drinks on any day or more than 14 per week for men. An estimated 9 percent of men consume an average of more than 3 drinks per day, and 4 percent of women consume an average of more than 1 drink per day (placing them in the "heavy or high-risk drinking" category) (Dietary Guidelines for Americans 2010). *Binge drinking* is the consumption, within 2 hours, of 4 or more drinks for women and 5 or more drinks for men. Binge drinking is the first behavior associated with problem drinking that we will examine.

Extreme Alcohol Use: Binge Drinking

Regardless of the tracking scheme—"problem drinking," "alcohol abuse," "AUD," or "alcoholism"—utilized by medical personnel or organizations that study alcohol use, "binge drinking" is considered a significant warning sign of dangerous levels of alcohol consumption. Modifying slightly the definition provided above by the Dietary Guidelines for Americans, the NIAAA (2015b) defines **binge drinking** as a pattern of drinking that brings blood alcohol concentration (BAC) levels to 0.08—which typically equals 4 drinks for women and 5 drinks for men—in about 2 hours.

Binge drinkers are the minority of drinkers. In the United States, nearly half of all adults are current regular drinkers and 14 percent are current infrequent drinkers. Of those American adults who drink, about 29 percent report binge drinking within the past month, usually on multiple occasions (Dietary Guidelines for Americans 2010). According to the New York State Department of Health, a binge drinker is someone who:

- Drinks heavily over a short period of time or drinks continuously over a number of days or weeks (see previously provided definition)
- Drinks to get drunk
- Will likely develop a number of alcohol-related problems (e.g., alcoholism, cirrhosis) later in life if binge drinking started at an early age
- May experience damage to the part of the brain that controls learning and memory, judgment, decision making, and impulse control if binge drinking started as a teen
- Will experience compromised physical health (to be discussed in greater detail later in this chapter)
- Is prone to injury due to risky behavior (e.g., engaging in unsafe sex, motor vehicle accidents)
- Will experience a great number of short-term physical health problems (e.g., hangover, headaches, nausea, shakiness, and vomiting)
- Is likely to develop a physical and psychological dependency on alcohol
- Increases the likelihood of victimization (e.g., approximately 75 percent of reported acquaintance rapes on North American college campuses start with excessive alcohol consumption)

Traditionally aged college students (those who start college shortly after graduating from high school) are stereotypically labeled as binge drinkers and abusers of alcohol. In 2013, nearly 60 percent (59.4 percent) of college students ages 18 to 22 drank alcohol in the past month compared with 50.6 percent of non-college students of the same age (NIAAA 2015b). For many college freshmen, the first year of college is their first introduction to freedom and independence from their parents and family. With this freedom, students often feel like they are free to participate in a great number of activities that were not available to them previously. Drinking is one of the favorite activities they are now free to participate in. Many students do not simply have an occasional drink, they binge drink. "Research suggests that a large percentage of college students who drink do so to excess" (Hingson and White 2012). In a study conducted from 1999 to 2007, it was revealed that nearly 43.8 percent of college students drank 5 or more drinks on an occasion in the previous 30 days (of the study) (Hingson and White 2012). In 2013, 39 percent of college students ages 18 to 22 engaged in binge drinking in the past month compared with 33.4 percent of non-college students of the same age (NIAAA 2015b). Binge drinking among college students contributes to poor academic performance. About 25 percent of college students report academic consequences from drinking, including missing class, falling behind in class, doing poorly on exams or papers, and receiving lower grades overall (NIAAA 2015b).

Although college students commonly binge drink, 70 percent of binge-drinking episodes involve adults age 26 years and older (CDC 2014h). The CDC (2014h) also reports that while binge drinking is most common among young adults aged 18 to 34, binge drinkers aged 65 years and older report binge drinking more often—an average of 5 to 6 times a month. Binge drinking is more common among those with household incomes of $75,000 or more than among those with lower incomes. Men are twice as likely as women to binge drink. Binge drinkers are 14 times more likely to report alcohol-impaired driving than non-binge drinkers. More than half of the alcohol consumed by adults in the United States is in the form of binge drinks. Binge drinking is also associated with many health problems, and that is the next topic we will review.

Alcohol Use and Health Problems

"If all drinkers limited themselves to a single drink a day, we probably wouldn't need as many cardiologists, liver specialists, mental health professionals, and substance abuse counselors" (Harvard T.H. Chan School of Public Health 2015). But people do not limit themselves to one drink per day and, as a result, there are many health problems associated with alcohol abuse. Alcohol is a toxin that is treated by the human body as a foreign substance. As alcohol goes through the digestive process, many issues may arise that contribute to short-term and long-term health problems. "Excessive (i.e., heavy, high-risk, or binge) drinking has no benefits, and the hazards of heavy alcohol intake are well known. Excessive drinking increases the risk for cirrhosis of the liver, hypertension, stroke, type 2 diabetes, cancer of the upper gastrointestinal tract and colon, injury, and violence. Excessive drinking over time is associated with increased body weight and can impair short-and long-term cognitive function" (Dietary Guidelines for Americans 2010).

Binge drinking is associated with many health problems, including:

- Liver disease
- Cirrhosis

- Heart disease
- Various forms of cancer (e.g., pharynx, larynx, esophagus, colon, and breast)
- Sudden deaths and injuries
- Alcohol poisoning
- Sexually transmitted disease
- Children born with fetal alcohol spectrum disorders
- High blood pressure, stroke, and other cardiovascular diseases
- Neurological damage
- Sexual dysfunction
- Poor control of diabetes

One of the major health issues resulting from alcohol abuse is liver disease. Alcohol is stored in the blood while people consume it, and as a result the liver is constantly working hard to filter and break down the alcohol in order to keep the blood natural and clean. Over an extended period of time, alcohol may destroy liver cells and compromise its functionality. In 2013, of the 71,713 total liver disease deaths among individuals aged 12 and older, 46.4 percent involved alcohol. In 2009, alcohol-related liver disease was the primary cause of almost 1 in 3 liver transplants in the United States. Among cirrhosis deaths in 2011, 48 percent were alcohol related (NIAAA 2015b). The American Heart Association (AHA) (2015) advises people not to drink. If you do drink, it recommends that you do so in moderation. Alcohol abuse contributes to heart disease primarily because alcohol can raise the levels of some fats in the blood (triglycerides), which contributes to such problems as high blood pressure, obesity, and hardening of the arteries and heart. The AHA also warns that binge drinking can lead to stroke, fetal alcohol syndrome, cardiomyopathy, cardiac arrhythmia, and sudden cardiac death. The American Cancer Society (2015) warns that cancers of the mouth, throat, voice box, and esophagus increase with the amount of alcohol consumed. The risk of getting these forms of cancer is even higher when drinking is combined with smoking, because alcohol can act as a solvent, helping harmful chemicals in tobacco to get inside the cells that line the digestive tract. Alcohol may also slow down these cells' ability to repair damage to their DNA caused by chemicals in tobacco.

Alcohol-related incidents are responsible for a great number of premature deaths each year. According to the NIAAA (2015b), 1,825 college students between the ages of 18 and 24 die each year from alcohol-related unintentional injuries, including motor-vehicle crashes; nearly 88,000 people (approximately 62,000 males and 26,000 females) die from alcohol-related causes annually, making it the third leading preventable cause of death in the United States; and in 2012, 3.3 million deaths, or 5.9 percent of all global deaths (7.6 percent for males and 4.0 percent for females) were attributed to alcohol consumption.

Alcohol Use and Crime

There is a great deal of data available on the relationship between alcohol use and crime, including domestic abuse, violent behavior, underage drinking, robbery and assault, and sexual assault. According to the National Council on Alcoholism and Drug Dependence (NCADD) (2015a), 5.3 million U.S. adults—36 percent of those under correctional supervision at the time—were drinking at the time of their conviction offense. In 40 percent of homicides, alcohol use was a factor for convicted murderers being held in either jail or state prison. Forty percent of violent crimes (about three million such offenses) committed today also involve alcohol use. Based on victim reports, alcohol use by the offender was a factor in:

- Thirty-seven percent of rapes and sexual assaults
- Fifteen percent of robberies
- Twenty-seven percent of aggravated assaults
- Twenty-five percent of simple assaults

Among violent crimes, the offender is far more likely to be under the influence of alcohol than any other drug, and alcohol is more likely to be a factor in violence where the attacker and the victim know each other. Two-thirds of victims who were attacked by an intimate partner reported that alcohol use had been involved at the time of the incident, compared to 31 percent of victimizations by strangers. Approximately 1.4 million incidents of alcohol-related violence are committed against strangers (NCADD 2015a).

With regard to college students, nearly 700,000 (696,999) students between the ages of 18 and 24 are assaulted each year by another student who has been drinking. Approximately 97,000 college students between the ages of 18 and 24 are annually victimized by an alcohol-related sexual assault or date rape (NIAAA 2015b).

Underage drinking is another criminal offense associated with alcohol use. According to the 2013 National Survey on Drug Use and Health (NSDUH), 35.1 percent of 15-year-olds reported that they have had at least 1 drink in their lives. About 8.7 million people ages 12 to 20 (22.7 percent of this total age group) reported drinking alcohol in the past month (23 percent of males and 22.5 percent of females) (NIAAA 2015b). Nearly 5.4 million people ages 12 to 20 were binge drinkers (15.8 percent of the males and 12.3 percent of the females in this age group). Among the consequences of underage drinking include the disruption of normal adolescent brain development and an increase in the risk of developing an AUD—not to mention the realization that the offender could be sent to a juvenile detention center and face a rash of criminal offenses both in the present and in the future if their behavior continues (NIAAA 2015b).

Drinking and Driving

Driving while under the influence of alcohol (DUI), commonly called "drunk driving," is one of the most talked-about criminal activities associated with alcohol use. **Drunk driving** can be defined as operating a motor vehicle while one's blood alcohol content is above the legal limit set by statute. Currently, all 50 states have set 0.08 percent blood alcohol concentration (BAC) as the legal limit for driving under the influence, or driving while impaired. For commercial drivers, a BAC of 0.04 percent is the established legal limit. Drinking and driving is a very serious form of deviant behavior. Drunk drivers not only put their own lives in danger, they also put innocent lives in danger. As the concept implies, drinking and driving occurs when an individual consumes alcohol and drives a motorized vehicle (e.g., car, truck, or motorcycle). It is illegal in all jurisdictions within the United States, though enforcement and penalties vary widely between and within states and territories. The specific criminal offense is usually cited as driving while impaired (DWI) or driving under the influence (DUI). Some jurisdictions used other terms such as operating while impaired (OWI) or operating a vehicle under the influence (OVI). There are also laws against drinking alcohol and then driving a boat or piloting an aircraft. Just like driving under the influence while on land, boating and drinking or flying and drinking can lead to fines and/or imprisonment, plus the loss of boating or flying privileges.

Attempting to drive a vehicle while under the influence of alcohol is not only against the law, it violates common sense and logic, as brain functioning (e.g., psychomotor and cognitive skills) has been compromised. Alcohol, a depressant, affects an individual's ability to concentrate and make split-second decisions

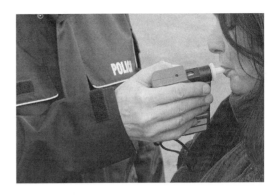

A woman's BAC level is tested to see if she was driving while impaired.

while driving a vehicle. An individual's hand-eye coordination is significantly affected by alcohol in a negative way as well. The .08 percent BAC level is believed to be the cutoff rate by which a person can safely perform the task of driving. However, long before the .08 percent level is reached, the driver's ability to operate a motor vehicle is believed to be compromised (see box 7.2).

A CLOSER LOOK

Box 7.2 How Alcohol Affects the Driver

According to the National Council on Alcoholism and Drug Dependence (2015b), a person's ability to drive is impaired even with a blood alcohol concentration (BAC) level of 0.02 percent. Listed below are three different BAC levels (0.02, 0.05, and 0.08 percent) and the corresponding impairment affecting motorized drivers.

  BAC of 0.02 percent—At this level, the driver begins to experience some loss of judgment, relaxation, and altered mood, which results in a decline in visual functions and inability to perform two tasks at the same time.
  BAC of 0.05 percent—Psychomotor performance is significantly impaired; slower eye movements occur; visual perception, reaction time, and information processing are adversely affected, resulting in reduced coordination, reduced ability to track moving objects, difficulty steering, and reduced response to emergency driving situations.
  BAC of 0.08 percent—The driver's motor coordination is poor (e.g., balance, speech, vision, reaction time, and hearing); it is harder to detect danger; and judgment, self-control, reasoning, and memory are impaired, resulting in reduced concentration, short-term memory loss, loss of speed control, reduced information processing capability (e.g., signal detection, visual search), and impaired perception.

While there is a great emphasis in contemporary society on eliminating drunk driving, this was not the case prior to 1980. This author remembers folks his parents' and grandparents' age using such expressions in the 1970s as "one more for the road" or "you better have a shot to wake up before you drive home." In other words, drinking and driving attitudes were far different in past generations than they are today. What changed this cultural norm and value? Many people point to the 1980 formation of Mothers Against Drunk Drivers (MADD), now known as Mothers Against Drunk Driving (the name change places the focus on drunk driving instead of on individuals) (MADD 2015). The Irving, Texas–based organization was founded in California by Candace Lightner after her 13-year-old daughter was killed by a drunk driver. Today, nearly everyone has heard of MADD, the grassroots organization that became a powerful lobbying force to help change the perception of drunk driving. The 1985 mission statement of MADD sums up their stand on drunk driving as it reads: "Mothers Against Drunk Driving mobilizes victims and their allies to establish the public conviction that impaired driving is unacceptable and criminal, in order to promote corresponding public policies, programs and personal responsibility" (MADD 2015). MADD claims that the incidence of drunk driving has been cut in half since its formation.

Despite the positive impact of MADD to cut down drunk driving, it remains far too commonplace. According to NCADD (2015b), nearly 13,000 people are killed each year in alcohol-related accidents and hundreds of thousands more are injured. The CDC (2015g) and NIAAA (2015b) cite 10,076 alcohol-impaired driving crashes (wherein more than one person per crash may die) in 2013, accounting for nearly one-third (30.8 percent) of all overall driving fatalities. Every day, nearly 30 people in the United States die in motor vehicle crashes that involve an alcohol-impaired driver. This amounts to 1 death every 51 minutes. The annual cost of alcohol-related crashes range from $60 billion to $100 billion per year (CDC 2015g; NCADD 2015b). In 2010, there were over 1.4 million arrests for DWI with over 780,000 convictions (NCADD 2015b).

Those most at risk of being involved in an alcohol-related crash are young people, motorcyclists, and drivers with prior DWI convictions. At all levels of BAC, the risk of being involved in a crash is greater for young people than for older people. For example, among drivers with BAC levels of 0.08 percent or higher involved in crashes in 2013, 1 out of every 3 were between 21 and 24 years of age; 29 percent were ages 25 to 34; and 24 percent were between 35 and 44 years of age (CDC 2015g). Riding a motorcycle comes with certain risks (e.g., many motorists cannot see bikers because of mirror "blind spots," and motorcycles offer very little protection in an accident), and this includes potential victimization due to drunk driving. Among motorcyclists killed in fatal crashes in 2013, 27 percent had BACs of 0.08 percent or greater. Older motorcyclists are more likely than younger bikers to be killed in alcohol-related deaths with nearly half age 40 or older; motorcyclists ages 40 to 44 have the highest percentage of deaths with BACs of 0.08 percent or greater (44 percent). Drivers with a BAC of 0.08 percent or higher involved in fatal accidents were six times more likely to have a prior conviction for DWI than were drivers with no alcohol in their system, and two-thirds of those sentenced to incarceration were repeat offenders (NCADD 2015b).

Interestingly, and as an example of statistical deviance, in some rare cases a person may have a genetic disorder known as auto-brewery syndrome, a rare intestinal disorder wherein a person's intestinal system sometimes converts ordinary food and beverages into alcohol (within the person's body). There is a case of a woman in Hamburg (outside of Buffalo), New York, who was arrested for aggravated driving while intoxicated with a BAC measurement at .33 percent. Her defense lawyer successfully argued in court (case was dismissed) that alcohol was not the contributing factor to her very high BAC. Limited research on this syndrome indicates that just 50 to 100 people have been officially diagnosed with the illness (Herbeck 2015).

"It Wasn't My Fault; I Was Drunk"

In the introductory story to this chapter the idea of people doing things while they were drunk but not wanting to take personal responsibility for them was first introduced. That people will deny responsibility for some act of deviance and attempt to deflect the blame has been a mainstream understanding in sociology since at least the time of Sykes and Matza's (1957) usage of the techniques of neutralization (see chapter 3). With this in mind, it is now time to look at some behaviors that, while they may be deviant and/or embarrassing to the subject, are not as serious as some of the previously discussed topics (e.g., driving under the influence or committing violent acts of assault and murder). In many cases, the drunk person may not realize until the next day—when informed by friends or family members—just exactly what they did while intoxicated. Perplexed by the retelling of certain stories, the subject is left dumbfounded in his or her rationalization or justification of such behavior, which leads to the cliché response, "It wasn't my fault; I was drunk." Let's look at some examples of drunk behaviors that lead to this response. (It should be noted that some of the examples used here come from interviews I conducted with people, both college students and non-college students, regarding their drunken escapades.)

Public Intoxication

One form of deviant drunken behavior involves public intoxication, otherwise known as "public drunkenness" and in some cases, being "drunk and disorderly." Definitions of public intoxication vary from country to country and from jurisdiction to jurisdiction, but they usually require some sort of obvious display of intoxicated behavior that is disruptive to the public order. For our purposes, **public intoxication** is defined as an intoxicated or drugged person in a public place who is disturbing the public peace and order. While public intoxication can be a relatively serious criminal offense, especially if the act disrupts the public peace or places people in potential harm, in many cases a public intoxication violation may occur simply because the drunk person was annoying. While many people who are *not* drunk are annoying, being drunk and annoying is a potentially punishable offense, generally a fine or maybe a few hours in jail. In the state of Virginia, for example, "Code of Virginia 18.2–388: Profane swearing and intoxication in public; penalty, transportation of public inebriates to detoxification center," states: "If any person profanely curses or swears or is intoxicated in public, whether such intoxication results from alcohol, narcotic drug or other intoxicant or drug or whatever nature, he shall be deemed guilty of a Class 4 misdemeanor. In any area in which there is located a court-approved detoxification center a law-enforcement officer may authorize the transportation, by police or otherwise, of public inebriates to such detoxification center in lieu of arrest; however, no person shall be involuntarily detained in such a center." We can imagine any person detained for public intoxication and then waking up in a detention center only to wonder what happened, having to call friends/family for help and when told the circumstances that led to his detainment, saying, "It wasn't my fault; I was drunk." In one case, a respondent informed me that she was having a lengthy argument with a tree in Hanover Square, located in Syracuse, New York. Hanover Square is a busy place with many bars and restaurants. People in the bar called police "out of concern" for her well-being. The police eventually took her under custody for her own safety. The next day she offered this excuse: "I just turned 21; what can I say?"

Public intoxication can be a serious offense and a sign of a drinking problem.

There are countless instances when people are publicly intoxicated but the police are not involved. These types of stories are generally funnier and less likely to be criminal. For example, the drunk person trying to sing in a bar or who tries to tell a joke to people on the sidewalk, or who spills food on herself after buying it from a street vendor. Waking up the next day, the person may wonder why there are stains on her favorite blouse only to be told that the sauce from her gyro (that she bought from a street vendor outside a bar) had dripped all over her. She initially denied ever having a gyro from a street vendor but had to relent after her friends showed her photos from their phones of her sloppily eating a gyro. She could then only smile and blame it on the alcohol.

Public Nuisance

When someone threatens the health, morals, safety, comfort, convenience, or welfare of a community, they have committed a public nuisance. Thus, **public nuisance** may be defined as an act, condition, or thing that is illegal because it interferes with the rights of the public generally. Violators may be sentenced to a criminal offense, a fine, or both. A nuisance may be private or public. A *private nuisance* is an unreasonable, unwanted, or unlawful interference with another person's private use and enjoyment of his or her property. The law has been used by law enforcement as a type of grab-bag way of dealing with a variety of issues. Specific nuisance abatement laws are often created to deal with gangbangers congregating on premises where they are unwelcomed, such as schools and other public places. Dade County (Miami), Florida, for example, enacted Ord. No. 99-43, Nuisance Abatement, with Section 2–98.4 declaring that "any places or premises which are used as the site of the unlawful sale or delivery of controlled substances, prostitution, youth and street gang activity, gambling, illegal sale or consumption of alcoholic beverages, or lewd or lascivious behavior may be a public nuisance that adversely affects the public health, safety, morals, and welfare." Reno, Nevada (Chapter 8.22, Sec. 8.22.020), has passed nuisance abatement ordinances as a means of keeping its community, including property, buildings, and premises within its limits, safe and as aesthetically pleasing as possible by forbidding a number of criminal activities, especially the use of graffiti by gang members. Nuisance abatement laws are certainly applicable to nongang members as well and may be used to curtail drunken activities of otherwise conventional people. One respondent told me that he attempted to spray-paint his and his girlfriend's initials inside a heart on a public building in order to "prove his love" to her. He was caught by the police halfway through his criminal act and offered no other excuse than he was "drunk with love" for his girlfriend. People who drink too much and congregate outside someone's home or office may also be subject to public nuisance laws.

Indecent Exposure as a Sex Offense

Among the more common deviant activities committed by drunk people is indecent exposure. **Indecent exposure** is the deliberate exposure in public or in view of the public by a person of a portion or portions of his or her body, causing others to be alarmed or offended. Indecent exposure also involves circumstances where the exposure is contrary to local moral or other standards of appropriate behavior. Indecent exposure is often committed for the sexual gratification of the offender or committed to entice a sexual response. Women who are drunk may "flash their breasts" in such a way as to gain sexual gratification or to entice a sexual response from others. Then again, a male may "flash his genitals" to shock observers as a means of gaining sexual gratification. Because many people who drink alcohol lose their inhibitions, flashing body parts is more than a rare event. In New Orleans during Mardi Gras it is in fact quite common for some women to flash their breasts for beads.

In some jurisdictions, to be convicted of indecent exposure, the prosecution must prove an intent to sexually arouse or sexually insult or offend on the part of the offender. This is an important consideration for the person who decides the line for the bathroom is too long and heads for an outdoor destination to relieve him- or herself. A respondent stated that she was drunk at a wedding reception and that the bathroom line was so long that she decided to go outside and urinate behind a dumpster. As she pulled up her bridesmaid dress, a local police officer drove by and asked her what she was doing. She replied, "What do you think I'm doing?" and proceeded to pee. The cop laughed and pulled away. Men have urinated in semi-public areas while drunk, most likely for as long as people have consumed alcohol. Generally, people are not overly concerned when a man urinates behind a tree or a dumpster and at least attempts to hide his activities, as it is clear he is not doing it to expose himself or to violate a local moral code of behavior; he simply wants to relieve himself.

There is something important to note with regard to indecent exposure that makes this relatively harmless drunken activity more serious. In some instances, indecent exposure may land the violator on a "sex offender" list. At least 13 states require sex offender registration for public urination, according to a Human Rights Watch comprehensive review of sex offender laws in 2007. Two of those states specify that the urination must happen in front of a minor. Flashing your breasts may also lead you to a sex offender list (Fuchs 2013). Landing on a sex offender list for urinating behind a dumpster seems quite tame compared to charges of pedophilia, and yet it can happen, depending on the laws of your jurisdiction. Even though the violator is a different-level offender, it would be tough to have to inform people you are on a sex offender list just because you were too drunk to urinate at a proper facility. Bear this in mind the next time you think "mooning" someone or showing someone the "full Monty" is excusable because you were just drunk and it wasn't really your fault.

Relationship Issues

As we have learned throughout this chapter, people who drink excessively risk many potential problems, some very serious, some relatively frivolous. Many relationships have started and many more have ended because of drunken escapades. Flirting with someone at a party or a bar is fine, but not so fine if you are involved in a relationship with someone and especially if that person is standing right next to you at the time of the flirtation. On a number of occasions, people who are in a serious relationship with another may go out drinking with friends. And sometimes, "mistakes are made." One mistake could be a one-night hookup. The topic of cheating on a significant other while drunk came up in one of my classroom discussions on deviant behavior. One student said that "if the one-night stand is with a random person and it is just for one night, it's excusable." She also added, "but if it's with a good friend or someone you care about, it's not a good excuse because the alcohol gave you the liquid courage to do something you wanted to do sober but you know it would be wrong." Some of her classmates agreed with her, while others vehemently argued that cheating is always cheating whether you are drunk or not. What do you think?

The topic of a one-night stand leads to the concept of the "walk of shame." While most college students have heard of the expression "walk of shame," let's elaborate here. According to the *Urban Dictionary*, the walk of shame occurs when a person walks home alone after a night of drinking and sex (the *Urban Dictionary* uses more colorful words), usually wearing the clothes they went out in the night before, or in the case of women, with the man's T-shirt on. The walk of shame is especially tough for college students who have to walk across the campus. Many respondents, both male and female, gave me examples of the walk of shame scenario. The *Urban Dictionary*, however, provides a couple of colorful descriptions from people who had done the walk: "I don't remember what his face looked like and I had to do the walk of shame" and "I don't remember if the sex was good enough for the walk of shame."

Another fairly common scenario for people out drinking with friends involves the person who misses her ex, or the person who misses his current partner, and then decides to make the late-night "drunk call" or the "drunk text." Depending on the context, the drunk call may involve any sort of conversation, or attempted conversation. It may involve sexting (sending a provocative photo via text) and pleading to get together. In many cases, the person who makes the drunk call forgets all about it; that is, until the next day. Once again, the plea for forgiveness is centered on the premise "It wasn't my fault; I was drunk."

Acting Impulsively

One thing that nearly all deviant drunk behaviors have in common is the impulse to act before thinking. Once again, because many people lose their inhibitions when drunk and many others act in a manner they never would sober, people may find themselves doing deviant or criminal acts. Listed below are some comments shared with me as respondents recalled their past drunk behaviors:

- As I walked home from a night of drinking, I passed a flower garden. I thought the flowers were pretty, so I picked half of them and ran off, dropping most of them along the way. I feel bad about it now, but I was drunk then.
- When we get drunk at frat parties, we like to steal their stuff.
- I stole a Christmas wreath from the front door of a bar because I forgot to buy one.
- I notice that the more people drink, the closer they get to your face to talk with you (the "close talker") and the louder they get.
- I challenged this big guy to a fight; I told him I could kick his ass. He knocked me out with one punch.
- I maxed out a credit card buying crap on TV.
- My friends and I pig out when we are bombed. Last Friday I had four Big Macs at one time.

As you read this material, did something come to mind wherein you recall yourself, or someone else, saying, "It wasn't my fault; I was drunk"? What do you think of trying to use such an excuse in light of the material discussed here?

Drunk Shamings

In my *Shameful Behaviors* (2008) book I first presented my original research on the phenomenon "drunk shamings." Drunk shamings are quite common on college campuses and with young people not in college. Drunk shamings are an example of an informal degradation ceremony designed to shame and embarrass the victim. (An example of a formal shaming would be a military court-martial.) Degradation ceremonies represent attempts by others to alter one's identity by means of embarrassment and shame. Degradation ceremonies force the victims to yield to the wishes of others who are in a position of authority. Drunk shamings are unique in that they generally are not planned; they are spontaneous degradation ceremonies. In my research, it was revealed that 95 percent of drunk shamings were not planned. The other 5 percent were planned retaliations for previous shaming victimizations.

What Is a Drunk Shaming?

A **drunk shaming** occurs when people become too drunk to defend themselves from a private or public shaming. (Note: See chapter 13 for a further discussion on shamings, including shameful behaviors.) A drunk shaming is an example of a quasi-degradation ceremony because it is conducted informally; usually by close friends and/or family members. Often the drunk person will have his or her photo taken and placed online. Drunk shamings entail a four-step process:

Step 1—A person(s) drinks excessively (in the company of a group of other people) to the point where he or she passes out drunk.
Step 2—Someone from the group of other people needs to take action. That is, he or she needs to start the drunk shaming process.
Step 3—Some application method(s) of drunk shaming must be conducted (e.g., using a permanent marker and drawing on the person's body or putting objects on top of the person).
Step 4—The drunk shaming is captured for posterity on film or video, which may then be posted online.

Step 3 is the key to any successful drunk shaming, as some sort of shaming method must be used. The most common method involves drawing on the victim's skin (especially derogatory and obscene messages). This type of drunk shaming was demonstrated in a scene from the movie *Garden State*. The character Andrew Largeman, played by Zach Braff, is on an MRI machine after a night of partying (drinking and taking other drugs), and he has drawings of male genitalia and other obscene things drawn on his body.

Other shaming methods include putting objects on/near the victim (e.g., clothing, beer bottles, sex toys); shaving eyebrows and/or hair; duct taping the shamee to toilets, walls, chairs, beds, and so on; wrapping the shamee in plastic wrap; and rearranging the shamee's body into embarrassing positions. In some cases, perpetrators of a drunk shaming may employ shaming techniques known as "antiquing" and "tar and feather." These two techniques are combination shamings. Antiquing involves wetting the victim's face with a washcloth and then throwing flour, baby powder, and/or powdered sugar all over them. The "tar and feather" technique does not, of course, involve pouring actual hot tar on the victim (remember, drunk shamings are done in fun and "victims" nearly always laugh it off by saying, you guessed it, "I was drunk; it wasn't my fault"), but instead, some sort of sticky substance (e.g., honey) is poured on the person and then feathers or pillow stuffing is dropped on them.

Drunk Shaming Rules

Interestingly, there are rules involved in drunk shamings, although it should be pointed out not everyone agrees with this. One of the chief rules is the idea that the victim is not to be physically harmed. Drunk shamings are designed to embarrass the victim (like initiation rites of passage), not injure the person. Nearly all drunk shaming participants recognize that the host of a party is not to be shamed—this is a sign of respect. If a person makes it to their own bed, they are not to be shamed; after all, they accomplished what they are supposed to do, get home safely. If a person falls asleep with their shoes on, they are fair game for a drunk shaming. If the drunk person's significant other is at the gathering, they are not to be shamed; however, if the significant other gives the green light, then they are fair game. Visitors to a party are always fair game. A person's private property, especially the car, is not to be violated. House rules can always supersede any of the above rules.

Drunk Shaming and Self-Esteem

In my research (124 respondents completed a questionnaire consisting of 63 open-ended and closed-ended questions), I measured many variables, including victim by sex (35 percent of males and 26 percent of females reported being a victim of a drunk shaming); perpetrator of a drunk shaming by sex (76 percent of males and 47 percent of females); and age category of drunk shaming victims (28 percent of 17- to 20-year-olds; 34 percent of 21- to 23-year-olds; 25 percent of 24- to 29-year-olds; 0 percent of those 29 and over). As a quasi-degradation ceremony, the drunk shaming is designed to embarrass the "victim." A little more than half (52 percent) of victims agreed that they experienced shame and embarrassment for having their shaming made public, and 29 percent of victims agreed they experienced moral indignation as a result of their shaming. Twenty-one percent of drunk shaming victims agreed they experienced a decrease in self-esteem due to the shaming, and nearly the same figure (25 percent) agreed that they felt remorse for their drunken behavior. (Note: Rosenberg's measurement of self-esteem was built into the questionnaire to ascertain respondents' self-esteem levels.) Among the respondents' most interesting replies to the question "Was your self-esteem compromised as a result of a drunk shaming?" one person stated, "Having photos of me posted online being a victim of a drunk shaming was the best thing that ever happened to me as years from now I can tell everyone what a great time I had in college." The statement seems as sad as anything else.

The lesson to be learned with drunk shamings is nearly the same as all the other lessons one should've learned from this chapter—drinking in moderation (for those of legal age) seems to be fine for most people, but drinking to the point of impairment may cause a slew of problems.

Summary

Alcohol (ethyl alcohol, ethanol) is an intoxicating ingredient found in beer, wine, and liquor. It is produced by the fermentation of yeast, sugars, and starches. People have been drinking fermented drinks for at least 10,000 years and perhaps longer. The earliest evidence of the consumption of fermented drinks is traced to China and the Middle East, where natural climatic conditions would most likely assist the fermentation process. European explorers brought alcoholic beverages with them on their travels to the New World. Many indigenous people in the Americas already had their own version of alcoholic beverages upon the arrival of Europeans. Americans love their alcohol as much as most people around the world, but in the early 1900s it was outlawed via the Eighteenth Amendment. Organized crime thrived during prohibition, and alcohol was legalized again via the Twenty-First Amendment.

The effects of alcohol are mixed, as some people become happy, others depressed; some become outgoing, others withdrawn; some vicious, others pleasant; and some become energetic, while others are more passive. Furthermore, some people can "hold their liquor" and others cannot. A common belief about the effect of alcohol on behavior is that alcohol automatically reduces inhibitions. The idea of "drunken comportment" suggests that the effects of alcohol on behavior are learned.

Alcohol abuse and alcoholism are among the potentially serious problems associated with alcohol consumption. Binge drinking is an example of a problem with extreme alcohol consumption. There are a number of health problems associated with drinking, including liver disease, cirrhosis, heart disease, various forms of cancer, sudden deaths and injuries, alcohol poisoning, and children born with fetal alcohol spectrum disorders. There is a great deal of data available on the relationship between alcohol use and crime, including domestic abuse, violent behavior, underage drinking, robbery and assault, and sexual assault. Drinking and driving is a particularly dangerous social problem.

People who drink too much and commit silly/deviant/criminal acts may attempt to shift responsibility by saying, "It wasn't my fault; I was drunk." Public intoxication, public nuisance, indecent exposure, relationship issues, acting impulsively, and being victimized by a drunk shaming are among the behaviors associated with excessive drinking.

Key Terms

Discussion Questions

1. Provide a brief review of the history of alcohol use.
2. Explain why people have historically drunk alcohol.
3. Why do people drink alcohol today? Why do people binge drink?
4. Describe the similarities and differences between a person with a drinking problem and an alcoholic.
5. Describe what is meant by alcohol abuse. Identify a number of health problems associated with alcohol use.
6. Provide a review of alcohol use disorder (AUD) and share statistics of AUD in the United States.
7. Describe a time when you (or someone close to you) used the excuse, "It wasn't my fault; I was drunk." Have you (or someone close to you) participated in a drunk shaming? Describe the circumstances.

CHAPTER 8

Drug Use and Abuse and Social Deviance

CHAPTER OBJECTIVES

After reading this chapter students should be able to:

- Define the term "drug" and explain why people take drugs
- Describe drug abuse and identify some of the leading abused drugs
- Explain the factors that influence drug effects
- Identify the major categories of drugs and provide examples of each

- Explain what is meant by prescription drug abuse and describe why this type of drug abuse is perceived differently than recreational drug abuse
- Explain what is meant by "Big Pharma" and "Big Data"

"High there!" The phrase "high there!" seems innocent enough and looks like a fairly typical greeting as it appears to be a variation of "hello" or "hi." But in this world of "there's an app for that," the "high there!" moniker takes on an entirely different meaning. And if you are among the cannabis-consuming subculture living in a state where marijuana is legal, you are likely aware of the fact that "high there!" is a greeting reserved for like-minded people who consume cannabis products and are looking for people to date.

Most marijuana smokers have long attempted to keep their cannabis consumption private for fear of being "outed" to authorities for their illegal activities. When talking with one another about people they did not know well, pot smokers would use such expressions as "Is he cool?"—an expression meant to ascertain whether or not the person in question was a pot smoker. Pot smokers have long been stigmatized and discriminated against by non–marijuana smokers, and this discrimination has often been extended to the world of dating. Pot smokers are generally okay with dating, marrying, and starting a family with non–pot smokers, but the opposite is generally less true. To avoid the hassles of dating non–marijuana users, pot smokers often prefer to date others who share their passion. Now, thanks to the High There! app, it is easier than ever before for pot smokers to find one another.

According to their website, High There! is currently (June 2015) only available for use in U.S. states where cannabis is legal. High There! solves the problem many cannabis consumers face in connecting with similar people. "Whether looking to connect with new friends, current friends, fellow patients, or simply to find that special someone who understands and supports your choice to consume, High There! helps by giving you a safe place to express yourself" (High There! 2015). The High There! app allows cannabis users a chance to meet on their own terms.

For example, many people don't like to go to bars to drink; they prefer to stay home and hang out and get high. This app also allows cannabis users to describe themselves and their current situations (e.g., energetic, hanging out and vegging, or munching out).

As the tide has recently turned with regard to marijuana and deviancy, the High There! app is far from the only mechanism available for pro-marijuana people; in fact, there are hundreds of apps designed for the cannabis-using market. Leafly, for example, is the "world's cannabis information resource" used by millions of people who seek to explore and consume the thousands of marijuana strains available throughout the world (Leafly 2015).

Why Do People Take Drugs?

Nearly everyone takes drugs. Some people take drugs that are designated as legal (e.g., alcohol, nicotine, caffeine, and prescription drugs), and some people take drugs designated as illegal (e.g., heroin, cocaine, and psychedelics). Most drug users have little say in which drugs are legal or not, so the legality of their consumption, and thus the designation of their behavior as deviant or not, is determined by others, generally those with socioeconomic and political motivations.

Defining Drug

Before we examine why people take any of the wide variety of drugs available to them, it is important to first define the term "drug." A **drug** is "any chemical substance other than food or water that affects the mind or body" (Macionis 2010:208). The *Business Dictionary* (2015) defines a drug as a "natural or synthetic substance which (when taken into a living body) affects its functioning or structure, and is used in the diagnosis, mitigation, treatment, or prevention of a disease or relief of discomfort." The U.S. Food and Drug Administration (2015a) provides a much lengthier definition of drug:

> The term "drug" means (A) articles recognized in the official United States Pharmacopoeia, official Homoeopathic Pharmacopoeia of the United States, or official National Formulary, or any supplement to any of them; and (B) articles intended for use in the diagnosis, cure, mitigation, treatment, or prevention of disease in man or other animals; and (C) articles (other than food) intended for use as a component of any article specified in clause (A), (B), or (C).

There are thousands of natural and synthetic drugs available for people to ingest. Humans not only consume millions of doses of drugs each year, we have created drugs for the well-being of our pets and to assist or control wild animals as well. It is no stretch to suggest that we live in a very pro-drug culture; that is to say, as long as we take socially approved drugs.

Explanations as to Why People Use Drugs

As described in our discussion on alcohol use in chapter 7, for millennia people have taken a wide variety of natural substances in an attempt to alleviate pain and/or heighten pleasure. And just as past cultures learned about the fermentation process as a means of creating a variety of alcoholic beverages, so too have we learned over the past centuries to create synthetic substances to be consumed as drugs designed to assuage pain and/or amplify pleasure.

The pro-drug culture we live in is demonstrated in a number of ways, and much of it centers on the realization that drug use contributes to a huge economic industry valued at hundreds of billions of dollars. According to WHO (2015d), "The global pharmaceuticals market is worth US$300 billion a year, a figure expected to rise to US$400 billion within three years." Drugs are popular because they are advertised as a solution for nearly everything, including a salvation from general aches and pains, serious injuries, allergies, and a means toward such desired goals as weight loss/gain and sexual potency. In 2012, the pharmaceutical industry alone spent $27 billion on promoting drugs; although most of this money was spent on direct marketing to physicians (who would then promote/recommend drugs to their patients), a significant portion was spent on various advertisements directly targeting consumers (Kessel 2014). Drugs, especially alcohol, are promoted as the perfect companion for college graduation parties, job promotions, personal achievements all of sorts, sports fans who are celebrating their favorite team's accomplishments, and so on. Drugs, then, are promoted for a number of reasons including medical and recreational.

Macionis (2010) believes that there are five common reasons that people use drugs:

1. Therapeutic uses—Some drugs offer medical benefits such as controlling seizures, lessening depression, or reducing pain. For example, in 2015 the FDA approved Corlanor (ivabradine) for the treatment of chronic heart failure and Prestalia for the treatment of hypertension (CenterWatch 2015).
2. Recreational uses—Many people routinely consume drugs such as marijuana, beer, caffeine, or wine for recreational purposes, because it makes them feel more relaxed, and because it helps them to "take the edge off" stressful events.
3. Spiritual or psychological uses—Some drugs, such as psychedelics, have properties that can alter human consciousness and distort perception. Some Native American societies, especially tribes in the Southwestern plains, use peyote as sacred medicine to sharpen their awareness and deepen their spiritual experiences, as the psychedelic properties of peyote create brilliantly colored visions (Waters 2003). In the 1960s, it was common for hippies to take LSD as a means of gaining enlightenment.
4. Escape—There are times when people turn to drug use because they want to escape, at least temporarily, from their problems in life. Alcohol and other recreational drugs are popular for this purpose.
5. Social conformity—Many people consume certain drugs to fit in socially and to conform to cultural norms. Young people feel peer pressure to smoke cigarettes, and a number of adults feel a certain level of cultural expectation to consume caffeine via coffee. Whenever the non–coffee drinker hears another say, "Let's meet for coffee to discuss business," especially in the work environment, an uneasiness settles in because of the uncomfortable situation of being the lone person at a table not having coffee or some other hot beverage. A number of people, including this author, do not consume hot beverages. Is that deviant? What do you think?

Factors That Influence Drug Effects

A number of factors influence the effectiveness of drugs and the possibility of continued use. Described below are a number of these factors:

1. Identity—Is the drug as advertised; that is to say, does it live up to its identity? People take certain drugs for specific reasons and expect corresponding results.

Performance-enhancing drugs, for example, are supposed to help improve endurance and build muscles. When combined with physical exercise, performance-enhancing drugs, such as anabolic steroids, *are* as advertised. As a result, the user is likely to continue using such drugs. The marijuana "high" meanwhile is a "learned" high, and some people simply do not get high when they first try it. Many users have to be told that the feelings of light-headedness and dizziness they are experiencing are an expected consequence of smoking pot, and when you feel that way, you are "high." (In this regard, the marijuana high is much like drunken comportment discussed in chapter 7.)

2. Dose—A **dose** refers to the "quantity" of something (e.g., a drug) that has been prescribed by a doctor or recommended by the drug provider. Chemicals and drugs in general are the most common things for which doses are measured. Over-the-counter cold medicine, for example, may come with the instruction of "take two pills every four hours." When it comes to prescription drugs, doses for individuals are based on individual characteristics (e.g., age and weight) and pharmacokinetic considerations (thus, some people need a varying amount of the drug in order to attain the intended effect). The person who continues to struggle with a cold may be tempted to increase the dosage of the cold medicine in an effort to more quickly fight off the cold, the misguided philosophy being, "If two every four hours is good, four every four hours is twice as good." People in a hurry to bulk up may take twice the recommended amount of anabolic steroids in an effort to get bigger and stronger twice as quickly.

3. Potency and purity—Potency is another type of quantitative measurement and refers to the amount of the drug required to produce a given percentage of its maximal effect. Generally speaking, the lower the dose of a drug, the higher the potency. Legalized marijuana is a good example of demonstrated potency, as the strains available for legal purchase are much more potent than most strains available illegally. Purity is a measurement of how much of some substance is actually as advertised. Cocaine, for example, is a drug that is very inconsistent in purity, as drug dealers routinely "cut" cocaine with some other substance in order to increase the quantity of cocaine that can be sold to users. People who buy drugs such as cocaine and heroin on the streets have no real idea what they are buying, and thus both the potency and purity are random variables that are capable of influencing the effects of the drugs.

4. Drug mixing—There is a reason why medical professionals ask patients what drugs they are currently taking before they prescribe a drug for treatment, as mixing drugs can alter the effects and may lead to dire consequences. Recreational drug users also need to be careful when they mix drugs. For example, combining cocaine (or crack cocaine) and heroin—known as "speedballing"—has been recognized to have deadly consequences. Among famous celebrities to die from speedballing are John Belushi, Chris Farley (cocaine and morphine sulfate), Zac Foley, Philip Seymour Hoffman, River Phoenix, and Joey Stefano.

5. Route of administration—The manner in which a drug is taken can dramatically alter the effects of drugs. Typically, drugs can be taken orally (e.g., swallowing pills or eating "edibles"); smoked (e.g., marijuana, crack cocaine); snorted (cocaine); inhaled (e.g., asthma inhalers); vaporized (e.g., electronic cigarettes and cigars); and injected (e.g., intravenous injections made into a vein

for therapeutic, experimental, or recreational purposes). The quicker the drug gets into the bloodstream, the quicker the results; thus, intravenous drug use provides the quickest results. Speedballing is usually done intravenously, but sometimes the cocaine is snorted and the heroin injected. Injecting cocaine is more effective than snorting it, and so on.

6. Habituation—How accustomed someone is to taking a particular drug will impact its effectiveness. A couple of terms are all relevant to the habituation variable—tolerance and dependency. **Tolerance** refers to the repeated use of a drug over a period of time, which diminishes its effectiveness. When someone regularly consumes a drug (e.g., heroin or alcohol) but no longer receives the desired effect from the drug, a tolerance has been built up. The user will now require a better-quality alternative or a larger quantity of the drug for the same desired results that once occurred before tolerance was established. **Dependency** refers to "a state in which a person's body has adjusted to regular use of a drug" (Macionis 2010:211). When a person becomes dependent on a drug, addiction has been established. Tobacco smokers and coffee drinkers are among the most common addicts dependent on a drug.

7. Set and setting—The set and setting refers to more than the physical environment where the user consumes drugs; it also refers to the psychic, mental, and emotional state of the user. This is especially true for someone who has consumed psychedelics. A person who takes LSD, for example, is very susceptible to the happenings of the environment and vibes of others. Some people may have a "good trip" or a "bad trip" based on the set and setting.

So far, we have established a definition for drugs, examined some possible explanations as to why people use drugs, and have a description of some of the factors that influence the effects of drugs. It is now time to learn about a number of different categories of commonly consumed drugs and their prevalence in society.

Categorizing Drugs

The effects drugs have on the human body and brain help to determine the categorization of drugs. Even so, there are some slight variations in these classification schemes. The International Drug Evaluation and Classification Program (DECP)—which has roots with the early 1970s Los Angeles Police Department (LAPD) and their efforts to identify individuals driving under the influence (DUI) of substances other than alcohol and the National Highway Traffic Safety Administration (NHTSA), who adopted the LAPD's first drug recognition Expert (DRE) program—have identified seven drug categories: (1) central nervous system (CNS) depressants (e.g., Valium, Librium, Xanax, Prozac, and Rohypnol); (2) CNS stimulants (e.g., cocaine/crack, amphetamines, and methamphetamine ["crank"]); (3) hallucinogens (e.g., LSD, peyote, psilocybin and MDMA [Ecstasy]); (4) dissociative anesthetics (e.g., PCP); (5) narcotic analgesics (e.g., opium, codeine, Demerol, Darvon, morphine, methadone, Vicodin, and OxyContin); (6) inhalants (e.g., plastic cement, paint, gasoline, paint thinners, and hair sprays); and (7) cannabis (e.g., cannabis) (DECP 2015).

The Centre for Education and Information on Drugs and Alcohol (CEIDA) (2013), an organization designed to provide a comprehensive guide for parents to educate their children about drugs and their effects, categorize drugs under three different groupings: (1) stimulants (e.g., Ecstasy, speed, methamphetamine, crystal methylamphetamine, cocaine, and crack cocaine); (2) depressants (e.g., cannabis, inhalants, heroin, morphine, codeine, and methadone); and (3) hallucinogens (e.g., LSD, psilocybin, phencyclidine [PCP], and mescaline).

Sociologist John J. Macionis (2010) utilizes a classification system that incorporates six categories of drugs: (1) stimulants (e.g., caffeine, nicotine, Ritalin, cocaine and crack, and amphetamines); (2) depressants (e.g., analgesics, sedatives, alcohol, and antipsychotics); (3) hallucinogens (e.g., LSD, PCP, Ecstasy, peyote, mescaline, and psilocybin); (4) cannabis (e.g., marijuana and hashish); (5) steroids (e.g., androgenic and anabolic); and (6) prescription drugs. Macionis's classification system places cannabis in its own category of drug, a practice employed by many sociologists and the DECP, but not by CEIDA.

Taking into consideration the strengths and weaknesses of the drug classification schemes described above, I have developed my own categorical listing of commonly used drugs. My scheme includes the following eight categories of drugs: stimulants, depressants, hallucinogens, narcotics, inhalants, cannabis, performance-enhancing drugs, and prescription drugs.

As we examine each category of drugs, we will also look at drug use and drug abuse. Drug use simply refers to the act of a person taking a particular drug. People may use drugs legally or illegally. Some people abuse the drugs they consume. Ramachandra and associates (2012) define **drug abuse** as "persistent or sporadic excessive drug use with or without acceptable medical practice. Thus, the intentional use of excessive doses, or the intentional use of therapeutic doses for purposes other than the indication for which the drug was prescribed" (p. 593). A **drug abuser** then, would be a person who consumes drugs beyond the prescribed allotment or who endangers themselves or the public safety and welfare of others (Catalano 2009).

We begin our look at the different types of drugs, their use, and their abuse by examining stimulants.

Stimulants

Stimulants are drugs that increase alertness, accelerate heart rate, elevate the blood pressure, and speed up or overstimulate the user's body by increasing one's energy level. Because achievement and success are so highly valued in the United States, many Americans consume stimulants. Some stimulants are legal, while others are not. Examples of stimulants are discussed below.

Caffeine

Caffeine is a stimulant substance found naturally in more than 60 plants, including coffee beans, tea leaves, kola nuts (cola), and cacao pods used to make chocolate products. Man-made caffeine may be added to soft drinks, foods, and medicines that make the user feel more awake. Caffeine is the most widely used and generally the safest psychoactive drug consumed by people. A **psychoactive drug** is a chemical substance that acts primarily upon the central nervous system, where it alters the perceptions, cognition, and/or moods of people who take it. Many of these substances (especially stimulants and depressants) can be habit forming, cause chemical dependency, and may lead to substance abuse.

The FDA (2007) estimates that 90 percent of people in the world use caffeine in one form or another. In the United States, 80 percent of adults consume caffeine every day with the average adult consuming 200 milligrams daily—the amount found in two 5-ounce cups of coffee or 4 sodas. While caffeine's main effect on your body is to heighten alertness and help you feel more awake, it can also cause a number of problems, including make you jittery and shaky; contribute to irritability, depression, and diarrhea; cause trouble falling asleep and staying asleep; make the heart beat faster; cause an uneven heart rhythm; raise blood pressure; cause headaches, nervousness, and/or dizziness; cause dehydration (especially after a workout); and cause dependency. That some people become addicted and dependent on caffeine is illustrated by such common expressions as "I can't get going without my morning coffee" or "Don't talk to me until I've had my coffee." Expressions such as these are a clear sign of chemical dependency.

In recent years it has become fairly common for manufacturers to add high amounts of caffeine to a variety of products. The FDA is especially concerned about powdered pure caffeine (in some cases sold in bulk bags over the Internet) being marketed directly to consumers. "These products are essentially 100 percent caffeine. A single teaspoon of pure caffeine is roughly equivalent to the amount in 25 cups of coffee. Pure caffeine is a powerful stimulant and very small amounts may cause accidental overdose" (FDA 2014).

Many people need coffee to start their day.

Nicotine

While caffeine is considered one of the safest psychoactive drugs, nicotine is among the most dangerous. **Nicotine** is a toxic colorless or yellowish oily liquid alkaloid, water-soluble, and is the chief active ingredient of tobacco. It acts as a stimulant in small doses but in larger amounts blocks the action of autonomic nerve and skeletal muscle cells. It is also valued as an insecticide. Nicotine, consumed primarily via tobacco products, is legal in the United States and almost everywhere else in the world, but one has to wonder why. It is a bit ironic that two of the most dangerous drugs in the world—nicotine and alcohol—are both legal, while other, much safer drugs (e.g., cannabis) are illegal. Among the simplest explanations for the legality of tobacco products is the fact that it has long served as a cash crop since the time Europeans settled in what is now the United States. The undeniable power of the tobacco industry is revealed in both the economic and political arenas. For decades, especially in the 1950s and 1960s, tobacco was portrayed positively in television and feature films. It seemed like all the coolest characters smoked cigarettes or cigars. Today, that perception has changed nearly 180 degrees as smokers are generally viewed in a negative, deviant light. This perception has changed because we are well aware of the harmful effects of smoking tobacco products. As a result, the number of smokers has decreased. (To learn more about the harmful effects of smoking cigarettes see box 8.1.)

A man smokes a cigarette despite the health risks.

A CLOSER LOOK

Box 8.1 The Harmful Effects of Smoking Cigarettes

There are an estimated 42.1 million adults in the United States currently smoking cigarettes, and most of them can expect a premature death as a result of their addiction. Cigarette smoking is the leading cause of preventable disease and death in the United States, accounting for more than 480,000 deaths every year, or 1 of every 5 deaths (CDC 2015h). To put this statistic in another form, if your Deviance class met for 1 hour today, more than 50 Americans died because of tobacco use while you were in class. Tobacco itself is not so harmful; it's the more than 7,000 chemicals, including hundreds that are toxic and about 70 that can cause cancer, that are added to tobacco (primarily to increase the addictive properties of tobacco) that make smoking so harmful (CDC 2015i).

More than 16 million Americans are afflicted with a smoking-related disease. Cardiovascular diseases (heart disease, hypertension, and stroke) cause the largest number of smoking-related deaths, followed by various cancers (e.g., lung and throat); respiratory diseases (e.g., chronic airway obstruction, pneumonia, bronchitis, and emphysema); and other causes, such as burn deaths.

Nearly half of all nonsmoking Americans are regularly exposed to secondhand smoke (Surgeon General 2006). Secondhand smoke (SHS) is smoke from burning tobacco products, such as cigarettes, cigars, or pipes, and the smoke that has been exhaled, or breathed out, by the person smoking (CDC 2015i). Since 1964, approximately 2.5 million nonsmokers have died from health problems caused by exposure to SHS (CDC 2015i). In children, SHS causes the following: ear infections; more frequent and severe asthma attacks; respiratory symptoms (e.g., coughing, sneezing, and shortness of breath); respiratory infections (bronchitis and pneumonia); and a greater risk for sudden infant death syndrome (SIDS). In adults who have never smoked, SHS can cause heart disease, lung cancer, and stroke (CDC 2015i).

Recently, a number of smokers have switched from traditional cigarettes to electronic cigarettes (e-cigarettes). E-cigarettes are battery-powered devices (e.g., personal vaporizers) that produce an odorless vapor that typically contains nicotine and flavorings. At this point, there is very little conclusive evidence about the pros and con of e-smoking. E-smokers believe that vaping (the process of smoking via an electronic vaporizer) is healthier than traditional smoking. Other potential benefits include the monetary savings with e-smoking versus traditional smoking; the lack of secondhand smoke; and the ability to avoid some smoking bans. Among the cons of e-smoking are the realization that e-smoking is not healthy, even if it may be safer than traditional smoking; e-cigarette powered batteries have been know to explode while in use; e-cigarettes don't taste as good as traditional cigarettes; lack of e-cigarette regulation (meaning smokers have no true idea what e-liquid manufacturers have conjured up); and the concern over the growing popularity of e-cigarettes with underage smokers. In a 2015 study, it was revealed that traditional smoking has decreased among high school students (from 13 percent to 9.2 percent), but e-smoking had increased to 13 percent (Associated Press 2015b).

The deadly effects of tobacco are certainly not limited to the United States. According to WHO (2015e), tobacco is the second major cause of death in the world, killing nearly 6 million people each year. It is estimated that this figure could reach 8 million by 2030. Nearly 80 percent of the world's 1 billion smokers live in low- and middle-income countries. "In some countries, children from poor households are frequently employed in tobacco farming to provide family income. These children are especially vulnerable to 'green tobacco sickness,' which is caused by the nicotine that is absorbed through the skin from the handling of wet tobacco leaves" (WHO 2015e). As found in the United States, SHS is also a significant killer of nonsmokers around the world.

If we examine the demographics of cigarette smokers, we find that today nearly 18 of every 100 U.S. adults aged 18 or older (17.8 percent) currently smoke cigarettes (CDC 2015h). By gender, more men (20.5 percent) than women (15.3 percent) smoke. By age, those aged 25 to 44 (20.1 percent) are the most likely to smoke, followed by those aged 45 to 64 (19.9 percent), those aged 18 to 24 (18.7 percent), and those aged 65 and older (8.8 percent) the least likely to smoke (by this age, many cigarette smokers have died). By race/ethnicity, the highest percentage of smokers are non-Hispanic multiple race individuals (26.8 percent); non-Hispanic American Indians/Alaska Natives (26.2 percent); non-Hispanic whites (19.4 percent); non-Hispanic blacks (18.3 percent); Hispanics (12.1 percent); and non-Hispanic Asians (9.6 percent). By education, those with a high school graduate education (GED) certificate had the highest percentage of smokers (41.4 percent); those without a high school diploma (24.2 percent); high school diploma (22.0 percent); some college, no degree (20.9 percent); associate's degree (17.8 percent); undergraduate degree (9.1 percent); and those with a graduate degree (5.6 percent) the least likely to smoke. Those living below the poverty level (29.2 percent) are more likely to smoke than those adults who live at or above the poverty level (16.2 percent). People living in the Midwest have the highest percentage of smokers (20.5 percent), followed by the South (19.2 percent); the Northeast (16.9 percent); and the West (13.6 percent). LGBT adults (26.6 percent) have a higher percentage of smokers than straight adults (17.6 percent) (CDC 2015h).

Cocaine/Crack Cocaine

While cocaine certainly has a more deviant image, the negative effects of cocaine and crack cocaine, like every other drug to be discussed in this chapter, pale in comparison to tobacco. However, unlike tobacco products, cocaine and crack cocaine are illegal in the United States, as with most nations across the globe. It is interesting to note, however, that cocaine, which wasn't illegal in the United States until 1914, was an original ingredient in Coca-Cola from circa 1885 until 1906 (Hamblin 2013). Coca-Cola was promoted as a "medicinal" product because of the stimulant properties of cocaine.

Cocaine (commonly called "coke") is a white powder that can be snorted up the nose, mixed with water and injected with a needle, or sprinkled on a joint or cigarette and smoked. When cocaine is mixed with either ammonia or sodium bicarbonate (baking soda) in a glass beaker, it can be "cooked" (boiled) into a solid, cooled, dried, and cut up into small pieces/nuggets, known as "rocks." These rocks, which are usually white or tan in color, are known as crack cocaine. The cooking process clears out most of the impurities (the "cut" added to the powder

Two young women snort lines of cocaine.

cocaine by dealers to increase the quantity of the product) in cocaine, making it nearly pure cocaine. Naturally, the user gets a much more intense high from crack cocaine than powder cocaine.

Cocaine was quite popular among recreational drug users, especially wealthy ones, in the 1970s and 1980s and was known as the "rich man's high" because of how expensive it was (generally $100 per gram). Eric Clapton's 1977 song "Cocaine" (originally released by J. J. Cale in 1976) described the popularity of the drug in the mid-1970s. Crack cocaine, meanwhile, which is sold by the rock (a small chunk of solid cocaine), was much cheaper and popular with street drug users and was all the rage in the 1980s. The stiffer penalties for crack cocaine use led to repeated claims of racism, as minorities were far more likely to use crack cocaine than whites. A popular accessory for the cocaine user of the 1970s was a decorative coke spoon necklace. Those "in the know" knew what this piece of jewelry meant, while others were oblivious. The coke spoon necklace gave people a chance to flaunt their deviancy.

Cocaine gives users a euphoric lift, a heightened sense of alertness and energy, and a feeling of confidence and mental sharpness. Depending on its route of administration (snorted or injected), the user feels the effects within 15 to 30 minutes but the "high" is short-lived, leaving the user wanting to do more to regain the original high. This leads to prolonged use and a slew of negative effects that may include paranoia, hallucinations, sleeplessness, weight loss, irritability, anxiety, panic, and depression. Users may also experience tremors, vertigo, and muscle twitches. Cardiovascular effects may include disturbances in heart rhythm and heart attacks; neurological effects may include strokes, seizures, headaches, and coma; and gastrointestinal complications may include abdominal pain and nausea.

Most of the cocaine found in the United States is smuggled in from South American nations such as Colombia, Bolivia, and Peru through Mexico and across the American border. Cocaine is the second most trafficked illegal drug in the world (behind marijuana). More than 756 metric tons have been intercepted in South America and North America (Foundation for a Drug-Free World 2015b). Currently, cocaine is the second most commonly used illegal drug in Europe. It remains relatively common in the United States (although nowhere near its popularity in the 1970s and 1980s) with 6.9 percent of Americans aged 18 to 25 surveyed reporting that they had used cocaine, or crack, at least once in the last year (Foundation for a Drug-Free World 2015b).

Methylphenidate (Ritalin), Amphetamines, and Methamphetamines ("Crank")

Among other stimulants worth mentioning are Ritalin, amphetamines, and methamphetamine ("crank"). *Ritalin* is the brand name for methylphenidate and is a legal drug used by doctors to treat children with attention-deficit hyperactivity disorder (ADHD). Nearly 5 percent of U.S. children are described as having ADHD, but critics believe that many children are simply "acting as children" and are not hyperactive to the point of needing medication. Some teenagers take excessive amounts of Ritalin (or take it as a recreational drug) because of its stimulant effects. (Its recreational popularity has led to such street names for Ritalin as "the poor man's cocaine," Skittles, vitamin R, kiddie cocaine, R-ball, and Diet Coke.) However, "even when used as a prescription drug, it may have severe effects including nervousness, insomnia, anorexia, loss of appetite, pulse changes, heart problems and weight loss. The manufacturer says it is a drug of dependency" (Foundation for a Drug-Free World 2015c). The FDA (2013) reports that methylphenidate products may, in rare instances, cause prolonged and sometimes painful erections, known as priapism. If not treated right away, priapism can lead to permanent damage to the penis. Preteens, teens, and adult males who take methylphenidate are all at a minimal risk for priapism.

Amphetamines are a group of synthetic psychoactive CNS stimulants prescribed to children, adolescents, or adults diagnosed with ADHD. Adderall is among the more popular amphetamines. Amphetamines are used to suppress appetite, increase wakefulness, and increase focus and attention. However, like methylphenidates, amphetamines are often used recreationally because they may produce feelings of euphoria due to the fact that they increase dopamine levels in the brain—dopamine is a neurotransmitter associated with pleasure, movement, and attention (National Institute on Drug Abuse 2014b). When used recreationally to gain euphoric effects, amphetamine pills are crushed and then snorted or mixed with water and injected.

Methamphetamines (also called meth, crystal, ice, crank, MDMA, Ecstasy, and Molly) are extremely addictive synthetic stimulant drugs that are chemically similar to amphetamines. They take the form of either a white, odorless, bitter-tasting crystalline powder or as capsules or tablets. Methamphetamines are illegal drugs used by individuals of all ages, but certain variations—known as "club drugs"—are especially popular with teens and young adults. Club drugs, such as MDMA, popularly known as Ecstasy, and more recently as Molly (slang for "molecular"), are taken in capsule or tablet form. The attractiveness of club drugs is directly tied to their ability to give users prolonged energy (approximately three to six hours) that allows for a full night of partying at night clubs or "raves." "The surge of serotonin caused by taking MDMA depletes the brain of this important chemical, however, causing negative aftereffects—including confusion, depression, sleep problems, drug craving, and anxiety—that may occur soon after taking the drug or during the days or even weeks thereafter" (NIDA 2013). Other methamphetamines, such as meth and crank, are taken orally, smoked, snorted, or dissolved in water or alcohol and injected. Like amphetamines, crystal meth also stimulates the release of dopamine, which provides the user with the experience of pleasure and produces immediate and intense euphoria. However, because the crash is equally quick, users often repeat the process of "binge and crash" (NIDA 2014c).

Crystal meth has a particularly deviant aura surrounding its manufacture, distribution, sale, and consumption. Because it is a synthetic drug and relatively easy to make, many inexperienced people participate in the "cooking" of meth. People have set up labs inside their homes and apartments, in their garages, and even in their vans (mobile, or transportable, laboratories). In many cases, because people are acting as amateur chemists, these labs blow up, injuring those cooking the meth or innocent neighbors. Chances are, you've heard news reports about such incidents. Rarely, however, do you hear of people being praised or admired for producing methamphetamine, but such is the case with the popular former TV show *Breaking Bad*. To learn more about *Breaking Bad* and its, more or less, positive portrayal of cooking meth, see box 8.2.

CONNECTING SOCIAL DEVIANCE AND POPULAR CULTURE

Box 8.2 Cooking Meth with a High School Chemistry Teacher: The Saga of *Breaking Bad*

Breaking Bad was a very popular TV show that aired on AMC for five seasons from January 2008 to September 2013. It remains popular in syndication and on certain streaming sites (e.g., Netflix). The show is about a high school chemistry teacher, Walter White (played by Bryan Cranston), who is diagnosed with inoperable lung cancer. Worried about how his family will survive financially without him, White and one of his former students, Jesse Pinkman (Aaron Paul), decide to turn to a life of crime centered on cooking and selling methamphetamine. (In season one, White learns that Pinkman had experience with meth.) The show is set and was filmed in Albuquerque, New Mexico. Among the regular characters are White's wife Skyler (Anna Gunn) and children Flynn (R.J. Mitte) and Holly (Elanor Anne Wenrich), and Skyler's sister Marie Schrader (Betsy Brandt) and her husband Hank (Dean Norris), who also happens to be a DEA agent.

The series begins with a relatively naïve White trying to learn the ropes of creating meth, something he knows he's capable of because he is a chemistry teacher, to trusting Pinkman to join him and then learning how to sell the drug, without drawing suspicion, and of course, without getting caught. In season two, White's bills continue to skyrocket, so they produce more and more meth. As the series progresses, so too does White's prowess to cook meth. They build their clientele numbers to the point where they are cutting into the profits of other drug dealers. They now have a territory,

and their territory must be protected. The Walter White character becomes increasingly darker and ethically questionable. It becomes difficult for the audience to "cheer" for White, a man who started cooking meth to take care of his family—something many people can relate to—as he has, essentially, developed into a morally bankrupt person.

As the show was airing original episodes, its popularity was undeniable. Real-life chemists (e.g., Donna Nelson, a professor of organic chemistry at the University of Oklahoma) reviewed scripts, provided dialogue, and examined the accuracy of the "cooking" formulas. By the seventh season of the show, White had to create a different synthetic formula because of the difficulty of acquiring enough pseudoephedrine to produce large-scale amounts of meth. This storyline reflects the real-life difficulty of purchasing the formerly over-the-counter cold medicine Sudafed. A person wishing to purchase this medicine (and any other drug product containing pseudoephedrine, ephedrine, and phenylpropanolamine) is now only allowed a certain amount over a certain period time. It is also necessary to show ID to the pharmacist working behind the counter (FDA 2015b).

No spoilers here, but suffice it to say, *Breaking Bad* was among the most successful and popular cable television shows of all time. Critics applauded the show as well, as *Breaking Bad* was nominated and won numerous awards, including Primetime Emmy Awards and Outstanding Drama Series in 2013 and 2014.

Depressants

While stimulants are known collectively as "uppers" because they provide the user with a lift in energy, depressants are known collectively as "downers" because they have the opposite effect. **Depressants**, then, are drugs that sedate neurotransmission levels; they depress or lower the vital activities of the central nervous system. The most common and popular depressant is alcohol, which was reviewed extensively in chapter 7. Other popular depressants include analgesics, sedatives, antipsychotics (antianxiety tranquilizers), and antidepressants.

Analgesics

Analgesics are pain relievers, including over-the-counter depressants such as aspirin, ibuprofen (Motrin and Advil), and acetaminophen (Tylenol, Paracetamol, and Panadol). Effective relief from minor aches and pains can be achieved with analgesics. Each type of pain reliever has benefits and risks, and some variations work for some people but not for others. Aspirin works by reducing substances in the body that cause pain, fever, and inflammation. However, people with bleeding disorders or a recent history of stomach or intestinal bleeding, stomach ulcers, liver disease, kidney disease, heart disease, or gout should not use aspirin. It is sometimes used to prevent heart attacks, strokes, and chest pain (angina). Ibuprofen treats minor aches and pains caused by the common cold, headaches, toothaches, backaches, or muscle aches. Ibuprofen may, however, cause ulcers, bleeding, or holes in the stomach or intestine. Acetaminophen is a non-aspirin pain reliever for those who cannot take aspirin and is used to relieve fever and headaches and other common aches and pains. It does not relieve inflammation, but it does not cause as many stomach problems as other pain medicines do. It is also safer for children. Acetaminophen is often recommended for arthritis pain because it has fewer side effects than other pain medicines (U.S. National Library of Medicine 2015a).

Sedatives

Sedatives are CNS depressants that slow normal brain function by affecting the neurotransmitter gamma-aminobutyric acid (GABA). By decreasing brain activity, sedatives produce a relaxing effect that is beneficial to those suffering from anxiety or sleep disorders. Among the common sedatives prescribed for this purpose are barbiturates (e.g., Mebaral and Nembutal), which are helpful in treating anxiety, tension, and sleep disorders, and benzodiazepines, such as diazepam (Valium, Librium, and Xanax), which can be prescribed to treat anxiety, acute stress reactions, and panic attacks (*Psychology Today* 2014). Despite the many potential benefits of sedatives such as barbiturates and benzodiazepines, there are numerous possible side effects: the user initially feeling drowsy, uncoordinated, and depressed; the body is likely to develop a tolerance, thus requiring larger doses to achieve the same initial effects; continued use can lead to physical dependency, and withdrawal when use is lessened or stopped; and because the brain's workings have been reduced, when the user stops taking the medication, their brain may race out of control, possibly leading to seizures and harmful consequences, including death (*Psychology Today* 2014).

A sedative that most college students have heard of, and have been warned about, is Rohypnol. Rohypnol (known as "Quaaludes of the '90s," Mexican Valium, forget-me pill, roche, rope, and "roofies") is the brand name for a drug called flunitrazepam, a powerful sedative that depresses the CNS. Rohypnol is manufactured in Mexico, South America, Europe, and Asia and is prescribed for insomnia. Rohypnol comes in pill form but is usually crushed into a powder to snort, sprinkled on marijuana and smoked, dissolved in a drink, or injected. Like other benzodiazepines, Rohypnol's effects include sedation, muscle relaxation, reduction in anxiety, and prevention of convulsions. "However, Rohypnol's sedative effects are approximately 7 to 10 times stronger than Valium. The effects of Rohypnol appear 15 to 20 minutes after administration and last approximately four to six hours" (Drugs.com 2015). It is because of these side effects that Rohypnol has the infamous nickname of the "date rape drug." Unscrupulous persons will place Rohypnol—which is not approved for medical use or manufactured in the United States and is not available legally—unknowingly in the drinks of victims, often at a bar or party, and then take the person to some location and take advantage of them. Because of the strong amnesia produced by the drug, victims have limited or no recollection of the assault.

Antipsychotics (Major Tranquilizers)

Antipsychotics, including lithium and haloperidol, are medications that affect neurotransmitters that allow communication between nerve cells in order to treat people suffering from psychosis (e.g., delusions, hallucinations, or disordered thought), schizophrenia, and bipolar disorder. Dopamine—which is involved with how we feel—is the main neurotransmitter affected by these medications. Antipsychotics are also involved in the control of muscle movements. In the past, these medications were known as "major tranquilizers," but today they are not designed to make the patient calmer or sleepy; the basic aim is to help you feel better, without making you feel slowed down or drowsy—even though high doses will make the user feel "drugged up" (Royal College of Psychiatrists 2015). Antipsychotics have been shown to be effective in treating most personality disorders (especially schizophrenia), but they do come with some potential serious side effects depending on the potency and dosage prescribed and whether or not the patient follows proper prescription directions. Most side effects are mild, however, including drowsiness, rapid heartbeat, and dizziness when moving around.

Antidepressants

Antidepressants, such as Zoloft and Prozac, are drugs used for the treatment of depression or to prevent it from recurring. Antidepressants may not cure depression, but they can reduce the symptoms of depression. The medical profession currently believes that depression can be triggered by a lack of the chemical serotonin and, as a result, antidepressants are essentially designed to increase or maintain higher levels of serotonin in the brain to correct the deficiency. The current class of antidepressant medications are known as selective serotonin reuptake inhibitors (SSRIs) and include such brand names as Prozac and Zoloft. Despite great competition, Prozac and its generic equivalents remain very popular in the United States with more than 24.4 million Americans with such prescriptions in 2010 (DrugWatch.com 2015). Zoloft is used to treat depression, obsessive-compulsive disorder, panic disorder, anxiety disorders, posttraumatic stress disorder (PTSD), and premenstrual dysphoric disorder (PMDD).

Among the possible side effects of antidepressants are sexual dysfunction, dry mouth, nausea, headache, diarrhea, nervousness, restlessness, agitation, increased sweating, weight gain, insomnia, drowsiness, probability of dependency, and withdrawal symptoms if treatment ends too quickly or abruptly. In 2004, the FDA issued a public warning that extended Prozac use could lead to increased suicidal thoughts and behavior (DrugWatch.com 2015). Prozac is not the only antidepressant that has been linked to suicidal thoughts and actions by its users; Zoloft and most other SSRIs have also been linked to such a side effect.

Hallucinogens

Hallucinogens are a category of drugs that cause the user to perceive things differently than they actually are. Hallucinogens are also known as psychedelics, a term that refers to "mind vision" and a profound sense of intensified sensory perception. People who consume hallucinogens might have hallucinations that can range from extremely pleasurable visions and distortions of reality to frightening distortions that cause despair and great anxiety. Hallucinogens come in both synthetic and natural forms.

Synthetic Hallucinogens

The first and perhaps most popularly known synthetic hallucinogen is LSD (lysergic acid diethylamide). LSD was first synthesized (as lysergic acid) in the 1930s by a Swiss chemist named Albert Hofmann. In 1938, Hofmann derived the 25th version of his lysergic acid, lysergic acid diethylamide, or LSD-25. He thought it might help stimulate breathing and circulation, but test results did not confirm his belief. However, over the years, a number of psychiatrists ran experiments with LSD-25 and by 1960, there had been hundreds of papers published in scientific and medical journals on the various uses of LSD. Among the earliest claims about LSD was the idea that the drug did not give people hallucinations (seeing things that are not really there), but rather people saw real things that were there differently because their perceptions of reality were altered by LSD (Freeman 2015). The reality is people on LSD and other hallucinogens can have both hallucinations and altered perceptions.

In the 1960s, a decade known for many things, including the hippie, free-love, and pro-drug culture, LSD-25 took on an entirely new role. Harvard professor Timothy Leary was promoting the benefits of LSD-25 and ran a research program known as the Harvard Psilocybin Project. The goal of the research project was to test the effects of psilocybin on human subjects (first prisoners and then students) from a synthesized version of the then-legal drug. As the years went by, Leary became associated with the counterculture movement by promoting such mantras as "turn on, tune in, drop out" (turn on to LSD, tune in to its effects, and drop out of conventional society), "set and setting" (a reference to the importance of taking LSD-25 in the proper setting in order to enhance the positive experience of LSD-25), and "think for yourself and question authority" (the "question authority" slogan was popularized by Leary). Leary would leave Harvard for UC Berkeley in time for the height of the Haight-Ashbury hippie movement in 1968. Leary became notorious in the recreational drug world as the LSD-25 guru. For many years (especially throughout the 1970s) it was relatively popular for college students to turn on to LSD-25 as a means of trying to find enlightenment by tapping into a part of the brain inaccessible by conventional (nonpsychedelic) means—or so was the belief among users.

LSD (also known as acid, blotter, tabs, microdots, window panes, and trips) is sold in tablet, capsule, and occasionally in liquid form; thus, it is generally taken orally. Sometimes the synthetic liquid form of LSD is placed on a thin, small piece of blotter paper that the user then places on their tongue. When people take LSD, their experiences are referred to as "trips." A pleasurable experience is a "good trip," while an unpleasant experience is a "bad trip." As previously mentioned, *the setting* of the LSD experience is a critical factor in whether or not the user is going to have a good or bad trip. Trips can last up to 12 hours (NIDA 2014d). Among the side effects of LSD use are feelings of euphoria, enlightenment, visual hallucinations, impaired depth perception, fear of losing control, panic attacks, terrifying thoughts and feelings, flashbacks (from trips taken years before), sleeplessness, and dry mouth.

Generally, the ideal setting for the LSD user involves a controlled environment that includes close friends (especially if they are also on LSD) and preferred comforts such as proper mood lighting, favorite music, and little interaction with others (who could possibly jeopardize the positive trip). With the importance of the setting in mind, imagine a Major League Baseball player pitching while on LSD. Would that be an example of deviant behavior? In a story retold many times in the sports world, Pittsburgh Pirates pitcher Dock Ellis not only pitched on June 12, 1970, while on LSD, he hurled a no-hitter. A no-hitter itself is difficult enough, but to pitch a no-hitter in front of tens of thousands of people, teammates, and opposing players, this was some feat. Years later, in *No No: A Dockumentary* (2014), Ellis described how he thought he scored a *touchdown* during the *baseball* game. "I was as high as a Georgia pine," Ellis stated (Nashawaty 2014).

PCP (phencyclidine) is another popular form of a synthetic hallucinogen. Originally developed in the 1950s as a general anesthetic for surgery (it has since been discontinued due to serious adverse effects), PCP can be found in a variety of forms including tablets or capsules, and is sold as a liquid or powder. PCP (also know as ozone, rocket fuel, and angel dust) can be snorted, smoked, injected, or swallowed. When it is sprinkled on a joint (marijuana cigarette), it is referred to as a "duster." It can also be sprinkled on tobacco and smoked. Depending on its route of administration, PCP's effects can last approximately four to six hours. PCP is known to give users a sense of euphoria that makes them feel bigger than life. If the PCP user becomes violent, a possible side effect, they become very difficult to control. Law enforcement officers in particular have a hard time dealing with people who commit crimes while high on PCP. Agitation, delusions, euphoria, intense anger, sedation, irrational thinking, and mood swings are among the side effects of PCP use.

Natural Hallucinogens

There are a number of natural sources of hallucinogens, including psilocybin ("magic mushrooms," shrooms), peyote (mescaline), DMT (dimethyltryptamine), and ayahuasca (hoasca, aya, and yage). Psilocybin (4-phosphoryloxy-N) is extracted from certain types of mushrooms found in tropical and subtropical regions of South America, Mexico, and the United States. These mushrooms typically contain less than 0.5 percent psilocybin plus trace amounts of psilocin, another hallucinogenic substance (NIDA 2014d). Psilocybin can either be dried or fresh and eaten raw, mixed with food, or brewed into a tea, and produces similar effects to LSD (NIDA 2015a). Psilocybin may be ingested during religious ceremonies by indigenous cultures in the Americas, but they are consumed mostly by people for recreational purposes. However, by 2010, scientists were regularly conducting experiments involving psilocybin as a means of treating depression. Retired clinical psychologist Clark Martin is among the volunteers who have taken part in the psychedelic clinical trials. Martin suffered depression after going through chemotherapy and other grueling regimens for kidney cancer. He credits the six-hour experience with helping him overcome his depression and profoundly transforming his relationships with his daughter and friends (Tierney 2010). The results have been positive for all volunteers, but the researchers are playing it cautiously because "they do not want to repeat the mistakes of the 1960s, when some scientists-turned-evangelists exaggerated their understanding of the drugs' risks and benefits" (Tierney 2010). In an attempt to assure a positive "trip" the researchers, following developed guidelines, create a setting to assure a comfortable environment with monitors in the room to address patient issues should they arise. As for Martin, he put on an eye mask and headphones and lay on a couch listening to classical music as he contemplated the universe (Tierney 2010).

Peyote (also known as buttons, cactus, and mesc) is a small, spineless cactus in which the principal active ingredient is mescaline. This plant has been used by indigenous people in northern Mexico and southwestern United States as part of religious ceremonies. The peyote plant is revered by some Native Americans as "the flesh of God" (Sahagun 1994). The Native American Church in the United States and Canada is the only group authorized by federal authorities to ingest peyote—which is considered a divine gift, a sacrament consumed to focus worshippers' prayers to the Creator (Sahagun 1994). The top, or "crown," of the peyote cactus has disc-shaped buttons that are cut out, dried, and usually chewed or soaked in water to produce an intoxicating liquid. Because the extract has such a bitter taste, some users prepare a tea by boiling the plant for several hours (NIDA 2015a). Mescaline can also be produced through chemical synthesis.

DMT is a powerful hallucinogenic found naturally in some Amazonian plant species and can also be synthesized in the laboratory. Ayahuasca is a hallucinogenic brew made from one of several Amazonian plants containing DMT along with a vine containing a natural alkaloid that prevents the normal breakdown of DMT in the digestive tract. Ayahuasca tea has traditionally been used for healing and religious purposes in indigenous South American cultures, mainly in the Amazon region (NIDA 2015a).

A peyote cactus.

Perhaps one of the more unusual ways of getting high on a hallucinogen is toad smoking. In the mid-1990s, toad smoking had become quite a craze. Toad smoking involves grabbing a Sonoran Desert toad and squeezing the glands near the eyes. Shortly thereafter, the glands pop and out oozes a milky substance with the consistency of rubber cement and a chemical makeup similar to LSD. You let the blob dry on glass, cut off a piece, stuff it into a pipe, and light up (Banks 1994). While the entire process may sound gross (and one has to wonder, who was the person that discovered this method of getting high?), it is important to note that the toxin this particular species of toad produces—bufotenine—is listed as a controlled substance with the California Department of Justice (Shoales 1994). In February 1994 a California man was arrested for smoking the toad venom. Referred to as a "toad toker," the man told police that he could hear "electrons jumping orbitally in his molecules" (Shoales 1994). In March 1994, two Sonora, California, people were arrested for possessing desert toad venom (*Las Vegas Review-Journal* 3/2/94).

As if toad smoking wasn't odd enough, another mid-1990s craze involving southwestern amphibians was "frog licking." The skin of a brightly colored Ecuadoran frog holds a powerful painkiller—epibatidine—that works without the addictive side effect of narcotics like morphine, researchers and recreational drug users have found (*Las Vegas Review-Journal* 4/27/94). Low doses of epibatidine are more potent than morphine in blocking pain in mice in clinical studies. In a 1994 episode of *Beavis and Butt-Head* the Butt-Head character is shown devouring a toad in an unsuccessful attempt to get high (Shoales 1994). *The Simpsons* also had an episode (2009) in which Homer Simpson licks a toad to get high. In a separate episode, the Lenny character also licks a toad and gets high.

Are toad smoking and frog licking deviant? What do you think? What other life-forms found in nature could possibly provide humans with an opportunity to get high?

Narcotics

Narcotics (also known as opioid pain relievers, opioids, painkillers, and analgesics) are drugs designed to help people who are experiencing severe pain. When used carefully and under a doctor's direct care, narcotics can be very effective at reducing pain. Narcotics work by binding to receptors in the brain, which blocks the feeling of pain (U.S. National Library of Medicine 2015b). In addition to blocking pain, narcotics induce euphoria and create mood changes in the user (DECP 2015). Narcotics can be abused, are highly addictive, and may lead to accidental overdose deaths. Among the side effects of narcotics are drowsiness, impaired judgment, nausea or vomiting, and withdrawal symptoms (e.g., craving for the drug, yawning, insomnia, restlessness, mood swings, and diarrhea) when the user attempts to stop using narcotic drugs (U.S. National Library of Medicine 2015b).

Narcotics are derived from one of nature's most addictive plants, opium poppies. The poppy plant, *Papaver somniferum*, produces opium, a powerful narcotic whose derivatives include morphine, methadone, Vicodin, codeine, heroin, and oxycodone. The poppy alkaloid morphine was isolated in 1804 by German pharmacist Friedrich Serturner, who dubbed the alkaloid *morphium* after Morpheus, the Greek god of dreams, for its capacity to induce sleep (Kilham 2013). Oxycodone is a semisynthetic narcotic analgesic and, like other narcotics, is prescribed for moderate to severe pain, chronic pain syndromes, and terminal cancers. While there are scores of oxycodone products on the market, OxyContin has generated the greatest attention both because of its general effectiveness and abuse (Inciardi and Goode 2010).

Medical Use Narcotics

Narcotics, as described above, are designed to be used in the treatment of pain while supervised by medical professionals. Morphine, methadone, Vicodin, and oxycodone (i.e., OxyContin), are all among the typical narcotics prescribed by doctors for patients suffering from moderate to severe pain. Each of these narcotics can be highly effective in relieving patient pain, but they are all potentially addictive and may cause breathing problems and behavioral changes. Narcotics are not limited to hospital use (inpatient), as many people may be prescribed such drugs for home recovery or treatment (outpatient). Medical use narcotics all run a high risk for addiction and abuse. If the dose is reduced, or if the user attempts to quit using the narcotic, withdrawal is quite possible. Common morphine side effects may include drowsiness, dizziness, constipation, stomach pain, nausea, vomiting, headaches, tired feeling, anxiety, and/or mild itching.

Opium and Heroin

As narcotics, heroin and opium have medical purposes, and in some countries such as the United Kingdom, India, and Turkey, heroin is available as a controlled prescription drug. Most narcotics, in fact, are derived from opium poppies. "Of all plants used in the field of medicine, none has been as widely employed—nor has helped to save as many lives and ease suffering—as the opium poppy, *Papaver somniferum*. The plant and its derivatives have been used since antiquity . . . and remnants of opium date back as far as 10,000 years" (Kilham 2013). Opium is an addictive narcotic drug that is derived from unripe seedpods of the opium poppy and contains alkaloids such as morphine, codeine, and papverine. While opium-derived products are used legally for medical purposes, opium has a long history of illegal use in the United States. The U.S. Drug Enforcement Agency (DEA) describes illegal opium use as "America's first drug epidemic (1850–1914)" (DEA Museum 2015a). "When Chinese immigrants came to California in the 1850s to work in gold mines and then on the railroads, they brought opium smoking with them. . . . As more and more Americans patronized opium dens and became addicted, communities responded with alarm and concern. . . . By the 1890s, opium dens were commonplace in American life" (DEA Museum 2015a). Opium smoking isn't nearly as popular today. Instead, most illegally grown and distributed opium is converted into heroin.

Heroin is a powerful, highly addictive drug processed from morphine (the opium alkaloid) that is used in the United States primarily as an illegal narcotic powder. Heroin has been around since 1895, when a German pharmaceutical company, Bayer, began selling an over-the-counter pain reliever called Heroin. The name "Heroin" was derived from the German word *heroisch*, or "heroic," to convey the drug's superhuman effects on its user. "Developed as a morphine substitute, Bayer marketed heroin as a 'non-addictive cough suppressant'" (Ralph 2014). That Bayer aspirin's primary ingredient was heroin and that it was promoted as nonaddictive would ultimately embarrass the pharmaceutical company and yet was on par with the promotion of cocaine products in that same era—cocaine was an original ingredient in Coca-Cola (with its label description of "Intellectual Beverage"), and pain relievers such as "Cocaine Toothache Drops" (Hamblin 2013; DEA Museum 2015a) were readily available, over-the-counter medicines.

Despite a great deal of research throughout the 20th century detailing the addictive and potentially deadly consequences of heroin use, the drug remained relatively popular among the hard-core recreational drug user subculture. Its image as a drug for junkies (because the most effective way to use heroin is intravenous injection coupled with the realization that users often share needles and acquire diseases because they share dirty needles) kept most younger white recreational drug users from using heroin. However, in the 21st century the demographics of the heroin user have changed. "In 2000, the highest death rate from heroin overdoses was in blacks ages 45 to 64. But in 2013, whites ages 18 to 44 had the highest rate. Whites in that age group accounted for more than half of heroin-related overdose deaths that year" (Associated Press 2015c).

There were about 44,000 drug overdose deaths in 2013, and more than 16,000 of them involved narcotics. Of these 16,000 narcotic overdoses, about half were from prescription painkillers such as Vicodin and OxyContin and about 8,200—an average of 23 people each day—died of heroin overdoses (Tonzi 2015; Associated Press 2015c). The heroin overdose numbers are particularly disturbing, as the 2013 figure represents a figure three times higher than in 2010. The shift in demographics of heroin addiction and death is now that of a young, white midwesterner (Associated Press 2015c).

Inhalants

Inhalants include a wide variety of breathable substances (e.g., plastic cement, paint, gasoline, paint thinners, and hair sprays) that produce mind-altering results and effects (DECP 2015). With this description in mind, **inhalants** can be defined as "the wide variety of substances—including solvents, aerosols, gases, and nitrites—that are rarely, if ever, taken via any other route of administration" (NIDA 2012). All sorts of products that most people would never consider sniffing can be used as inhalants. There are home and workplace items such as spray paints, markers, glues, and cleaning fluids—all of which contain volatile substances that have psychoactive (mind-altering) properties when inhaled—that may entice certain people as an acceptable, or affordable, way of getting high. Inhaling some items catches on as a fad. When I was in high school there was a craze of sniffing the cooking spray Pam. This was the same era that young people sniffed ditto sheets—copies made with purple-ink sheets that teachers regularly cranked out on low-tech ditto machines. I can vividly remember teachers giving copies of worksheets to the student in the first seat of each row, who would then pass it to the person sitting behind and so on down the line, but with nearly every kid sniffing the paper before they passed it backward. The ditto machine fluid had excessive amounts of methanol, a highly volatile alcohol with a high odor threshold (meaning that by the time you smelled it, you've already been exposed) (Henry 1995).

High school–age youths are among the most likely age categories of people to abuse inhalants. According to NIDA (2012), among the people most likely to abuse inhalants are new users ages 12 to 15 who commonly abuse glue, shoe polish, spray paints, gasoline, and lighter fluid; while 16- to 17-year-olds most commonly abuse nitrous oxide or "whippets." Adults who abuse inhalants are most likely to take nitrites, such as amyl nitrites or "poppers." Nitrites are generally used by adults because the inhalant is known to enhance sexual pleasure by dilating and relaxing blood vessels. Most other forms of inhalants, however, depress the central nervous system much in the same manner as alcohol. The effects are similar too, including slurred speech, lack of coordination, feelings of euphoria, and dizziness. Inhalant abusers may also experience light-headedness, hallucinations, and delusions. Some users may experience extended periods of drowsiness and a lingering headache. Inhalants can also be deadly. Sniffing highly concentrated amounts of the chemicals in solvents or aerosol sprays can directly cause heart failure within minutes. This syndrome, known as sudden sniffing death, can result from a single session of inhalant use by an otherwise healthy young person (NIDA 2012).

People who regularly use inhalants are often referred to as huffers, and when they abuse inhalants they are said to be **huffing**. Huffers use inhalants by sniffing a product directly through their noses. In some circles, huffing refers to a specific type of inhaling; that is to say, when a chemically soaked rag is held to the face or stuffed in the mouth and the substance is inhaled (Inhalant Abuse Prevention 2012a). Another variation of abuse inhalants is called "bagging." Bagging involves spraying a substance into a plastic or paper bag, placing the bag over the user's head, and sniffing the vapors. This method can result in suffocation because the user's supply of oxygen is cut off. Over 2.6 million children aged 12 to 17 use inhalants each year to get high. One out of 4 American students has intentionally abused a common household product to get high by the time they reach the 8th grade. Sniffing can begin at age 10 or earlier. The number of lives claimed by inhalant abuse is unknown because these types of deaths tend to be attributed to other causes (Inhalant Abuse Prevention 2012b).

Inhalants may not be the first category of drugs that draws the attention of parents, medical professionals, and law enforcement officials, but they likely represent the first foray into future drug abuse for millions of people.

Cannabis

Cannabis is a category of psychoactive drugs that includes three different species, sativa, indica, and ruderalis. Cannabis is the scientific name for marijuana (other names for marijuana include pot, weed, grass, reefer, ganja, and Mary Jane). The active ingredient in cannabis is delta-9 tetrahydrocannabinol, or THC (DECP 2015). Cannabis is a fast-growing plant with dense, sticky flowers that produce the psychoactive THC. Cannabis has a long history of uses, including as hemp fiber and hemp oils; for medical purposes; and as a recreational drug. Marijuana use is very popular; in fact, it is the most commonly used illicit drug in the world. Its popularity makes it the third most prevalent drug in the world behind only alcohol and nicotine (tobacco) (Global Drug Survey 2015; *Huffington Post* 2014). In the United States, marijuana is the most popular recreational drug, and as recently as two decades ago it was described as the "most widely used psychoactive substance in the world" (Daly, Holmen, and Fredholm 1998:5878). Recreational marijuana can be smoked (e.g., rolled in paper, called "joints," or in a pipe, such as a "bong"); consumed as an edible (oral consumption, items such as brownies, candies, and cookies); and vaporized (inhaled as a gas after the marijuana has been processed through a vaporizer).

Marijuana

Marijuana use has a long history, dating back to ancient Mesopotamia, Persia, Egypt, Arabia, China, India, and many parts of Europe (Murrell 2008). The Europeans that settled the New World brought with them cannabis products, and hemp was a cash crop much as tobacco from the 1600s through the early years of the United States. Benjamin Franklin started one of the first American paper mills using hemp. This allowed the United States to produce its own supply of paper free from dependency on England. In the 1930s, the Federal Bureau of Narcotics ran a successful campaign against hemp. The propaganda used against hemp coincided with the legal action of a number of states (i.e., California, 1915; Texas, 1919) that had already outlawed marijuana. U.S. government propaganda movies of the 1930s, including *Teach Your Children* (1936) (better known as *Reefer Madness*); *Devils*

A marijuana bud growing in the wild.

Weed (1936); and *Marijuana: Assassin of Youth* (1937) all attempted to portray marijuana as a narcotic that could cause hallucinations and would corrupt the youth of America. For the past multiple decades, these movies (especially *Reefer Madness*) have been viewed, mostly by pot smokers, as cult films because of their blatant lies and stupidity.

Marijuana's popularity as a recreational drug began in the 1920s, in part because of Prohibition. However, its recreational use was primarily restricted to jazz musicians, their fans, and people in show business. Marijuana clubs, called "tea pads," sprang up in every major city and were ignored or tolerated by authorities because marijuana was not illegal and not considered a social threat. As stated above, the antimarijuana campaign of the 1930s changed the legality and perception of pot. The 1950s–early 1960s "Beat Generation," a counterculture group consisting mostly of literary authors that influenced American culture following World War II, was fond of marijuana and reintroduced its consumption as a pleasurable, recreational drug (PBS 2007). In the 1960s, marijuana became popular with college students and "hippies," and the drug became a symbol of rebellion against authority. Government propaganda once again prevailed with the passage of the Controlled Substances Act of 1970, which classified marijuana along with heroin and LSD as a Schedule 1 drug (meaning that it has the highest abuse potential and no accepted medical use). The United States declared a "war on drugs" in an ill-fated attempt to curb Americans' desires to consume pot and other recreational drugs. Nonetheless, marijuana's popularity as a recreational drug led to a description of "everyone smokes it"—meaning that people from all walks of life and regardless of SES enjoyed partaking in marijuana use.

At present, the laws and legality and the perception of marijuana as an example of deviant behavior are radically different from past generations. In fact, trying to keep information on marijuana up-to-date in a contemporary textbook is a difficult challenge due to the fluid nature of marijuana's legal and medical status. As of June 2015 there were four states, Alaska, Colorado, Oregon, and Washington, and the District of Columbia, where marijuana was legal for recreational purposes and five other states (Nevada, California, Arizona, Maine, and Massachusetts) that were projected to legalize marijuana in 2016 (Steinmetz 2015). In addition, there were 23 states that allow for the medical use of marijuana (National Conference of State Legislatures 2015a). The laws for medical marijuana use vary quite a bit from state to state. In California, people need a registry ID card to purchase marijuana products, but the conditions by which one can attain an ID card are very loose. In New York State, on the other hand, only patients with cancer, AIDS, Parkinson's disease, and certain other medical conditions are eligible, and even then, marijuana can only be ingested (edibles) or vaporized (it cannot be smoked) (National Conference of State Legislatures 2015a).

Marijuana users have long known that smoking cannabis makes them feel better. *How* does it make people feel better? "When THC hits brain cells, it causes them to release dopamine, a feel-good brain chemical . . . when over-excited by drugs, the reward system creates feelings of euphoria" (Welsh and Astaiza 2014). Marijuana also spurs creativity in the brain. For example, the late astronomer and author Carl Sagan was a secret but avid marijuana smoker and credited it with inspiring essays and scientific insight (*Buffalo News* 8/22/99). Among the medical uses of marijuana: it may reverse the carcinogenic effects of tobacco use; it is used to treat glaucoma; it helps to reduce anxiety; it decreases the symptoms of the severe seizure disorder known as Dravet's syndrome; the drug eases the pain of multiple sclerosis; helps to stop muscle spasms in other diseases such as Leeuwenhoek's disease; it lessens side effects from treatments for hepatitis C and increases treatment effectiveness; it improves the symptoms of lupus, an autoimmune disorder; it may be effective in fighting Crohn's disease; pot soothes tremors for people with Parkinson's disease; marijuana helps to control epileptic seizures; it relieves arthritis discomfort; treats inflammatory bowel diseases; slows the progression of Alzheimer's disease; it can help to stop cancer from spreading; it provides relief from nausea caused by cancer treatments (e.g., chemotherapy); it may help people suffering from PTSD; marijuana protects the brain after a stroke; it can help eliminate nightmares; and it can help people trying to cut back on drinking (Welsh and Astaiza 2014; Welsh and Loria 2014). Medical marijuana is also used to wean people off opioid addiction, thus becoming a "gateway" drug away from harder drugs.

As with any drug, there are a number of potential negative side effects of marijuana use: it may cause apathy; block memory formation; lead to intense anxiety, fear, and distrust; or rob you of your sleep (THC interrupts REM sleep). Smoking marijuana may cause an increase in heart rate; may cause red eyes; can lead to dry mouth (the result of inhaling hot smoke); and it may give you the munchies (a craving for "junk food") (Welsh and Astaiza 2014).

Hashish

Another popular version of cannabis is hashish, also known simply as hash. Hashish is the most concentrated and potent form of cannabis, containing high levels of THC. Hashish, a sticky, thick, dark-colored resin (like sap) is derived from the flowers of the female cannabis plant and is compressed into a variety of forms such as balls, cakes, or sticks. Hash is generally smoked in a pipe, similar to marijuana. A variation of hash is hash oil. Hash oil is the refined oily extract of the cannabis plant. Depending on the refining technique, the oil can vary in color from amber to dark brown with an average THC content at about 15 percent. The oil is usually mixed with tobacco or marijuana and smoked (DEA Museum 2015b).

Performance-Enhancing Drugs

Performance-enhancing drugs refer to a category of drugs generally consumed by athletes who hope to improve their athletic performance levels. (They are also used for medical purposes and by nonathletes who want to gain muscle mass.) The use of performance-enhancing techniques (e.g., **blood doping**, which does not involve taking drugs but rather entails infusing/injecting extra units of blood into the competitor's body in hopes of improving performance via the above-average level of blood cells and oxygen in the body that the blood produces) and drugs (e.g., anabolic steroids) in sport competitions generally connotes deviant, illegal, or unethical behavior. The use of performance-enhancing drugs in sports is a part of the culture of "win-at-any-costs" and is prevalent in any society that measures success in terms of winning. Success in sport, as with success in business and many other social institutions, is often a matter of achieving an "edge" over the competition. On many occasions, this edge is achieved through deviant means. Athletes, and nonathletes alike, have sought means to gain an edge over opponents in athletic competition for as long as there have been sporting events. Even young friends who decide to race each other to see who is faster look for some sort of edge, such as "jumping the gun" in the race (e.g., before someone says "go") or when one competitor tries to distract the other (e.g., "Hey, your shoes are untied"). Athletes, because they want to achieve peak levels of athletic performance, sometimes turn to deviant or illegal techniques in addition to athletic training in order to achieve the success goal. Performance-enhancing drugs (PED), such as anabolic steroids, have an aura of success and therefore pose a temptation to athletes, athletic medical personnel, coaches, and team officials.

Anabolic Steroids

Anabolic steroids are drugs that resemble androgenic hormones such as testosterone. Testosterone is a naturally synthesized hormone that is present in the male at significantly higher levels than in females. Testosterone's main effects are androgenic, which controls the secondary sexual characteristics in the male, and anabolic, which controls the growth and development of many body tissues, the most obvious being muscles (Lenehan 2003). Any anabolic steroid that builds up muscle tissue will also cause secondary sexual changes, and therefore, as Lenehan (2003) suggests, steroids should really be referred to as anabolic-androgenic steroids. Nonetheless, most people simply use the term "anabolic steroid."

Anabolic steroids are synthetic versions of naturally occurring hormones. Athletes use steroids in hopes of gaining weight, strength, power, endurance, and aggressiveness and because they help speed the recovery process when athletes get injured (quicker recovery equals a longer athletic career). The anabolic effects help to speed up the growth of muscle, bone, and red blood cells. The process works something like this: when anabolic steroids are infused into the body, the steroid hormone enters cells and binds to receptor molecules; the bound hormone enters the nucleus and activates specific genes to produce proteins; and these proteins, in turn, bring about the cellular changes triggered by the hormone. Proteins are an important aspect for building muscle tissue. Muscle growth will occur under two conditions: (1) with heavy training and weight-lifting, the testosterone binding capacity increases—aiding the user in reaching the goal of added strength, quickness, and bulk muscle; and (2) the body must retain more nitrogen (from protein) than it loses through the ongoing process of nitrogen excretions. In short, taking anabolic steroids represents an unnatural approach to muscle gain. The fact that steroids do assist in muscle growth, add strength and quickness, and speed the recovery process from injury, creates an "aura of success" that is attractive to many athletes (Delaney and Madigan 2015).

However, the excessive amount of testosterone provided to athletes through illegitimate means gives them an unfair advantage over the competition. When this testosterone is introduced into the body in an unnatural manner, it becomes a form of cheating, or social deviance. Ideals of fair play and good sportsmanship are compromised when people use banned performance-enhancing drugs. It does not measure true athletic ability. It is illegal to take PED without proper medical supervision and authorization. Still, many athletes, including bicyclists Lance Armstrong and Floyd Landis; track and field stars Marion Jones and Ben Johnson; and countless Major League Baseball stars such as Alex Rodriguez, Ryan Braun, Nelson Cruz, and so on, have all fallen for the aura of success that surrounds anabolic steroid use.

It is against federal law to possess and distribute steroids in the United States unless it is under direct medical supervision and for rehabilitative purposes. Under medical supervision steroids are used for a variety of reasons, including to build muscle; help repair tissue damage; treat inflammatory conditions such as systemic vacuities (inflammation of blood vessels); and selectively to treat inflammatory conditions such as rheumatoid arthritis, lupus, and gout. Steroids can be found in many over-the-counter products, often unbeknownst to those who take them. Corticosteroids, which may reduce inflammation associated with allergies, may be found in nasal sprays to treat nasal stuffiness, sneezing, and itchy, runny nose due to seasonal or year-round allergies. The FDA has approved the steroid nasal spray triamcinolone for over-the-counter use (American Academy of Allergy, Asthma and Immunology 2015). Systematic steroids may also be found in pills, liquids, or creams used to treat such ailments as symptoms from asthma and dry, itchy skin (especially for seniors).

While steroids can be quite effective as a treatment, there are many possible negative side effects, especially for those who take them for nonmedical purposes: in men prominent breasts, baldness, shrunken testicles, infertility, impotence, and prostate gland enlargement; in women a deeper voice, an enlarged clitoris, increased body hair, baldness, and infrequent or absent periods; and in both men and women severe acne, increased risk of tendonitis and tendon rupture, liver abnormalities and tumors, increased low-density lipoprotein (LDL, the "bad" cholesterol), decreased high-density lipoprotein (HDL, the "good" cholesterol), high blood pressure (hypertension), heart and circulatory problems, aggressive behaviors, rage of violence, psychiatric disorders such as depression, drug dependence, infections or diseases such as HIV or hepatitis for those who inject the drugs, and inhibited growth and development and risk of future health problems in teenagers (Mayo Clinic 2015d).

Human Growth Hormone (HGH)

HGH is a synthetic human growth hormone that has generally been used as a therapy technique for nonathletes. For example, parents of short children are increasingly turning to HGH in an attempt to stimulate their growth. HGH has become increasingly popular with athletes because it has the same aura of success as steroids but is much harder to detect via drug testing. "HGH is an endogenous peptide hormone involved in the regulation of diverse physiological processes including linear growth; protein, carbohydrate, and lipid metabolism (which includes effects on body composition such as anabolic and lipolytic actions); cardiovascular health; physical performance; and well being" (Evans-Brown and McVeigh 2009:268).

Prescription Drugs and Big Pharma

Prescription drugs (also known as prescription medication or prescription medicine) are pharmaceutical drugs that can only be legally obtained and consumed by means of a properly authorized person (e.g., a physician). A number of prescription drugs were discussed earlier in this chapter, including those from the categories of opioids, depressants, and narcotics. Prescription drugs are more likely to be abused than recreational drugs, although less likely to be abused than such legal drugs as alcohol and nicotine (tobacco products). Prescription drug abuse, or "problematic use," includes everything from taking a friend's prescription painkiller for your backache to snorting or injecting ground-up pills to get high. Prescription drug abuse can affect all age groups, but it's more common in young people. The prescription drugs most often abused include painkillers, sedatives, antianxiety medications, and stimulants (Mayo Clinic 2015e).

According to NIDA (2014e), an estimated 52 million people (20 percent of those aged 12 and older) have used prescription drugs for nonmedical reasons at least once in their lifetimes. Young people are strongly represented in this group. Data collected from a NIDA survey "found that about 1 in 12 high school seniors reported past-year nonmedical use of the prescription pain reliever Vicodin in 2010, and 1 in 20 reported abusing OxyContin—making these medications among the most commonly abused drugs by adolescents" (NIDA 2014e). The Foundation for a Drug-Free World (2015d) also reports that a teen is more likely to have abused a prescription drug than an illegal street drug because many teens mistakenly believe that prescription drugs are safe just because they were prescribed by a doctor. But taking them for nonmedical use to get high or "self-medicate" can be just as dangerous and addiction-forming as taking illicit street drugs.

A consumer culture amenable to the idea of "taking a pill for what ails you" has led to a general perception of prescription drugs as less harmful than illicit drugs. This perception, combined with the dramatic increase (since the 1990s) in the number of prescriptions for opioid painkillers, has contributed heavily to prescription drug abuse (NIDA 2014; Kristof 2015). Kristof (2015) specifically blames reckless marketing by pharmaceutical companies (Big Pharma) and overprescribing by doctors for the rise in prescription drug abuse in general and heroin use and abuse specifically. It is Kristof's research that sets the tone for the link between prescription drug abuse and Big Pharma.

Big Pharma

Big Pharma is a term that encompasses the largest global corporations in the pharmaceutical industry, including AstraZeneca, Bristol-Myers Squibb, GlaxoSmithKline, Maxim, Merck, Monsanto, Pfizer, Roche, Tanabe, and Wyeth. According to WHO (2015f), the global pharmaceuticals market is worth US$300 billion a year, a figure expected to rise to US$400 billion within 3 years. The 10 largest drug companies control over one-third of this market, several with sales of more than US$10 billion a year and profit margins of about 30 percent. Six of the 10 largest Big Pharma companies are based in the United States and 4 in Europe. For the past few decades, Big Pharma companies have strayed away from producing and discovering lifesaving drugs and started becoming more concerned about making money. Consider, for example, that Big Pharma currently spends about one-third of all sales revenue on marketing their products—roughly twice what they spend on research and development (WHO 2015f). This focus on profit has led to many charges, including those from WHO (2015f) that there is "an inherent conflict of interest between the legitimate business goals of manufacturers and the social, medical, and economic needs of providers and the public to select and use drugs in the most rational way." WHO does acknowledge that some Big Pharma companies, such as SmithKline, which made a US$500 million commitment to WHO of its drug albendazole (used to treat lymphatic filariasis), support health development through public-private partnerships.

The "Big Pharma" nickname is meant to demonize an industry under increasing scrutiny by the general public, consumer watchdog groups, and governments. Consumer mistrust is driven by Big Pharma's aggressive marketing practices that, at times, have been "reckless, deceptive and criminal" (Kristof 2015:A-14). "In a 3-year period (2012–2014), global Big Pharma giants paid fines to the tune of $11 billion for criminal wrongdoing, including withholding safety data and promoting drugs for use, beyond any licensed condition" (Bio Spectrum 2015). Consider these instances of Big Pharma fraud over the past decade:

- The GlaxoSmithKline office in Beijing was the center of a 2013 scandal in which local managers were accused of paying millions of dollars in bribes to Chinese doctors to prescribe the company's drugs (Kessel 2014; Bio Spectrum 2015).
- Before the China bribery scandal, GlaxoSmithKline, became a part of the largest health care fraud settlement in U.S. history; the drug maker paid $3 billion for promoting 2 drugs for unapproved uses and failing to report safety data about a diabetes drug to the U.S. FDA (Bio Spectrum 2015).
- Merck was involved in a case of fraudulently representing the mumps component of its MMR vaccine Pluserix as an effective vaccine after studies proved its ineffectiveness (Bio Spectrum 2015).
- The U.K. medicines regulatory body MHRA claims that European medicines giant Roche did not evaluate about 80,000 reports, including over 15,000 death reports, suspecting that adverse patient reactions were caused by Roche drugs (Bio Spectrum 2015).
- In 2012, Pfizer paid $60.2 million to the United States to settle charges that the company bribed government officials, including hospital administrators, government doctors, and members of regulatory and purchasing committees in China, Russia, Italy, and a number of other European countries to approve and prescribe Pfizer products (Bio Spectrum 2015).
- Abbott Laboratories pleaded guilty and paid $1.5 billion for unlawfully promoting the prescription drug Depakote for uses not approved safe and effective by the U.S. FDA (Bio Spectrum 2015).
- Top executives of Purdue Pharma, which made OxyContin, pleaded guilty in 2007 to criminal charges for their role in deceptive marketing that downplayed the risk of abuse (Kristof 2015).

Let's return to Kristof's accusation that reckless marketing by pharmaceutical companies and overprescribing by doctors have contributed to the current heroin epidemic. In 2015, Kristof stated that "heroin is out of control, with deaths nearly tripling in three years" (p. A-14). The push by pharmaceutical companies for doctors to prescribe opioids as pain relievers resulted in health care providers writing 259 million prescriptions for opioid painkillers in 2012—enough for a bottle for every American adult. "Many Americans, often military veterans, get hooked on pills, and then, unable to afford prescription painkillers, turn to heroin as a much cheaper alternative. We talk about personal irresponsibility as a factor in drug abuse, and that's real; so is corporate irresponsibility" (Kristof 2015:A-14). While Kristof makes some valid points, he failed to emphasize that many heroin dealers are "cutting" heroin with toxic substances, such as fentanyl, which is much stronger than street heroin. Heroin laced with fentanyl has led to many recent deaths (Drugs-Forum 2014). The CDC (2015j) reports that heroin-related drug-poisoning deaths have increased fourfold from 2000 to 2013 and just between 2010 and 2013, heroin deaths due to drug lacing have tripled. It is so recognized that heroin deaths have increased in recent years—both in general and because of drug lacing—that police, ambulance services, and paramedics carry Narcan or naloxone to successfully treat heroin overdoses (Leger 2014; Barker 2015; Ross 2013). Kristof, like many others, however, are calling out Big Pharma to be responsible citizens. Will they heed the call? What do you think?

In 2016, the CDC recommended that doctors limit opioid prescription painkillers especially as a first choice for treating common ailments like back pain and arthritis. The CDC suggests that primary care doctors should first try physical therapy and over-the-counter pain medication. The CDC reports that in 2014, U.S. doctors wrote nearly 200 million prescriptions for opioid painkillers, while deaths linked to the drugs climbed to roughly 19,000—the highest number on record.

To heed the call for responsibility will mean that Big Pharma will have to change its Wall Street practices and its "profit for stockholders over patient needs" business model. Big Pharma is facing many patent expirations on their blockbuster drugs, and this will lead to, among other things, a slash in their profits, but more than likely, a continued increase in the cost of generics. Some Big Pharma companies have seen the handwriting on the wall and have begun to purchase the generic manufacturers as a means of eliminating competition and regaining control of the market. Meanwhile, consumers want affordable medicine, and medicine that does what it claims to do.

Big Data

One last topic worth describing is "Big Data." **Big Data** is an evolving term, or catchphrase, that describes any massive volume of both structured and unstructured data that is so large it is difficult to process and also has the potential to be mined (or hacked) for information. Large, electronic data will be a topic of discussion in chapter 9 with cyberhacking, but its relevancy here is predicated on the fact that patient privacy protections are at risk as a result of burgeoning electronic medical records. In 2013, corrective action was required in nearly 3,500 cases (affecting millions of patients) of privacy protection violations. In 2015, a case of Big Data privacy protections came to light when a new employee—a nurse practitioner from the University of Rochester (New York) Medical Center—brought thousands of patient records with her. The medical center did not have a clear policy that governs whether or how a provider leaving for another practice can contact soon-to-be-former patients, according to the head of the center (Singer 2015). Perhaps the ethical thing to do would have been for the medical center to instruct the nurse to delete the files. Instead, they opened up the records and used them for potential gain, sending letters to advise patients that they could follow the nurse practitioner to her new job.

As technology advances, the need to update policy to protect patients must evolve with it; otherwise, we have, as in this case, another gray area in the study of social deviance.

Summary

A drug is any natural or synthetic chemical substance that affects the functioning of the mind or body. People take drugs for a variety of reasons, including therapeutic, recreational, spiritual or psychological, escape, and social conformity. There are many factors that influence drug effects, including identity, dose, potency and purity, drug mixing, route of administration, habituation, and set and setting.

Eight different categories of drugs—stimulants, depressants, hallucinogens, narcotics, inhalants, cannabis, performance-enhancing drugs, and prescription drugs—are described, in detail, in this chapter. While describing each category of drugs, drug use and drug abuse were also examined.

Stimulants include the most commonly used drug among Americans—caffeine—and the deadliest drug—nicotine (via tobacco use). Stimulants also include cocaine and crack cocaine, methylphenidate (Ritalin), amphetamines, and methamphetamines. Depressants, known collectively as "downers," sedate, or depress, neurotransmission levels in users. Hallucinogens, also known as psychedelics, have a profound effect on sensory perception. Narcotics, also known as opioids, are designed to help people who are experiencing severe levels of pain. Inhalants include a variety of breathable substances, some legally prescribed and others that are common household or work products. Cannabis, the scientific name for marijuana, is among the most popular drugs in the world and the most commonly used illicit drug in the world. The legality of cannabis is very fluid in the United States, as a number of states have legalized pot for either recreational or medical purposes. Performance-enhancing drugs are used by people, especially a number of athletes, who hope to gain muscle mass, run faster, and increase overall athletic performance. Prescription drugs are legal drugs that are prescribed by properly authorized persons to treat a wide range of ailments, pain, and diseases. The growing role of Big Pharma in the drug market was also explored.

Key Terms

anabolic steroids, 228

Big Data, 232

Big Pharma, 230

blood doping, 227

cannabis, 225

dependency, 209

depressants, 216

dose, 208

drug, 206

drug abuse, 210

drug abuser, 210

hallucinogens, 218

huffing, 224

inhalants, 224

narcotics, 222

nicotine, 211

performance-enhancing drugs, 227

prescription drugs, 229

psychoactive drug, 210

stimulants, 210

tolerance, 209

Discussion Questions

1. Define the term "drug." Why do people take drugs? Explain what is meant by drug abuse and (if relevant) share stories of a drug abuser who has affected your life.

2. Is caffeine use safe? Can caffeine be abused? Explain your answer.

3. Should tobacco use be legal? How does society justify the loss of hundreds of thousands of lives each year due to the consumption of the drug nicotine?

4. Saving marijuana for a later discussion, do you believe other recreational drugs (e.g., cocaine, heroin, LSD) should be legalized? If yes, which ones and why? If no, why not?

5. Do you believe marijuana should be legalized throughout the United States? Why or why not? Should people be allowed to use cannabis products for medical purposes? Explain your answer.

6. Are collegiate and professional athletes who take performance-enhancing drugs deviant? Are they violating codes of fair play, ethics, and/or morality? Explain your answer.

7. Explain the role of Big Pharma with the pharmaceutical drug industry. In general, do you think Big Pharma has the best interest of patients in mind? Explain.

CHAPTER 9

Cybertechnology and Social Deviance

CHAPTER OBJECTIVES

After reading this chapter students should be able to:

- Explain how technology led to the rise of the Internet
- Compare and contrast catfishing and cyberbullying
- Analyze the methods used for cyberstalking
- Describe how banks/financial institutions are vulnerable to cyberattacks
- Explain what is meant by intellectual property rights
- Provide specific examples of cyberattacks against the private sector
- Detail the increasing threat of cyberattacks against government agencies

If you are a fan of college football, the NFL, or the University of Notre Dame, chances are you've heard of Manti Te'o. Even if none of these three characteristics that are applicable to Te'o are of interest or relevance to you, perhaps you've heard of him because he was infamously duped as a victim of catfishing. If the concept of "catfishing" is new to you, this chapter will really open your eyes to a whole new world of social deviance. If you know what catfishing is all about, this chapter should be particularly interesting to you.

Manti Te'o (born January 26, 1991) is a native-born Hawaiian of Hawaiian-Samoan descent who left his island home in the Pacific as an all-state football player and as a person who was also highly ranked as a college football linebacker prospect. Te'o, a Mormon, decided to play football at the famed University of Notre Dame, a Catholic university. During his four years at Notre Dame, Te'o excelled on the football field and in the classroom, earning All-American and Academic All-American status. In 2012, Te'o was heading into his senior season at Notre Dame with the unranked Fighting Irish facing the toughest schedule in America. On September 15, the Irish beat recent nemesis Michigan State, 20–3. Te'o had an outstanding performance—12 tackles—and was asked by a TV sideline reporter how he managed to play such an inspired game, given the fact that—as reported in *Sports Illustrated* the day before the Michigan State game—he had just learned earlier in the week that he lost both his grandmother, Annette Santiago (from complications stemming from diabetes), and his girlfriend, Lennay Kekua, to leukemia. The two deaths occurred in a span of six hours. Te'o replied, "They were with me. I'm just so happy that I had a chance to honor my grandmother and my girlfriend and my family" (Zeman 2013). The *Sports Illustrated* article reported that Kekua had been in a serious car accident in California, and that she had been diagnosed with leukemia (Polzer 2012; Burke and Dickey 2013). Many people found it odd that Te'o never went to his girlfriend's funeral in California. Te'o stated that Kekua made him promise he wouldn't miss a game. "All she wanted was some white roses. So, I sent her roses and sent her two picks [interceptions] along with that" (Zeman 2013).

Te'o would go on to play inspired football the rest of the season, leading the Irish to a number one national ranking and a date against the University of Alabama in the national championship game. All season long Te'o received all sorts of accolades for his play on the field and the manner in which he held himself up despite the loss of his grandmother and girlfriend. But the storyline would change a couple of days after 'Bama's crushing victory over Notre Dame. Deadspin, a less than fully reputable website, broke its biggest story ever, claiming that Te'o never had a girlfriend and that Lennay Kekua was a fictional person; at least fictional in the sense that she did not exist in reality. But Kekua did exist in "virtuality." As it turned out, Te'o was the victim of a "catfishing" scheme—being duped into thinking you are having a virtual relationship with someone online. Te'o was deceived by a man, Ronaiah Tuiasosopo, who was pretending, online, to be Kekua. Tuiasosopo, the "catfish"—the person who sets up a false social networking profile for deceptive purposes—sent photos of Kekua (they were photos of a different young woman) to Te'o to keep the story going (Goodman 2013). Eventually Te'o found out that he was a victim of an online prank. In an attempt to lessen any further embarrassment (e.g., people asking him about his girlfriend) he decided to make up a story that she died. Further details of the Te'o catfishing tale will be presented later in this chapter.

"Catfishing" is only possible in a world where technology has led to the creation of cyberworlds and cyber forms of communications. That someone would dupe another person into thinking that they were involved in a real personal relationship is just the beginning of the world of cybertechnology social deviance.

Technology and the Rise of the Internet

So how did we get to this point, where people can claim to have a virtual significant other and yet the only interactions between the two are in cyberspace? It began with the development of technology that gave rise to computers, which led to the use of the Internet and fueled our fascination with virtual worlds.

Technology—the branch of knowledge that deals with the creation and practical use of technical means to solve problems or invent useful tools—is stimulated by progressive, creative thought that allows for the creation of new technologies in the many spheres of social life, including forms of communications. Long ago, if we wanted to communicate with persons not in our immediate vicinity, we would have to send messages via long-distance runners, or in some cases carrier pigeons or smoke signals. Over time, humans found other ways to communicate across long distances, including the introduction of the Pony Express, telegraph wires, telephones, radio and television, and then computers. The creation of computers led to the formation of the Internet, which now allows for immediate long-distance social interactions through a series of networking sites.

The Internet is a relatively new, but very influential and prevalent aspect of human life in contemporary society. To underscore the importance of the Internet it might be helpful to think of it as the electronic nervous system of the planet. The Internet was created in an effort to speed communication between people separated by long distances. While there might be some debate as to who exactly created the Internet (remember, Al Gore told CNN's Wolf Blitzer on March 9, 1999, that he created the Internet), many people have contributed to its creation and growth. Al Gore, for example, *did* help pass legislation that advanced the information technology highway, but he was not the person who "created" it.

According to Leiner and associates (2014), "the first recorded description of the social interactions that could be enabled through networking was a series of memos written by J.C.R. Licklider of MIT in August 1962 discussing his 'Galactic Network' concept. He envisioned a globally interconnected set of computers through which everyone could quickly access data and programs from any site." Thus, the Internet was intended to be a widespread information infrastructure designed to help speed up communication, especially among intellectuals conducting scientific research. And while the Internet still helps intellectuals conduct research, its everyday usage is far removed from such lofty endeavors.

A global perspective of the galactic network.

Today, some of us use the Internet to conduct research; it sure does make it easier to write papers and books. Most people, however, use the Internet for its social component, especially via social network sites that allow us to engage in such virtual social interactions as sharing photos (including "selfies") and videos (especially popular are cat videos), wishing people a "happy birthday," and bragging about our latest vacation or favorite sports team victory. In some instances, people have used the Internet to achieve more ambitious goals, such as organizing flash mobs, protests, or revolutions. In brief, nearly everyone uses the Internet.

A growing characteristic of contemporary society is virtual reality. Virtual reality refers to technology that allows users to interact with a computer-simulated environment. Simulated environments, accessible as visual experiences via display technology, are utilized by a variety of social institutions, organizations, groups, and individuals. The medical community uses virtual medicine to train surgeons for surgery and to experiment, virtually, with new radical procedures before subjecting humans to potentially harmful and untried techniques of treatment. The field of psychology also utilizes virtual reality to treat people who suffer from phobias. Engineers use virtual reality in a wide variety of designs to test their functionality before proceeding to implementing their construction in the real world. Hollywood has increasingly employed virtual reality with filmmaking. Among their newest tricks is "digital cloning." Digital cloning was used in the blockbuster film *Maleficent* to affix "pixie-perfect" human faces on tiny fairies. The military uses virtual reality to train pilots, parachutists, and combat soldiers. Soon they may add cloned personnel to their drones.

And then there are individuals who want to transcend the confines of reality for a fantasy world. In these fantasy worlds, participants can create a whimsical version of themselves through such mechanisms as avatars. In the fantasy escapism world of virtual reality, individuals can essentially create a "virtual self"—a sort of alter ego and an identity hidden from others in the real world. Individuals can also carry on relationships with people they have never met. It's because so many people are finding the virtual world as a better alternative to the real world that phenomena like catfishing and a slew of deviant and criminal activities such as cyberstalking, online bullying, cyberporn, revenge porn, large-scale hacking of financial institutions, and so on, can exist.

There were warnings about the potential problems associated with cybertechnology decades ago. And still, many of us have fallen victim to cyberdeviancy.

Heed the Warning: Crime and Deviancy in Cyberspace Will Rise

There were warnings from academics and law enforcement agencies about the potential for computer-related crime dating back since the introduction of microcomputers on the public market in the late 1970s, when the access to and the volume of personal computing grew (Carter and Bannister 2002). One of the earliest authors sounding the alarm about the potential threat of computer-related crime was Donn Parker. The subtitle to his 1976 publication, *Crime by Computer: Startling New Kinds of Million-Dollar Fraud, Theft, Larceny and Embezzlement*, neatly sums up his concerns about the possibility for cybercrime. For decades Parker attempted to warn people about the growing threat of cybercriminality. Parker not only addressed many of the major concerns we still have today, he touched upon another tricky topic of relevancy in contemporary society—how do we best secure ourselves from hackers? In his foreword to Parker's 1998 publication *Fighting Computer Crime*, William Hugh Murray cites a quote from the book wherein Parker states, "Given the choice of criminals abusing my information in absolute secrecy and the FBI eavesdropping on my information, I choose the FBI" (p. viii). Parker's version of such a "law and order" approach to cybercrime is voiced by many today (with the NSA replacing the FBI as the main culprit of government agencies spying on citizens today). Then again, Murray also counters with another prevalent contemporary perception of the role of government and their intrusion on citizens' private lives when he cites a quote from Benjamin Franklin, "Those who would give up essential liberty for a little temporary safety deserve neither liberty nor safety" (p. viii). As Murray explains, "While I can rely upon the FBI to protect me from the lawless, I have only the Constitution to protect me from the state" (p. viii). While Parker (1998) was correct in his warning of the potential growth of cybercriminal activity, he never quite truly understood its magnitude, insisting that far more damage to information is caused by error than by crime. It is true that individuals accidentally delete files or leave important cyberinformation improperly protected, but the greatest cyberthreat today clearly comes from the outside.

Among the early U.S. government agencies exploring computer crime was the Bureau of Justice Statistics (BJS). During the late 1970s and early 1980s, the BJS released a number of publications—beginning with the 1979 publication *Computer Crime: Criminal Justice Resource Manual*—on the growing threat of cybercrime. A number of academic publications cited the BJS reports and statistics, and the term "hacker" was already being used in the late 1970s.

Carter and Bannister (2002) describe a number of 1980s publications on the emerging threat of cybercrime that focused on such details as dealing with logistical issues associated with computer-related criminality; methods to prevent computer crimes; practices for effectively investigating and prosecuting computer crime cases; classification systems for computer crimes (which quickly became outdated as a result of significant changes in computing capabilities); and the need for dedicated computer crime units. And while some of these issues were addressed, for the most part, private citizens, businesses, and government agencies basked in the developing technology of computers and computer programs while treating the threat of cybercrime as a secondary concern. Little wonder then that a study conducted by the American Bar Association (ABA) in 1987 found that 72 (24 percent) of the 300 corporations and government agencies surveyed claimed to have been a victim of computer-related crime in the 12 months prior to the survey (ABA 1987; Carter and Bannister 2002). In 1989, the Florida Department of Law Enforcement (FDLE) found that 403 (44.9 percent) of the 898 surveyed public and private sector organizations that conducted business by computer had been victimized by computer criminals (FDLE 1989; Carter and Bannister 2002).

During the 1990s, when the Internet experienced explosive growth compared to the previous two decades, computer-related crime began to increase dramatically. This is true both in terms of the character and nature of computer-related crimes and in their frequency of occurrence. Carter and Bannister (2002) described how computers via the Internet were being used to commit white-collar crimes but also described how they were being used in occupational settings by employees and customers, while others were committing fraud and other offenses against corporations. Carter and Bannister also stated that the bulk of the law-enforcement establishment in the United States was still ill-prepared to investigate or otherwise deal with computer crime. As we shall learn throughout this chapter, the wide variety and vast number of cybercrimes being committed today would seem to indicate that U.S. law enforcement agencies and private-sector businesses are still ill-equipped to handle the challenge of hackers, let alone develop safeguards to protect individuals from victimization of cybercrimes. To be fair, Carter and Bannister (2002) point out that the challenge facing law enforcement with regard to computer crime was especially challenging in the 1990s due to "the global character of networking offenses—transactions and behavioral interactions that can occur between people worldwide, from their homes, with no scrutiny by the immigration, customs, or other government entity" (p. 184). The Internet provided criminals an opportunity to commit crime in such a manner that never existed in any time during history prior to the development of computer technology.

The Australian Federal Police (AFP) was among the early law enforcement agencies to address the emerging trend of computer-related crime in the late 1990s. Glenn Wahlert, who undertook a study for the Office of Strategic Crime

Assessments, where he was a senior analyst at the time, provided an early warning call for Australian law enforcement and national security agencies. Wahlert warned, "The increasing dependence of business on computer systems has made many more organizations vulnerable to the impact of computer crime. Indeed, more companies are worried about the risk of computer crime than they are about product liability, fraud and theft" (Australian Federal Police 1998). Based on Wahlert's study, the AFP warned that Australian companies remain most vulnerable to computer misuse from their own employees, contractors, consultants, or anyone else with knowledge of and access to their computer systems. The AFP also concluded that there was enough evidence to suggest that the external threat had increased substantially over the past five years and that it is likely to continue to do so in at least the medium term (three to five years). The AFP (1998) cited three factors that would create an environment conducive to further external threats of cybercrime:

1. The first generation of computer-literate citizens will reach adulthood shortly after the turn of the century and may open a new age in the annals of crime and crime fighting. In the future, it is likely there will be more users who will have skills far beyond those of today's hackers/crackers.

2. Hackers are using the Internet chat rooms and discussion groups to share information on system vulnerabilities. Essentially, the Internet has become one big laboratory where hackers share information, hone their skills and techniques, and develop tools. The Internet has proven to be an almost ideal learning environment for existing and future hackers.

3. The growing concern that the benign "hacker" is being replaced by the menacing "cracker"—an individual or member of a group intent on using cyberspace for illegal profit.

While the term "cracker" is not used in the same manner in the United States as described by the AFP ("cracker" is a slang term to refer to those of European ancestry and usually meant as an insult much like the "n-word" is used as an insult against African Americans), all three of their major points have come to fruition. The first generation of hackers were replaced by a much more sophisticated breed of hackers with skills (and technological advancements at their disposal) beyond that of the first generation; the Internet has become a place where individuals can find information on any topic; and third, groups of hackers from remote places in the world are capable of breaking into nearly any cybersecurity system.

"Hackers" and "hacking" are concepts that nearly everyone in the contemporary era has heard referenced in the news, popular culture, work environments, and discussed by friends and family because of their preponderance. Even so, let's take a quick and closer look at the computer hacking phenomenon. A **computer hacker** is a person who illegally gains access to a computer system in order to get information (e.g., data or top secrets), cause damage (e.g., deleting important files or stealing bank account numbers), or create havoc (e.g., releasing a virus in the network system). The initial unauthorized access is generally done covertly and may remain covert; then again, the hacker may leave a "calling card" to self-identify and take credit for their devious acts. **Computer hacking** is the process of intentionally accessing a computer without authorization or exceeding authorized access. Individuals or small groups of people with hacking skills can cause all sorts of problems to individuals, businesses, and/or governments, as the cybercrimes and forms of deviancy to be discussed in this chapter will reveal. The critically acclaimed *Mr. Robot* (USA

Network) provides an outstanding insight into the world of computer hacking and provides proper warnings to viewers just how serious computer hacking can be. In its first season (2015), *Mr. Robot* not only mirrored real-life hacking schemes, it also aired episodes previous to real-life hacking plots. The show points out how large corporations and banks control society via monetary manipulation and leads the audience into cheering for the main character, Elliot Alderson (Rami Malek) and his group of hackers known as "F--- Society." At the conclusion of season one, Elliot and "F--- Society" manage to hack the powerful E Corporation (which Elliot refers to as Evil Corp.) and cause a "cyber Pearl Harbor" by erasing everyone's debts. While people in debt are initially happy about this, the debt erase causes a devastating ripple effect to the economy and to those people who were owed money for services already rendered and especially to those who were debt-free and retired.

Mr. Robot helps us to understand the sometimes-gray area of hacking and makes us realize that the absolutist perspective (that hacking is always wrong) is not necessarily the best viewpoint. In fact, the relativist perspective on deviance comes into play with hacking, as the seriousness and high frequency rate of hacking in the contemporary era have led some government agencies to employ hackers to protect their own interest. For example, the FBI has hired technology experts—including those with experience in "ethical hacking"—to become "cyber special agents" (Yerak 2014). Hackers hired by the FBI generally assist the policing agency with its counterterrorism criminal investigations or traditional cyberattacks. The FBI is looking for agents who have the skills to "conduct multi-faceted investigations of high-tech crimes, including cyber-based terrorism, computer intrusions, online exploitation and major cyber fraud schemes" (Yerak 2014). This leads us to an interesting question: if the government hires someone to illegally access computer networks, is this deviant? Most would say it is not if the hacking is designed to "protect the citizenry" of the United States; but what if the hacking is being conducted to spy on citizens and residents of the United States? What do you think?

Getting back to the Australian policing efforts, the AFP also correctly identified a number of other trends in cybercrime back in the 1990s that still exist, and cause trouble for victims, today. Here is a sampling of their computer-related crime warnings:

1. Potential vulnerability of the banking and finance sector—Although the AFP were specifically concerned with Australian banks, they correctly reported that "attacks on financial institutions are not only increasing but are also becoming more sophisticated."
2. Reporting—The AFP found that many financial institutions work under a veil of secrecy and fail to report all instances of cybercrime victimization, and because of this, they cannot create a reliable threat assessment or establish accurate databases on cybercrime.
3. Plastic payment cards—Counterfeit and stolen plastic payment cards (e.g., credit and debit cards) assist organized crime enterprises that operate across national borders. The AFP recommended chip card technology to cut down on this type of cybercrime—a move that most of the world, but surprisingly not the United States, has embraced (by 2015 a few credit cards had finally started offering customers cards with chips inserted).
4. Intellectual property—Corporate espionage has led to the theft of a wide range of private and confidential information from businesses. Today, the intellectual

property of individuals, businesses, and government agencies are all at risk of cybercriminality.

5. Identities—In the mid-1990s, Australian law enforcement agencies had already found a dramatic increase in the use of counterfeit documents (e.g., certificates of identification, ownership, and origin) that are used in a variety of fraud- and deception-related activities, such as opening up bank accounts (for money laundering, tax evasion, and fraud), obtaining loans, securing hire purchase agreements, and supporting documentation for stolen cars and other property.

6. Sexually related commerce—Today, everyone knows that the Internet is filled with pornography, but there was a time when this was new. The AFP documented many complaints concerning online pornography.

7. Cyberscams—It was already abundantly clear by the 1990s that the Internet would replace the more traditional means of committing fraud because of its speed and anonymity.

All of the computer-related deviant trends identified by the AFP described above are still relevant today, and examples of each will be provided in the following pages. A number of other, newer categories of cyberdeviancy will also be discussed. We begin our examination of cyberdeviancy in the contemporary era with cyberdeviancy and crime that primarily affects individuals.

Cyberdeviancy: Individual-Level Victimization

There are a number of examples of acts of cyberdeviancy wherein the intended victim is an individual; thus, these actions are described as instances of "individual-level" victimization. While the behaviors described here generally target individual victims, they may affect large numbers of people in total. Discussion begins with the topic of catfishing.

Catfishing

As described in the chapter's introductory story, former Notre Dame, and current (as of summer 2015) San Diego Chargers, football player Manti Te'o was a victim of a catfishing scheme wherein he was duped into thinking he had an ongoing relationship with a young woman. The *Urban Dictionary* (2015) defines **catfishing** as "The phenomenon of internet predators that fabricate online identities and entire social circles to trick people into emotional/romantic relationships over a long period of time." The person who pretends to be someone they're not and who creates false identities on Facebook or other social networking sites for deceptive purposes is known as the "catfish." Catfish was added to the *Merriam-Webster Dictionary* in May 2014. Possible motivations for catfishing include revenge, loneliness, curiosity, boredom, and blackmail.

Catfishing is a slang term, and its origins are connected to the 2010 film *Catfish*, a "pseudo-documentary that chronicled a young man's online friendship with a woman that turned out to be very different from her Facebook profile" (Palmer 2013). (The film was a critical and commercial success and led to an MTV reality TV series called *Catfish: The TV Show*.) Another plausible explanation for the term "catfishing" is related to real-life scenarios wherein seafood restaurants fraudulently pass off a cheaper fish for a higher-priced fish. Thus, customers are being duped into thinking they are purchasing and eating a higher-quality fish product than they really are. For example, a 2011 *Boston Globe* investigation of seafood mislabeling at local restaurants and markets found that patrons of a Dorchester restaurant were paying $23 for flounder fillet, but they were actually being served a Vietnamese catfish known as swai—nutritionally inferior and often priced at under $4 a pound (Palmer 2013; Abelson and Daley 2011). The *Globe* collected fish from 134 restaurants, grocery stores, and seafood markets from Leominster to Provincetown and hired a laboratory in Canada to conduct DNA testing on the samples. Analyses by the DNA lab and other scientists found that 87 of 183 samples (48 percent) were sold with the wrong species' name. All 23 white tuna samples tested as some other type of fish, usually escolar, which is nicknamed the "ex-lax" of fish by some in the industry because of the digestion problems it can cause (Abelson and Daley 2011).

Victims of online catfishing often feel sick to their stomachs too. They may also feel embarrassed, angry, upset, and a number of other emotions when they learn they were duped into thinking they had a relationship with someone who turned out not to be real. Te'o has explained that he met a woman online with whom he maintained what he thought was an authentic relationship through frequent phone calls (Ronaiah Tuiasosopo, the catfish, disguised his voice to sound like a woman) and online conversations and fell in love with her. "He called himself the victim of 'someone's sick joke'" (Brady and George 2013). To be kind, Te'o was naïve; to be blunt, he was foolish to think he was in an actual relationship with a young woman, Lennay Kekua, someone he never met. The young woman who was used in the catfishing scheme was Diane O'Meara, and she claims that her pictures were stolen and that she never met Te'o (Goodman 2013).

In a very bizarre case of catfishing, a 41-year-old man pretended to be a 16-year-old boy and established a relationship with a 14-year-old girl. While the two never met, they referred to each other as boyfriend and girlfriend while texting one another. The "boyfriend" was able to convince the girl to send pornographic pictures of herself to him. The boyfriend later threatened to send the photos of the girl to her father if she resisted sending more sexually explicit photos to him. She broke up with him and hoped that would be the end of it. However, the girl then received a text from the boy's account from a woman who claimed to be the boy's mom. The text read that the boy had committed suicide because he was distraught over the breakup. And this is when the case turns quite deviant. The girl's father told her that her boyfriend had indeed sent him photos. The father then told his daughter how much he enjoyed the photos of her. In addition, the father admitted to being the boyfriend that catfished her all along. The father then blackmailed his daughter into having sex with him or else he would make the sexually explicit photos public. Eventually the girl reported the sexual abuse she was enduring from her father to her school nurse, and her father was arrested and charged with such offenses as 12 counts of enticing a child to produce child pornography and receiving and sending child porn (O'Brien 2016).

Being a victim of catfishing is a contemporary phenomenon, as the key elements have only existed in recent years. First, there have to be social networking sites. Second, there have to be people who are willing to consider strangers as "friends," something that is often the case on Facebook. Ask people today how many friends they have on Facebook and then ask a follow-up question: "How many of these people do you actually *know*, or have a face-to-face relationship with?" It is likely there is a big gap in these numbers. Third, there has to be someone willing to victimize another person. And fourth, there has to be a willingness among people to think that it is possible to have a dating relationship with someone strictly in the cyberworld. These four elements combined explain why catfishing is possible today but was never possible in the past, as previous generations would say it's only possible to have a relationship with someone whom you have met.

But these are different times. For well over a decade now, people have used online dating sites as a means to find someone special. And because it is far easier to lie about one's true appearance online than it is in person, the likelihood that someone may get duped by a fabricated online profile is correspondingly higher. A study conducted at the University of Wisconsin–Madison, for example, found that 81 percent of people misrepresent their height, weight, or age in their online profiles (Rosenbloom 2011). In a Pew Research Center study, it was found that more than half of online daters (54 percent) state that a web crush has "seriously misrepresented" themselves in a profile (*Inquisitr* 2013). The lesson to be learned with catfishing is, if the online person seems too good to be true, that just may be the case.

The discussion of catfishing serves as a nice transition to the topic of cyberbullying as, according to the CyberBully Hotline (2013), catfishing is an example of cyberbullying.

Cyberbullying

Cyberbullying is the act of harassing someone online by sending or posting embarrassing photos/videos or mean-spirited messages, including spreading rumors/gossip, about a person, often done anonymously. Catfishing is considered an example of cyberbullying because someone had to create a false identity online, and they did so for bullying purposes (CyberBully Hotline 2013). Teens suffering from angst may be susceptible to catfishing schemes because they often turn to websites that foster connections with strangers. The bullying form of catfishing has been increasing over the past few years. "Several teens have committed suicide after a 'catfish' in their school or community targeted them for abuse. Many more have experienced the pain of being deceived, abused, and teased after falling for the deceptive moves of a 'catfish'" (CyberBully Hotline 2013). The CyberBully Hotline provides three suggestions to parents to help keep their teens safe from catfish cyberbullying:

1. Know all of the websites and mobile apps that your teen is using to network with others.
2. Encourage your teen to connect only with people they know in real life.
3. Keep your teens from disclosing personal information on social media sites.

As described by StopBullying.gov (a website managed by the U.S. Department of Health and Human Services), cyberbullying is different than face-to-face bullying, and these points are emphasized:

- Kids who are being cyberbullied are often bullied in person as well.
- Kids who are cyberbullied have a harder time getting away from the behavior, as it can happen 24 hours a day, 7 days a week.
- Cyberbullying messages and images can be posted anonymously and distributed quickly to a very wide audience. It is often difficult to trace the source.
- Deleting inappropriate or harassing messages, texts, and pictures is extremely difficult after they have been posted or sent (StopBullying.gov 2015).

StopBullying.gov (2015) points out that cybertechnology (e.g., smartphones and computers) is not to blame for cyberbullying, as social media sites are often used for positive activities; but they warn that these same tools can be used to hurt other people. The effects of cyberbullying can be devastating to young people (and adults). Kids who are cyberbullied are more likely to:

- Use alcohol and drugs
- Skip school
- Experience in-person bullying
- Be unwilling to attend school
- Receive poor grades
- Have lower self-esteem
- Have more health problems

How prevalent is cyberbullying? According to the National Center for Education Statistics (NCES) (2014), approximately 9 percent of students ages 12 to 18 reported being cyberbullied in 2011. More girls than boys reported being cyberbullied. The 2013 Youth Risk Behavior Surveillance Survey found that 15 percent of high school students (grades 9–12) were electronically bullied in the past year (StopBullying.gov 2015). Statistics gathered by Enough Is Enough (a website funded by the Office of Juvenile Justice and Delinquency Prevention) provide an overview of cyberbullying that includes such information as:

- Of social media–using teens, 95 percent have witnessed cruel behavior on social networking sites; 55 percent report seeing cruel and mean behavior being directed toward others on a frequent basis.
- Eighty-four percent of social media–using teens report that they have defended the person being harassed, and the same percentage report telling cyberbullies to stop bullying.
- Sixty-six percent of teens who have witnessed online cruelty have also witnessed others joining in on the harassment.
- Only 7 percent of U.S. parents are worried about cyberbullying, even though 33 percent of teenagers have been victims of cyberbullying.
- One million children were harassed, threatened, or subjected to other forms of cyberbullying on Facebook during the past year.
- Bullying over texting is becoming more common.
- While girls are more likely to be cyberbullied than boys, more girls are cyberbullies than boys.
- Eighty-one percent of youth agree that bullying online is easier to get away with than bullying in person (Enough Is Enough 2013).

Trying to eliminate cyberbullying is as difficult of a challenge as trying to stop face-to-face bullying—something that has likely occurred throughout humanity. Parents are encouraged to talk to their children about cyberbullying and have them inform their parents if they are being victimized. Those being bullied should keep bullying messages as proof that cyberbullying is occurring. Efforts should be made to block the person sending the messages, even if that means getting a new phone number or social network account. School administrators, teachers, and staff are encouraged to help identify cases of cyberbullying. In one instance, a Utah high school football coach suspended his entire team after learning of his players' off-the-field deviant behavior that included cyberbullying. Matt Labrum, football coach at Union High School in Roosevelt, who made his 80 players help out in the community instead of going to practice, said, "We felt like everything was going in a direction that we didn't want our young men going. We felt like we needed to make a stand" (Choe 2013).

As a final note, it is important to point out that cyberbullying certainly does not end in high school or in one's teens. Cyberbullying occurs in college, outside of college, and after college years of age. One must be careful about their social networking, as many sites and apps perpetuate cyberbullying, even when it's their intent to simply foster sociability. Consider, for example the Yik Yak app. In October 2013, two Furman University students launched the popular app Yik Yak in an effort to connect people through anonymous location-based posts. While the Yik Yak app rules allow for communication of almost any kind, they specifically state that there is a zero-tolerance policy on bullying. Nonetheless, the site is a place where the trend of cyberbullying exists alongside the proper usage of sharing ideas, having fun, and meeting people (Inguaggiato 2014).

A teenage girl is distraught over the electronic messages she is receiving from online bullies.

Cyberstalking

The Internet affords people an opportunity to communicate with a wide variety of people including friends, family, business associates, acquaintances, and long-lost people from our past. Conversely, it provides a series of networks that allow people an opportunity to track others who may not want anything to do with specific others. This negative aspect of tracking down others leads us to cyberstalking, or cyberharassment. The repeated act of following, watching, harassing, or trying to communicate with someone who does not want your attention is known as stalking. When stalking is done in the cyberworld, it is known as cyberstalking. **Cyberstalking** involves the use of electronic forms of communication (e.g., social networking sites, e-mail, or smartphones) to track or harass a person. Cyberstalking can be combined with traditional forms of stalking, and either deviant instance is a criminal offense.

Some U.S. states have enacted cyberstalking or cyberharassment laws that specifically deal with electronic forms of stalking or harassment, while other states have added components to existing laws against traditional forms of stalking and harassment to include electronic forms. While the terms of "cyberstalking" and "cyberharassment" are fairly similar, there are differences. According to the National Conference of State Legislatures (2015b), cyberstalking is the use of the Internet, e-mail, or other electronic communications to stalk, and generally refers to a pattern of threatening or malicious behaviors. Depending on the credible threat of harm, sanctions against cyberstalking may range from misdemeanors to felonies. Cyberharassment differs from cyberstalking in that such actions do not involve a credible threat. **Cyberharassment** usually pertains to threatening or harassing e-mail messages, instant messages, or to blog entries or websites dedicated solely to tormenting an individual.

Working with these parameters of cyberstalking and cyberharassment, read the two "Closer Look" boxes provided below and try to ascertain whether these are examples of cyberstalking, cyberharassment, or both.

A CLOSER LOOK

Box 9.1 "I'm Trying to Find Him"

On the June 18, 2015, episode of ESPN's *Highly Questionable*, cohost Dan Le Batard interviewed former Dallas Cowboys running back and current MMA fighter Herschel Walker about his upcoming MMA fight. Le Batard asked Walker when he was last afraid of another man (presumably to ask a follow-up question about his forthcoming MMA fight). Walker responded that it was when he was in eighth grade and a man named Anthony Logan beat him up. Le Batard and his cohosts were surprised that Walker remembered the man's name and specifically mentioned it on air. Walker continued and said that he's been looking for him (Logan). "I tried to find him on Facebook, I've tried Googling him, tweeting about him, and I can't find him. But I'm trying to find him." Cohost Bomani Jones appeared quite taken aback about Walker's bluntness, and in an attempt to lessen the perception of viewers (such as myself) who were probably

thinking, "He sounds like a cyberstalker," Jones asked Walker if he was serious about pursuing his childhood tormentor. Walker just smiled and said that he wouldn't do anything about the past beating he took, and then he gave a smile that was hard to interpret. Walker's words would likely send shivers down the backs of people who have actually been victimized by a cyberstalker, because they know there are people who use any electronic means possible to keep tabs on another.

So does it sound to you like Walker is a cyberstalker? Or was he mostly fooling around? What if a person made comments similar to Walker's in a different context? Would that sound like cyberstalking or cyberharassment? If someone you feared and were making every attempt to avoid said that they were trying every form of electronic communication available to track you down, would that concern you?

A CLOSER LOOK

Box 9.2 Frequent Location

If someone is stalking you, they are likely to track you at locations you are known to frequently visit. This helps to explain why long before cybertechnology existed, so many stalking victims were harassed or stalked at work, home, or their favorite hangouts. In the electronic world in which we live today the number of ways to track someone's every move has increased and become more stealthy. For example, if the person being stalked regularly uses social networking sites to publicly post or tweet their activities, they have given the stalker a location. If you are tagged in a photo, the stalker may be able to track you down. If you once dated, or are/were friends or coworkers with, the person who is stalking you, it is possible that the stalker may have placed a tracer on your automobile or smartphone. Even if the stalker did not place a tracking device in your smartphone, if they know of a little "secret" utilized by phone providers, they can retrieve your entire location history.

As reported by Jeff Rossen on NBC's *Today* show (April 28, 2015), if you have an iPhone or an Android, chances are that every single move you make is being tracked, location by location, minute by minute, including the exact times you were there, via a "Frequent Location" setting. So who is getting this information? According to Apple, this frequent location information is used solely to personalize services for each individual user. Apple states that "it's kept solely on your device and won't be sent to Apple without your consent" (Rossen and Billington 2015). If you use an Android, all that frequent location tracking data is being sent straight to Google. And because Google has this frequent location information, that means it is readily available online and susceptible to hackers, including stalkers, or anyone who has, or can gain, access to your phone's password. Google is known for their maps, and that means addresses of locations, along with a tracking map, can also be pulled up because of this frequent location setting. Stalkers can find out where you live, where you have lunch, work out, go to movies, and so on, and they know exactly how long you have been there.

If this information is new to you, it is highly likely you may want to know how to turn this setting off. The directions are simple: Go to "Settings" and scroll to "Privacy" and then go to "Location Services." Next, scroll all the way down to "System Services" and then scroll to "Frequent Locations," as this is the site that shows you every location you have been to and for how long you were there. Click "Clear History" and then slide to the "off" position. (Note: Chances are, by the time you read this text, technology has already moved on to the next step of secretly tracking your frequent locations, so keep alert!)

During his *Today* show report, Rossen interviewed a number of people in a park. They were all quite surprised by the frequent location setting and naturally wanted to learn how to turn it off. One woman remarked to Rossen, "I can take my husband's phone and look at all the places he's been recently. . . . So maybe I won't tell him how to turn it off." This woman has just learned how to check her husband's location history but doesn't want to tell him that she has this information. Is this an example of cyberstalking? Apple and Google have built into their smartphones a setting that, until turned off, tracks phone users' every move. Is that stalking? When Apple creates "personalized services" (which means advertisements to post on your phone), is that a form of cyberharassment? If you do not tell your significant other about the frequent location setting and how to turn it off so that you can review her or his location history, does that make you a cyberstalker?

Swatting

Like catfishing, cyberbullying and cyberstalking, swatting is an example of recent individual-level victimizations that were not conceived of decades ago when the AFP described their trends in cyberdeviancy. Swatting is a phenomenon known to people who study social deviance, law enforcement, and video gamers. **Swatting** is the act of pranking or tricking an emergency service dispatcher (e.g., 911 opera-tors) into deploying a Special Weapons and Tactics (SWAT) unit to an unsuspecting victim's home under false pretenses. Swatting has become increasingly popular with online gamers (but is certainly not limited to online gamers), especially those who play *Mortal Kombat*, *Call of Duty*, and *Counter-Strike*.

Swatting typically occurs when an online user has a problem with another online user and tries to find personal information on the target, which will then be used to call the emergency services to file a fake report of an emergency. The reported emergency leads to emergency response teams appearing at the address of the targeted user, who is, of course, a victim of the vengeful gamer. The term "swat-ting" is derived from the tactical response typically generated by such calls, which usually includes SWAT. The vengeful gamer has, of sorts, performed a nonlethal, real-world "fatality." "Fatalities" is an integral aspect of *Mortal Kombat* wherein the gamer is required to push a sequence of buttons to perform a signature "finale" to the game. For players of *Mortal Kombat* the thrill of the game is the fatalities, because this provides the gamer a chance to demonstrate his or her virtual skills.

Call of Duty is a violent video game that can be played as a first-person or third-person shooter. There are many variations of *Call of Duty* with the earlier ones consisting of World War II scenarios. *Counter-Strike* is a first-person shooter game in which the player takes on various combat teams throughout the world involved in terrorism and counterterrorism. In August of 2014, Jordan Mattherson from Littleton, Colorado, was playing *Counter-Strike* while causing a "swatting" incident. He recorded himself playing the game and live streamed his play. The cam-era caught the SWAT team entering his room as they arrested him. One of my stu-dents in my fall 2014 Introductory Sociology class told me that he was watching the streamed video live and saw Mattherson get arrested.

Swatting has become increasingly popular, and it's not an isolated incident of one upset gamer perpetrating a hoax. Swatters, the people who commit the crime of reporting a false emergency, have also turned swatting into a type of game by keeping track of how many emergency response vehicles and personnel respond. The swatting gamer with the highest number of responding emergency vehicles and personnel "wins."

As a sign of the growing popularity of swatting hoaxes, a privately owned video game store in Clifton, New Jersey, was the site of a massive swatting hoax during its monthly meeting of the North Atlantic Video Game Aficionados in March 2015. A swatter had called emergency responders that suspicious activities were occur-ring at the video store, prompting a massive law enforcement response. The swatter also called the video store pretending to be from the Clifton Fire Department and ordered them to lock down the store and close their blinds due to the event outside (that was supposed to be unrelated to the video store). The threat level increased correspondingly among law enforcement due to the activity in the video store. The people inside realized they were being victimized by a swatting hoax and dialed 911 to explain everything to the police. Eventually, law enforcement determined that it was indeed a hoax (Ledford 2015; Pugliese and Villeneuve 2015).

The swatting "win," while enjoyed by a very small number of gamers, comes at a potentially great cost, as emergency crews responding to a false call are not avail-able to respond to a real emergency. If swatting incidents were part of a game and restricted to the virtual world, law enforcement and the general public would not care, but because swatting interferes with the overall functioning of the real world, it is a growing nuisance and an example of social deviance.

A SWAT team prepares to move in on a home.

Cyberscams

Interestingly, and certainly reflective of the nature of cyberscams, while I searched for reputable sites to define the term "cyberscam," I clicked on one seemingly reliable site that set off my computer's scam alert. **Cyberscams**, also referred to as Internet fraud, are crimes in which the perpetrator develops a scheme using one or more elements of the Internet in an attempt to defraud people with the goal of acquiring/stealing personal property, money, or any other asset by means of false representation, whether by providing misleading information or by concealment of information. (Note: Identity theft and fraud are examples of cyberdeviancy/cyberscams but were already discussed in chapter 4.)

Perhaps the most common example of cyberscams is the Nigerian letter or "419" scam. The Nigerian scam is so well-known it is surprising that anyone would still fall victim to this scam, and yet it is estimated that Nigerian cybercriminals have illegally attained multi-billions of dollars. The "419 fraud" term is connected to a formerly relevant section of the Criminal Code of Nigeria numbered 419. The 419 scam is a modern version of traditional, centuries-old West African scams and pranks designed to defraud people of their assets (The 419 Coalition Website 2015).

The FBI (2015j) warns us to be skeptical of individuals representing themselves as Nigerian or foreign government officials asking for your help in placing large sums of money in overseas bank accounts. Individuals should heed simple, specific warnings: (1) do not believe the promise

A phishing e-mail purporting to be from PayPal.

of large sums of money for your cooperation and (2) guard your account information carefully. These two warnings are applicable for all suspicious forms of communication, whether they originate from cyber or traditional sources.

The FBI states that it does not send mass e-mails to private citizens about cyber-scams, so if you receive an e-mail that claims to be from the FBI director or some other top official, it is likely a scam. The FBI also states that any unsolicited e-mail offers or spam should be sent to the Federal Trade Commission. The FBI does, however, keep a list of the latest e-scams and warnings via its Internet Crime Complaint Center. In June 2015, the FBI had listed the following examples of current cyber-scams: gift card scams; threats to target law enforcement personnel and public officials; fake government services that attempt to attain personal information and to collect fraudulent fees; tax refund frauds; university employee payroll scams; and scams targeting university students (The Internet Crime Complaint Center 2015).

As we transition to large-scale examples of cyberdeviancy, Homeland Security (2015) advises that individuals and social institutions are all susceptible to cyber-scams. "The growing number of serious attacks on essential cyber networks is one of the most serious economic and national security threats our nation faces. An important way to protect yourself and others from cyber security incidents is to watch for them and report any that you find" (Homeland Security 2015).

Cyberdeviancy: Large-Scale Victimization

We have learned some of the many ways in which individuals can be harmed by cyberdeviancy. Just as we, as individuals, are vulnerable to cyberattacks, so too are commercial enterprises and government agencies—which also affects many individuals either directly or indirectly. Our reliance and dependence on the digital realm make us extremely vulnerable to cyberdeviancy. The evidence of this vulnerability is all around us, as cyberattacks are happening at an alarming frequency. While I write this first draft, I can hear the televised news in the background reporting on hackers who successfully grounded around 1,400 passengers at the Warsaw Chopin airport. The hackers breached the airport's base computers and managed to ground LOT Polish Airways (the national airline of Poland). Poland's national flag carrier was forced to cancel 20 flights, and several others were delayed on June 21, 2015, after suffering an attack on its IT system. As Sebastian Mikosz, CEO of LOT, warned, "This is an industry problem, not a LOT problem but an industry problem on a much wider scale, and for sure we have to give it more attention" (Marsh 2015). Anyone who has flown realizes the hassles involved when flights are delayed, but they also understand (or should comprehend) that a hacked flight already airborne poses far greater concerns.

As with cyberdeviancy at the individual level, there are many examples of large-scale versions of cyberdeviancy. In the following pages we will take a look at a sampling of these threats.

Banks/Financial Institutions

As we learned in chapter 4, banking and financial institutions control a huge percentage of the world's total assets. And while it is fashionable to condemn the banks, much like many people condemn "Big Oil," their assets include the mortgages, savings, retirement funds, and much more, of us everyday citizens. Thus, it is not in the best interest of nearly all of us to have banking and financial institutions vulnerable to cyberattack. We should also be concerned that if the largest banks in the world cannot protect their (and our) financial assets, who can?

In February 2015 the largest (to date) bank hacking scheme took place. An international band of cybercrooks (referred to as Carbanak by Russian computer security) looted as much as $1 billion worldwide; and this time, the hackers stole directly from the banks, instead of their customers (Associated Press 2015d; Whitehouse 2015; Reuters 2015). Some experts are saying this crime represents a new era of cybercrime (certainly compared to two decades ago) where criminals steal directly from banks instead of their customers (Whitehouse 2015). Moscow-based security firm Kaspersky Lab released a report indicating that a gang of international hackers had stolen as much as $1 billion from 100 banks across 30 countries by installing malware that allowed them to take control of the banks' internal operations (Whitehouse 2015). It is the scale and level of sophistication of the attacks that has experts concerned that this form of cyberhacking represents a new trend. Previously, the biggest cyberthreat to banks was of hackers going after customers, including stealing their personal financial information and skimming their bank cards. Still, customers are at risk, as the cyberthieves had access to all of the banking infrastructures and therefore were able to get the data of any banking customer. In this particular breach, American banks were safe and there was no evidence that U.S. banking customers had their information stolen. American banking customers are also protected from financial losses up to $250,000 thanks to the Federal Deposit Insurance Corporation. Nonetheless, their personal information is still potentially vulnerable.

There is a reason why we are warned to never open an attachment from an e-mail that was sent to us by an unknown sender, as it appears as though the hacker gang accessed computers by having bank employees click on e-mail attachments. The hackers relied on a technique known as "spear phishing." **Spear phishing** is a targeted e-mail scam sent from a fake account that looks familiar but is sent with the sole purpose of obtaining unauthorized access to sensitive data. Once the hackers gain access to bank employees' computer systems they lie in wait, often for months, watching how employees operate until they figure out for themselves how to transfer money to an outside account. This phishing scheme represents an evolutionary approach to cybertheft, and it is certainly not limited to the banking industry.

Prior to the banking scheme described above, a number of other significant bank theft schemes occurred that resulted in the loss of tens of millions of dollars. For example, in 2013, a worldwide gang of hackers stole $45 million in a matter of hours by hacking their way into a database of prepaid debit cards and then draining cash machines around the globe (Long 2013). In 2009, money mule scams netted more than $100 million. According to the FBI, criminals used Trojans like Zeus and URLZone to steal victims' online banking credentials and wire money to so-called "mules." Consumers were tricked into agreeing to work-from-home scams and tasked with withdrawing cash and sending it to scammers via Moneygram. The targeted malware used in these cybercrimes could cover the cybercriminals' tracks in some cases by rewriting the online banking statement (Costa 2015).

Plastic Cards/Credit Cards

While credit card fraud was discussed in chapter 4, cyberdeviancy and plastic cards/credit cards represent a different type of crime and one (like banking and intellectual property cybercrime) that was discussed by the AFP two decades ago.

Echoing the belief among experts in the banking industry that worry cyber-hacking has reached a new era of sophistication and a corresponding record high amount of financial loss, the credit card industry is also equally vulnerable. Federal prosecutors announced in July 2013 that they charged five men responsible for a hacking and credit card fraud spree that cost companies more than $300 million. At the time, the case represented the biggest cybercrime case filed in U.S. history (Jones and Finkle 2013). Authorities had been pursuing the hackers for years, and while some of breaches they were responsible for were released to the public, the breach on NASDAQ OMX Group was disclosed for the first time. The hackers targeted Visa Inc., J.C. Penney Co., Jet Blue Airways Corp., and French retailer Carrefour SA, according to the indictment released in July 2013. Prosecutors said that the hacker group, who were from Russia and Ukraine, helped steal at least 160 million payment cards, resulting in losses in excess of $300 million. The five-member hacking crew had specialized jobs that included hacking into networks, mining them for data, and selling stolen data and distributing the profits (Jones and Finkle 2013).

The U.S. Attorney's Office in Manhattan announced that the NASDAQ breach occurred from November 2008 through October 2010 and said that malicious software was installed that enabled the hackers to execute commands to delete, change, or steal data. This breach was separate from the one NASDAQ had acknowledged occurred in 2010 (Jones and Finkle 2013).

When it comes to using plastic cards (credit and debit), the user is, essentially, always at risk at of being a victim of fraud every time their card is swiped. The hacking of Target, Home Depot, Staples (to be discussed shortly), and other top retailers involved two separate crimes with two sets of criminals—sophisticated cyberthieves who stole credit card information as part of a criminal syndicate and common criminals who used the stolen cards to purchase items for personal use. *60 Minutes* referred to 2014 as the "year of the data breach," citing the theft of 40 million credit cards from Target; 2.6 million stolen credit cards at Michaels stores; and the theft of another 56 million credit cards from those who shopped Home Depot (Whitaker 2014). Dave DeWalt, CEO of FireEye, a cybersecurity company that gets hired to keep hackers from getting into a company's network or getting them out after there's been a breach, told *60 Minutes* that 97 percent of all companies are getting breached (Whitaker 2014). Trying to keep up with the hackers is a difficult challenge as they work 24–7 and are always trying new ways to breach security systems.

Credit card companies in the United States are finally starting to catch up with much of the rest of the industrialized world that incorporates the use of "chip technology" in its credit cards as a means of trying to reduce fraud. These new cards are known as EMV-enabled (Europay) and come with an embedded chip and a PIN. By the end of 2015, 70 percent of U.S. credit cards and 41 percent of U.S. debit cards will have these security chips (Groenfeldt 2014). Despite the enthusiasm for credit cards with chips and PIN, hackers have shown that they do not need the actual plastic card in hand, they just need certain bits of information. The lesson here is, be very careful every time you swipe your card, and try to keep it to a minimum to reduce your chances of being victimized by a credit card hacker.

It should be noted that plastic credit cards are slowly becoming obsolete, as an increasing number of people are using their cell phones for purchases. This will not, however, diminish the threat of fraud, as it would stand to reason that the theft of smartphones and information from smartphones will also increase correspondingly.

Instead of using cash for inexpensive purchases, many people use credit cards, thus increasing their chances of being a victim of credit card fraud and identity theft.

Intellectual Property Rights

Intellectual property refers to a wide variety of products of the intellect (creations of the mind) that have commercial value, including copyrighted property such as literary or artistic works, and ideational property, such as patents, business methods, and industrial processes. In most instances intellectual property is intangible and available as cybertechnology, thus making it open to cybertheft. **Intellectual property rights (IPR) theft** is the stealing of any intellectual property ranging from songs and movies to machine tools and pharmaceuticals (U.S. Department of State 2015a). The FBI (2015k) describes intellectual property theft as robbing people of their ideas, inventions, and creative expressions, including everything from trade secrets to proprietary products and parts to movies and music and software.

The Department of State reports that IT-enabled crimes are increasing dramatically given the borderless nature of cyberspace. The FBI (2015k) also believes that intellectual property theft is a growing threat because of the rise of digital technologies and Internet file-sharing networks. "And much of the theft takes place overseas, where laws are often lax and enforcement more difficult. All told, intellectual property theft costs U.S. businesses billions of dollars a year and robs the nation of jobs and lost tax revenue" (FBI 2015k). The U.S. Department of Justice's Computer Crime and Intellectual Property Section (CCIPS) is responsible for implementing the department's national strategies in combating computer and intellectual property crimes worldwide. CCIPS prevents, investigates, and prosecutes computer crimes by working with other government agencies, the private sector, academic institutions, and foreign counterparts. The concern over IPR theft centers on its role as one of the principal U.S. economic engines; in turn, its value makes it an attractive target for hackers worldwide.

The CCIPS releases regular press releases of IPR theft. By mid-June 2015 it had released 17 press releases describing such IPR thefts as a New Orleans man charged with conspiracy to commit wire fraud and conspiracy to commit trademark counterfeiting; Chinese professors among six defendants charged with economic espionage and theft of trade secrets; a former PPG employee charged with theft of trade secrets; Kolon Industries Inc. pleading guilty for conspiracy to steal DuPont trade secrets involving Kevlar technology; a man charged with recording movies in a local theater and criminal infringement of a copyright; and a pharmacist pleading guilty to trafficking in counterfeit Viagra (U.S. Department of Justice 2015d).

A couple of unusual cases of IPR theft include the June 2015 federal investigation of Major League Baseball's St. Louis Cardinals for allegedly illegally hacking into a computer database of the Houston Astros to obtain information on players. Both the FBI and the Justice Department were investigating whether the Cardinals' front-office officials were behind the effort to steal information from the Astros' database, called Ground Control (Associated Press 2015e). One final example to be discussed—the hacking of Sony Corporation—is examined in box 9.3.

CONNECTING SOCIAL DEVIANCE AND POPULAR CULTURE

Box 9.3 James Franco and Seth Rogen Almost Start World War III and Sony Gets Hacked

James Franco and Seth Rogen are among the more popular, and sometimes controversial, celebrities of contemporary society. In 2014 they were involved in an action comedy, *The Interview*. Franco plays the character Dave Skylark and Rogen plays Aaron Rapoport. In the film, Skylark is the host of a celebrity tabloid show, *Skylark Tonight*, and Rapoport is the producer of the show. Known mostly for fluff pieces, much like real entertainment/variety shows, Skylark and Rapoport are surprised when they learn that North Korean dictator Kim Jong-un, who is a big fan of the show, wants to be interviewed by Skylark. Skylark and Rapoport must go to North Korea to conduct the interview, which they are happy to do, as both characters want to improve the show's image as a more credible news show. The CIA learns of the planned interview and recruits Skylark and Rapoport to assassinate the dictator.

As a comedy, especially a Franco/Rogen comedy, it is clear to everyone, including North

Koreans, that Kim Jong-un will be depicted in a less than flattering manner. It is this realization that connects *The Interview* and Sony Pictures Entertainment (the parent company of Columbia Pictures, the film's distributor) with IPR theft and far-fetched worries about the beginning of World War III if the film was released. In June 2014, the North Korean government threatened the United States if Columbia Pictures went ahead with the release. Suddenly, a movie that would have drawn modest interest among moviegoers had now gained the attention of the governments of North Korea and the United States. Furthermore, threats of hacking drew the attention of numerous U.S. law enforcement agencies.

On November 24, 2014, an image of a stylized skull with long, skeletal fingers flashed on every employee's computer screen at the same time at Sony Headquarters in Culver City, California, with a threatening message warning, "This is just the beginning. We've obtained all your internal data" (Robb 2014). The hackers, who called themselves "Guardians of Peace," further warned Sony that if they did not abide by their demands, they would release the company's "top secrets." In a little more than a week, hackers released numerous Sony films so that they could be downloaded illegally for free. The Sony computer system was still down. E-mail and voice mail were inoperable. Hackers released pre-bonus salaries of top Sony executives and thousands of other employees. Hackers release private e-mails of top executives, and some of the e-mails included celebrity bashing and politically incorrect jokes and commentary that was very embarrassing. The FBI launched a full investigation, initially thinking it was the work of North Korean terrorists. On December 5, 2014, the hackers threatened the lives of Sony family members. On December 14, North Korea denied any involvement in the hacking while praising it as a "righteous deed." The next day, the Guardians of Peace warned that if the film was shown, they would blow up movie theaters and claimed the film's release would be treated as an act of war (Robb 2014). *The Interview* premiered amid tight security at the Ace Hotel's theater in downtown Los Angeles on December 11. A week later, however, Sony, under threat of terrorist attacks from hackers and major movie theater chains' refusal to show the film, announced that the December 25 release of *The Interview* had been canceled (Coyle 2014). Sony's announcement not to show the film at the theater met with additional threats as the hackers demanded that *The Interview* never come out on DVD, pay-per-view, or VOD (TMZ 2014).

President Obama criticized Sony's decision and stated that the United States "will respond proportionally" to the cyberattack on the studio and American moviegoers. On December 20, North Korea proclaimed its innocence and invited the United States to take part in a joint investigation of the Sony attack, and counterwarned of "serious consequences," including a threat to attack the White House, the Pentagon, and the whole U.S. mainland, if the U.S. retaliated (Robb 2014). On December 23, Sony announced it would release *The Interview* as originally scheduled on Christmas Day. On December 26, waiting a day to make sure everything was safe, this author attended the movie.

The movie is funny, especially if you like Franco and Rogen, but in reality, the depiction of Kim Jong-un and of the Korean regime in *The Interview* is reflective of all news media outlets; nonetheless, Jong-un is assassinated. As for IPR theft, however, as stated by Sony president and CEO Kazuo Hirai, the attack on Sony is "one of the most vicious and malicious cyber attacks in recent history" (BBC News 2015). What concerns U.S. government law enforcement agencies is the fact that not only was intellectual property stolen, but property (Sony computer operating systems) was also destroyed. The stealing of property combined with wanton destruction of property could represent the new era of cybertheft.

Cyberattacks Against the Private Sector

Riley Walters of the Heritage Foundation wrote in 2014 that "the spate of recent data breaches at big-name companies such as JPMorgan Chase, Home Depot, and Target raises questions about the effectiveness of the private sector's information security" (Walters 2014). Speaking to CBS's *60 Minutes*, James Comey, the director of the FBI, commented on the prevalence of Chinese hackers against the U.S. private sector, "There are two kinds of big companies in the United States. There are those who've been hacked by the Chinese and those who don't know they've been hacked by the Chinese" (Cook 2014). Comey went on to say that Chinese hackers are motivated primarily by finding trade secrets of U.S. businesses so that they can be used in China; this saves the Chinese the time of having to invent their own products.

If FBI director Comey is correct about the prevalence of Chinese cyberattacks against the U.S. private sector, it would be impossible to chronicle every

TABLE 9.1	Sampling of U.S. Private Sector Companies That Were Victimized by Cyberattack, 2014

January:

Target (retail)—The retail giant announced that an additional 70 million individuals' contact information was taken during the December 2013 breach, in which 40 million customers' credit and debit card information was stolen.

Neiman Marcus (retail)—Sophisticated code written by hackers in their 2013 breach, which led to over 350,000 individuals having their credit card information stolen, continued to plague the retailer's customers in 2014.

Michaels (retail)—The payment cards of 2.6 million Michaels customers were affected from May 2013 through January 2014. Attackers targeted the Michaels POS system to gain access to their system.

Yahoo! Mail (communications)—The e-mail service for 273 million users was reportedly hacked in January, although information on specific accounts was not released.

April:

Aaron Brothers (retail)—The credit and debit card information for roughly 400,000 customers of Aaron Brothers, a subsidiary of Michaels, was compromised by the same POS system malware.

AT&T (communications)—For two weeks AT&T was hacked from the inside by personnel who accessed user information, including Social Security information.

May:

eBay (retail)—Cyberattacks in late February and early March led to the compromise of eBay employee log-in information (passwords).

June:

Feedly (communications)—Feedly's 15 million users were temporarily affected by three distributed denial-of-service attacks.

Evernote (technology)—One hundred million users faced denial-of-service attacks.

P.F. Chang's China Bistro (restaurant)—Between September 2013 and June 2014, credit and debit card information from 33 P.F. Chang's restaurants was compromised and reportedly sold online.

August:

U.S. Investigations Services (services)—A subcontractor for federal employee background checks was breached, which led to the theft of employee personnel information.

Community Health Services (health care)—The personal data for 4.5 million patients was compromised for any patient who visited any of its 206 hospital locations over the past five years. The FBI warns that other health care firms may have also been attacked by the same Chinese sophisticated malware.

September:

Home Depot (retail)—Cybercriminals reportedly used malware to compromise the credit card information for roughly 56 million Home Depot shoppers.

Google (communications)—Five million Gmail usernames and passwords were compromised.

Apple iCloud (technology)—Hackers gained access to Apple users' online data storage, leading to, among other things, the subsequent posting of celebrities' private photos online.

October:

JPMorgan Chase (financial)—Information from 76 million households and 7 million small businesses was compromised.

Source: The Heritage Foundation/Walters 2014

example; indeed, we might as well simply list every single major company that operates in the United States. Nonetheless, there are specific cases of cyberterrorism worth mentioning. The list provided in table 9.1 represents a sampling of the data breaches in the calendar year 2014 compiled by the Heritage Foundation (see table 9.1).

The magnitude of cyberattacks against the private sector cannot be overstated, as clearly the hacking examples shown in table 9.1 represent a mere sampling of the breaches that are constantly occurring and being reported. As I wrote the first draft of this chapter in June 2014, it was reported that every Samsung Galaxy device—from the S3 to the latest S6—has a significant design flaw in its keyboards (which cannot be deleted) that allows hackers to spy on anyone using such a device. The seriousness of this cyberattack is underscored by the reality that there are an estimated 600 million Samsung devices that are affected. Among other things, the breach may allow hackers to gain access to users' Wi-Fi or cell networks and take control of the microphones and cameras (Pagliery 2015; Gibbs 2015).

Cyberattacks Against Government Agencies

While it is bewildering to think of the ineffectiveness of the private sector to guard against cyberattacks, what is more disconcerting is the realization that federal agencies are also just as incompetent when it comes to protecting their databases from cyberattack. In June 2015 the House Oversight and Government Reform Committee (the main investigative committee in the U.S. House of Representatives) took to task the federal government for using outdated antivirus software and lax policies on securing passwords, leaving it vulnerable to cyberattacks. The federal government, which holds secrets and sensitive information ranging from nuclear blueprints to the tax returns of hundreds of millions of Americans, has for years failed to take basic steps to protect its data from hackers, according to Representative Jason Chaffetz (R-UT), chairman of the House Oversight and Government Reform Committee. Chaffetz states, "Last year [2014], across government, we the American people spent almost $80 billion on information technology, and it stinks" (Associated Press 2015f).

In June 2015, the Office of Personnel Management (OPM) was under fire for allowing its databases to be plundered by suspected Chinese cyberspies in what U.S. officials say is the "worst ever breach of U.S. government data" (Perez and LoBianco 2015). OPM repeatedly neglected to implement basic cybersecurity protections, which allowed hackers linked to China to steal private information on nearly every federal employee—and detailed personal histories of millions with security clearances—officials acknowledged to Congress (Associated Press 2015f; Dilanian 2015). The OPM director, Katherine Archuleta, testified before the House Oversight and Government Reform Committee (June 16, 2015) that she believed just 4 million federal employees had their information stolen by cyperspies, but Chaffetz said the number of affected federal employees was actually a total of 32 million people (Perez and LoBianco 2015). "Representatives from Homeland Security Department, Office of Management and Budget, Interior Department—where the OPM's hacked servers are housed—and OPM all said they were taking steps to upgrade systems and boost security protocols" (Katz 2015). Trying to defend herself, Archuleta pointed out that she inherited "decades old" legacy systems and that she was doing her best to modernize them in an attempt to halt cyberbreaches.

The Departments of Treasury, Transportation, State, and Health and Human Services have much worse records than the OPM, according to a 2015 administration report to Congress under the Federal Information Security Management Act. Each of these agencies has been hacked in the last few years. The IRS is another federal agency that was hacked in 2015, and simple upgrades to its computer systems could have helped to prevent the breach and the theft of tax information from more than 334,000 taxpayers, a government investigator told Congress (Associated Press 2015g; Ohlemacher 2015). Congress cannot solely blame federal agencies for their lapse in cybersecurity. "While President Barack Obama's latest [2015] budget plan called for a $14 billion increase for cyberdefenses, the House proposed a budget in March that didn't include specific funding for cybersecurity. Nor has Congress imposed much accountability on agencies that suffer breaches" (Associated Press 2015f).

The prevalence of security lapses at federal agencies alone should serve as a red flag that serious measures need to be taken to curtail cyberhacking. In the 2014 fiscal year, the federal government dealt with 67,196 cyberincidents, up from 57,971 incidents the year before, according to a White House report (Associated Press 2015f). And if the prevalence of cyberattacks against federal agencies wasn't a loud enough warning siren, the consistency of the problem should have been. The Government Accountability Office (GAO) has labeled federal information security a "high-risk area" since 1997. In 2003, the GAO expanded its high-risk designation to include computer networks supporting critical infrastructure. "This year [2015], it added 'personally identifiable information' to the list, just in time to see hackers steal the Social Security numbers and other private information of nearly every federal worker" (Associated Press 2015f). Clearly, federal agencies are at high risk of cyberattack. To date, such breaches have led to substantial financial losses. Future breaches may lead to deadly consequences.

The Future of Cyberdeviancy

The threat of cyberdeviancy and crime to society is very real. According to a recent RAND report, cyber black markets are now more profitable than the illegal drug trade (Ablon, Libicki, and Golay 2015). "Experts agree that the coming years will bring more activity in darknets, more use of crypto-currencies, greater anonymity capabilities in malware, and more attention to encrypting and protecting communications and transactions; that the ability to stage cyberattacks will likely outpace the ability to defend against them; that crime will increasingly have a networked or cyber component, creating a wider range of opportunities for black markets; and that there will be more hacking for hire, as-a-service offerings, and brokers" (Ablon et al. 2015). At present, there is a site called Infosec Institute that teaches people how to hack professionally for private companies, intelligence agencies, and criminal gangs. The organization describes hacking services as among the most attractive commodities in the underground market. It also describes prices that hackers can charge for per-hire hacking (e.g., $90 to hack someone's Gmail account) (Infosec Institute 2015). If we are at the point where hackers can be openly hired for their services, private and government anti–cyber attack systems are primitive and outdated and easily hacked, and a slew of people exist around the world with the skills to penetrate defense systems, we can only imagine that the future might be dominated by cyber chaos.

So far, hackers have primarily limited their cyberdeviancy to theft of goods and services, private information, and so on in order to attain financial gain. One form of attempted cyberdeviancy we can expect more of in the future is cybertheft followed by a ransom demand if the victim wishes to retrieve their data information. This type of extortion is explained by the term "ransomware." **Ransomware** is a type of cyberscam that involves trying to extort money from individuals and business owners by infecting and taking control of the victim's computer (Tompor 2015). The FBI warns that ransomware is typically spread through a threat called CryptoWall and its variants. In addition to ransom dollars, many victims of ransomware face costs associated with network mitigation, network countermeasures, loss of productivity, legal fees, IT services, and the purchase of credit monitoring services for employees or customers (Tompor 2015).

Future concerns over cyberdeviancy are centered on the realistic threat that such deviants will shift their efforts from theft to destruction. We learned that the cyberbreach of Sony not only involved the theft of intellectual property, it also included the destruction of part of their network. What if hackers decide to take down the power grid or take down planes in the air instead of keeping them grounded so that they cannot fly? Businesses and government agencies both need to be proactive instead of reactive in their attempts to eliminate the dangers associated with cyberdeviancy.

Summary

In this chapter the many forms of cyberdeviancy and crime are discussed. Analysis begins with a brief overview of the role of technology and the development of the Internet. Since the early stages of cyber forms of communications and technology, there have been warnings about the potential danger from cyberdeviants, including hackers. As presented in this chapter, we can divide cyberdeviancy into two primary categories: cyberdeviancy at the individual level of victimization and cyberdeviancy at the large-scale level of victimization.

Cyberdeviancy at the individual level of victimization refers to acts wherein the primary targeted victims are individuals. While such behaviors generally target individual victims, they may affect large numbers of people in total. Among the topics discussed were catfishing; cyberstalking; cyberbullying; swatting; identity theft and identity fraud; cyberpornography, including revenge porn; and cyberscams. Variations of these deviant acts (e.g., stalking, bullying, identity theft, pornography, and scams) existed long before the introduction of the Internet, while others (e.g., catfishing, cyberstalking, and swatting) are a unique by-product of the cyberworld. In all cases, the cyberworld has created an environment that fosters a great deal of social deviance.

Large-scale variations of cyberdeviancy place large numbers of people, financial institutions, private businesses, and government agencies at risk of being victimized by cyberattacks. Our reliance and dependence on the digital realm make us extremely vulnerable to cyberdeviancy. The evidence of this vulnerability is all around us as cyberattacks are happening at an alarming frequency. Specific examples of large-scale versions of cyberdeviancy discussed in this chapter include cyberattacks against banks/financial institutions; cyberattacks against plastic card/credit card users; the cybertheft of intellectual property rights; and cyberattacks, primarily as result of hacking, against the private sector and against government agencies.

The chapter concludes with a look at the future of cyberdeviancy. It is clear that our dependency on cybetechnology will assure that cyberdeviancy will not only continue but actually increase in the future. That is, unless there comes a time when we no longer rely on cybertechnology either because we voluntarily stop using such technology (which will not be the case) or involuntarily due to hackers bringing down the grid (and then no one has access to the cyberworld). Private and government agencies must step up their commitment to combat cyberdeviancy, or the worse-case scenario presented here is a real possibility.

Key Terms

catfishing, 242

computer hacker, 240

computer hacking, 240

cyberbullying, 244

cyberharassment, 247

cyberscams, 250

cyberstalking, 247

intellectual property, 254

intellectual property rights (IPR) theft, 254

ransomware, 260

spear phishing, 252

swatting, 248

technology, 236

Discussion Questions

1. People of a certain age remember a time without cybertechnology. Would it be a tough transition for you if suddenly cybertechnology of all forms ceased to exist? Explain.

2. Decades ago there were those who sounded the alarm that cybertechnology could lead to a great deal of cyberdeviancy and crime, and yet those warnings were mostly ignored. Why do you think that is the case?

3. Explain the social phenomenon of "catfishing." Why do you think it occurs? Have you or anyone you know been a part of catfishing, either as victim or perpetrator?

4. Describe the serious nature of cyberstalking, cyberbullying, swatting, and cyberporn. What would you do if you were a victim of cyberstalking?

5. Explain the risks involved every time you have your credit or debit card swiped. Why do you suppose people have abandoned the relative safety of a cash society for the relatively unsafe cyber-purchasing society?

6. What is your reaction to the realization that the federal government is so vulnerable to cyberattack?

7. If hackers reach the point where they can take control of the cyberworld, what would some of the possible consequences be?

CHAPTER 10

Mental Illness and Disorders and Social Deviance

CHAPTER OBJECTIVES

After reading this chapter students should be able to:

- Explain what is meant by good mental health and poor mental health
- Describe mental illness and mental disorders
- Describe the role of stigma on mental illness
- Provide a review of seven major types of mental illness and disorders
- Provide a brief history of the treatment of mental illness

- Describe the three major approaches to treating mental illness
- Demonstrate the ability to describe the major approaches to treating mental illness to specific types of mental illness
- Apply the five perspectives of social deviance to the study of mental illness

There are many times in our daily activities when we place our trust, and in some instances our lives, in the hands of others. If we have a surgical procedure, we have to rely on the professionalism of medical caregivers (including surgeons, nurses, and anesthesiologists); when we drive our cars, we have to assume that other motorists will abide by the laws of the road; when we take a ferry or subway ride, we have to trust that the operator is competent; and when we fly we are dependent upon the professionalism, competency, and skill of the pilots. There are people who get nervous when they have to fly, but most fliers block out the anxiety or simply assume and/or trust that the pilot is capable of handling the duties associated with piloting a plane. I have flown well over a half-million miles in my lifetime and recall years ago on one of my first flights a passenger sitting next to me who said, "You don't have to worry about pilots of planes because they don't want to crash either." The implication was quite clear—the pilot will do all they can in order to assure a safe flight. I found my fellow passenger's comment reassuring and comforting.

But what if the pilot does *not* want a safe flight and, worse, what if the pilot actually wants to end his own life by purposively crashing the plane? It seems absurd that a pilot would want to intentionally crash a plane filled with passengers, but such is the potential case if the pilot is suffering from mental illness. (In another scenario, a terroristic pilot may also want to purposively crash a plane.) A rare example of a pilot suffering from a mental illness ("severe depression") who deliberately crashed the plane he was piloting occurred on March 24, 2015, when

Andreas Lubitz intentionally used the controls to speed up the plane's descent, sending Germanwings Flight 9525 into a mountainside in the French Alps (Smith-Spark and Haddad 2015). Germanwings is a wholly owned subsidiary of Lufthansa. After the fatal crash of Flight 9525, Lufthansa revealed that it knew copilot Lubitz suffered from an episode of "severe depression" before he finished his flight training with the German airline; in fact, Lubitz had sent e-mails to the Lufthansa flight school informing them that he had suffered a "previous episode of severe depression," which had since subsided (Associated Press 2015h:A6). The airline said that Lubitz subsequently passed all medical checks. Evidence from the plane's cockpit voice recorder ("black box") led investigators to believe that Lubitz deliberately crashed the Airbus A320, killing all 150 people on board. Furthermore, prosecutors in Germany announced that an analysis of a tablet device retrieved from the 27-year-old Lubitz's apartment in Düsseldorf revealed that he had researched suicide methods and cockpit door security on the Internet (Smith-Spark and Haddad 2015).

We will revisit this tragic incident and the mental illness of severe depression later in this chapter. We will also examine a number of examples of mental illness and a number of related topics throughout this chapter.

Mental Health

Just as we would prefer good physical health to poor health, we would also prefer good mental health over poor mental health. From a normative perspective of social deviance, to have a mental illness would be equated to violating the social norm expectation of good mental health. It is generally believed that people with good mental health are more stable, reasonable, and pleasant to be around. This helps to explain why some people hide their mental disorders in order to appear to be "normal" and to avoid the negative stigmatization associated with mental illness. (As described in chapter 1, a person is **stigmatized** after being characterized or branded as "disgraceful" or "ignominious.") Some people seek treatment for mental abnormalities, and others are forced to receive medical treatment intervention. Treatment represents attempts to "normalize" people. As we shall learn in this chapter, however, the topic of mental illness is far too complicated to be summarized in such a manner as people with good mental health are "normal" and people with poor mental health are "abnormal" or "deviant." Nonetheless, a quick look at the meaning of good mental health and poor mental health provides an excellent starting point for the discussion of mental illness.

Good Mental Health

The very implication of the concepts of "mental illness" and "mental disorders" presupposes the existence of a more desired form of mental health—good mental health. **Good mental health**, among other things, offers feelings of well-being, inner strength, emotional functionality, and the ability to cope and manage change and uncertainty. According to the Mental Health Foundation (2015), you are in good mental health if you can:

- Make the most of your potential
- Cope with life
- Play a full part in your family, workplace, community, and among friends

Some people refer to mental health as "emotional health" or "well-being." It is generally recognized that good mental health is as important as good physical health for the overall well-being (functioning) of the individual. The Mental Health Foundation (2015) states that good mental health is characterized by a person's ability to fulfill a number of key functions and activities, including:

- The ability to learn
- The ability to feel, express, and manage a range of positive and negative emotions
- The ability to form and maintain good relationships with others
- The ability to cope with and manage change and uncertainty

The Mental Health Foundation also states that our mental health is not static and is subject to change when confronted with changes in circumstances. And while all of us have experienced times when we feel down, stressed, or anxious, most of us can cope with such challenges, and before too long these feelings pass and we are soon happy, upbeat, and relaxed. But not everyone bounces back so quickly, if at all, when confronted with adverse situations or conditions, and for them, attaining good mental health represents a greater challenge.

Martin Seligman, a psychologist who promotes the idea of positive psychology via a number of self-help books, details his notion of good mental health in his 2011 book *Flourish*. In *Flourish*, Seligman promotes his "Well-Being Theory" via the acronym PERMA. PERMA contains five key aspects necessary for good mental health:

Positive emotion—Includes behaviors that leave individuals feeling good about themselves, which can only be evaluated subjectively via such means as asking oneself, "How happy do I feel?"
Engagement—Involvement with others, work, and general activities that bring enrichment
Relationships—Maintaining a sense of closeness with significant others (people you care about and who care about you) such as family, friends, intimacy, or social connections with others
Meaning—Involved with activities that are bigger than the individual; a sense of purpose or a calling
Achievement—A sense of fulfillment that brings about a sense of emotion

Felicia Huppert, director of the Well-Being Institute at the University of Cambridge, has studied mental well-being for more than two decades. She describes mental health as a spectrum with positive mental health on one end and mental disorders (e.g., anxiety and depression) at the other end (ABC Health & Wellbeing 2015). In order to flourish with good mental health, Huppert promotes a list of 10 features of positive well-being, which includes Seligman's PERMA attributes as well as emotional stability, optimism, resilience, self-esteem, and vitality.

Good mental health is, of course, very important to each of us, as it helps us to enjoy life and cope with problems. The Office on Women's Health (a subsidiary of the U.S. Department of Health and Human Services) provides us with tips on how to keep our mind healthy:

1. Nutrition—The food that one eats can have a direct effect on one's energy level, physical health, and mood.
2. Exercise—Regular physical activity is important to the physical and mental health of almost everyone. Being physically active can help one continue

their pursuits of activities that bring happiness as well as provide a sense of independence.

3. Sleep—The body needs time to rest and heal every day; this helps to explain why people who have trouble sleeping generally have other mental health issues (Office on Women's Health 2015).

A number of mental health experts have ideas about how to best achieve good mental health. ABC Health & Wellbeing (2015) recommends:

- Mindfulness—The practice of drawing one's attention to the present moment, focusing on emotions, thoughts, and sensations in a nonjudgmental way; often achieved through some variation of meditation.
- Gratitude diary—A good way to foster optimism is to keep a "gratitude diary" wherein at the end of each day the individual lists in a private journal/diary the positive things that happened that day.
- Optimism—Focusing on the positive but in a grounded-to-reality mode.
- Realistic expectations—It is important to realize that it's virtually impossible to be happy all the time or to expect that every encounter with others will be positive.
- Social engagement—Being involved in the positive development of others can foster a sense of positive well-being. Volunteerism is a great way to become socially or civically engaged.

Perhaps one of the greatest detractors of good mental health and leading contributors to poor mental health is stress. Stress may occur for many reasons, including everyday challenges brought about due to the pressures of school, work, or family responsibilities and more serious traumatic events such as a car accident, states of emergencies, and the death of a loved one. Trying to stay calm during stressful situations is one of the biggest challenges each of us is likely to face in our pursuit of good mental health. Common symptoms of stress include headache, sleep disorders, difficulty concentrating, short temper, upset stomach, job dissatisfaction, low morale, anxiety, and depression (Office on Women's Health 2015).

Poor Mental Health

Poor mental health is generally expressed in terms of mental illness or mental disorder and refers to conditions that negatively impact a person's ability to cope with everyday events or stressful situations. Generally, the two terms of "mental illness" and "mental disorder" are used interchangeably. The World Health Organization more often than not uses the term "mental disorder." According to WHO (2014) a **mental disorder** refers to a mental or bodily condition marked primarily by insufficient organization of personality, mind, and emotions that impairs the normal functioning of the individual. Mental disorders are generally characterized by a combination of abnormal thoughts, perceptions, emotions, behavior, and relationships with others. The National Alliance on Mental Illness (NAMI) (as its name would imply) generally discusses the term "mental illness" when describing poor mental health. According to NAMI (2015a), a **mental illness** is a condition that impacts a person's thinking, feeling, or mood and may affect his or her ability to relate to others and function on a daily basis. As we can see, the definitions used by WHO and NAMI are nearly the same even though they are defining two different terms.

Certainly, the common thread between the two terms of "mental illness" and "mental disorder" is the realization that we are talking about poor mental health as opposed to good mental health. And challenging the statistical perspective of social deviance as that which is unusual, rare, or uncommon, there are many people suffering from poor mental health. According to NAMI (2015a), 1 in 5 adults experiences a mental health condition every year and 1 in 20 lives with a serious mental illness such as schizophrenia or bipolar disorder. NAMI points out that in addition to the person directly experiencing a mental illness are his or her close associates (family members, friends, and caregivers). Roughly half of mental health conditions begin by age 14, and 75 percent of mental health conditions develop by age 24. "The normal personality and behavior changes of adolescence may mimic or mask symptoms of a mental health condition. Early engagement and support are crucial to improving outcomes and increasing the promise of recovery" (NAMI 2015a).

Despite the seriousness of poor mental health, a disproportionately small amount of governmental money is allocated to help and support those suffering from mental illnesses or mental disorders. According to WHO (2014), in low- and middle-income countries, between 76 percent and 85 percent of people with mental disorders received no treatment for their disorder. In high-income countries, between 35 percent and 50 percent of people with mental disorders are in the same situation. Furthermore, WHO reports that the quality of care, for those who do receive it, is generally very poor. In the United States, a glance at the 2015 Federal Budget Spending Estimates would seem to reveal, on the surface, that the government is allocating a proportionately fair amount of money on good mental health. The 2015 estimated budget allocated 28 percent of the budget toward health care but, upon closer examination, we see that of the more than $1.1 trillion directed toward health care, over $576 billion was allocated for medical service to seniors, $502 million for vendor payments (welfare), and nearly $33 million for research and development (Chantrill 2015). This leaves very little money for the development of good mental health for all U.S. citizens.

WHO recommends the full implementation of its Mental Health Action Plan 2013–2020, endorsed by the World Health Assembly in 2013, which recognizes the essential role of mental health in achieving good mental health for all people. The plan includes four major objectives:

- More effective leadership and governance for mental health
- The provision of comprehensive, integrated mental health and social care services in community-based settings
- The implementation of strategies for promotion and prevention
- Strengthened information systems, evidence, and research

This concludes our look at mental health. It is now time to focus on specific examples of mental illnesses and disorders.

Types of Mental Illness and Disorders

There are many types of mental illness and disorders, and different organizations have their own manner of categorizing them. There are over 200 classified forms of mental illnesses (Mental Health Association 2011), so it would be impossible to cover them all here. Instead, in the following pages a number of the more significant and prevalent types of mental illnesses and disorders will be reviewed. Our review begins with depression.

Depression

According to the Mayo Clinic (2015f), "**depression** is a mood disorder that causes a persistent feeling of sadness and loss of interest." Also known as "major depressive disorder" or "clinical depression," it affects how one feels, thinks, and behaves "and can lead to a variety of emotional and physical problems." Depression is more than just feeling sad or going through a rough patch. It's a serious mental health condition that requires understanding, treatment, and a good recovery plan (NAMI 2015b). Like many forms of mental illness, people suffering from depression can learn to cope and/or overcome depression. "With early detection, diagnosis and a treatment plan consisting of medication, psychotherapy and lifestyle choices, many people get better. But if left untreated, depression can be devastating, both for the people who have it and for their families" (NAMI 2015b).

WHO (2014) reports that depression is a common mental disorder and one of the main causes of disability worldwide, with approximately 400 million people of all ages suffering from the illness. An estimated 16 million American adults had at least 1 major depressive episode in 2014 (NAMI 2015b). Both men and women may suffer from depression, but women are 70 percent more likely than men to experience depression, and young adults aged 18 to 25 are 60 percent more likely to have depression than people aged 50 or older (NAMI 2015b). Among the symptoms of depression are changes in sleep (especially trouble falling asleep, staying asleep, sleeping too much, and waking up early in the morning); changes in appetite (some people stop eating and lose a lot of weight while others overeat as a coping mechanism); lack of concentration (unable to focus even on simple tasks); loss of energy (prolonged fatigue); lack of interest (lose the capacity to experience pleasure); low self-esteem (dwelling on losses or failures); hopelessness (including suicidal thoughts); changes in movement (includes extreme examples of physical depletion to angrily pacing for hours at a time); and complaining about physical aches and pains rather than discussing emotions (NAMI 2015b). Causes of depression may include trauma (especially early-age trauma); genetics (while mood disorders and risk of suicide tend to run in families, studies of identical twins reveal that both develop depression only about 30 percent of the time); life circumstances, such as financial or marital troubles (research cannot definitively show a causal effect, and therefore life circumstances may be an example of "the chicken or the egg" scenario as to which came first); brain structure (e.g., the frontal lobe is less active in depressed people; depression is also associated with changes in how the pituitary gland and hypothalamus respond to hormone stimulation); other medical conditions that may contribute to depression; and drug and alcohol abuse (NAMI 2015b).

As described above, suicide is a possible outcome of depression. If we revisit this chapter's introductory story about Andreas Lubitz, the copilot who deliberately steered Germanwings Flight 9525 into the French Alps, we gain a glimpse of major depression and how it can lead to an act of suicide. More than 40,000 people commit suicide annually in the United States, and most of those cases involve major depression. However, it is immensely rare for depression to result in violence to others (Sapolsky 2015). It is true that instances occur of deeply depressed individuals killing their family members and then themselves, but such acts usually involve a mixture of revenge and/or a disintegration of ego boundaries (wherein the sufferer cannot clearly distinguish where his ego ends and where loved ones' begin) (Sapolsky 2015). But these variables would not appear to be applicable to Lubitz. Nonetheless, data gained from the on-flight black box and subsequent investigations into Lubitz's apartment, electronic footprint, and so forth has led to the presumption that Lubitz did indeed plan to commit suicide, as well as mass murder. German officials said that his search-engine history on his computer tablet from March 16 to March 23 revealed that he searched for medical treatment methods but also ways of going about a suicide. He also searched terms about cockpit doors and their security arrangements (Hassan and Willsher 2015). Just prior to crashing into the mountain, Lubitz had locked the pilot out of the cockpit after he went to the restroom. Documents from Germany's air transportation regulator also revealed that Lubitz had sought psychiatric help for a bout of serious depression in 2009 and that he was still getting assistance from doctors (Hassan and Willsher 2015).

People who suffer from depression will experience a persistent feeling of sadness and loss of interest and may suffer from a variety of emotional and physical problems.

The Lubitz case provides us with another cautionary warning about the difficulty of diagnosing depression, as some mental health experts say that it was aggression—not just depression—that would have driven the 27-year-old Lubitz to deliberately crash a Germanwings airliner into a mountainside. Among the noises picked up in the recovered black box was an evenly breathing Lubitz while passengers screamed and the plane's frantic captain pounded helplessly on the cockpit door. Unless investigators recognize the toxic role of aggression and hostility in some patients' depression, some mental health experts warn, such troubled individuals (as Lubitz) will continue to elude detection (Healy 2015).

Bipolar Disorder

Bipolar disorder, formerly known as manic depression, is a chronic mental illness that is characterized by alternating periods of mood changes of elation and depression and causes changes in sleep, energy, thinking, and behavior. This disorder affects about 60 million people worldwide (WHO 2014). People with a bipolar disorder have high and low moods, known as mania and depression, which differ from the usual ups and downs most people experience. Although bipolar affective disorder can occur at any point in one's life cycle, the average age of onset is 25. Approximately 3 percent (2.9) of the U.S. population is diagnosed with bipolar disorder, with nearly 83 percent of cases being classified as severe. The disorder affects men and women equally (NAMI 2015c).

Symptoms of a bipolar disorder can include distinct states of mania (an abnormally elated mental state, typically characterized by feelings of euphoria, lack of inhibitions, racing thoughts, and overactivity) or depression or mixed episodes of both extremes simultaneously or in rapid sequence. Severe bipolar episodes of mania or depression may also include psychotic symptoms such as hallucinations or delusions. Usually, these psychotic symptoms mirror a person's extreme mood (e.g., someone who is manic might believe she has special powers while someone who is depressed might feel hopeless or helpless). If left untreated, the symptoms usually get worse; however, with a strong lifestyle that includes self-management and a good treatment plan, many people live effectively with the condition (NAMI 2015c). The causes of bipolar affective disorder include genetics (as with depression, the role of genetics is not definitive, but is a risk factor); stress (a stressful event may trigger the first bipolar episode); and brain structure (there are some conditions in which damaged brain tissue can contribute to bipolar disorder) (NAMI 2015c).

Some people live with a bipolar disorder and are not even aware of being bipolar. Consider the case of Demi Lovato, an American singer, songwriter, and actress. For years, Lovato could not understand her own feelings. She reports self-abusing, self-medicating, dragging other people down around her, and generally growing up very depressed. She always wondered why she felt so alternately confused and depressed while also ecstatic that she was living her dream as an entertainer. After a family intervention, she sought professional help and was diagnosed with bipolar disorder. She reports feeling relieved to learn that she was bipolar because it explained so much of her behavior. Lovato has since become one of the faces of mental illness health campaigns with her "Be Vocal: Speak Up for Mental Health" (Friedman 2015). Her campaign, initiated in May 2015, is run by a pharmaceutical company, the National Alliance on Mental Illness, and four other mental-health advocacy groups. The campaign encourages people struggling with mental illness to seek assistance (e.g., by calling the National Alliance on Mental Illness).

From an absolutist perspective on deviance, there are certain behaviors that are inherently deviant regardless of context. However, what if a person is suffering from a mental illness? Are they to be held responsible for their bipolar or delusional behavior? Absolutists would say yes, especially if serious breaches of social norms occur. Some people with bipolar disorder may be prone to commit acts of deviancy or even extreme forms of criminal behavior. Two sensationalized examples of individuals with mental illness causing serious harm to innocent individuals at movie theaters are discussed in box 10.1.

A CLOSER LOOK

Box 10.1 Is It Safe to Go to the Movie Theater?

Millions of people love going to the movie theater to watch a new movie release. The movie experience provides people with an opportunity for a couple of hours of escape from everyday life. High-quality video imaging on large screens and distortion-free sound quality in a darkened theater help to assist and enhance our escapism. Movie patrons also enjoy munching on their favorite snacks (e.g., popcorn, sweets, nachos, and hot dogs) and beverages (e.g., soda, water, and at some locations, alcohol). And while there are a number of minor irritants such as people making a lot of noise eating and drinking, people getting up from their seats to go to the bathroom, and the dreaded cell phone user, in addition to the occasional more serious irritant such as patron verbal or physical confrontations, for the most part going to the movies is a very pleasant experience.

However, over the course of the past few years an extreme form of deviant behavior has invaded the movie theater experience—a mentally ill person who decides to attack and attempts to hurt or kill innocent patrons. Three examples in particular have caught the public's attention. On August 5, 2015, Vincente David Montano, a man with a history of mental illness (he had been committed to mental institutions four times, according to local police) armed with pepper spray, a hatchet, and an airsoft pellet gun, unleashed a volley of pepper spray at audience members inside a movie theater during a showing of *Mad Max: Fury Road*, in the Nashville, Tennessee, suburb of Antioch. There were just eight people in the theater, but three people were hit with the spray. The attacker fled out the back of the theater, where he encountered and exchanged gunfire with a SWAT team before he was shot dead (Almasy and Marco 2015). As disturbing as this incident of a movie theater attack is, it pales in comparison to the next two examples.

On July 23, 2015, John Russell Houser fired on theater audience members during the airing of the film *Trainwreck* at a movie theater in Lafayette, Louisiana. Houser had a long history of mental illness and in 2008 was ordered by Carroll County (Georgia) Probate Judge Betty Carson to be committed for mental treatment. Carson's April 22, 2008, order authorized deputies to detain Houser and take him, against his will if necessary, to a treatment facility for a mental health evaluation. While at the West Central Regional Hospital, Houser was listed as being admitted voluntarily (Henry 2015b). If he had been listed as being hospitalized involuntarily, his name would have been added to the Georgia database that feeds the FBI's background check system (Perez-Pena 2015). Under federal law, the list of prohibited buyers is supposed to include people convicted of felonies and certain misdemeanors, drug abusers, and those convicted of certain drug crimes, and anyone whom a court has involuntarily committed for being dangerously mentally ill (Perez-Pena 2015). It should be noted that there is no requirement that the states participate in adding names to the federal database, and thus the system to check gun buyers is flawed.

In 2008, Houser's family had accused him of threatening behavior and displays of erratic behavior, warning authorities that he had a history of bipolar disorder and was making ominous statements in Carroll County objecting to the pending marriage of his daughter. His wife removed his guns from their home and together, the family persuaded Carroll County Probate Judge Carson to issue a protective order keeping him away once he left the hospital. Despite his history of mental illness, Houser legally purchased a .40-caliber handgun at an Alabama pawn shop in 2014—it was the same weapon he used to kill two people and wound nine others before killing himself on that fateful night at the Lafayette movie theater (Henry 2015a). Following the arrest of Houser, a search of his home led to the discovery of a rambling, hate-filled journal in which the shooter referred to the United States as a "filth farm" and railed against women, gays, and blacks and thanked Dylann Roof (the young man who shot churchgoers in South Carolina) for his "wake up call" (Kunzelman 2016).

Questions about gaps in the system that allow individuals with mental illness to purchase guns had already arisen after James Holmes bought firearms to kill 12 people and wound 70 others in a Denver suburb (Aurora) movie theater in a chilling 2012 attack on moviegoers at a midnight premiere of *The Dark Knight Rises*. Unlike Houser, Holmes did not kill himself, nor was he killed by police after his violent onslaught, and thus provides us with a rare glimpse into the mind of a mass shooter. Holmes graduated from the University of California, Riverside, with a B.S. in neuroscience in 2010 and in 2011 enrolled in the Ph.D. neuroscience program at the University of Colorado's Anschutz Medical Campus in Aurora. Months after beginning a relationship with Gargi Datta, another first-year student in the program, the two broke off their relationship (February 2012). Holmes began to see psychiatrist Lynne Fenton on March 2012 and informed her that he was having homicidal thoughts. Fenton informed campus police about Holmes's homicidal statements and that he sent her a threatening e-mail. His last meeting with Fenton occurred June 11, 2012. Having already purchased tear gas canisters online, handguns, a shotgun, an assault rifle, and 6,295 rounds of ammunition and body armor, either online or in person, Holmes slipped through a back door of the Century 16 Theater in Aurora, where about 420 people were watching *The Dark Knight Rises*. Dressed head-to-toe in body armor and blasting techno music through earphones so that he wouldn't hear his victims scream, he opened fire. Ten people died at the scene and two died

James Holmes appears with defense attorney Tamara Brady before Arapahoe County District Court Judge William B. Sylvester in Centennial, Colorado, July 23, 2012.

at hospitals. Another 70 were wounded. Officers found Holmes leaning against his car behind the theater and arrested him without a struggle. Later, police found booby-trapped bombs and a Batman mask at Holmes's apartment. The bombs were defused (ABC News 2015).

Holmes made his first court appearance on July 23, 2012. His hair was dyed orange-red, face unshaven, and his eyes appeared dazed. He was charged with 24 counts of murder (two counts for each person murdered), 140 counts of attempted murder, and possession of explosives (165 charges in total). The judge ordered Holmes to a hospital psychiatric ward, and he was held for several days, sometimes in restraints. In March 2013, Holmes's attorneys said that he was willing to plead guilty in exchange for avoiding the death penalty. Prosecutors later rejected the plea offer and said that they would seek the death penalty. June 4, 2013, the judge accepted Holmes's insanity plea and ordered Holmes to undergo a mental evaluation. On July 10, 2013, defense lawyers acknowledged that Holmes was the shooter but claimed that he was "in the throes of a psychotic episode." His lawyers later claimed that Holmes was driven

to murder by delusions (Associated Press 2015i). In April 2015, Holmes's jury trial began. Numerous theater shooting survivors gave testimony, and psychiatrists that interviewed Holmes provided their accounts over a period of two months. On July 16, 2015, jurors found Holmes guilty on all 165 criminal charges. Prosecutors announced that they would seek the death penalty for Holmes. His lawyers, seeking to avoid the death penalty for their client, countered, "The only reasonable explanation here is a psychotic break, a broken mind. We are not going to ask you to forgive Mr. Holmes. We are going to ask for your compassion, your understanding, your mercy . . . because all that aggravation was born of disease, and we don't kill people for being sick" (Associated Press 2015j). On August 7, 2015, a jury sentenced Holmes to life in prison without parole after they failed to unanimously agree on whether he should get the death penalty for his murderous attack. Holmes got the verdict he wanted, and many people wondered whether justice was served. As it turned out, the issue of mental illness was the determinant factor in deciding the punishment, as one juror was solidly opposed to death (9 were in favor and 2 unsure) for someone who was mentally ill (Healy 2015). In August 2015 Holmes was sentenced to serve life in prison without parole plus 3,318 years—the maximum allowed by law.

Many survivors of the deadly theater shootings stated that they would never return to a movie theater out fear of some sort of reoccurrence. In response to the growing public concern with safety issues at movie theaters Regal Entertainment Group, the largest movie theater chain in the United States, implemented a bag inspection policy at the end of August 2015. On its website, Regal posted admittance procedures that read in part "To ensure the safety of our guests and employees, backpacks and bags of any kind are subject to inspection prior to admission" (Loman 2015).

Schizophrenia and Other Psychoses

Schizophrenia is a severe mental disorder that interferes with a person's ability to correctly interpret reality, to think clearly, manage emotions, make decisions, and relate to others. "Contrary to popular belief, schizophrenia isn't a split personality or multiple personality. The word 'schizophrenia' does mean 'split mind,' but it refers to a disruption of the usual balance of emotions and thinking" (Mayo Clinic 2015g). *Psychoses* (including schizophrenia) are characterized by distortions in thinking, perception, emotions, language, sense of self, and behavior. Common psychotic experiences include hearing voices and delusions; consequently, the disorder can prevent people from being able to work or study normally. People with psychosis are at high risk of exposure to human rights violations, such as long-term confinement in institutions (WHO 2014).

Schizophrenia is a complex, long-term medical illness that affects about 21 million worldwide and about 1 percent of Americans. Although schizophrenia can occur at any age, it typically begins in late adolescence or the early 20s for men and the late 20s to early 30s for women (WHO 2014; NAMI 2015d). Diagnosing symptoms of schizophrenia in teens is challenging, as the characteristics—a change of friends, a drop in grades, sleep problems, and irritability—are common among many teenagers. Other symptoms of schizophrenia include isolating oneself from others, an increase in unusual thoughts and suspicions, and a family history of psychosis. When some of the following symptoms occur for at least 6 months, there is an increased likelihood that the person is suffering from schizophrenia: hallucinations (e.g., hearing voices, seeing things, or smelling things others do not); delusions (false beliefs); negative symptoms (e.g., unemotional, failure to follow through with tasks, little interest in life, or the lack of sustaining relationship); and cognitive issues/disorganized thinking (e.g., struggle to remember things, organize thoughts, or complete tasks). As with most mental illnesses, the causes of schizophrenia and other psychoses may be the result of genetics (a family history increases the odds), environment (exposure to viruses or malnutrition before birth, inflammation, or autoimmune diseases); brain chemistry (problems with certain brain chemicals, including neurotransmitters called dopamine and glutamate); and substance use (e.g., consumption of mind-altering hallucinogens) (NAMI 2015d).

Dementia

Dementia is a chronic disorder of the mental processes caused by brain disease or injury and is characterized by memory disorders, personality changes, and deterioration in cognitive function (e.g., impaired reasoning). The Mayo Clinic (2015h) states that dementia, per se, isn't a specific disease; instead, it describes a group of symptoms affecting memory, thinking, and social abilities severely enough to interfere with daily functioning. Dementia indicates problems with at least two brain functions, such as memory loss and impaired judgment or language, and the inability to perform some daily activities such as paying bills or becoming lost while driving in familiar areas. The Mayo Clinic (2015h) cautions that while memory loss is a characteristic of dementia, memory loss alone doesn't mean you have dementia, as a certain amount of memory loss is a normal part of aging.

WHO (2014) estimates that dementia affects over 35 million people worldwide.

There are many symptoms of dementia, including cognitive changes: memory loss, difficulty communicating or finding words, difficulty with complex tasks, difficulty with planning and organizing, difficulty with coordination and motor functions, and problems with disorientation, such as getting lost; and psychological changes: personality changes, inability to reason, inappropriate behavior, paranoia, agitation, and hallucinations (Mayo Clinic 2015h). Dementia is caused by damaged nerve cells in the brain. Dementias can be classified in a variety of ways and are often grouped by what they have in common (e.g., what part of the brain is affected). Dementias may affect people differently depending on the area of the brain affected. Some dementias, such as those caused by a reaction to medications or an infection, are reversible with treatment. At this point in time in medical treatment a number of progressive dementias are not reversible and worsen over time. Examples of progressive dementias include Alzheimer's disease (the most common cause of dementia; caused by plaques [clumps of protein called beta-amyloid] and tangles [fibrous tau proteins] found in the brain); vascular dementia (second most common type of dementia; caused by brain damage due to a reduced or blocked blood flow in blocked vessels leading to the brain); Lewy body dementia (caused by abnormal clumps of protein found in the brain); and frontotemporal dementia (caused by the degeneration of nerve cells in the frontal and temporal lobes of the brain). Other disorders linked to dementia include Huntington's disease (an inherited disease that causes certain nerve cells in the brain and spinal cord to waste away); traumatic brain injury (caused by repetitive head trauma); Creutzfeldt-Jakob disease (a rare disease usually found in people without risk factors); and Parkinson's disease (chronic and progressive movement disorder) (Mayo Clinic 2015h).

Dissociative Disorders

Dissociative disorders are characterized by an involuntary escape from reality highlighted by a disconnection between thoughts, identity, consciousness, and memory (NAMI 2015e). People from all age groups and racial and ethnic and socioeconomic backgrounds can experience a dissociative disorder. Approximately 2 percent of Americans suffer from a dissociative disorder. Dissociative disorders usually develop as a response to a traumatic event, such as abuse or military combat. Stressful situations can worsen the symptoms and cause problems with functioning in everyday activities.

Symptoms and signs of dissociative disorders include significant memory loss of specific times, people, and events; out-of-body experiences, such as feeling as though you're watching a movie of yourself; mental health problems such as depression, anxiety, and thoughts of suicide; a sense of detachment from your emotions, or emotional numbness; and a lack of sense of self-identity. The symptoms of dissociative disorders depend on the type of disorder that has been diagnosed by medical professionals (NAMI 2015e). The *Diagnostic and Statistical Manual of Mental Disorders* (DSM) recognizes three types of dissociative disorders: dissociative amnesia (the main symptom is difficulty remembering important information about one's self); depersonalized disorder (the main symptom involves ongoing feelings of detachment from actions, feelings, thoughts, and sensations, such as watching a movie about oneself rather than self-experiencing events); and dissociative identity disorder, formerly known as multiple personality disorder (the main symptom involves the individual alternating between multiple identities). Dissociative disorders are usually a result of trauma, especially with children who were exposed to long-term physical, sexual, or emotional abuse. Natural disasters and combat can also cause dissociative disorders (NAMI 2015e).

Posttraumatic Stress Disorder (PTSD)

The previous discussion on dissociative disorders being caused by a traumatic event such as military combat or surviving a natural disaster (as well as man-made disasters) might have made you think of posttraumatic stress disorder (PTSD). **Posttraumatic stress disorder** is a mental health condition that's triggered by a highly stressful or terrifying event, either by experiencing it or witnessing it. While it is natural for people to be afraid when confronted with dangerous situations—because such a fear triggers many split-second changes in the body to prepare to defend against danger or to avoid it ("fight-or-flight" response)—people who have PTSD may feel stressed or frightened even when they're no longer in danger (National Institute of Mental Health 2015a).

PTSD was first brought to public attention in relation to war veterans, but it can occur as a result of a variety of traumatic incidents, such as a mugging, rape, torture, being kidnapped or held captive, child abuse, car accidents, train wrecks, plane crashes, bombings, or natural disasters such as floods or earthquakes (NIMH 2015a). Immediately after a traumatic experience, the mind and body experience shock as a result of our biological responses to a life-threatening crisis. The body increases the heart rate, pumps blood to muscles for movement and preparing the body to fight off infection and bleeding in case of a wound, and essentially focuses bodily resources and energy toward dealing with the stressful event (NAMI 2015f). People with PTSD, however, experience psychological shock and remain in that state for a prolonged period of time. Their memory of what happened and their feelings about it are disconnected. To move on, people who experience PTSD must face and confront their memories and emotions. PTSD affects 3.5 percent of the U.S. adult population (approximately 7.7 million Americans), and 37 percent of those with PTSD are classified as severe. PTSD can occur at any age, but the average age of onset is when one reaches their early 20s (NAMI 2015f).

There are numerous symptoms of PTSD, and generally these symptoms are grouped into three categories (Smith and Segal 2015; NIMH 2015a):

1. *Reexperiencing Symptoms*

   - Flashbacks—reliving the trauma over and over, including physical symptoms like a racing heart or sweating
   - Bad dreams/nightmares—either of the event itself or of other frightening things
   - Frightening thoughts—daytime fears of the event or of other things
   - Feelings of intense distress when reminded of the trauma

2. *Avoidance Symptoms*

- Staying away from places, events, or objects that are reminders of the experience
- Feeling emotionally numb
- Feeling strong guilt, depression, or worry—survivors of traumatic events wherein many others died are especially prone to "survivor's guilt"
- Losing interest in activities that were enjoyable in the past
- Having trouble remembering the dangerous event
- Sense of a limited future—the PTSD person doesn't expect to live a normal life span, get married, or have a career

3. *Hyperarousal (Anxiety and Emotional) Symptoms*

- Being easily startled, feeling jumpy
- Feeling tense or "on edge" ("red alert")
- Having difficulty sleeping and/or having angry outbursts
- Irritability or outbursts of anger
- Difficulty concentrating

It is important to try and help someone you suspect of suffering from PTSD, as the sooner it is confronted, the easier it is to overcome. Some people, especially military personnel, may be reluctant to seek help because they may view PTSD as a sign of weakness. However, the only way to overcome PTSD is to confront what happened (to the person suffering from PTSD) and learn to accept it as a part of the past. This process is easier with assistance from professional and experienced therapists and medical personnel. In a number of instances, military people try to help fellow military victims of PTSD. The results are often mixed. (See box 10.2 to see how a real-life scenario of soldiers suffering from PTSD comes to life in the hugely successful box office film *American Sniper*.)

CONNECTING SOCIAL DEVIANCE AND POPULAR CULTURE

Box 10.2 PTSD, Reactivist Deviance, and *American Sniper*

American Sniper (2014) is a story about Navy SEAL Chris Kyle. Directed by Clint Eastwood and starring Bradley Cooper as Kyle, *American Sniper* pulled in a record-breaking $105 million in its first full weekend release (January 16, 2015) and went on to garner a domestic total gross of over $350 million (plus a nearly additional $200 million in foreign earnings). The film received six Oscar nominations (including Best Picture, Best Adapted Screenplay, and Best Actor for Cooper), winning one (Best Sound Editing). Screenwriter Jason Hall states that, despite the film's success, there was "a bittersweet quality" as "We intended to make this movie with Chris, and he died in the middle of all this. There's a sadness in it, knowing that

his wife and kids will carry on without him" (Baker 2015a). Kyle had already begun work on the film, which was based on his own bestselling memoir—*American Sniper: The Autobiography of the Most Lethal Sniper in U.S. Military History* (2013)—about his four tours in Iraq, when he died at age 38 on a Texas gun range in 2013. Kyle is considered by the U.S. government as the deadliest marksman (sniper) in U.S. military history with 255 kills from 4 tours in the Iraq War, with 160 confirmed by the Department of Defense.

As the most lethal sniper in U.S. history, Kyle saw a great deal of combat and, of course, death. It is not surprising that by the time Kyle went back home to his wife and kids in Texas that he suffered from PTSD. "While Kyle served in some of the world's most dangerous war zones for the better part of eight years, Taya [Kyle's wife] feared for his safety every day—especially after insurgents had placed a bounty on his head—and always wondered if he would make it home for the next Christmas. . . . Still, it wasn't until he left the military and came home for good in 2009 that their relationship began to crack under the strain of what he had endured" (Baker 2015b:70). Taya Kyle states, "The war hardened his soul in different ways. There were times we did not think we were going to make it" (Baker 2015b:70). Taya, who has since written her own book, *American Sniper Widow* (2015), about her life with Chris Kyle, is hesitant to say outright that Chris suffered from PTSD because he never publicly used the label, but admits that there is no question that he wrestled with the aftereffects of war. Taya says about her husband's struggle with PTSD, "It's what a lot of the guys struggle with. It's missing the brotherhood, because that is something you can't get anywhere else in life, where your coworkers will die for you. There were so many things, and that manifested in sleepless nights and a detachment you see in the movie" (Baker 2015b:72).

It wasn't until Kyle began to help other veterans cope with PTSD that he was able to finally reclaim his purpose. Taya believes that Chris's helping other veterans is what brought him back to his family. Rick Kell, the cofounder of Troops First, a group that Chris Kyle worked with closely, said that whether hunting with them or knocking back a beer, "he wanted to talk about the things that were on their minds" (Baker 2015b:72). Tragically, it was one of these veterans, Eddie Ray Routh, whom Kyle was working with, and who suffered from PTSD, who ended Kyle's life by shooting him and his friend, Chad Littlefield, on February 2, 2013, at an upscale shooting range near Fort Worth. Two years later, Routh was found guilty of capital murder for the shooting deaths of Kyle and Littlefield (Jervis 2015).

It is interesting to note that the *American Sniper* movie and the legendary status of Chris Kyle as the deadliest sniper in American history provide us with an example of reactivist deviance. If you recall, this perspective of social deviance takes into consideration the idea that deviance can be positive. Generally speaking, taking another person's life is considered deviant and criminal. However, as we have already learned, there are many occasions wherein taking another's life is labeled as justified, and a soldier killing an enemy soldier is one of these examples. But some critics of the *American Sniper* film say the idea of killing someone while hidden a relatively great distance away is actually a form of deviant behavior. Filmmaker Michael Moore (director of such films as *Fahrenheit 9/11* and *Bowling for Columbine*) tweeted (on Twitter) on January 18, 2015, that "snipers aren't heroes" and are actually "cowards" (Baker 2015a; LeTrent 2015). Bill Maher is another critic of Kyle and *American Sniper*. On his January 23, 2015, episode of *Real Time with Bill Maher* (HBO), Maher referred to Kyle as a "psychopath patriot" and criticized his claim to be a Christian in light of his describing Iraqis as "damn savages" (Karlin 2015).

Military leaders and personnel, along with a seemingly vast majority of Americans, however, view Chris Kyle as a hero because he helped to save the lives of American military personnel, thus making his actions positive. Defenders of Kyle's status as a hero also point out that combatants on each side of a war all use snipers. The film *American Sniper* also acknowledged Kyle's counterpart, "Mustafa," a highly trained sniper who had picked off numerous U.S. Army combat engineers who were attempting to build a barricade.

Readers can decide for themselves whether or not Chris Kyle is a hero or a coward, or even a psychopath, and chime in on whether or not the validation of his actions (killing enemy soldiers) constitutes justifiable actions (positive deviance). But let's not forget the main aspect of this Popular Culture box, the role of PTSD and the effects of living through a traumatic event and its consequences on later life.

Developmental Disorders

Developmental disorders is an umbrella term used to cover a number of chronic disabilities that affect the mental and/or physical development (e.g., receptive and expressive language, learning, and mobility) of the afflicted. Such impairments are generally manifested in childhood or by the early 20s and are likely to persist into adulthood, causing a delay in functions related to the central nervous system maturation. Developmental disorders generally follow a steady course rather than periods of remissions and relapses that characterize many other mental disorders (WHO 2014). Developmental delay (impairment) is defined as the failure to meet expected developmental milestones in one or more of the following areas: physical, social, emotional, intellectual, speech and language, and/or adaptive development (sometimes called self-help skills, which include dressing, toileting, feeding, etc.). A developmental disorder is diagnosed when a child performs approximately 25 to 30 percent below age norms in one or more of these areas (with adjustment for prematurity in affected children). Developmental progress occurs at a slower-than-expected rate following anticipated sequence (Kennedy Krieger Institute 2012). According to WHO (2014), lower intelligence diminishes the ability to adapt to the daily demands of life.

Potential causes of developmental disorders are both medical and environmental, including:

- Chromosomal abnormalities
- Genetic or congenital disorders
- Severe sensory impairments, including hearing and vision
- Inborn errors of metabolism
- Disorders reflecting disturbance of the development of the nervous system
- Congenital infections
- Disorders secondary to exposure to toxic substances, including fetal alcohol syndrome (Kennedy Krieger Institute 2012)

The verification of developmental impairment can be obtained through an evaluation process, which includes at least three of the following: informed clinical opinion to include observational assessment, standardized development test(s), developmental inventory, behavioral checklist, adaptive behavior measure, and parent interview (Kennedy Krieger Institute 2012). Family involvement in care of people with developmental disorders is very important (WHO 2014).

Two of the more common examples of developmental disorders are **attention-deficit hyperactivity disorder (ADHD)** and autism. ADHD is a developmental disorder where there are significant problems with attention, hyperactivity, or acting impulsively. **Autism spectrum disorder (ASD)** is a developmental disorder that makes it difficult to socialize and communicate with others (NAMI 2015a).

ADHD is most commonly diagnosed in young people, with an estimated 9 percent of children between ages 3 and 17 afflicted by it; however, an estimated 4 percent of adults have ADHD (NAMI 2015g). A number of symptoms associated with ADHD are normal for any active child, but someone with ADHD will have trouble controlling these behaviors and will show them much more frequently. Signs of inattention include:

- Becoming easily distracted and jumping from activity to activity
- Becoming bored with a task quickly
- Difficulty focusing attention or completing a single task or activity
- Trouble completing or turning in homework assignments
- Losing things such as school supplies or toys
- Not listening or paying attention when spoken to
- Daydreaming or wandering with lack of motivation
- Difficulty processing information quickly
- Struggling to following directions (NAMI 2015g)

Signs of hyperactivity include:

- Fidgeting and squirming, having trouble sitting still
- Nonstop talking
- Touching or playing with everything
- Difficulty doing quiet tasks or activities (NAMI 2015g)

Signs of impulsivity include:

- Impatience
- Acting without regard to consequences, blurting things out
- Difficulty taking turns, waiting, or sharing
- Interrupting others (NAMI 2015g)

There are several causes or factors that contribute to ADHD, including genetics (it runs in the family) and environmental factors (e.g., if a child is exposed to lead, or if the child's mother drank alcohol and/or smoked tobacco while pregnant with the child).

Autism spectrum disorder (ASD) is a developmental disorder that, in addition to affecting an afflicted person's ability to socialize and communicate with others, can result in restricted, repetitive patterns of behavior, interests, or activities (NAMI 2015h). The term "spectrum" refers to the wide range of symptoms, skills, and levels of impairment or disability that people with ASD can display. Some people are mildly impaired by their symptoms, while others are severely disabled. The growing awareness of ASD in the past decade or so has greatly contributed to the rising prevalence rate of 1 in 68 children. Boys are 4 times more likely than girls to develop autism, but people from all racial, ethnic, and social backgrounds can be afflicted with ASD (NAMI 2015h).

Symptoms of autism can occur in the first few months of life for the baby (e.g., difficulty engaging in the give-and-take of everyday human interactions, such as turning toward voices, grasping a finger, and smiling by 2 to 3 months of age). Among the more common symptoms of autism are:

- Delay in language development—such as not responding to their own name, speaking only in single words, if at all
- Repetitive and routine behaviors—such as walking in a specific pattern or insisting on eating the same meal every day
- Difficulty making eye contact—such as focusing on a person's mouth when that person is speaking instead of their eyes, as is usual in most young children
- Sensory problems—such as experiencing pain from certain sounds (e.g., telephone ringing) or not reacting to intense cold or pain
- Difficulty interpreting facial expression—such as misreading or not noticing subtle facial cues, like a smile, wink, or grimace, that could help understand the nuances of social communication
- Problems with expressing emotions—such as facial expressions, movements, tone of voice, and gestures that are often vague or do not match what is said or felt
- Self-harm behavior—such as hitting his or her head against a wall as a way of expressing disapproval
- Absence of pretend play—such as taking a long time to line up toys in a certain way (NAMI 2015h)

As with ADHD, a combination of genetics (e.g., if one child in the family has ASD, another sibling is more likely to develop it too) and environment (e.g., the mother's health) factors can cause ASD. As mentioned in chapter 1, strong evidence has been shown that vaccines do not cause autism (NAMI 2015h).

A Brief Sociohistorical Review of the Treatment of the Mentally Ill

As described in chapter 3, one of the earliest diagnoses of deviancy and mental illness resulted in the conclusion that the afflicted must be possessed by demons or evil spirits. The belief in demonic possession dates back at least to 5000 BCE as evidenced by archaeological discoveries of trephines (surgical instruments with a cylindrical blade) and skulls found with drill holes in them (Porter 2002). It is believed that humans drilled holes in the skulls of individuals who engaged in odd and bizarre behaviors because they were believed to be possessed by demons or sorcery. In ancient Mesopotamia, priest-doctors treated the possessed with pseudo-religious ritualistic procedures such as exorcisms, incantations, prayer, atonement, and other unusual mystical means in an attempt to drive out evil spirits from the afflicted person (Alexander and Selesnick 1966). The ancient Hebrews also believed that demons could possess humans and the afflicted were being punished by God because they had committed sin (Alexander and Selesnick 1966). All of the afflicted persons subjected to demonic possession treatments involving such techniques as drilling holes in skulls are likely to simply have suffered from mental illness and certainly were not possessed. The idea that people could be possessed by demons existed in many parts of the ancient world and in many societies. This belief would continue through the Middle Ages, Renaissance Europe, and until the time of the Salem, Massachusetts, witch hunts.

400 BCE–1800s CE

However, around 400 BCE Greek physician Hippocrates began treating mental disorders as diseases to be understood in terms of disturbed physiology and not the reflections of demonic possession or evidence of displeased gods. Hippocrates prescribed a treatment that involved mentally ill people being placed in quiet environments and peaceful pursuits and also prescribed drugs such as the purgative hellebore. Family members generally took care of people with mental illness in this era (PBS 2002).

Despite the enlightened treatment perspective introduced by Hippocrates in 400 BCE, for the next 2,000 years or so, the mentally ill were mostly left alone (not offered treatment), so long as they were not a deemed dangerous; treated as if they were possessed by demons; labeled as witches (e.g., Salem, Massachusetts); or placed in asylums (Muslim Arabs had established asylums as early as the eighth century; the first European establishment for people with mental illness was likely in Valencia, Spain, in 1407) (PBS 2002). Throughout the 1600s, Europeans increasingly began to isolate mentally ill people, often housing them with handicapped people, vagrants, and delinquents—and clearly they were not receiving the treatment they needed to help cope. Those considered insane were increasingly treated inhumanely, often chained to walls and kept in dungeons. By the late 1700s there was a growing concern in Europe about the treatment of mentally ill people. For example, following the French Revolution, physician Phillippe Pinel took control of the Bicetre insane asylum and forbade chains and shackles, removed the mentally ill from dungeons, and provided them with sunny rooms and allowed them to exercise on the grounds. In most other societies, however, mistreatment persisted (PBS 2002). In colonial American society, for example, mentally ill persons were labeled as "lunatics" with the word derived from the root word *lunar*, meaning "moon." It was believed that lunacy was caused by a full moon at the time of the baby's birth or if the baby slept under the light of a full moon. These lunatics were presumed by colonists to be possessed by the devil and were usually removed from society and locked away (Leupo 2008).

Throughout the 1800s, a number of reformers would work diligently in an attempt to change the manner in which the mentally ill were treated. Dorothea Dix, for example, lobbied for 40 years to help establish 32 state hospitals for the mentally ill in the United States after studying and reporting on the cruel treatment facilities in Massachusetts (PBS 2002). The rise of psychiatry in the 1800s further assisted in the movement to better treat the mentally ill (Porter 2002). In 1883, for example, Emil Kraepelin distinguished mental disorders, and although subsequent research will disprove some of his findings, his fundamental distinction between manic-depressive psychosis and schizophrenia would hold true through the modern era.

1900s CE–Early 2000s CE

Arguably, the 1900s represent the century with the greatest improvement, to date (presumably far greater improvements in treatment techniques will be developed in the 2000s), on the treatment of the mentally ill. Sigmund Freud and Carl Jung identified various psychoses and treatment procedures in the early 1900s, and drugs and electroconvulsive therapy along with surgical procedures were introduced in the 1930s. In 1949, Australian psychiatrist J. F. J. Cade introduced the use of lithium to treat psychosis. Before this, drugs such as bromides and barbiturates had been used to quiet or sedate patients, but they were ineffective in actually treating the basic symptoms of those suffering from psychosis. Prescribing lithium would become quite popular by the mid-1960s to treat those with bipolar disorder. During the 1950s a series of antipsychotic drugs were introduced to control the symptoms of psychosis, rather than cure it. By the mid-1950s, the number of mentally ill people receiving treatment in Europe and the United States reaches unprecedented numbers.

Many of the techniques embraced in the first half of the 1900s, however, were challenged in the 1960s. Social thinkers such as Thomas Szasz and Michel Foucault employed the relativist perspective of deviance, suggesting that the concept of "mental illness" only exists because people established social norms that led to parameters of "normal" behavior and "deviant" behavior, or mental illness. In his 1961 book *The Myth of Mental Illness*, psychiatrist Thomas Szasz questioned psychiatry's foundations, argued against the tendency of psychiatrists to label some people as "mentally ill," and argued that there is no such disease as schizophrenia. Szasz (1961) suggested that psychiatry is in the company of alchemy and astrology and is nothing more than a pseudoscience. The relativist stand taken by Szasz reflected sociology's conflict theory that states special interest groups and those in power dictate what is right and what is normal while the rest of society must go along with such distinctions or risk being labeled a deviant, or in this case, mentally ill. To support his premise, Szasz noted how psychiatry had until recently described homosexuality, delinquency, and divorce as the result of mental illness.

Szasz was not alone in his critique of psychiatry, as the renowned Michel Foucault similarly argued in his 1961 publication *Madness and Civilization* that the evolving meaning of "madness" in European culture was a result of social construction. As explained by Porter (2002), Foucault argued that mental illness must be understood not as a natural fact but as a cultural construct, sustained by a grid of administrative and medico-psychiatric practices. Another criticism of the mental health establishment created and sustained by psychiatry came from sociologist Erving Goffman and his 1961 book, *Asylums*. Goffman had conducted field work research at St. Elizabeth's Hospital in Washington, D.C., a federal institution of over 7,000 inmates. In this groundbreaking publication, Goffman, among other things, coined the term "total institutions" to express the reality that the rules of the everyday life outside the asylum have no validity for the members inside the asylum and that their every activity is highly structured to conform with the large number of like-situated individuals. Goffman found that most people in mental hospitals exhibit their psychotic symptoms and behavior as a direct result of being hospitalized (Goffman 1961). Goffman's ideas would be very influential in developing the labeling theory and the dramaturgical perspective. People who do not properly fall into set parameters of acceptable behavior are labeled as deviant or mentally ill, and because of the stigma (a mark of disgrace or dishonor) attached to being labeled mentally ill, such people lack full acceptability in society. Before long, these otherwise unique people come to see themselves as deviant and conform to the deviant label. Contemporary labeling theorists believe that "individuals are aware of their label and use stigma management strategies to cope with the perceived threat of rejection or social exclusion that might come from the label" (Ray and Dollar 2014:720).

In 1962, counterculture author Ken Kesey wrote a best-selling novel, *One Flew Over the Cuckoo's Nest*, which would later be adapted into a very influential film in 1975, to reveal his experiences working in the psychiatric ward of a Veterans Administration hospital. Kesey put forth the notion that patients do not really have mental illnesses; rather, they simply behave in ways the rigid society is unwilling to accept (PBS 2002). Thus, mental illness is a matter of social construction, and anyone who does not fit into a predetermined mode of expected behavior is automatically labeled as deviant, or in these cases, as mentally ill.

Continued criticism of the manner in which people were treated in mental institutions led to the deinstitutionalization of hundreds of thousands of patients from the mid-1960s through 1980. **Deinstitutionalization** refers to the release of institutionalized individuals from institutional care (e.g., psychiatric hospital) to care, treatment, support, or rehabilitation primarily through community resources under the supervision of health-care professionals or facilities. "The number of institutionalized mentally ill people in the United States [dropped] from a peak of 560,000 to just over 130,000 in 1980" (PBS 2002). Care for the deinstitutionalized mentally ill was supposed to come from community-based facilities. In support of that effort, in 1963, the United States passed the Mental Retardation Facilities and Community Health Centers Construction Act, which was to provide federal money for the development of a network of community-based mental health services facilities. Advocates of deinstitutionalization first believed that the released patients would voluntarily seek treatment at these facilities if they needed it. As it turned out, this was not always the case.

Many of the formerly institutionalized persons were able to live successfully and independently because of antipsychotic drugs. Conversely, many mentally ill people were not able to adjust to life outside the total institution and became home-less. Thus, while deinstitutionalization was the goal of many early 1960s reformers, many of the deinstitutionalized patients struggled with freedom because there was generally a lack of adequate follow-up and outpatient care. In the 1980s, another wave of deinstitutionalization occurred. Once again, many of these former patients refused or failed to seek treatment at local facilities. As a result, it was estimated that in the 1980s one-third of all homeless people were considered seriously men-tally ill, the vast majority of them suffering from schizophrenia (PBS 2002).

By the early 2000s, a number of new-generation drugs (medication), psycho-therapy techniques, and complementary and alternative approaches of treatments were introduced to help treat mental illness. In the remainder of this chapter we will revisit each type of mental illness and disorders previously discussed and examine treatment approaches utilized. There are two main reasons for utilizing this approach. First, because we have learned about each of the categories of mental illness, includ-ing their symptoms and causes, discussing the various treatments for each example of mental illness completes the review. Second, as we apply the treatment techniques to the study of each type of mental illness, we will see examples of new medications, psychotherapy techniques, and complementary and alternative approaches in action.

Before we shift our attention to specific treatment strategies used to help people with mental illness, let's make sure we have a clear understanding of what is meant by medicalization of treatment, psychotherapy, and complementary and alternative medicine approaches to treatment.

Contemporary Treatment Approaches

Medicalization can be defined as the process of increasingly treating aspects of human life as medical problems rather than social problems. Among the leading consequences of the increasing medicalization of treatment for mental illness is the "manipulation and transformation of human nature by biomedical technology" and an increased perspective of "biology and genetics [as the] main forces which affect human life, with social factors playing a minor role" and ultimately leading soci-ety to become "increasingly bionic" (Maturo 2012). The medicalization of mental illness goes against sociological ideas that people are responsible for their actions and notions that social reality is socially constructed not medically constructed. For example, alcoholism has gone from being seen primarily as a personal deficiency to a medical condition, and as a medical condition, individual responsibility can be reduced or eliminated and treatment may proceed along medical lines (e.g., insur-ance companies can cover treatment and pharmaceutical companies can develop medications for treatment) (Medley-Rath 2012).

In an attempt to eliminate or minimize dependency on drugs as a form of treatment, a number of people turn to psychotherapy. Psychotherapy involves talking with a men-tal health professional as a means of treating illness (NIMH 2015a). The Mayo Clinic (2015i) defines **psychotherapy** as a general term for treating mental health problems by talking with a psychiatrist, psychologist, or other mental health provider. Ideally, during a therapy session patients, with the help of the therapist, learn more about their condi-tion, moods, feelings, thoughts, and behaviors and how to take control of their lives by responding to challenging situations with healthy coping skills. There are a wide variety of psychotherapy techniques, including "talk therapy," counseling, psychoso-cial therapy, or, simply, therapy. Psychotherapy can be helpful in treating most mental health problems, including anxiety disorders (e.g., obsessive-compulsive disorder, phobias, panic disorder, and PTSD); mood disorders (e.g., depression); addictions (such as alcoholism, compulsive gambling); personality disorders (e.g., borderline personality disorder); and schizophrenia (psychotic disorders) (Mayo Clinic 2015i).

Complementary and alternative medicine (CAM) approaches to treatment involve embracing new ideas to treat mental illness and often combining them with mainstream medical therapies—spawning the term "integrative medicine" (Mayo Clinic 2015j). Some of the examples of CAM therapies include whole medical systems (e.g., ancient healing systems, homeopathy, and naturopathy); mind-body medicine (e.g., meditation, prayer, relaxation, and art therapies); biologically based practices (e.g., dietary supplements and herbal remedies); manipulation and body-based practices (e.g., chiropractic and osteopathic manipulation and massage); and energy medicine (e.g., getting in touch with one's aura, chi, or life force) (Mayo Clinic 2015j). Many traditional medical doctors do not have training in CAM therapies and as a result are often reluctant to prescribe such a treatment. Additionally, there is little empirical research to indicate the effectiveness of CAM therapies.

A customer in a drugstore looks over the labels of medication boxes.

The Treatment of Mental Illness

When someone becomes physically ill, they generally seek medical attention and help from trained professionals. Then again, some people, especially those without health care or those who feel they simply need to bear the discomfort and pain they are experiencing, will not seek help. In still other cases, others (e.g., family members, friends, neighbors, and officials) may intervene and force the ill person to see a medical professional. For example, even complete strangers are likely to call 911 for ambulance service if they come across someone bloody and unconscious lying on the street. These same scenarios are applicable to mental illness as well; that is to say, some people realize there is something wrong with them, so they seek help. Some are afraid of the stigma attached to being labeled "mentally ill" and therefore avoid treatment, while in some additional scenarios others may become so concerned about the mental health of another, they intervene and make sure the "ill" person seeks a diagnosis. For example, loved ones and strangers alike are apt to call the police if a person acting erratically and yielding a knife attempts to randomly stab people on a busy city street. Sociologists, among others, are concerned about the increased role of psychiatrists and psychologists, especially in light of the ever-expanding list of what constitutes mental illness found in the most recent

Diagnostic and Statistical Manual of Mental Disorders (DSM-5). An ever-growing number of children are being diagnosed with a mental illness and given medications. For example, the frequency of bipolar disorder in children has jumped fortyfold in the last two decades, according to Dr. Bernard Carroll, a former Duke University psychiatry department chairman. As a result, he states, "You've got all these young kids running around with diagnosis, yet many of them have never, ever had a manic episode, which is the hallmark of bipolar disorder" (Gray 2013).

Regardless of the conditions that lead one to treatment for mental illness, a number of options exist, depending on the disorder. Our review begins with the treatment options available for depression.

Depression

The Anxiety and Depression Association of America (ADAA) (2015) reminds us that, as with any illness, treatment should be tailored to a specific diagnosis. For example, if a person who is highly depressed is unable to begin treatment for an anxiety disorder, which requires a great deal of motivation and energy, it may be necessary to treat the depression first before addressing any corresponding anxiety issues. The ADAA recommends either medications or psychotherapy. Among the useful medications designed to address the symptoms of depression (and anxiety disorders) are such options as a selective serotonin reuptake inhibitor (SSRI) and serotonin norepinephrine inhibitor (SNRI). Reflective of the medicalization of mental illness, more than 1 in 10 Americans take antidepressants, the number one type of medication used by people ages 18 to 44 (ADAA 2015). Among the forms of psychotherapies recommended by the ADAA to treat depression are cognitive behavioral therapy (CBT), which works to replace negative and unproductive thought patterns with more realistic and useful ones; interpersonal therapy; and problem-solving therapies. Complementary and alternative medicine (CAM) approaches include such options as joining a support group; relaxation techniques, meditation, and breathing exercises; talking with family members and friends and explaining how they can help; and regular exercise (ADAA 2015).

In addition to the recommendations of the ADAA described above, the NAMI (2015b) recommends such medication approaches as taking benzodiazepines such as alprazolam (Xanax) or antidepressants. The NAMI also recommends CBT as a psychotherapy approach and as CAM approaches suggest, self-management (e.g., allocating specific periods of time for worrying) and stress and relaxation techniques (e.g., breathing exercises), yoga, and exercise.

Bipolar Disorder

With proper treatment, most people with a bipolar disorder can gain control of their mood swings and related symptoms, but because it is a lifelong illness, long-term treatment is needed to control symptoms (NIMH 2015b). The NIMH states that treatment is more effective if the patient works closely with a doctor and is open about concerns and options of treatment. Many people who opt for medication as a form of treatment discover that they have to make changes in order to find the ones that work best. Among the medications available are mood stabilizers (e.g., lithium); anticonvulsants (e.g., valproic acid or divalproex sodium (Depakote); lamotrigine (Lamictal); and gabapentin (Neurontin, Topamax, and Trileptal);

atypical antipsychotics (e.g., Zyprexa, Abilify, and Seroquel); and antidepressants (e.g., Prozac, Paxil, Zoloft, and Wellbutrin). Psychotherapy techniques include cognitive behavioral therapy, family-focused therapy, interpersonal and social rhythm therapy, and psychoeducation. CAM approaches include electroconvulsive therapy (ECT), sleep medications (people with bipolar disorder have trouble sleeping and may need sedatives or other sleep medications), and herbal supplements (e.g., St. John's wort, or *Hypericum perforatum*) (NIMH 2015b).

Schizophrenia and Other Psychoses

Most people diagnosed with schizophrenia or some other psychoses can be integrated in society and lead productive lives when they receive appropriate treatment. Medication treatments include first-generation (typical) antipsychotics and second-generation (atypical) antipsychotics. First-generation antipsychotic medications have been available since the mid-1950s and include chlorpromazine (Thorazine), haloperidol (Haldol), perphenazine (Etrafon, Trilafon), fluphenazine (Prolixin), loxapine (Loxitane), thiothixene (Navane), and trifluoperazine (Stelazine) (NAMI 2015d; NIMH 2015c). Second-generation antipsychotics were developed in the 1990s. One of these medications, clozapine (Clozaril), is an effective medication that treats psychotic symptoms, hallucinations, and breaks with reality, but it can sometimes cause a serious problem called agranulocytosis—the loss of white blood cells (that help a person fight infection) (NIMH 2015c). Other atypical antipsychotics include risperidone (Risperdal), olanzapine (Zyprexa), ziprasidone (Geodon), lurasidone (Latuda), and paliperidone (Invega).

Both psychotherapy and psychosocial therapy treatments may be an effective way to treat schizophrenia and other psychoses. Among the psychotherapy techniques are cognitive behavioral therapy, supportive psychotherapy, and cognitive enhancement therapy (CET). Psychosocial treatments include assertive community treatment (ACT) (highly individualized services connecting people with mental health services found within local communities); illness management skills; integrated treatment for co-occurring substance abuse; rehabilitation (e.g., emphasizing social and vocational training, job counseling, money management counseling, and help in learning to use public transportation); family education; and self-help groups. Complementary and alternative treatments include combining a number of the therapies, combining medicines with therapy, and the consumption of omega-3 fatty acids, commonly found in fish oil. In general, omega-3 may help treat mental illness because of its ability to replenish neurons and connections in affected areas of the brain (NAMI 2015d; NIMH 2015c).

Dementia

The treatment of dementia is so challenging that WHO (2014) proclaims that there is no treatment currently available to cure dementia or to alter its progressive course, but reports that many treatments are in various stages of clinical trials. The United Kingdom's National Health Service (NHS), however, states that there are important exceptions. For example, dementia caused by vitamin and thyroid deficiencies can be treated with supplements. Some forms of dementia (caused by brain tumors, excess fluid on the brain, or head injuries) can be treated surgically. For types of dementia that involve degeneration of nerve and brain tissue it is possible to reduce further damage by managing high blood pressure, high cholesterol, type 1 diabetes, and by stopping smoking (NHS 2015).

The NHS agrees with WHO that dementia cannot currently be cured but believes that medicine may prevent symptoms from getting worse for a period of time. These medicines need to be given to patients in the early and middle stages of the disease to have any chance of being effective. A number of medicines have been shown to be effective in treating mild, moderate, and severe dementia. They include: Aricept (donepezil) and other acetylcholinesterase inhibitors (used to treat Alzheimer's, dementia with Lewy bodies, and for treating hallucinations); memantine hydrochloride (blocks the effects of a chemical in the brain and is used when inhibitors do not work); antipsychotics; and antidepressants. While the NHS has not found psychological treatments to be effective in slowing down the progression of dementia, they do believe such treatments can help with the symptoms. Three therapies recommended by NHS (2015) are cognitive stimulation and reality orientation (e.g., taking part in activities and exercises designed to improve memory, problem-solving skills, and language ability); validation therapy (a focus on the emotional aspects of dementia); and behavioral therapy (tries to find the reasons for difficult behavior demonstrated by the person with dementia—for example, a person with dementia who tends to wander out of their home or care center may actually be feeling restless).

Dissociative Disorders

"The goals of treatment for dissociative disorders are to help the patient safely recall and process painful memories, develop coping skills, and, in the case of dissociative identity, to integrate the different identities into one functional person" (NAMI 2015e). At this time, there are no drugs that deal specifically with treating dissociation itself. Still, some medications, such as antidepressants, antianxiety medications, or antipsychotic medications may be prescribed to combat additional symptoms that commonly occur with dissociative disorders (Mayo Clinic 2015k).

Psychotherapy is the primary treatment utilized in the treatment of dissociative disorders. Among the psychotherapies used to treat dissociative episodes are cognitive behavioral therapy (designed to help change the negative thinking and behavior associated with depression); dialectical behavioral therapy (with a focus on teaching coping skills to combat destructive urges, regulate emotions, and improve relationships); eye movement desensitization and reprocessing (EMDR) (designed to alleviate the distress associated with traumatic memories via a number of CBT techniques and visual stimulation exercises to access traumatic memories and replace the associated negative beliefs with positive ones); and talk therapy (counseling and psychosocial therapy between the patient and mental health provider) (NAMI 2015e; Mayo Clinic 2015k).

Posttraumatic Stress Disorder (PTSD)

All three categories of treatment are applicable to treating people suffering from PTSD. The earlier treatment begins, the more effective it is likely to be. Among the medicines available to treat PTSD are antidepressants (e.g., selective serotonin reuptake inhibitors, Zoloft, Paxil, Prozac, and Celexa); alpha- and beta-blockers (e.g., Prazocin); and mood stabilizers and antipsychotic medications (to treat the symptoms of aggression, mood instability, or dissociation) (NAMI 2015f; NIMH 2015a).

Psychotherapy treatments may be an effective way to treat people with PTSD. Among the treatments available are cognitive behavioral therapy (designed primarily to replace negative thoughts with positive thoughts); eye movement desensitization and reprocessing; exposure therapy (safely exposes PTSD sufferers to similar stimuli that initially caused the trauma that triggered PTSD); and stress inoculation training (teaching a person how to reduce anxiety) (NAMI 2015f; NIMH 2015a). CAM treatments include group therapy (a support group can help a PTSD sufferer realize that others share their sense of trauma); service dogs (especially helpful for veterans); yoga; aqua therapy, such as flotation chambers and surfing; acupuncture; and mindfulness and meditation.

Developmental Disorders

Treatment plans for developmental disorders should be crafted to meet the individual's needs and will be most affected if it is implemented early on. The two developmental disorders discussed earlier in this chapter were attention-deficit hyperactivity disorder (ADHD) and autism spectrum disorder (ASD). There are different strategies in the treatment of each of these disorders both regardless of the treatment method used, behavioral therapy should be incorporated (NAMI 2015g).

Medication is used to improve the symptoms of ADHD so that people can focus more on the things that provide enjoyment; it improves the quality of life of the afflicted person. The most widely prescribed medications for ADHD are stimulants. Stimulants make it easier for nerve receptors in the brain to communicate with each other. Stimulants such as Ritalin, Daytrana, Dexedrine, Adderall, and dimesylate are generally the first choice of medication to use for the management of ADHD. In other cases, nonstimulants, such as Strattera, Intuniv, and Kapvay, may be used to treat ADHD. Someone living with ADHD and depression may be prescribed antidepressants (Pamelor, Aventyl, Norpramin, Tofanil, or Effexor) as a medical treatment (NAMI 2015g).

The NAMI (2015h) states that, as of now, there are no FDA-approved medications for the core symptoms of autism. Two antipsychotic medicines—aripiprazole (Abilify) and risperidone (Risperdal)—have been approved for irritability associated with autism. Some medications may be prescribed off-label (drugs approved by the FDA to treat other disorders that are similar to autism) for children with ASD, including antipsychotic medications, antidepressant medications, and stimulant medications (Ritalin) (NIMH 2015d).

Behavioral treatment is very important as a treatment method when treating ADHD, as it can help the afflicted person improve social skills (such as sharing and interacting with peers) and learn appropriate responses to everyday situations, especially in schools. The CDC (2015k) recommends that the following strategies be incorporated into a child's behavioral therapy:

- Create a routine—Try to follow the same schedule every day, from wake-up to bedtime.
- Get organized—Put schoolbags, clothing, and toys in the same place every day so your child will be less likely to lose them.
- Avoid distractions—When the child is doing homework, he or she should turn off the TV, headphones, and computer.
- Use goals and rewards—Set up a chart and list goals and track positive behavior and then reward the child's efforts. Make sure the goals are realistic.
- Discipline effectively—Instead of yelling or spanking, use time-outs or removal of privileges as consequences for inappropriate behavior.

As with treating ADHD, psychotherapy is an important treatment strategy used to treat autism. There are many options, including applied behavioral analysis (ABA), which teaches children positive behavior while discouraging the negative; floor time, a therapy that targets speech, motor, or cognitive skills through focus on emotional development through interactive play between parents and children; and education and development therapy, which involves creating a highly structured and specialized treatment plan, something autistic children respond to positively (NAMI 2015h).

Complementary approaches to the treatment of ADHD include elimination diets (some people with ADHD are sensitive to sugar and artificially added colors, flavors, and preservatives); nutritional supplements (e.g., omega-3); interactive metronome training (a computerized metronome produces a rhythmic beat that individuals attempt to match by tapping their hand or foot); chiropractic medicine (addresses muscle tone imbalance that can affect imbalances in brain activity); and neurofeedback (teaches individuals how to increase arousal levels in the frontal areas of the brain) (NAMI 2015d).

CAM approaches for people with ASD include melatonin, a natural sleep supplement; nutritional supplements, like multivitamins to replenish nutrients; and gluten- and casein-free diets (foods with wheat or dairy may irritate the GI tract, which in turn increases ASD symptoms) (NAMI 2015h).

This concludes our examination of mental illness. Undoubtedly, an increasing number of people will be diagnosed with mental illness in the future, and it is up to health professionals to come up with strategies for those suffering with a mental illness to cope with their illness and the realities of the social world.

Summary

In this chapter, the topic of mental illness and disorders was discussed. As a means of providing a starting point, good (or "normal") mental health was first discussed. Good mental health, among other things, offers feelings of well-being, inner strength, emotional functionality, and the ability to cope and manage change and uncertainty. Contrastingly, poor mental health is generally expressed in terms of mental illness or mental disorder and refers to conditions that negatively impact a person's ability to cope with everyday events or stressful situations. A mental illness or disorder is a condition that impacts a person's thinking, feeling, or mood and may affect his or her ability to relate to others and function on a daily basis.

There are over 200 classified forms of mental illness and disorders, and this chapter examined seven of the more common ones: depression, bipolar disorder, schizophrenia and other psychoses, dementia, dissociative disorders, posttraumatic stress disorder (PTSD), and developmental disorders (ADHD and autism spectrum disorder). An analysis, description of the symptoms, and causes of each type of mental illness were provided.

A brief sociohistorical review of the treatment of the mentally ill illustrates that humanity has come a long way since the early days (circa 5000 BCE) through the contemporary era. While the mentally ill are no longer subjected to having their skulls drilled in an effort to release evil spirits or demons and women are not burned at the stake as witches, there are concerns over the primary method of treatment today—medicalization. Increasingly, the mental health profession has diagnosed a growing number of people as suffering from a mental illness or disorder and then prescribed drugs often to the point of increasing dependency. In an attempt to eliminate or minimize the dependency on drugs as a form of treatment, a number of people turn to psychotherapy. Psychotherapy involves talking with a mental health professional as a means of treating illness. A third option as a contemporary approach to treating mental illness involves complementary and alternative medicine (CAM) approaches, which often involve embracing new ideas to treat mental illness and combining them with mainstream medical therapies—spawning the term "integrative medicine." The three treatment options are then applied to the seven major types of mental illness and disorders described throughout the chapter.

Key Terms

attention-deficit hyperactivity disorder (ADHD), 277

autism spectrum disorder (asd), 277

bipolar disorder, 268

deinstitutionalization, 281

dementia, 272

depression, 267

developmental disorders, 276

dissociative disorders, 273

good mental health, 263

medicalization, 282

mental disorder, 265

mental illness, 265

poor mental health, 265

posttraumatic stress disorder (PTSD), 274

psychotherapy, 282

schizophrenia, 272

Discussion Questions

1. Would you consider yourself to have good mental health or poor mental health? Why?

2. Explain the relationship between social deviance and mental illness.

3. Do you believe that the trend of increasingly diagnosing people with a mental illness or disorder will continue to increase? Why or why not?

4. What sort of mental health evaluation should pilots go through before they are allowed to fly a plane? Do you think other professionals should have to undergo a mental evaluation? Explain.

5. Do you think James Holmes should have received the death penalty for committing mass murder at an Aurora, Colorado, movie theater? Why or why not?

6. Is Chris Kyle an American hero? Explain. Describe the impact of PTSD on Kyle's life and ultimate death.

7. If you had a friend or relative with a young child that appeared to be developmentally challenged, would you point that out and recommend the child get evaluated by a mental health professional?

CHAPTER 11

Sexual Social Deviance

CHAPTER OBJECTIVES

After reading this chapter students should be able to:

- Explain what is meant by sexual social deviance
- Describe why some people are homophobic and explain conversion therapy
- Describe what is meant by a hostile workplace and give examples
- Provide different examples of pornography

- Compare and contrast sexual assault and rape
- Explain the relationship between human trafficking and prostitution
- Demonstrate knowledge of a variety of sexual fetishisms

Since the 1990s, the adage of "no means no" was promoted on college campuses as a means of stopping unwanted sexual advances. Nothing could possibly be clearer as proponents of this motto repeatedly asked, "What part of 'no' don't you understand?" The adage and implication were as straightforward as any slogan could possibly be. If someone says no to a sexual advance, of any kind, the other person is supposed to immediately stop any continued action and behavior. The primary goal of the "no means no" policy was to cut down on, or ideally eliminate, sexual assaults and rape, especially "date rape," on college campuses. (A number of businesses and corporations also have related "no means no" policies to address sexual harassment in the workplace.) College football fans may recall University of Oregon football players using the Florida State University tomahawk chop to the tune of the "war chant" used by FSU fans while they repeated "no means no," directed toward FSU star quarterback Jameis Winston (who was accused of sexual assault in December 2012) following their 2015 New Year's Day Rose Bowl victory. Winston, the 2013 Heisman Trophy winner (an award given to the top Division I football player) and current NFL player, was never charged with rape following a woman's highly publicized accusation. Winston was cleared of violating FSU's student code of conduct, but the controversy continued to surround him. Oregon athletes (three former basketball players were suspended in June 2014) have also faced sexual assault allegations, but prosecutors decided there wasn't enough evidence to charge the players, who said the sexual contact was consensual (ESPN 2015a).

While the Oregon players involved in the taunting of Winston were disciplined, proponents of ending sexual assaults were dismayed and discouraged that so many cases of rape go unpunished. To that end, the "no means no" policy has recently been replaced by the "yes means yes" policy on many college campuses. In September 2014, California Governor Jerry Brown signed legislation requiring colleges in the state to adopt sexual assault policies that shifted the burden of proof in campus sexual assault cases from those accusing to the accused. Thus, the accused would have to prove that he or she had consent to engage in a sexual encounter with the accusing person. Consent at California colleges is now "an affirmative, unambiguous, and conscious decision by each participant to engage in mutually agreed-upon sexual activity," and the consent has to be "ongoing" throughout any sexual encounter (New 2014). California college students must receive an enthusiastic yes, either verbally or physically; if the student is intoxicated, there is no consent.

In October 2014, the State University of New York system, the largest in the nation, adopted the same uniform definition at all of its 64 campuses. In July 2015, Governor Andrew Cuomo signed a measure into law requiring that New York State's private colleges and universities must also abide by the "yes means yes" policy. The law also created a victim's bill of rights and boosted training for law enforcement, faculty, and students. The bill of rights guarantees students the right to report any incident to campus police or local law enforcement. Fordham University student Monica Sobrin, a member of the group Students United for Safer Schools in New York, said that the new law and bill of rights make New York a "national leader in the fight against campus sexual assault" and "will greatly impact the way that sexual assault is discussed, taught and handled in colleges and universities state-wide" (Associated Press 2015l). It's just a matter of time before we find out whether or not the new "yes means yes" policy will replace the "no means no" policy on all college campuses and whether or not this initiative will be effective in combating sexual assault and rape on college campuses.

The topics of sexual assault and rape, along with sexual harassment, pornography, prostitution, and sexual fetishism, are among those to be discussed in this chapter.

What Is Sexual Deviance?

Sexual deviance includes a wide range of unusual or abnormal forms of sexually related behaviors that are outside of the culturally and historically determined social norms and expectations of a society. A **sexual deviant** is a person who finds pleasure in and/or participates in acts of sexual deviancy.

The five perspectives of deviant behavior (normative, absolutist, statistical, reactivist, and relativist) are very applicable to the study of sexual deviancy. The idea that deviance is something that violates a social norm (normative deviance) is applicable in a wide variety of instances, including such behaviors as incest and pedophilia. Many people claim the absolutist position (certain behaviors are inherently deviant regardless of context, times, and the diversity of the members of a society) when discussing topics such as sexual orientation and prostitution. The statistical perspective of deviance, which focuses on that which is unusual, rare, or uncommon, is often applied to examples of sexual fetishism. Reactivist deviance takes into consideration the idea that deviance can be positive, and this perspective is applicable to those who fought for the rights of gay people to get legally married. And the relativist perspective of deviance, which examines the manner in which social norms are created and the people who create them, is particularly relevant to sexual harassment and a slew of other sexually related forms of deviancy.

We begin our discussion on what constitutes sexual deviance by examining a few specific examples. In each case, you should determine which of the five perspectives of deviant behavior are applicable.

Infidelity

Infidelity involves the act of behaving unfaithfully and cheating (e.g., sexual or emotional betrayal) on a spouse or significant other. When married people cheat on their spouses, they are said to have committed adultery. When someone in a committed relationship cheats, they are said to be cheating on their partner. Infidelity, while it refers to a specific behavior, is an interesting phenomenon in that no one wants to be victimized by an unfaithful significant other, as they tend to feel that their trust in someone special has been violated. And yet infidelity is so common that it is likely more than half of the readers of this text have not only been cheated on, they have cheated on their partner. Thus, the expectation, moral or otherwise, is for the significant other not to engage in infidelity, while the statistical reality is, the vast majority of us have either been cheated on, have cheated on the other, or both.

Above, the term "statistical reality" was used. It seems obvious that infidelity is fairly common in contemporary American society, but given the secretive nature of infidelity, coming up with precise data on cheating and extramarital affairs is nearly impossible. Nonetheless, based on data compiled by researchers in a variety of fields, the following facts and statistics from two separate sources are presented:

- Percentage of marriages where one or both spouses admit to infidelity, either physical or emotional: 41 percent
- Percentage of men who admit to committing infidelity in any relationship they've had: 57 percent
- Percentage of women who admit to committing infidelity in any relationship they've had: 54 percent
- Percentage of men and women who admit to having an affair with a coworker: 36 percent
- Percentage of men and women who admit to infidelity (emotional or physical) with a brother-in-law or sister-in-law: 17 percent
- Percentage of men who say they would have an affair if they knew they would never get caught: 74 percent
- Percentage of women who say they would have an affair if they knew they would never get caught: 68 percent (Infidelity Facts 2006)

Truth about Deception (2015) provides us with additional facts and statistics about infidelity:

- Roughly 30 to 60 percent of all married individuals in the United States will engage in infidelity at some point during their marriage.
- Nearly 2 to 3 percent of all children are the product of infidelity.
- Infidelity is becoming more common among people under 30.
- As more and more women have entered the workforce, "office romances" have become more common.
- Infidelity is usually driven by emotion rather than by a rational choice.
- Some people find their more suitable mate (someone they love more than their spouse) after they are already married.

- Biological evidence indicates that long-term monogamy is difficult for many humans to achieve.
- Almost everyone admits to having fantasies that involve someone other than a spouse.

In this world of social networking it should not come as a surprise that it has become easier to cheat on your spouse, as there are specific websites, such as Ashley Madison, that are specifically designed to bring would-be cheaters together. See box 11.1 for a description of Ashley Madison, the Internet's leading facilitator of extramarital affairs, and the trouble they faced when hackers known as the "Impact Team" infiltrated their site.

CONNECTING SOCIAL DEVIANCE AND POPULAR CULTURE

Box 11.1 Want to Cheat? There's an App for That

With the advancement of technology and social networking during the early 21st century came the expression, "There's an app for that." Apps are computer programs designed to run on mobile devices such as smartphones and tablet computers. There are free apps and apps that have to be purchased. There are apps that allow you to follow your favorite sports teams, find restaurants and gas stations, receive the latest weather information, and so on. There are even apps designed to make it easier for you to find someone to hook up with (e.g., Tinder) or to have an affair with (Ashley Madison). Tinder is a dating profile site that allows people to search for other like-minded people. Individuals set up a profile page with a photo (Tinder states that all profiles that do not have a profile photo will be deleted as well as those that have obscene pictures) and scan pages of others, swiping left if they are not interested in that person or swiping right if they are interested in that person. If both parties swipe right, there is a match, and a get-together is set up between the two. Tinder promotes itself as a fun way to connect with new and interesting people around you. While people in a relationship may use Tinder, it is more popular with single people looking for fun.

The global network site Ashley Madison, on the other hand, is specifically designed for married people who are looking to cheat on their spouse. Their motto of "Life is short. Have an affair" is the first thing people see when they go to the Ashley Madison site. AshleyMadison. com and a similar site, EstablishedMen.com, are sites owned by Toronto-based Avid Life Media Inc. Ashley Madison proudly proclaims to be "the Internet's leading facilitator of extramarital liaisons, boasting having nearly 39 million members and that 'thousands of cheating wives and cheating husbands sign up every day looking for an affair'" (Associated Press 2015n). Ashley Madison also claimed that their site was 100 percent secure, but as we know, no site is secure from hackers.

In July 2015, hackers, going by the name of "Impact Team," threatened to expose the Ashley Madison client list in one month's time, making the information available to the public so that anyone could search for those using the site to cheat on their spouses. Ashley Madison (and Avid Life) mostly ignored the hackers' threats but did offer clients an opportunity to have their information wiped clean from the site for a fee of $19. As it turned out, Ashley Madison did not wipe clean the records of those who paid the extra security fee. And, true to their word, a month later (August 2015) the Impact Team did make public the client list of Ashley Madison. In addition to naming names, contact information such as the users' passwords, street addresses, credit card information, height, weight, and GPS coordinates was also released (Associated Press 2015n).

The FBI is among the government agencies investigating the hacking of Ashley Madison and not just because hacking and blackmailing are crimes, but because an estimated 15,000 accounts included .gov email addresses.

Government workers, especially military personnel, could be subject to a slew of punishments (for using a .gov address), including dishonorable discharge and court-martial proceedings (*CBS This Morning* 2015a).

The prospect of millions of adulterous partners being publicly shamed obviously concerned many Ashley Madison users. The hackers, meanwhile, seem to be happy about exposing adulterers.

As this short look at infidelity would seem to indicate, many people cheat on their significant others and many more would cheat if they knew they could get away with it. And yet none of us wants to be cheated on because of the pain and embarrassment generally associated with being the partner who was victimized by infidelity. After all, we enter romantic relationships with love and excitement and the hope that we may have "found the one" we can form a lasting relationship with for a lifetime. Less than one-third (31 percent) of marriages last after an affair has been admitted to or discovered (Infidelity Facts 2015). While many of these fractured relationships will cause a lifetime rift between the two persons involved, some couples attempt to be civil to one another, especially if children are involved. This more civil approach to treating one another after a breakup has been addressed in a number of ways, and one variation is known as *conscious uncoupling*. The term "conscious uncoupling" was introduced to the world of popular culture by Gwyneth Paltrow's announced breakup with husband Chris Martin, the lead singer of Coldplay. While the phrase "conscious uncoupling" went viral immediately afterward, Paltrow, interestingly, became the butt of jokes for using such a term rather than the standard phrases of "breaking up" or "getting a divorce." As it turns out, Paltrow never used the term; rather her editorial director, Elise Loehnen, borrowed the "conscious uncoupling" term from a psychologist and titled her blog about Paltrow's breakup *Conscious Uncoupling* (Takeda 2015). The term "conscious uncoupling" comes from Catherine Woodward Thomas, who has since published a book by the same title. In her book, Thomas provides a five-step process designed to steer the victim of a breakup from a bitter end and instead toward a new life that's empowering and flourishing (Thomas 2015).

Teenage Pregnancy

Teenage pregnancy while a straightforward concept that involves pregnancy of a female, age 13 to 19, is a topic generally considered deviant in American and other Western societies, especially when the female in question is under the age of consent. But is it deviant for an 18- or 19-year-old teenage woman to be pregnant? The answer to that question often has a lot to do with specific circumstances that surround the pregnancy.

Teenage pregnancy is generally considered a form of social deviance when it is the result of other deviant behaviors (e.g., alcohol and/or other drug use and underage sexual intercourse). Teenage pregnancy may also be considered deviant because it often contributes to a number of social and economic costs through the immediate and long-term impacts on teen parents and their children:

- In 2010, teen pregnancy and childbirth accounted for at least $9.4 billion in costs to U.S. taxpayers for increased health care and foster care, increased incarceration rates among children of teen parents, and lost tax revenue because of lower educational attainment and income among teen mothers.

- Pregnancy and birth are significant contributors to high school dropout rates among girls—only about 50 percent of teen mothers receive a high school diploma by 22 years of age compared to the approximate 90 percent high school graduation rate of women who had not given birth during adolescence.

- The children of teenage mothers are more likely to have lower school achievement and drop out of high school, have more health-problems, be incarcerated at some time during adolescence, give birth as a teenager, and face unemployment as a young adult (CDC 2015l).

A number of risk factors contribute to the likelihood that a teenager will become pregnant, including growing up in poverty, having parents with low levels of education, growing up in a single-parent family, and having poor performance in school. Teenagers who have sexual intercourse are often lacking in knowledge of sexual issues (e.g., HIV and other STDs), how to avoid places and situations that might lead to sex, and the value of using condoms (CDC 2015l).

A pregnant teen contemplates her baby's future life.

In 2013, there were a total of 273,105 babies born to females aged 15 to 19 years, for a live birth rate of 26.5 per 1,000. Nearly 89 percent of these births occurred outside of marriage. One in six (17 percent) of teen births were to females who already had one or more babies (Office of Adolescent Health 2015). On the plus side, 73 percent of teenage births occurred to 18- and 19-year-olds, and the overall teen birth rate has declined almost continuously over the past 20 years for whites, blacks, and Hispanics (see table 11.1).

TABLE 11.1	Birth Rates per 1,000 Females Ages 15 to 19, by Race/Ethnicity			
Year	Total	White	Black	Hispanic
1990	59.9	42.5	116.2	100.3
1995	56.0	39.3	97.2	99.3
2000	47.7	32.6	79.2	87.3
2005	39.7	26.0	59.4	76.5
2010	34.3	23.3	51.5	55.7
2013	26.5	18.8	39.0	41.7

Source: Office of Adolescent Health, 2015

In 2013, the lowest teen birth rates (less than 20 per 1,000) were reported in the Northeast (i.e., New York, Vermont, Maine, Massachusetts, and New Hampshire), while rates were highest (40.0 to 49.9 per 1,000) in states across the southern part of the country (i.e., Texas, Oklahoma, Mississippi, New Mexico, and Arkansas).

Sexting

Sexting refers to sending, receiving, or forwarding sexually suggestive text messages that generally include sexually suggestive nude or nearly nude photos (Delaney 2012b). Sexting is a type of playful flirting. Sociologist Georg Simmel (1858–1918) discussed flirting in his work on sociability. According to Simmel (1972), sociability is the association of people for its own sake and for the delight of interacting with others. The limits of sociability rest purely with the participating interactants. Flirting is an excellent example of sociation because so many people flirt and do so in different ways. Flirting can range from the pure fun of flirting with others (e.g., smiling at strangers just to make oneself or others happy) to flirting for some specific end goals, such as preferential treatment, romance, or sex (Delaney 2012b).

Simmel (1972) described many categories of sociability, and the one that is most relevant here is his concept of coquetry. Coquetry represents the play form of eroticism (Wolff 1950). It is this type of flirting that has for an end goal, sex. In this type of flirting, the two individuals playfully tease an "offer" while countering with a "refusal." This give-and-take represents flirtation. Simmel believed that the nature of flirting is to play up alternately allusive promises and allusive withdrawals—to attract the other but stopping short of flat-out decision, or commitment. Flirting also involves swings back and forth between offers of enticement while keeping the other at bay with a playful no. That the two people have a mutual attraction will eventually lead to the fulfillment of the coquetry interaction (Delaney 2012b). If, however, we revisit this chapter's introductory story and the "yes means yes" policy on a growing number of college campuses, flirting may become a thing of the past, as such playful advances of coquetry may be viewed as sexual harassment. If coquetry on college campuses can be viewed as a form of social deviance, then sexting most definitely runs that risk.

By definition, sexting involves "sex" and "texting." Sexting is very common in this, the era of electronic social networking. As we can see from the sexting example of a newly developing relationship provided below, a simple opening text message can quickly transform flirting to sexual desire:

> He: "Hey. What's up?"
> She: "I'm failing at making cupcakes."
> He: "I'd like to try your cupcakes."
> She: "Well, I'd love for you to try them."
> He: "I want to try everything of yours."
> She: "I'd love for you to try everything of mine. My body is yours."

Beyond its flirtatious nature for couples in the early stages of a relationship, sexting has been shown to provide benefits for committed couples as well. Researchers at Drexel University's Women's Health Psychology Lab report that 88 percent of adults ages 18 to 82 have sexted at least once, while approximately 82 percent report having sexted in the past year (Grinberg 2015). The researchers hoped to show that sexting, which generally has a bad rap because of its association with adolescent use, has positive benefits for adults in committed relationships. Among the preliminary results of the Drexel research: the existence of a positive correlation between couples who sext one another and overall satisfaction within the relationship; partners who sext one another are more open to sexual conversations, which can lead to better communication; and sending and receiving sexy messages can keep the sparks of romance alive in a relationship. The research also indicates that people who are cheating on their significant other are far less likely to sext their relationship partner (*CBS This Morning* 2015b).

While sexting among adults in a committed relationship may have some positive consequences, sexting among underage teens remains as an example of sexual deviance. The prevalence of teenagers sexting has increased over the years, rising from an estimated 20 percent of all teens in 2010 (*Parade* 2010) to 25 percent in 2012 (Castillo 2012). There is every reason to believe that the percentage of teenagers sexting has increased since 2012. Although sexting is meant as flirtatious fun, a number of potential deviant and possible criminal issues arise when such behavior involves minors, including charging teens who send and receive such images with child pornography and possible felony obscenity charges (Delaney 2012a). Depending on particular jurisdictions, someone who receives a sext photo of an underage person may face sex offender status. Other issues include the embarrassment and shame that someone may experience if a sext photo meant for one person is shared with others. In Ohio in 2008, a teenage girl hanged herself after an ex-boyfriend sent naked photos of her to students at their school (*Parade* 2010). Research conducted by Temple and associates (2012) found a number of relationships between teen sexting and sexual behaviors, including 81.8 percent of boys who sent a sext reported that they already had sex, while only 45.4 percent of boys who had never sent a sext reported that they had sex; and of those who reported that someone had asked them to send a sext, 76.2 percent had sex while just 38.2 percent of those who reported not having been asked to sext had already had sex.

Sexually Transmitted Diseases (STDs) and Sexually Transmitted Infections (STIs)

Sometimes referred to as venereal diseases or sexually transmitted infections (STIs), **sexually transmitted diseases** (STDs) are infections that are generally acquired via sexual contact with someone who has the infection. Some infections can be transmitted nonsexually, such as from a mother to infant during pregnancy or childbirth, or through blood transfusions or shared needles. The organisms that cause STDs may be passed from person to person in blood, semen, or vaginal and other bodily fluids (Mayo Clinic 2015l). The term STIs is more popular than STDs with some professionals because many STDs cause no symptoms in some people. Among the noticeable symptoms and signs of STDs and STIs are sores or bumps on the genitals or in the oral or rectal area; painful or burning urination; discharges from the penis; unusual or odd-smelling vaginal discharge; unusual vaginal bleeding; pain during sex; sore, swollen lymph nodes, particularly in the groin but sometimes more widespread; lower abdominal pain; and a rash over the trunk, hands, or feet (Mayo Clinic 2015l).

The causes of STDs are bacteria (e.g., gonorrhea, syphilis, and chlamydia); parasites (trichomoniasis); and viruses (human papillomavirus, genital herpes, HIV). If you have an STD caused by bacteria or parasites, your health care provider can treat it with antibiotics or other medicines; however, if you have a sexually transmitted disease caused by a virus, there is no cure. There are more than 20 types of STDs, including chlamydia, gonorrhea, genital herpes, HIV/AIDS, human papillomavirus (HPV), syphilis, and trichomoniasis (also known as trich). Most STDs affect both men and women, but in many cases the health problems they cause can be more severe for women, and if the inflicted woman is pregnant, serious health problems can be transmitted to the child (U.S. National Library of Medicine 2015c).

It is beyond the scope of our coverage here to explore the prevalence of all STDs and STIs; thus, a sampling of data will be provided. STIs affect people of all ages, genders, races/ethnicities, and social backgrounds, totaling approximately 19 million new cases each year, with about half occurring among those ages 15 to 24 (American University 2015). More than 1.2 million people in the United States are living with the HIV virus, and almost 1 in 8 (12.8 percent) are unaware of their infection. Gay, bisexual, and other men who have sex with men (MSM), particularly young black MSM, are most seriously affected by HIV. By race, blacks face the most severe burden of HIV (CDC 2015m). Chlamydia is the most prevalent bacterial STI in the United States with over 1 million cases reported per year (1,401,906 cases in 2013), followed by gonorrhea (333,004 reported cases in 2013) and syphilis (primary and secondary, with 17,375 reported cases in 2013) (CDC 2014i). The highest rates of chlamydia infections occur between the ages of 18 and 24. While younger people represent the highest risk group for acquiring an STD, such diseases are increasing at a rapid rate among senior citizens. The rate of STDs among senior citizens has doubled from 2000 to 2010 with rates the highest in the retirement state of Florida. Diseases such as syphilis and chlamydia have increased by 52 and 31 percent respectively from 2007 to 2011. This rate of increase puts seniors in competition with young people between the ages of 20 and 24 in terms of the biggest increase in STDs (Savastio 2014). Among the primary reasons for the increase in STDs among the elderly is the increased availability and use of erectile dysfunction drugs such as Viagra and Cialis and the fact that senior citizens are far less likely to use condoms than their younger counterparts (Savastio 2014).

Most people realize that whenever they have sex, especially with an unknown partner, they run the risk of acquiring an STD or STI. The Mayo Clinic (2015l) recommends several ways to avoid or reduce the risk of becoming inflicted, including abstaining from sex; maintaining a mutually monogamous relationship with an uninfected partner; using condoms and dental dams consistently and correctly; getting vaccinated; not drinking alcohol excessively or using drugs (people under the influence are more likely to take sexual risks); and communicating with your partner ahead of time about their sexual history (as it pertains to the potential risk of STDs). As the cliché goes—"You don't just have sex with your partner but every one of their partners as well."

Engaging in sexual contact with another is generally not considered deviant. Engaging in sexual relations with someone underage is considered both deviant and criminal. Purposively hiding or lying about having an STD with a sexual partner is certainly deviant and in some circumstances may come under the "depraved indifference" criminal umbrella. There is a case, currently still in progress, in Syracuse, New York, where a man has been charged with a felony for recklessly inflicting his partner with HIV. The case involves Terrance Williams, who was charged with the felony in 2010 for knowing he had HIV and having unprotected sex with another man. A local judge and an appeals court reduced the charge to a misdemeanor, but in 2015 the court of appeals took an interest in the case, focusing on the state's "depraved indifference" statute, as well as whether or not giving someone HIV constitutes a "grave risk" of death. As a case of "depraved indifference," the court is essentially comparing having sexual relations with another person while hiding the fact that one has hidden the truth about having an STD to a game of Russian roulette, a drunk driver going at a high rate of speed, or distributing a dangerous drug (Dowty 2015). What do you think? Is hiding the truth of having an STD a matter of depraved indifference, a simple matter of social deviance, or neither?

Gender Identity and Sexual Orientation

Traditionally, one's gender identity and sexual orientation was predicated on their sexual categorization. Such a perspective, however, is a matter of social construction. Social construction refers to the idea that all concepts exist because humans created or built them. In this manner, concepts are not defined by laws of nature but rather, they are socially constructed and dependent upon human social experiences, needs, values, and interests. Thus, social construction is contingent not only on ideas about things but on beliefs that have been shaped by social forces. Socially constructed reality is also viewed as an ongoing, dynamic process rather than a static perspective on social reality. This is certainly true with regard to the concepts of sex, gender, gender roles, and gender identity.

People who use the absolutist perspective of deviancy would generally not agree with the social constructionist perspective that one can choose to identify by any other means than the biological classification of male or female (based on genitalia at the time of birth) and thus, would also have a far more narrow view of gender and gender roles.

Sex, Gender, and Gender Roles

Sex refers to an individual's biological classification (e.g., male or female). Males and females differ biologically with regard to their internal and external reproductive organs, types and levels of hormones, and chromosomal structure (females have an XX and males an XY design). Some people, however, may be born with both male and female genitalia, and in such cases, the term "intersex person" is applied. (The term "hermaphrodite" was once used to describe persons with mixed sexual physiology but has fallen out of favor in describing humans.) An intersex person is born with or develops mixed sexual physiology (e.g., an abnormally small penis and a large clitoris). Some individuals do not discover they are intersex until they reach puberty. Throughout history, intersex persons have generally been treated as deviants because they did not neatly fit the preconceived notion that everyone is either a male or female. The designation of male or female has historically been important because the prevailing culture of societies assigned gender roles based on one's sex.

Gender refers to socially determined expectations placed on individuals because of their sexual category. In most societies, the prevailing culture expects males to display certain "masculine" behaviors and females to display certain "feminine" behaviors. Each society will decide what it means to be masculine and what it means to be feminine, and thus what is "appropriate" and "inappropriate." These gender ideals extend to all sorts of realms of social life, including emotional-response patterns, mannerisms, tone of voice, body language, style of dress and ornamentation, and so on. Such expectations lead to the construction of "gender roles." Thus, gender roles can be defined as sets of cultural expectations associated with being a male (masculinity) or female (femininity). Sociologists, however, point out that gender roles are learned and culturally defined, vary from one culture to the next, and therefore are not innate but socially constructed.

Gender Identity

Most people identify primarily with their biological sex; others, however, do not believe that the sexual category assigned to them at birth corresponds with how they view themselves. As a result, sexual identity is far more complicated for some individuals than it is for others. **Gender identity**, then, can be defined as the way in which a person conceives of their sexual self. It is a label that people adopt in order to signify to others who they are as a sexual being. In 2015, the University of California admissions department adopted a policy effective for the fall 2015 semester that allows students to choose from six categories of gender identity. UC applicants can choose any of the following:

1. Male
2. Female
3. Trans male/trans man
4. Trans female/trans woman
5. Gender queer/gender nonconforming
6. Different identity

Other questions on the UC admissions form include "What sex were you assigned at birth?" with two possible responses—male or female; and "What is your sexual orientation?" with three possible responses—heterosexual or straight, gay or lesbian, or fill-in-the-blank (Fox News 2015; Chan 2015). Among the practical concerns with allowing for six different gender identities are the designation of gender-neutral restrooms and changing rooms. The alterations made to the admissions forms and university facilities are the result of UC President Janet Napolitano's formation of a council to advise her on how to best address LGBT issues in 2014. Napolitano states, "UC is working hard to ensure our campuses model inclusiveness and understanding" (Fox News 2015).

College campuses are not the only entities trying to break down gender identity walls. Many businesses have embraced and fully accept people who identify in ways beyond male and female. In August 2015, Target initiated a policy that will stop separating toys and bedding into girls' and boys' sections. Thus, if you go to the toy section at Target, you will find that all toys are lumped together without a boys' or girls' section. And the aisles will no longer have colored backdrops to indicate gender, such as pink and yellow for girls or blue and green for boys (Contrera 2015). Other retailers are expected to follow Target's initiative. While some people will applaud such a movement, others will view it in a more negative light.

Sexual Orientation

An important aspect of sexual identity is sexual orientation. **Sexual orientation** refers to a person's physical, romantic, and emotional attraction to another person. People may be drawn to partners of the opposite sex (the most common form of sexuality), same sex, both sexes, or neither sex (asexuality). Data on sexual orientation generally reveals that between 1 and 5 percent of Americans report being gay (same-sex orientation) with fewer people describing themselves as bisexual or asexual. In their report on sexual orientation and health among U.S. adults, researchers at the CDC found that, among all U.S. adults aged 18 and over, 96.6 percent identified as straight, 1.6 percent identified as gay or lesbian, and 0.7 percent identified as bisexual (Ward et al. 2014).

Until fairly recently, American and Canadian society held such negative attitudes toward gay, lesbian, and bisexual people that such sexual orientations were not only viewed as deviant but as a mental disorder (Society of Obstetricians and Gynaecologists of Canada 2012). The American Psychiatric Association (APA) (2015) labeled homosexuality as a mental disorder until 1972. Because of the negative attitudes and behaviors directed toward being gay, many people decided to hide their true sexual identities and orientations. The idea of keeping such identities private was known as "hiding in the closet." However, since the early 1970s, an increasing number of people came out of the closet and proclaimed to others (e.g., friends and family members) that they were gay or bisexual. The term used to describe this process is known as "coming out" (Stambolis-Ruhstorfer and Saguy 2014). The APA (2015) describes coming out not as a onetime event, but a lifelong process of identifying as gay, lesbian, or bisexual to family, friends, and other significant members of one's social world. Each person's experience with coming out is unique, and the process generally stimulates anxiety and risks (e.g., not everyone will be accepting; some relationships may permanently change; some may experience harassment or discrimination; personal safety may be put at risk; and some young people have been thrown out of their family home) as well as providing challenging possibilities for personal empowerment and emotional growth and personal benefits (e.g., living an open and whole life; developing closer, more genuine relationships; gaining self-esteem; reducing the stress of hiding the true identity; becoming a part of a new, strong, and vibrant community; and becoming a role model for others) (Society of Obstetricians and Gynaecologists of Canada 2012).

LGBTQ

As described above, one of the benefits of "coming out" is the opportunity to become a part of a new, strong, and vibrant community, a community often referred to as LGBTQ (although more commonly known as LGBT). Sociologists have long studied the lesbian, gay, bisexual, transgender, and queer (LGBTQ) "community." While the acronym LGBTQ has automatic meaning to sociologists, it is important to realize that not all LGBTQ persons share similar life experiences, and thus it is not necessarily the inclusive community the acronym might seem to indicate (de Vries 2007).

The *L-G-B* of LGBTQ is quite clear to readers as, assumingly, everyone understands what the terms lesbian, gay, and bisexual mean. The *T* is fairly well understood, while the *Q* may not be as clear. Transgender people have a unique status that does not seem to fit the LGBTQ collective category, as "they include people who present themselves as male or female, or both, in varying situations. They

A transgender high school student from Michigan urges the State Board of Education to approve LGBT guidelines for schools during a school board meeting.

include people who may be postoperative, preoperative (e.g., transitioning), or nonoperative male-to-female (MTF) or female-to-male (FTM) in status" (de Vries 2007:20). Transgender people believe that they were born into the opposite-sex body to the gender with which they identify. A transgender person may eventually reach a point in his or her life when a sex change operation is deemed necessary to stop "living a lie." (See box 11.2 for a further look at the transitionary process of a transgender person.)

A CLOSER LOOK

Box 11.2 Keeping Up with Transitioning

Typically, a transgender person struggles internally with his or her sexual identity. Such individuals may experience emotional distress that most others cannot understand. If a transgender person begins to experiment with behaviors characteristically expected of an opposite-sex person, family members and friends may react negatively. Transgender persons may eventually reach a point when they deem a sex change procedure as their only viable option to claim their true gender identity. Once the decision is made to have a sex change, hormone therapy and psychological counseling, sometimes spanning several years, begin (Young 2000). This eventually leads to sex-reassignment surgery (the existing genitals are removed and replaced with those of the new sex). Next, the transgender person faces the need to change his or her forms of identification (e.g., driver's license, passport, Social Security card, etc.), which accompanies a name change. For example, I know of a person born as a biological male named Daniel, who, after a sex-change operation, changed her name to Danielle. That Danielle chose a name so close to her original name is not necessarily common. (To learn more about Danielle's change from Daniel, read her book, *It's Always Okay to Be Me*.)

In 2015, the most popularly known person to transition from male to female was William Bruce Jenner (1949–). Jenner became an American athlete icon after winning a gold medal in the 1976 Olympics as a decathlete. Jenner's fame was further immortalized by appearing on the cover of Wheaties boxes following Olympic success (in those days, earning the cover of the Wheaties box was a huge deal and increased tremendously one's popular culture appeal). Jenner's victory in the decathlon made him an American hero during the Cold War period (a Soviet athlete had won the title in 1972). American interest in Jenner never faded, even after his athletic career ended.

Jenner is the father of six children from marriages to Chrystie Crownover, actress Linda Thompson, and most recently to reality TV matriarch Kris Jenner. Jenner also considers himself to be father to Kourtney, Kim, Khloe, and Rob Kardashian, Kris's children from her marriage to the late Robert Kardashian (Nahas and Gomez 2015). Marrying into the Kardashian family would make Jenner famous to a younger generation that embraces "reality" television due to the popularity of *Keeping Up with the Kardashians*. Despite his new television fame, Jenner was never completely happy, as behind closed doors "he dressed as a woman" and was "always very closeted [having] other people buy him [women's] clothes" (Nahas and Gomez 2015:58). Following his 2013 split from Kris Jenner, Bruce underwent subtle but significant emotional and physical changes. In December 2013, Jenner underwent a laryngeal shave to minimize the appearance of his Adam's apple (a biological trait of males is the Adam's apple, a feature missing from biological females). Jenner embraced a number of traditionally feminine activities including having his nails manicured, putting highlights in his hair, wearing diamond ear studs, wearing lip gloss, changing the manner in which he walked (to be more feminine), and speaking in a softer tone (Nahas and Gomez 2015:58). Jenner was transitioning. He informed his family and then the public that he wanted to become a woman. Bruce Jenner announced that his new name would be Caitlyn Jenner and he would become a she.

The news made headlines around the world. The transgender community embraced Jenner as a champion and hoped that his public transition would foster greater understanding of the estimated 700,000 transgender Americans (Nahas and Gomez 2015). Although his days as an athlete were long behind him, in July 2015, ESPN awarded Jenner the Arthur Ashe Courage Award during its annual ESPY Award ceremonies. Caitlyn Jenner accepted the award and during her acceptance speech urged acceptance for others who are transgender. Her 10-minute speech included many moments of huge applause from the audience of athletes and celebrities. Addressing the transition from male to female, Jenner stated, "This transition has been harder on me than anything I can imagine," and she vowed "to do whatever I can to reshape the landscape of how transgender people are viewed and treated" (ESPN 2015b).

In an effort to further highlight the transitioning process, Jenner created her own reality TV show for E!—*I Am Cait*. The show lost almost half of its audience in its second episode (from 3.892 million to 2.256 million) (Rosenfeld 2015), leading *Entertainment Weekly* to proclaim, "The former *Keeping Up with the Kardashians* wallflower may have a tough time transitioning into a full-time star" (Hibberd and Abrams 2015:9). While the viewing numbers were much lower than *Keeping Up with the Kardashians*, the show has generally been praised for its approach to the social issues facing the transgender community. In the show's eighth and final episode of the 2015 summer season (7/26/15–9/13/15), Caitlyn was joined by former wife Kris, who expressed a variety of emotions with regard to her relationship with Bruce and his transformation to Caitlyn, but was mostly supportive of Caitlyn. *I Am Cait* closed as it opened, with Jenner speaking directly into a small camera, stating, "I want to help people" (Lowry 2015).

The idea of being "queer" was discussed in box 2.2. As a brief reminder, the term "queer" was once used as an offensive insult against members of the LGBT community, but gay-rights advocates of the early 1990s began the process of claiming the term "queer" as a badge of honor (a sort of taking ownership of the word). The term "queer" now includes gay men, lesbians, bisexuals, transgender persons, and other "sexual radicals (those who practice sadomasochism, bondage and discipline, etc.)" and serves to rally LGBT under an umbrella identity (Howe 2004:251).

Homophobia and Conversion Theory

Homophobia is an aspect of sexism. **Sexism** refers to behaviors, conditions, or attitudes that foster stereotypical social roles based on sexual identity and orientation and that lead to prejudice and discrimination against members of one sex due to preferential treatment for members of the offending sex. Transgender persons, like other members of LGBTQ, often face prejudice and discrimination just because of their sexual identity and orientation. Sociologists typically use the term **homophobia** to describe the bigotry directed toward people simply because of their LGBTQ identity and orientation. As Lincoln (2013) explains, homophobia is the fear or hatred of homosexuals, with such fear leading to expressions of disgust, hostility, as well as some acts of violence—sometimes by organized hate groups that aim to attack, harass, or bring down the esteem of LGBTQ folks through the use of violence and violent language in an attempt to intimidate or persecute them. As explained by the University of Texas at Dallas Student Counseling Center (2015), homophobia is connected to heterosexism, with heterosexism defined as the belief that heterosexuality is the only normal sexual orientation and those falling outside this norm are abnormal or flawed. This leads to a perspective of homophobia as a fear of homosexuality that entails negative feelings and attitudes about LGBT people. With all of these ideas in mind, homophobia can be defined as an irrational and unreasoning fear of, aversion to, or antipathy toward members of the LGBTQ community manifested via prejudice, discrimination, and sometimes acts of violence and expressions of hostility.

Kantor (2009) believes that homophobia exists because of homophobes who live in a world of their own where they find fault in those who don't fit their model of how the world should operate. "Homophobes are obsessive hairsplitters who favor seemingly weighty ideological differences without true distinctions, such as 'love the sinner, but hate the sin.' They also use gross or subtle cognitive errors to develop homohating stereotypes as they create singularly homogeneous groups out of heterogeneity, leading them to wax monothematic in an age of diversity" (p. 4). Their hatred or disgust toward the LGBTQ lifestyle allows homophobes to see the world in extremes, such as only heterosexuals should be allowed to marry and homosexuality is something that needs to be changed.

With regard to gay marriage, attitudes have changed dramatically in the United States over the course of the past few decades. In 1988, just 11 percent of Americans said they agreed with the idea that gays should be allowed to marry; in 2015, only a third of Americans were opposed to gay marriage (Associated Press 2015m). In 2004, only Massachusetts allowed an actual gay marriage (as opposed to such alternatives as "civil unions"); by June 1, 2015, 37 states allowed legal same-sex marriage (26 by court decision, 8 by state legislature, and 3 by popular vote). On June 26, 2015, in a landmark opinion, a divided Supreme Court ruled that states cannot ban same-sex marriage, essentially making gay marriage legal in the United States. The United States became the 21st country to legalize same-sex marriage nationwide. With this decision, married same-sex couples gained the same legal rights and benefits as married heterosexual couples (CNN 2015). Among these rights are adoptive rights (Raleigh 2012); full consideration in child-custody cases; hospital visitation rights; the power to make medical decisions with regard to a partner; access to health insurance coverage offered by employers to workers' spouses; and the right to be recognized on official documents such as birth and death certificates. It should be noted that some of these rights were being challenged at the state level. For example, in August 2015, a gay couple in Mississippi sued the state, seeking to overturn its law banning gay couples from adopting or taking children into foster care. At this time, Mississippi was the last state to still ban adoptions by same-sex couples (Amy 2015).

As for the homophobic idea that homosexuality is something that needs to change, we find a variety of therapies designed to convert gay people into straight people. Among the most controversial methods is sexual conversion therapy. *Sexual conversion therapy* refers to a range of dangerous and discredited practices that falsely claim to change a person's sexual orientation or gender identity or expression (Human Rights Campaign 2017). These therapies have been rejected by every mainstream medical and mental health organization, but due to continued homophobia against LGBTQ people, some practitioners continue to conduct conversion therapy. Minors are especially vulnerable to conversion therapy by homophobic parents. Minors forced to endure conversion therapy often suffer from depression, anxiety, drug use, homelessness (parents kick them out of the house for failing to convert or failing to go through with the therapy), and suicide. While a number of conservative religious groups promote the concept that an individual can change his or her sexual orientation, either through prayer or other religious efforts, or through "reparative" or "conversion" therapy, a number of states have signed into law legislation that prevents licensed providers from offering conversion therapy to minors. In April 2015, the Obama administration spoke out against conversion therapy on minors, saying that the practice is "neither medically nor ethically appropriate" (*Los Angeles Times* 2015).

Sexual Harassment

Sexual harassment refers to any uninvited or unwelcome sexual advances, requests for sexual favors, and other verbal or physical conduct of a sexual nature that tends to create an uncomfortable environment. Sexual harassment occurs for many reasons but often begins with the realization that sexual harassers are willing to objectify others. Objectification is the term used when humans are treated as objects rather than as unique individuals. Sexual objectification is the act of treating a person as a tool of sexual pleasure because of their sexual attributes. While anyone can be a victim of sexual objectification, women are more likely to be objectified and judged by a perceived sexual attractiveness rather than by their other attributes (e.g., intelligence, kindness, leadership skills, and coolness under pressure).

There are two generally recognized types of sexual harassment, quid pro quo and a hostile work environment. Quid pro quo (meaning "this for that") sexual harassment occurs when it is stated or implied that an individual must submit to conduct of a sexual nature (e.g., go out on a date or perform some sexual act) in order to receive some other benefit (e.g., a promotion, salary increase, or time off). Refusing a quid pro quo offer may result in the targeted victim losing her or his job, demotion, bad performance review, or a failing grade in a class. Quid pro quo advances, like all forms of sexual harassment in the workplace and academic environment, are illegal, and the person guilty of such actions may suffer severe consequences such as losing their job.

The second type of sexual harassment involves the creation of a hostile work environment and is discussed below.

The Hostile Work Environment

The hostile work environment version of sexual harassment is different from the quid pro quo primarily because there is no "this for that" scenario involved; furthermore, it can be perpetrated by a person at any level of employment (not just a person in a position of authority controlling the allocations of work benefits). Hostile work environment sexual harassment occurs when unwelcome conduct of a sexual nature creates an intimidating, threatening, or abusive working or learning environment or is so severe, persistent, or pervasive that it affects a person's ability to participate in or benefit from normal work programs or activities (Sexual Assault Prevention and Awareness Center 2015).

According to the U.S. Department of State (2015b), any of the following actions may be considered inappropriate and, depending on the circumstances, may meet the definition of sexual harassment or contribute to a hostile work environment:

* Sexual pranks, or repeated sexual teasing, jokes, or innuendo, in person or via e-mail
* Verbal abuse of a sexual nature

- Touching or grabbing of a sexual nature
- Repeatedly standing too close to or brushing up against a person
- Repeatedly asking a person to socialize during off-duty hours when the person has said no or has indicated he or she is not interested
- Giving gifts or leaving objects that are sexually suggestive
- Making or posting sexually demeaning or offensive pictures, cartoons, or other materials in the workplace
- Off-duty, unwelcome conduct of a sexual nature that affects the work environment

The victim of sexual harassment can be a man or a woman. The victim can be of the same sex as the harasser. The harasser can be a supervisor, coworker, or a non-employed who has a business relationship with the work environment in question.

According to the U.S. Equal Employment Opportunity Commission (EEOC) (2015), sexual harassment is a form of sex discrimination that violates Title VII of the Civil Rights Act of 1964. Title VII applies to employment agencies and to labor organizations, as well as to the federal government. The EEOC (2015) states that unwelcome sexual advances, requests for sexual favors, and other verbal or physical conduct of a sexual nature constitutes sexual harassment when this conduct explicitly or implicitly affects an individual's employment, unreasonably interferes with an individual's work performance, or creates an intimidating, hostile, or offensive work environment.

Sexual harassment and objectification can lead to many other problems beyond the creation of a hostile environment. Among these problems are stalking and sexual assault and rape.

Stalking

There are occasions when sexual harassment extends to stalking. **Stalking** involves the willful and repeated following, watching, and/or harassing of another person. The stalker often treats the object of desire as prey to be hunted. According to the DOJ (2014), stalking is a pattern of repeated and unwanted attention, harassment, contact, or any other course of conduct directed at a specific person that would cause a reasonable person to feel fear. Stalking can include:

- Repeated, unwanted, intrusive, and frightening communications from the perpetrator by phone, mail, and/or e-mail
- Repeatedly leaving or sending the victim unwanted items, presents, or flowers
- Following or lying in wait for the victim at places such as home, school, work, or recreation place
- Making direct or indirect threats to harm the victim, the victim's children, relatives, friends, or pets
- Damaging or threatening to damage the victim's property
- Harassing victim through the Internet
- Posting information or spreading rumors about the victim on the Internet, in a public place, or by word of mouth
- Obtaining personal information about the victim by accessing public records, using Internet search services, hiring private investigators, going through the victim's garbage, following the victim, contacting the victim's friends, family, work, or neighbors, etc.

The DOJ recommends victims of stalking call 911 if in immediate danger and contact the local police department to report stalking and stalking-related incidents and/or threats, as this helps to create a file against the stalker that may be used if legal action is required (e.g., a restraining order). Each state has its own laws regarding stalking, and the federal government has its own laws when stalking involves travel in interstate or foreign commerce.

A man stalks a woman as she walks down a dimly lit street.

Sexual Assault and Rape

Sexual assault is any type of sexual contact or behavior that occurs without explicit consent of the recipient, including such behaviors as sexual intercourse, forcible sodomy, child molestation, incest, fondling, and attempted rape (DOJ 2015e). The Rape, Abuse and Incest National Network (RAINN) (2009) states that sexual assault is a crime of power and control and points out that regardless of the form of sexual assault, the victim is never at fault.

Sexual assault takes many forms and is often prevalent in hazing. (Note: Hazing was described in chapter 6 as a form of violence; here we are examining hazing from a sexual assault perspective.) **Hazing** is "an encompassing term that covers silly, potentially risky, or degrading tasks required for acceptance by a group of full-fledged members" (Nuwer 2004:xiv). Crow and Rosner (2004) incorporate the aspects of humiliation and shaming in their legal interpretation of hazing. They define hazing as "any activity expected of someone joining a group that humiliates, degrades, abuses, or endangers, regardless of the person's willingness to participate" (p. 200). Hazing is fairly common in sports, fraternities and sororities, the military, and street gangs and generally operates under the cloak of secrecy.

Proponents of hazing argue that such ritualistic behaviors stimulate loyalty, bonding, and solidarity. Opponents, which include nearly all schools, colleges, and universities, argue that there is no place for degrading or humiliating activities in team building. Despite opposition, hazing remains fairly common, and humiliating newcomers is a big part of hazing. In fraternities and on sports teams, newcomers are often humiliated in a sadomasochistic manner. Nuwer (1999) argues that sadomasochistic sexual assaults or threats of such assaults in fraternal hazing may be performed by older members to demonstrate their dominance over newcomers. In September 2014, abusive initiation rites at sororities were thrust into the spotlight following the revelation that newly crowned Miss America 2015 Kira Kazantsev was forced out of her Hofstra University sorority over hazing concerns (McKay 2014). (Note: Kazantsev admits to being a part of hazing and that she was kicked out of the sorority, but she denies taking part in "abusive" hazing. Her platform, interestingly enough, was domestic violence.) In her book, *Pledged: The Secret Lies of Sororities* (2011), Alexandra Robbins describes a wide variety of humiliating acts at sororities, including:

- Women being branded with cigarettes
- Being forced to do underwear runs across campus
- Standing in pools of water others had defecated in
- Pledges being forced to stand unclothed on running washing machines so their "jiggly" spots can be marked
- Subjected to a "boob ranking," an activity wherein pledges had to rush around examining each other topless so that they were lined up in order of chest size when the sisters called "time" (time was up). The sisters would then inspect the order and tell the girls why they were wrong.

Other examples of hazing, including those that involve sexual assault, are too numerous to document. But hazing continues to exist for many reasons, especially because many victims speak fondly of being a part of a tradition while others are afraid to speak out over fears of social embarrassment, ostracism, or retaliation. But colleges and universities are intent on ending hazing, and most have very specific student conduct policies that address hazing of all kinds, including sports and the Greek system.

Arguably, the most vicious form of sexual assault is rape. Rape, and to a lesser extent sexual assault, were discussed in chapter 5. Among other things, rape has been a characteristic of human history since the dawn of humanity and is commonly associated with warfare. Rape is still a major component of present-day warfare. Consider, for example, in August 2015, the parents of 26-year-old Kayla Mueller (an American aid worker in Syria who was captured by ISIS) revealed that their daughter was a sex slave and repeatedly raped by Abu Bakr al-Baghdadi, the top leader of the Islamic State. Two Yezedi girls who escaped the compound where Mueller was being held revealed details of the sexual abuse (Collman 2015). Before the girls escaped, ISIS had claimed that Mueller was killed during a U.S. air strike, but when they learned the United States was about to launch a rescue attempt of the American, she was killed.

Rape should not be a part of any civil society, and yet it occurs far too often. Rape is commonly viewed as unwanted sex forced by one person(s) on another. The FBI (2014e), in its Uniform Crime Reports (UCR), provides an official definition of **rape** as "penetration, no matter how slight, of the vagina or anus with any body part or object, or oral penetration by a sex organ of another person, without the consent of the victim." Rape, like all forms of sexual assault, is a serious problem in many communities and college campuses and is underreported. (See chapter 5 for statistics on rape.)

While it would seem safe to say everyone is against rape, there are those who make different distinctions of rape than does the FBI (forcible rape, statutory rape, and attempted forcible rape). There are a few conservative politicians (and many of their supporters) who view rape as acceptable in some conditions, primarily when the woman gets pregnant. Because these politicians are against abortion and know that they will be asked such questions as "Are you in favor of abortion if the pregnancy is a result of rape?" they have redefined rape. Consider the following examples:

- Former Senator Todd Akin (MO) has said that women cannot get pregnant from "legitimate" rape. Akin told a St. Louis TV station in 2012 that "If it's a legitimate rape, the female body has ways to shut the whole thing down" (Alter 2014).
- Texas Senator Ted Cruz, a 2016 presidential candidate, continued Akin's idea of a woman's ability to shut down her reproductive system during a "legitimate rape" and therefore opposes abortion for victims of rape and incest (Chapin 2015).
- Richard Mourdock (IN) has described a pregnancy as a result of a sexual assault as something God intended. Mourdock said, "I struggled with it myself for a long time, but I came to realize life is that gift from God. And I think even when life begins in that horrible situation or rape, that is something that God intended to happen" (Madison 2012).
- Ron Paul (TX) has attempted to make a distinction between rape and "honest rape" (Johnson 2012).
- Brian Kurcaba, a state legislator from West Virginia, said, "While rape is awful, a child that results from a rape is beautiful." He later apologized for the statement (Groppe 2015).
- In August 2015, Mike Huckabee, a 2016 presidential candidate, was asked if he would support abortion in a case involving a 10-year-old rape victim (an unidentified girl in Paraguay was raped by her stepfather in a case that drew national and worldwide attention at that time), and he responded, "I wouldn't pretend it's anything other than a terrible tragedy, but let's not compound the tragedy by taking yet another life" (Worland 2015).

Sociologists consider rape to be a violent, coercive act of aggression against individuals as a means of forcible dominance having little or nothing to do with sexual attraction. Sociologists are very concerned about all forms of rape and especially date rape on college campuses, which is so prevalent that it's televised in after-school specials as a social problem (Polletta and Tomlinson 2014). College students might want to check with their specific campus for information on date rape and methods utilized on their campus to help protect students from being victimized by date rape.

Pornography

Pornography, more commonly known as porn, is defined as words or images (generally found in books, magazines, photographs, film, art, and cyberspace) intended to cause sexual arousal. Such a vague definition leaves open to debate what precisely constitutes material that is pornographic. The classification of a material as pornographic reflects the greater community's standards of decency. As with most broad topics, there is often a debate among community members as to what exactly should be considered as pornographic, erotic, or acceptable. Erotic images are those that spark sexual feelings and may involve the portrayal of nudity but not necessarily sexual activity. Erotica is generally considered artistic and classy, as opposed to pornography, which is usually "trashy." Pornography is often divided into two categories: soft-core porn, which shows or describes nudity and suggests sexual activity; and hard-core porn, which contains explicit descriptions or images of sexual acts.

The First Amendment, which protects many things, including the freedom of speech or expression, is generally invoked by those who believe pornography should be protected. The U.S. Supreme Court has established that pornography is deemed obscene, and it is not protected by the First Amendment. One of the earliest decisions concerning the issue of obscenity and pornography dates back to 1957 in the *Roth v. United States*, 354 U.S. 476, 77 S. Ct. 1304, 1 L. Ed. 2d 1498, case when the court ruled obscenity is "utterly without redeeming social importance" and is therefore not protected by the First Amendment. Later cases would elaborate on the parameters of obscenity, but the basic idea that not all forms of pornography are legal remains (*The Free Dictionary* 2015).

There are a number of issues related to pornography, including possible addiction to pornography, the idea that pornography is a type of cheating on a significant other, revenge porn, and the most serious concern when discussing deviant pornography, child porn.

Porn Addiction

There is a concern that some people may become addicted to porn. For some people, this addiction is similar to drug addiction and may be just as difficult to break. According to Focus on the Family (2015), there are five stages of addiction:

1. Early exposure—Most people who get addicted to porn start early in life.
2. Addiction—The person keeps coming back to porn, it becomes a regular part of life, and there is no desire to quit.
3. Escalation—Over time, the addiction grows to the point where the addict looks for a higher level of porn, including images that once seemed disgusting.
4. Desensitization—The pornographic images begin to lose their appeal, and the addict no longer finds them exciting.
5. Acting out sexually—At this point the addict may seek to act out the viewed pornographic images in the real world.

Sex compulsivity is a progressive intimacy disorder in which the individual cannot control his or her sexual impulses and/or actions. As an addiction, it is likely that sexual compulsivity will have a negative impact on the individual and his or her family that over time could develop to such deviant behaviors as exhibitionism, voyeurism, child molestation, or rape.

Is Viewing Porn an Example of Cheating?

There are some people who consider viewing porn as an adulterous act. "Polls show that Americans are almost evenly divided on questions like whether porn is bad for relationships, whether it's an inevitable feature of male existence, and whether it's demeaning to women. This divide tends to cut along gender lines" (Douthat 2008).

While there are more women who view porn today than in the past, the gender line still existed in 2007, with 70 percent of women saying they never looked at pornography while just 14 percent of males said they never looked at porn (Douthat 2008). When one person in a committed couple spends time viewing porn, the other partner may feel cheated from intimacy and sexual fantasy desires that are instead directed toward a pornographic image. So what do you think? Is viewing porn an example of cheating?

Revenge Porn

There are many occasions wherein people who have sexted one another end their relationship and yet the former partner now possesses nude photos of the other. If the lover felt jilted, he or she may resort to "revenge porn." **Revenge porn** involves the cybersharing of sexually explicit photo(s)/videos of another person (generally an ex-lover or ex-friend) by an angered ex-partner without the consent of the person(s) in the photo/video for the purpose of spiteful humiliation. We are likely witnessing the beginning of a new trend in cyberpornography, the revenge porn industry. On the other hand, there is a national push to punish jilted lovers and others who distribute revenge porn racy photos online. In 2015, former NFL (New York Jets) linebacker Jermaine Cunningham became the most recognizable defendant to face revenge porn charges. "The decade old New Jersey law being used to prosecute Cunningham was the first of its kind in the country, and 16 more states have passed laws since, including 14 in the past two years. At least 10 additional legislatures are considering revenge porn laws" (*The Daily News* 5/14/15). Although Cunningham may be among the most well-known "revenge porn" defendants, he will not be the first to be prosecuted under this new legislation. A Los Angeles man was sentenced to a year in prison for posting a topless photo of his ex on her employer's website and urging that she be fired (*The Daily News* 5/14/15). Anyone who has, or is thinking about, sexting a current significant other should consider revenge porn as among the potential deviant outcomes of such behavior.

Child Pornography

The issue of obscenity and pornography is especially relevant when discussing child porn. The DOJ (2015f) articulates that images of child pornography are not protected under the First Amendment rights and are therefore deemed illegal contraband under federal law. Child pornography is a form of child exploitation. Federal law defines child pornography as any visual depiction of sexually explicit conduct involving a minor (persons less than 18 years old). Images of child pornography are also referred to as child sexual abuse images (DOJ 2015c). **Cyber child pornography** refers to the sexually explicit content made available online in various formats, including images, video files, video games, and streaming videos.

As described by the Australian Federal Police (AFP), sexually related commerce (e.g., pornography, especially child pornography) was identified as a growing trend in the 1990s. Some Australian law enforcement agencies had described cyberpornography as the fastest-growing single area of computer-related crime. The unprecedented growth of cyber child pornography was also identified in the United States at this same time by a number of U.S. authorities and scholars (Armagh 1998). More than a decade later, under the American Recovery and Reinvestment Act of 2009, the Office of Justice Programs (OJP), which administers more than $2.76 billion in awards for state and local law enforcement and for other criminal justice activities that prevent and control crime, allocated $48.5 million for the Internet Crimes Against Children Task Force Program and $97.5 million for local and national mentoring initiatives (Office of Juvenile Justice Delinquency Prevention 2010a). More recently, the Child Pornography Victim Assistance (CPVA) program is in existence to ensure that victims have access to victim assistance services no matter how much time has passed since the original abuse took place (FBI 2014d). Today, the Internet Crimes Against Children Task Force Program (ICAC program) helps state and local law enforcement agencies develop an effective response to technology-facilitated child sexual exploitation and Internet crimes against children (OJJDP 2015).

The child pornography market exploded with the advent of the Internet and advanced digital technology. Child pornography images are readily available at the click of a button. While some child sexual abuse images depict children in great distress and the sexual abuse is self-evident, other images may depict children that appear complacent. However, just because a child victim may not appear to be in distress, that does not mean that sexual abuse did not occur. Victims of child pornography not only suffer from the sexual abuse inflicted upon them to produce the images, but also from knowing that their images can be traded and viewed by others worldwide (DOJ 2015c).

Prostitution

Prostitution refers to the act of offering one's self for hire to engage in sexual relations of any kind. A prostitute is a person who offers sexual acts for the gratification of a customer in exchange for money or something else of value. Sexual acts can include, but are not limited to, intercourse, penetration, fellatio, cunnilingus, assisted masturbation, or any other form of contact between the breast, genitals, pubic area, or buttocks. There are three primary components to prostitution: sexual activity (an individual has agreed to perform or has actually performed any sexual act with another); compensation (money or some other form of consideration); and intent (simple negotiation of the act or performing the act for compensation) (Smith and Villaamil 2012).

Prostitution has occurred throughout history in nearly all societies and as a result is often described as "the world's oldest profession" (Smith 2012; Smith and Villaamil 2012). Early forms of prostitution involved "sacred prostitution," in which the sexual act was performed for a religious purpose with a person other than one's spouse. Major world religions have consistently condemned other forms of prostitution in which the activity is purely for personal pleasure, and severe penalties have been imposed on the prostitutes while lesser penalties have generally been applied to their clients (*New World Encyclopedia* 2014).

Illegal in every state in the United States, except parts of Nevada, prostitution is generally categorized as a "victimless crime" in some criminal categorical schemes. It is considered a victimless crime only when all the direct participants are willing and consenting adults. If a minor is involved or if any of the parties involved are not willing participants, it is not a victimless crime. Still, even when all parties are consenting adults, participants can be victimized, such as in cases when one (or both) persons involved are physically harmed or when an STD is transmitted from one person to the other. When one is victimized because of the act of prostitution, their spouses or significant others may also be indirectly victimized (e.g., stigmatized if the act of prostitution is revealed, feelings of betrayal, acquiring an STD, and so on).

Most prostitutes are females, and there exists a tragic link between prostitution and child abuse. As described by Julian Sher (2013), many adult prostitutes who recount their stories of their lives as a street-level prostitute acknowledge that that they were runaways or throwaways (thrown out of the house by their parents/guardians), and they had experienced some form of child physical, emotional, or sexual abuse. Many female prostitutes also grew up in homes without fathers, and they attested to this being a major factor into why they felt no remorse or guilt for what they were doing. Some females become prostitutes in order to support a drug and/ or alcohol addiction. In some instances, the drug and alcohol addiction keeps them in the profession of prostitution (Wiechelt and Shdaimah 2011). Once involved in prostitution, many women experience mental health troubles (e.g., depression and PTSD) and psychological illnesses as a result of the trauma from their lived experiences. Wiechelt and Shdaimah found that 75 percent of prostitutes had attempted suicide and that 15 percent of all suicide victims are prostitutes. Because they lack the self-confidence and funds to leave prostitution, most prostitutes find it very difficult to leave the grip of their pimps (a type of sexual manager who controls the business aspects of the acts of prostitution). Andrea Cimino (2012), among others, recommends that rehabilitation programs need to be made available to these victims so that they can successfully exit prostitution.

Prostitution is one of the major components of the commercial sex industry, an enterprise that has witnessed a dramatic growth in the past few decades in the United States. The commercial sex industry, which has led to the privatization of commercial sex services, includes such deviant sexual activities as pornography, stripping, phone and Internet sex, and escort services (Smith and Villaamil 2012). While there a number of possible ways of categorizing the umbrella term of "prostitution," we will briefly examine four categories: street prostitution, brothel prostitution, escort services, and human sex trafficking.

Street Prostitution

Street prostitution, as the name implies, involves prostitutes, generally women, who walk the streets soliciting customers for sexual favors. "Street prostitution varies with the type of prostitutes involved and their commitment to prostitution, the market size, the community's tolerance levels, the degree to which prostitutes are organized, and the relationship of prostitution to drug use and trafficking. Street prostitution accounts for perhaps only 10 to 20 percent of all prostitution, but it has the most visible negative impact on the community" (Scott 2002:1). Because they are out on the streets, streetwalkers are more susceptible to the risk of negative encounters, especially violence from pimps and customers ("Johns").

Brothel Prostitution

A brothel is a place of prostitution. Brothels are essentially community homes that can house any number of prostitutes. Unlike the streets, customers enter the domain of prostitutes, making it a relatively safer environment (for the prostitute and customer). A brothel can be legally or illegally operated. In the United States, legal brothels can only be found in parts of Nevada, excluding Las Vegas, a city where many tourists are surprised to learn that prostitution is *not* legal. Legal brothels are regulated and must comply with health and safety standards and government policies. Most legal brothels have security guards and are equipped with emergency buttons and microphones in case the employed prostitute needs help. Most importantly—for both the prostitute and the customer—the prostitutes are subject to regular health checks that test for STDs and infections. If a test comes back positive for a disease, the prostitute cannot return to work, and it is a crime to knowingly prostitute an employee who has an

Prostitutes lined up for customers at the Bunny Ranch, a legal brothel outside of Carson City, Nevada.

STD or infection (Sullivan 2010). Illegal brothels, on the other hand, are not regulated and are less safe and subject to police raids.

Escort Services

Escort services are a unique component to the commercial sex industry in that specifically designed companies provide the prostitutes, known as escorts, for clients, generally for sexual services. Escorts may also be hired for longer durations to serve as companions for clients who travel or attend business trips. Escort agencies receive a fee from the client, but the escort negotiates for any additional fees or arrangements (e.g., sexual favors) directly with the client. Unlike other prostitutes, escorts operate mostly invisible from the law. They are often very well paid and thus perceived in a more prestigious manner than other prostitutes. Escorts do not have to worry about many of the same problems as streetwalkers, but most will find it hard to maintain a real, committed romantic relationship, which takes a toll on both their personal and social life (McLaren 2010).

Human Sex Trafficking

Arguably the most deviant form of commercial sex involves the human trafficking of women and underage girls into prostitution. **Human trafficking** involves the illegal trade of human beings and is considered a modern version of slavery. "The United States government considers trafficking in persons to include all of the criminal conduct involved in forced labor and sex trafficking, essentially the conduct involved in reducing or holding someone in compelled service" (U.S. Department of State 2015c). As it pertains specifically to prostitution, we can distinguish between adult and child sex trafficking. Adult sex trafficking occurs when an adult is coerced, forced, or deceived into prostitution—or maintained in prostitution through coercion. All of those involved in recruiting, transporting, harboring, receiving, or obtaining individuals for the purpose of performing sexual acts have committed a sex trafficking crime (U.S. Department of State 2015c). Child sex trafficking follows the same parameters as described above for adults except that minors are now involved. "According to UNICEF, as many two million children are subjected to prostitution in the global commercial sex trade. . . . The use of children in the commercial sex trade is prohibited under both U.S. law and the Palermo Protocol as well as by legislation in countries around the world" (U.S. Department of State 2015c). The Department of State states that "sex trafficking has devastating consequences for minors, including long-lasting physical and psychological trauma, disease (including HIV/AIDS), drug addiction, unintended pregnancy, malnutrition, social ostracism, and death." Human trafficking is not just a problem for people in foreign nations, as "the United States is a source and transit country, and is also considered one of the top destination points for victims of child trafficking and exploitation" (UNICEF 2015b).

Sexual Fetishisms

A **fetish** refers to a strong desire or fixation for some object. There are sexual fetishes and nonsexual fetishes (e.g., the obsessive baseball fan who desperately tries to catch a home-run or foul ball). The sexual meaning of a fetish is the most commonly described version and the one of relevance here. **Sexual fetishism** refers to the desire to engage in specific forms of sex-related activities that bring satisfaction to the participants. Most likely, there are thousands of sexual fetishes, and the extensive coverage of such a topic is beyond our scope of concern. Examples of sexual fetishes include exhibitionism/flashing, toe sucking, spanking, group sex, cross-dressing, spanking, sexual role-play, voyeurism, and domination and submission.

10 of the Most Popular Sexual Fetishes

Distinguishing nearly and clearly between fetishisms and kinks or preferences presents some gray areas. It is also relatively difficult to ascertain just how popular any given fetish may be. Nonetheless, Jean Ferraiuolo (2014) has complied a list of 10 of the most popular sexual fetishes:

10. *Adult babies*—Individuals who enjoy being a baby again. They may enjoy regressing partially or completely, participating in the act of wearing diapers, being fed by an adult, sucking a baby bottle or pacifier, and so on. Individuals who engage in such behavior enjoy being nurtured, may be seeking attention, or are trying to escape from the responsibilities of their daily lives.

9. *Swinging and group sex*—Swingers are people who engage in sex with other couples or groups of people with the full consent of both partners. It all depends on the couple and the reasons for participating as to whether the relationship will remain strong or dissolve after engaging in swinging or group sex.

8. *Water sports*—Include having sex in a shower but generally means urolagnia, the act of being aroused by urine, whether it is the feel or smell of it, and often referred to as a "golden shower." Water fetishes may also include a desire to urinate in public, wetting oneself, or watching another urinate. It involves elements of control and humiliation, especially when someone enjoys having another relieve themselves on them.

7. *Cross-dressing*—Individuals who like to wear clothing and accessories generally associated with the "opposite sex." As it has become increasingly common for people to act and dress in nontraditional, gender-specific manners, cross-dressing has become more popular over the course of the past couple decades.

6. *Foot worship*—Perhaps the most common fetish of the nongenital body parts and nonsexual objects. Freud addressed the idea of foot worship as due to the belief that the human foot resembles a penis. Foot worship fetish is generally manifested via toe sucking. (Note: While foot fetishism is very real for a number of people, not all scholars accept the Freudian explanation.)

5. *Spanking*—The buttocks is considered an erogenous zone, and if contact is made with the right amount of pressure and frequency, it can result in arousal for many people. People who like to experiment with domination and submission are especially turned on by spanking.

4. *Voyeurism and exhibitionism*—A significant number of people (perhaps one in three adults) enjoy watching sex or exposing themselves in public. There may be a bit of exhibitionism in all of us when one considers that at some point in time (e.g., when we feel good about how we look) we have worn clothing that shows off our best attributes. Many people enjoy Mardi Gras, where women often flash their breasts, while others love Halloween, where they can dress provocatively for the pleasure of others who like looking at exhibitionists.

3. *Rubber/latex/leather*—Referred to as "rubberists," some people enjoy tight materials, as they represent a type of sexual bondage. For some, the smell of rubber/latex/leather is a turn-on. This helps to explain why some people love wearing leather jackets.

2. *Sexual role-play*—Couples may choose to act out roles at home in order to spice up their love lives. Some couples may go to public places, such as a bar, pretend to be strangers, tease others at the bar, and then "allow" their partner to "pick them up." Once again, Halloween becomes the perfect time for people to act out a role they fantasize about playing in real life.

1. *Domination and submission*—A number of people enjoy the sexual fetish known by its acronym—BDSM—which stands for bondage, domination and submission, sadism, and masochism. BDSM activities include a wide range of behavior, including such things as being tied up, wearing fuzzy handcuffs, the use of whips and chains, and so on. As evidenced by the popular movie *Fifty Shades of Grey*, BDSM has a mainstream appeal.

15 of the Strangest Sexual Fetishes

While the list above includes popular forms of sexual fetishes, CBS News (2015b) compiled a list of the 15 strangest sex fetishes that include agalmatophilia (mannequin love); ursusagalmatophilia or plushies (people who like to dress up like animals, calling themselves "furries" or "plushies"); partialism/gas pedal honeys (a woman's high-heeled foot, including images of stilettos on a gas pedal found on some truckers' mud flaps); salirophilia (liking their partners literally dirty); paraphilic infantilism (adults who wear diapers and pretend to be an infant); hybristophilia (an attraction to criminals); hematolagnia or vampire sex (having erotic thoughts about blood; which became increasingly popular due to the *Twilight* movies); mechanophilia (an erotic love for gadgets such as cars); claustrophilia (a love of being in tight places); odaxelagnia (an erotic pleasure in biting or being bitten by another); dacryphilia (being turned on by making someone cry); masks (wearing masks for sexual pleasure); autoandrophilia (women who enjoy dressing up as and/or imagining themselves as

Fetishists wearing leather bondage dog hoods participate in a parade in Toronto, Canada.

men); acrotomophilia (being turned on by a lover with a missing limb); and somno-philia (the sexual enjoyment from watching one's partner sleep).

As we can see from this sampling of sexual fetishisms, people are turned on by many things other than what might constitute "normal" turn-ons. A discussion of sexual fetishisms, unlike topics such as child prostitution and pornography, sexual harassment, and prejudice and discrimination against LGBTQ people, clouds the entire topic of what constitutes sexual social deviance.

Summary

Sexual social deviance was the topic of this chapter. *Sexual deviance* includes a wide range of unusual or abnormal forms of sexually related behaviors that are outside of the culturally and historically determined social norms and expectations of a society. A *sexual deviant* is a person who finds pleasure in and/or participates in acts of sexual deviancy. The topics of infidelity, teenage pregnancy, sexting, and the transmission of sexually transmitted disease (STDs) and sexually transmitted infection (STIs) were dis-cussed as a means of introducing some of the complexities of sexual social deviance.

Primary topics examined include gender identity and sexual orientation; sexual harassment; pornography; prostitution; and sexual fetishisms. Traditionally, one's gender identity and sexual orientation was predicated on their sexual categoriza-tion. Such a perspective, however, is a matter of social construction. Most people identify primarily with their biological sex; others, however, do not believe that the sexual category assigned to them at birth corresponds with how they view them-selves. As a result, sexual identity is far more complicated for some individuals than it is for others. An important aspect of sexual identity is sexual orientation. Sexual orientation refers to a person's physical, romantic, and emotional attraction to another person. People may be drawn to partners of the opposite sex (the most common form of sexuality), same sex, both sexes, or neither sex (asexuality). The LGBTQ community, homophobia, and the conversion theory were also looked at as a means of further exploring sexual identity and orientation.

Sexual harassment refers to any uninvited or unwelcome sexual advances, requests for sexual favors, and other verbal or physical conduct of a sexual nature that tends to create an uncomfortable environment. Sexual harassment occurs for many reasons but often begins with the realization that sexual harassers are willing to objectify others. Pornography, more commonly known as porn, is defined as words or images (generally found in books, magazines, photographs, film, art, and cyberspace) intended to cause sexual arousal. Such a vague definition leaves open to debate what precisely constitutes material that is pornographic. Prostitution refers to the act of offering one's self for hire to engage in sexual relations of any kind. A prostitute is a person who offers sexual acts for the gratification of a customer in exchange for money or something else of value. A fetish refers to a strong desire or fixation for some object. Examples of sexual fetishes include exhibitionism/flashing, toe sucking, spanking, group sex, cross-dressing, spanking, sexual role-play, voyeurism, and domination and submission.

Key Terms

cyber child pornography, 311

fetish, 315

gender, 299

gender identity, 300

hazing, 307

homophobia, 303

human trafficking, 314

infidelity, 292

pornography, 309

prostitution, 312

revenge porn, 311

sex, 299

sexism, 303

sexting, 296

sexual assault, 307

sexual deviance, 291

sexual deviant, 291

sexual fetishism, 315

sexual harassment, 305

sexually transmitted diseases (STDs), 297

sexual orientation, 300

stalking, 306

Discussion Questions

1. What do you think of the "yes means yes" policy? Is it better than the "no means no" policy?

2. How would you explain the meaning of sexual social deviance to a friend or family member who has not taken a sociology course on deviant behavior? Which of the five perspectives of deviance would you emphasize over the others?

3. Is cheating on a significant other a form of sexual deviance? Explain.

4. What do you think of the University of California's admissions policy of allowing students to choose between six different categories for gender identity? With which category do you identify?

5. Explain the relationship between sexual objectification and sexual harassment. Are women the only victims of sexual harassment, or the most likely to be victimized?

6. Do you believe all images and expressions of individuality should be protected by the First Amendment, or are there some things that are simply obscene? If there are things you deem obscene, what are they?

7. What can be done to stop human trafficking, especially trafficking of children into a life of prostitution?

CHAPTER 12

Environmental Social Deviance

CHAPTER OBJECTIVES

After reading this chapter students should be able to:

- Explain what is meant by environmental social deviance
- Describe the concepts of "carrying capacity" and "mass extinctions"
- Identify and explain the causes of mass extinctions
- Demonstrate the ability to apply the environmental imagination to the study of the environment

- Compare and contrast fossil fuels used for energy to alternative forms of energy
- Explain how climate change occurs
- Demonstrate knowledge of multiple human behaviors that have a negative impact on the environment

For a very long time now, humans have been draining natural resources from the environment with little regard to the consequences of such behaviors. We take and we take energy and have so taken for granted the idea that the environment will continue to serve our every need that most of us are oblivious to the dangers lurking right around the corner. These dangers come in many forms but are highlighted by the fact that there is a limited **carrying capacity**, or maximum feasible load just short of the level that would end the environment's ability to support life, and still we continue to waste resources and pollute the environment. When the planet exceeds its carrying capacity, *all* living species risk extinction.

In addition to the threat of a mass extinction brought about by our reaching and surpassing the earth's carrying capacity is the scenario wherein the "power grid" goes down. Without our human-made power grid humanity faces a complete societal breakdown. Think about it: without the power grid we wouldn't have electricity and the means to provide heat and cooling for our homes; there would be no way to power our electronic devices; mass transportation systems would become inoperable; food supplies for the masses (especially in large urban areas) would become exhausted in a short period of time; and there would be a slew of other problems that most people choose to ignore at the present time. Adding to the problem of the grid going down is the realization that at the current time there isn't a proper public emergency contingency plan to deal with the inevitable chaos that would be caused by humans as they panic in their feeble attempts to adjust to the new world order caused by the lack of a sustained power grid.

Human ignorance combined with a hubristic way of thinking has led to countless forms of behaviors that have a negative impact on the physical environment. Our "environmental-awareness" intelligence has not grown correspondingly with our level of technological advancements, especially since the time of early industrialization. The warning signs that we are in the midst of the sixth mass extinction era are evident all around us, and still most people choose to ignore the warning signs. The idea that the planet is facing its sixth mass extinction, the first one that will involve humans, highlights just how important the study of environmental social deviance truly is.

What Is Environmental Deviance?

As this is a text on social deviancy, the focus of this chapter centers on the behaviors of people that affect local ecosystems and the environment in its totality. Beginning with the term "environment," we should acquaint ourselves with some key concepts. The **environment** refers to the totality of social and physical conditions that affect nature (land, water, air, plants, and animals) and humanity and their influence on the growth, development, and survival of organisms found in a given surrounding (e.g., a limited proximity or the earth as a whole) (Delaney and Madigan 2014). The **ecosystem** refers to the ecological network of interconnected and interdependent living organisms (plants, animals, and microbes) in union with the nonliving aspects found in their immediate community, including air, water, minerals, and soil (Delaney and Madigan 2014). Although it could be argued that the entire planet is an ecosystem, the term is generally applied to limited areas. In this regard, the concepts of "ecosystem" and "environment" are similar but not necessarily interchangeable. As Charles Harper (2012) explains, "An ecosystem means the community of things that live and interact in parts of the geophysical environment" (p. 3). Thus, ecosystems are generally considered parts of the greater planetary whole environment.

An ecosystem consisting of a reef and a school of fish.

Because of the concern that the earth's environment has been compromised due to, at least in part, human activity, two other important and related terms—"sustainability" and "thrivability"—to the study of environmental deviancy need to be defined. **Sustainability** refers to the ability of the environment to hold, endure, or bear the weight of a wide variety of social and natural forces that may compromise its functionality. Delaney and Madigan (2014), among others, however, argue that merely sustaining the environment is too insignificant of a goal and point out that sustaining a compromised environment is akin to sustaining poverty, poor health, homelessness, hunger, and the slew of other social problems that exist in society. Why would anyone want to sustain a dire situation? The goal then should be to encourage thrivability. **Thrivability** refers to a cycle of actions that reinvest energy for future use and stretch resources further; it transcends sustainability by creating an upward spiral of greater possibilities and increasing energy. This idea is similar to the reality that people living in poverty or with poor health would much rather live a life where they thrived with economic riches and excellent physical health. As will be demonstrated in this chapter, the environment is so compromised due to deviant human activity that emphasizing sustainability alone is not nearly as important as promoting thrivability.

Limited Carrying Capacity and Mass Extinctions

Of all the earth's organisms, humans place the highest demands on the environment, and yet we also represent a great threat to its sustainability and thrivability. While many people are afraid or too naïve to consider the ramifications of a compromised environment due to human activity, a number of scientists and conscientious people are acutely in tune with the limited carrying capacity of the planet's environment. The carrying capacity is tied to the number of organisms that can be supported in a given area based on the natural resources available without compromising present and future generations. While research has been conducted on a number of animal species with respect to a specific area's carrying capacity, the concept of a limited carrying capacity has been applied to the human population since the 1960s. Because the consumption habits of humans are much more variable than those of most other animal species, it is more difficult to determine or predict the carrying capacity of earth for human beings. As a result, the IPAT equation is applied to study the carrying capacity for humans. The IPAT formula is expressed as I (Environmental Impact) = P (Population) $\times$ A (Affluence) $\times$ T (Technology) (The Sustainability Scale Project 2003). This formula reveals that the carrying capacity for any specific area is not necessarily fixed, as food production, for example, can be improved through technology. Nonetheless, once the environment has been sullied, the carrying capacity shrinks, thus negatively altering its ability to sustain life. Biologist Peter C. Schulze (2002) puts forth that "the IPAT equation is particularly useful as a starting point for disentangling the determinants of per capita impact, either of a group of people, such as a nation, or of an individual, such as one's self" (p. 149). As an illustration of how the formula works, consider the following: the larger the population (P) of a given society, the greater the environmental impact (I) because large numbers of people draw more resources; the greater the affluence (A) of a society, the greater the I because affluence places greater demands on the environment, as people with extra income and wealth will purchase and consume goods and services beyond their survival needs; and the greater the level of technology (T) of society, the more resources it will draw from the environment (I), or technological ability may create means to sustain the environment (e.g., improve our ability to mass-produce food and develop energy sources that are not dependent upon fossil fuels). Schulze (2002) and his colleagues introduced the variable of Behavior expressed as B in their adapted formula of environmental impact leading to I = PBAT. With this modified equation, the question of whether or not humanity will exceed the earth's carrying capacity is answered by examining human behavior itself. For example, if everyone on Earth managed to do more with less, the earth's carrying capacity could more easily be sustained (Layton 2015). Conversely, if human behavior leads to negative action against the environment, the greater the likelihood the carrying capacity will be exceeded.

Exceeding the earth's carrying capacity is a potentially huge problem for humanity, but it's not the only major hurdle facing the human species. Another problem that humans must come to grips with is their own extinction. Every species, including humans, has a limited shelf-life. Mammals, the best-studied species, are likely to exist for about one-quarter million years, and since there are about 5,500 mammal species on the planet today, we would expect one species to disappear every 700 years. This type of extinction is known as a background extinction (Kolbert 2014). Mass extinctions are much different. "Instead of a background hum there's a crash, and disappearance rates spike" (Kolbert 2014:15–17). Stuart Pimm, a conservation biologist at Duke University and president of the Saving Species organization, has published research in such journals as *Nature* and *Science* for decades, warning that the extinction rate is 100 to 1,000 times faster than the normal pace of evolution would dictate, thus supporting the notion that disappearance rates have indeed spiked (Saving Species 2015; Pimm and Raven 2000; Saul 2015). A **mass extinction** (ME) occurs when the planet loses more than three-quarters of its species in a geologically short interval of time, usually a few hundred thousand to a couple of million years (Barnosky et al. 2011). However, a critical event such as a meteorite impact may trigger a mass extinction in a much shorter period of time. While everyone is aware of the most recent ME—the one that killed the dinosaurs over 65 million years ago as a result of meteorites/asteroids—there have been a total of five MEs in the past 540 million years (see table 12.1).

TABLE 12.1   **Mass Extinctions (ME)**

The 1st ME (the late-Ordovician period, beginning nearly 440 million years ago)—Caused by glaciation, killed off nearly two-thirds of all land and marine animal life and most plant life worldwide.

The 2nd ME (the late-Devonian period, about 365 million years ago)—Caused by glaciation resulting in the destruction of nearly 85 percent of marine and land species.

The 3rd ME (end-Permian era, about 250 million years ago)—Caused by asteroids and volcanoes, killed off approximately 80 to 95 percent of all marine species. It would take 10 million years for coral reefs to reappear.

The 4th ME (end-Triassic period, about 200 million years ago)—Caused by volcanoes, killed off half of all marine invertebrates and approximately 80 percent of all land quadrupeds (4-legged animals, especially mammals that use all 4 limbs for walking).

The 5th ME (end-Cretaceous era, about 65 million years ago)—Caused by meteorites/asteroids, made famous because of the demise of dinosaurs but in addition, nearly all land animals perished.

The 6th ME (current period, Cenozoic)—In progress as evidenced by such occurrences as: every 20 minutes we lose an animal species (Corwin 2009); every thousand years we lose an amphibian species (Kolbert 2014); in the past 40 years the number of wild animals has been cut in half and the marine species are being decimated (Carrington 2014); and predictions that within 300 years three-quarters of today's animal species could vanish (Barnosky et al. 2011). This is the first ME that will impact humans and, ironically, it is being sped up by human activity.

Source: Delaney and Madigan 2014

A mass extinction occurs about every 70 million years and as table 12.1 reveals, we are currently in the sixth ME period. Obviously, this is the first time humans will be impacted by a ME, and while the previous five MEs were caused by forces of nature (worldly or celestial), this mass extinction is being assisted by deviant human behaviors, especially our behaviors since industrialization.

Environmental Sociology and the "Environmental Imagination"

The environment is compromised in a number of ways, and because the compromised environment is, at the very least, a partial result of human behavior, and because a compromised environment affects humanity, sociology is perfectly fitted to study the environment. While "Earth Day 1970 is often said to represent the debut of the modern environmental movement" (Hannigan 2014:18), sociologists had been studying the relationship between human behavior and the physical environment since at least the mid-1930s. For example, a number of sociologists, some belonging to the Rural Sociological Society (RSS), established in December 1937 (Rural Sociological Society 2015), examined food production and agriculture within given ecosystems; the effect of "boomtown" development on the physical environment; and the social disruption on nature via such human activities as forestry, mining, and fishing.

Sociologists continued to examine the role of humans and their impact on the environment throughout the 20th century, and in the late 1990s Lawrence Buell modified C. Wright Mills's famous term of the "sociological imagination" (see chapter 2) to create his concept of the "environmental imagination." Among other things, Mills (1959) had stated that the **sociological imagination** "enables its possessor to understand the larger historical scene in terms of its meanings for the inner life and the external career of a variety of individuals" (p. 5), the implication being that individuals are influenced by social forces that, while created by humans, come to exert power over individuals, rendering them powerless to control events of potentially great magnitude. Buell applied this idea to the role of humans and their impact on the physical environment while pointing out that eventually the environment would, in turn, impact humanity. Buell (1995) identified four key aspects of the environmental imagination:

1. The nonhuman environment is present not merely as a framing device but as a presence that begins to suggest that human history is implicated in natural history.
2. The human interest is understood not to be the only legitimate interest.
3. Human accountability to the environment is an ethical concern.
4. The environment should be viewed as a process in flux rather than as a constant.

Today, environmental sociologists examine how humans waste or conserve resources; track public opinions on issues such as climate change, the dependency on fossil fuels, and hydraulic fracturing; examine social movements (e.g., "going green" and "freeganism"); and acknowledge the role of nature on the environment but focus on human factors (e.g., the use of plastics, agricultural mismanagement, and the creation of medical waste and e-waste) that impact the environment.

The Study of Deviancy and the Environment

Throughout this text we have looked at social deviancy in terms of five different perspectives (normative, absolutist, statistical, reactivist, and relativist), and that will remain the case here. A number of human behaviors can have a negative impact on the environment, while others may have a positive impact on our attempt to help the environment thrive. The focus of the remainder of this chapter centers on specific human behaviors that impact the environment in general and specific ecosystems. It is worth noting here that nature itself, as demonstrated in table 12.1, can be the primary culprit in compromising the environment, but because we are concerned with social deviance, the focus will be on human behavior and its impact on the environment. In his coauthored (with Tim Madigan) *Beyond Sustainability: A Thriving Environment* book, Tim Delaney fully acknowledges the role of nature on the environment but explains that human behavior has accelerated the sixth ME process. As we shall see in the following pages, human impact on the environment is often as extreme as nature.

Human Behaviors That Have a Negative Impact on the Environment

To this point in the chapter, the idea that humans can have a negative impact on the environment has been described in generalities. We will now look at some specific examples of the negative impact humans have on the environment.

Human Dependency on Fossil Fuels

Certainly one of the most discussed human behaviors that has a negative impact on the environment is our dependency on fossil fuels. The major forms of fossil fuels are coal, oil, and natural gas. Fossil fuels were formed in the Carboniferous Period (approximately 360 to 286 million years ago and part of the Paleozoic Era)—a period named for carbon, the basic element in coal and natural gas—as the result of the decomposition of ancient living things such as animals and plant life that after millions of years turned into organic materials that formed fossil fuels (California Energy Commission 2012; U.S. Department of Energy 2013).

For the past century, humanity has been highly dependent upon the burning of fossil fuels for its energy needs. In fact, as described in box 12.1, humans would likely be "lost" and spiral into chaos without their current energy grid. According to the Institute for Energy Research (IER), a not-for-profit organization founded in 1989, the consumption of fossil fuels across the globe continues to increase; the 2014 consumption rate grew 0.9 percent (IER 2015). The U.S. Energy Information Administration (EIA) reports that the United States meets its energy needs from three primary sources: (1) fossil fuels, (2) nuclear power, and (3) renewable energy (EIA 2012). In 2011, approximately 83 percent of its total energy sources were fossil fuels (petroleum, 36 percent; natural gas, 26 percent; and coal, 20 percent); followed by renewable energy (9 percent) and nuclear electric power (8 percent). The primary sources of renewable energy are hydroelectric (35 percent of the total); wood (22 percent); biofuels (21 percent); wind (13 percent); waste (5 percent); geothermal (2 percent); and solar/PV (2 percent) (EIA 2012).

CONNECTING SOCIAL DEVIANCE AND POPULAR CULTURE

Box 12.1 What Happens When the "Grid" Goes Down?

The expression "grid" refers to the power grid that the vast majority of Americans are dependent on. According to the Trustworthy Cyber Infrastructure for the Power Grid's (TCIPG) Office for Mathematics, Science and Technology Education (MSTE), the *power grid* refers to the system of producers and consumers of electricity; it includes the sources of power or power generators (e.g., fossil fuels, nuclear, and renewable); the system of substations, power lines, and transformers that deliver electricity; and the consumers of that electricity (TCIPG 2015). A number of homes, schools, and businesses supplement the grid and lessen their dependence on power being transported to them by adding features such as solar panels. All such activities, however, are still connected to the grid.

One of the ultimate questions regarding our dependency on the power grid is, what happens if the grid goes down for an extended period of time, say for months or years? In other words, what happens to humanity if there is no electrical power source available to feed our humongous hunger for energy? We know how uncomfortable it is when the power goes out for a few hours because of a storm, and we have witnessed what happens when a community or region loses power for a few days, but an extensive power outage for a long period of time is quite different. A number of scenarios of prolonged power outages have been played out in a variety of popular culture venues, including television's *Revolution* (2012–2014), which powerfully demonstrated the downfall of humanity from the time the worldwide grid collapsed at its inception, highlighted by scenes of airplanes falling from the sky, cell phones that no longer worked, people trapped in emergency situations, and public reactions that were mostly expressed by shock or denial. The show quickly fast-forwarded to years later, and we saw a world that included collapsed societies and militias that had emerged to control geographic regions. Movies such as the 2008 *The Day the Earth Stood Still* depicted a helpless humanity that needed to be saved by the very alien

that turned the power off. And many books, including Ted Koppel's 2015 *Lights Out*, clearly point out that a cyberattack on America's power grid is not only possible but is likely to occur and present society with a devastating shot of reality—a type of "survival of the fittest" scenario. Even without a cyberattack, the grid risks going down via a meteor/asteroid or some other natural power. Furthermore, we should be concerned about such things as general maintenance (e.g., keeping aging power lines up-to-date). New York State, for example, is in a drastic need of power line upgrades, as some sections of power lines are nearly 80 years old and are barely able to meet the energy needs of the largest urban areas (Skerpon 2015). Thus, terrorists, forces of nature, and a near obsolete grid system all pose potential threats to the power grid.

The Internet, a major source for popular culture, is filled with sites that attempt to paint a scenario of what happens when the grid goes down. Here is a sampling of what would occur if the power grid goes down: our key infrastructure, including the Internet, would cease to operate; no electricity would mean no lights, no refrigeration, no heat or cooling; ATMs would not work, rendering credit and debit cards useless; people would need large sums of cash to buy what food and supplies were available to purchase before looting occurred; travel as we know it would cease to exist (this includes no mass transit and inoperable automobiles once existing gas supplies are exhausted); running water would become scarce, so people would need to live near freshwater supplies; food supplies would disappear quickly, especially in large urban areas; people who could hunt and fish would need to have access to such places to have food to eat; traditional cooking methods, such as on a stove, in an oven, or in a microwave, would no longer exist; people would need guns to protect themselves once humanity fell into complete chaos; people would go without heat in the winter months and without air-conditioning in the summer; hand tools would be invaluable; large urban areas would be the first to collapse and small rural communities would be the safest, at least for a while; and people would have to form tight-knit groups, similar to clan behavior, in an attempt to survive.

The above descriptions are just a mere sampling of what would happen if the power grid were to go down for an extended period of time so long as humanity remains dependent upon a grid fueled primarily by fossil fuels. We would have a *Mad Max* type of world without a power grid. Most people would not be able to handle a world without power, while a select few would thrive. People should heed the warning presented by many from the world of popular culture that a collapse in the power grid is akin to a collapse of human society as we know it.

A major aspect of our current power grid consists of the transportation of electricity via high-voltage pylons.

Although fossil fuels are finite, a great deal of them still remain to be extracted. Along with their relative abundance, fossil fuels are relatively cheap and yield a high net useful energy quotient. "Net useful energy is the total useful energy left from the resource after subtracting the amount of energy used and wasted in finding, processing, concentrating, and transporting it to users" (Harper 2012:111). Among the positive aspects of using fossil fuels is the realization that oil is easy to transport and can be used as fuel for a wide variety of devices (e.g., to propel vehicles, heat buildings and water, and supply high-temperature heat for industrial and electricity production); natural gas is cleaner-burning than oil or coal and there appears to be a huge amount of it in the United States and other parts of the world; and coal, while very "dirty" (in terms of mining, transporting, and burning it), is economically cheap and abundant supplies still exist.

The burning of fossil fuels comes at a great cost to the environment, however. It would be impossible, and outside of the scope of this text, to provide even a fraction of the evidence of harm caused by burning fossil fuels. Suffice it to say that among the costs are a compromised ozone layer, poorer air quality, glacier thawing, climate change, and the greenhouse effect. The *ozone layer* is the earth's upper atmosphere, which screens out a great deal of the sun's harmful ultraviolet rays. It extends about 10 to 30 miles above the earth. The ozone risks compromise when harmful chemicals and contaminants (e.g., emissions from burning fossil fuels) are released into the atmosphere. Scientists first became concerned with ozone in the mid-1970s because of human use of chlorofluorocarbons (CFCs). CFCs were widely used as aerosol propellants in consumer products such as hairsprays and deodorants, and as coolants in refrigerators and air conditioners. In 1978, the U.S. government banned CFCs as propellants in most aerosol uses. The U.S. Environmental Protection Agency (EPA) (2015a) reports that depleted ozone has led to more cases of skin cancer, cataracts, and many other health and environmental problems for humans (e.g., especially for people with asthma) and causes damage to crops, trees, and other vegetation. Humanity's continued reliance on burning fossil fuels compromises the ozone and the air we breathe on a regular basis. And while the ozone often finds a way to refurbish itself, the continued expansion of fossil fuel usage can cause lasting damage.

The effects of the compromised ozone layer are made evident in a number of ways, including the ice cap and glacier thawing in Greenland and the Arctic. The Arctic acts as the earth's refrigerator, cooling the planet. According to the National Oceanic and Atmospheric Administration (NOAA) (2015a), a deteriorating ozone layer interferes with this process and contributes to permafrost loss, changing Arctic wind patterns, glacier shrinkage, reduction in the total numbers of Arctic species, a "browning" tundra, and rising sea levels. The **greenhouse effect** refers to circumstances where the short wavelengths of visible light from the sun pass through the atmosphere, but the longer wavelengths of the infrared reradiation from the heated objects are unable to escape the earth's atmosphere. The trapped long-wavelength radiation (infrared light) leads to more heating and a higher resultant temperature, thus contributing to global warming. The infrared light is felt as heat similar to the heat lamps used by, for example, fast food restaurants that keep foods hot (NOAA 2004). The major greenhouse gases are carbon dioxide, CFCs, methane, and nitrous oxide—all of which contribute to climate change. The burning of fossil fuels was responsible for 79 percent of the U.S. greenhouse gas emission in 2010. These gases insulate the planet and can potentially cause catastrophic changes in the earth's climate (Environmental and Energy Study Institute 2015). Coal alone is responsible for 32 percent of the greenhouse gases, and natural gas is responsible for 27 percent (EESI 2015).

Despite the harm caused by fossil fuels (and we will revisit the negative effects of burning fossil fuels in later discussions with such topics as climate change and hydraulic fracturing), it is considered the norm among the public to consume them; thus, the relativist perspective on social deviance is applicable here. Correspondingly, people who promote a rapid departure from fossil fuel dependency are deemed as the deviants (the statistical perspective on social deviance). We can assume that for as long as large corporations profit from fossil fuels, the masses will be put into a situation where they are, more or less, dependent upon them. Environmentalists would prefer that large oil companies allocate a significant portion of their huge profits into the development of alternative energy sources, thus helping the environment to sustain itself or perhaps even thrive.

Climate Change

Related to the discussion of human dependency on the burning of fossil fuels is its effect on climate change. **Climate change** refers to a long-term change in the earth's climate, especially due to shifts in average atmospheric temperatures. Climate change includes both global warming and global cooling. In the 1970s, scientists were worried about potential global cooling; however, for the past few decades, scientists have become very concerned with global warming trends. The biggest concern with climate change is the realization that extreme forms of both global cooling and global warming have contributed to or caused previous mass extinctions. It is logical to reason that climate change may contribute to a future mass extinction, including the current sixth ME. Humans certainly had nothing to do with contributing to climate change millions of years ago, but it is just as certain that human behavior has an impact on the climate today. The only question with regard to humanity's impact on climate change is the degree of our impact.

Nearly all scientists around the world, including those from NASA, NOAA, and major universities, put forth the notion that human behavior has a significant impact on the climate, while a vocal minority protests such a notion. In his 2015 State of the Union Address, President Obama stated, "No challenge—no challenge—poses a greater threat to future generations than climate change" (The White House 2015). In August 2015, President Obama's sweeping new power plant regulations—power plants account for roughly one-third of all U.S. emissions of the heat-trapping gases blamed for global warming, making them the single largest source—spearheaded a divisive debate over climate change among mostly Republican politicians and big-business executives who question not only the legitimacy of human-caused climate change but also warn that such regulations are bad for the economy (Lederman 2015; Associated Press 2015o). Consider, for example, Cal Thomas, a conservative national columnist who had this to say about climate change: "In my opinion, belief in 'climate change' is on par with childhood faith in Santa Claus and the tooth fairy" (Thomas 2015:A-14).

In November 2015, Obama joined world leaders from nearly 200 countries gathered in Paris to discuss ways in which humans can help save the planet. Convened by the United Nations, the meeting (which is known by its shorthand name, COP21, for the 21st Conference of Parties to the United Nations Framework Convention on Change, or UNFCCC) continued the process that began at the Rio Earth Summit in Rio de Janeiro in 1992, culminating in the Kyoto Protocol in 1997 (Goodman 2015a). The COP21 meetings described climate change as a very real global threat and acknowledged the increasing scientific consensus that global warming is caused by human activity, especially since the time of the industrial age. Since the rise of industrialization, humans have continuously dumped pollutants into the sky as if the atmosphere can absorb an infinite amount of our smoke and exhaust (Goodman 2015a).

At the conclusion of the COP21 conference the nearly 200 nations adopted the first global pact to fight climate change, calling on the world to collectively cut and then eliminate greenhouse gas pollution but imposing no sanctions on countries that don't comply. The "Paris agreement" aims to keep global temperature from rising another 1.8 degrees Fahrenheit between now and 2100, a key demand of poor nations ravaged by rising sea levels and other effects of climate change. In order to reach this goal, nations that rely on burning fossil fuels for energy will have to nearly completely stop doing so (Associated Press 2015p:A-19).

We know that the earth's climate has changed throughout its long history, and in just the past 650,000 years there have been seven cycles of glacial advance and retreat, with the abrupt end of the last ice age about 7,000 years ago marking the beginning of the modern climate era (NASA 2015a). "Most of these changes are attributed to very small variations in the Earth's orbit that change the amount of solar energy our planet receives" (NASA 2015a). NASA reports, however, that the current warming trend is mostly caused by human activity and particularly because of our dependency on burning fossil fuels since industrialization. NASA (2015a) states that evidence for rapid climate change is compelling and includes the following examples:

- Sea level rise—Global sea level rose about 17 centimeters (6.7 inches) in the last century, with the rate in the last decade nearly double that of the last century.
- Global temperature rise—Most warming has occurred since 1880, with 10 of the warmest years occurring in the past 12 years.
- Warming oceans—The oceans are absorbing much of this increased heat, with the top 700 meters (about 2,300 feet) of ocean showing warming of 0.302 degrees Fahrenheit since 1969.
- Shrinking ice sheets—The Greenland and Antarctic ice sheets have decreased in mass.
- Declining Arctic sea ice—Both the extent and thickness of Arctic sea ice have declined rapidly over the last several decades.
- Glacial retreat—Glaciers are retreating almost everywhere around the world, including the Alps, Himalayas, Andes, Rockies, Alaska, and Africa.
- Extreme events—The number of record high temperature events in the United States has been increasing, while the number of low temperature events has been decreasing since 1950. The United States has also witnessed increasing numbers of intense rainfall events.
- Ocean acidification—Since the beginning of the Industrial Revolution, the acidity of surface ocean waters has increased by about 30 percent. The increased carbon dioxide into the atmosphere is being absorbed into the oceans. The upper layers of the oceans are absorbing about 2 billion tons of CO_2 per year.
- Decreased snow cover—Satellite observations reveal that the amount of spring snow cover in the Northern Hemisphere has decreased over the past five decades and that snow is melting earlier.

NOAA (2013) warns of extreme climate and weather events, long-term droughts, coastal infrastructure collapse, and increased risks to marine ecosystems as a result of climate change. Other examples of climate change come in the form of a *coral bleaching* (occurs when coral lose their color as they expel the symbiotic algae living in their tissues due to stress caused by changes in conditions such as temperature, light, or nutrients) crisis that has spread worldwide (Borenstein 2015) and bird species leaving specific wetlands (e.g., the boreal chickadee showing signs of extinction possibilities in the Adirondack wetlands) (Associated Press 2014b).

The prime human contribution to global warming is the output of carbon dioxide (CO_2), which is measured in terms of parts per million (ppm). The measurement of CO_2 is significant because carbon dioxide is the chief greenhouse gas that results from human activities. Scientists warn that the atmospheric CO_2 count needs to be at 350 ppm (maximum) in order to halt global warming and avoid catastrophic weather patterns that could spell the demise of human civilization (Delaney and Madigan 2014). The COP21 convention concluded that the planet's temperature has far exceeded this 350 ppm safety figure, and NASA (2015b) reported that at the time of this convention the CO_2 level was 401.58 ppm. NASA also reports that global temperature has risen 1.4 degrees Fahrenheit since 1880.

Methane (CH_4) is the second most prevalent greenhouse gas emitted in the United States from human activities (EPA 2015b) and is, therefore, another contributor to global warming. A hydrocarbon gas, produced both through natural sources and human activities, methane is a far more active greenhouse gas that CO_2, but also one that is much less abundant in the atmosphere (NASA 2015b). Methane can trap as much as 30 times the amount of heat per molecule (Lutter 2015). Methane is produced via the decomposition of wastes in landfills, agriculture, and especially rice cultivation, as well as ruminant digestion and manure management associated with domestic livestock (NASA 2015b). According to the EPA (2015b), over 60 percent of CH_4 emissions come from human activities. U.S. methane emissions by source include industry, natural gas, and petroleum systems (29 percent); enteric fermentation (fermentation of feed as part of the normal digestive processes of livestock) (26 percent); landfills (waste from homes and businesses) (18 percent); coal mining (19 percent); manure management (10 percent); and other sources (8 percent) (EPA 2015b).

Other human activities that contribute to climate change include nitrous oxide, a powerful greenhouse gas produced by soil cultivation practices, especially the use of commercial and organic fertilizers, fossil fuel combustion, nitric acid production, and biomass burning; and CFCs (previously discussed), synthetic compounds entirely of industrial origin used in a number of applications (NASA 2015b).

The consequences of climate change are immense and include changes in precipitation patterns, more droughts and heat waves, hurricanes that will become stronger and more intense, increased sea level rise (perhaps as much as 1 to 4 feet by 2100), and a possible ice-free Arctic. Climate change threatens public health in a variety of ways, including the growth and spread of pathogenic organisms; the spread of intestinal diseases such as dysentery, cholera, and typhoid fever; and increased numbers of people suffering from asthma, emphysema, and chronic obstructive pulmonary disease (COPD). Massive disruptions in the climate will also trigger greater migration, conflict, and hunger around the globe, leading to deviant global unrest and violence.

Hydraulic Fracturing

Hydraulic fracturing, commonly known as hydrofracking, or simply fracking, involves a controversial method of drilling for natural gas. Although natural gas is a fossil fuel, it represents a cleaner energy source than crude oil or coal. As a result, natural gas is in high demand (Delaney and Madigan 2014). The EPA (2015c) acknowledges that natural gas plays a key role in our nation's "clean energy" future. The EPA also points out that the key to natural gas serving as viable clean energy is a matter of responsible extraction processes. And therein lies the controversy of fracking. The extraction process involves a well stimulation (drilling) process that creates fractures within a reservoir that contains oil or natural gas and allows for maximum extraction. A hydraulic fracture is formed when a fracking fluid is pumped down the well at pressures that exceed the rock strength, causing open fractures to form in the rock. Once a rock formation has been breached, the natural gas is released and, ideally, caught within the well system. The fracking fluid consists of a mixture of water, sand, and hundreds of chemicals (many of which are not identified by extraction companies). If a sufficient amount of sand grains are trapped in the fractures, the fractures will remain propped open after the pressure of the fracking fluid is reduced. This process increases the permeability of the shale, which allows much greater flow of gas back up the well bore (Nersesian 2010).

Among the known risks of fracking are:

- Stress on surface water and ground water supplies from the withdrawal of large volumes of water used in drilling and hydraulic fracturing;
- Contamination of underground sources of drinking water and surface waters resulting from spills, faulty well construction, or by other means;
- Adverse impacts from discharges into surface waters or from disposal into underground injection wells; and
- Air pollution resulting from the release of volatile organic compounds, hazardous air pollutants, and greenhouse gases (EPA 2015c).

There is concern with undersurface disturbances (earthquakes) and fracking. The U.S. Geological Survey's (USGS) analysis of earthquake data indicates that there has been a dramatic increase in the number of undersurface disturbances in areas where fracking is common. "Within the central and eastern United States, the number of earthquakes has increased dramatically over the past few years. Between the years 1973–2008, there was an average of 21 earthquakes of magnitude three and larger in the central and eastern United States. This rate jumped to an average of 99 M3+ earthquakes per year in 2000–2013, and the rate continues to rise. In 2014, alone, there were 659 M3 and larger earthquakes" (USGS 2015). Previous USGS studies have shown a strong connection in many locations between the deep injection of fluids and increased earthquake rates.

There are undeniable examples of surface land disturbances as a result of high-volume hydraulic fracturing, beginning with the construction of gravel access roads, well pads, and utility corridors to the clearing and leveling of an area of adequate size in preparation of the surface to support the movement of heavy equipment and the establishing of erosion and sediment control structures and constructing pits that (in theory) are used for the retention and maintenance of fracking fluid wastes. In addition, the land disturbances caused by drilling wells and support activities have a negative aesthetic impact on the site.

While natural gas does not create CO_2 emissions like coal and oil do, it does produce methane pollution. During fracking procedures it is highly possible for methane leakage to occur at wells and along aging pipelines and at other points in the fracking process (e.g., the transportation of natural gas). In a study conducted by two groups of scientists at Cornell University, it was reported that methane leakage causes a worse greenhouse gas footprint than that of coal. The scientists estimate that as much as 8 percent of methane from shale gas production escapes into the atmosphere, where it is a far more potent greenhouse gas than carbon dioxide (Esch 2012). In recent years methane leaks at gas drilling sites have led to mass community evacuations following complaints from citizens that have experienced such ailments as nausea, dizziness, headaches, and nosebleeds. A leak at Southern California Gas Company's Aliso Canyon storage facility near the San Fernando Valley community of Porter Ranch in the Santa Susana Mountains that began on October 23, 2015, emitted methane at a rate of about 50,000 kilograms per hour, accounting for about one-quarter of all methane emission in California (Sewell 2015). Months later, and following the evacuation of Porter Ranch residents, the leak still had not been contained; furthermore, the gas company was sure of the exact location of the leak. By the end of December 2015, it was estimated that between 70,000 and 110,000 pounds of methane gas per hour were being released from the 8,700-foot-deep well (Barragan 2015). The leak was finally contained 4 months after it was first detected. Nearly 100,000 tons of methane were released into the atmosphere in all. The leaked methane was visible from space (Walton 2016).

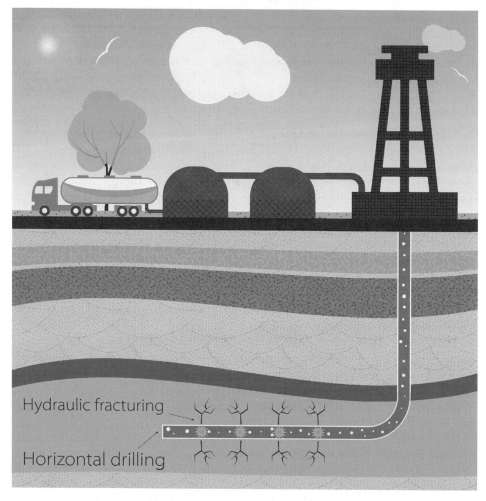

An illustration of the hydraulic fracturing extraction process.

Plastics

Depending upon one's perspective, the use of plastics is either deviant or not. Nearly all people use some plastic product every day, thus making it the norm to do so. On the other hand, plastic products take centuries to decompose and are a leading cause of waste, thus representing a significant threat to the environment and another contributor to the sixth mass extinction.

Plastics come under a very broad category of materials known as polymers. Polymers are substances made up of a large number of smaller molecules that link together to form larger molecules, which, in the case of plastics, are primarily made of carbon (Knight 2014). The word *plastic* originally meant "pliable and easily shaped," and such characteristics make this polymer valuable for a wide variety of industries. For the past century and a half, humans have used synthetic polymers, sometimes using natural substances like cellulose, but more often using carbon atoms provided by petroleum and other fossil fuels. The first synthetic polymer was invented in 1869 by John Wesley Hyatt, who created the product as a substitute for ivory (Chemical Heritage Foundation 2015). In 1907, Leo Baekeland invented Bakelite, the first fully synthetic plastic, meaning it contained no molecules found in nature. World War II necessitated a great expansion of the plastics industry in the United States, as there was a concerted effort to preserve scarce natural resources. Among the synthetic products produced during this era was nylon, a synthetic silk used for parachutes, ropes, body armor, helmet liners, and more. Plexiglas, another synthetic product, provided an alternative to glass for aircraft windows. During World War II plastic production increased 300 percent. The use of plastics continued to expand following World War II with "unblemished optimism" (Chemical Heritage Foundation 2015).

By the 1960s, plastic debris was noticeable on land and sea. The pro-Earth environmental movement of the 1960s and 1970s began to question the continued and expanded use of plastics as an endless stream of new commercial products. In the 1980s, the plastics industry led an influential drive to encourage municipalities to collect and process recyclable materials as part of their waste-management systems (Chemical Heritage Foundation 2015). While it is commendable that many people recycle plastics and other products still today, we are not doing a very good job of it. The EPA (2014) reports that Americans recycled and composted 1.51 pounds of individual waste per day in 2012; however, individuals generate 4.38 pounds of waste per day. When controlling for plastics, Americans only recovered 8.8 percent of the 31.75 million tons of weight generated from plastics (EPA 2014).

One of the oddest plastic products that Americans purchase is bottled water. In a nation where most people (especially those outside the Southwest region) enjoy easy access to an abundance of fresh, clean water via water fountains inside nearly all public and private buildings, many people insist on buying bottled water. In 2009, Americans consumed over 1,500 plastic water bottles per second (Scholtus 2009). That number has only increased as the reported sales of bottled water tripled from 2003 to 2013 (Natural Resources Defense Council 2013). The vast majority of single-use plastic water bottles are made out of polyethylene terephthalate, better known as PET plastic (Gleick 2009). PET is a thermoplastic polymer resin. It takes a great deal of oil and energy to produce and transport plastic bottles for consumer consumption. The production, distribution, and sale of bottled water has alarmingly been privatized to the point that major corporations such as Nestlé, Coca-Cola, and Pepsi control the vast majority of water supplies.

Perhaps the most critical issue related to the deviancy of bottled water specifically, and plastics in general, is decomposition. It takes about 450 years for non-biodegradable plastic bottles to decompose. Some other facts about plastics and decomposition include:

- Nearly every piece of plastic ever made still exists today.
- A plastic cup can take 50 to 80 years to decompose.
- Plastic garbage in the ocean kills as many as 1 million sea creatures every year.

- The global fishing industry dumps an estimated 150,000 tons of plastic into the ocean each year, including packaging, plastic nets, lines, and buoys (Institute for Sustainable Communication 2012).

The great amounts of plastic waste created by humans is just the beginning of how much waste we generate. Among other types of waste created by humans are marine debris, food waste, electronic waste (e-waste), nuclear waste, and medical waste. Each of these topics will be discussed in the following pages.

Marine Debris

Marine debris includes any form of manufactured or processed material discarded, disposed of, or abandoned in the marine environment (Scientific and Technical Advisory Panel 2011). Marine debris can be found from the poles to the equator and from shorelines, estuaries, and the sea surface to the depths of the ocean, making this a global issue. NOAA (2015b) describes marine debris as a global problem because it affects everything from the environment to the economy; from fishing and navigation to human health and safety; from the smallest coral polyps to giant blue whales. Marine debris comes in many forms and sizes, from a cigarette butt tossed on the beach to a 4,000-pound tangle of derelict fishing nets caught on a coral reef (NOAA 2015b). Marine debris has many detrimental impacts on ecosystems, including habitat degradation, entanglement, ingestion, and transportation of nonnative species.

Plastics are among the items that contribute to marine debris. Plastic marine debris includes various domestic and industrial products such as bags, cups, bottles, balloons, strapping bands, plastic sheeting, hard hats and resin pellets, and discarded fishing gear. A great deal of marine debris also includes harmful chemicals that cause a loss of biodiversity, increase acidification, and contribute to the rise in the sea level (Scientific and Technical Advisory Panel 2011).

Perhaps the best example of the seriousness posed by marine debris is the "Great Pacific Garbage Patch," or the "Garbage Island" for short. The Garbage Island is like a floating landfill of trash and marine debris found in the Pacific Ocean north of Hawaii and is larger than the size of Texas. The Great Pacific Garbage Patch is a loose collection of islands in close proximity that sometimes links together into large pieces and other times floats apart into smaller islands, many of which are larger than the Hawaiian Islands. The debris is continuously mixed by wind and wave action and widely dispersed both over huge surface areas and throughout the top portion of the water column. At some points in time it is actually possible to sail through the garbage patch (NOAA 2015c).

A characteristic of the Great Pacific Garbage Patch or Eastern Garbage Patch is a loose collection of islands of rubbish.

The floating islands of trash are harmful to the environment in general but also to a great number of specific sea creatures, such as sea turtles, seabirds, and seals, and marine vegetation life such as coral reefs (Howell, Bograd, Morishige, Seki, and Polovina 2012). Because most of the trash in the garbage island is not biodegradable (a great deal of the garbage is plastics), these islands are destined to float long into the foreseeable future. This implies that this part of the Pacific Ocean will be compromised for hundreds of years as well.

Food Waste

People in technologically advanced societies tend to waste a great deal of food, and this is coupled with their knowledge that over a billion people around the world are malnourished or face starvation. Roughly one-third of the food produced in the world for human consumption every year—approximately 1.3 billion tons—gets lost or wasted (Blomberg 2011). Food waste includes uneaten portions of meals; trimmings from food preparation in kitchens, restaurants, fast food chains, and cafeterias; and food thrown away by grocery stores because it is deemed unsellable. Food waste is the second largest component of generated waste by weight and the largest component of discarded waste by weight (Miller 2009). (Paper waste represents the largest material category of waste that Americans generate.)

According to Food and Drink Europe (2015), an organization that represents the European food and drink industry, there are many possible causes of food loss and food waste. Food loss may occur during agricultural production and harvest because of such factors as premature harvesting; excess production; noncompliance with regulations, standards, and food safety (e.g., size specification); climate and environmental factors leading to spoilage or unsafe food; poor storage; lack of adequate infrastructure; lack of processing facilities (in developing and low-income countries); lack of cold chain (the series of storage and distribution of food); and pests, diseases, and spoilage. Food loss may occur during processing because of rejected primary resources that do not comply with standards (e.g., bacterial levels too high for human consumption); rejected products; spoilage or contamination; food sent back to the manufacturer (or not sold because of durability demands) close to the best-before sold date; process interruptions; and packaging errors. Food waste may occur at three distinct locations. First, food waste may occur at distribution and retail sources because of inaccurate order forecasting and management of stocks; deterioration of products and packaging; and noncompliance with regulations, standards, and food safety (e.g., lack of adequate temperature control due to power outage). Food waste may occur at restaurants and bars because of consumer preferences for some food items offered but not for others; errors in food storage; poor food stock management; hygiene and food safety measures (e.g., food that falls on the floor cannot be sold); and the "just in time" principle whereby meals must be delivered on demand without prior knowledge of how many consumers can be expected or their purchasing decisions. Food waste may occur during domestic consumption because of excess portions prepared; excess purchases; difficulty correctly interpreting date labels; food not used in time; errors in food storage; poor food management; difficulty removing all the product from the packaging; and errors in food preparation.

When considering food waste as a form of deviant behavior, it becomes necessary to examine the many possible causes of food losses and food waste described above. Nonetheless, in a world filled with starving and malnourished people it is important for all those involved in food production, distribution, sale, and consumption to be diligent and avoid being wasteful.

E-Waste

Since industrialization, humans have increasingly found ways to produce devices and materials that make life easier. Among the items that humans have found useful are a slew of electronic devices. Electronic devices are used for multiple purposes, including communications and entertainment, and in nearly every industry. Unfortunately, just as easily as new electronic devices are produced, they are thrown away by consumers to be replaced by new and improved versions. This results in a great deal of electronic waste. **E-waste** is a popular, informal name for electronic products that have been deemed obsolete because they are outdated and are discarded. E-waste represents more than just solid waste materials; it is an environmental hazard because of its toxins. E-waste consists of any combination of toxins including lead, mercury, nickel, cadmium, arsenic, beryllium, and brominated flame retardants. The toxic materials found in electronics can cause cancer, reproductive disorders, endocrine disruption, and many other health problems (Mulvaney and Robbins 2011; Causes International 2014). Causes International (2014) provides us with a sampling of the potential health problems that face humans because of e-waste:

- Lead is toxic to the kidneys, accumulating in the body and eventually affecting the nervous and reproductive systems. Children's mental development can be impaired by low-level exposure to lead.
- When burned, PVC produces dioxins, some of the most hazardous carcinogens known.
- Brominated flame retardants have been linked to fetal damage and thyroid problems.
- Barium produces brain swelling after a short exposure. It may cause weakness in muscles as well as heart, liver, and spleen damage.
- Hexavalent chromium damages kidneys, the liver, and DNA. Asthmatic bronchitis has been linked to this substance.
- Mercury is known to harm developing fetuses and is passed through mothers' milk to newborns. In adults, it can cause brain and kidney damage.
- Beryllium causes acute or chronic beryllium disease, a deadly ailment affecting the lungs.
- Cadmium is a carcinogen, and long-term exposure leads to kidney and bone damage.

Virtually all electronics contain toxic materials that can be harmful to people and the planet. Improperly disposing of electronic devices contributes to damage to the environment. Under the Toxic Substances Control Act (TSCA) and the Pollution Prevention Act, the EPA evaluates potential risks from new and existing chemicals and finds ways to prevent or reduce pollution before it gets into the environment. The proper disposal and recycling of electronics helps to minimize the damage caused by e-waste. There is ample reason to be concerned about e-waste as, despite legislation, less than a third of electronics are properly discarded. Consider, for example, that over 2.4 million tons of electronics (e.g., computers, monitors, hard copy devices, keyboards and mice, televisions, and mobile devices) were disposed of in 2010 but just 27 percent were properly recycled (Electronics TakeBack Coalition

2014). While e-waste comprises just 2 percent of America's trash in landfills, it accounts for 70 percent of the overall toxic waste (Causes International 2014).

Nuclear Waste

The previously discussed concern over our reliance on burning fossil fuels could be alleviated if we used nuclear energy or alternative energies (to be discussed later in this chapter). Nuclear energy has one big advantage over the burning of fossil fuels; that is, it does not release carbon dioxide into the atmosphere. Nuclear-fueled power plants, like plants that burn coal, oil, and natural gas, produce electricity by boiling water into steam. This water is turned into steam, which in turn drives turbine generators to produce electricity. The difference is the source of heat—fission, which is created when uranium atoms split. The uranium fuel consists of small, hard ceramic pellets that are packaged into long, vertical tubes. Bundles of this fuel are inserted into the reactor (Nuclear Energy Institute 2015; Duke Energy 2015). Commercial nuclear power plants in the United States are either boiling water reactors (BWRs) or pressurized water reactors (PWRs). In BWRs, the water heated by fission actually boils and turns into steam to turn the turbine generator, while PWRs keep water under pressure so that it heats but does not boil—this heated water is circulated through tubes in steam generators, which then turns the turbine generator.

Nuclear waste is the material that nuclear fuel becomes after it is used in a reactor; this spent fuel material contains radioactive and extremely toxic by-products. Nuclear wastes may remain radioactive for thousands of years, and therein lies one of the primary concerns with nuclear waste—how can we properly dispose of nuclear waste? Should we bury it (in thick concrete or metal containers) deep underground and risk a leak that can reach the topsoil? Or do we bury it at sea and risk a leak that causes damage to marine ecosystems? And do we have containers that will last long enough to store nuclear waste? The answer is, no one really knows for sure how to handle the waste problem. So while nuclear energy does not produce the dangerous CO_2 toxin or any other greenhouse gas emission, it does produce radioactive waste—something that fossil fuels do not.

From an environmental standpoint radioactive waste may be the biggest issue with nuclear energy, as meltdowns and major nuclear accidents, although rare, do occur. The Hanford nuclear power plant in Washington, a facility that was a part of the government's top secret "Manhattan Project," had six underground radioactive waste tanks leaking in 2013. The tanks, which were already long past their intended 20-year life span, hold millions of gallons of a highly radioactive stew left from decades of plutonium production for nuclear weapons (Associated Press 2013). (Note: The threat of nuclear weapons in the "wrong hands" is another major concern with nuclear energy but beyond the scope of this discussion.) Major nuclear meltdowns gain so much notoriety that, like hurricane, earthquakes, and major snowstorms, their names become synonymous with devastating nightmares. For example, most people recognize the names "Three Mile Island" (a U.S. nuclear plant in Pennsylvania that allowed radioactive gases to escape) and "Chernobyl" (a nuclear power plant in the former Ukrainian Soviet Socialist Republic, now the Ukraine, which experienced a complete meltdown). The crippled Fukushima Daiichi nuclear power plant in Japan, which was breached due to a tsunami in 2011, left radioactive contaminated debris that made its way to the American western coastline, killing marine life caught in its path. In August 2012, Connecticut's Unit 2 of Millstone

Power Station nuclear power plant had to be shut down because the seawater used to cool it was too warm—the warm ocean water blamed on climate change.

It is noteworthy to mention that the planning, building, and maintaining of nuclear power plants is very expensive and is therefore deemed by the government and private companies as a poor economic investment. In comparison, a state-of-the-art, coal-fired plant is a much less costly way to generate electricity (Harper 2012). As the price of gas dropped in 2014 and 2015, nuclear power plants were deemed non-cost-effective. The FitzPatrick nuclear power plant, for example, located in Scriba, New York (very close to my university), was deemed cost inefficient in 2015 by its owner, Entergy Corporation (The plant is scheduled to be shut down by early 2017—although as of this writing [late 2015] New York State officials were trying to find a way to keep it open because the four upstate New York nuclear power reactors are responsible for $3 billion in economic activity and nearly 25,000 jobs [Knauss 2015a].) Among the concerns of the closing of the FitzPatrick plant was the spent fuel stored in dry cask containers (carbon steel casing with 26-inch-thick concrete, each 20 feet in height and weighing 180 tons) and the realization that the plant would have to sit dormant for 50 years before the Entergy Corporation would begin to tear down and clean up the site (Knauss 2015b).

Medical Waste

Medical waste pales in comparison to most forms of waste caused by humans, but it is a growing concern as having a negative impact on human health and the environment in general. **Medical waste,** or health care waste, includes waste generated by health institutions, research institutions, and laboratories, as well as waste originating from health care done at home (e.g., dialysis, insulin injections, and blood sugar test strips) (Brasovean et al. 2010). Most medical waste (between 75 percent and 90 percent) can be treated as household waste and transported to the landfill, but the remainder should be considered hazardous to health and places the environment at risk (Brasovean et al. 2010).

Among the waste items generated by health care activities are used needles and syringes, soiled dressings, body parts, diagnostic samples, blood, chemicals, pharmaceuticals, medical devices, and radioactive materials (World Health Organization 2015g). WHO (2015g) warns that "Poor management of health care waste potentially exposes health care workers, waste handlers, patients and the community at large to infection, toxic effects and injuries, and risks polluting the environment. It is essential that all medical waste materials are segregated at the point of generation, appropriately treated and disposed of safely."

After medical wastes were found among other wastes washing up on several East Coast beaches in the 1980s, concern over the potential health hazards prompted Congress to enact the Medical Waste Tracking Act (MWTA) in 1988. The act empowered the EPA to define medical waste and to identify wastes to be regulated; establish a "cradle to grave" tracking system utilizing a generator-initiated tracking form; establish management standards for segregation, packaging, labeling and marking, and storage of medical waste; and establish record-keeping requirements and penalties that could be imposed for mismanagement (EPA 2015d). The regulations promulgated under the MWTA expired in 1999, but the EPA continues to monitor medical waste. Much medical waste is incinerated, and alternatives to incineration include thermal treatment, such as microwave technologies; steam sterilization, such as autoclaving; electropyrolysis; and chemical mechanical systems, among others (EPA 2015d).

Harmful Agricultural Practices

As the world's population continues to explode, the need comes to produce enough food to feed everyone. To meet the growing demand, crop and livestock farms have expanded (and will continue to expand), and scientists have incorporated genetic manipulations in an effort to increase food yield. Finding the balance between feeding billions of people while preserving the environment's natural resources has become increasingly problematic. On the plus side, modern agricultural systems are very technologically advanced both in terms of the tools and techniques used to cultivate crops and in terms of genetic technology that helps to modify the maximum possible yield. Genetically modified organisms (GMOs) have been introduced to assist in the growth of food supplies. However, environmentalists and many citizens are concerned about the precise genetic makeup of the altered food being grown and served to consumers. They see such techniques as GMOs as an example of harmful agricultural practices. Harmful agricultural practices refer to the many unsustainable techniques and practices utilized by humans in relation to food production, distribution, and consumption.

When there were fewer people on the planet, it was more common for family farms to grow food for themselves and local communities. Family farms have all but disappeared and have been replaced by industrial farms (or factory farms) and animal feeding operations (AFOs). Industrial farms operate over a large land area and often specialize in planting a specific crop, creating a monoculture farming environment. Monoculture farming poses many problems, including decreasing the diversity of the land considerably and eliminating natural biological controls that would maintain levels of pests and diseases (Mission 2014: Feeding the World 2014). The monoculture of farming is highlighted by the realization that there are over 50,000 varieties of edible plants, and yet only 15 varieties provide 90 percent of the world's food energy intake; just three of these plants (rice, wheat, and corn) are the staple foods for nearly two-thirds of the world's population. A quarter of the neglected edible plants risk extinction by 2025 (Mission 2014: Feeding the World 2014). The failure to rotate crops (in favor of monoculture farming) also interferes with nature's way of sustaining topsoil. Instead, monoculture farming becomes dependent upon the mass use of pesticides, herbicides, and insecticides, resulting in more chemicals seeping into food supplies. As is the case with nature, many insects have evolved to the point where they have become resistant to chemicals, leading scientists to develop even stronger chemical pesticides to keep up with the rapidly evolving pests (Mission 2014: Feeding the World 2014). The use of synthetic chemical pesticides and fertilizers also pollutes the soil, water supplies (due to runoff), and air, harming both the environment and human health (Organic Consumers Association 2002). The amount of water consumed by factory farms often exceeds sustainable rates too, as large-scale farms also require extensive irrigation systems that pump out water at incredibly fast rates. Water used for irrigation is being extracted from reservoirs faster than it is being regenerated.

Animal feeding operations are farms or feedlots where animals are kept and raised in confined areas for at least 45 days over a 12-month period. AFOs pose many of the same types of problems as factory farms but also cause such problems and concerns as manure and urine waste disposal, contaminated wastewater, and dead animal disposal; they involve an environment wherein feed is brought to the animals rather than the animals grazing in pastures (a much more natural way of raising farm animals) (EPA 2015f). The EPA (2015f) estimates that there are 450,000 AFOs in the United States. The most common types of AFOs include dairies, cattle feedlots, and poultry farms. Animal waste and waste management are among the chief concerns of AFOs as the waste produced per day by one dairy cow is equal to that of 20 to 40 people. On the plus side, manure can be used in digesters (machines that decompose manure to capture the methane gas emitted) to produce electricity and other useful by-products such as ethanol. However, if not managed properly, the waste produced by AFOs can pollute the environment—especially water supplies (e.g., lakes and streams) (EPA 2015f). The microorganisms found in animal wastes, such as cryptosporidium, can pose significant public health threats. A severe rainstorm can cause an overflow of wastewater at AFOs that seeps into drinking supplies of nearby communities. The air quality near AFOs can be compromised as well due to the decomposition of animal wastes and the dust generated by animal activity and farming practices. These air pollutants can cause respiratory illness and lung inflammation and increase vulnerability to respiratory diseases, such as asthma (EPA 2015f).

Western societies and an increasing number of non-Western societies have incorporated meat into their daily diets. Environmentalists, vegetarians, and vegans point to the "law of thermodynamics," which reveals that it takes more energy to eat higher up on the food chain than it does at the lower end (Puskar-Pasewicz 2010). This concept can be applied in two different scenarios. First, a simpler creature such as a grasshopper expends less energy to eat grass than a bird expends to eat a grasshopper, and it takes even more energy for a predator to eat a bird (Puskar-Pasewicz 2010). Secondly, it takes less energy, or fewer resources (e.g., fuel, land, and water) to produce lower levels of food, such as grains, than it does to produce meat from livestock (Bittman 2009). A diet that consists of meat involves the use of a great deal of energy both in terms of production and in terms of distribution. Additionally, livestock (in non-AFOs) do much more than simply graze; they overgraze. Overgrazing causes 34 percent of the world's soil degradation, putting it ahead of deforestation, cropland agriculture, overexploration, and industrialism (Withgott and Brennan 2007).

Deforestation

A different type of waste caused by human activity involves deforestation. **Deforestation** refers to the clearing, or permanent removal, of the earth's forests on a massive scale. According to the Rainforest Concern (2008) organization, "Tropical rainforests took between 60 and 100 million years to evolve and are believed to be the oldest and most complex land-based ecosystem on earth, containing over 30 million species of plants and animals. That's half of the Earth's wildlife and at least two-thirds of its plant species." The importance of the Amazon rain forest, in particular, is powerfully expressed by its description as the "lungs of the planet."

Deforestation is a serious problem around the world but especially in tropical areas. Countries with significant deforestation include Thailand, Brazil, the Congo, and Indonesia, as well as parts of eastern Europe (Smith 2012b). There are many causes of deforestation, including the following:

- The trees are used as fuel (about half of all trees illegally removed from forests are used for fuel).
- To make more land available for housing and urbanization

- To create ingredients that are highly prized consumer items, such as the oil from palm trees
- To create room for cattle ranching (Bradford 2015) and agriculture (Pachamama Alliance 2015)

While forests still cover about 30 percent of the world's land area, an estimated 18 million acres (7.3 million hectares) of forest, which is roughly the size of the country of Panama, are destroyed each year (Bradford 2015). At this rate of deforestation the rain forests would completely vanish within 100 years; however, before that would happen humans would die off because the lack of oxygen and increased CO_2 counts would lead to our premature extinction. With this in mind, let's identify some of the negative effects of deforestation:

- Seventy percent of the earth's land animals and plants reside in forests; thus, the destruction of rain forests would lead to the loss of habitat and the demise of countless other species in addition to the human species (Pachamama Alliance 2015; Bradford 2015).
- Trees are natural consumers of carbon dioxide—one of the prime causes of greenhouse gases that contribute to global warming. The destruction of trees not only removes these "carbon sinks," but tree burning and decomposition pump even more CO_2, along with methane, into the atmosphere (*National Geographic* 2015).
- Trees are important to the water cycle. They absorb rainfall and produce water vapor that is released into the atmosphere (Bradford 2015). Trees, then, provide clean water, but they also help with flood control (EPA 2015e).
- Tree roots anchor the soil; thus, they help to control soil erosion and coastal flooding (Pachamama Alliance 2015; Bradford 2015; EPA 2015e).
- The rain forest provides a home for indigenous people (Rainforest Concern 2008; Pachamama Alliance 2015). The loss of rain forest homelands contributes to migration to large cities (Smith 2012b).
- The rain forest is a type of pharmacy, as more than 25 percent of our modern medicines originate from tropical forest plants. And this is just the beginning, as researchers are looking into the possibility that rain forest plant life might provide medical benefits in an infinite number of ways (Rainforest Concern 2008; EPA 2015e).

In short, tropical forests are a critical element in the survival of the earth's diverse ecosystems, as globally, they store huge quantities of carbon and regulate the climate, and locally, they provide a home for many species, clean water, flood control, food, fuel, and medicine for adjacent populations (EPA 2015e). However, just as with the case of harmful agricultural practices and with the many forms of waste described in this chapter, the ever-expanding human population necessitates continually taking from the environment more than we give back. Eventually, we will reach the brink of the earth's carrying capacity, and all the combined deviant activities of humans will greatly contribute to the sixth mass extinction.

Overpopulation

A critical element in calculating the earth's carrying capacity is population. (See the earlier review of the IPAT formula.) Many social thinkers, especially since the time of industrialization, have put forth the notion that there are too many people in the world. Add to this notion the reality that every environmental problem discussed in this chapter is the result of human activity and the fact that all these problems will only get worse as the number of people increases, and it is easy to understand why some social thinkers believe that overpopulation is the biggest threat to the environment.

At the end of 2015 there were over 322 million Americans and nearly 7.4 billion people worldwide (U.S. Census 2015; WorldOMeters 2015). The WorldOMeters website provides running totals (counters) of the number of people in the world and a slew of other interesting demographic data, including "population growth today," which tracks the number of births, deaths, and net population growth for each day and "population growth this year." It is fascinating to watch before our eyes the number of people around the world rapidly increasing. The net population growth on any given day is approximately 200,000. As the year 2015 drew near an end, there was a net population growth of roughly 80 million people (WorldOMeters 2015). As an interesting note, the WorldOMeters tracks such things as the hectares of forest lost each year (in 2015 the figure was roughly 5 million) and the tons of CO_2 emissions each year (over 35 billion). Disturbingly, the site also runs totals on the number of undernourished people in the world (nearly 800 million); overweight people in the world (roughly 1.7 billion); number of obese people in the world (over 540 million); and the number of people who died of hunger today (nearly 30,000).

The data cited above helps to illustrate the concerns of social thinkers who worry about overpopulation. Thomas Malthus, for example, in his *An Essay on the Principles of Population* (1798), claimed that the world's population was growing too quickly in proportion to the amount of food available. His theory suggested that the world's population grew geometrically while the ability to produce food grew arithmetically. His theory is not correct, but his concerns are not without merit. Consider that at the dawn of agriculture (circa 8000 BCE), the world's population was approximately 5 million. Over the 8,000-year period up to 1 CE, the population grew to approximately 200 million, although some estimates are higher. One thousand years later and the total world population is estimated at 275 million and by 1750, a date just prior to the beginning of industrialization, there were approximately 750 million people (Delaney and Madigan 2014). Thomas Malthus, who lived from 1766 to 1834, was alive when the world's population reached its first 1 billion mark (1804). Since the time of industrialization, the world's population has not grown geometrically, but it certainly has sped its pace. While it took all of human history to reach 1 billion in 1804, the 2nd billion was reached in just 123 years (1927); the 3rd billion in less than 30 years; the 4th billion in 15 years; the 5th billion in only 13 years. It is estimated that we will reach 8 billion by 2025 and 9 billion by 2045. So it is clear that the number of people in the world has increased tremendously since industrialization. And while there is enough food for roughly 1.7 billion people to be overweight, there are over 1 billion people facing malnourishment and hunger.

Sociologist Herbert Spencer, in an attempt to update Thomas Malthus's theorem of overpopulation, was inspired to create the term "survival of the fittest" to explain the struggle societies face when attempting to secure enough natural resources to continue to evolve and avoid dissolution. Spencer first used the concept of survival of the fittest in his *Principles of Biology* (1864). Spencer attempted to update Malthus's population theory, which also included the idea that nature would keep the population "in check" via the "Four Horsemen"—war, famine, pestilence, and disease (a concept described in Revelation, the last book in the Bible). As a social theorist myself, I was influenced by Spencer's and Malthus's notions but realized that the Four Horsemen are not forces of nature but rather, forces created mostly by humanity. My updated version of the Four Horsemen comes in the form of the Five Horrorists—a concept first introduced in *Contemporary Social Theory: Investigation and Application* (2005). It has been my contention that the Five Horrorists represent the greatest threat to humanity, and if left unchecked, will spell the doom of human existence as we know it. See box 12.2 for a brief synopsis of the "Five Horrorists" concept.

A CLOSER LOOK

Box 12.2 The Five Horrorists: Destroyers of Humanity and the Environment

The "Five Horrorists" represent an advanced evolutionary interpretation and development of the Four Horsemen concept. Breaking completely from the religious roots and deemphasizing the natural component of the Four Horsemen, the Five Horrorists emphasize social forces that will lead to the destruction of humanity and ultimately the physical environment, if left unchecked by global powers. The original four concepts of war, famine, pestilence, and disease are maintained, but a fifth and more deadly concept of the **enviromare** is added. (Note: The descriptions below are a mere summary of the full description of the Five Horrorists.)

War—One of the most devastating forces facing humanity and the environment is war, so it is listed as the first horrorist. As sociologist C. Wright Mills (1958) states, "To reflect upon war is to reflect upon the human condition" (p. 1). And what does it say about humanity that war is so common? War results in the loss of life for countless humans but also contributes to a number of negative impacts on the environment. When humans go to war, they defoliate jungles; burn oil wells; use uranium-enriched weapons; cause general degradation to local ecosystems; ruin water supplies with bombs, chemicals, and decaying bodies; devastate biodiversity of local ecosystems; destroy wetland ecosystems; cause deforestation; and so on. The potential threat for all-out nuclear or hydrogen world war should be enough to scare any rational human being.

Famine—From the Latin *fames*, meaning "hunger," this second horrorist is the result of both natural and social forces. The word "famine" is used to describe conditions in which a large number of people are drastically affected by a severe scarcity of food, resulting in mass malnutrition, starvation, and death. Forces of nature that can contribute to famine include floods, droughts, hurricanes, and earthquakes, but as we have learned in this chapter, even these natural forces can be negatively influenced by humans. Social forces that cause famine are wars and deliberate crop destruction. Famine leads to social unrest and contributes to disease. There is a constant state of famine somewhere on the planet nearly at all times.

Pestilence—The third horrorist of pestilence refers to plagues caused by swarms of locusts, grasshoppers, and other insects. Malthus was partially correct in identifying this horrorist as a force of nature as locusts, grasshoppers, and other insects are parts of the natural world that constantly consume vegetation. However, social forces also contribute to conditions favorable to pestilence, as deforestation and the draining of marshlands have led to the increasing migratory behavior of locusts and other insects. When insects cannot find food in their environment, they will seek it elsewhere, usually resulting in crop and vegetation devastation (Delaney 2005). Agricultural practices that fail to heed natural biodiversity place crops and livestock at risk, which could trigger the growth and increase the danger posed by insects that become immune to certain pesticides. Insects that survive may multiply and cause harm to the environment and humanity (UNEP 2010). Global warming, which humans contribute to, will also contribute to pestilence, as well as famine, death, and war (Delingpole 2014).

Disease—Despite modern technology, disease, the fourth horrorist, is as prevalent today as in the past, although the specific diseases that kill people have changed over the years. Disease is also the result of natural and social forces. Societal and environmental changes such as a worldwide, explosive population growth; expanding poverty; urban migration; and a dramatic increase in international travel and commerce are all factors that increase the risk of exposure to infectious agents. New diseases causing death and human destruction are so prevalent that health officials have utilized the phrase "emerging infectious diseases," or EIDs. EIDs refer to infectious diseases that have emerged since the mid-1980s, or are likely to emerge in the near future. Still, it is many of the long-existing diseases (e.g., heart disease and cancer) that continue as the leading causes of death. The CDC (2015n) reports that leading causes of death in 2013 were heart disease (611,105 deaths); chronic lower respiratory disease (149,205); accidents, unintentional injuries (130,557); stroke, cerebrovascular diseases (128,978); Alzheimer's disease (84,767); diabetes (75,578); and influenza and pneumonia (56,979). The causes of diseases are diverse, but in many cases it was a matter of human lifestyle choices (e.g., choosing to smoke cigarettes despite the known risks).

Enviromares—The fifth horrorist is a new addition to the Four Horsemen concept. An enviromare is defined as an environmentally produced nightmare that causes great harm to humanity and the physical environment. In Malthus's era (as with nearly every era until the past half century or so) it would appear that there was relatively little concern about protecting the environment, as it was in fairly good shape and had been barely exposed to the harmful effects of industrialization. However, in the nearly 250 years of industrialization, humans have come perilously close to altering the earth's fragile ecosystem in a very harmful manner (Delaney 2005). Enviromares are all connected to the various forms of pollution, and although they are connected to nature (the ecosystem, the biosphere, etc.), they are primarily the result of social/human forces. Enviromares include air pollution; water pollution; land pollution; chemical and nuclear pollution; solid waste pollution; noise pollution; e-waste; medical waste; and celestial pollution (space junk). In recent years, terrorism has been added to the list of enviromares because of the damage terroristic acts can have on the environment (see chapter 14 for a discussion on terrorism).

Human Behaviors That Have a Positive Impact on the Environment

While humans commit a number of acts that have a negative impact on the environment, there are a number of people who are engaging in behaviors that are designed to help protect the environment. In some cases these behaviors involve acts of conservation that have become mainstreamed; however, in other cases some behaviors might seem a bit odd to conventional folks. Thus, there are human behaviors that have a positive impact on the environment that could be described as examples of positive deviance. In the following pages we will take a brief look at some of the measures people have taken to be good stewards of the environment. Many of these examples of attempting to protect the environment come under the collective umbrella of "going green"—a social movement promoting environmentally friendly decisions such as "reduce, reuse, and recycle." Original members in the "going green" social movement were once openly mocked as "tree huggers," implying that anyone who expressed eco-friendly behaviors was a deviant, as in, "Go hug a tree if you love trees so much." (Original tree huggers participated in the practice of embracing a tree in an attempt to prevent it from being felled.) We are now at the point where tree huggers are admired by many and are no longer a very small minority within society.

Freeganism

Freeganism, sometimes called dumpster diving, refers to the anticonsumerist movement wherein people reclaim and eat food that has been discarded. Freegans (from the two words "free" and "vegan"), the people who participate in dumpster diving for dining purposes ("dumpster diners"), are scavengers of the developed world who live on consumer waste in an effort to minimize their own spending and to deny their support of corporations (More 2011). Freegans have embraced a subcultural perspective on values; they do not value how much something is worth based on conventional standards, but rather, they value using and consuming goods that have now become reused. As stated on the website Freegan.Info (2015), freegans are people who employ alternative strategies for living based on limited participation in the conventional economy and minimal consumption of resources. Freegans embrace community, generosity, social concern, freedom, cooperation, and sharing in opposition to a society based on materialism, moral apathy, competition, conformity, and greed. Eating food that others consider trash and not being involved in the production of food or other goods used in the economy are among the reasons conventional society considers freegans as deviants. They, however, would consider their behaviors as positive deviance, at the very least.

Freegans sort through garbage in a dumpster, looking for edible food items.

Green Roofs/Living Roofs

Green roofs, or living roofs, are a part of the overall "going green" movement and, in particular, a part of the greening of urban areas. Green roofs are a growing phenomenon designed to help protect the environment. Green roofs provide many benefits, including aesthetic improvement; waste diversion (e.g., prolonging the life of waterproofing membranes; reducing associated waste; using recycled materials in the growing medium; and prolonging the service life of heating, ventilation, and HVAC systems through decreased use); stormwater management (e.g., water is stored by the substrate and then taken up by the plants from where it is returned to the atmosphere through transpiration and evaporation and reduces the amount of stormwater runoff); moderation of urban heat island effect (through the daily dew and evaporation cycle, plants on vertical and horizontal surfaces are able to cool cities during hot summer months and reduce the urban heat island effect); improved air quality (e.g., the plants on green roofs can capture airborne pollutants and atmospheric deposition and they can filter noxious gases); create new amenity spaces (e.g., community gardens and food production); local job creation (transforming rooftops to living roofs will put people to work); fire retardation (green roofs have a much lower burning heat load); reduction of electromagnetic radiation; and noise reduction (Green Roofs 2015).

In 2015, France decreed that all buildings built in commercial zones must either be partially covered in plants or in solar panels. While many applauded this landmark legislation, environmentalists wanted the legislation to state that green roofs cover the entire surface (*The Guardian* 2015).

Urban Farms and Urban Agriculture

The idea of turning rooftops into something green, useful and productive, and functional has also been applied to ground-level urban areas. In many instances empty city lots, especially where abandoned houses have been demolished, have been transformed into urban farms or urban agricultural sites. While urban farms and urban agriculture are similar, there is a distinction. An urban farm grows food in an urban area on land—usually a backyard or a vacant lot—that would not typically be dedicated to producing food and may also involve tending to animals such as chicken coops, beehives, and rabbit warrens (Watson 2015). Urban farms, where city ordinances allow, may also involve raising turkeys, goats, and pigs; space is too limited to graze sheep or cattle. Urban agriculture involves a level of commerce, the growing of a product to be sold as opposed to being grown for personal consumption or sharing (as with urban farms) (Greensgrow 2015). Urban farms and agriculture provide the means to increase access to locally grown food and a way of reintroducing to the public the knowledge of where food comes and the labor involved to produce the foods that people eat. Providing knowledge to others underscores the reality that some urban farms are built primarily for education, training, or reentry programs (Greensgrow 2015). Cities across the nation are involved with urban farming and agriculture. In Los Angeles, for example, there is a project called L.A.'s First Urban Fruit Trail (in the MacArthur Park area) that uses art and fruit trees to encourage the public to walk more, eat more healthfully, and save money. In all, 150 fruit trees were expected to be planted, offering folks plenty more shade and a chance at free snacks year-round (Bermudez 2014).

Alternative Forms of Energy

As described earlier in this chapter, humans around the world are primarily dependent upon burning fossil fuels for their energy needs. Such dependence comes at a great environmental cost, and yet it is considered the norm. When individuals, groups, companies, or governments attempt to introduce alternative forms of energy, they are often looked upon as the deviants. If it is deviant to develop alternative forms of energy that do not involve fossil fuels, we should look upon such quests as, at the very least, positive forms of deviance.

We have already examined one type of alternative form of energy—nuclear power—and realized that it comes with as many potential problems as fossil fuels. Another type of alternative form of energy often suggested and sometimes utilized that may also have unforeseen pitfalls is wind power. Wind power operates on a simple principle: windmills are equipped with turbines that work opposite of fans—instead of using electricity to make wind, the wind turbines use wind to make electricity. The wind turns the blades, which spin a shaft, which connects to a generator and makes electricity (U.S. Department of Energy 2015a). While one drawback of wind power is the lack of wind, Marilyn vos Savant (2014) states that as wind farms become more widespread, they can contribute to climate change beyond ground warming and drying for miles around: "Even improved engineering of the turbines (to reduce turbulence, etc.) cannot eliminate the fact that the machines remove energy from the wind, and this will have an impact on the weather and ultimately the climate" (p. 7).

A variation of turbine-generated power is being developed in Scotland that harnesses the power of ocean currents into a clean and limitless form of renewable energy (Lewis 2014a). The idea centers on the use of giant underwater turbines to capture the energy from deep-ocean currents where the force of the ocean tidal waves turns their rotors to make electricity. Northern Scotland is particularly suited for this type of power because the waves from the Atlantic Ocean and the North Sea guarantee a continuous source of powerful waves. Other parts of the world, such as Nova Scotia and the San Francisco Bay, are also well suited for such a clean alternative source of energy.

Solar power is another relatively popular form of alterative energy used by individual homeowners as well as businesses and government office buildings. *Solar power* uses the sun's energy either directly as thermal energy (heat) or through the use of photovoltaic cells in solar panels and transparent photovoltaic glass to generate electricity (Tech Target 2015). A variation of solar power that involves mirrors is utilized in the Mojave Desert, close to Interstate 15, near the California-Nevada border. The Ivanpah Solar Electric Generating System consists of nearly 350,000 software-controlled helostat mirrors, each focusing sunlight toward one of the three "LPT 550" solar receivers sitting atop centralized towers. "The receivers use the sunlight to superheat steam and to spin a specially-adapted turbine, creating electricity. The steam is then reclaimed using an air-cooled condenser" (Tarantola 2011). The Ivanpah system became operational in 2014 after years of regulatory court battles.

Stressing Environmental Rights

For far too long, humans have purposively and accidentally harmed the environment. To counter the harm caused by humanity a great deal of legislation has been passed that is designed to protect the environment; often, to little or no avail. In most societies, especially democratic ones, citizens have rights that are guaranteed. If the environment is to survive, and ideally thrive, perhaps it too should be granted rights. After all, humans have violated the environment in many ways, including dumping their trash on land; discarding so much trash into bodies of water that garbage islands have formed in the Pacific Ocean; burning contaminants into the sky; dumping toxins into the ocean via such means as oil spills; destroying marine life and vegetation; compromising the ozone layer to a potential point of deterioration;

and so on. All of these deviant behaviors have compromised the vitality of Earth's ecosystems to the point that we have entered the sixth mass extinction period. Perhaps it is a little far-fetched to suggest that the environment has actual rights of protection from humanity, but shouldn't humans have the right to reside in a thriving environment?

Summary

In this chapter we examined the topic of environmental social deviance. The evidence presented throughout the chapter made clear the notion that humans often have a negative impact on the environment. We not only drain natural resources, we also cause direct and indirect harm to ecosystems in particular and the earth's environment in general. Our behaviors are not only threatening the earth's carrying capacity; we are speeding the sixth mass extinction period.

A great number of human behaviors have a negative, or deviant, impact on the environment. Among the most harmful human behaviors discussed were human dependency on fossil fuels as a primary source of energy; our contributing role in causing climate change; hydraulic fracturing, or fracking; the development, production, and overreliance on the use of plastics; marine debris; food waste; electronic waste, more commonly known as e-waste; nuclear waste; medical waste; harmful agricultural practices; deforestation; and overpopulation.

Humans have engaged in efforts to make a positive impact on the environment as well. In some cases these behaviors involve acts of conservation that have become mainstreamed; however, in other cases some behaviors might seem a bit odd to conventional folks. Thus, there are human behaviors that have a positive impact on the environment that could be described as examples of positive deviance. Freeganism would fall under the positive deviance realm, while green roofs and living roofs have become slightly mainstreamed. Urban farms and urban agriculture are still on the fringe but perhaps becoming more mainstreamed.

Key Terms

carrying capacity, 319

climate change, 328

deforestation, 340

ecosystem, 320

enviromare, 343

environment, 320

e-waste, 336

freeganism, 345

greenhouse effect, 327

hydraulic fracturing, 330

marine debris, 334

mass extinction, 322

medical waste, 338

sustainability, 320

thrivability, 321

Discussion Questions

1. What is meant by the term "the grid"? What does it mean to say "the grid is down"? How would you survive an extended period of time in a world without a power grid?
2. Explain how the topic of deviancy is relevant to the study of the physical environment.
3. Describe the first five mass extinctions. Explain why, or why not, we are currently in the era of the sixth mass extinction.
4. Why are humans so dependent upon fossil fuels? Is this the most efficient form of attaining power?
5. Describe what is meant by climate change. Is climate change a reality? Explain your answer. Why do some people refuse to accept all the evidence that supports the notion that our planet is experiencing a significant climate change?
6. Do the positive aspects of plastic products outweigh the negative? Why or why not?
7. Should the environment have rights? Explain your answer.

CHAPTER 13

Social Control and Social Deviance

CHAPTER OBJECTIVES

After reading this chapter students should be able to:

- Explain the connection between social control and deviant behavior
- Describe the socialization process
- Identify the agents of socialization and their role in shaping behavior
- Provide a description and understanding of the "culture of shamelessness"
- Compare and contrast the concepts of "embarrassment" and "shame"
- Explain how informal social control operates
- Demonstrate knowledge of the major aspects of formal social control

A young family is taking a car ride in the countryside when one of the parents notices a roadside sign that reads "Fresh Fruit Stand Ahead." The two parents look at each other and decide to pull over and check out the fruit stand. They notice plenty of delicious-looking fruits. One child excitedly shouts out, "May we get the watermelon?" The other child asks for grapes. The parents decide to get a water-melon, grapes, and some apples. They look around for someone to pay for the fruit when they notice a handmade sign over a drop box that reads, "Please deposit payment here." The oldest child, about seven years old, asks her parents, "Where is the person to pay for the fruit?" The mother explains that no one is there and that they will leave the money in the drop box. The child is puzzled and asks, "If no one is here, why do we have to pay?" The father answers by saying, "Just because no one is here to take the money doesn't mean that we can take the food for free. That would be stealing, wouldn't it?" The daughter replies, "Oh, I see." Her brother also acknowledges it is the right thing to do. The parents have taught their children an important message—just because no one is around to observe your behavior does not mean you can violate the rules. On the drive home, the parents reiterate why they paid for the fruit even though no one was there. They explained that it was part of an "honor system." The young children acknowledge that they understand the valuable life lesson they just learned.

Shortly after the first family pulls away from a fruit stand another car pulls over. The second car also has a young family in it, and they too bag up a variety of fruits. Noticing that no one is around to take their money, they decide to drive off quickly without paying. The driver abruptly stops the car and returns to the stand and takes the drop box containing money left behind by others who abided by the honor system. As the driver returns to the car and quickly drives away, one of the children asks, "Isn't that stealing?" The parent driving justifies his behavior by saying, "It's not stealing if no one sees you take the food and money." The oldest child is confused by this, and the other parent states, "Your father is correct; the fruit farmer should have been at the stand to make sure no one takes the fruit without paying." These children have also learned a lesson, but not the type of lesson society would prefer.

These two situations, with different outcomes, help to illustrate an informal social control scenario. They also help to introduce the role of socialization with regard to social control and deviancy.

An honor-code country roadside vegetable stand.

Social Control and the Role of Socialization

Deviant behavior is associated with violating societal or group norms and expectations. Every society has cultural norms. In chapter 1, the three categories of social norms identified by sociologists were introduced—folkways, mores, and laws. **Laws,** the most serious social norms, are enforced by agents of the judicial system (e.g., the police, prosecutors, criminal court, corrections). Because laws are formalized norms determined by a political authority, the enforcement of laws is accomplished via formal social control methods. Social control enforcement of *mores* (norms that constitute the basic judgments of a society) may come under the jurisdiction of either formal or informal social control efforts depending upon the seriousness of the specific more violated. Folkways (the conventional rules of everyday life that people follow almost automatically) are a little more challenging in that violating an informal norm does not lead to criminal prosecution. For example, a person who picks his nose in public is guilty of violating basic standards of etiquette, but he is not guilty of committing a crime. Because the police do not arrest people for violating folkways, it is up to members of the general public to "punish" inappropriate behaviors. Violations of folkways are enforced in such mundane manners as mild joking or ridicule. At the very least, "punishment" may involve pointing out the transgression; for example, giving someone "the stare" or clearing one's throat with a "harrumph" to draw attention to patrons who are talking or texting during a movie at the theater. Ideally, people learn not to commit violations of social norms via the socialization process. In some cases, embarrassment and shame have traditionally been used as tactics to motivate people to conform to cultural norms, both informal and formal.

The importance of conforming to social norms is infused in every perspective of social deviance. The normative perspective on deviance includes in its definition the parameter of a social norm being violated; the absolutist perspective argues that certain behaviors are inherently deviant, regardless of context, because they go against ideals deemed obvious that people must adhere to; the statistical perspective focuses on behaviors that are unusual, rare, or uncommon, thus implying they go against what most people would consider the norm; the relativist perspective of social deviance, while it takes into consideration the manner in which social norms are created, still centers on the idea that some standard of expectation has been violated; and the **reactivist** perspective takes into account the idea that some deviant forms of behavior can be positive but still works with the basic assumption that expectations of "normal" behavior have been established and ultimately violated. Thus, it can be argued that all forms of deviancy boil down to the realization that people strayed away from the ideals of what society, or a particular group, has taught to be the norm. In other words, there was a disconnect between actual behavior and expected behavior, and such a disconnection is often the result of a breakdown in the socialization process. In this regard, among other goals, the socialization process represents our first indoctrination into the world of social control. **Social control** itself refers to all the processes, formal or informal, used to prevent deviant behavior.

The Socialization Process

Sociologists view socialization as a lifelong process of learning—one that spans from infancy to old age. Like psychologists, sociologists acknowledge the importance of early childhood development as a critical phase of learning; however, sociologists also emphasize that, ideally, each of us will continue to learn throughout our lifetimes. We learn by interacting with others. The importance of learning is a focal point in the definition of **socialization**, which is defined as "a process of social development and learning that occurs as individuals interact with one another and learn about society's expectations for acceptable behavior" (Delaney 2012a:146). Parents, guardians, or other primary caregivers are responsible for loving, nurturing, protecting, and teaching children, especially young children, the ways of the world. Infants are especially vulnerable and consequently dependent upon caregivers for their very survival. Caregivers not only have to help assure the survival of infants and young children, they must also find a way to break them of their self-centeredness that results from their survival dependency. Think about it: infants cannot feed or bathe themselves; they must rely on others. Infants learn to manipulate caregivers via a number of techniques, especially crying and throwing temper tantrums. And because others take care of their every need, infants and young children become quite narcissistic and demand immediate gratification. If they are hungry or thirsty, they will usually cry and scream (as if dying!), regardless of the time of day or night, or whether other family members are trying to sleep. They do, after all, have biological needs that they cannot fulfill themselves. So instead, they rely on others. The role of caregivers, then, continues from taking care of the basic needs of infants to trying to break young children from the habit of being waited on by others. Children must learn to take care of themselves and to consider the needs of others. They learn such things through the socialization process.

One of the early goals of the socialization process is to tame narcissism and to teach children that they cannot have whatever they want whenever they want it. The real world seldom provides instant gratification for all individual needs, biological or social. For example, young children have to learn to control their bodily functions via "potty training" and learn that just because they are hungry or thirsty does not mean they instantly receive food and drink; instead, they must wait to have dinner, for example, when the rest of the family has dinner. They must learn that temper tantrums no longer work and that proper behavior is expected at all times. Ideally, children learn such things before they reach school age.

In order for the socialization process to be effective, individuals must learn to internalize the messages being sent to them. In this regard, the expectations of society are added to the "script" of response patterns of individuals; they have learned to respond to various stimuli in a routine fashion (e.g., everyday courtesy and manners, formal etiquette, and knowing when to speak and when to remain quiet). Individuals who are properly socialized and have internalized the cultural expectations of the greater society are able to function properly in a variety of social settings. The socialization process, then, prepares individuals to perform appropriately in all social settings. In a broader sense, the socialization process is critical for the survival and stability of the greater society itself. After all, if everyone behaved in a narcissistic manner or acted as they pleased in every social situation, it would be difficult for any sort of maintenance or growth of society to occur; civil society itself would likely cease to exist. Conversely, a general adherence to societal rules and expectations does not preclude any chance of social change, as changing beliefs, norms, and values as the result of significant social events and technological advancements can alter a given society's ideology and operating structure.

Primary Groups

Socialization is most effective within primary groups. Sociologist Charles Horton Cooley (1909) describes **primary groups** as "those characterized by intimate face-to-face association and cooperation. . . . The result of intimate association, psychologically, is a certain fusion of individualities in a common whole, so that one's very self, for many purposes at least, is the common life and purpose of the group" (p. 23). These associations are primary in many ways, but especially in that they are fundamental in shaping the social individual. For Cooley, primary groups are intimate, face-to-face groups that play a key role in linking the individual to the larger society. The primary group is relatively small, informal, involves close personal relationships, and has an important role in shaping the self. Primary groups are such groups from which individuals receive their earliest and most basic experiences of social unity. They are the sources of the individual's ideals, which derive from the moral and ethical unity of the group itself. Cooley stated that the most important primary groups are the family, the playgroup of children, and the neighborhood or community of elders. (Society has changed since the time of Cooley, as in most modern societies a "community of elders," if it even exists, generally has little or no impact on young individuals—children and young people seldom are taught to respect the advice of unknown elders.)

Close relations with primary groups help give individuals a sense of "we" or "belonging," as members of a primary group share a sense of "we-ness"—a sort of sympathy and mutual identification for which "we" is a natural expression. In the context of deviancy, the messages individuals receive from primary groups are especially important in shaping one's perception of "right" and "wrong." Thus, if we revisit the introductory story of this chapter, the children in story one were taught that you heed honor codes and that it is not right to steal unattended food, that you still must pay for it; conversely, the children in the second scenario were taught that it is okay to steal food, and money, if it is unattended.

Agents of Socialization

Primary groups are an example of agents of socialization. **Agents of socialization** are sources of culture; they are people, groups, organizations, and institutions that teach us what we need to know in order to function properly in society. In addition to our primary agents of socialization—parents and the family—are peer groups, schools, mass media, social media, religion, employers, and the government.

The first primary group encountered by most individuals is the family—especially the parents. Siblings, grandparents, and other close family members of the child may also be considered members of the initial primary agent of socialization. It is within the family structure that most of us first experience face-to-face associations. Raised within the family structure, the young child receives mostly consistent messages about social expectations and concepts of "right" and "wrong."

When children start going to school (or even earlier, if they are in day care during the infant and toddler years), they begin to interact with a number of other children and adults with potentially different outlooks on what constitutes "proper" behavior. These others may even have different ideas on norms, values, and cultural beliefs. These different outlooks on life may confuse the child, but they may also enhance an appreciation for diversity of thought and action. Attending school represents the beginning of secondary socialization. This is because parental influence usually declines as the child progresses through school.

As the young child grows older, the opinions, values, and norms of peers become increasingly important; consequently, peer groups come to have a strong influence on individuals. A peer group consists of close associates of a similar age and usually from the same social status and background. Peers enjoy a certain amount of autonomy and egalitarianism as each friend possesses relatively equal status with the group. Peer group participation affords members an opportunity to explore the limits of adult rules and expectations. In this manner, the child is being socialized into accepting the idea that norms, values, and beliefs are not fixed entities. This newfound freedom is exciting to most children and helps to explain why they value praise and acknowledgment from their peers. This newfound freedom also underscores the concern that parents have for the friendships their children establish and maintain, as most parents are wary of their children hanging out with other kids who might be a "bad" influence.

The mass media, in addition to being a source of news, information, and entertainment, may also display a significant influence over aging children. The mass media includes television, radio, motion pictures, newspapers, books, magazines, and sound recordings. It also consists of such things as video and computer games that may consume a great deal of time and thus have a moderate to great influence on children and young adults. Some adolescents are more susceptible to the advertising associated with the mass media that is geared toward their generation.

For some people, religion is a highly influential agent of socialization. Religious leaders and doctrines of moral and ethical teachings can have a great influence on the behavior of religious adherents. For many religious people, certain behaviors carry with them automatic ideals of matters of "right" and "wrong." In this regard, the advice and teachings of religious leaders serve as beacons of truth that must be followed. Other people, however, lead a more secular, or less religious, lifestyle, and religion has little significance for them.

Most people work because they have to, and even if they are lucky enough to have a job they truly love and enjoy being a part of, employers play an important role in their lives. Employers provide a wage or salary that allows us to secure the resources necessary to survive. In turn, employers can have an influence over people and alter they manner in which they behave, perhaps to the point of influencing cultural and idealistic belief systems.

The role of government is quite profound on the lives of people, and this is true whether someone lives under a dictatorship or resides within a democratic society. It is the government that dictates what is legal and what is illegal and therefore has a strong influence in determining what is "right" and "wrong." Thus, while someone may find it perfectly acceptable to smoke marijuana, if the government has labeled the consumption, possession, and sale of marijuana "illegal," individuals must realize that there are consequences if their behaviors involve consuming marijuana.

People of most ages spend a great deal of time communicating with one another in the virtual world (cyberspace) rather than in face-to-face interactions. This process is called virtual socialization, and its influence on our lives is increasing. The amount of time spent in the cyberworld generally comes at the cost of less time spent with personal relationships in the real world. Today, socializing online is a norm of behavior and as a result, the virtual world can have a great influence on one's outlook of proper behavior. Consider, for example, that Americans aged 18 and older use electronic media on average 11-plus hours per day (Richter 2015). The average time American adults (18-plus) spent with electronic media during the 4th quarter of 2014: live television (4 hours and 51 minutes); radio (2:43); smartphone (1:25); Internet on a PC (1:06); time-shifted TV (:33); game console (:13); DVD/Blu-ray (:09); and multimedia device (:07) (Richter 2015). In a study conducted in the United Kingdom, it was revealed that young people aged between 16 and 24 spend more than 27 hours a week on the Internet (Anderson 2015). This figure is an increase double from 10 years ago and is fueled by the increasing use of tablets and smartphones. The biggest increase has been among young adults, with time spent online almost tripling from 10 years ago (Anderson 2015). Younger people are watching television programming, but they are increasingly watching it streamed online rather than on television. The most popular websites accessed from mobile phones among young people in the United Kingdom are Facebook, Twitter, Google+, LinkedIn, and Myspace (Anderson 2015).

Almost 70 percent of Internet users in the U.K. study cited above report that they feel comfortable giving away personal information on the Net, including their home addresses, and a quarter say they don't read website terms and conditions or privacy statements at all. Two-thirds of Internet users use the same passwords for most or all websites. Such lax attitudes contribute to the high frequency of cyber-crime (see chapter 9) and cyberbullying. **Cyberbullying** refers to the use of technologies such as the Internet, cell phones, or other devices to send or post text or images with the intent of intimidating, hurting, or embarrassing another person. Cyberbullying and cybercrime are among the deviant behaviors being learned, or endured, online.

Adult Socialization

Sociologists are quick to point out that the socialization process continues throughout adulthood. Children become young adults, young adults become middle-agers, and the middle-agers become elderly. The adult life cycle presents new situations that require the learning of new roles. High school graduates may go to college, find a job, or join the armed services, and each of these life course paths comes with social expectations of new and often particular lessons to learn. Agents of socialization will teach, either directly or indirectly, the norms and values of that particular social environment. College graduates will seek a career. Those who started working right after high school or those that joined the armed services may transition to new roles or continue on the life course they chose at an early age. Many young adults will get married and start a family, resulting in the sudden realization that they are now primary agents of socialization to the next generation. There's a near equal chance that the marriage will not last as there is of it continuing on. Divorced adults must now find a way to cope with new life challenges and social expectations. Some divorced people will marry a second or third time and will face the reality that divorce rates are higher than for first marriages. Many will change careers and jobs, some voluntarily, some not. Some will move away from the geographic area of their birth and start new lives in new social environments. Parents with aging children will eventually cope with the "empty nest" syndrome as their children move out of the home and start their own lives. Retirement and old age bring all sorts of new scenarios for the aging adult. The bottom line is, there is no end to the possibilities for life-learning situations and the corresponding changes in role expectations that confront us as we go through life. In each case, a socialization process accompanies the transition in the life cycle (Delaney 2012a).

While a great deal of attention is focused on young people who commit acts of deviance—juvenile delinquency—adult deviancy is just as, if not more, prevalent. In fact, at every stage of life development come societal expectations as to what constitutes "proper" behavior. There also comes a point in time when individuals can no longer blame a poor socialization (e.g., via a "tough" childhood or the lack of proper role models) for their rule-breaking behavior. Instead, it is up to each of us to take personal responsibility for our actions and realize that if we violate societal or group rules, norms, values, and beliefs, we may have to face sanctions, or punishments.

Most people will abide by social norms in most situations. People who attempt to follow the rules and expectations of society do so because they were socialized to do the "right" thing. We also tend to do the "right" thing because we do not want to face the negative consequences associated with committing acts of deviancy. Among these negative consequences is the risk of being stigmatized as a "deviant."

Stigmatization and the Culture of Shamelessness

Historically, when someone was labeled a "deviant," there was a corresponding stigma attached to the deviant identity. Going back to the days of colonial America, when people were modest, hard workers who went about their business without drawing attention to themselves or asking anything from others, members of a community adhered to the prevailing moral codes of conduct. Puritan values included a strong sense of family, and while there were likely those who cheated on their spouses, such indiscretions were kept quiet so as to avoid public humiliation (stigmatization). As per the common ideological belief among patriarchal societies, the Puritans treated female adulteresses worse than male adulterers. The Puritan perspective of adultery of the 17th century is neatly described by Nathaniel Hawthorne (1850) in *The Scarlet Letter*, where "adulteress" Hester Prynne (there is great debate over the historic accuracy of her being an adulteress) is publicly shamed and forced to wear a patch of fabric in the shape of an *A*, signifying that she was an adulterer. The scarlet letter *A* indicated that she had sinned, and her punishment included public ridicule and scorn as a moral sinner. Designating certain behaviors and attitudes as sinful is a community's way of trying to encourage, or force, compliance to a specific code of communal behavior.

Today, there are still local community codes of conduct that citizens are expected to abide by, and there are greater societal norms and values as well. Violations of these codes may also lead to public scorn via the traditional and social media and through judicial public shamings (examples to be provided later in this chapter). However, while deviants and criminals may be subjected to a metaphoric scarlet letter and subject to public shame and ridicule, there are a growing number of people who do not feel shame. In fact, some of the same behaviors that in the past would have elicited great shame and embarrassment are treated with indifference today and have led to what can be described as a growing **culture of shamelessness** (Delaney 2008). The culture of shamelessness is further fueled by the realization among many in society that the basic rules of etiquette, decorum, and proper behavior are disappearing from American culture. This digression away from traditional norms and toward a blasé attitude in regard to behaviors formerly described as shameful leads to the realization that many people today are not experiencing shame for behaviors traditionally described as shameful (Delaney 2008). Many readers of this text may be aware of Showtime's *Shameless*, a TV show that has aired since 2011 and features William H. Macy and Emmy Rossum. The network's home page for *Shameless* sums up the Chicago-based Gallagher family by saying, "They may not be like any family you know, but they make no apologies for being exactly who they are" (Showtime 2016).

Building off the chapter 10 discussion on the growing number of recognized mental illnesses and disorders and the increasing number of psychological syndromes that enable people to avoid taking responsibility for their actions is the "affluenza" defense. The public first heard of this "psychological problem" when a Texas teenager, Ethan Couch, who killed four people in a drunken-driving crash, was given probation (Couch's punishment prohibits him from driving, drinking, or using drugs, and he must check in with his probation officer) after a defense witness suggested he suffered from **affluenza**—a term used to describe psychological problems that can afflict children from wealthy families (Hauser 2015). Essentially Couch's lawyers argued that his sense of entitlement kept him from seeing the consequences of his bad behavior. (If we are going to create syndromes, we could try "povertitis"—an affliction that affects the poor and clouds their judgment, thus giving them a free pass from committing crime and deviancy. Chances are the public, let alone the judicial system, would not accept this defense.) Public debate did ensue as to whether this wealthy teenager got off lightly and shamelessly got away with murder/manslaughter. In December 2015, these concerns resurfaced when Couch appeared in a six-second video posted on Twitter, which appeared to show Couch at a drinking party with other youths. Immediately after the Twitter post Couch went on the run and his juvenile probation officer was unable to make contact with him (Hauser 2015). Couch's mother, Tonya, also disappeared at the same time. By the end of December 2015, Couch and his mother were detained in Puerto Vallarta, Mexico. Shameful behaviors such as those displayed by Couch and his legal defense, in addition to the other examples of shameful behaviors to be discussed throughout this chapter, help to fuel the growing culture of shamelessness; and it further clouds the issue of describing certain behaviors as deviant. (Sociologically speaking, the affluenza defense is really an example of poor socialization on the part of primary caregivers.) It should be pointed out that Couch was eventually punished for his shameful behavior, as in April 2016, Texas Judge Wayne Salvant sentenced the affluenza teen to spend nearly two years in jail, the maximum allowable punishment per state law (Richter 2016).

Arguably, the culture of shamelessness began in earnest in the 1960s when many traditions were being challenged by ideals of women's equality, civil rights for minorities, anti–Vietnam War protests, draft dodgers, the hippie movement, and participants in premarital sex, all of whom failed to experience a sense of shame for their behaviors. In the 1970s, there was preponderance toward the "sex, drugs, and rock and roll" behavior of young people. Proponents of this lifestyle were also shame-free. They played music loudly, dressed provocatively, freely engaged in premarital sex, and consumed recreational drugs. The 1980s brought us the iconic Madonna, a performer who raised the bar on shamelessness with "S&M"-inspired costumes and, later, by publishing a pornographic book. In 1983, Madonna famously stated that "I have no shame" (Delaney 2008). The 1990s brought us shock jocks and rap music that pushed the envelope on issues of freedom of speech and expression. The 2000s have played witness to an increasing number of shameless behaviors, including an avoidance to abide by ideals of everyday etiquette and an acceptance to do nearly anything to become famous. TV shows like *The Jerry Springer Show* pushed the envelope of shameful behaviors, and that was replaced by reality TV, wherein people either don't care they are being foolish or they don't realize just how idiotic they appear to be. In 2006, Jean Twenge, author of *Generation Me* (2006), said that young people today are less concerned about social approval and society's standards than their peers of generations past. Twenge notes that in the late 1950s, only 30 percent of young people approved of sex before marriage (just 12 percent of women); now 75 percent (80 percent of women) approve. Twenge reports that among college students today, 62 percent say they pay little attention to social conventions; in 1958, an average of 50 percent did.

Part of the idea of punishing violators of codes of conduct is to stigmatize them. As Erving Goffman (1963a) explains, a **stigma** makes reference to a damaged self. "Stigma is a term that describes a mark of disgrace or dishonor. Persons who are stigmatized are lacking in full social acceptance, and their self-identity is negatively affected by this label" (Delaney 2005:125). Goffman traced the term "stigma" to the ancient Greeks, who used visible signs to disgrace dishonored members of society. "The signs were cut or burnt into the body and advertised that the bearer was a slave, a criminal, or a traitor" (Goffman, 1963b:1). Stigmas are designed to be blemishes on an individual character. Goffman (1963a) also distinguished between discredited and discreditable individuals. Individuals who have been discredited have already been labeled as deviants; they are stigmatized/tainted (disqualified from full social acceptance). The discredited deviant's characteristics or behaviors are known about; hence they cannot pass themselves off as "creditable." Thus, a discredited deviant labeled as a "sex offender" cannot pass him/herself off as a trustworthy babysitter. Discreditable persons are those who potentially can be discredited, but their deviant behavior has not become known to others. A shoplifter who has yet to be caught is a discreditable person.

In the culture of shamelessness, however, it is harder to stigmatize deviants because they do not experience embarrassment and shame as easily as people in the past. Embarrassment reflects a failure to present oneself in the way one would have wished, but if one does not experience embarrassment over a deviant deed (e.g., being yelled at by your boss for being incompetent while your coworkers are standing nearby), then one has not damaged their sense of self. Shame goes beyond the level of embarrassment, as it has moral implications. Thus, a shameful behavior involves judgment from others expressed in some fashion similar to "You ought to be ashamed of yourself" (e.g., for sleeping with your best friend's significant other). Some researchers suggest that shame is one of the most painful emotions and that it is generally repressed, with anger emerging to take its place (Turner 2007; Abrutyn and Mueller 2014).

It is not suggested here that people today are free from embarrassment, shame, or stigma altogether. Furthermore, there are plenty of informal and formal shamings conducted on a regular basis. Formal shamings include the military court-martial (a classic example of a degradation ceremony designed to bring shame to the discredited person); judicial shamings (e.g., being labeled a "sex offender"); sports shamings (e.g., an athlete's transgressions aired to the public via the media); religious shamings, (e.g., the Amish shame adherents via a religious shunning—they are excommunicated); and workplace shamings (wherein individuals in the workplace are targeted by others for termination for reasons that are not related to poor job performance). Informal shamings, like formal shamings, are designed to alter (degrade) the identity of the targeted person(s). The 2004 movie *Mean Girls* is often cited to demonstrate how cliques of friends pick on others in school in an attempt to embarrass and humiliate them. Pulling pranks and practical jokes on others is informal shaming because it is designed to embarrass others. Social network sites are often used as public means to shame people either by stories or shameful photos. However, it should be noted that college students from the 1960s to the 1970s did whatever they could to keep certain behaviors secret and rarely took photos of each other in compromising positions; today, it is like a badge of honor to post on social media photos of oneself drunk or wearing provocative outfits while engaged in questionable behaviors. The culture of shamelessness would suggest that while people are quite capable of being embarrassed, they are not as likely to experience shame.

Embarrassment

The distinction between the terms "embarrassment" and "shame" seems to underscore the culture of shamelessness. That is, people are capable of being embarrassed over relatively informal breaches of social norms, but that does not mean they experience shame. As described earlier, **embarrassment** reflects a failure to present oneself in the manner that one would have wished, and because of this, they feel foolish and self-conscious and perhaps confused, flustered, or mortified. Embarrassment generally occurs following the breach of folkway norms. Examples of embarrassing moments include:

- Realizing your zipper is down while in public.
- A cell phone goes off during class and it's the professor's phone! To make matters worse, the professor has just warned students to keep their cell phones off during class.
- While on a first date at a restaurant, you suddenly realize that you forgot your wallet and have no means of paying the bill.
- Discovering that you had a piece of food stuck in between your teeth after you leave a job interview or after you asked someone out on a first date.
- Calling someone by the wrong name while on a date; or worse, during a moment of intimacy.
- Having a visible urine stain (or water stain from the sink splashing that looks like a urine stain) on your pants.
- A student who falls asleep in class.
- Parents who cannot control their unruly children in public, especially in grocery or shopping stores.
- As a waiter or waitress you trip and fall, spilling multiple plates of food and glasses of beverages.

A student embarrasses herself by sleeping at her desk during class.

These are just a few examples of embarrassing situations that people may find themselves in. In each of these cases, the individual has failed in an aspect of their role performance and feels, at least temporarily, foolish, self-conscious, flustered, or mortified because they breached a social norm. This awareness triggers sociological, psychological, and physiological reactions. Sociologically, embarrassed persons will experience social anxiety and may fear future public engagements. Psychologically, embarrassed people have their self-esteem and self-identities compromised. Physiologically, embarrassed people may blush, stutter, sweat, experience an increased heart rate, and fumble about.

Embarrassment "reflects a failure to present oneself in the way one would have wished" (Edelmann 1987:14). Embarrassment is usually regarded as a form of social anxiety closely related to shyness, audience anxiety, and shame (Buss 1980; Schlenker and Leary 1982; Edelmann 1987). The fear of embarrassment plays a central role in the experience of social anxiety, as embarrassing behaviors can cause discrepancy between one's current unintended self-presentation and one's desired self (Asendorpf 1984). Goffman points out that we can recognize embarrassment in ourselves and in others by objective signs of emotional disturbance: blushing, fumbling, mumbling, stuttering, an unusually low- or high-pitched voice, quavering speech or breaking of the voice, sweating, tremor of the hand, and absentmindedness.

Embarrassing situations usually involve people who have violated minor social norms; they have committed a faux pas (a slip or blunder in etiquette, manners, or conduct; an embarrassing social blunder or indiscretion) or an impropriety. Thus, while it is understandable why the embarrassed person may experience anxiety, she should not necessarily feel ashamed for her behaviors. After all, accidents and minor transgressions will occur, and we have all experienced embarrassing moments in our lives. As a result, it is not necessary to experience shame over embarrassing situations. Shame, then, is a stronger emotion than embarrassment (Delaney 2008).

Shame

Shame involves intense negative emotion having to do with the self in relation to societal standards and responsibilities (Lewis 1998). Buss (1980) argues that shame is a more severe feeling because it has "moral implications," whereas embarrassment does not. Shame, then, involves painful feelings of guilt, regret, or sadness because you know you have done something morally wrong, dishonorable, improper, or ridiculous. As an example of the distinction between feelings of embarrassment—which violate folkways—and shame—which usually violate mores—a person who slips and falls in a mud puddle in front of others will experience embarrassment, but not shame. Falling in mud is embarrassing, but it is hardly a behavior that one needs to feel ashamed of committing. A traitor should experience shame (especially when caught) because of the built-in moral implication of betraying one's country. The traitor should feel ashamed because he has brought dishonor and disgrace upon himself. Conditions of disgrace and dishonor are beyond those of simple embarrassment; they involve guilt.

Guilt, then, is a component of shame. Guilt involves feelings of remorse and regret for one's actions, and shame refers to the feelings that one has about the guilt for violating a social norm. Joyce Brothers (2005) explains, "While guilt is the feeling that you have done something wrong, shame is the feeling that there's something wrong with you. Nothing could be more all-encompassing. When we've had too much exposure to shame, our joy in life is severely diminished. That's why the self-esteem movement declared war on shame decades ago" (p. 5). Guilt is something that develops from one's conscience and is typically expressed by such sentiments as "I did something morally wrong" or "I did something very bad."

Guilt can lead to consequences beyond feelings of shame; it may lead to suicide. Such is the case with John Gibson, a pastor and seminary professor who was "outed" by hackers who exposed the names of millions of people who had signed up for Ashley Madison, the website designed to help married people have affairs (see chapter 11 for a description of the hacking of Ashley Madison). Gibson was married with two children. Gibson felt so guilty and ashamed by having his name leaked from a cheater's site that he committed suicide. In his suicide note, Gibson chronicled his demons, spoke about the depression he was experiencing, and expressed great sorrow (Segall 2015). Despite all the people that Gibson had helped in his life, he could not "see past a single mistake, or a single flaw, or to see beyond the darkness of the present moment into a better future" (Roberts 2015). Shame can clearly have some serious consequences.

Gibson experienced deep shame; he acknowledged that he violated a societal more by his willingness to sign up for a website designed to help people cheat on their spouses (we do not know if Gibson actually committed adultery, but he did feel guilty enough to kill himself). In contrast to Gibson, who felt guilt for his behavior, there are people such as Edward Snowden who do not take ownership for shameful behaviors. Snowden has been labeled as a traitor to his country because of his behaviors, but he feels no remorse or guilt whatsoever; instead, he appealed to a higher loyalty and proclaimed that he was a whistle-blower and not a traitor. Snowden is a computer professional, former CIA employee, and former government contractor who copied classified information from the U.S. National Security Agency (NSA) (while working as a subcontractor for Booz Allen) in the NSA's Oahu office in 2013. He began to collect top-secret documents regarding NSA domestic surveillance practices (under the umbrella of programs such as PRISM), which he found troubling. He then released the information to the media. In 2014, the U.S. government charged Snowden with violating multiple laws under the Espionage Act. Snowden, after having fled to Hong Kong in 2013, remained in hiding and then fled to Moscow, Russia (where he still resided at the end of 2015). Some people describe Snowden as a hero for sticking up for U.S. citizens (the higher authority to whom he proclaimed an allegiance). The *New York Daily News* described Snowden as a "know-it-all millennial who arrogated to himself the right to determine what secrets, if any, our government should be allowed to keep" (Kirchick 2014). Clearly, the *Daily News* is taking the perspective that Snowden is a product of the culture of shamelessness, as he not only refuses to accept the label of traitor or feel remorse or guilt for releasing government secrets that put certain government employees in danger, he views himself as a hero. Readers can determine for themselves whether Snowden is a hero or traitor.

Issues related to embarrassment and shame as well as the culture of shamelessness are aspects of social control and social deviancy. In some instances, people should have learned self-control because they should have learned from agents of socialization the difference between right and wrong. In other instances, people engage in behaviors with little or no regard to how society views such acts. If people do not experience a sense of shame, embarrassment, or guilt over their deviant behaviors, how is society to exert any influence over them? We will find out the answer to this question in the following pages with our review of informal and formal social control.

Informal (Internal) Social Control

Informal, or internal, social control regulates behavior through ideological or cultural manipulation. It is accomplished through the internalization of norms, values, and beliefs via the socialization process wherein people learn to accept the rules presented to them. When individuals accept the ideas and norms introduced to them, they have internalized society's expectations. Agents of socialization (informal social control), throughout one's life cycle, will often exert pressure on us in an attempt to force, or encourage, compliance. Socialized to conform to the norms of society, individuals exert self-control; that is, we stop ourselves from engaging in improper/deviant behavior because we have learned to control our own behaviors (internal social control).

A great deal of conformity comes about as a result of internalizing norms, values, and beliefs; thus, through the process of socialization, most of us learn to follow most of the laws of society routinely without having to be told to do so. Violations of social norms are usually matched by appropriate sanctions (punishments) such as a frown, a heavy sigh, verbal putdowns, and sometimes via a shaming of some sort (e.g., on social media). Proper displays of behavior, however, are generally reinforced via such methods as a smile or nod of approval or gratitude. Since most people seek the approval of others, internal social control can be very effective.

Whether it's because we seek the approval of others or that we have developed a social conscience, most social control is accomplished through informal means. After all, think about on any given day the vast number of deviant behaviors each of us could commit, and yet we rarely, if ever, do so. For example, most of us do not steal our neighbor's newspaper, we do not cause random acts of violence or paint graffiti on buildings, we do not run red lights and do come to a complete stop at a stop sign, we do not litter, we do not assault people, we do not steal from classmates or professors, we honor someone's space when they put a blanket down on a part of the beach, we dress appropriately for specific social events, and so on. The possibilities and opportunities to commit social deviance are almost infinite, and yet nearly all the time, nearly all of us conform to the norms and values of the greater society and/or the most significant social institutions and groups to which we belong. And we do this because we are socialized to do so and we have learned self-control.

Honor Codes

Honor codes are an example of informal social control wherein participants are expected to be trusted to adhere to a set of ideals governing a body. These ideals are based on what group members consider to be important and virtuous. When a group institutes an honor code, it is based on the idea that people within the group can be trusted to act honorably. In this chapter's introductory story the concept of an honor code was implemented by the farmers who set up an unattended fruit stand and entrusted random passersby to honor the system set up that if you take fruit, you leave money for the fruit in a drop box. Most people—with the implication being those who were raised to respect other people's property—will abide by such a concept as a fruit-stand honor system. However, as in the example provided in the introductory story, not all people can be trusted to abide by codes of honor.

An honor code system implemented by a fruit stand farmer compared to that of a specific work site or college has a greater chance of failure because people do not have the same type of involvement/investment in the fruit farmer's activities and goals as they would at their place of employment. Consider the office kitchen area in contrast to the fruit stand. If the place of work has an honor system wherein workers are expected to clean up after themselves and not to take each other's food from the refrigerator, such a system is more likely to be adhered to because everyone knows each other and has an investment in the success of the honor system. The threat of sanctions, if one is caught violating the workplace honor system, is a very real possibility. Furthermore, fellow workers will exert informal social control over one another if they notice a violation. At the roadside fruit stand the customers do not know the owners of the stand and therefore have no investment in its successful and smooth operation. Furthermore, there is no chance of informal social control from others if there are no other customers at the fruit stand. The fruit thief is likely never to return to the scene of the crime, whereas an office worker who violates the kitchen honor system will have to return to the scene of the "crime" repeatedly. Anyone who has ever worked at an office or work site with a kitchen/refrigerator honor system is, however, likely to tell stories of people who violate this trust. Like a chain, an honor system is only as strong as its weakest link.

Many colleges have an honor code system. The University of Virginia's honor code is described as both an injunction and an aspiration. "The injunction is simple: students pledge to never lie, cheat or steal, and accept that the consequence for breaking this pledge is permanent dismissal from the University. It is for this aspirational quality, however, that the Honor Code is so cherished: in leading lives of honor, students have continuously renewed that unique spirit of compassion and interconnectedness that has come to be called the Community of Trust" (University of Virginia the Honor Committee 2012). At the University of Virginia, students are expected to honor the code of conduct of the university, and they are also expected to report others' wrongdoing to an honor advisor. Once the honor advisor has been contacted, an official report begins and the reported incident cannot be rescinded.

At Elon University (a selective private liberal arts university in North Carolina), students sign the honor pledge when they join the Elon community to "publicly affirm their intent to behave according to the values of the Elon community. They also sign this pledge on papers, tests, assignments and other documents when requested. The honor pledge is printed in classrooms and residence halls throughout campus" (Elon University 2015). The honor code itself entails that every member of the university uphold four main values: Honesty (Be truthful in your academic work and in your relationships); Integrity (Be trustworthy, fair, and ethical); Responsibility (Be accountable for your actions and your learning); Respect (Be civil. Value the dignity of each person. Honor the physical and intellectual property of others).

If is fairly common for colleges and universities across the United States, and in other nations, to adopt an honor code system of some sort. Perhaps there is good reason to have honor codes, as numerous reports indicate that cheating, especially on tests and term papers, is running rampant on college campuses. Following a cheating scandal at Harvard University—one of the most prestigious universities in the world—wherein a professor found that nearly half of his 250 students had cheated on a final exam (Buchmann 2014), the *Boston Globe* reported that the rate of students who admit to cheating at least once in their college careers has held steady somewhere around 75 percent since the first major survey on cheating in higher education in 1963 (Lang 2013). This figure is disheartening, to say the least, for faculty, future employers, and the parents who pay hefty tuition bills. It is also an indication that self-control mechanisms have failed. Cheating is certainly not restricted to Harvard. At Stanford University, 45 percent of undergraduates said they would not report cheating in a 2010 survey, and at Princeton University only 4 of 85 students who witnessed cheating reported it (Cheung 2014). More than 100 Stanford University students in an introductory computer science course found themselves under investigation for academic dishonesty following their return from spring break in March 2015. Infractions ranged from outright plagiarism to "unpermitted collaboration" (Greenberg 2015). Instead of being upset with students who cheated, *Washington Post* writer Susan Greenberg argued for doing away with honor codes and claimed that punishing "cheating" in classrooms has become impractical and antiquated. Greenberg claims that "in an age in which collaboration and interpersonal skills are increasingly valued in the workplace, honor codes that rigidly define and punish 'cheating' in classrooms" are a thing of the past. Greenberg (2015) also believes that it is wrong to put pressure on students to succeed and to turn in their peers for cheating and adds that because of this, honor codes have fallen out of step with the values of the modern college student. Greenberg's attitude goes against the perspective of college professors and universities' standards of conduct. However, if students believe that concepts such as honor are no longer important, they will not feel as though they have committed an act of deviance, and it becomes much easier to justify cheating.

Informal Shaming

Earlier in this chapter, the idea that there is a growing culture of shamelessness in society was presented. A great number of people share this sentiment, and in many instances they have attempted to bring about shame on violators of cultural norms by stigmatizing them. Part of the goal of shaming is to compromise the intended victim's self-identity and sense of self-worth. Attempts to shame others in an unofficial capacity come under the domain of an informal shaming. Informal shamings may be instituted by anyone and are designed to embarrass the intended victims. **Informal shamings** contain elements of moral indignation, shame, ridicule, stigmatism, and attempts to compromise the victim's identity and self-esteem and are used by people against others in an attempt to alter their behavior.

Informal shamings may be conducted by nearly anyone in any given social environment. For example, colleagues, friends, and intimate partners may attempt to shame one another in a variety of ways. When a work colleague goofs up and is embarrassed, his face may turn red. A fellow worker may attempt to shame his colleague by yelling, "Look! His face is turning red!" This comment is usually followed by gawking audience members who laugh at the shamed person. The shamed person turns a brighter color red and wishes he could run and hide his embarrassment. After all, he was publicly shamed and already felt bad enough for causing the original transgression that was called out. Drawing attention to someone blushing is, in itself, a shameful behavior, but it is the person who was targeted by this comment that will feel the most shame and embarrassment.

Pointing to someone who turns red after saying or doing something embarrassing and then making a joke at his expense is an example of an emergent, unplanned informal shaming because such an opportunity has to present itself. On the other hand, there are also planned informal shamings, such as when a group of people get together to conduct an intervention. Interventions involve friends and family members coming together at a planned time and place, but in an informal capacity, to draw attention to the self-destructive behavior (e.g., substance abuse, eating disorders, and gambling addiction) of a targeted person. When done properly, an intervention is an effective way to get people to conform to the norm and seek help for their deviant behavior. Some people might wonder whether an intervention really qualifies as a shaming. However, when we realize that the primary purpose of an intervention is to draw attention to the targeted person that her behaviors are destructive and counter to the norms of the group and that those involved with the intervention *are* trying to alter the identity of the targeted person, it is safe to refer to intervention as a type of planned informal shaming (Delaney 2008).

Informal shamings are very prevalent. They are popular because people seem to enjoy informally shaming others. Finding joy at the expense of others is an aspect of the concept of "schadenfreude." Schadenfreude refers to gaining satisfaction, pleasure, or joy at someone else's misfortune, especially a friend's or close associate's. Schadenfreude is an aspect of the growing culture of shamelessness. Whether it involves schadenfreude or not, chances are everyone has been victimized numerous times by some sort of informal shaming. Informal shamings begin early in life. For example, when a child misbehaves and is given a "time-out" or sent to his or her room, the child is being socially isolated. The punishment is designed to draw attention to misbehavior in an attempt to point out to the punished child that he or she needs to conform to social expectations. Children, like adults, may also be subject to informal shamings from their peers. Neighborhood kids playing a game may mock and tease a child who does not fully understand the rules of the game. Acquaintances and friends alike may use hurtful words (e.g., "slut," "whore," "redneck," "moron," "hick," and a slew of other words) in an attempt to shame and embarrass others. A member of an intimate couple who attempts to fulfill a sexual fetishism by trying a new sexual act may be rebuffed by the partner who calls him a "pervert" or "sicko." Subcultural groups reinforce group norms and expectations among their members in a variety of shameful ways, including initiations and unique punishments for violating group norms. Pulling pranks on friends and family members is designed to embarrass unsuspecting others and thus is a form of informal shaming.

The mass media may shame people as well. The manner in which news stories are broadcast can be designed to make fun of someone who engaged in some sort of transgression (that has nothing to do with criminal issues), or they can be outright vicious in their attack against someone who engaged in behavior they deemed vile. For example, one of the big shaming news stories of 2015 was directed against Walter Palmer, a Minnesota dentist and big-game hunter who killed a beloved wild animal in Zimbabwe, the lion known as Cecil. Palmer and his family faced threats—including death threats—and saw worldwide protests unfold, including demonstrations outside his Bloomington dentist office after the Zimbabwe Conservation Task Force reported that Cecil was lured out of Hwange National Park and shot with a compound bow. Palmer had a permit to hunt in Zimbabwe and stated, "I had no idea that the lion I took was a known, local favorite, was collared and part of a study until the end of the hunt. I relied on the expertise of my local professional guides to ensure a legal hunt" (McLaughlin 2015). Palmer did not face any formal (legal) charges in Zimbabwe, but he was certainly shamed by the media and social media alike. In addition to news reporters, sports commentators on televised sports broadcasts often make fun of people, especially those who cannot catch a foul ball or who have fallen asleep during a game. A number of musicians and singers (e.g., Taylor Swift, Carly Simon, Alanis Morissette, No Doubt, The Notorious B.I.G., and Tupac Shakur) have written songs about past lovers or musical rivals in an attempt to publicly but informally shame them. Jimmy Kimmel, the host of ABC's *Jimmy Kimmel Live*, started a campaign in April 2015 that asked viewers to send him photos of people doing annoying and inappropriate things while making sure that the photographer pointed a finger of shame toward the transgression that would be a part of the photo. (Using a finger gesture of shame is the theme of a *Simpsons* episode that is described in box 13.1.) He referred to this campaign as the "Finger of Shame" (Sedgwick 2015). Kimmel crossed his mass media Finger of Shame campaign over to social media as well by having people send their photos to his Twitter or Instagram account with the hashtag#FingerOfShame. From time to time, Kimmel airs photos on his TV show.

CONNECTING SOCIAL DEVIANCE AND POPULAR CULTURE

Box 13.1 "Shame On You! Shame On Your Whole Ill-Mannered Town"

In *The Simpsons* episode "There's Something about Marrying" (#345), Bart Simpson and his best friend Milhouse Van Houten attempt to trick Barney Gumble, the Springfield town drunk, with a beer inside a trap. But Barney is wise to the pranking behaviors of the two boys and manages to avoid being shamed by them. Bart tells Milhouse, "We need someone new we can prank." At that moment, a turnip truck drives past Bart and Milhouse and a man falls off the back of it (full pun intended by *The Simpsons* writers, as now Bart and Milhouse had a bumpkin, an unsophisticated and naïve person, who literally fell off a turnip truck!). The man's name is Howell Huser. Huser introduces himself to the boys and explains that he is a traveler who likes to learn about local folklore. Bart and Milhouse quickly sum up Huser as an easy "mark" in their need to shame and embarrass someone for their own shameless joy.

Huser falls victim to one prank after another. The boys laugh hysterically at his follies. Huser is so humiliated and upset with Bart and Milhouse that he "shames" them. Shaking his hand with the index finger raised (the "classic" shaming gesture), Huser looks at Bart and states, "Shame on you." He then turns to Milhouse and proclaims, "And shame on you." Huser turns away from the boys and aims his shaming gesture toward various Springfield buildings and yells, "Shame on your whole ill-mannered town." While Huser is shaming the entire town, he points toward a group of Springfield tough kids, Jimbo, Dolph, and Kearney. They overhear everything Huser is spouting and they do not take too kindly to being shamed. Dolph angrily points out, "My self-esteem sure didn't need that."

Sensing impending danger from the tough kids, Huser runs away. The boys taunt Huser by saying things like "loser" and "Get out, shamer." The rowdies throw rocks at Huser, who is saved when the same turnip truck, which is now heading out of town, drives by. Huser jumps on the back of the truck and makes the other "classic" shaming gesture of rubbing one index finger over the other, toward the whole town of Springfield as he rides away. Bart comments, "I don't think we'll be hearing from him again." A few days later, however, while the Simpson family is watching television, Huser appears on the Soft News Network. Huser, as it turns out, is actually a reporter for the network who tours small towns and writes fluff stories about his travels. He is clearly upset and blasts Springfield in his report. Huser gives Springfield his lowest score. As a result of Huser's media shaming, Springfield's tourism suffers tremendously.

As we know, social media plays a huge role in the daily lives of most people and is certainly the site of countless acts of informal shaming. As with other forms of informal shaming, both individuals and other social institutions, such as the mass media, may utilize social media in an attempt to informally shame others who have breached social norms and etiquette. Individuals may make posts that are meant to jokingly embarrass others, such as posting a compromising photo of someone and creating a meme with degrading comments. Birthday wishes are sometimes borderline brutal, especially the older someone turns. Do a Google search of "Internet shaming, images" and you will find a wide variety of photos of people who have shamed their friends, children, pets, and just about anyone else. Among the photos I found was one of a girl who looked like a young teenager standing next to what appears to be her dad with her holding a big sign that reads, "I sneak boys in at 3am and disrespect my parents and grandparents." Another image showed a baby sleeping in a crib with a sign that read, "I fart like an adult." The number of photos is nearly endless. And it does not end with photos; posting videos is also very popular. Among the more popular shaming videos that trended in 2015 was the "ugly haircut" video. In these videos, parents take electric razors to the heads of their misbehaving tweens and teens to create ugly cuts as a form of punishment, then publicly post the handiwork on YouTube, Facebook, and elsewhere (Associated Press 2015q). Anyone who has a Facebook, Twitter, Instagram, or any other social media account has surely seen a wide variety of these types of informal Internet posts and videos. In many instances, people use social media sites to shame people they do not know. They may do this just to be mean or vindictive or because they are trying to draw attention to a more serious norm violation. For example, while California was suffering through a severe drought in 2015 (continuing years of severe drought), and new rules were implemented in an attempt to get people to conserve water (e.g., you cannot hose down the sidewalk, you cannot wash your car with a hose that doesn't have a shutoff nozzle, and you cannot water your lawn between 9 a.m. and 5 p.m.), it became commonplace for the public to use a Twitter hashtag #droughtshaming, which is designed to embarrass people caught needlessly wasting water (Sternheimer 2015).

As this quick look at informal social control reveals, there are a great number of people, in a wide variety of ways, attempting to exert pressure and influence in hopes of influencing people to conform to social norms. In all of these cases, the people doing the shaming have no real power, and that is why their form of social control is informal. In the following pages, we will examine formal, or external, social control.

Formal (External) Social Control

With **formal social control** (sometimes called external or direct social control) regulation of behavior comes from exterior social control agents, such as law enforcement, the judicial system, the legislative system, and other authority figures (in contrast to informal social control, which is accomplished via self-control mechanisms). The common thread among these external social control agents is the realization that there are people in our lives who are watching our behavior. External social control agents not only observe our behavior, they have the right to dictate our behavioral choices because they have been given the authority to do so (e.g., law enforcement agencies have been given the right to enforce laws on behalf of the community in accordance to recognized political authorities). Those with legitimate authority are also in the position to levy sanctions against norm violators (e.g., law enforcement agents have the legal right to arrest lawbreakers). Formal sanctions (punishments) can be used for violations of specific rules and laws. The major reason for the use of formal sanctions is deterrence. *Deterrence* refers to the idea that the threat of punishment alone should be enough to stop individuals from breaking the law. Deterrence, then, is a type of prevention strategy designed to help stop people from violating social norms or breaking the law.

Prevention Strategies

Prevention strategies refer to the various techniques used to steer individuals away from the temptations of committing deviancy and crime and to keep them on the straight path toward law-abiding lifestyles. Prevention strategies, in general, fall into two categories: community programs and national programs. Community crime prevention programs or strategies target changes in community infrastructure, culture, or the physical environment in order to reduce crime. "The diversity of approaches include neighborhood watch, community policy, urban or physical design, and comprehensive or multi-disciplinary efforts. These strategies may seek to engage residents, community and faith-based organizations, and local government agencies in addressing the factors that contribute to the community's crime, delinquency, and disorder" (National Institute of Justice 2015a). Lowell, Massachusetts, for example, first instituted in 2005 the "Hot Spots Policy" crime reduction policing strategy that uses a disorder policy approach to concentrate on improving physical and social order in high-crime locations in its city. The strategy uses three approaches to reduce disorder-related crime:

- Increased misdemeanor arrests—This component entails the use of aggressive order maintenance techniques by police (e.g., making arrests for public drinking, conducting "stop and frisks" of suspicious individuals, and conducting foot patrol in high-crime areas) as a means of taking high-risk individuals off the street to reduce disorder-related crimes.
- Situational prevention strategies—This component involves a variety of measures broadly designed to improve physical and social disorder in target areas (e.g., installation of improved street lighting, implementation of video surveillance, dispersing groups of loiterers, performing code inspections, cleaning up vacant lots, razing abandoned buildings, and evicting problem residents) by promoting a generalized sense of order in problem areas.
- Social services actions—This component entails assistance from social service agencies to help police increase social order (e.g., providing youth with recreational opportunities, working with local shelters to provide housing for homeless individuals, and connecting problem tenants to mental health services) in order to create opportunities for high-risk individuals in targeted locations to assist police efforts to promote social order (National Institute of Justice 2015b).

The Hot Spots Policy program is based on the "broken windows" theory of crime, which postulates that crime is likely to flourish in areas with high levels of physical and social disorder.

One of the most well-known national deviance and crime prevention programs is the Boys and Girls Clubs of America (BGCA). The BGCA has been in existence for over a century and currently includes more than 1,140 independent organizations across the nation. In 2013, the BGCA provided youth developmental programs and training services to nearly 4 million children and teens (Boys and Girls Clubs of America 2015). The BGCA maintains a commitment to its core beliefs of character development and keeping kids off the streets and to provide them with a safe community facility under adult supervision. Clubs provide a wide variety of activities, including sports, recreation, arts and science education, and opportunities to learn life skills that will help form a solid foundation for youths as they become adults. The BGCA serves youths of all racial and ethnic backgrounds and partners with formal social control agents, such as the police, probation officers, and school officials, in an attempt to both help steer youths away from delinquency and crime (prevention) and to provide youths with useful skills (e.g., job interviewing and training) that will help them as they become adults.

While the two programs described above were quite specific examples of prevention strategies programs, the Center for Problem-Oriented Policing (2015) provides a more general scheme for a variety of situational prevention needs. That is to say, some of these prevention techniques might be applicable in addressing crime, while others might be more applicable for various forms of deviancy. These techniques of situational prevention are found in table 13.1.

Parents and guardians are the first direct social-control agents in the life of individuals. However, as we learned in the discussion of informal social control, while individuals are expected to internalize the socialization efforts introduced to them by the agents of socialization and learn to abide by the rules, not everyone willingly goes along with all the rules of society. Furthermore, the threat of punishment and implementation of a number of prevention programs and strategies is not enough deterrence to halt all deviant and criminal behavior. As a result, any given society will establish various suppression efforts in an attempt to ensure, or force, compliance.

Suppression Strategies

Suppression strategies are any attempts by law enforcement and the full force of the law to forcibly end, dissolve, or prohibit criminal activities. Suppression efforts generally come from three sources: law enforcement, the judicial system, and the legislative system.

Law Enforcement

The first line of defense against lawbreakers is law enforcement. The police are responsible for the suppression of street crime, while specific government regulatory agencies (e.g., the EPA, IRS, and FDA) are responsible to make sure various entities are not breaking other types of crimes (e.g., white collar crime, political crime, and organized crime). The suppression process generally includes police getting to know the nature and scope of criminal activity within their jurisdictions, gathering information and intelligence, creating a comprehensive database, and developing strategies to eliminate, or at least reduce, criminal activity. Law enforcement suppression efforts are rather involved and start with the allocation of personnel (to deal with a particular set of problems in the community), receiving and managing calls for service or the identification of problems while on patrol, deploying personnel to a call, methods of patrol (e.g., foot, horse, bicycle, aircraft,

TABLE 13.1	Twenty-Five Techniques of Situational Prevention			
Increase the Effort	**Increase the Risks**	**Reduce the Rewards**	**Reduce Provocations**	**Remove Excuses**
1. Harden Targets * Steering column locks and immobilizers * Antirobbery screens * Tamper-proof packaging	*6. Extend Guardianship* * Take routine precautions (i.e., go out in groups) * Establish neighborhood watch	*11. Conceal Targets* * Off-street parking * Use unmarked cars	*16. Reduce Frustrations and Stress* * Efficient queues and polite service * Expanded seating * Soothing music/ muted lights	*21. Set Rules* * Rental agreements * Harassment codes * Hotel registration
2. Control Access to Facilities * Entry phones * Electronic card access * Baggage screening	*7. Assist Natural Surveillance* * Improved street lighting * Defensible space design * Support whistle-blowers	*12. Remove Targets* * Removable car stereos/radios * Prepaid cards for pay phones	*17. Avoid Disputes* * Separate sections for rival sports fans * Reduce crowding in pubs/bars * Fixed cab fares	*22. Post Instructions* * "No Parking" * "Private Property" * "Extinguish camp fires"
3. Screen Exits * Ticket needed for exit * Export documents * Electronic merchandise tags	*8. Reduce Anonymity* * Taxi driver IDs * "How's my driving?" decals	*13. Identify Property* * Property marking * Vehicle licensing and parts marking * Cattle branding	*18. Reduce Emotional Arousal* * Controls on violent pornography * Enforce good behavior at sporting events * Prohibit racial slurs	*23. Alert Conscience* * Roadside speed display boards * Signatures for customs declarations
4. Deflect Offender * Street closures * Separate bathrooms for women * Disperse pubs/ bars	*9. Utilize Place Managers* * Two clerks for convenience stores * Reward vigilance * Closed-circuit TV	*14. Disrupt Markets* * Monitor pawn shops * License street vendors * Controls on classified ads	*19. Neutralize Peer Pressure* * Remove troublemakers * "It's OK to say no" * "Idiots Drink and Drive"	*24. Assist Compliance* * Easy library checkout * Public lavatories * Litter bins
5. Control Tools/ Weapons * "Smart" guns * Disabling stolen cell phones * Restrict spray paint sales to juveniles	*10. Strengthen Formal Surveillance* * Red-light cameras * Burglar alarms * Security guards	*15. Deny Benefits* * Ink merchandise tags * Graffiti cleaning * Speed bumps	*20. Discourage Imitation* * Rapid repair of vandalism * V-chips in TVs * Censor details of modus operandi	*25. Control Drugs and Alcohol* * Breathalyzers in pubs/bars * Server intervention * Alcohol-free events

Source: Center for Problem-Oriented Policing 2015

watercraft, cruiser, and one-person or two-person patrols), deciding whether or not force is necessary and what type of force (e.g., use of a Taser, nightstick, or firearm), investigating a call or crime, deciding when to use discretion in making an arrest, booking and fingerprinting, incarceration, and turning the case over to prosecutors (Delaney 2014b).

How the police are perceived by citizens varies "based on global attitudes toward crime and social justice, past experiences with governmental agencies, and social status" (Gaines and Kappeler 2011:12). Research indicates that people who do not have contact with the police, presumably because they are law-abiding, have more favorable views of the police than citizens who do not have contact with them (Gaines and Kappeler 2011). Thus, with such incidents as riots (discussed in chapter 6), the manner in which the police are viewed by the public has a lot to do with one's past experience with law enforcement as to whether police actions are viewed as "acceptable" or as "out of line" and "unacceptable."

Law enforcement suppression efforts generally take two forms: proactive strategies and reactive strategies (Sanders 1994). Proactive strategies center on fact gathering so that the police can stop crime before it occurs. Most law enforcement agencies will enter data gathered into a computer program, such as COMPSTAT (an acronym for "computer statistics"). Reactive strategies involve the everyday interaction between law enforcement and law violators. Most police work is reactive. The typical police response involves answering a call of a reported crime or coming across a crime in progress. Many police agencies, especially those in large cities, have specialized task forces designed to combat specific types of criminal activity, such as a street gang task force or a SWAT (i.e., Special Weapons and Tactics) unit. Some law enforcement jurisdictions have some version of community policing. Community policing represents a shift in thinking of law enforcement as the sole watchmen over neighborhoods by giving local community members an active role as overseers. "Community policing is people-based as opposed to being bureaucratic or militaristic. It is about improving people's quality of life" (Kappeler and Gaines 2011:165).

A police officer arrests a driver for violating the law.

Judicial System

After a law enforcement officer makes an arrest, it is up to prosecutors to try and convict the perpetrator in a court of law in front of a judge (and perhaps a jury, depending on the type of case). Just as law enforcement may use discretion (personal judgment) when making an arrest, prosecutors sometimes use their own discretions as to whether to proceed to trial in specific cases. They may feel that the evidence is too weak or will not hold up in court; the suspect's prior arrest record is clean; the seriousness of the violation is too light; and whether or not they feel they can get a conviction (e.g., in cases where public sentiment is overwhelmingly with the accused).

Prosecution is a critical element in suppression efforts. The prosecutor is supposed to act in the best interest of the state (or "the people"). The prosecutor is also expected to support law enforcement suppression efforts and find additional information, when necessary, to gain a conviction. The prosecutor, then, is the second line of defense against crime, or "the regulator within the criminal justice system" (Shelden, Tracy, and Brown 2001:253).

The courts are, ideally, the legitimate segment of the criminal justice system. The court is presumed to consist of an unbiased judge, preexisting legal norms and rules that do not change depending on who is on trial, due process, and (typically) a jury of peers. The court is supposed to be a place where objectivity prevails. However, most judges in U.S. jurisdictions are elected and wish to be reelected. With that in mind, a judge's personal bias, subjectivity, and political ambition may at times interfere with the objectivity of judicial proceedings and sentencing. The latitude that judges enjoy during sentencing procedures has led a number of them to turn to alternative forms of punishment (especially for low-level offenders) that focus on shaming. Earlier in this chapter the topic of informal shamings was discussed. Within the context of judicial suppression efforts, formal shaming is applicable.

The purpose of any **formal shaming** is to make the offender feel extreme guilt for violating a law. In this regard, traditional punishment is not good enough. A formal shaming is used when a judge considers an offense so distasteful that the whole community should be made aware of it. Communal involvement reaffirms what Emile Durkheim labeled the "collective conscience." Durkheim (1938/1895) defines the collective conscience as "the totality of beliefs and sentiments common to average citizens of the same society" (p. 79). Durkheim believed that public ceremonies of punishments help to strengthen communal bonds. However, Durkheim also argued that public shamings are more characteristic of primitive societies than they are of modern societies.

Formal shamings can be viewed as degradation ceremonies. Degradation ceremonies represent attempts by others to alter one's identity. As with any ritualistic behavior, communication plays a role in degradation ceremonies. Harold Garfinkel (1956) states, "Any communicative work between persons, whereby the public identity of an actor is transformed into something looked on as lower in the local scheme of social types, will be called a 'status degradation ceremony'" (p. 420). Garfinkel, in contrast to Durkheim, suggests that all moral societies have degradation ceremonies and only those with total anomie (a sense of normlessness) do not. Garfinkel also believed that someone who goes through a degradation ceremony is stigmatized and should experience shame. There are many forms of degradation ceremonies in the United States, including the military (e.g., court-martial); the workplace (e.g., a "workplace mobbing"—a sinister form of psychological abuse conducted through innuendo, intimidation, harassment, badgering, humiliation, degradation, and rumor); religious formal shamings (e.g., being "excommunicated" from the church; the Amish "shunning" ceremony); sports shamings (e.g., being "cut" from the team via a press release; sports announcers that point out mistakes and mock the player); and judicial shamings. Some examples of judicial shamings include:

- In April 2014, Ohio Municipal Court Judge Gayle Williams-Byer order defendant Edmond Aviv to remain on a street corner for 5 hours with a sign that read, "I AM A BULLY! I pick on children that are disabled, and I am intolerant of those that are different from myself. My actions do not reflect an appreciation for the diverse South Euclid community that I live in" (*Prison Legal News* 2015).
- In November 2012, Shena Hardin, who was caught on camera passing a school bus by driving on a sidewalk, was ordered by Cleveland Ohio Municipal Court Judge Pinkey Carr to stand at an intersection wearing a sign that read, "Only an idiot would drive on the sidewalk to avoid a school bus" (*Prison Legal News* 2015).
- A Georgia judge gave Natasha Freeman, 38, a choice of spending 4 weekends in jail or wearing a sign to resolve charges related to her boarding a school bus to assault her 11-year-old cousin. Freeman chose to wear a sign that read, "I made a fool of myself on a Bibb County Public Schools' bus" for 1 week, starting on December 10, 2012 (*Prison Legal News* 2015).
- In a case of a more serious infraction, Montana District Judge G. Todd Baugh ordered Pace Anthony Ferguson, 27, to write "Boys do not hit girls" 5,000 times as part of his punishment for punching his girlfriend. The punishment took place 2 days before Christmas in 2013. Ferguson was also ordered to serve 6 months in jail and pay $3,800 in medical bills for fracturing the woman's face in three places (*Prison Legal News* 2015).

As part of her punishment for driving on a |sidewalk to avoid a Cleveland school bus that was unloading children, this woman was sentenced to hold a sign of her transgression in public and open to shaming by others.

- As another example of public shamings being utilized for offenses more serious than petty crimes, in 2012 a Texas man on probation for drunk driving was ordered to return to the scene of a crash he caused for 4 Saturdays from 9 a.m. to 5 p.m. with a sign reading, "I killed Aaron Coy Pennywell while driving drunk." The punishment only lasted a day, after the driver said he received death threats (The Marshall Project 2015).
- Many judges and jurisdictions post the names of violators for a variety of offenses on shaming websites. (In some cases these sites may only last for a short period, such as a year or two.) For example, in Boston, men who missed child-support payments found their photos displayed on subways and buses (Shipman 2006); in 2005, Tennessee passed legislation requiring convicted drunken drivers to wear orange vests reading "I am a Drunk Driver" while doing 24 hours of roadside trash pickup (Redhage 2006); and in 2010, Mayor Tom McMahon of Reading, Pennsylvania, created an online "Wall of Shame" feature blighted properties (Associated Press 2010).

Ideally, the judicial system works to keep innocent people found not guilty, and guilty people incarcerated. Unfortunately, this is not always the case. The U.S. judicial system has, however, used incarceration as a form of punishment so frequently, it leads the world in incarceration rates. (See box 13.2 for a look at incarceration in the United States.)

A CLOSER LOOK

Box 13.2 United States Correctional Population

The United States has the highest correctional population in the world. According to the Bureau of Justice Statistics (BJS) (2015), "The total correctional population consists of all offenders under the supervision of adult correctional systems, which includes offenders supervised in the community under the authority of probation or parole agencies and those held in the custody of state or federal prison or local jails." With this description in mind, the total number of people to make up the correctional population of the United States in 2012 was over 2.2 million, which equates to slightly more than 700 per 100,000 population (World Prison Brief 2015). The American Psychological Association (APA) reports that in comparison, the Russian Federation has 474 per 100,000, followed by Ukraine, 286; Iran, 284; Poland, 209; Turkey, 188; Hungary, 186; and estimates for China at 124 to 173 per 100,000. On the opposite end of the spectrum, Finland has just 58 per 100,000 population in the correctional population; Sweden, 67; Norway, 73; Denmark, 73; Germany, 77; Switzerland, 82; and the Netherlands, 82 (APA 2014).

This 2.2 million correctional population figure equates to nearly 25 percent of the world's total correctional population despite the fact that the United States has only 5 percent of the world's population (APA 2014). Slightly more than 20 percent of the total correctional population are pretrial detainees/remand prisoners. A little more than 9 percent (9.3) are females, and the percentage of foreigners in the total U.S. correctional population is around 5.5 percent (World Prison Brief 2015). Over the past four decades, the nation's "get-tough-on-crime" policies are a contributing factor to the large correctional population in the United States. A closer look at this population reveals that the prisons and jails consist largely of poor, under-educated people of color, about half of whom suffer from mental health problems (APA 2014).

In 2010, the number of people actually incarcerated in U.S. jails and prisons was about 1.6 million, for a rate of about 500 per 100,000 residents. Since 2002, the United States has had the highest incarceration rate in the world (Tsai and Scommegna 2015). The American judicial system's tough sentencing laws and record number of imprisoned nonviolent drug offenders contribute to the high incarceration rate found in the United States. According to data provided by Congress's Joint Economic Committee, drug offenders constitute nearly 33 percent of the prison population. An estimated 60 percent of the incarcerated drug offenders are nonviolent (passive users or minor dealers) (Webb 2009). "The continued incarceration of drug offenders has done nothing to break-up the power of the multibillion-dollar illegal drug trade" (Webb 2009:5).

The BJS (2015) reported that the United States held an estimated 1,561,500 prisoners in state and federal custody at the end of 2014, down 1 percent from the previous year (and down from the 2010 figure cited previously). This was the smallest incarceration rate in the United States since 2005 and the second largest decline in more 35 years. The BJS (2015) reports that of those in custody, an estimated 37 percent were black males, followed by 32 percent white males and 22 percent Hispanic males. The number of drug offenders incarcerated remains startling high with 50 percent of federal inmates and 16 percent of state prisoners convicted of drug offenses. In comparison, only 53 percent of state prisoners and 7 percent of federal prisoners were serving time for violent offenses.

Legislative System

While law enforcement and prosecutors represent the "first and second lines of defense" in suppression efforts, they must all work within the framework of the law; in other words, they must "play the hand they were dealt." Both law enforcement and the judicial system must uphold the laws passed by the legislative system. The legislative system is the branch of the government that is empowered to make laws that are then enforced by law enforcement and interpreted by the judicial branch. Legislative bodies respond to the requests/demands of both law enforcement and the judicial system as well as the general public. The will of the people is very important, especially considering that the general public elected legislators to represent their needs.

Legislators make laws for a variety of reasons, including to suppress crime. Sociologists view the creation of laws as part of an ongoing social process that, ideally, entails representing the needs of the people. However, a number of sociologists, especially those that utilize the conflict perspective, would argue that those in power use the justice system to maintain their social status while at the same time keeping others subservient. Conflict theorists would point to the fact that a disproportionate number of racial minorities and lower-SES persons are arrested for criminal activities as partial evidence in support of their perspective. Structural functionalists would argue that the judicial system operates to help maintain the functioning of the social system (society) in its entirety. Symbolic interactionists would look at the symbolic meaning behind the creation of laws. In fact, every theoretical perspective would offer an interpretation of how and why laws are created.

The one thing that is universally understood about U.S. laws is that there are a lot of them. There are so many federal and state laws and ordinances that no single reporting entity seems to know exactly how many total laws exist. And yet we are supposed to live by the creed that "ignorance of the law is not a valid excuse for violating a law." Reynolds (2015) reports that estimates of the number of federal statutes that impose criminal sanctions during the years 2000–2015 alone range from 3,600 to approximately 4,500. On January 1, 2010, it is estimated that a total of 40,627 new laws went into effect (Search Amelia 2010). On January 1, 2012, an estimated 40,000 new laws were put on the books (Ashford-Grooms 2012). As this snapshot view of the number of laws on the books reveals, there are a lot of laws we are expected to abide by. Furthermore, with so many total laws on the books it is safe to say that from a statistical standpoint each of one of us is more likely to break a law today than we are not to break a law today. We are also very likely to violate a law of some sort nearly every day. If we combine this idea with the realization that we are all more likely to commit an act that someone considers deviant than we are to break a law, it should be clear that there is a great deal of social deviancy in society.

Treatment Strategies

Despite all efforts to prevent and suppress social deviancy, as the implication above indicates, society is never going to stop crime, let alone social deviancy. Additionally, the policy of incarcerating lawbreakers does not appear to be working, as it has not served as an effective deterrent. Because of this, a variety of treatment strategies have been established primarily as alternatives to imprisonment. (Note: Other forms of norm violation such as drug abuse have their own versions of treatment programs.)

In some instances, court officials may opt to employ such alternatives to secure detention (e.g., jails) and secure confinement (e.g., prisons/correctional facilities) as outright release. As the term "outright release" implies, law violators will not serve time behind bars or within confinement facilities but will instead be released upon making restitution or performing community services. In cases where offenses committed involve property damage, property loss, or personal injuries to victims, restitution may be deemed appropriate. Restitution programs have been designed to help offenders pay for the damage they caused. One option involves violators working at specific job sites chosen by the court where the offender does not receive a salary; instead, the money is taken by the court for payment to the victim. This is a good option for violators who deface property, especially with graffiti. Community service programs are a good option too, as they are less expensive to operate than restitution programs and involve far less paperwork for administrators.

Supervised release is applicable when outright release is deemed too risky because the offender is either unlikely to appear for adjudication or is likely to commit new offenses (Austin, Johnson, and Weitzer 2005). Supervised release comes in many forms, including home detention, probation, and electronic monitoring. Home detention requires offenders to remain at home during specified time periods: (1) at all times; (2) at all times except when in school or working; (3) at night (curfews). Supervisory conditions, such as drug testing, may also apply to home detention release. Probation can be either informal (when compliance is voluntary) or formal (when the court requires mandatory compliance in lieu of formal adjudication). Electronic monitoring (usually via an ankle or wrist attachment) is utilized when the court decides that the offender is a potential risk to cause more harm/offenses (Austin et al. 2005). Supervised release is a very good alternative to incarceration for deserving offenders because it allows offenders an opportunity to remain in the community. If their behavior is positive, and they meet all the requirements of probation, offenders are free at the end of a designated period of time without having served jail/prison time.

Day and evening reporting centers represent another alternative to secure detention. They are nonresidential treatment programs that require offenders to report daily activities to case managers. Skills training programs are another example of a nonresidential alternative to secure detention and confinement. These programs are designed to teach offenders specific skills that will help them find work and, ideally, cut down on repeat law violations. Another alternative to secure detention is the residential programs. Residential programs are for youths awaiting adjudication and include home programs, detention homes, and programs for runaways that serve as alternatives to secure detention.

A number of social control agents are in a position to divert offenders, especially youths, away from formal court action. Law enforcement, for example, may, at their discretion, decide to "give a break" to certain offenders, such as juvenile delinquents, in the hope that eventually they will grow out of their delinquent ways and become productive members of society. While their discretion may be flawed at times, social control agents can help "save" the lives of offenders who did break the law. Diversion, then, takes place when law enforcement and court personnel exercise their discretion to keep an individual from entering the judicial system. One variation of a diversionary treatment program is sentencing violators to a "boot camp" or a "shock therapy" program. **Parole** is a common type of "aftercare" treatment program in that offenders who were incarcerated are released early but must meet a number of criteria while released in order to avoid being sent back to a detention or confinement facility.

There are a number of treatment programs and therapies designed to help keep offenders out of trouble. Some examples include:

- Transactional analysis—A treatment approach primarily concerned with evaluating and interpreting interpersonal relationships and the dynamic transactions between the client (e.g., the offender) and the environment.
- Cognitive therapies—Cognitive therapy concentrates on thoughts, assumptions, and beliefs. With cognitive therapy approaches, people are encouraged to recognize and to change faulty or maladaptive thinking patterns. The cognitive behavioral therapy/treatment (CBT) approach involves patients identifying and changing their dysfunctional beliefs, thoughts, and patterns of behavior that contribute to problems. Thus, CBT is a problem-focused approach form of treatment. Its underlying principle is that thoughts affect emotions, which then influence behaviors (OJJDP 2010b).
- Vocational training—An atypical treatment approach that does not address the interpersonal dynamics of human behavior or spend a large time on diagnosis. Vocational training provides the client with vocational counseling in order to increase the client's knowledge of career choices and how to address job specifications and qualification requirements (Trojanowicz, Morash, and Schram 2001).
- Behavior therapy, better known as behavior modification—This treatment approach is based on principles of learning theory as well as of experimental psychology and attempts to modify the undesired behaviors of offenders through a series of therapeutic sessions (Trojanowicz, Morash, and Schram 2001).

There are any number of other treatment approaches beyond those described above, including community-based treatment and therapy programs and a wide variety of prison/correctional facility treatment programs designed to modify undesired behaviors and replace them with desired behaviors and/or vocational skills training.

Summary

Deviant behavior is tied to the violation of societal or group norms and expectations. It follows that if any group, organization, or society takes the time to establish rules, norms, and laws, it will also find a way to try and enforce them. The methods used in attempts to encourage, or force, compliance are accomplished via various social control mechanisms. Most people conform to the vast majority of rules and laws because we were socialized to do so. As a result, the socialization process is a critical element of social control. People who deviate from cultural expectations are generally stigmatized and punished. Stigmatization is coupled with feelings of shame and embarrassment. A growing number of people, however, do not feel the same sense of shame and embarrassment for their deviant behaviors, which, in turn, has fueled a growing culture of shamelessness.

Social control is accomplished informally and formally. Informal, or internal, social control regulates behavior through ideological or cultural manipulation. It is accomplished through the internalization of norms, values, and beliefs via the socialization process wherein people learn to accept the rules presented to them. When individuals accept the ideas and norms introduced to them, they have internalized society's expectations. Informal social control is a type of self-control. Examples of informal social control include honor codes and informal shamings.

The second type of social control is formal, sometimes called external or direct social control. Formal social control is in contrast to informal social control, which is accomplished via self-control mechanisms. With formal social control, regulation of behavior comes from exterior social control agents, such as law enforcement, the judicial system, legislative system, and other authority figures. The common thread among these external social control agents is the realization that there are people in our lives who are watching our behavior. External social control agents not only observe our behavior, they have the right to dictate our behavioral choices because they have been given the authority to do so. Those with legitimate authority are also in the position to levy sanctions against norm violators (e.g., law enforcement agents have the legal right to arrest lawbreakers). Formal sanctions (punishments) can be used for violations of specific rules and laws. The major reason for the use of formal sanctions is deterrence. In this chapter we learned about prevention strategies, suppression strategies (law enforcement, judicial system, and the legislative system), and treatment strategies.

Key Terms

affluenza, 357

agents of socialization, 354

culture of shamelessness, 357

formal shaming, 373

formal social control, 368

honor codes, 363

informal shamings, 365

informal, or internal, social control, 363

parole, 377

prevention strategies, 369

primary groups, 353

social control, 352

socialization, 352

stigma, 358

suppression strategies, 370

Discussion Questions

1. How has socialization affected the manner in which you view social norms and societal law? What agents of socialization have had the most profound effect in your life?

2. Do you believe there is a growing culture of shamelessness in society? Explain.

3. Which variation of social control—informal or formal—do you believe is the most effective in curbing deviant behavior?

4. Identify and describe at least three types of informal shamings that you have been a part of and describe three types of formal shamings.

5. Explain the various prevention strategies utilized in society.

6. Describe the role of law enforcement in society. Do you believe they are doing an effective job in curtailing criminal behavior?

7. What is your reaction to learning about the high rate of incarceration in the United States compared to other countries?

CHAPTER 14

Social Deviance and Its Omnipresence

CHAPTER OBJECTIVES

After reading this chapter students should be able to:

- Explain how social deviance is omnipresent
- Describe various trending forms of social deviance
- Provide examples of serious variations of trending social deviance

- Explain what is meant by a desnuda and how it is an example of a trending form of social deviance
- Demonstrate a knowledge of examples of less serious, frivolous variations of trending social deviance

In *The Rules of Sociological Method*, Emile Durkheim (1938/1895) proclaims that even in a society of saints there will be "sinners." This idea regarding social deviance comes about as a result of the realization that those in power will always find fault in the attitudes, behaviors, and conditions ("ABCs of Deviance") of others. Furthermore, this notion of social deviance underscores Durkheim's overall sentiment of deviance—following years of study of human behavior in his own society, neighboring, and past societies—that deviance is a common thread shared by all cultures. Durkheim found that all societies have determined that certain human behaviors are deviant, and therefore he put forth the view that the commonness of deviance was most likely associated with its necessity. Utilizing a functionalist perspective, Durkheim argued that deviance, and crime, serve a valuable function in society (e.g., reaffirm the common morality and collective conscience), as they bring together the members of society who share a common notion of "right" and "wrong," thus reaffirming society's bond and its adherence to certain standards of expected behavior. The existence of laws and norms represents a shared sense of morality within society. Durkheim (1984/1893) argued that certain acts go against the collective conscience not because they are criminal, but rather they are criminal because they counter the collective conscience. In addition, we do not condemn specific acts because they are crimes, but rather they are crimes because we condemn them.

In an effort to support his outlook on deviant behavior Durkheim argued that even in a society of monks (or what he refers to as "saints"), deviance would not disappear. Instead, certain behaviors among the saints, such as eating too much, speaking too loudly or softly, or failing to clean one's own room in a timely manner would come to be defined as "deviant." Thus, a society consisting of saints, who committed no criminal offenses or acts that outside societies would consider deviant, would still find characteristics of human behavior that would be labeled as deviant. Petty deviant behaviors such as those committed by "saints" but mostly ignored by societies with more serious issues of social deviance (e.g., murder, robbery, and bullying) would attract reactions worthy of serious punishment. This notion supports the realization that in large cities law enforcement pays close attention to more serious crimes while paying far less attention to petty crimes; while smaller towns, mostly devoid of serious crimes, place a high focus on curtailing petty offenses and variations of social deviance.

Interestingly, Durkheim also believed that deviant behavior helps to stimulate innovation and social change. The idea of thinking "outside of the box" (innovation) is based on the notion that if everyone followed all the established rules of conduct and behavior, thought processes would become devoid of creativity. For example, less than a century ago the notion of humans walking on the moon was considered ludicrous by the vast majority of people, and yet humans *have* walked on the moon and are likely to soon walk on Mars. As demonstrated by the reactivist perspective of deviance, thinking and acting outside the norm may lead to positive change. Durkheim believed that social deviance can lead to social change, as it may stimulate a reevaluation of certain behaviors on the part of the members of that society. Therefore, an activity that was once considered deviant (e.g., tattoos and piercings) may be reconsidered and become part of the norm simply because it gained support from a large portion of the society. In short, deviance can help a society to rethink its boundaries, and ignite social change.

Social Deviance *Is* Omnipresent

Durkheim's idea that social deviance exists in all societies, past, present, and future, leads to the realization that it is **omnipresent**. The previous chapters pay testament to the realization that social deviance is very diverse and widespread. A quick review of the previous chapters is provided below.

The Deviant World We Live In

In chapter 1, we learned about the difficulty in defining "deviance," and as a result five perspectives were presented and applied throughout the text. We also learned that deviance involves the judgment and evaluation of the behaviors of others; morality; a matter of context; what is considered deviant changes over time; and it varies from one culture and subculture to the next. In chapter 2, social deviance was connected to social problems, both subjective and objective variations. Among the specific topics discussed were unemployment; social stratification and poverty; and obesity and the associated health concerns associated with obesity. A wide variety of examples of deviance were discussed in chapter 3 when social deviance was explained via a number of sociological, psychological, biological, and demonic possession perspectives.

Chapters 4 and 5 discussed a large number of deviant behaviors that are labeled criminal. In chapter 4, we looked at white collar crime (securities fraud, identity fraud and theft, credit and debit card fraud, health care and health insurance fraud, extortion, forgery, insider trading, occupational crime, and unsafe products); political crime (political corruption, bribery, espionage, treason, and political torture); and organized crime (Italian Mafia and Russian Mafia). Chapter 5 examined the two major subcategories of street crime: violent offenses (homicide, robbery, assault and battery, and rape/sexual assault), including the demographic characteristics of violent crime victims; and property offenses (burglary, larceny-theft, motor vehicle theft, arson, and vandalism).

The many forms of violence found in society warranted their own chapter. As explained in chapter 6, violence takes many forms, some of which are criminal and some of which are not. The chapter began with a quick look at some of the theories that attempt to explain why violence occurs, and continued with a discussion of some broad categories and specific examples of violence that included self-directed violence (self-harm, suicide, and suicide by cop); interpersonal violence (bullying, hazing, "bum fights," and intimate interpersonal violence); and collective violence (riots and war).

Chapters 7 and 8 focused on two longtime standard topics in the study of social deviance: alcohol and other drugs. Chapter 7 discussed alcohol and its effects, including a brief history of alcohol use and the effects of alcohol; alcohol abuse and alcoholism, including the causes of alcoholism and alcohol use disorder (AUD) in the United States; behaviors associated with problem drinking (binge drinking, health problems associated with problem drinking, alcohol use and crime, and drunk driving); a number of deviant behaviors associated with alcohol use that are "justified" by drunk persons and therefore brushed aside as excusable (public intoxication, public nuisance, indecent exposure, relationship issues, and acting impulsively); and research on drunk shamings conducted by the author. In chapter 8 we explored explanations as to why people use drugs, factors that influence drug effects, and the categorization of drugs. We looked at specific categories of drugs including stimulants (caffeine, nicotine, cocaine/crack cocaine, methylphenidate, amphetamines, and methamphetamines); depressants (analgesics, sedatives, antipsychotics, and antidepressants); hallucinogens (both synthetic and natural); narcotics (medical use narcotics, opium, and heroin); inhalants; cannabis (marijuana and hashish); performance-enhancing drugs (anabolic steroids and human growth hormone); and prescription drug abuse and the role of Big Pharma.

With the advent of technology in nearly every sphere of life comes a corresponding dramatic increase in cybertechnology, the primary topic of chapter 9. Among the topics discussed in this chapter were cyberdeviancy and the individual level of victimization (catfishing, cyberbullying, cyberstalking, swatting, identity theft and fraud, and cyberscams); and cyberdeviancy at the large-scale level of victimization (e.g., banks/financial institutions, plastic cards/credit cards, and intellectual property rights victimization).

Mental illnesses and disorders were the topic of chapter 10. The idea of good mental health was contrasted with poor mental health. Other primary topics included various types of mental illnesses and disorders (depression, bipolar disorder, schizophrenia and other psychoses, dementia, dissociative disorders, posttraumatic stress disorder, and developmental disorders); a brief sociohistorical review of the treatment of the mentally ill was provided; and treatment procedures of the specific types of mental illness previously reviewed were provided.

Sexual social deviance was discussed in chapter 11. This is a particularly interesting topic, as some forms of sexual deviance are serious issues that may involve criminal activity while other forms may best be described as fetishisms. The topic of gender identity and sexual orientation was discussed, including such subject areas as LGBTQ and homophobia and conversion theory. Sexual harassment (the hostile work environment, stalking, and sexual assault and rape); pornography (porn addiction, is viewing porn an example of cheating, revenge porn, and child pornography); prostitution (street prostitution, brothel prostitution, escort services, and human sex trafficking); and sexual fetishism (the most popular sexual fetishes and the strangest sexual fetishes) were all reviewed.

The very important (and yet often-ignored subject matter in most social deviance books) topic of environmental social deviance was discussed in chapter 12. The chapter began with a discussion on the earth's limited carrying capacity and mass extinctions, the application of the environmental imagination, and the study of deviancy and the environment. The majority of the chapter focused on human behaviors that have a negative impact on the environment (human dependency on fossil fuels, climate change, hydraulic fracturing, the use of plastics, marine debris, food waste, e-waste, nuclear waste, medical waste, harmful agricultural practices, deforestation, and overpopulation) and human behaviors that have a positive impact on the environment (freeganism, green roofs/living roofs, urban farms and urban agriculture, and alternative forms of energy). The idea of stressing "rights" for the environment is presented at the end of the chapter.

The topic of social control was saved for chapter 13 so that the reader had time to acquaint him- or herself with the many broad and specific examples of social deviance. As presented in this chapter, the role of socialization, especially primary groups and the agents of socialization, have a significant role in whether individuals are likely to conform or deviate from the norm. The role of stigmatization and the culture of shamelessness were presented in an attempt to show the manner in which a growing number of people in contemporary society have attempted to avoid taking personal responsibility for their deviant behaviors. The two primary topics reviewed in this chapter were informal (internal) social control (honor codes and informal shaming) and formal (external) social control (prevention strategies, suppression strategies, and treatment strategies).

Trending Forms of Social Deviance

Despite the extensive coverage of various forms of social deviance provided throughout the text's first 13 chapters, there are still a number of other trending forms of deviant behaviors that range from serious violations (e.g., mass shootings) to less serious breaches of norms and etiquette (e.g., inappropriate selfies). In the following pages, a sampling of trending forms of deviance will be acknowledged.

Active and Mass Shootings, Terrorism, and Drones

Despite the relatively extensive coverage of the variations of homicide discussed in chapter 5 and the many variants of violence discussed in chapter 6, there are still a number of serious deviant subject areas that were saved for here. Perhaps the most serious violation of all is the topic of mass shootings. A **mass shooting** is a term used to refer to an incident involving multiple victims of gun violence. While mass shootings are not new, the number of incidents of this violent phenomenon has increased dramatically. The prevalence of mass shootings has led to a reexamination of how law enforcement agencies should describe such incidents. In 2014, the FBI (2014f) initiated the usage of the term "active shooting" incidents. **Active shooting** describes "a situation in which a shooting is in progress and an aspect of the crime may affect the protocols used in responding to and reacting at the scene of the incident" (FBI 2014f). Unlike other shooting incidents, an active shooting "inherently implies that both law enforcement personnel and citizens have the potential to affect the outcome of the event based upon their responses" (FBI 2014f). An active shooter is "an individual actively engaged in killing or attempting to kill people in a confined and populated area" (FBI 2014f).

The FBI reports that there were 45 active shooting incidents in the years 2000–2006 and 115 active shooting incidents in the years 2007–2013. The 160 total active shooting incidents between 2000 and 2013 resulted in an average of 11.4 incidents annually. Seventy percent of these incidents occurred in either a commerce/business or educational environment; 60 percent of the incidents ended before police arrived (FBI 2014f). The active shooting trend increased substantially in 2014 with nearly 1 active shooting incident every 3 weeks (Ingraham 2014). In 2015, the number of active shootings increased dramatically with an average at just about one per day (355 by December 2, 2015) for the entire calendar year (*CBS This Morning* 2015c). The December 2, 2015, San Bernardino active shooting incident, the deadliest on American soil since the December 14, 2012, Sandy Hook incident, resulted in 14 deaths and more than a dozen wounded during a workplace banquet at a social services center for the disabled. The frequency at which active shooting incidents occur is not only trending but has led law enforcement to encourage potential victims at the shooting site to either run away (if possible) or if possible attempt to take the shooter out of commission (by attacking the shooter/s). An active shooting incident typically lasts about 10 to 15 minutes.

In some cases, the active shooting incidents are linked to terrorist attacks. Terrorism, like active shootings, is not new but is a trending form of violent social deviance. The FBI (2015l) defines **terrorism** as "the unlawful use of force or violence against persons or property to intimidate or coerce a government, the civilian population, or any segment thereof in furtherance of political or social objectives." The FBI (2015l) further classifies terrorism as either domestic or international, depending on the origin, base, and objectives of the terrorist organization. The trending nature of terrorism has led the FBI to consider terrorism as its top priority in protecting U.S. citizens. Protecting the United States against foreign intelligence operations and espionage and against cyber-based attacks (see chapter 9) and high technology are the FBI's next two top priorities (FBI 2015m). The sociopolitical climate of the contemporary era has fueled an increasing number of threats of terrorism and incidents of terrorism. There are many complicated and not so complicated causes of terrorism, including political dimensions (e.g., instability and opportunity; superpower foreign policies that lead to global resentment; political repression and violent rebellion; and the rejection of political institutions) and religious and socioeconomic dimensions (e.g., religious intolerance; doomsday predictions; dependency on fossil fuels and the associated power by those who control them; and the drug trade) (Forest 2006).

One weapon the U.S. military and other nations across the globe use to combat terrorism is drones. Drones are the nickname for **unmanned aerial vehicles (UAVs)**. They are controlled by "pilots" from the ground sometimes, especially in the case of military use, autonomously following a preprogrammed mission. Military personnel justify the use of drones because they help to keep soldiers safe and because of the tasks that they can perform—close air support (giving support to troops on the ground by firing from the air); elimination of specific targets; and continuous surveillance of a specific area to allow suspected objects to be attacked immediately (Reaching Critical Will 2015). Some people, including drone protesters who have gone to jail to protest the use of drones, consider the use of drones as an example of social deviancy on the grounds that by removing one of the key restraints to warfare—the risk to one's own forces—unmanned systems make undertaking armed attacks too easy and will make waging war more likely to occur and because drones have been responsible for large numbers of civilian casualties. As early as 2010,

A private citizen flies his commercial drone.

more than 40 countries utilized drone technology, some of which had the capability to shoot laser-guided missiles ranging in weight from 35 pounds to more than 100 pounds (Reaching Critical Will 2015).

Consumer use of drones has also become increasingly popular. They've become so popular that the Federal Aviation Administration requires that all drones, not just those used for commercial purposes (e.g., companies use drones for delivering packages), be registered. Drones generally come equipped with cameras, but many people have modified them to carry weapons. The potential threat from drones is just beginning to trend. Rogue drone operators are rapidly becoming a national nuisance, invading sensitive airspace (one landed on the White House lawn) and private property (they have been used to spy on neighbors and to peep into bedroom windows and on sunbathers in private lawns). In 2015 alone, drones were used to smuggle illegal drugs, tobacco, and pornographic videos into prisons; they have smashed against buildings, including a Cincinnati skyscraper; impeded efforts to fight wildfires in California; and nearly collided with three airliners over New York City (Whitlock 2015). If everyday citizens can make such intrusions into the social fabric of society, imagine what drones can do when used as terroristic weapons. The deviant and criminal behaviors that could be associated with drone use are nearly limitless—think of such things as gang drive-by drone shootings as part of their initiation ceremonies and terrorists flying them into the engines of commercial airplanes.

An addition to the threat posed by drones to airliners is the use of laser pointers. Laser pointers as small as pocket-sized can reach helicopters and aircraft flying overhead. In fact, ever since laser pointers were first introduced as a cheap, consumer-use device in the 1990s, they have been used in a variety of deviant ways, including pointing them at other people, animals, and most recently toward aircraft. "The light originating from the ground reaches the cockpit of planes; it's also magnified considerably by their Plexiglas windows. The pilot's field of vision is compromised as the light comes in bursts, a strobe effect the FBI compared to setting off a camera flash in a dark room. At distances of up to 1200 feet, it can engulf a cockpit. It remains a distraction hazard all the way up to 12,000 feet" (Rossen 2015). A federal law passed in 2012 made **lasing** (the act of pointing a laser at a specific object) aircraft punishable by up to 5 years in prison. The FBI pays up to $10,000 for information leading to the arrest of any individual who intentionally aims a laser at an aircraft (FBI 2014g).

U.S. Secretary of Transportation Norman Mineta learns about the problem of lasers being aimed at commercial aircraft during a 747 simulator demonstration at the Mike Monroney Aeronautical Center in Oklahoma City.

Nothing in Particular (Nones) and Swearing

As we learned in chapter 1, deviance has a great deal to do with judging and evaluating the behavior of others. In many instances, deviance is also associated with ideals of morality. We also know that culture is subject to constant change. Often, constructs of morality and proper behavior among the masses lag behind those who move beyond the traditional way of thinking. As a result, emerging forms of behavior may conflict with the established, socially preferred expectations of behavior. The examples discussed below fall into this category of trending social deviance because they are not nearly as serious as such things as active shootings and drone attacks but more serious than someone who checks their smartphone for messages while at a movie theater.

Consider for example the growing number of "nones" in the United States. The term **nones** is used by the Pew Research Center to describe Americans who have identified themselves as believing in "nothing in particular" when it comes to religious identification. While the United States was founded on the principle of secular idealism and freedom of, and freedom from, religion, many citizens have very strong beliefs about the role of religion, Christianity in particular, as a basis of morality. The Pew Research Center reports, "Religious 'nones' are not only growing as a share of the U.S. population, they are becoming more secular over time by a variety of measures, a fact that also is helping to make the U.S. public overall somewhat less religious, according to surveys done as part of our Religious Landscape Study" (Lipka 2015). The nones include people who self-identify as atheists or agnostics, as well as those who say their religion is "nothing in particular," and now make up 23 percent of U.S. adults, up from 16 percent in 2007; most of the nones, however, say that they do believe in God. Still, the Pew Research Center reports that only 27 percent of the nones are absolutely certain about God's existence, down from 36 percent in 2007. And fully a third of religiously unaffiliated Americans (33 percent) now say they do *not* believe in God, up 11 percentage points over that time (Lipka 2015). Other 2014 characteristics of the nones include 65 percent who report that religion is "Not too/not at all" important; 62 percent "Seldom/never" pray; and 91 percent attend religious services "A few times a year or less."

The United States is a nation of moderate modesty when it comes to how people dress in public. Women, and men, are allowed to wear relatively skimpy and revealing outfits in public. This is certainly not the case in Muslim nations, where women are not only expected to cover their bodies but in many cases cover their hair and face. Research conducted by the University of Michigan's Institute for Social Research conducted in seven Muslim-majority countries (Tunisia, Egypt, Iraq, Lebanon, Pakistan, Saudi Arabia, and Turkey) finds that most people prefer that a woman completely cover her hair but not necessarily her face (Poushter 2014). Muslims, and a number of Americans alike, would be alarmed with some of the street performers found in New York's Times Square, especially the daily routine of desnudas. **Desnuda** is a Spanish word meaning naked/nude that has been embraced by the women who strut around the Times Square pedestrian plaza topless and covered in body paint to pose for photos in exchange for tips (Wright 2015). The earliest sighting of a desnuda in Times Square would appear to date to the summer of 2013. They are primarily Latina women who make about $300 a day in tips from taking photos with tourists. The desnudas have joined a slew of other street entertainers, such as Disney and superhero characters, as well as the famous "Naked Cowboy" (Robert Burck) and "Naked Cowgirls" (Burck's wife and female associates). The "painted ladies," as desnudas are also known, have their critics, most of

A street performer dressed up as the Statue of Liberty in Times Square, New York.

whom object to their scanty attire, their paint rubbing off on their clothing, or being aggressively asked for money to have their photo taken with them. While it is legal for women to go topless in New York City (as well as in most states and jurisdictions that allow men to go shirtless), some people consider this a form of deviant behavior. At present, however, desnudas and women going topless is a trendy phenomenon.

The public use of cuss, or curse, words (profanity) is generally considered in poor taste and therefore deviant; this is true despite the common usage of swear words. But why do some people swear in public, and why do others condone the use of vulgar words? As for the origin of swear words used by English-speaking people, we must take into account that the English language is the result of pillaged words from Latin, Greek, Dutch, Arabic, Old Norse, Spanish, Italian, Hindi, and other influences. Following the Norman Conquest of England nearly 1,000 years ago, a two-tiered linguistic society emerged, with the nobles speaking old English with a Gallo-Roman dialect that descended from Latin and was spoken in northern France, the ancestor of modern French, and the peasants speaking a dialect influenced from German origins. The nobles would describe the peasants' way of talking as "vulgar"—a word derived from Latin and meaning "of the crowd"—with certain words, which we now call swear words, considered to be of especially poor taste because of cultural prejudice (*Oxford Dictionaries* 2015). As a result, the English would consider certain words and ways of talking as "high talk" (high culture) and others as "low talk" (low culture). For example, the words we use to describe one's residence reflect a cultural divide. The German word *haus* (house) can mean anything from a ramshackle hut to 1600 Pennsylvania Avenue and would be used by common people, while the word "mansion," from the French word *maison*, would refer to a grand residence of the wealthy (*Oxford Dictionaries* 2015).

In the 18th and 19th centuries, the English were expected to embrace linguistic delicacy, which meant, among other things, the avoidance of taboo swear words. As a form of revolt from such conditions of repression, obscene words came into their own and were used in nonliteral ways. The use of swear words was meant to shock and offend others (Mohr 2013). Among the earliest swear words used by the English was the term "bloody"—as in, "He was bloody drunk." Words such as "bloody," "f**k," and "c*nt" were used in English plays and publications during the 18th and 19th centuries, but they became increasingly associated with a negative connotation during the Victorian era. The English of this era also used the term "bugger" in a nonliteral manner (it is a direct word for anal intercourse, or for the person who does the penetrating during said anal intercourse) and could be applied to men and women. Today, the term "bugger" is used almost exclusively toward men. The words "b*tch" and "c*nt" were once directed toward women only but today are applied to men and women in England. The word "sh*t" used to be applied to men only—as in "He's a regular sh*t"—but now can be applied to men and women.

The progression of the usage of swear words as a means of expressing a rejection of the status quo and the power elites has only expanded in the more recent era. Many people swear today not only as an expression against authority figures but because it makes us feel better. Psychologist Timothy Jay believes that swearing is positively correlated with extraversion and "Type A" hostility but negatively correlated with agreeableness, conscientiousness, religiosity, and sexual anxiety. Jay (2009) further argues that "swearing persists because taboo words can communicate emotion information (anger, frustration) more readily than nontaboo words, allowing speakers to achieve a variety of personal and social goals with them (utility)" (p. 153). Swearing may represent an attempt by people to take ownership of certain words that were directed toward them and meant to cause harm. In this manner, taking ownership is a means of regaining power. Among the examples are women who have claimed ownership of such words as "b*tch" and "c*nt" and African Americans who have claimed ownership of "n*gger." When groups take ownership of divisive words, they not only own the term, they have lessened the negative harmful impact on the group. Perhaps the best way to determine whether someone has truly gained ownership of offensive terms is to see how they react when called names by people outside their identifying group; for example, when a man calls a woman a "b*tch" or "c*nt" or a white person calls an African American a "n*gger." If the targets of these words react angrily, they have not truly taken ownership of these offensive terms; otherwise, it would not have bothered them. As we learned in chapter 2, a number of LGBTQ persons have embraced the term "queer" and are not offended by people who call them queer. Thus, they have successfully taken ownership of the term "queer."

Today, swearing is so commonplace that people of all ages, but especially young adults, and people of all social classes, but especially those from the lower and middle classes, and females as commonly as males swear in public settings. It is so common it can be described as trending. Despite its statistically commonplace status, it is still considered a deviant form of communication, especially in polite and proper settings. It is especially considered deviant on public broadcasts. The use of vulgarity on public airways was cleverly articulated by comedian George Carlin's routine on the "Seven Dirty Words" and is still relevant today (see box 14.1).

CONNECTING SOCIAL DEVIANCE AND POPULAR CULTURE

Box 14.1 The Seven Dirty Words

Throughout the early 1960s, comedian Lenny Bruce (Leonard Alfred Schneider) was arrested on obscenity charges following his stand-up routines, which included the use of such obscenities as "c**ks*cker," f**k," and "tits." Bruce was eventually blacklisted from performing in most U.S. clubs because of his use of profanity. Bruce attempted, and succeeded, in shocking and offending countless Americans. During one of Bruce's performances in 1966, he used nine words—ass, balls, c**ks*cker, c*nt, f**k, motherf**ker, p*ss, sh*t, and tits—that would lead to his arrest. (Note: Later that year, Bruce died at age 40, following a drug overdose.)

Bruce influenced many young comedians, including George Carlin. On May 27, 1972,

Carlin took to the stage for a show at the Santa Monica (California) Civic Auditorium to record his *Class Clown* album, which was scheduled to be released that fall. Carlin, as much a counterculture force as Bruce, with his long hair, a thick beard, earrings, and propensity for recreational drugs, wrote material that was designed to upset some people and appease others (Bella 2012). One of his tracks on *Class Clown* was titled "Seven Words You Can Never Say on Television." The seven words Carlin employed were the last seven of those previously used words by Bruce. On his next album, *Occupation: Foole* (1973), Carlin performed a similar routine titled "Filthy Words" that dealt with the same list of seven dirty words. Following a complaint about Carlin's seven dirty words routine to the Federal Communications Commission (FCC), the Supreme Court ruled in 1978 (*Federal Communications Commission v. Pacifica Foundation*, 438 U.S. 726), in a 5–4 decision, that the FCC had the right to bar the use of the seven dirty words, stating that it did not violate the First or Fifth Amendments. The decision formally established indecency regulation in American broadcasting.

Since the Supreme Court's landmark decision that gave the FCC the right to regulate the content on public airways, many entities have challenged the ruling. The FCC (2015) reports that it receives numerous complaints that television and/or radio networks, stations, or their employees or guests have broadcast extreme, incorrect, or somehow improper political, economic, or social statements. Some complaints claim that the content of specific broadcasts may endanger the United States or its people, or threaten our form of government, our economic system, or established institutions like the family or marriage. The FCC claims that it does not want to impede the rights of people to express opposing viewpoints and instead is primarily concerned with assuring that profane material is not aired between 6 a.m. and 10 p.m. (FCC 2015).

Shock jocks like Howard Stern, who was subject to constant scrutiny while on celestial airwaves, moved to paid radio so that his programming is not subject to the FCC. Many television programs that wish to run "adult content material" have also moved to paid stations in order to avoid government control of their content. As a result, while the seven dirty words are seldom heard on public airwaves, they are alive and well on paid airways. The trend of people using vulgar language continues stronger than ever.

The Trending Culture of Narcissistic Behaviors

A number of relatively less serious variations of social deviance exist in society, some that are trending (e.g., inappropriate selfies) and others that have existed for a long time (e.g., parents who lie to their children by telling them that such magical creatures as Santa Claus, the Tooth Fairy, and the Easter Bunny exist). As for inappropriate selfies, this trending phenomenon is an extension of the narcissistic behavior displayed by an increasing number of people who insist on documenting every aspect of their life with themselves as the center of attention. By definition, **narcissism** refers to a pattern of traits and behaviors that signify infatuation and obsession with one's self, often to the exclusion of all others, and the egotistic and ruthless pursuit of one's gratification, dominance, and ambition (Healthy Place 2015). Whether or not taking inappropriate selfies is a matter of social deviance reflects one's attitude (the *A* in the ABCs of Deviance) on such behaviors.

In chapter 13, we learned that individuals are supposed to learn—via the socialization process—to break away from such childish and self-centered behavior. However, with the ever-expanding popularity of smartphones and many people's infatuation with chronicling their every move via selfies, this behavior is not only expanding but is encouraged by the agents of socialization, including parents, peers, the media, and so on. While the narcissistic nature of taking selfies is of concern in varying degree among sociologists and psychologists, it is the inappropriate selfie that brings trepidation. Most assuredly, everyone has viewed inappropriate selfies online, and chances are a number of people reading this text are guilty of this act themselves. A Google search of "inappropriate selfies" will enlighten anyone who is unaware of this trending form of social deviance. Among the photos found on one site:

- Countless examples of a mother taking a "sexy" photo of herself in the bathroom with her young children in the background looking into the mirror, bathing, or being made to stand in the corner.
- A young man who took a selfie from the gas chamber in Auschwitz.

- Two young women who took a selfie at the Berlin Wall (the monument that remains).
- A male firefighter taking a photo of himself with a house on fire in the background.
- A young man grinning widely with the Chernobyl power plant in the background.
- A young couple who took a photo of themselves at the Holocaust memorial site.
- A tourist who took a photo of himself smiling at Pearl Harbor with the *USS Arizona* in the background.
- A young man who took a photo of himself giving the "peace sign" with a down-and-out homeless man in the background.
- Tourists smiling while taking a selfie in front of the 9/11 Memorial.

A smiling young man takes a selfie while defecating. Sharing this photo will make such an act even more inappropriate.

- A preteen smiling while taking a photo of his grandmother lying in her coffin at a funeral (Opposing Views 2015).

The examples described above are a mere sampling of all the vast number of self-ies that have been posted online. In the grand scheme of things, these are relatively minor violations, especially compared to homicide, environmental degradation, and fraud, but they do represent a growing trend in social deviance.

People often tell "tall tales" that consist of half-truths or perhaps no truth at all, but in this day and age of social media, a number of such stories spread quickly and are consumed by a mass audience who seem eager to believe them. Anyone on social networks has read about a number of hoaxes. For example, at the end of 2015, there was a rumor circulating on Facebook that CEO Mark Zuckerberg was giving away $4.5 million to 1,000 users who repost a notification on their feeds. The post claims that the giveaways will continue until 10 percent of the $45 billion Zuckerberg is donating to charity is given to random Facebook users (Stoffers 2015). Many people naïvely (to put it nicely) not only reposted this claim but also "testified" to its apparent authenticity. A number of other people on Facebook created **memes**—an idea, concept, activity, or catchphrase superimposed on a photo, often as a mimicry, from person to person via the Internet—mocking those who fell for the false Zuckerberg giveaway story by posting such things as Zuckerberg giving away unicorns and trips to Mars.

A nonfiction story to gain mass media attention in 2015 was told by NASCAR driver Kurt Busch. Busch, known as the "Outlaw," broke up with his then-girlfriend Patricia Driscoll in the fall of 2014. She claimed that he "grabbed her by the throat and slammed her head against the wall of his motor home" (Helling 2015:58). His response was that he could not possibly physically harm Driscoll because she is a "trained assassin" (Lawrence 2015:16). Busch claimed that Driscoll conducts assassin missions across Central and South America. "Everyone on the outside can tell me that I'm crazy, but I lived on the inside and saw it firsthand" (Helling 2015:58). Busch also claims that Driscoll flaunts cell phone pictures of her kills and darts across the Mexican border to execute missions (Lawrence 2015). He also states that a character in the movie *Zero Dark Thirty* was based on her and other women (Helling 2015). Driscoll—who runs a defense contracting company in Washington, D.C., and is the president of a military-focused charity that partners with NASCAR—called the claims "ludicrous and cast Busch as a drunk and a depressive who has hurt her before" (Lawrence 2015:16).

In an attempt to be civil and not offend others—and no, this is not a reference to "political correctness"—it has often been said that there are certain topics one should attempt to avoid discussing in polite company (the company of people with whom you are not really familiar). These topics are religion and politics. Some people also warn you not to discuss personal financial matters (money). I have found that discussing sports with people who do not share your passions is also a good topic to avoid. The primary reason for avoiding such topics is because they generate heated and passionate defenses among those who have strong feelings. Thus, if you are at a social gathering at your boss's home and you do not know most of the people there, it is advised not to discuss politics, for example, as your passionate support of a particular candidate or political issue may come in direct conflict with someone else's, perhaps even your supervisor(s)'. Thus, the longtime recommendation was to avoid certain topics altogether. One of the most annoying aspects of social media centers on people who insist on constantly expressing their narrow political views. Social media sites such as Facebook are not a good place to try and change someone's opinions about a particular candidate, and it is likely that friendships will be severed. Still, some people insist on telling everyone else that their opinion is correct and everyone else's is wrong. Learning when to speak one's mind and learning when to keep quiet is practically an art form and another example of something that should be learned during the socialization process (especially during adult socialization). In box 14.2, a number of things that should not be said on your first day of work are shared.

A CLOSER LOOK

Box 14.2 Things You Should Never Say on Your First Day at Work

There are a number of websites that offer sage advice for people who are just starting a new job. I share these bits of information with my soon-to-be-graduating students in my department's Senior Capstone course as I prepare them for life after undergraduate school. The 13 suggestions listed below are a modification of a list provided by *Business Insider* (2015).

1. "At my last company . . ." or . . . "At my last job . . ."—Seldom, if ever, does a new boss want to hear how you "used to do things." It makes one look like a know-it-all.

2. "When do I get a raise?"—It is best to put in a significant amount of time on the job before asking this question. I advise students that during the interviewing process, the salary should be one of the last questions they ask.

3. "I need to leave early on Fridays."—Even if there is a legitimate reason for needing to leave

early on Fridays, this is a topic that needed to be introduced prior to starting the job.

4. "Who should I meet and who should I avoid around here?"—While it is helpful to eventually ascertain this information, such a question on the first day of work (or any time very early in the employment stage) is likely to come across as gossipy or crass.

5. "That's not how I learned how to do it."—Similar to #1, this bit of advice refers to the idea that employers want you, at the very least, to be open to their ideas and ways of doing things.

6. "What's the holiday party like? Do we get bonuses or a ham or something?'—Just wait and see what happens. Or, if this is the type of company/industry where bonuses are commonly handed out, discuss this issue prior to employment (after discussing salary).

7. "I need an upgrade on my phone/computer, etc."—Asking for an upgrade on your first day of work will likely alienate you from coworkers who may already be waiting for upgrades and may make you look pushy to your employer.

8. "That makes no sense."—Whether a certain suggestion or course of action on the part of your employer seems illogical or not, it is not a good idea to rock the boat on your first day of work.

9. "My prior boss was clueless."—Badmouthing your previous boss and other such negative comments about your past employer are rarely welcomed.

10. "I'd like to invite you all to my church this Sunday." Or . . . "I'd like to invite you all to join me on the political campaign of X."—Unless it has something directly to do with your job it is best to heed the advice given in this chapter: avoid discussing certain topics in polite company—religion and politics being the top two topics to avoid.

11. "In my opinion . . ."—As a general rule, it is best to keep your personal opinions to yourself, especially when new to the job.

12. "What's the employee discount like?"—If your job entails retail sales and you are interested in things like employee discount, it is best to look at the company's employee (policies and procedures) manual.

13. "Hey, Donna, working hard or hardly working?!"—Comments like that are lame. Also as the new person on the job it is best to avoid joining in with coworkers ribbing each other until you get to know them and they get to know you. (One should also watch out for sexist or racist comments.)

In box 14.2, we were given some advice about how to behave on the first day of work. Another bit of good advice, for the workplace or in the company of others in any capacity, is to avoid engaging in or discussing the general topic of bodily functions (e.g., puking and farting). And yet an increasing number of vulgar behaviors are appearing on television, film, and the mass media in general. For example, for decades now, people have had a fascination with zombies, and yet they are trending more now than ever before. The popular TV show *The Walking Dead* has depicted countless, brutal ways to kill zombies. They have even shown characters cutting open a zombie to see what they have recently eaten (one of their friends or an animal). In a wide variety of shows and films actors have had to fake vomit (actors utilize a small tube that starts from a hidden container filled with fake barf that snakes through his/her clothing and then jags into the side of the mouth and points outward). Shows that include forensic labs often portray bodies in various stages of decomposition (in most cases organs are sculpted in silicone and then covered in fake blood and methyl cellulose—a food thickener—to create a gooey substance). And there are shows like *Hannibal* that depict scenes of cannibalism (pig organs are the most commonly used because of their similarity to human organs). The depictions of killing zombies, people vomiting, and others committing acts of cannibalism are not only trending; they seem to challenge long-held beliefs that airing such gross subject matters is taboo.

In the contemporary era in which we live, deciding what is and what is not an example of social deviance has become increasingly challenging to ascertain.

Summary

As demonstrated throughout this text and as articulated in this chapter, social deviance is omnipresent in society. This chapter began with a review of the previous chapters and then proceeded to give examples of trending forms of social deviance to help demonstrate the fact that social deviance is omnipresent in society. Three categories of trending forms of deviance were covered, ranging from serious variations (e.g., active shootings, terrorism, and the use of drones and lasers to cause harm) to middle-range variations (e.g., the growing number of "nones," desnudas, and public swearing) to less serious, frivolous variations (e.g., inappropriate selfies, social media rumors, and topics to avoid in polite company).

Key Terms

active shooting, 383

desnuda, 387

lasing, 385

mass shooting, 383

memes, 391

narcissism, 390

nones, 386

omnipresent, 381

terrorism, 384

unmanned aerial vehicles (UAVs), 384

Discussion Questions

1. Do you believe that Emile Durkheim was correct when he said that even in a society of saints there will still be "sinners"? Explain.

2. How is social deviance omnipresent?

3. Identify examples of trending variations of social deviance not discussed in this chapter (and feel free to send them to the author for future editions of this text!).

4. Is it ethical for governments to use drones in war? Why or why not?

5. Why do so many people so easily use profanity in public places? Should profanity be allowed on public airways?

6. Have you ever taken inappropriate selfies? Have you ever witnessed someone take an inappropriate selfie in a public place?

7. Are there any topics that you try to avoid when in "polite company" (a group of people that consists of individuals you do not know, or do not know very well)?

Glossary

absolutist deviance A perspective of deviance that argues that certain behaviors *are* inherently deviant regardless of context, times, and the diversity of the members of a society.

active shooting A situation in which a shooting is in progress and an aspect of the crime may affect the protocols used in responding to and reacting at the scene of the incident.

affluenza A term used to describe psychological problems that can afflict children from wealthy families.

agents of socialization Sources of culture; they are people, groups, organizations, and institutions that teach us what we need to know in order to function properly in society.

aggravated assault An attempt to purposely inflict serious bodily harm or injury to another.

alcohol (ethyl alcohol or ethanol)—Is an intoxicating ingredient found in beer, wine, and liquor. It is produced via the fermentation process.

alcohol abuse The pattern of drinking that results in harm to one's health, interpersonal relationships, or ability to work.

alcoholism A chronic and often progressive disease that includes problems controlling your drinking, being preoccupied with alcohol even when it causes problems, having to drink more to get the same effect (physical dependence), or having withdrawal symptoms when you rapidly decrease or stop drinking.

anabolic steroids Drugs that resemble androgenic hormones such as testosterone.

application fraud Occurs when an unauthorized person opens up a credit card account in another person's name.

arson Any willful or malicious burning or attempting to burn, with or without intent to defraud, a dwelling house, public building, motor vehicle or aircraft, personal property of another, etc.

assault An act of violence that creates an apprehension in another of an imminent harmful, unwanted, or offensive contact.

attention-deficit hyperactivity disorder (ADHD) A developmental disorder where there are significant problems with attention, hyperactivity, or acting impulsively.

autism spectrum disorder (ASD) A developmental disorder that in addition to affecting an afflicted

person's ability to socialize and communicate with others, can also result in restricted, repetitive patterns of behavior, interests, or activities.

battery The harmful or offensive touching of another.

Big Data A term that describes any massive volume of both structured and unstructured data that is so large it is difficult to process and also has the potential to be mined (or hacked) for information.

Big Pharma A term that encompasses the largest global corporations in the pharmaceutical industry.

binge drinking A pattern of drinking that brings blood alcohol concentration (BAC) levels to 0.08—which typically equals 4 drinks for women and 5 drinks for men—in about 2 hours.

bipolar disorder (formerly known as manic depression)—A chronic mental illness that is characterized by alternating periods of mood changes of elation and depression and causes changes in sleep, energy, thinking, and behavior.

blood doping Introducing a surplus of one's own blood into his or her body in hopes of improving performance, especially athletic performance.

body mass index (BMI) A method used to measure whether an individual weight is underweight, healthy weight, overweight, obese, or morbidly obese.

bootlegging The unlawful production, sale, and transportation of alcoholic liquor without registration or payment of taxes.

born criminal A person born with a predisposition to commit crime and social deviance.

breaching experiment A quasi-experiment that seeks to examine people's reactions to violations of commonly accepted social rules, or norms in order to shed light on the methods by which people construct social reality.

bribery Involves the offering of money or gifts to a person in power, especially a public official in the discharge of his or her legal duties, in an effort to entice that public official to do something on behalf of the briber.

burglary (breaking or entering) The unlawful entry of a structure to commit a felony or a theft.

cannabis The scientific name for marijuana; it is a category of psychoactive drugs that includes three different species: sativa, indica, and ruderalis.

cannibalism The act of one individual of a species consuming all or part of another member of the same species.

carrying capacity The maximum feasible load just short of the level that would end the environment's ability to support life.

catfish The person who pretends to be someone they're not and who creates false identities on social networking sites for deceptive purposes.

catfishing Internet predators that fabricate online identities and entire social circles to trick people into emotional/romantic relationships over a long period of time.

claims making The process of trying to convince the public and important officials that a particular issue or situation should be defined as a social problem.

climate change A long-term change in the earth's climate, especially due to shifts in average atmospheric temperatures.

collective conscience The totality of beliefs and sentiments common to average citizens of the same society forms a determinate system that has its own life.

collective violence Violence committed by larger groups of individuals and political states.

computer hacker A person who illegally gains access to a computer system in order to get information (e.g., data or top secrets), cause damage (e.g., deleting important files or stealing bank account numbers), or create havoc (e.g., releasing a virus in the network system).

computer hacking The process of intentionally accessing a computer without authorization or exceeding authorized access.

corporate deviance Acts of immense physical, financial, and moral harm committed by wealthy and powerful corporations no longer being constrained by government in their relentless pursuit of profits.

credit card fraud A form of identity theft that involves the unauthorized taking of another's credit card information for the purpose of charging purchases to the account or removing funds from it.

crime Any deviant behavior or omission of behavior that violates a law of the land.

crimes of omission The failure to act when called upon to do so either by law or by law enforcement representatives; such acts constitute an *actus reus* (Latin for "guilty act").

criminal intent (in legal terminology, *mens rea*, or "guilty mind") Varies by degree, ranging from willful conduct (the perpetrator had full intention to commit the crime, such as robbery, aggravated assault, and murder) at one extreme to negligence (meaning that the criminal act was not deliberate) at the other end.

culture The shared knowledge, values, norms, and behavioral patterns of a given society that are passed on from one generation to the next, forming a way of life for its members.

culture of shamelessness A term used to describe the phenomenon of changing cultural norms wherein behaviors that in the past would have elicited great shame and embarrassment are treated with indifference in contemporary society.

cyberbullying The act of harassing someone online by sending or posting embarrassing photos/videos or mean-spirited messages, including spreading rumors/gossip about a person, often done anonymously.

cyber child pornography The sexually explicit content made available online in various formats including images, video files, video games, and streaming videos.

cyberharassment Threatening or harassing electronic messages (e.g., emails, instant messages, blogs, and websites) designed to torment and harm the targeted person.

cyberscams, also referred to as Internet fraud Crimes in which the perpetrator develops a scheme using one or more elements of the Internet in an attempt to defraud people with the goal of acquiring/stealing personal property, money, or any other asset by means of false representation, whether by providing misleading information or by concealment of information.

cyberstalking The use of electronic forms of communication (e.g., social networking sites, e-mail, or smartphones) to track or harass a person.

cyclical unemployment Occurs when there is not enough demand for goods and services in the market to provide enough employment opportunities for all who want to work.

deforestation The clearing, or permanent removal, of the earth's forests on a massive scale.

deinstitutionalization The release of institutionalized individuals from institutional care (e.g., psychiatric hospital) to care, treatment, support, or rehabilitation primarily through community resources under the supervision of health care professionals or facilities.

dementia A chronic disorder of the mental processes caused by brain disease or injury and characterized by memory disorders, personality changes, and deterioration in cognitive function (e.g., impaired reasoning).

demonic possession Refers to being under the power or influence of a demon or evil spirit to the point where one cannot control their mind or actions.

dependency A state in which a person's body has adjusted to regular use of a drug.

depressants Drugs that sedate neurotransmission levels; they depress or lower the vital activities of the central nervous system.

depression A mood disorder that causes a persistent feeling of sadness and loss of interest that can lead to a variety of emotional and physical problems.

desnuda Spanish for naked, nude, or ill-clothed.

developmental disorders An umbrella term used to cover a number of chronic disabilities that affect the mental and/or physical development (e.g., receptive and expressive language, learning, and mobility) of the afflicted.

deviance Any behavior that is labeled by some members of society, especially those in a position of authority or power, or specific subcultural groups, as an unacceptable violation of social norms and codes of morality that may elicit negative reactions from others.

deviant A person who violates the social norms or cultural codes of morality.

differential association A theory that proposes that through interaction with others, individuals learn their norms, values, and attitudes.

discouraged workers Persons not currently looking for work because they believe no jobs are available for them.

dissociative disorders Are characterized by an involuntary escape from reality highlighted by a disconnection between thoughts, identity, consciousness, and memory.

dissociative identity disorder A psychological perspective that puts forth the notion that any given individual can possess multiple and distinct personalities.

dose Refers to the quantity of a drug that has been prescribed by a doctor or recommended by the drug provider.

drinking problem Occurs when alcohol consumption causes problems for the drinker.

drive-by shootings The combined use of firearms and automobiles in a mobile attempt by assailants to kill targeted victims.

drug Any natural or synthetic chemical substance that affects the functioning of the mind or body.

drug abuse Persistent or sporadic excessive drug use with or without acceptable medical supervision.

drug abuser A person who consumes drugs beyond the prescribed allotment or who endangers themselves or the public safety and welfare of others.

drunk driving Operating a motor vehicle while one's blood alcohol content is above the legal limit set by statute.

drunken comportment The idea that people are not simply under the control of alcohol, but instead act as they have been taught to act when drunk.

drunk shaming A quasi-degradation ceremony that occurs when people become too drunk to defend themselves from a private or public shaming.

ecosystem The ecological network of interconnected and interdependent living organisms (plants, animals, and microbes) in union with the nonliving aspects found in their immediate community, including air, water, minerals, and soil.

enviromare An environmentally produced nightmare that causes great harm to humanity and the physical environment.

environment The totality of social and physical conditions that affect nature and humanity and their influence on the growth, development, and survival of organisms found in a given surrounding.

espionage The act of spying or of using spies to obtain, deliver, or transmit secret or confidential information, especially regarding a government or business, without the target's permission or knowledge.

ethics Having the ability to distinguish between right and wrong courses of actions and the ability to understand the difference between the virtuous and the nonvirtuous aspects of human behavior.

e-waste A popular, informal name for electronic products that have been deemed obsolete because they are outdated and are discarded.

extortion The criminal behavior of trying to get money, property, or some other sort of favors from a person, entity, or institutions through coercive means.

felony murder The killing of an individual(s) during the commission of a felony such as rape or robbery.

fetish A strong desire or fixation for some object.

folkways The conventional rules of everyday life that people follow almost automatically, such as holding a door open for the person behind you.

food neophobia The fear of trying new foods.

forgery The altering, copying, or imitating of something, without authority or right, with the intent to deceive or defraud by passing the copy of thing altered or imitated as that which is original or genuine.

formal shaming Efforts used by formal entities to make the offender feel extreme guilt for violating a law or significant social norm.

formal social control (sometimes called external or direct social control) Regulation of behavior comes from exterior social control agents, such as law enforcement, the judicial system, the legislative system, and other authority figures.

freeganism (sometimes called "dumpster diving") The anticonsumerist movement wherein people reclaim and eat food that has been discarded.

frictional unemployment Stems from the temporary transitions that people take when graduating from college and looking for employment or when workers leave one job in search of a better one.

gender Socially determined expectations placed on individuals because of their sexual category.

gender identity The way in which a person conceives of their sexual self.

good mental health Offers feelings of well-being, inner strength, emotional functionality, and the ability to cope and manage change and uncertainty.

greenhouse effect The circumstances where the short wavelengths of visible light from the sun pass through the atmosphere, but the longer wavelengths of the infrared reradiation from the heated objects are unable to escape the earth's atmosphere.

hallucinogens A category of drugs (also known as psychedelics) that cause the user to perceive things differently than they actually are; they provide a profound sense of intensified sensory perception.

hazing An all-encompassing term that covers silly, potentially risky, or degrading tasks as a means of initiating a person into a group, with or without the consent of the participates, that is required for acceptance by a group of full-fledged members.

hedonism Seeking pleasure and attempting to avoid pain in one's activities.

homelessness People who lack a fixed, regular, and adequate nighttime residence.

homicide The killing of one human being by another. Homicides can be criminal or noncriminal.

homophobia An irrational and unreasoning fear of, aversion to, or antipathy toward members of the LGBTQ community manifested via prejudice, discrimination, and sometimes acts of violence and expressions of hostility.

honor codes An example of informal social control wherein participants are expected to be trusted to voluntarily adhere to a set of ethical principles, ideals, rules, values and norms.

honor killings The homicide of a female member of a family by her male family members because she has "dishonored" or shamed the family because of her behavior.

huffing The inhaling of substances (e.g., spray paint, oven cleaners or gasoline) in an attempt to get "high."

human cannibalism The consuming of human flesh by another human.

human trafficking The illegal trade of human beings, it is considered a modern version of slavery.

hydraulic fracturing Commonly known as hydrofracking, or simply fracking, involves a controversial method of drilling for natural gas wherein hundreds of unidentified chemicals are used during the extraction process.

identity fraud A crime in which a criminal uses a victim's personal data through fraud or deception for economic gain or other deceitful purposes.

identity theft The fraudulent appropriation and use of someone else's personal identification information, personal data, or documents for the purpose of assuming that person's name or identity in order to make transactions or purchases.

ideology A set of beliefs, values, norms and doctrines that characterize a particular group, institution, organization or society.

illegal insider trading Buying or selling a security, in breach of fiduciary duty or other relationship of trust and confidence, while in possession of material, nonpublic information about the security.

indecent exposure The deliberate exposure in public or in view of the public by a person of a portion or portions of his or her body, causing others to be alarmed or offended.

infidelity The act of behaving unfaithfully and cheating (e.g., sexual or emotional betrayal) on a spouse or significant other.

informal shamings A type of social control that contains elements of moral indignation, shame, ridicule, stigmatism, and attempts to compromise the victim's identity and self-esteem; they are used by people against others in an attempt to alter their behavior.

informal, or internal, social control Methods used to regulate behavior through ideological or cultural manipulation.

inhalants Include a variety of breathable substances, some legally prescribed and others that are common household or work products.

inner containments Self-controls (e.g., self-concept, ego strength, tolerance of frustration, goal-directedness, and identification with lawfulness) that develop during the socialization process.

insider trading The trading of securities or stocks by "insiders" with material, nonpublic information pertaining to significant, often market-moving developments to benefit themselves or others financially.

intellectual property Includes a wide variety of products of the intellect (creations of the mind) that have commercial value, including copyrighted property such as literary or artistic works, and ideational property, such as patents, business methods, and industrial processes.

intellectual property rights (IPR) theft The stealing of any intellectual property ranging from books, songs and movies to machine tools and pharmaceuticals.

interpersonal violence Violence between individuals, individuals and groups, groups and individuals, and groups against groups.

intimate interpersonal violence Acts carried out with the intention of, or perceived as having the intention of, physically or emotionally hurting one's partner (in marriage, cohabitation, or dating); child; parent; sibling; or some other intimate person (e.g., close family member such as a niece or nephew, aunt or uncle, or grandparent).

labor force The measure of the sum of the employed and unemployed persons in a society.

larceny-theft The unlawful taking, carrying, leading, or riding away of property from the possession or constructive possession of another.

lasing The act of pointing a laser at a specific object.

laws Formalized norms, as determined by a political authority.

marine debris Includes any form of manufactured or processed material discarded, disposed of, or abandoned in the marine environment.

mass extinction An event that occurs when the planet loses more than three-quarters of its species in a geologically short interval of time, usually a few hundred thousand to a couple of million years.

mass shooting An incident involving multiple victims of gun violence.

medicalization The process of increasingly treating aspects of human life as medical problems rather than social problems.

medical waste Also known as health-care waste, includes waste generated by the health institutions, research institutions and laboratories, as well as waste originating from health care done at home (e.g., dialysis, insulin injection devices, and blood sugar test strips).

memes An idea, concept, activity, or catchphrase superimposed on a photo, often as a mimicry, from person to person via the Internet.

mental disorder A mental or bodily condition marked primarily by insufficient organization of personality, mind, and emotions that impairs the normal functioning of the individual.

mental illness A condition that impacts a person's thinking, feeling, or mood and may affect his or her ability to relate to others and function on a daily basis.

modeling Occurs by watching and listening to significant others and then copying their behaviors and attitudes.

moderate alcohol consumption Up to one drink per day for women and up to two drinks per day for men.

modes of adaptation Manners in which individuals adjust to strain caused by anomic conditions.

morality A code of conduct that includes ideals of proper and ethical behavior used to guide human behavior and to develop or maintain good character.

mores Norms that constitute the basic moral judgments of a society, such as the taboos against incest, pedophilia, and cannibalism.

motor vehicle theft The theft or attempted theft of a motor vehicle; a motor vehicle is defined as a self-propelled vehicle that runs on land surfaces and not on rails.

narcissism A pattern of traits and behaviors that signify infatuation and obsession with one's self, often to the exclusion of all others, and the egotistic and ruthless pursuit of one's gratification, dominance, and ambition.

narcotics (also known as opioid pain relievers, opioids, painkillers, and analgesics) Are drugs designed to help people who are experiencing severe pain.

neurosis A relatively mild personality disorder typified by excessive anxiety and social maladjustment.

nicotine A toxic colorless or yellowish oily liquid alkaloid, water-soluble, that is the chief active ingredient of tobacco. It acts as a stimulant in small doses but in larger amounts blocks the action of autonomic nerve and skeletal muscle cells. It is also valued as an insecticide.

noncriminal homicides Include excusable and justifiable homicide wherein the death of another person was not the result of wanton disregard, malice aforethought, premeditation, or during the commission of a felony.

nones A term used by the Pew Research Center to describe Americans who have identified themselves as believing in "nothing in particular" when it comes to religious identification.

normative deviance A focus on deviant behavior from the perspective that a social norm has to be violated in order for deviance to have occurred.

norms Socially defined rules and expectations regarding human behavior.

obesity Having a body mass index (BMI) score measuring between 30 and 40.

objective social problems Harmful social situations or issues acknowledged to exist within society.

objectum sexuality An orientation to love objects, including inanimate objects.

occupational crime Deviant or criminal behavior committed during the course of one's occupation for the purpose of seeking ill-gotten personal gain.

omnipresent Present in all places at all times.

organized crime Also known as syndicate crime, involves criminal activity committed by members of criminal enterprises that exist to operate profitable illicit enterprises (e.g., insurance fraud, counterfeiting, tax evasion, and money laundering).

outer containments The social control agents found in society (e.g., law enforcement, the judicial systems, and others in a position of authority).

outsourcing Occurs when a company moves its operations away from one market to another, generally to another country where labor and/or raw materials are cheaper.

parole A common type of "aftercare" treatment program in that offenders who were incarcerated are released early but must meet a number of criteria while released in order to avoid being sent back to a detention or confinement facility.

performance-enhancing drugs Are drugs used by people who hope to rehabilitate, gain muscle mass, run faster, and increase overall athletic performance.

physiognomy Involves the study of faces and skulls and other physical features in order to reveal an individual's natural disposition.

political crime Refers to acts perpetrated by, or against, a government or state.

poor mental health Generally expressed in terms of mental illness or mental disorder and refers to conditions that negatively impact a person's ability to cope with everyday events or stressful situations.

pornography (more commonly known as porn) Words or images (generally found in books, magazines, photographs, film, art, and cyberspace) intended to cause sexual arousal.

positive deviance Behaviors that violate a rule that other people find desirable that may or may not bring about positive consequences.

posttraumatic stress disorder (PTSD) A mental health condition that's triggered by a highly stressful or terrifying event either by experiencing it or witnessing it.

poverty The lack of basic necessities, goods, or financial means of support.

power elites The set of people with a disproportionate amount of influence over public policy who are found atop the major power structure of American society—business, military, and politics.

prescription drugs (also known as prescription medication or prescription medicine) Are pharmaceutical drugs that can only be legally obtained and consumed by means of a properly authorized person (e.g., a physician).

prevention strategies The various techniques used to steer individuals away from the temptations of committing deviancy and crime and to keep them on the straight path toward law-abiding lifestyles.

primary groups Those characterized by intimate face-to-face association and cooperation.

product recall The process of retrieving defective products from consumers and providing those consumers with compensation (e.g., monetary compensation or product replacement).

property offenses Involve offenses committed against the property of others and include such crimes as burglary, larceny-theft, motor vehicle theft, arson, and vandalism.

prostitution The act of offering one's self for hire to engage in sexual relations of any kind.

psychoactive drug A chemical substance that acts primarily upon the central nervous system where it alters the perceptions, cognition and/or moods of people who take it.

psychosis A symptom or feature of mental illness that affects the mind and is typically characterized by dramatic changes in personality, impaired functioning, and a distorted or impaired relationship with reality.

psychotherapy A general term for treating mental health problems by talking with a psychiatrist, psychologist, or other mental health provider.

public intoxication An intoxicated or drugged person in a public place that is disturbing the public peace and order.

public nuisance An act, condition, or thing that is illegal because it interferes with the rights of the public generally.

ransomware A type of cyberscam that involves trying to extort money from individuals and business owners by infecting and taking control of the victim's computer.

rape The unlawful compelling of a person, or persons, through the use of physical force, or the threat of physical force, or duress to have unwanted vaginal, anal, and/or oral sex, without the consent of the victim.

reactivist deviance A perspective of social deviance that takes into consideration the idea that deviance can be positive.

reinforcement A term used in operant conditioning, referring to the manner in which behaviors are rewarded or punished with its consequence of strengthening or weakening a behavior in the future.

relativist deviance The perspective on social deviance that examines the manner in which social norms are created and the people who create them.

revenge porn The cybersharing of sexually explicit photos/videos of another person (generally an ex-lover or ex-friend) without their consent for the purpose of spiteful humiliation.

riot A violent public disorder involving a large number of people assembled together and acting with a common intent—the wanton destruction of human life and/or property.

robbery The completed or attempted theft, directly from a person, of property or cash by force or threat of force, with or without a weapon, and with or without injury.

schizophrenia A severe mental disorder that interferes with a person's ability to correctly interpret reality, to think clearly, manage emotions, make decisions, and relate to others.

scratchiti A version of graffiti that involves using a sharp object like a knife to scratch painted surfaces, wood, and glass windows.

securities fraud A type of serious white-collar crime in which a person(s) or company misrepresents information that investors use to make decisions.

self-directed violence Violence in which the perpetrator and the victim are the same individual.

self-harm (also known as self-injury and/or self-mutilation) Occurs when a person purposively inflicts physical harm to self via such methods as self-cutting, head banging, self-biting, and self-scratching.

sex A biological classification (e.g., male or female).

sexism Behaviors, conditions, or attitudes that foster stereotypical social roles based on sexual identity and orientations and that lead to prejudice and discrimination against members of one sex due to preferential treatment for members of the offending sex.

sexting The sending, receiving, or forwarding of sexually suggestive text messages that generally include sexually suggestive nude or nearly nude photos.

sexual assault Any type of sexual contact or behavior that occurs without the explicit consent of the recipient including such behaviors as sexual intercourse, forcible sodomy, child molestation, incest, fondling, and attempted rape.

sexual deviance Includes a wide range of unusual or abnormal forms of sexually related behaviors that are outside of the culturally and historically determined social norms and expectations of a society.

sexual deviant A person who finds pleasure in and/or participates in acts of sexual deviancy.

sexual fetishism The desire to engage in specific forms of sex-related activities that bring satisfaction to the participants.

sexual harassment Any uninvited or unwelcome sexual advances, requests for sexual favors, and other verbal or physical conduct of a sexual nature that tends to create an uncomfortable environment.

sexual orientation A person's physical, romantic, and emotional attraction to another person.

sexually transmitted diseases (STDs) Infections that are generally acquired via sexual contact with someone who has the infection.

simple assault Acts of violence against a person that inflict less than serious bodily harm without a deadly weapon.

social construction of reality The perspective that our world is a social creation, originating and evolving through our everyday thoughts and actions.

social control The processes, formal or informal, used to prevent deviant behavior.

social deviance The study of human deviant behavior within a social context.

social disorganization Disruption or breakdown of the structure of social relations as the result of the contrasting values and norms of the established residents and the new values and norms of immigrants; the breakdown of social cohesion; high rates of unemployment; and a disregard for established social control agents (e.g., existing community leaders and law enforcement).

socialization A process of social development and learning that occurs as individuals interact with one another and learn about society's expectations for acceptable behavior.

social problem A social situation found in society that at least some people view as undesirable and/or harmful.

social stratification A system for ranking members of a social system into levels with different or unequal evaluations.

sociological imagination The awareness that an individual's private life is often influenced/shaped by the social environment and the existing societal forces.

spear phishing A targeted e-mail scam sent from a fake account that looks familiar but is sent with the sole purpose of obtaining unauthorized access to sensitive data.

stalking Involves the willful and repeated following, watching, and/or harassing of another person.

statistical deviance Deviance is that which is unusual, rare, or uncommon.

statutory rape Any sexual contact with an underage person.

stigma A mark of disgrace or dishonor.

stigmatized Characterized or branded as disgraceful or ignominious.

stimulants Drugs that increase alertness, accelerate heart rate, elevate the blood pressure, and speed up or overstimulate the user's body by increasing one's energy level.

street crime An umbrella term used by sociologists, criminologists, and law enforcement agencies to describe criminal acts committed in public outdoor places, including the streets, playgrounds, shopping areas, business districts, and residential neighborhoods, including private homes, and encompasses violent offenses and property offenses.

structural unemployment The mismatch of skills in the labor force to the composition of the local industry.

subculture A category of people found within the greater society who share a distinctive set of cultural beliefs and behaviors that distinguish them from the larger society.

subjective social problems Social situations or issues acknowledged by segments of society as harmful.

suicide by cop (SBC) A situation where individuals deliberately place themselves or others at grave risk in a manner that compels the use of deadly force by police officers.

suppression strategies Attempts by law enforcement and the full force of the law to forcibly end, dissolve, or prohibit criminal activities.

sustainability The ability of the environment to hold, endure, or bear the weight of a wide variety of social and natural forces that may compromise its functionality.

swatting The act of pranking or tricking an emergency service dispatcher (e.g., 911 operators) into deploying a SWAT unit to an unsuspecting victim's home under false pretenses.

techniques of neutralization Methods used by norm violators in their attempt to rationalize their deviant behaviors, thus freeing them from their commitment to societal values and norms.

technology The branch of knowledge that deals with the creation and practical use of technical means to solve problems or invent useful tools.

terrorism The unlawful use of force or violence against persons or property to intimidate or coerce a government, the civilian population, or any segment thereof in furtherance of political or social objectives.

theory A statement that proposes to explain or relate observed phenomena or a set of concepts via a collection of interrelated statements and/or arguments that seek to described and explain cause-effect relationships.

thrivability A cycle of actions that reinvest energy for future use and stretch resources further; it transcends sustainability by creating an upward spiral of greater possibilities and increasing energy.

tolerance The repeated use of a drug over a period of time, which diminishes its effectiveness.

torture The act of causing excruciating pain as a form of punishment or revenge or as a means of forcing someone to give up information or a confession.

treason The offense of the betrayal of one's own country by waging war against it or by consciously or purposely acting to aid its enemies.

unemployment The condition of being jobless, looking for a job, and being available for work.

unmanned aerial vehicles (UAVs), known as *drones* Airborne devices controlled by "pilots" from the ground, sometimes, especially in the case of military use, autonomously following a preprogrammed mission.

unsafe products Those products that cause undue or unexpected harm, including death, to those who use them.

utilitarianism The idea of doing what is best for the greatest number of people.

vandalism The willful or malicious destruction, damaging, or defacing of public or private property.

violence The intentional use of physical force or power, threatened or actual, against oneself, another person, or against a group or community, that either results in or has a high likelihood of resulting in injury, death, psychological harm, maldevelopment, or deprivation.

violent offenses Involve offenses committed against other persons and include such crimes as homicide, robbery, assault and battery, and rape/sexual assault.

war A state or period of collective fighting between large groups or countries via the use of armed combat.

white collar crimes Crimes that are typically nonviolent, nonstreet crimes committed by someone, generally a professional of high status, in commercial situations for financial gain.

working poor Persons who spent at least 27 weeks in the labor force (either working or looking for work) but whose incomes still fell below the official poverty level.

workplace bullying The repeated, health-harming mistreatment of one or more persons (the targets) by one or more perpetrators in the work environment.

Bibliography

Abbey-Lambertz, Kate. 2015. "These Are the Major U.S. Cities with the Highest Murder Rates, According to the FBI." *Huffington Post*, November 12. Retrieved April 15, 2015 (http://www.huffingtonpost.com/2014/11/12/highest-murder-rate-us-cities-2013_n_6145404.html).

Abbott, Andrew. 2014. "The Problem of Excess." *Sociological Theory*, 32(1):1–26.

ABC Health & Wellbeing. 2015. "What Is Good Mental Health?" Retrieved July 25, 2015 (http://www.abc.net.au/health/features/stories/2014/09/11/4085497.htm).

ABC News. 2005. "'Excusable Homicide' in McDonald's Parking Lot." August 24. Retrieved April 11, 2015 (http://abcnews.go.com/GMA/story?id=1064137).

———. 2015. "Timeline of Events Leading to James Holmes' Guilty Verdicts." July 16. Retrieved July 27, 2015 (http://abcnews.go.com/US/wireStory/theater-shooting-key-events-life-james-holmes-32506142).

Abelson, Jean, and Beth Daley. 2011. "On the Menu, But Not on Your Plate." *Boston Globe*, October 23. Retrieved June 18, 2015 (http://www.boston.com/business/articles/2011/10/23/on_the_menu_but_not_on_your_plate/).

Ablon, Lillian, Martin C. Libicki, and Andrea A. Golay. 2015. "Markets for Cybercrime Tools and Stolen Data." Rand Corporation. Retrieved June 22, 2015 (http://www.rand.org/pubs/research_reports/RR610.html).

Abrutyn, Seth, and Anna S. Mueller. 2014. "The Socioemotional Foundations of Suicide: A Microsociological View of Durkheim's Suicide." *Sociological Theory*, 32(4):327–51.

Adler, Patricia, and Peter Adler. 2011. *The Tender Cut: Inside the Hidden World of Self-Injury.* New York: New York University Press.

———. 2016. *Constructions of Deviance: Social Power, Context, and Interaction, 8th edition.* Boston, MA: Cengage.

Aircraft Interiors International. 2015. "The True Costs of Heavier Passengers: Part One." Retrieved February 16, 2015 (http://www.aircraftinteriorsinternational.com/articles.php?ArticleID=422).

AlcoholPolicyMD.com. 2005. "Alcohol & Health: The Effects of Environmental Factors on Alcohol Use and Abuse." Retrieved May 27, 2015 (http://www.alcoholpolicymd.com/alcohol_and_health/study_env.htm).

Alexander, Franz G., and Sheldon T. Selesnick. 1966. *The History of Psychiatry: An Evaluation of Psychiatric Thought and Practice from Prehistoric Times to the Present.* New York: Harper and Row.

ALS Association. 2014. "The ALS Association Announces Initial Commitment of $21.7 Million from the Ice Bucket Challenge Donations to Expedite Search for Treatments and a Cure for ALS." Retrieved February 13, 2015 (http://www.alsa.org/news/media/press-releases/ibc-initial-commitment.html).

Alter, Charlotte. 2014. "Todd Akin Still Doesn't Get What's Wrong with Saying 'Legitimate Rape.'" *Time*, July 17. Retrieved August 16, 2015 (http://time.com/3001785/todd-akin-legitimate-rape-msnbc-child-of-rape/).

Altman, Larry. 2014a. "Weeping Mother Said She Was Tired Just Hours before Daughters Were Found Slain." *The Daily Breeze*, May 22. Retrieved February 28, 2015 (http://www.dailybreeze.com/general-news/20140522/weeping-mother-said-she-was-tired-just-hours-before-daughters-were-found-slain).

———. 2014b. "Carole Coronado, Accused of Killing 3 Daughters, Told Their Grandmother, "I Had a Bad Day,' Report Says." *The Daily Breeze*, October 13. Retrieved February 28, 2015 (http://www.dailybreeze.com/general-news/20141013/carol-coronado-accused-of-killing-3-daughters-told-their-grandmother-i-had-a-bad-day-report-says).

American Academy of Allergy, Asthma and Immunology (AAAAI). 2015. "Over-the-Counter Allergy Nasal Spray Triamcinolone—What Does It Mean for Patients?" Retrieved June 15, 2015 (http://www.aaaai.org/conditions-and-treatments/library/allergy-library/triamcinolone-nasal-spray.aspx).

American Association for Marriage and Family Therapy. 2014. "Sibling Violence." Retrieved May 24, 2015 (http://www.aamft.org/iMIS15/AAMFT/Content/Consumer_Updates/Sibling_Violence.aspx).

American Bar Association (ABA). 1987. *Report on Computer Crime.* Chicago, IL: American Bar Association.

American Cancer Society. 2015. "Alcohol Use and Cancer." Retrieved May 28, 2015 (http://www.cancer.org/cancer/cancercauses/dietandphysicalactivity/alcohol-use-and-cancer).

American Heart Association. 2015. "Alcohol and Heart Health." Retrieved May 28, 2015 (http://www.heart.org/HEARTORG/GettingHealthy/NutritionCenter/HealthyEating/Alcohol-and-Heart-Health_UCM_305173_Article.jsp).

American Psychiatric Association (APA). 2015. "LGBT-Sexual Orientation." Retrieved August 14, 2015 (http://www.psychiatry.org/lgbt-sexual-orientation).

American Psychological Association (APA). 2014 (October). "Incarceration Nation" 45(9). Retrieved December 20, 2015 (http://www.apa.org/monitor/2014/10/incarceration.aspx).

American University. 2015. "Concerning Sexually Transmitted Infections (STI)." Retrieved August 13, 2015 (http://www.american.edu/ocl/wellness/Sexually-Transmitted-Diseases.cfm).

America's Health Rankings. 2014. "Physical Inactivity United States." Retrieved February 15, 2015 (http://www.americashealthrankings.org/ALL/Sedentary).

Amy, Jeff. 2015. "Gay Couples Sue over Adoption Ban." *The Post-Standard*, August 13:A-13.

Anderson, Elizabeth. 2015. "Teenagers Spend 17 Hours a Week Online: How Internet Use Has Ballooned in the Last Decade." *The Telegraph*, May 11. Retrieved December 14, 2015 (http://www.telegraph.co.uk/finance/newsbysector/mediatechnologyandtelecoms/digital-media/11597743/Teenagers-spend-27-hours-a-week-online-how-internet-use-has-ballooned-in-the-last-decade.html).

Anxiety and Depression Association of America (ADAA). 2015. "Depression." Retrieved August 2, 2015 (http://www.adaa.org/understanding-anxiety/depression/treatment).

AOL News. 2015. "'My Strange Addiction': Florida Woman Marries a Carnival Ride." January 15. Retrieved January 16, 2015 (http://www.aol.com/article/2015/01/15/my-strange-addiction-florida-woman-marries-a-carnival-ride/21130207/).

Armagh, Daniel. 1998. "A Safety Net for the Internet: Protecting Our Children." *Juvenile Justice Journal*, 5(1). Retrieved June 20, 2015 (http://www.ojjdp.gov/jjjournal/jjjournal598/net.html).

Asendorpf, J. 1984. "Shyness, Embarrassment, and Self-Presentation: A Control Theory Approach," pp. 109–14 in *The Self in Anxiety, Stress, and Depression*, edited by Ralf Schwarzer. Amsterdam: North Holland.

Ashford-Grooms, Meghan. 2012. "Ron Paul Says 40,000 New Laws Were 'Put on the Books' on the First Day of 2012." *Politifact Texas*. Retrieved December 20, 2015 (http://www.politifact.com/texas/statements/2012/apr/27/ron-paul/ron-paul-says-40000-new-laws-were-put-books-first-/).

Associated Press. 2010. "Web Shaming for Neglectful Owners." As it appeared in *The Citizen*, August 4:A2.

———. 2013. "US Nuclear Waste Tanks Leaking." As it appeared in *The Citizen*, February 23:A5.

———. 2014a. "Corporal Punishment Used, but Declining." As it appeared in *The Citizen*, September 14:A6.

———. 2014b. "Environment: Bird Species Leaving Adirondack Wetlands." As it appeared in *The Post-Standard*, April 20:A-6.

———. 2015a. "Girls to Be Tried as Adults in Stabbing." As it appeared in *The Citizen*, March 14:A5.

———. 2015b. "Smoking Falls as E-cigs Boom." As it appeared in *The Citizen*, April 17:A6.

———. 2015c. "U.S. Heroin Overdoses Are Shifting." As it appeared in *The Citizen*, March 4:A2.

———. 2015d. "Hackers' $1 Billion Bank Theft May Still Impact Consumers." As it appeared in *The Citizen*, February 17:A6.

———. 2015e. "Source: Hacking Probe Begins." As it appeared in *The Citizen*, June 17:B1.

———. 2015f. "Federal Agencies Are Wide Open to Hackers, Cyberspies." As it appeared in *The Citizen*, June 24:A6.

———. 2015g. "IRS Failed to Upgrade Security Ahead of Cyberattack Threat." As it appeared in *The Citizen*, June 3:A6.

———. 2015h. "Lufthansa: Co-pilot Disclosed He Had 'Severe Depression.'" As it appeared in *The Citizen*, April 1:A6.

———. 2015i. "Jury Convicts Theater Shooter." As it appeared in *The Citizen*, July 17:A6.

———. 2015j. "Death Penalty Remains an Option." As it appeared in *The Citizen*, July 24:A5.

———. 2015k. "Baltimore Killings Most in Decades." As it appeared in *The Citizen*, August 1:A5.

———. 2015l. "State Expands 'Yes Means Yes' Policy to Private Colleges." As it appeared in *The Citizen*, July 8:A5.

———. 2015m. "Poll: Most Support Same-Sex Marriage." As it appeared in *The Citizen*, March 6:A6.

———. 2015n. "Millions on Cheating Site May Be Exposed." As it appeared in *The Citizen*, August 20:B6.

———. 2015o. "Obama Power Plant Rules Spark Fight over Climate Change." As it appeared in *The Citizen*, August 4:A6.

———. 2015p. "Historic Pact to Slow Global Warming Is Celebrated in Paris." As it appeared in *The Post-Standard*, December 13:A-19.

———. 2015q. "Ugly Hair Cut Videos Shaming Kids Are Going Viral." As it appeared in *The Post-Standard*, June 12:A-9.

———. 2016a. "GM Ignition Switch Trial Abruptly Called Off." As it appeared in *The Citizen*, January 23:A3.

———. 2016b. "CDC Suggests Doctors Limit Opioid Prescriptions." *The Citizen*, March 16:A6.

Austin, James, Kelly Dedel Johnson, and Ronald Weitzer. 2005 (September). "Alternatives to the Secure Detention and Confinement of Juvenile Offenders." OJJDP, Washington, D.C.: U.S. Department of Justice.

Australian Federal Police (AFP). 1998. "Crime in Cyberspace." *Platypus Magazine*, June. Retrieved June 16, 2015 (http://www.afp .gov.au/media-centre/publications/platypus/ previous-editions/1998/june-1998/cyber).

Avramescu, Catalin. 2011. *An Intellectual History of Cannibalism*. Princeton, NJ: Princeton University Press.

Baker, K. C. 2015a. "The Real Story of *American Sniper*: A Dangerous Life, A Family's Grief." *People*, February 2:24.

———. 2015b. "*American Sniper* Widow: Taya Kyle." *People*, February 9:68–72.

Bandura, Albert, and Richard Walters. 1963. *Social Learning and Personality Development*. New York: Holt, Reinhart and Winston.

Banks, Leo W. 1994. "Fads: Toads." *The Los Angeles Times*, April 19:E1, E3.

Barker, Karen. 2015. "Meet Narcan: The Amazing Drug That Helps Save Overdose Patients." *Journal of Emergency Medical Services*. Retrieved June 14, 2015 (http:// www.jems.com/articles/print/volume-33/ issue-8/patient-care/meet-narcan-amazing- drug-helps.html).

Barnes, Ann Smith, and Stephanie A. Coulter. 2012. "Obesity and Sedentary Lifestyles: Risk for Cardiovascular Disease in Women." *Texas Heart Institute Journal*, 39(2):224–27.

Barnosky, Anthony D., Nicholas Matzke, Susumu Tomiya, Guinevere O. U. Wogan, Brian Swartz, Tiago B. Quental, Charles Marshall, Jenny L. McGuire, Emily L. Lindsey, Kaitlin C. Maguire, Ben Mersey, and Elizabeth A. Ferrer. 2011. "Has the Earth's Sixth Mass Extinction Period Already Arrived?" *Nature*, 471 (7336):51–57.

Barragan, Bianca. 2015. "New Aerial Video Shows the Terrifying Hugeness of the Porter Ranch Gas Leak." *Los Angeles Curbed*, December 28. Retrieved December 29, 2015 (http://la.curbed .com/archives/2015/12/porter_ranch_aliso _canyon_gas_leak_aerial_video_size.php).

Barro, Josh. 2014. "Here's Why Stealing Cars Went Out of Fashion." *The New York Times*, August 11. Retrieved April 19, 2015 (http:// www.nytimes.com/2014/08/12/upshot/heres- why-stealing-cars-went-out-of-fashion.html? _r=0&abt=0002&abg=1).

Bartol, Curt, and Anne M. Bartol. 2005. *Criminal Behavior: A Psychological Approach*, 7th edi- tion. Upper Saddle River, NJ: Prentice Hall.

BBC News. 2015. "CES 2015: Sony Condemns 'Vicious' Cyber Attack." January 6. Retrieved June 24, 2015 (http://www.bbc.com/news/ technology-30692105).

———. 2016. "Qandeel Baloch: Pakistan Social Media Celebrity 'Killed by Brother.'" July 16. Retrieved July 17, 2016 (http://www.bbc.com/ news/world-asia-36814258).

Beccaria, Cesare. 1963. *On Crimes and Punishments*, translated, with an intro- duction by Henry Paolucci. Indianapolis, IN: Bobbs-Merrill.

Becker, Howard S. 2010 [1963]. "Labeling Theory," pp. 39–41 in *Readings in Deviant Behavior*, edited by Alex Thio, Thomas C. Calhoun, Addrain Conyers. Boston: Allyn & Bacon.

Begley, Sharon. 2012. "As America's Waistline Expands, Costs Soar." *Reuters*, April 30. Retrieved February 16, 2015 (http://www .reuters.com/article/2012/04/30/us-obesity- idUSBRE83T0C820120430).

Bella, Timothy. 2012. "The '7 Dirty Words' Turn 40, but They're Still Dirty." *The Atlantic*, May 24. Retrieved December 30, 2015 (http://www .theatlantic.com/entertainment/archive/2012/ 05/the-7-dirty-words-turn-40-but-theyre-still- dirty/257374/).

Berger, Peter, and Thomas Luckmann. 1966. *The Social Construction of Reality: A Treatise in the Sociology of Knowledge.* Garden City, NY: Doubleday.

Bermudez, Esmeralda. 2014. "For Trail, Time Is Ripe." *The Los Angeles Times*, July 8:A1.

Best, Joel and David F. Luckenbill. 1994. *Organizing Deviance, 2nd edition.* Englewood Cliffs, NJ: Prentice Hall.

Billings Gazette. 1995. "Nude Photos of Students Off Limits." January 21:1A.

Bio Spectrum. 2015. "Recent 6 'Big Pharma' Frauds." Retrieved June 13, 2015 (http://www.biospectrumasia.com/biospectrum/analysis/192973/worlds-big-pharma-frauds/page/1?WT.rss_a=recent+6+%E2%80%98big+pharma%E2%80%99+frauds&WT.rss_f=pharma).

Bishaw, Alemayehu, and Kayla Fontenot. 2014. "Poverty: 2012 and 2013." *U.S. Census*, September 2014. Retrieved February 14, 2015 (http://www.census.gov/content/dam/Census/library/publications/2014/acs/acsbr13-01.pdf).

Bittman, Mark. 2009. *Food Matters: A Guide to Conscious Eating with More Than 75 Recipes.* New York: Simon and Schuster.

Blomberg, Lindsey. 2011. "Mountains of Food Waste." *The Environmental Magazine.* Retrieved December 7, 2015 (http://www.emagazine.com/daily-news/mountains-of-food-waste).

Borenstein, Seth. 2015. "Scientists: Coral Bleaching Crisis Spreads Worldwide." *The Post-Standard*, October 8:A-21.

Boston Tea Party. 2015. "The Tea Act." Retrieved April 29, 2015 (http://www.bostonteaparty-ship.com/the-tea-act).

Botelho, Greg. 2014. "9 Air Force Commanders Fired from Jobs over Nuclear Missile Test Cheating." *CNN.com*, March 27. Retrieved January 19, 2015 (http://www.cnn.com/2014/03/27/us/air-force-cheating-investigation/).

Boys and Girls Clubs of America (BGCA). 2015. "Our Facts and Figures." Retrieved December 17, 2015 (http://www.bgca.org/whoweare/Pages/FactsFigures.aspx).

Bozza, Anthony. 1999. "The Fragile World of Trent Reznor." *The Rolling Stone*, October 14. Retrieved May 2, 2015 (http://www.rollingstone.com/music/news/the-fragile-world-of-trent-reznor-19991014).

Bradford, Alina. 2015. "Deforestation: Facts, Causes & Effects." *Live Science.* Retrieved December 10, 2015 (http://www.livescience.com/27692-deforestation.html).

Brady, Erik, and Rachel George. 2013. "Manti Te'o 'Catfish' Story Is a Common One." *USA Today*, January 18. Retrieved June 18, 2015 (http://www.usatoday.com/story/sports/ncaaf/2013/01/17/manti-teos-catfish-story-common/1566438/).

Bragg, Rick. 2002. "Enron's Collapse: Workers; Workers Feel Pain of Layoffs and Added Sting of Betrayal." *The New York Times*, January 20. Retrieved March 19, 2015 (http://www.nytimes.com/2002/01/20/us/enron-s-collapse-workers-workers-feel-pain-layoffs-added-sting-betrayal.html).

Brasovean, I., I. Oronian, C. Ideran, C. Oroian-Mihai, A. Fleseriu, and P. Burduhos. 2010. "Legislative Framework and Objectives of Medical Waste Management." *Pro Environment*, 3:301–4.

Breiding, Matthew J., Sharon G. Smith, Kathleen C. Basile, Mikel L. Walters, Jieru Chen, and Melissa T. Merrick. 2014. "Prevalence and Characteristics of Sexual Violence, Stalking, and Intimate Partner Violence Victimization—National Intimate Partner and Sexual Violence Survey, United States, 2011." *Centers for Disease Control and Prevention*, September 5. Retrieved May 24, 2015 (http://www.cdc.gov/mmwr/preview/mmwrhtml/ss6308a1.htm?s_cid=ss6308a1_e).

Brothers, Joyce. 2005. "Shame May Not Be So Bad after All," *Parade*, February 27:4, 6–7.

Buchmann, Bryce. 2014. "Cheating Iin College: Where It Happens, Why Students Do It and How to Stop It." *Huffington Post*, April 22. Retrieved December 16, 2015 (http://www.huffingtonpost.com/uloop/cheating-in-college-where_b_4826136.html).

Buell, Lawrence. 1995. *The Environmental Imagination.* Cambridge, MA: Harvard University Press.

Buffalo News. 1999. "Tennessee Man's Dream to Marry Car Thwarted." March 6:A5.

———. 1999. "Marijuana Enhanced Sagan's Intellectual Efforts, Biographer Says." August 22:A12.

Bullying Statistics. 2013. "School Bullying Statistics." Retrieved May 2, 2015 (http://www.bullyingstatistics.org/content/school-bullying-statistics.html).

Bureau of Justice Statistics (BJS). 1979. *Computer Crime: Criminal Justice Resource Manual.* Washington, D.C.: U.S. Department of Justice.

———. 2004. "Carjacking, 1993–2002." Retrieved April 19, 2015 (http://www.bjs.gov/index.cfm?ty=pbdetail&iid=476).

———. 2013. "Robbery." Retrieved April 11, 2015 (http://www.bjs.gov/index.cfm?ty=tp&tid=313).

———. 2015 (September). "Prisoner in 2014." *Summary/NCJ248955*. Retrieved December 20, 2015 (http://www.bjs.gov/content/pub/pdf/p14_Summary.pdf).

Burger, Jerry M. 2014. *Personality*. Stamford, CT: Cengage.

Burke, Timothy, and Jack Dickey. 2013. "Manti Te'os Dead Girlfriend, the Most Heartbreaking and Inspirational Story of the College Football Season, Is a Hoax." *Deadspin*, January 16. Retrieved June 15, 2015 (http://deadspin.com/manti-teos-dead-girlfriend-the-most-heartbreaking-an-5976517).

Business Dictionary. 2015. "Drug." Retrieved June 3, 2015 (http://www.businessdictionary.com/definition/drug.html).

Business Insider. 2015. "13 Things You Should Never Say on Your First Day at Work." Retrieved December 31, 2015 (http://www.businessinsider.com/things-you-never-say-on-your-first-day-2015-4#at-my-last-company-or-in-my-last-job-1).

Buss, Arnold. H. 1980. *Self-Consciousness and Social Anxiety*. San Francisco: W.H. Freeman.

Butcher, James N., Susan Mineka, and Jill M. Hooley. 2007. *Abnormal Psychology*, 13th edition. Boston: Pearson.

Calderone, Ana. 2015. "Bryn Mawr College Accused of Fat-Shaming After Inviting Students with High BMI to Join Weight-Loss Program." *People*, February, 2. Retrieved February 22, 2015 (http://www.people.com/article/bryn-mawr-fat-shaming-high-bmi-rudrani-sarma).

California Department of Transportation (Caltrans). 2015. "Caltrans Workers Hit the Highways to Clean Up California." Retrieved April 20, 2015 (http://www.dot.ca.gov/hq/paffairs/news/pressrel/13pr033.htm).

California Energy Commission. 2012. "Where Fossil Fuels Come From." Retrieved November 8, 2015 (http://www.energyquest.ca.gov/story/chapter08.html).

Canadian Association for Equality. 2014. "Don't Allow the Ban on 'Man Spreading' on the Bus/Train to Pass." December 23. Retrieved January 15, 2015 (https://www.change.org/p/toronto-transit-comission-don-t-allow-the-ban-on-man-spreading-on-the-bus-train-to-pass).

Carrington, Damian. 2014. "The Earth Has Lost Half of Its Wildlife in the Past 40 Years, Says WWF." *The Guardian*, September 30. Retrieved November 7, 2015 (http://www.theguardian.com/environment/2014/sep/29/earth-lost-50-wildlife-in-40-years-wwf).

Carter, David, and Andra J. Bannister. 2002. "Computer-Related Crime," pp. 183–201 in *Readings in White-Collar Crime*, edited by David Shichor, Larry Gaines, and Richard Ball. Prospect Heights, IL: Waveland.

Caruso, Kevin. 2015. "Suicide by Cop." *Suicide.org*. Retrieved May 2, 2015 (http://www.suicide.org/suicide-by-cop.html).

Castillo, Michelle. 2012. "One in Four Teens Admit to Sexting, Study Finds." *CBS News*, July 3. Retrieved August 12, 2015 (http://www.cbsnews.com/news/one-in-four-teens-admit-to-sexting-study-finds/).

Catalano, Jeannine. 2009. "Pain Management and Substance Abuse: A National Dilemma." *Social Work in Public Health*, 24:477–90.

Causes International. 2014. "E-Waste Facts." Retrieved December 9, 2015 (https://www.causesinternational.com/ewaste/e-waste-facts).

CBS. 2015. "News at Noon" (Syracuse, NY). Airdate: April 15.

CBS News. 2015a. "Right-to-Die Advocate's Mom: Vatican Remarks 'More than a Slap in the Face.' " November 18. Retrieved January 27, 2015 http://www.cbsnews.com/news/brittany-maynard-death-mom-of-right-to-die-advocate-calls-vatican-remarks-a-slap-in-the-face/).

———. 2015b. "15 Strangest Sex Fetishes: Do You Have One?" Retrieved August 22, 2015 (http://www.cbsnews.com/pictures/15-strangest-sex-fetishes-do-you-have-one/).

CBS This Morning. 2015a. "Cheating Site Exposed." Original airdate August 20.

———. 2015b. "The Joy of Sexting." Original airdate August 10.

———. 2015c. "Surviving a Shooter." Original airdate December 3.

Center for Constitutional Rights. 2015. "Report: Torture and Cruel, Inhuman, and Degrading Treatment of Prisoners at Guantanamo Bay." Retrieved March 21, 2015 (http://ccrjustice.org/learn-more/reports/report:-torture-and-cruel,-inhuman,-and-degrading-treatment-prisoners-guantanamo-).

Center for Problem-Oriented Policing. 2015. "Twenty-Five Techniques of Situational Prevention." Retrieved December 17, 2015 (http://www.popcenter.org/25techniques/).

Centers for Disease Control and Prevention (CDC). 2010. "Suicide: Facts at a Glance." Summer 2010. Retrieved May 1, 2013 (http://www.cdc.gov/violenceprevention/pd/Suicide_DataSheet-a.pdf.)

———. 2011. "Quick Facts about Suicide." Retrieved April 29, 2013 (http://www/spanusa.org/index.cfm?fuseaction=home.viewPage&page_id=0D213AD4-C50A-1085-4D96CE0EEED52A0).

———. 2012. "Defining Overweight and Obesity." Retrieved February 15, 2015 (http://www.cdc.gov/obesity/adult/defining.html).

———. 2013. "Suicide and Self-Inflicted Injury." Retrieved May 2, 2015 (http://www.cdc.gov/nchs/fastats/suicide.htm).

———. 2014a. "Adolescent and School Health: Nutrition and Health of Young People." Retrieved January 22, 2015 (http://www.cdc.gov/healthyyouth/nutrition/facts.htm).

———. 2014b. "Homelessness Is a Risk Factor for TB." Retrieved January 22, 2015 (http://www.cdc.gov/features/dsTB2011Data/).

———. 2014c. "Obesity and Overweight." Retrieved February 14, 2015 (http://www.cdc.gov/nchs/fastats/obesity-overweight.htm).

———. 2014d. "Adult Obesity Facts: Obesity Is Common, Serious and Costly." Retrieved February 15, 2015 (http://www.cdc.gov/obesity/data/adult.html).

———. 2014e. "Basics about Diabetes." Retrieved February 15, 2015 (http://www.cdc.gov/diabetes/basics/diabetes.html).

———. 2014f. "Understanding Suicide: Fact Sheet." Retrieved May 2, 2015 (http://www.cdc.gov/violenceprevention/pdf/suicide_factsheet-a.pdf).

———. 2014g. "Alcohol and Public Health: Frequently Asked Questions." Retrieved May 26, 2015 (http://www.cdc.gov/alcohol/faqs.htm#whatAlcohol).

———. 2014h. "Fact Sheets—Binge Drinking." Retrieved May 28, 2015 (http://www.cdc.gov/alcohol/fact-sheets/binge-drinking.htm).

———. 2014i. "CDC Fact Sheet: Reported STDs in the United States."

———. 2015a. "Measles Cases and Outbreaks." Retrieved January 14, 2015 (http://www.cdc.gov/measles/cases-outbreaks.html).

———. 2015b. "Fast Stats: Assault or Homicide." Retrieved April 11, 2015 (http://www.cdc.gov/nchs/fastats/homicide.htm).

———. 2015c. "Self-Directed Violence and Other Forms of Self-Injury." Retrieved May 1, 2015 (http://www.cdc.gov/ncbddd/disabilityandsafety/self-injury.html).

———. 2015d. "Suicide Prevention." Retrieved May 2, 2015 (http://www.cdc.gov/violenceprevention/suicide/).

———. 2015e. "Intimate Partner Violence." Retrieved May 24, 2015 (http://www.cdc.gov/violenceprevention/intimatepartnerviolence/).

———. 2015f. "Child Maltreatment Prevention." Retrieved May 24, 2015 (http://www.cdc.gov/violenceprevention/childmaltreatment/).

———. 2015g. "Impaired Driving: Get the Facts." Retrieved May 28, 2015 (http://www.cdc.gov/motorvehiclesafety/impaired_driving/impaired-drv_factsheet.html).

———. 2015h. "Current Cigarette Smoking among Adults in the United States." Retrieved June 6, 2015 (http://www.cdc.gov/tobacco/data_statistics/fact_sheets/adult_data/cig_smoking/).

———. 2015i. "Secondhand Smoke (SHS) Facts." Retrieved June 6, 2015 (http://www.cdc.gov/tobacco/data_statistics/fact_sheets/secondhand_smoke/general_facts/).

———. 2015j. "Drug-Poisoning Deaths Involving Heroin: United States, 2000–2013." Retrieved June 14, 2015 (http://www.cdc.gov/nchs/data/databriefs/db190.htm).

———. 2015k. "Attention-Deficit/Hyperactivity Disorder (ADHD): Treatment." Retrieved August 3, 2015 (http://www.cdc.gov/ncbddd/adhd/treatment.html).

———. 2015l. "Teenage Pregnancy in the United States." Retrieved August 11, 2015 (http://www.cdc.gov/teenpregnancy/about/index.htm).

———. 2015m. "HIV in the United States: At a Glance." Retrieved August 13, 2015 (http://www.cdc.gov/hiv/statistics/basics/ataglance.html).

———. 2015n. "Number of Deaths for Leading Causes of Death." Retrieved December 11, 2015 (http://www.cdc.gov/nchs/fastats/leading-causes-of-death.htm).

CenterWatch. 2015. "FDA Approved Drugs for Cardiology/Vascular Diseases." Retrieved June 4, 2015 (http://www.centerwatch.com/drug-information/fda-approved-drugs/therapeutic-area/1/cardiology-vascular-diseases).

The Centre for Education and Information on Drugs and Alcohol (CEIDA). 2013. "The Three Main Categories of Drugs." Retrieved June 5, 2015 (http://www.ceida.net.au/drugs .asp).

Chambliss, William. 1964. "A Sociological Analysis of the Law of Vagrancy." *Social Problems*, 12:67–77.

Chambliss, William, and Robert Seidman. 1971. *Law, Order, and Power*. Reading, MA: Addison-Wesley.

Champion, Dean John. 2004. *The Juvenile Justice System, 4th edition*. Upper Saddle River, NJ: Prentice Hall.

Chan, Alex. 2015. "Applying to a UC Campus? Now You Can Choose among Six Gender Identities—If You Want To." *The Los Angeles Times*, August 6. Retrieved September 5, 2015 (http://www.latimes.com/local/lanow/la-me-ln-uc-gender-20150806-story.html).

Chantrill, Christopher. 2015. "Federal Budget: FY 13 Federal Budget Spending Estimates for Fiscal Years 2012—2017." *USGovernmentSpending.com*. Retrieved July 27, 2015 (http://www.usgovernmentspending.com/health_care_budget_2013_1.html).

Chapin, Laura. 2015. "A Race to the Bottom on Women's Rights." *U.S. News & World Report*, March 23, 2015. Retrieved August 18, 2015 (http://www.usnews.com/opinion/blogs/laura-chapin/2015/03/23/ted-cruz-ignites-2016-race-to-the-bottom-on-abortion-and-womens-health).

Chemical Heritage Foundation. 2015. "Conflicts in Chemistry: The Case of Plastics." Retrieved December 7, 2015 (http://www.chemheritage.org/discover/online-resources/conflicts-in-chemistry/the-case-of-plastics/all-history-of-plastics.aspx).

Chesney-Lind, Meda. [1989] 2012. "Feminist Theory," pp. 98–104 in *Constructions of Deviance: Social Power, Context, and Interaction*, edited by Patricia A. Adler and Peter Adler. Belmont, CA: Wadsworth.

Cheung, Jessica. 2014. "The Fading Honor Code." *The New York Times*, April 11. Retrieved December 16, 2015 (http://www.nytimes.com/2014/04/13/education/edlife/the-fading-honor-code.html?_r=0).

Cheverere, Dillon. 2015. "Top 10 College Movies of All Time." Frat House Move. Retrieved May 30, 2015 (http://totalfratmove.com/top-10-college-movies-of-all-time/).

Child Help. 2015. "Child Abuse Statistics & Facts." Retrieved May 24, 2015 (https://www.childhelp.org/child-abuse-statistics/).

China Daily (Hong Kong edition). 2016. "China Tackles Growing Identity Crisis." May 25:6.

Choe, Jonathan. 2013. "Utah Coach Suspends Entire Football Team to Build Character." *Fox10Phoenix.com*, September 26. Retrieved July 14, 2014 (http://www.fox10phoenix.com/story/23540191/utah-coach-suspends-entire-football-team).

Churchland, Patricia S. 2012. *Braintrust: What Neuroscience Tells Us about Morality*. Princeton, NJ: Princeton University Press.

Cimino, Andrea N. 2012. "A Predictive Theory of Intentions to Exit Street-Level Prostitution." *Violence Against Women*, 18(10):1235–52.

The Citizen. 2014. "Maynard Galvanizes Right-to-Die Efforts." November 14:A6.

Civil Rights Digital Library. 2015. "Watts Riots." Retrieved April 29, 2015 (http://crdl.usg.edu/events/watts_riots/?Welcome&Welcome).

Clarke, Alan W. 2012. *Rendition to Torture*. Rutgers, NJ: Rutgers University Press.

Clear, Todd R., Michael D. Reisig, and George F. Cole. 2012. *American Corrections, 10th edition*. Belmont, CA: Wadsworth/Cengage.

Cloward, Richard, and Lloyd Ohlin. 1960. *Delinquency and Opportunity: A Theory of Delinquent Gangs*. New York: Free Press.

CNN. 2015. "Map: Same-Sex Marriage in the United States." June 26. Retrieved August 15, 2015 (http://www.cnn.com/interactive/us/map-same-sex-marriage/).

Cohan, Peter. 2010. "Today's Financial Meltdown vs. the 1990s S&L Crisis: Which Was Worse?" *Daily Finance*, July 3. Retrieved March 19, 2015 (http://www.dailyfinance.com/2010/07/03/financial-meltdown-vs-savings-loan-crisis-recession/).

Cohen, Albert. 1955. *Delinquent Boys: The Culture of the Gang*. New York: Free Press.

Collins, Randall. 1999. *Macro-History: Essays in Sociology of the Long Run*. Stanford, CA: Stanford University Press.

———. 2009. *Conflict Sociology: A Sociological Classic Updated*. Boulder, CO: Paradigm.

Collman, Ashley. 2015. "ISIS Leader 'Repeatedly Raped and Kept 26-Year-Old American Aid Worker Hostage Kayla Mueller as His Personal Sex Slave' before She Was 'Killed by US Air Strike.'" *Daily Mail*, August 16. Retrieved August 16, 2015 (http://www.dailymail.co.uk/

news/article-3198571/Islamic-State-ruler-kept-26-year-old-American-air-worker-personal-sex-slave-killed-February.html).

Conley, Mikaela. 2012. "Nip/Tuck Nations: 7 Countries with Most Cosmetic Surgery." *ABC News*, April 25. Retrieved February 1, 2015 (http://abcnews.go.com/Health/niptuck-nations-countries-cosmetic-surgery/story?id=16205231).

Constantine, Peter. 2009. *A History of Cannibalism: From Ancient Cultures to Survival Stories and Modern Psychopaths*. New York: Chartwell.

Constitution Society. 2015. "Cesare Beccaria." Retrieved March 7, 2015 (http://www.constitution.org/cb/beccaria_bio.htm).

Contrera, Jessica. 2014. "Joshua Bell's Metro Encore Draws a Crowd." *The Washington Post*, September 30. Retrieved February 5, 2015 (http://www.washingtonpost.com/lifestyle/style/joshua-bells-metro-encore-draws-a-crowd/2014/09/30/c28b6c50-48d5-11e4-a046-120a8a855cca_story.html).

———. 2015. "Target Will Stop Separating Toys and Bedding into Girls' and Boys' Sections." *The Washington Post*, August 9. Retrieved August 14, 2015 (https://www.washingtonpost.com/news/style-blog/wp/2015/08/09/target-will-stop-separating-toys-and-bedding-into-girls-and-boys-sections/).

Cook, James. 2014. "FBI Director: China Has Hacked Every Big US Company." *Business Insider*, October 6. Retrieved June 25, 2015 (http://www.businessinsider.com/fbi-director-china-has-hacked-every-big-us-company-2014-10).

Cooke, Lucy J., Claire M. A. Haworth, and Jane Wardle. 2007. "Genetic and Environmental Influences on Children's Food Neophobia." *The American Journal of Clinical Nutrition*, 86:428–33.

Cooley, Charles. 1909. *Social Organization*. New York: Scribners.

Cornell University Law School. 2015. "White Collar Crime." *Legal Information Institute*. Retrieved March 16, 2015 (https://www.law.cornell.edu/wex/white-collar_crime).

Corwin, Jeff. 2009. "The Sixth Extinction." *The Los Angeles Times*, November 30. Retrieved November 7, 2015 (http://articles.latimes.com/2009/nov/30/opinion/la-oe-corwin30-2009nov30).

Coser, Lewis. 1967. *Continuities in the Study of Social Conflict*. New York: Free Press.

Costa, Chloe Della. 2015. "3 Global Cyber Crimes That Had Huge Payoffs." *Business Cheat Sheet*, April 21. Retrieved June 22, 2015 (http://www.cheatsheet.com/business/3-global-cyber-crimes-that-had-huge-payoffs.html/?a=viewall).

Coyle, Jake. 2014. "Sony Cancels 'Interview.'" *The Post-Standard*, December 18:A-15.

Crisis Intervention Center. 2011. "What Is Sexting?" Retrieved September 16, 2011 (http://www.crisisinterventioncenter.org/index.php?option=com_content&view=article&id=147:what-is-sexting&catid=39:teens&Itemid=79).

Crow, R. Brian, and Scott R. Rosner. 2004. "Hazing and Sport and the Law," pp. 200–223 in *The Hazing Reader*, edited by Hank Nuwer. Bloomington, IN: Indiana University Press.

CTV News Toronto. 2014. "Movement to Ban 'Man-Spreading' on Transit Picks Up Speed in Toronto." December 22. Retrieved January 5, 2015 (http://toronto.ctvnews.ca/movement-to-ban-man-spreading-on-transit-picks-up-speed-in-toronto-1.2158517).

Curran, Daniel, and Claire Renzetti. 1994. *Theories of Crime*. Boston, MA: Allyn & Bacon.

CyberBully Hotline. 2013. "Catfishing: A Growing Trend in Cyberbullying." Retrieved June 19, 2015 (http://www.cyberbullyhotline.com/catfishing.html).

Daily Mail. 2012. "'I Had to Eat Piece of my Friend to Survive': Torment of 1972 Andes Plane Crash Survivor Still Haunted by His Ordeal 40 Years Later." October 13. Retrieved January 12, 2015 (http://www.dailymail.co.uk/news/article-2217141/I-eat-piece-friend-survive-Torment-1972-Andes-plane-crash-survivor-haunted-ordeal-40-years-later.html).

The Daily News. 2015. "Former Jets Linebacker Jermaine Cunningham to Face 'Revenge Porn' Charges in Court on Wednesday." May 4. Retrieved June 15, 2015 (http://www.nydailynews.com/sports/football/jets/ex-jet-jermaine-cunningham-face-revenge-porn-charges-article-1.2209657).

Daly, J. W., J. Holmen, and B. B. Fredholm. 1998. "Is Caffeine Addictive? The Most Widely Used Psychoactive Substance in the World Affects Same Parts of the Brain as Cocaine." *Lakartidningen*, Dec (51–52):5878–83.

Day, Michael. 2014. "Global Demonic Possessions Are Reaching 'Emergency Levels,' Exorcism Expert Warns Pope." *Sunday Express*, October 28.

Retrieved March 1, 2015 (http://www.express .co.uk/news/weird/528622/Devil-Woman-Demonic-Possession-Pope-Francis).

Dearing, Eric, and Christine Wade. 2006. "Poverty," pp. 1014–16 in *Encyclopedia of Human Development*, Vol. 3, edited by Neil J. Salkind. Thousand Oaks, CA: Sage.

Death with Dignity National Center. 2015. "Death with Dignity around the U.S." Retrieved January 18, 2015 (http://www.deathwithdig nity.org/advocates/national).

Delaney, Tim. 2004a. *Classical Social Theory: Investigation and Application*. Upper Saddle River, NJ: Prentice Hall/Pearson.

———. 2004b. "The Russian Mafia in the United States," pp. 6–17 in *Social Diseases: Mafia, Terrorism, and Totalitarianism*, edited by Tim Delaney, Valerii Kuvakin, and Timothy Madigan. Moscow: Russian Humanist Society.

———. 2005. *Contemporary Social Theory: Investigation and Application*. Upper Saddle River, NJ: Prentice Hall/Pearson.

———. 2006. *Seinology: The Sociology of Seinfeld*. Amherst, NY: Prometheus.

———. 2008. *Shameful Behaviors*. Lanham, MD: University Press of America.

———. 2012a. *Connecting Sociology to Our Lives: An Introduction to Sociology*. Boulder, CO: Paradigm.

———. 2012b. "Georg Simmel's Flirting and Secrecy and Its Application to the Facebook Relationship Status—It's Complicated." *Journal of Journalism and Mass Communication*, 2(5):637–47.

———. 2014a. *Classical and Contemporary Social Theory: Investigation and Application*. Upper Saddle River, NJ: Prentice Hall/Pearson.

———. 2014b. *American Street Gangs, 2nd edition*. Upper Saddle River, NJ: Pearson.

Delaney, Tim, and Tim Madigan. 2014. *Beyond Sustainability: A Thriving Environment*. Jefferson, NC: McFarland.

———. 2015. *The Sociology of Sports: An Introduction, 2nd ed*. Jefferson, NC: McFarland.

Delingpole, James. 2014. "Global Warming Will Cause War, Pestilence, Famine and Death, Says New IPCC Report Inevitably." *Brietbart*, March 31. Retrieved December 11, 2015 (http://www.breitbart.com/london/2014/03/ 31/global-warming-will-cause-war-pestilence-famine-and-death-says-new-ipcc-report-inevitably/).

Demetriou, Danielle. 2008. "Japanese Launch Campaign to Marry Comic Book Characters." *The Telegraph*, October 30. Retrieved January 8, 2015 (http://www.aol.com/article/2015/ 01/15/my-strange-addiction-florida-woman-marries-a-carnival-ride).

Depression Connect. 2011. "Q&A: Patricia Adler, Author of 'The Tender Cut.'" Retrieved July 22, 2016 (http://www .depressionconnect.com/depression-articles/ 9-q-amp-a-patricia-adler-author-of-the-tender-cut#41G8TRJlWO6ZcMs3.97).

DeSilver, Drew. 2014. "Who's Poor in America? 50 Years into the 'War on Poverty,' a Data Portrait." *Pew Research Center*, January 13. Retrieved February 14 (http://www .pewresearch.org/fact-tank/2014/01/13/whos-poor-in-america-50-years-into-the-war-on-poverty-a-data-portrait/#more-253059).

de Vries, Brian. 2007. "LGBT Couples in Later Life: A Study in Diversity." *Generations* (Fall):8–23.

Dietary Guidelines for Americans. 2010. "Alcohol Guideline." Retrieved May 28, 2015 (http:// www.drinkiq.com/DrinkiQ%20Documents/ en-US/2010%20alcohol%20DG%20tear%20 pad%20final%20Sep%2024%202012.pdf).

Digital History. 2014. "The Espionage Act of 1917." Retrieved March 21, 2015 (http:// www.digitalhistory.uh.edu/disp_textbook .cfm?smtID=3&psid=3904).

Dilanian, Ken. 2015. "Years of 'Neglected' Security Left Door Open to Hack Millions of Fed Workers' Info." *U.S. News & World Report*, June 16. Retrieved June 25, 2015 (http://www .usnews.com/news/politics/articles/2015/06/ 16/cybertheft-of-personnel-info-rips-hole-in-espionage-defenses).

DMV.org. 2013. "Top 10 Most Stolen Vehicles by Year (2003–2012)." Retrieved April 19, 2015 (http://www.dmv.org/insurance/most-stolen-cars-and-other-vehicles.php).

Doksone, Thanyarat, and Jocelyn Gecker. 2014. "'Bumfights' Producers Accused of Mailing Body Parts." *San Diego Times Union*, November 18. Retrieved May 3, 2015 (http://www .utsandiego.com/news/2014/nov/18/bumfights-producers-stolen-body-parts-thailand/).

Domhoff, G. William. 1970. *The Higher Circles*. New York: Random House.

Domhoff, G. William, and Thomas R. Dye. 1987. "Introduction," 7–17 in *Power Elites and*

Organizations, edited by G. William Domhoff and Thomas R. Dye. Newbury Park, CA: Sage.

Doran, Elizabeth. 2014. "Bullied, Not Broken." *The Post-Standard*, September 9:A-3.

————. 2016. "Manlius Town Computer Attacked by Russian 'Ransomware.'" *The Post-Standard*, March 15:A-4.

DoSomething.org. 2015. "11 Facts about Bullying." Retrieved May 2, 2015 (https://www.dosome thing.org/facts/11-facts-about-bullying).

Douthat, Ross. 2008. "Is Pornography Adultery?" *The Atlantic*, October. Retrieved August 21, 2015 (http://www.theatlantic.com/magazine/archive/2008/10/is-pornography-adultery/306989/).

Dowie, Mark. 1977. "Pinto Madness." *Mother Jones*, 2 (September-October):18–32.

Dowty, Douglas. 2014. "Judge: 25 Years Is Not Enough for Killer of Elmwood's Beloved Jim Gifford." *The Post-Standard*, October 23:A-3.

————. 2015. "How a Syracuse Case Could Define 'Depraved Indifference.'" *The Post-Standard*, January 27:A-4.

Drug Enforcement Administration Museum (DEA Museum). 2015a. "Illegal Drugs in American: A Modern History—America's First Drug Epidemic, 1850–1914." Retrieved June 9, 2015 (http://www.deamuseum.org/museum_idaafde.html).

————. 2015b. "Cannabis, Coca & Poppy: Nature's Addictive Plants." Retrieved June 11, 2015 (http://www.deamuseum.org/ccp/cannabis/history.html).

Drugs.com. 2015. "Rohypnol." Retrieved June 7, 2015 (http://www.drugs.com/illicit/rohypnol.html).

Drugs-Forum. 2014. "Heroin." Retrieved June 14, 2015 (https://drugs-forum.com/forum/showwiki.php?title=Heroin).

DrugWatch.com. 2015. "Prozac." Retrieved June 7, 2015 (http://www.drugwatch.com/prozac/).

Duke Energy. 2015. "How Do Nuclear Plants Work?" Retrieved December 9, 2015 (https://www.duke-energy.com/about-energy/generating-electricity/nuclear-how.asp).

Durkheim, Emile. 1938 [1895]. *The Rules of Sociological Method*. New York: Free Press.

————. 1951 [1897]. *Le Suicide*. New York: Free Press.

————. 1973 [1925]. *Moral Education: A Study in the Theory and Application of the Sociology of Education*. New York: Free Press.

————. 1984 [1893]. *The Division of Labor in Society*, translated by W. D. Halls. New York: Free Press.

Edelmann, Robert J. 1987. *The Psychology of Embarrassment*. New York: Wiley & Sons.

Electronics TakeBack Coalition. 2014. "Facts and Figures on E-Waste and Recycling." Retrieved December 9, 2015 (http://www.electronic stakeback.com/wp-content/uploads/Facts_and_Figures_on_EWaste_and_Recycling.pdf).

Ellis, Ralph. 2015. "Oklahoma Approves Nitrogen Gas as Backup Execution Method." *CNN*, April 17. Retrieved April 18, 2015 (http://www.cnn.com/2015/04/17/us/oklahoma-executions/).

Elon University. 2015. "Elon Honor Code, Pledge, and Policies." Retrieved December 16, 2015 (http://www.elon.edu/e-web/students/hand book/honor.xhtml).

Enough Is Enough. 2013. "Cyberbullying Statistics." Retrieved June 20, 2015 (http://www.internet safety101.org/cyberbullyingstatistics.htm).

Environmental and Energy Study Institute (EESI). 2015. "Fossil Fuels." Retrieved November 8, 2015 (http://www.eesi.org/topics/fossil-fuels/description).

Envision Counselling and Support Centre. 2014. "Parent Abuse." Retrieved May 24, 2015 (http://www.envisioncounsellingcentre.com/resources/parent_abuse.html).

Esch, Mary. 2012. "Cornell Debates Evils of Fracking vs. Coal Mining." *The Post-Standard*, January 25:A-4.

ESPN. 2015a. "Coach: Ducks Will Be Disciplined." January 2. Retrieved August 10, 2015 (http://espn.go.com/college-football/bowls14/story/_/id/12110366/rose-bowl-oregon-ducks-players-face-discipline-no-means-no-chant).

————. 2015b. "Caitlyn Jenner Vows to 'Reshape the Landscape' in ESPY's Speech." July 16. Retrieved August 15, 2015 (http://espn.go.com/espys/2015/story/_/id/13264599/caitlyn-jenner-accepts-arthur-ashe-courage-award-espys-ashe2015).

Evans-Brown, Michael, and Jim McVeigh. 2009 (October). "Injecting Human Growth Hormone as a Performance-Enhancing Drug—Perspectives from the United Kingdom." *Journal of Substance Use*, 14(5):267–88.

Farganis, James. 2011. *Readings in Social Theory: The Classic Tradition to Post-Modernism*, 6th edition. Boston: McGraw-Hill.

Federal Bureau of Investigation (FBI). 2009. "Bernard L. Madoff Pleads Guilty to 11-Count Criminal Information and Is Remanded into Custody," *U.S. Attorney's Office, Southern District of New York*, March 12. Retrieved March 16, 2015 (http://www.fbi.gov/newyork/press-releases/2009/nyfo031209.htm).

———. 2010. "Public Corruption: Why It's Our #1 Criminal Priority." Retrieved March 21, 2015 (http://www.fbi.gov/news/stories/2010/march/corruption_032610).

———. 2011a. "Crime in the United States: Burglary." Retrieved April 18, 2015 (http://www.fbi.gov/about-us/cjis/ucr/crime-in-the-u.s/2010/crime-in-the-u.s.-2010/property-crime/burglarymain).

———. 2011b. "Crime in the United States: Larceny-Theft." Retrieved April 18, 2015 (http://www.fbi.gov/about-us/cjis/ucr/crime-in-the-u.s/2010/crime-in-the-u.s.-2010/property-crime/larcenytheftmain).

———. 2011c. "Crime in the United States: Motor Vehicle Theft." Retrieved April 18, 2015 (http://www.fbi.gov/about-us/cjis/ucr/crime-in-the-u.s/2010/crime-in-the-u.s.-2010/property-crime/mvtheftmain).

———. 2011d. "Crime in the United States: Arson." Retrieved April 19, 2015 (http://www.fbi.gov/about-us/cjis/ucr/crime-in-the-u.s/2011/crime-in-the-u.s.-2011/property-crime/arson).

———. 2012. "Insider Trading: Proactive Enforcement Paying Off." Retrieved April 20, 2016 (https://www.fbi.gov/news/stories/insider-trading).

———. 2014a. "'Virtual Kidnapping' Extortion Calls on the Rise." Retrieved March 21, 2015 (http://www.fbi.gov/sanantonio/press-releases/2014/virtual-kidnapping-extortion-calls-on-the-rise).

———. 2014b. "Frequently Asked Questions about the Change in the UCR Definition of Rape." December 11. Retrieved April 17, 2015 (http://www.fbi.gov/about-us/cjis/ucr/recent-program-updates/new-rape-definition-frequently-asked-questions).

———. 2014c. "Suicide by Cop: Broadening Our Understanding." Retrieved May 2, 2015 (http://leb.fbi.gov/2014/september/suicide-by-cop-broadening-our-understanding).

———. 2014d. "Child Pornography Victim Assistance (CPVA)." Retrieved June 20, 2015 (https://www.fbi.gov/stats-services/victim_assistance/overview/child-pornography-victim-assistance).

———. 2014e. "Frequently Asked Questions about the Change in the UCR Definition of Rape." Retrieved August 16, 2015 (https://www.fbi.gov/about-us/cjis/ucr/recent-program-updates/new-rape-definition-frequently-asked-questions).

———. 2014f. "A Study of Active Shooter Incidents in the United States Between 2000 and 2013." Retrieved December 29, 2015 (https://www.fbi.gov/news/stories/2014/september/fbi-releases-study-on-active-shooter-incidents/pdfs/a-study-of-active-shooter-incidents-in-the-u.s.-between-2000-and-2013).

———. 2014g. "Laser Pointers." Retrieved December 29, 2015 (https://www.fbi.gov/news/stories/2014/february/protecting-aircraft-from-lasers).

———. 2015a. "Insider Trading: Proactive Enforcement Paying Off." Retrieved March 18, 2015 (http://www.fbi.gov/news/stories/2012/august/insider-trading-enforcement-paying-off).

———. 2015b. "White Collar Crime: Corporate Fraud." Retrieved March 16, 2015 (http://www.fbi.gov/about-us/investigate/white_collar/corporate-fraud).

———. 2015c. "Securities Fraud Awareness & Prevention Tips." Retrieved March 17, 2015 (http://www.fbi.gov/stats-services/publications/securities-fraud/securities-fraud-awareness-prevention-tips).

———. 2015d. "Crime in the United States: Offense Definitions." Retrieved March 18, 2015 (http://www.fbi.gov/about-us/cjis/ucr/crime-in-the-u.s/2010/crime-in-the-u.s.-2010/offense-definitions).

———. 2015e. "It's Our Top Priority Among Criminal Investigations—and for Good Reason." Retrieved March 21, 2015 (http://www.fbi.gov/about-us/investigate/corruption).

———. 2015f. "What We Investigate." Retrieved March 21, 2015 (http://www.fbi.gov/albuquerque/about-us/what-we-investigate).

———. 2015g. "Asian Criminal Enterprises." Retrieved March 27, 2015 (http://www.fbi.gov/about-us/investigate/organizedcrime/asian).

———. 2015h. "Italian Organized Crime: Overview." Retrieved March 28, 2015 (http://www.fbi.gov/about-us/investigate/organizedcrime/italian_mafia).

———. 2015i. "Victim Assistance: Financial Crime and You." Retrieved June 20, 2015 (https://www.fbi.gov/stats-services/victim_assistance/fincrime_vic).

———. 2015j. "Common Fraud Schemes." Retrieved March 17, 2015 (http://www.fbi .gov/scams-safety/fraud).

———. 2015k. "Common Fraud Schemes: Internet Fraud." Retrieved June 22, 2015 (https://www .fbi.gov/scams-safety/fraud/internet_fraud).

———. 2015l. "Intellectual Property Theft." Retrieved June 23, 2015 (https://www.fbi.gov/ about-us/investigate/white_collar/ipr/ipr).

———. 2015m. "What We Investigate." Retrieved December 29, 2015 (https://www.fbi.gov/ albuquerque/about-us/what-we-investigate).

Federal Communications Commission (FCC). 2015. "The FCC and Freedom of Speech." Retrieved December 30, 2015 (https://www.fcc.gov/consumers/guides/fcc-and-freedom-speech).

Ferraiuolo, Jean. 2014. "10 of the Most Popular Sexual Fetishes." *The Richest*, June 3. Retrieved August 23, 2015 (http://www .therichest.com/rich-list/most-popular/10-of-the-most-popular-sexual-fetishes/).

Finckenauer, James. 1998. *Russian Mafia in America*. Boston: Northeastern University Press.

———. 2002. "Russia," pp. 1423–29 in *Encyclopedia of Crime and Punishment*, Vol. 3, edited by David Levinson. Thousand Oaks, CA: Sage.

Fink, Arthur E. 1938. *Causes of Crime*. New York: A. S. Barnes.

Finkelstein, Eric A., Justin G. Trogdon, Joel W. Cohen, and William Dietz. 2009. "Annual Medical Spending Attributable to Obesity: Payer- and Service-Specific Estimates." *Health Affairs*, 28(5):822–31.

Fire Science. 2015. "Investigator." Retrieved April 20, 2015 (http://www.firescience.org/how-to-become-an-arson-investigator/).

Fitzsimmons, Emma G. 2014. "A Scourge Is Spreading. M.T.A.'s Cure? Dude, Close Your Legs." *The New York Times*, December 20. Retrieved January 8, 2015 (http://www.nytimes .com/2014/12/21/nyregion/MTA-targets-manspreading-on-new-york-city-subways .html?_r=0).

Florida Department of Law Enforcement (FDLE). 1989. *Computer-Crime in Florida*. An unpublished report prepared by the Florida Department of Law Enforcement, Tallahassee, Florida.

Focus on the Family. 2015. "The Stages of Pornographic Addiction." Retrieved August 21, 2015 (http:// www.focusonthefamily.com/marriage/divorce-and-infidelity/pornography-and-virtual-infidelity/ stages-of-porn-addiction).

Fontana, Andrea. 1973. "Labeling Theory Reconsidered," pp. 177–212 in *Outsiders: Studies in the Sociology of Deviance*, edited by Howard Becker. New York: Free Press.

Food and Beverage Underground. 2014. "The History of Vodka and Its Production Then and Now." Retrieved January 4, 2016 (http://www .food and beverage underground.com/history-of-vodka.html).

Food and Drink Europe. 2015. "Possible Causes of Food Loss and Food Waste." Retrieved December 7, 2015 (http://www.fooddrinkeu rope.eu/our-actions/foodwaste-toolkit/ possible-causes-of-food-loss-and-food-waste/).

Forest, James J. F. (Editor). 2006. *The Making of a Terrorist: Recruitment, Training, and Root Causes*, Vol. 3. Westport, CT: Praeger.

Foucault, Michel. 1961 [1965]. *Madness and Civilization: A History of Insanity in the Age of Reason*, translated by R. Howard. London: Tavistock.

Foundation for a Drug-Free World. 2015a. "The Truth about Alcohol." Retrieved May 30, 2015 (http:// www.drugfreeworld.org/drugfacts/alcohol/ a-short-history.html).

———. 2015b. "The Truth about Cocaine: International Statistics." Retrieved June 6, 2015 (http://www.drugfreeworld.org/drugfacts/ cocaine/international-statistics.html).

———. 2015c. "What Is Ritalin?" Retrieved June 6, 2015 (http://www.drugfreeworld.org/drugfacts/ ritalin.html).

———. 2015d. "The Truth about Prescription Drug Abuse." Retrieved June 12, 2015 (http://www .drugfreeworld.org/drugfacts/prescription-drugs.html).

The 419 Coalition Website. 2015. "We Fight the Nigerian Scam with Education." Retrieved June 22, 2015 (http://home.rica.net/alphae/ 419coal/).

Fox News. 2015. "University of California Offers Six Choices for 'Gender Identity.'" July 28. Retrieved August 14, 2015 (http://www.foxnews.com/ us/2015/07/28/university-california-offers-six-choices-for-gender-identity/).

The Free Dictionary. 2015. "Pornography." Retrieved August 21, 2015 (http://legal-dictionary.thefreedictionary.com/pornography).

Freedman, Estelle B. 2013. *Redefining Rape: Sexual Violence in the Era of Suffrage and Segregation*. Cambridge, MA: Harvard University Press.

Freegan.Info. 2015. "What Is a Freegan?" Retrieved December 11, 2015 (http://freegan.info/).

Freeman, Shanna. 2015. "How LSD Works." Retrieved June 7, 2015 (http://science.how stuffworks.com/lsd1.htm).

Friedman, Megan. 2015. "Demi Lovato Says She's 'Living Well' with Bipolar Disorder." *Cosmopolitan*, May 28. Retrieved August 3, 2015 (http://www.cosmopolitan.com/enter tainment/celebs/news/a41103/demi-lovato-says-shes-living-well-with-bipolar-disorder/).

Fuchs, Erin. 2013. "7 Surprising Things That Could Make You a Sex Offender." *Business Insider*, October 9. Retrieved May 30, 2015 (http://www.businessinsider.com/surprising-things-that-could-make-you-a-sex-offender-2013-10).

Gaines, Larry K., and Victor E. Kappeler. 2011. *Policing in America, 7th edition*. Waltham, MA: Elsevier/Anderson Publishing.

Gardner, Greg. 2015. "Deaths Tied to Defective GM Switches Rise to 84." As it appeared in *The Post-Standard*, April 14:B-3.

Garfinkel, Harold. 1956. "Conditions of Successful Degradation Ceremonies." *American Journal of Sociology*, 61:420–24.

Garratt v. Dailey. 1955. "Garratt v. Dailey—Case Brief Summary." 46 Wash. 2d 197, 279 P .2d 1901. Retrieved April 16, 2015 (http://www .lawnix.com/cases/garratt-dailey.html).

Geis, Gilbert. 2002. "White Collar Crime: What Is It?" pp. 7–25 in *Readings in White-Collar Crime*, edited by David Shichor, Larry Gaines, and Richard Ball. Prospect Heights, IL: Waveland Press.

Gert, Bernard. 2011. "The Definition of Morality." *Stanford Encyclopedia of Philosophy*. Retrieved January 28, 2015 (http://plato.stanford.edu/entries/morality-definition/).

Gibbs, Samuel. 2015. "Samsung Keyboard Bug Leaves 600m Android Devices Exposed to Hackers." *The Guardian*, June 17. Retrieved June 25, 2015 (http://www.theguardian.com/technology/2015/jun/17/samsung-keyboard-bug-android-hack).

Giddens, Anthony. 1972. *Emile Durkheim: Selected Writings*. Cambridge: Cambridge University Press.

Gleick, Peter. 2009. "Energy Implications of Bottle Water." *Environmental Research Letters*, 4:664–70.

Global Drug Survey. 2015. "The Global Drug Survey 2014 Findings." Retrieved June 9, 2015 (http://www.globaldrugsurvey.com/facts-figures/the-global-drug-survey-2014-findings/).

Goffman, Erving. 1961. *Asylums: Essays on the Social Situation of Mental Patients and Other Inmates*. Garden City, NY: Anchor.

———. 1963a. *Stigma: Notes on the Management of a Spoiled Identity*. Englewood Cliffs, NJ: Prentice Hall.

———. 1963b. *Behavior in Public Places: Notes on the Social Organization of Gatherings*. Glencoe, IL: Free Press.

Goldstein, Arnold. 1991. *Delinquent Gangs: A Psychological Perspective*. Champaign, IL: Research Press.

Gongloff, Mark. 2002. "Bush Seeks New Business Ethic." *CNN Money*, July 9. Retrieved March 16, 2015 (http://money.cnn.com/2002/07/09/news/bush/).

Goodman, Amy. 2015a. "Storming the Bastille at Paris Climate Summit." As it appeared in *The Citizen*, October 31:A-4.

———. 2015b. "Trans-Pacific Partnerships Should Get Flushed." Syndicated column as it appeared in *The Citizen*, March 21:A4.

Goodman, Tim. 2013. "Manti Te'o, 'Catfish,' Katie Couric, Oprah and the Sports World: Paging Dr. Phil!" *The Hollywood Reporter*, January 24. Retrieved June 18, 2015 (http://www .hollywoodreporter.com/bastard-machine/manti-teo-story-hooks-media-415094).

Gorzelany, Jim. 2014. "The Most-Stolen New and Used Cars in America." *Forbes*, August 18. Retrieved April 19, 2015 (http://www.forbes .com/sites/jimgorzelany/2014/08/18/the-most-stolen-new-and-used-cars-in-america/).

Gosztola, Kevin. 2013. "Snowden Becomes Eighth Person to Be Charged with Violating the Espionage Act Under Obama." *Dissenter*, June 21. Retrieved March 21, 2015 (http://dissenter .firedoglake.com/2013/06/21/snowden-becomes-eighth-person-to-be-indicted-for-espionage-by-the-obama-justice-department/).

Gould, Jennifer, and Bruce Golding. 2016. "'Wolf of Wall Street' Film Was Financed with Stolen Money: Feds." *New York Post*, July 20. Retrieved July 22, 2016 (http://nypost.com/2016/07/20/wolf-of-wall-street-was-financed-with-stolen-money-feds/).

GraffitiHurts.com. 2015. "Fast Facts about Graffiti." Retrieved April 20, 2015 (http://www.graffitihurts.org/getfacts/fastfacts.jsp).

Gratz, Kim, and Alexander Chapman. 2009. *Freedom from Self-Harm: Overcoming Self-Injury*. Oakland, CA: New Harbinger.

Gray, Katti. 2013. "Are We Over-diagnosing Mental Illness?" *CNN*, March 18. Retrieved August 1, 2015 (http://www.cnn.com/2013/03/16/health/mental-illness-overdiagnosis/).

Greenberg, Susan H. 2015. "Why Colleges Should Ditch Honor Codes." *The Washington Post*, May 28. Retrieved December 16, 2015 (https://www.washingtonpost.com/posteverything/wp/2015/05/28/why-colleges-should-ditch-honor-codes/).

Green Roofs. 2015. "Green Roof Benefits." Retrieved December 11, 2015 (http://www.greenroofs.org/index.php/about/greenroofbenefits).

Greensgrow. 2015. "What Is Urban Farming?" Retrieved December 12, 2015 (http://www.greensgrow.org/urban-farm/what-is-urban-farming/).

Grinberg, Emanuella. 2015. "Online Survey Finds 8 in 10 Adults Have Engaged in Sexting." *CNN*, August 8. Retrieved August 12, 2015 (http://www.cnn.com/2015/08/08/health/sexting-adults-online-survey-feat/).

Groenfeldt, Tom. 2014. "More Secure Credit Cards with Chips Coming to the U.S." *Forbes*, June 23. Retrieved June 23, 2015 (http://www.forbes.com/sites/tomgroenfeldt/2014/06/23/more-secure-credit-cards-with-chips-coming-to-the-u-s/).

Groppe, Maureen. 2015. "Lawmaker Sorry for Saying Having Child from Rape is 'Beautiful.'" *USA Today*, February 7. Retrieved August 16, 2015. (http://www.usatoday.com/story/news/politics/2015/02/07/rape-kurcaba/23042669/).

The Guardian. 2015. "France Decrees New Rooftops Must Be Covered in Plants or Solar Panels." March 19. Retrieved December 11, 2015 (http://www.theguardian.com/world/2015/mar/20/france-decrees-new-rooftops-must-be-covered-in-plants-or-solar-panels).

Hadden, Richard W. 1997. *Sociological Theory*. Orchard Park, NY: Broadview.

Haddock, Deborah. 2001. *The Dissociative Identity Disorder*. New York: McGraw-Hill.

Haidt, Jonathan. 2013. *The Righteous Mind: Why Good People Are Divided by Politics and Religion*. New York: Vintage.

Haiken, Melanie. 2012. "5 Deadliest Diet Trends: Pills That Really Can Kill." *Forbes*, April 19. Retrieved August 19, 2015 (http://www.forbes.com/sites/melaniehaiken/2012/04/19/5-deadliest-diet-trends/print/).

Hamblin, James. 2013. "Why We Took Cocaine Out of Soda." *The Atlantic*, January 31. Retrieved August 19, 2015 (http://www.theatlantic.com/health/archive/2013/01/why-we-took-cocaine-out-of-soda/272694/).

Hammond, Ross A., and Ruth Levine. 2010. "The Economic Impact of Obesity in the United States." *Diabetes, Metabolic Syndrome and Obesity: Targets and Therapy*, 3 (August): 285–95.

Hannigan, John. 2014. *Environmental Sociology, 3rd edition*. New York: Routledge.

Hanson, David J. 2013. "Historical Evolution of Alcohol Consumption in Society," pp. 3–12 in *Alcohol: Science, Policy and Public Health*, edited by Peter Boyle, Paolo Boffetta, Albert B. Lowenfels, Harry Burns, Otis Brawley, Witold Zatonski, and Jurgen Rehm. Oxford: Oxford University Press.

Harper, Charles. L. 2012. *Environment and Society, 5th edition*. Boston: Pearson.

Hartl, Emil M., Edward P. Monnelly, and Roland D. Elderkin. 1982. *Physique of Delinquent Behavior: A Thirty-Year Follow-Up of William H. Sheldon's Varieties of Delinquent Youth*. New York: Academic Press.

Harvard T.H. Chan School of Public Health. 2015. "Alcohol: Balancing Risks and Benefits." Retrieved May 28, 2015 (http://www.hsph.harvard.edu/nutritionsource/alcohol-full-story/).

Hassan, Amro and Kim Willsher. 2015. "Chilling Internet Searchers: Officials Say the German Copilot Explored Suicide and Cockpit Security Systems." *The Los Angeles Times*, April 3:A3.

Hauser, Christine. 2015. "Teenager Who Used 'Affluenza' Defense in Fatal Crash Is Missing." *The New York Times*, December 16. Retrieved December 17, 2015 (http://www.nytimes.com/2015/12/17/us/ethan-couch-missing-texas-affluenza-case.html?_r=0).

Hawkins, Derek, Lynh Bui, and Peter Hermann. 2016. "Baltimore Prosecutors Drop All Remaining Charges in Freddie Gray Case." *The Washington Post*, July 27. Retrieved July 29, 2016 (https://www.washingtonpost.com/local/public-safety/baltimore-prosecutors-drop-all-remaining-charges-in-freddie-gray-case/2016/07/27/b5c10f34-b655-4d40-87e6-80827e2f0e2d_story.html).

Health Central. 2015. "Causes of Obesity—Biological and Medical Causes." Retrieved February 15, 2015 (http://www.healthcentral

.com/obesity/complications-000053_2-145_1.html).

Healthy Place. 2015. "Narcissistic Personality Disorder (NPD) Definition." Retrieved December 31, 2015 (http://www.healthyplace.com/personality-disorders/malignant-self-love/narcissistic-personality-disorder-npd-definition/).

Healy, Jack. 2015. "Life Sentence for James Holmes, Aurora Theater Gunman." *The New York Times*, August 7. Retrieved August 8, 2015 (http://www.nytimes.com/2015/08/08/us/jury-decides-fate-of-james-holmes-aurora-theater-gunman.html?_r=0).

Healy, Melissa. 2015. "Beyond Average Depression." *The Los Angeles Times*, April 5:A4.

Heckert, Alex, and Druann Maria Heckert. 2002. "A New Typology of Deviance: Integrating Normative and Reactivist Definitions of Deviance." *Deviant Behavior*, 23(5):449–79.

Heiner, Robert. 2002. *Social Problems: An Introduction to Critical Constructionism*. New York: Oxford University Press.

Held, David. 1980. *Introduction to Critical Theory*. Berkeley, CA: University of California Press.

Helling, Steve. 2015. "Drama off the Track: NASCAR's Bizarre Split." *People*, February 2:58.

Henry, Ray. 2015a. "Shooter's Mental Illness Didn't Stop Gun Buy." *The Post-Standard*, July 26:A-13.

———. 2015b. "Judge Says She Did Not Commit Theater Gunman." *The Post-Standard*, July 28:A-11.

Henry, Tamara. 1995. "Ditto Sheets in Schools Hazardous." *USA Today*, March 21:1D.

Henshaw, Sophie. 2015. "Bullying at Work: Workplace Mobbing Is on the Rise." Retrieved May 2, 2015 (http://psychcentral.com/blog/archives/2013/12/28/bullying-at-work-workplace-mobbing-is-on-the-rise/).

Hensley, Nicole. 2014. "Firefighters Rescue Stuck Burglar from California Chimney." *Daily News*, October 19. Retrieved April 18, 2015 (http://www.nydailynews.com/news/crime/firefighters-rescue-stuck-burglar-cali-chimney-article-1.1979854).

Henslin, James M. 1994. *Social Problems, 3rd edition*. Englewood Cliffs, NJ: Prentice Hall.

Herbeck, Dan. 2015. "Woman's Body Acts as 'Brewery,' So Judge Dismisses DWI." *Buffalo News*, December 26. Retrieved January 4, 2016 (http://www.buffalonews.com/city-region/police-courts/womans-body-acts-as-brewery-so-judge-dismisses-dwi-20151226).

Hewitt, John, and Randall Stokes. 1975. "Disclaimers." *American Sociological Review*, 40(1):1–11.

Hibberd, James, and Natalie Abrams. 2015. "News + Notes: Scoring Summer TV." *Entertainment Weekly*, August 21/29:8–9.

High There! 2015. Website home page. Retrieved June 3, 2015 (https://play.google.com/store/apps/details?id=com.happyfuncorp.highthere&hl=en).

Hingson, Ralph W. and Aaron M. White. 2012. "Prevalence and Consequences of College Student Alcohol Use," pp. 3–24 in *College Student Alcohol Abuse: A Guide to Assessment, Intervention, and Prevention*, edited by Christopher J. Correia, James G. Murphy, and Nancy P. Barnett. Hoboken, NJ: John Wiley & Sons.

Hirschi, Travis. 1969. *Causes of Delinquency*. Berkeley, CA: University of California Press.

History.com. 2015. "Trail of Tears." Retrieved February 7, 2015 (http://www.history.com/topics/native-american-history/trail-of-tears).

Hoebel, E. Adamson. 1964. *The Law of Primitive Man: A Study in Comparative Legal Dynamics*. Cambridge, MA: Harvard University Press.

Hollywood.com. 2015. "*Jaws, The Exorcist* and *The Sixth Sense* Rank as Highest Grossing Horror Films of All Time in Hollywood.com Report." Retrieved March 1, 2015 (http://www.prnewswire.com/news-releases/jaws-the-exorcist-and-the-sixth-sense-rank-as-highest-grossing-horror-films-of-all-time-in-hollywoodcom-report-55638142.html).

The Holy Bible: King James Version. 2000. "The First Epistle of Paul the Apostle to Timothy 3." New York: Bartleby.com.

Homeland Security. 2015. "Report Cyber Incidents." Retrieved June 22, 2015 (http://www.dhs.gov/how-do-i/report-cyber-incidents).

Hough, Andrew, Claire Duffin, and Hayley Dixon. 2013. "'Burglar' Found Stuck in Chimney of Derby Grade II Listed Building." *The Telegraph*, May 3. Retrieved April 18, 2015 (http://www.telegraph.co.uk/news/uknews/crime/10034410/Burglar-found-stuck-in-chimney-of-Derby-Grade-II-listed-building.html).

House, Samantha. 2015. "Auburn Man Charged with Stealing Friend's Debit Card." *The Citizen*, March 17:A3.

Howe, Alyssa Cymene. 2004. "Queer Pilgrimage: The San Francisco Homeland and Identity

Tourism," pp. 248–64 in *Life in America*, edited by Lee D. Baker. Malden, MA: Blackwell.

Howell, Evan A., Steven J. Bograd, Carey Morishige, Michael P. Seki, and Jeffrey J. Polovina. 2012. "On North Pacific Circulation and Associated Marine Debris Concentration." *Marine Pollution Bulletin*, 65:16–22.

Howerton, Jason. 2014. "A Real-Life Demon Possession Is Being Reported in Indiana—The Details Are Almost Too Horrifying to Believe." *The Blaze*, January 27. Retrieved March 1, 2015 (http://www.theblaze.com/stories/2014/01/27/a-real-life-demon-possession-is-being-reported-in-indiana-the-details-are-almost-too-horrifying-to-believe/).

Huffington Post. 2014. "The Most Used Drugs According to the 2014's Global Drug Survey." Retrieved June 9, 2015 (http://www.huffingtonpost.com/2014/04/14/most-used-drug_n_5147042.html).

Human Rights Campaign. 2017. "Policy and Position Statements on Conversion Therapy." Retrieved January 21, 2017 (http://www.hrc.org/resources/policy-and-position-statements-on-conversion-therapy).

IMDb. 2015. "Wedding Crashers." Retrieved January 20, 2015 (http://www.imdb.com/title/tt0396269/).

Inciardi, James A., and Jennifer L. Goode. 2010. "OcyContin: A Prescription for Disaster," pp. 223–28 in *Readings in Deviant Behavior, 6th edition*, edited by Alex Thio, Thomas C. Calhoun, and Addrain Conyers. Boston: Allyn & Bacon.

Infidelity Facts. 2006. "Infidelity Statistics." Retrieved August 10, 2015 (http://www.infidelityfacts.com/infidelity-statistics.html).

Infosec Institute. 2015. "Hacking Communities in the Deep Web." Retrieved June 25, 2015 (http://resources.infosecinstitute.com/hacking-communities-in-the-deep-web/).

Ingraham, Christopher. 2014. "FBI: U.S. Now Has One Active Shooter Incident Every Three Weeks." *The Washington Post*, September 25. Retrieved December 29, 2015 (https://www.washingtonpost.com/news/wonk/wp/2014/09/25/fbi-u-s-now-has-one-active-shooter-incident-every-three-weeks/).

Inguaggiato, Brodie. 2014. "Yik Yak App May Perpetuate Cyberbullying." *The Stylus*, October 1:10.

Inhalant Abuse Prevention. 2012a. "Huffing, Sniffing, Dusting & Bagging." Retrieved June 9, 2015 (http://www.inhalants.org/inhalant-abuse/huffing-sniffing-dusting-bagging/).

———. 2012b. "Inhalant Statistics and Reports." Retrieved June 9, 2015 (http://www.inhalant.org/media/inhalant-statistics-and-reports/).

Inquisitr. 2013. "Catfishing 'Rampant,' but Online Dating Is Here to Stay." Retrieved June 18, 2015 (http://www.inquisitr.com/1003352/catfishing-rampant-but-online-dating-is-here-to-stay/).

Inside Hazing. 2014. "Statistics: High School Hazing, College Hazing, Hazing Trends." Retrieved May 2, 2015 (http://www.insidehazing.com/statistics_25_high.php).

Institute for Energy Research (IER). 2015. "Global Consumption of Fossil Fuels Continues to Increase." Retrieved November 8, 2015 (http://instituteforenergyresearch.org/analysis/global-consumption-of-fossil-fuels-continues-to-increase/).

Institute for Sustainable Communication. 2012. "Plastic Garbage." Retrieved December 7, 2015 (http://www.sustainablecommunication.org/eco360/what-is-eco360s-causes/plastic-garbage).

International Association of Arson Investigators (IAAI). 2015. "About IAAI." Retrieved April 20, 2015 (https://www.firearson.com/).

The International Drug Evaluation and Classification Program (DECP). 2015. "Drug Recognition Experts (DRE): The 7 Drug Categories." Retrieved June 5, 2015 (http://www.decp.org/experts/7categories.htm).

International Rehabilitation Council for Torture Victims. 2013. "Defining Torture." Retrieved March 21, 2015 (http://www.irct.org/what-is-torture/defining-torture.aspx).

Internet Crime Complaint Center (IC3). "Welcome to the IC3: Alerts." Retrieved June 22, 2015 (http://www.ic3.gov/default.aspx).

Jacobson, Louis. 2011. "Bernie Sanders Says Six Bank Companies Have Assets Equaling 60 Percent of U.S. GDP." *Tampa Bay Times*, March 16. Retrieved March 16, 2015 (http://www.politifact.com/truth-o-meter/statements/2011/oct/06/bernie-s/bernie-sanders-says-six-bank-companies-have-assets/).

Jaffe, Matthew. 2012. "Thieves Cracking Security Codes to Get into Cars." *ABC News*, October 1. Retrieved April 18, 2015 (http://abcnews.go.com/Technology/breaking-cars-thieves-crack-wireless-security-codes/story?id=17367442).

Jay, Mary Lou. 2015. "Drivers Who Can No Longer Afford Their Cars Turn to Auto Theft

Fraud." *Insure Me*. Retrieved April 19, 2015 (http://www.insureme.com/auto-insurance/auto-theft-fraud).

Jay, Timothy. 2009. "The Utility and Ubiquity of Taboo Words." *Perspectives on Psychological Science*, 4(2):153–61.

Jervis, Rick. 2015. "'American Sniper' Trial Likely to Increase Stigma of PTSD." *USA Today*, February 26. Retrieved August 1, 2015 (http://www.usatoday.com/story/news/2015/02/25/american-sniper-murder-trial-ptsd/24008739/).

Johnson, Luke. 2012. "Ron Paul Pressed on Abortion in the Case of Rape." *Huffington Post*, February 26. Retrieved August 16, 2015 (http://www.huffingtonpost.com/2012/02/06/ron-paul-abortion-rape_n_1257324.html).

Jones, Corey, and Phil Anderson. 2012. "Tow Trucks Used in Latest Auto Theft Trend." *The Topeka Capital-Journal*, April 4. Retrieved April 19, 2015 (http://cjonline.com/news/2012-04-04/tow-trucks-used-latest-auto-theft-trend).

Jones, David, and Jim Finkle. 2013. "Largest Hacking Fraud Case Launched after Credit Card Info Stolen from J.C. Penney, Visa Licensee." *Reuters*. July 25. Retrieved June 23, 2015 (http://www.huffingtonpost.com/2013/07/25/credit-card-stolen-visa_n_3653274.html).

Kantor, Martin. 2009. *Homophobia: The State of Sexual Bigotry Today, 2nd edition*. Westport, CT: Praeger.

Kappeler, Victor E., and Larry K. Gaines. 2011. *Community Policing: A Contemporary Perspective, 6th edition*. Boston: Elsevier/Anderson Publishing.

Karlin, Lily. 2015. "Bill Maher Says 'American Sniper' Is About a Psychopath Patriot." *The Huffington Post*, January 24. Retrieved August 3, 2015 (http://www.huffingtonpost.com/2015/01/24/bill-maher-american-sniper_n_6537880.html).

Katz, Eric. 2015. "OPM Will Soon Notify New Wave of Workers Their Data Was Hacked." *Government Executive*, June 16. Retrieved June 25, 2015 (http://www.govexec.com/pay-benefits/2015/06/opm-will-soon-notify-new-wave-workers-their-data-was-hacked/115441/).

Kellaway, Jean. 2000. *The History of Torture and Execution*. New York: Lyons Press.

Kendall, Diana. 2013. *Social Problems: In a Diverse Society*. Upper Saddle River, NJ: Pearson.

Kennedy Krieger Institute. 2012. "Developmental Disorders." Retrieved July 30, 2015 (http://www.kennedykrieger.org/patient-care/diagnoses-disorders/developmental-disorders).

Kenney, Dennis J., and James O. Finckenauer. 1995. *Organized Crime in America*. Belmont, CA: Wadsworth.

Kenny, Robert Wade. 2010. "Beyond the Elementary Forms of Moral Life: Reflexivity and Rationality in Durkheim's Moral Theory." *Sociological Theory*, 28(2): 215–44.

Kessel, Mark. 2014. "Restoring the Pharmaceutical Industry's Reputation." *Nature Biotechnology*, 32:983–90.

Keyworth, Richard J. 2010. *Fires . . . Accidental or Arson?" Fire Investigations*. Denver, CO: Outskirts Press.

Kiely, David, and Christina McKenna. 2007. *The Dark Sacrament: True Stories of Modern-Day Demon Possession and Exorcism*. New York: HarperCollins.

Kilham, Chris. 2013. "Opium: A Powerful Medicine for Pain Relief." *FoxNews.com*, July 24. Retrieved June 9, 2015 (http://www.foxnews.com/health/2013/07/24/opium-powerful-medicine-for-pain-relief/).

Kirchick, James. 2014. "Edward Snowden, Traitor." *New York Daily News*, June 1. Retrieved December 15, 2015 (http://www.nydailynews.com/opinion/edward-snowden-traitor-article-1.1811878).

Knauss, Tim. 2015a. "Report: Upstate Nukes Support 25,000 Jobs." *The Post-Standard*, December 8:B-4.

———. 2015b. "After FitzPatrick: Spent Fuel Stored on Site for Decades." *The Post-Standard*, November 10:A-1.

Knight, Laurence. 2014. "A Brief History of Plastics, Natural and Synthetic." *BBC News*, May 17. Retrieved December 7, 2015 (http://www.bbc.com/news/magazine-27442625).

Kolbert, Elizabeth. 2014. *The Sixth Extinction*. New York: Picador.

Kratcoski, Peter, and Lucille Dunn Kratcoski. 1996. *Juvenile Delinquency, 4th edition*. Upper Saddle River, NJ: Prentice Hall.

Krisher, Tom. 2016. "12M More Takata Air Bags Recalled." *The Post-Standard*, May 31:B-3.

Kristof, Nicholas. 2015. "Heroin Doesn't Have to Be a Killer." Syndicated column as it appeared in *The Post-Standard*, June 11:A-14.

Krulos, Tea. 2013. *Heroes in the Night: Inside the Real Life Superhero Movement*. Chicago: Chicago Review Press.

Kunzelman, Michael. 2016. "La. Theater Shooter Calls America a 'Filth Farm.'" *The Post-Standard*, January 14:A-12.

Kurlantzick, Joshua. 2014. "The CIA Torture Report Is Causing Political Ripples Overseas." *Bloomberg Business*, December 11. Retrieved March 21, 2015 (http://www.bloomberg.com/bw/articles/2014-12-11/the-senate-torture-report-is-causing-political-ripples-overseas).

Kwan, Samantha, and Jennifer Graves. 2013. *Framing Fat: Competing Constructions in Contemporary Culture*. New Brunswick, NJ: Rutgers University Press.

Lang, Alan R. 1992. *The Encyclopedia of Psychoactive Drugs: Alcohol and Teenage Drinking*, introduction by Jack H. Mendelson and Nancy K. Mello. New York: Chelsea House.

Lang, James M. 2013. "How College Classes Encourage Cheating." *The Boston Globe*, August 4. Retrieved December 16, 2015 (http://www.bostonglobe.com/ideas/2013/08/03/how-college-classes-encourage-cheating/3Q34x5ysYcplWNA3yO2eLK/story.html).

Las Vegas Review-Journal. 1994. "Couple Charged for Frog Venom." March 2:10A.

———. 1994. "Frog Produces Potent Painkiller." April 27:3A.

Lavrinc, Damon. 2015. "Thieving Teens Likely Used $17 Gadget to Break into NYT Columnist's Car." *Jalopnik*, April 15. Retrieved April 18, 2015 (http://jalopnik.com/thieving-teens-likely-used-17-gadget-to-break-into-ny-1698036188).

Lawrence, Andres. 2015. "Strange Case: The Hearing." *Sports Illustrated*, January 26:16.

Layton, Julia. 2015. "Has Earth Reached Its Carrying Capacity?" *Science: How Stuff Works*. Retrieved November 7, 2015 (http://science.howstuffworks.com/environmental/green-science/earth-carrying-capacity2.htm).

Leafly. 2015. "Most Popular Strains on Leafly." Retrieved June 3, 2015 (https://itunes.apple.com/en/app/leafly-marijuana-strain-dispensary/id416456429?mt=8).

Leavenworth, Jesse. 2012. "Heavy Lifting for Ambulance Crews." *Hartford Courant*, October 20. Retrieved February 15, 2015 (http://articles.courant.com/2012-10-20/health/hc-ct-obese-transport-1014-20121012_1_obese-patients-dave-skoczulek-ambulance-service).

Lederman, Josh. 2015. "Obama Tries to Clinch Climate Pact in Paris." *The Post-Standard*, November 29:A-17.

Lederman, Linda C. and Lea P. Stewart. 2005. *Changing the Culture of College Drinking: A Socially Situated Health Communication Campaign*. Cresskill, NJ: Hampton Press.

Ledford, Jon. 2015. "Video Game Store Swatting Victims Tricked into Making Things Worse." *Arcade Sushi*, March 30. Retrieved June 20, 2015 (http://arcadesushi.com/clifton-nj-video-game-store-swatting/).

Leger, Donna Leinwand. 2014. "Police Carry Special Drug to Reverse Heroin Overdoses." *USA Today*, February 3. Retrieved June 14, 2015 (http://www.usatoday.com/story/news/nation/2014/01/30/police-use-narcan-to-reverse-heroin-overdoses/5063587/).

Leiner, Barry M., Vinton G. Cerf, David D. Clark, Robert E. Kahn, Leonard Kleinrock, Daniel C. Lynch, Jon Postel, Larry G. Roberts, and Stephen Wolff. 2014. "Brief History of the Internet." *Internet Society*. Retrieved September 16, 2014 (http://www.internetsociety.org/internet/what-internet/history-internet/brief-history-internet).

Leising, Daniel, Anne-Marie B. Gallrein, and Michael Dufner. 2014. "Judging the Behavior of People We Know: Objective Assessment, Confirmation of Preexisting Views, or Both?" *Personality and Social Psychology Bulletin*, 40(2):153–63.

Lenehan, Pat. 2003. *Anabolic Steroids: And Other Performance Enhancing Drugs*. New York: Taylor and Francis.

Leon-Guerrero, Anna. 2013. *Social Problems: Community, Policy, and Social Action*. Thousand Oaks, CA: Sage.

LeTrent, Sarah. 2015. "Michael Moore Calls Snipers 'Cowards' on Twitter." *CNN*, January 19. Retrieved August 1, 2015 (http://www.cnn.com/2015/01/19/entertainment/feat-michael-moore-sniper-tweet-feat/).

Leupo, Kimberly. 2008. "The History of Mental Illness." Retrieved August 1, 2015 (http://www.toddlertime.com/advocacy/hospitals/Asylum/history-asylum.htm).

Lewis, Michael. 1998. "Shame and Stigma," pp. 126–40 in *Shame: Interpersonal Behavior, Psychopathology, and Culture*, edited by Paul Gilbert and Bernice Andrews. New York: Oxford University Press.

Lewis, Tanya. 2014a. "Underwater Ocean Turbines: A New Spin on Clean Energy?" *Live Science*, August 5. Retrieved December 12, 2015 (http://www.livescience.com/47188-ocean-turbines-renewable-energy.html).

Lewis, Tanya. 2014b. "Casting Out Demons: Pope Francis Declares Support for Exorcisms." *Live*

Science, October 31. Retrieved March 1, 2015 (http://www.livescience.com/48563-pope-francis-supports-exorcisms.html).

Lilly, J. Robert, Francis T. Cullen, and Richard A. Ball. 2015. *Criminological Theory: Context and Consequences, 6th edition*. Thousand Oaks, CA: Sage.

Lincoln, Caesar. 2013. *Homophobia: The Ultimate Guide for How to Overcome Homophobic Thoughts Forever*. Amazon Digital Services.

Lipka, Michael. 2015. "Religious 'Nones' Are Not Only Growing, They're Becoming More Secular." *Pew Research Center*, November 11. Retrieved December 30, 2015 (http://www.pewresearch.org/fact-tank/2015/11/11/religious-nones-are-not-only-growing-theyre-becoming-more-secular/).

Lipkins, Susan. 2009. *Preventing Hazing*. New York: Jossey-Bass.

Llorens, Ileana. 2012. "Man Marries Dead Girlfriend in Joint Funeral and Wedding Ceremony in Thailand." *Huffington Post*, January 19. Retrieved January 27, 2015 (http://www.huffingtonpost.com/2012/01/18/man-marries-dead-girlfriend-thailand_n_1211497.html).

Loman, Christine. 2015. "Regal Entertainment Group Movie Theaters Start Bag, Purse Inspections." *The Post-Standard*, August 30:A-8.

Lombroso, Cesare. 2006 [1876]. *Criminal Man* translated with a new introduction by Mary Gibson and Nicole Hahn Rafter. Durham, NC: Duke University Press.

Long, Colleen. 2013. "Feds in NYC: Hackers Stole $45M in ATM Card Breach." *AP News*, May 9. Retrieved June 22, 2015 (http://bigstory.ap.org/article/feds-nyc-hackers-stole-45m-atm-card-breach).

Longhi, Silvia and Giorgio Radetti. 2013. "Thyroid Function and Obesity." *Journal of Clinical Research in Pediatric Endocrinology*, (1): 40–44.

Los Angeles Times. 2015. "White House Backs Banning Gay Conversion Therapy for Minors." April 8. Retrieved August 15, 2015 (http://www.latimes.com/nation/nationnow/la-na-nn-conversion-therapy-20150408-story.html).

Lovejoy, Bess. 2014. "The Gory New York City Riot That Shaped American Medicine." *Smithsonian*, June 17. Retrieved April 29, 2015 (http://www.smithsonianmag.com/history/gory-new-york-city-riot-shaped-american-medicine-180951766/?no-ist).

Lowry, Brian. 2015. "'I Am Cait' Displays Strengths, Weaknesses in Season Finale." *Variety*, September 13. Retrieved September 15, 2015 (http://variety.com/2015/tv/columns/i-am-cait-season-finale-review-e-caitlyn-enner-spoilers-1201591396/).

Lutter, Stefan. 2015. "Methane Becoming Bigger Worry than CO2." *The Citizen*, October 16:A8.

Lyman, Michael D. and Gary W. Potter. 2000. *Organized Crime, 2nd edition*. Upper Saddle River, NJ: Prentice Hall.

MacAndrew, Craig and Robert B. Edgerton. 1969. *Drunken Comportment*. New York: Aldine.

Macionis, John J. 2010. *Social Problems, 4th edition*. Upper Saddle River, NJ: Pearson.

Mackey, Robert. 2015. "Michelle Obama Praised for Bold Stand She Didn't Take in Saudi Arabia." *The New York Times*, January 28. Retrieved January 29, 2015 (http://www.nytimes.com/2015/01/29/world/middleeast/michelle-obama-praised-for-bold-stand-she-did-not-take.html?_r=0).

Madison, Lucy. 2012. "Richard Mourdock: Even Pregnancy from Rape Something 'God Intended.'" *CBS News*, October 24. Retrieved August 16, 2015 (http://www.cbsnews.com/news/richard-mourdock-even-pregnancy-from-rape-something-god-intended/).

Mancini, Vince. 2014. "The Guys Behind 'Bumfights' Got Arrested for Trying to Mail Infant Body Parts from Thailand." *UPROXX.com*, November 18. Retrieved May 3, 2015 (http://uproxx.com/filmdrunk/2014/11/the-guys-behind-bumfights-got-arrested-for-trying-to-mail-infant-body-parts-from-thailand/).

Marsh, Rene. 2015. "Hackers Successfully Ground 1,400 Passengers." *CNN Politics*, June 22. Retrieved June 22, 2015 (http://www.cnn.com/2015/06/22/politics/lot-polish-airlines-hackers-ground-planes/).

The Marshall Project. 2015. "Public Shamings." Retrieved December 20, 2015 (https://www.themarshallproject.org/2015/03/31/public-shamings#.XQrKnRAlo).

Marx, Karl and Friedrich Engels. [1845–46] 1970. *The German Ideology, Part 1*, edited by C. J. Arthur. New York: International Publishers.

Matthews, Chris. 2014. "Wealth Inequality in America: It's Worse Than You Think." *Fortune*,

October 31. Retrieved January 30, 2015 (http://fortune.com/2014/10/31/inequality-wealth-income-us/).

Maturo, Antonio. 2012 (Jan-Dec). "Medicalization: Current Concept and Future Directions in a Bionic Society." *Mens Sana Monographs*, 10(1):122–33. Retrieved August 1, 2015 (http://www.ncbi.nlm.nih.gov/pmc/articles/PMC3353591/).

Matza, David. 1964. *Delinquency and Drift*. Englewood Cliffs, NJ: Prentice Hall.

Mayo Clinic. 2015a. "Diseases and Conditions: Measles." Retrieved January 7, 2015 (http://www.mayoclinic.org/diseases-conditions/measles/basics/definition/con-20019675).

———. 2015b. "Diseases and Conditions: Alcoholism." Retrieved May 26, 2015 (http://www.mayoclinic.org/diseases-conditions/alcoholism/basics/definition/con-20020866).

———. 2015c. "Healthy Lifestyle: Nutrition and Healthy Eating." Retrieved May 28, 2015 (http://www.mayoclinic.org/healthy-lifestyle/nutrition-and-healthy-eating/in-depth/alcohol/art-20044551).

———. 2015d. "Performance-Enhancing Drugs: Know the Risks." Retrieved June 12, 2015 (http://www.mayoclinic.org/healthy-lifestyle/fitness/in-depth/performance-enhancing-drugs/art-20046134).

———. 2015e. "Prescription Drug Abuse." Retrieved June 12, 2015 (http://www.mayoclinic.org/diseases-conditions/prescription-drug-abuse/basics/definition/con-20032471).

———. 2015f. "Depression (Major Depressive Disorder): Definition." Retrieved July 26, 2015 (http://www.mayoclinic.org/diseases-conditions/depression/basics/definition/con-20032977).

———. 2015g. "Schizophrenia." Retrieved July 27, 2015 (http://www.mayoclinic.org/diseases-conditions/schizophrenia/basics/definition/con-20021077).

———. 2015h. "Dementia." Retrieved July 29, 2015 (http://www.mayoclinic.org/diseases-conditions/dementia/basics/definition/con-20034399).

———. 2015i. "Psychotherapy." Retrieved August 1, 2015 (http://www.mayoclinic.org/tests-procedures/psychotherapy/basics/definition/prc-20013335).

———. 2015j. "Complementary and Alternative Medicine." Retrieved August 1, 2015 (http://www.mayoclinic.org/healthy-lifestyle/consumer-health/in-depth/alternative-medicine/art-20045267).

———. 2015k. "Dissociative Disorders." Retrieved August 3, 2015 (http://www.mayoclinic.org/diseases-conditions/dissociative-disorders/basics/treatment/con-20031012).

———. 2015l. "Sexually Transmitted Diseases (STDs)." Retrieved August 13, 2015 (http://www.mayoclinic.org/diseases-conditions/sexually-transmitted-diseases-stds/basics/definition/con-20034128).

Mazza, Sandy. 2014. "Carol Coronado, Indicted in Murder of Her 3 Children, Invokes Insanity Plea." *The Daily Breeze*, September 29. Retrieved February 28, 2015 (http://www.dailybreeze.com/general-news/20140929/carol-coronado-indicted-in-murder-of-her-3-children-invokes-insanity-plea).

McCool, Grant and Martha Graybow. 2009. "Madoff Gets 150 Years for Massive Investment Fraud." *Reuters*, June 29. Retrieved March 16, 2015 (http://www.reuters.com/article/2009/06/29/us-madoff-idUSTRE55P6O520090629).

McCutcheon, Chuck. 2006. "Feeling the Strain." *The Post-Standard*, September 18:D2.

McFadden, Robert D. 2014. "Charles Keating, 90, Key Figure in '80s Savings and Loan Crisis, Dies." *The New York Times*, April 2. Retrieved March 19, 2015 (http://www.nytimes.com/2014/04/02/business/charles-keating-key-figure-in-the-1980s-savings-and-loan-crisis-dies-at-90.html?_r=0).

McKay, Hollie. 2014. "Mean Girls: Humiliating Hazing Still a Problem at College Sororities." *Fox News*, September 25. Retrieved August 15, 2015 (http://www.foxnews.com/entertainment/2014/09/25/mean-girls-dangerous-hazing-growing-problem-at-college-sororities/).

McKenzie, John L. 1965. *Dictionary of the Bible*. Milwaukee: Bruce Publishing.

McLaren, Leah. 2010. "The Secret Life of a Bay Street Hooker." *Toronto Life*. Retrieved August 22, 2015 (http://www.torontolife.com/informer/features/2010/12/08/the-secret-life-of-a-bay-street-hooker/).

McLaughlin, Eliott C. 2015. "Zimbabwe Won't Press Charges against Cecil the Lion's Killer." *CNN World*, October 12. Retrieved December 16, 2015 (http://www.cnn.com/2015/10/12/africa/zimbabwe-cecil-lion-walter-palmer-no-charges/).

McLean, Bethany and Peter Elkind. 2013. *The Smartest Guys in the Room*. New York: Penguin.

McNally, Siobhan. 2014. "Fatkini Trend Inspiring and Empowering Curvy Women Everywhere." *Mirror*, August 18. Retrieved March 6, 2015 (http://www.mirror.co.uk/news/weird-news/).

Medley-Rath, Stephanie. 2012. "The DSM-IV & The Medicalization of Behavior." *Sociology in Focus*. Retrieved August 1, 2015 (http://www.sociologyinfocus.com/2012/07/18/the-dsm-iv-the-medicalization-of-behavior/).

Mental Health Association (Forsyth County, NC). 2011. "The Five (5) Major Categories of Mental Illness." Retrieved July 26, 2015 (http://triadmentalhealth.org/the-five-5-major-categories-of-mental-illness/).

Mental Health Foundation. 2015. "What Is Mental Health?" Retrieved July 25, 2015 (http://www.mentalhealth.org.uk/help-information/an-introduction-to-mental-health/what-is-mental-health/).

Merriam-Webster Dictionary. 2015. "Poverty." Retrieved February 7, 2015 (http://www.merriam-webster.com/dictionary/poverty).

Merrills, Andrew and Richard Miles. 2014. *The Vandals*. Malden, MA: Wiley-Blackwell.

Merton, Robert K. 1938 (October). "Social Structure and Anomie." *American Sociological Review*, 3(5):672–82.

Meyers, Laura Marie. 2015. "What?! Maroon 5 Crashed Real Weddings for a Surprise-Filled Music Video." *Pop Sugar*, January 15. Retrieved January 28, 2015 (http://www.popsugar.com/entertainment/Maroon-5-Sugar-Music-Video-36574650).

Miller, Chaz. 2009. "Food Waste." *Waste 360*. Retrieved December 7, 2015 (http://waste360.com/Collections_And_Transfer/food-waste-facts-200909).

Miller, Laurence. 2006. "Suicide by Cop: Causes, Reactions, and Practical Intervention Strategies." *International Journal of Emergency Mental Health*, 8(3):165–74.

Miller, Walter. 1958. "Lower Class Culture as a Generating Milieu of Gang Delinquency." *Journal of Social Issues*, 14(3):5–19.

Mills, C. Wright. 1956. *The Power Elite*. New York: Oxford University Press.

———. 1958. *The Causes of World War Three*. New York: Simon and Schuster.

———. 1959. *The Sociological Imagination*. New York: Oxford University Press.

Mission 2014: Feeding the World. 2014. "Ineffective/Inadequate Agricultural Practices." Retrieved December 10, 2015 (http://12.000.scripts.mit.edu/mission2014/problems/ineffectiveinadequate-agricultural-practices).

Mizruchi, Mark S. 1987. "Why Do Corporations Stick Together? An Interorganizational Theory of Class Cohesion," pp. 204–18 in *Power Elites and Organization*, edited by G. William Domhoff and Thomas R. Dye. Newbury Park, CA: Sage.

Mohr, Melissa. 2013. "The Modern History of Swearing: Where All the Dirtiest Words Come From." *Salon*, May 11. Retrieved December 30, 2015 (http://www.salon.com/2013/05/11/the_modern_history_of_swearing_where_all_the_dirtiest_words_come_from/).

Monaghan, Angela. 2014. "US Wealth Inequality—Top 0.1% Worth as Much as the Bottom 90%." *The Guardian*, November 13. Retrieved January 28, 2015 (http://www.theguardian.com/business/2014/nov/13/us-wealth-inequality-top-01-worth-as-much-as-the-bottom-90).

More, Victoria C. 2011. "Dumpster Dinners: An Ethnographic Study of Freeganism." *Journal for Undergraduate Ethnography*, June, No. 1:1–13.

The Most. 2014. "10 Most Cannibalistic Animals." Retrieved May 9, 2015 (http://www.themost10.com/most-cannibalistic-animals/)

Mothers Against Drunk Driving (MADD). 2015. "Mission Statement." Retrieved May 28, 2015 (http://www.madd.org/about-us/mission/).

Mulvaney, Dustin, and Paul Robbins. 2011. *Green Technology: An A-to-Z Guide*. Thousand Oaks, CA: Sage.

Murano, Grace. 2010. "10 Hilarious Robbery Stories." *Oddee*, February 19. Retrieved April 15, 2015 (http://www.oddee.com/item_96979.aspx).

———. 2012. "10 Craziest Plastic Surgeries to Look like Someone Else." *Bizarre Medical Stories*. Retrieved January 23, 2015 (http://www.oddee.com/item_96941.aspx).

Murrell, Nathaniel Samuel. 2008. "Medicated Ganja and Rasta Rituals." *IDEAZ*, (7):115–37.

Nahas, Aili, and Patrick Gomez. 2015. "Bruce Jenner: Happy at Last." *People*, February 16:56–60.

Nashawaty, Chris. 2014. "No No: A Dockumentary." *Entertainment Weekly*, September 12:46.

National Aeronautics and Space Administration (NASA). 2015a. "Global Climate Change: Vital Signs of the Planet." Retrieved December 6, 2015 (http://climate.nasa.gov/evidence/).

———. 2015b. "Global Climate Change: Vital Signs of the Planet." Retrieved December 6, 2015 (http://climate.nasa.gov/).

National Alliance on Mental Illness (NAMI). 2015a. "Mental Health Conditions." Retrieved July 26, 2015 (https://www.nami.org/Learn-More/Mental-Health-Conditions).

———. 2015b. "Depression." Retrieved July 26, 2015 (https://www.nami.org/Learn-More/Mental-Health-Conditions/Depression/Overview).

———. 2015c. "Bipolar Disorder." Retrieved July 26, 2015 (https://www.nami.org/Learn-More/Mental-Health-Conditions/Bipolar-Disorder/Overview).

———. 2015d. "Schizophrenia." Retrieved July 27, 2015 (https://www.nami.org/Learn-More/Mental-Health-Conditions/Schizophrenia/Overview).

———. 2015e. "Dissociative Disorders." Retrieved July 29, 2015 (https://www.nami.org/Learn-More/Mental-Health-Conditions/Dissociative-Disorders/Overview).

———. 2015f. "Posttraumatic Stress Disorder." Retrieved July 29, 2015 (https://www.nami.org/Learn-More/Mental-Health-Conditions/Posttraumatic-Stress-Disorder/Overview).

———. 2015g. "ADHD." Retrieved July 30, 2015 (https://www.nami.org/Learn-More/Mental-Health-Conditions/ADHD/Overview).

———. 2015h. "Autism." Retrieved July 30, 2015 (https://www.nami.org/Learn-More/Mental-Health-Conditions/Autism/Overview).

National Archives. 2015a. "Confrontations for Justice." Retrieved January 29, 2015 (http://www.archives.gov/exhibits/eyewitness/html.php?section=3).

———. 2015b. "Teaching with Documents: The Volstead Act and Related Prohibition Documents." Retrieved May 30, 2015 (http://www.archives.gov/education/lessons/volstead-act/).

National Association of Addiction Treatment Providers (NAATP). 2015. "Seven Stages of Alcohol Addiction." Retrieved May 26, 2015 (http://www.carontexas.org/treatment-programs/assessment/seven-stages-of-alcohol-addiction).

National Association of People Against Bullying (NAPAB). 2015. "Advocating for Children's Rights." Retrieved May 2, 2015 (http://www.napab.org/).

National Association to Advance Fat Acceptance (NAAFA). 2015. "NAAFA Homepage." Retrieved February 22, 2015 (http://www.naafaonline.com/dev2/).

National Center for Education Statistics (NCES). 2014. *Indicators of School Crime and Safety: 2013.* "Key Findings." Retrieved June 20, 2015 (http://nces.ed.gov/programs/crimeindicators/crimeindicators2013/key.asp).

National Conference of State Legislatures. 2015a. "State Medical Marijuana Laws." Retrieved June 11, 2015 (http://www.ncsl.org/research/health/state-medical-marijuana-laws.aspx).

———. 2015b. "State Cyberstalking and Cyberharassment Laws." Retrieved June 20, 2015 (http://www.ncsl.org/research/telecommunications-and-information-technology/cyberstalking-and-cyberharassment-laws.aspx).

National Council on Alcoholism and Drug Dependence (NCADD). 2015a. "Alcohol and Crime." Retrieved May 28, 2015 (https://ncadd.org/learn-about-alcohol/alcohol-and-crime).

———. 2015b. "Drinking and Driving." Retrieved May 28, 2015 (https://ncadd.org/learn-about-alcohol/drinking-and-driving).

National Energy Institute. 2015. "How Nuclear Reactors Work." Retrieved December 9, 2015 (http://www.nei.org/Knowledge-Center/How-Nuclear-Reactors-Work).

National Fire Protection Association. 2014. "Intentional Fires." Retrieved April 20, 2015 (http://www.nfpa.org/research/reports-and-statistics/fire-causes/arson-and-juvenile-firesetting/intentional-fires).

National Geographic. 2015. "Forest Holocaust." Retrieved December 10, 2015 (http://www.nationalgeographic.com/eye/deforestation/effect.html).

National Health Service (NHS). 2015. "How Is Dementia Treated?" Retrieved August 3, 2015 (http://www.nhs.uk/conditions/dementia-guide/pages/dementia-treatment.aspx).

National Heart, Lung, and Blood Institute (NHLBI). 2012. "What Are the Health Risks of Overweight and Obesity?" Retrieved February 15, 2015 (http://www.nhlbi.nih.gov/health/health-topics/topics/obe/risks).

National Highway Traffic Safety Administration (NHTSA). 2013. "NHTSA Letter to Chrysler

Group, LLC." June 3. Retrieved March 23, 2015 (http://www-odi.nhtsa.dot.gov/acms/cs/jaxrs/download/doc/UCM439144/INRM-EA12005-2111.pdf).

National Information Center. 2015. "Holding Companies with Assets Greater than $10 Billion." Retrieved March 16, 2015 (http://www.ffiec.gov/nicpubweb/nicweb/top50form.aspx).

National Institute of Justice. 2015a. "Community Crime Prevention Strategies." Retrieved December 17, 2015 (https://www.crimesolutions.gov/TopicDetails.aspx?ID=10).

———. 2015b. "Program Profile: Hot Spots Policing (Lowell, Mass.)." Retrieved December 17, 2015 (https://www.crimesolutions.gov/ProgramDetails.aspx?ID=208).

National Institute of Mental Health (NIMH). 2015a. "What is Post-traumatic Stress Disorder (PTSD)?" Retrieved July 30, 2015 (http://www.nimh.nih.gov/health/topics/post-traumatic-stress-disorder-ptsd/index.shtml).

———. 2015b. "Bipolar Disorder in Adults." Retrieved August 2, 2015 (http://www.nimh.nih.gov/health/publications/bipolar-disorder-in-adults/index.shtml).

———. 2015c. "What Are the Symptoms of Schizophrenia?" Retrieved August 3, 2015 (http://www.nimh.nih.gov/health/publications/schizophrenia/index.shtml).

———. 2015d. "What Is Autism Spectrum Disorder?" Retrieved August 3, 2015 (http://www.nimh.nih.gov/health/topics/autism-spectrum-disorders-asd/index.shtml).

National Institute on Alcohol Abuse and Alcoholism (NIAAA). 2000 (June). *Special Report to the U.S. Congress on Alcohol and Health*. U.S. Department of Health and Human Services. Retrieved May 27, 2015 (http://pubs.niaaa.nih.gov/publications/10report/intro.pdf).

———. 2008. "Genetics of Alcohol Use Disorder." Retrieved May 27, 2015 (http://www.niaaa.nih.gov/alcohol-health/overview-alcohol-consumption/alcohol-use-disorders/genetics-alcohol-use-disorders).

———. 2015a. "Alcohol's Effects on the Body." Retrieved May 26, 2015 (http://www.niaaa.nih.gov/alcohol-health/alcohols-effects-body).

———. 2015b. "Alcohol Facts and Statistics." Retrieved May 27, 2015 (http://www.niaaa.nih.gov/alcohol-health/overview-alcohol-consumption/alcohol-facts-and-statistics).

———. 2015c. "Alcohol Use Disorder." Retrieved May 27, 2015 (http://www.niaaa.nih.gov/alcohol-health/overview-alcohol-consumption/alcohol-use-disorders).

National Institute on Drug Abuse (NIDA). 2012. "Drug Facts: Inhalants." Retrieved June 9, 2015 (http://www.drugabuse.gov/publications/drugfacts/inhalants).

———. 2013. "Drug Facts: MDMA (Ecstasy or Molly)." Retrieved June 7, 2015. (http://www.drugabuse.gov/publications/drugfacts/mdma-ecstasy-or-molly).

———. 2014a. "Alcohol: Brief Description." Retrieved May 26, 2015 (http://www.drugabuse.gov/drugs-abuse/alcohol).

———. 2014b. "Drug Facts: Stimulant ADHD Medications: Methylphenidate and Amphetamines." Retrieved June 6, 2015 (http://www.drugabuse.gov/publications/drugfacts/stimulant-adhd-medications-methylphenidate-amphetamines).

———. 2014c. "Drug Facts: Methamphetamine." Retrieved June 6, 2015 (http://www.drugabuse.gov/publications/drugfacts/methamphetamine).

———. 2014d. "Drug Facts: Hallucinogens—LSD, Peyote, Psilocybin, and PCP." Retrieved June 7, 2015 (http://www.drugabuse.gov/publications/drugfacts/hallucinogens-lsd-peyote-psilocybin-pcp).

———. 2014e. "Prescription Drug Abuse." Retrieved June 12, 2015 (http://www.drugabuse.gov/publications/research-reports/prescription-drugs/director).

———. 2015a. "What Are Hallucinogens and Dissociative Drugs?" Retrieved June 7, 2015 (http://www.drugabuse.gov/publications/research-reports/hallucinogens-dissociative-drugs/what-are-hallucinogens).

National Oceanic and Atmospheric Administration (NOAA). 2004. "Greenhouse Effect." Retrieved November 8, 2015 (http://www.oar.noaa.gov/k12/html/greenhouse2.html).

———. 2013. "Climate." Retrieved December 6, 2015 (http://www.noaa.gov/climate.html).

———. 2015a. "What's New in 2014?" *Arctic Report Card: Update for 2014*. Retrieved November 8, 2015 (http://www.arctic.noaa.gov/reportcard/).

———. 2015b. "Marine Debris." Retrieved December 7, 2015 (http://response.restoration.noaa.gov/marine-debris).

———. 2015c. "Great Pacific Garbage Patch." Retrieved December 7, 2015 (http://marinedebris.noaa.gov/info/patch.html).

National Park Service. 2015. "Selma-to-Montgomery March: National Historic Trail & All-American Road." U.S. Department of the Interior. Retrieved January 18, 2015 (http://www.nps.gov/nr/travel/civilrights/al4.htm).

National Public Radio (NPR). 2015. "The Fall of Enron." Retrieved March 19, 2015 (http://www.npr.org/news/specials/enron/).

Natural Resources Defense Council. 2013. "Bottled Water." Retrieved December 7, 2015 (http://www.nrdc.org/water/drinking/bw/exesum.asp).

Naylor, R. T. 2002. *Wages of Crime: Black Markets, Illegal Finance, and the Underworld Economy*. Ithaca, NY: Cornell University Press.

NBC News. 2015. "Bernie Madoff Responds to Trustee Representing Fraud Victims." January 23. Retrieved March 16, 2015 (http://www.nbcnews.com/news/us-news/bernie-madoff-responds-trustee-representing-fraud-victims-n292211).

Neighborhood Scout. 2015. "Neighborhood Scout's Murder Capitals of America—2015." Retrieved April 14, 2015 (http://www.neighborhoodscout.com/top-lists/highest-murder-rate-cities/).

Nersesian, Roy L. 2010. *Energy for the 21st Century: A Comprehensive Guide to Conventional and Alternative Sources, 2nd edition*. London: Routledge.

New, Jake. 2014. "More College Campuses Sway 'No Means No' for 'Yes Means Yes.'" *Inside Higher Education*, October 17. Retrieved August 10, 2015 (http://www.pbs.org/newshour/rundown/means-enough-college-campuses/).

New World Encyclopedia. 2014. "Prostitution." Retrieved August 22, 2015 (http://www.newworldencyclopedia.org/entry/Prostitution).

New York State Department of Health. 2015. "10 Facts about Binge Drinking and Your Health." Retrieved May 28, 2015 (http://www.activebeat.co/your-health/10-facts-about-binge-drinking-and-your-health/?utm_medium=cpc&utm_source=google&utm_campaign=AB_GGL_US_DESK&utm_content=test&utm_term=binge%20drinking).

News Service Reports. 2014. "When Your Best Friends Become the Boogeyman: 12-Year-Old Didn't Know Sleepover Plans Included Her Murder to Impress Slenderman." *The Post-Standard*, June 8:B-1, B-3.

Nuwer, Hank. 1999. *Wrongs of Passage*. Bloomington, IN: Indiana University Press.

———, ed. 2004. *The Hazing Reader*. Bloomington, IN: Indiana University Press.

O'Brien, John. 2016. "Father Posed as Boyfriend to Trick Daughter into Porn." *The Post-Standard*, March 15:A-3.

Office of Adolescent Health. 2015. "Trends in Teen Pregnancy and Childbearing," *U.S. Department of Health and Human Services*. Retrieved August 11, 2015 (http://www.hhs.gov/ash/oah/adolescent-health-topics/reproductive-health/teen-pregnancy/trends.html).

Office of Juvenile Justice and Delinquency Prevention (OJJDP). 2010a. "Recovery Act." Retrieved June 20, 2015 (http://www.ojjdp.gov/recoveryact.html).

———. 2010b. "Cognitive-Behavioral Treatment." Washington, D.C.: U.S. Department of Justice. Retrieved December 21, 2015 (http://www.ojjdp.gov/mpg/litreviews/Cognitive_Behavioral_Treatment.pdf).

———. 2015. "Program Summary: Internet Crimes against Children Task Force Program." Retrieved June 20, 2015 (http://www.ojjdp.gov/programs/progsummary.asp?pi=3).

Office on Women's Health (U.S. Department of Health and Human Services). 2015. "Mental Health." Retrieved July 25, 2015 (http://womenshealth.gov/mental-health/good-health/).

Ohlemacher, Stephen. 2015. "IRS Reveals Hackers Stole Data from 220,000 More Victims." *The Post-Standard*, August 18:A-9.

Opposing Views. 2015. "25 Incredibly Inappropriate Selfies." Retrieved December 31, 2015 (http://www.opposingviews.com/i/gallery/entertainment/25-incredibly-inappropriate-selfies).

Organic Consumers Association. 2002. "What's Wrong with Industrial Agriculture." Retrieved December 10, 2015 (https://www.organicconsumers.org/old_articles/Organic/IndustrialAg502.php).

Organization for Economic Cooperation and Development. 2015. "Average Annual Hours Actually Worked Per Worker," *OEDC. Stat Extracts*. Retrieved January 22, 2015 (http://stats.oecd.org/index.aspx?DataSetCode=ANHRS).

Orlove, Raphael. 2015. "Tech Blogger Says He Watched As Youths Wirelessly Broke into His Car." *Jalopnik*, April 6. Retrieved April 18, 2015 (http://jalopnik.com/tech-blogger-says-he-watched-as-youths-wirelessly-broke-1696012518#kxsegs=o7mp4e3md,o9i68fk9g,pexi6me2k).

Orshansky, Mollie. 1963. "Children of the Poor." *Social Security Bulletin*, 26 (July):3–13.

———. 1965. "Children of the Poor." *Social Security Bulletin*, 28 (January):3–29.

Orthmann, Christine Hess and Karen Matison Hess. 2013. *Criminal Investigation, 10th edition*. Clifton Park, NY: Delmar/Cengage.

Ospina, Marie Southard. 2013. "My Name Is Marie, and I Love My Fat." *Huffington Post*, December 13. Retrieved February 16, 2015 (http://www.huffingtonpost.com/bustle/my-name-is-marie-and-i-love-my-fat_b_4400890.html).

Oxford Dictionaries. 2015. "Curse Words, Etymology, and the History of English." Retrieved December 30, 2015 (http://blog.oxforddictionaries.com/2015/06/swear-words-etymology-and-the-history-of-english/).

Pachamama Alliance. 2015. "Effects of Deforestation." Retrieved December 10, 2015 (http://www.pachamama.org/effects-of-deforestation).

Pagliery, Jose. 2015. "600 Million Samsung Galaxy Phones Exposed to Hackers." *CNN Money*, June 17. Retrieved June 19, 2015 (http://money.cnn.com/2015/06/17/technology/samsung-galaxy-hack/).

Palmer, Ewan. 2014. "'Bumfights' Creators Flee Thailand after Arrest for Posting Baby's Head and Body Parts to U.S." *International Business Times*, November 17. Retrieved May 3, 2015 (http://www.ibtimes.co.uk/bumfights-creators-flee-thailand-after-arrest-posting-babys-head-body-parts-us-1475211).

Palmer, Roxanne. 2013. "Where Does 'Catfish' Come From? Online Hoax Movie Inspired by Fisherman's Lore." *International Business Times*, January 17. Retrieved June 18, 2015 (http://www.ibtimes.com/where-does-catfish-come-online-hoax-movie-inspired-fishermans-lore-1022374).

Parade. 2010. "Intelligence Report: Should Sexting Be a Crime?" April 4:10.

Parker, Donn B. 1976. *Crime by Computer: Startling New Kinds of Million-Dollar Fraud, Theft, Larceny and Embezzlement*. New York: Charles Scribner and Sons.

———. 1998. *Fighting Computer Crime: A Framework for the Protection of Information*. New York: John Wiley & Sons.

Patrick, Clarence H. 1952. *Alcohol, Culture and Society*. Durham, NC: Duke University Press.

Pegues, Jeff. 2015. "Chrysler Recall Investigation." *CBS This Morning*, March 23.

Perez, Evan and Tom LoBianco. 2015. "U.S. Government Hacking Number Sparks Unusual Drama at Senate Briefing." *CNN Politics*, June 24. Retrieved June 25, 2015 (http://www.cnn.com/2015/06/24/politics/opm-hacking-senate-briefing/).

Perez-Pena, Richard. 2015. "Problems Plague System to Check Gun Buyers." *The New York Times*, July 27. Retrieved July 27, 2015 (http://www.nytimes.com/2015/07/28/us/problems-riddle-system-to-check-buyers-of-guns.html?_r=0).

Pero, Cheryl S. 2013. *Liberation from Empire: Demonic Possession and Exorcism in the Gospel of Mark*. New York: Lang.

Phillips, John. 1993. *Sociology of Sport*. Boston: Allyn & Bacon.

Phillips, Rod. 2014. *Alcohol: A History*. Chapel Hill, NC: University of North Carolina Press.

Pimm, Stuart L. and Peter Raven. 2000. "Biodiversity: Extinction by Numbers." *Nature*, 403:843–45.

Platts. 2015. "Global Energy Company Rankings: Exxon Mobil Corp." Retrieved March 16, 2015 (http://top250.platts.com/Top250Companies/1).

Polletta, Francesca and Christine Tomlinson. 2014. "Date Rape after the Afterschool Special: Narrative Trends in the Televised Depiction of Social Problems." *Sociological Forum*, 29(3):527–48.

Polzer, Tim. 2012. "Notre Dame LB Manti Te'o to Play While Mourning Two Deaths." *Sports Illustrated*, September 14. Retrieved June 15, 2015 (http://www.si.com/si-wire/2012/09/14/notre-dame-manti-teo-mourning-grandmother-girlfriend-death).

Pope, Nicole. 2011. *Honor Killings in the Twenty-First Century*. New York: Palgrave Macmillan.

Popular Culture Association/American Culture Association (PCA/ACA). 2013. "National Conference Program." March 27–30, 2013. Hoboken, NJ: Wiley-Blackwell.

Porter, Roy. 2002. *Madness: A Brief History*. New York: Oxford University Press.

Positive Deviance Initiative. 2014. "What Is Positive Deviance?" Retrieved January 8, 2015. (http://www.positivedeviance.org/).

The Post-Standard. 1996. "Bride Weds Man of Her Dreams—Except He's Dead." September 1:A-6.

———. 2003. "German Says Victim Wanted to Be Eaten." December 4:A-4.

———. 2007. "Man Hopes His Luck Will Improve after He Marries Dog to Atone." November 14:A-2.

———. 2013. "Police Still Seething after Teen's Arrest." September 24:A-3.

Poushter, Jacob. 2014. "How People in Muslim Countries Prefer Women to Dress in Public." *Pew Research Center*, January 8. Retrieved December 30, 2015 (http://www.pewresearch.org/fact-tank/2014/01/08/what-is-appropriate-attire-for-women-in-muslim-countries/).

Powell, Hannah Lyons. 2014. "Tearing It Up." Glamour, November 28. Retrieved January 17, 2015 (http://www.glamourmagazine.co.uk/fashion/celebrity-fashion/2014/05/celebrities-wearing-ripped-jeans).

Powell, Lisa, Jennifer L. Harris, and Tracy Fox. 2013. "Food Marketing Expenditures Aimed at Youth: Putting the Numbers in Context." *American Journal of Preventive Medicine*, 45(4):453–61.

Prisbell, Eric, and Brent Schrotenboer. 2014. "Adrian Peterson Avoids Jail Time in Child Abuse Case." *USA Today*, November 4. Retrieved May 24, 2015 (http://www.usatoday.com/story/sports/nfl/vikings/2014/11/04/adrian-peterson-minnesota-vikings-child-abuse-plea-deal-misdemeanor/18466197/).

Prison Legal News. 2015. "For Shame! Public Shaming Sentences on the Rise." Retrieved December 20, 2015 (https://www.prisonlegalnews.org/news/2015/feb/4/shame-public-shaming-sentences-rise/).

Psychology Today. 2014. "Sedatives." Retrieved June 7, 2015 (https://www.psychologytoday.com/conditions/sedatives).

Public Broadcast Service (PBS). 2002. "Timeline: Treatments for Mental Illness." Retrieved August 1, 2015 (http://www.pbs.org/wgbh/amex/nash/timeline/index.html).

———. 2007. "Mid-1950s–1960s Beat Generation." Retrieved June 11, 2015 (http://www.pbs.org/wnet/americannovel/timeline/beatgeneration.html).

Pugliese, Nicholas, and Marina Villeneuve. 2015. "Police: Reported Hostage Situation in Clifton Was Hoax." *NorthJersey.com*, March 29. Retrieved June 20, 2015 (http://www.northjersey.com/news/police-reported-hostage-situation-in-clifton-was-hoax-1.1298190).

Puskar-Pasewicz, Margaret, editor. 2010. *Cultural Encyclopedia of Vegetarianism*. Santa Barbara, CA: Greenwood.

RT America. 2014. "State Dept. Contractor to Go to Jail under Espionage Act for Tipping Off Journalist." February 7. Retrieved March 21, 2015 (http://rt.com/usa/stephen-kim-espionage-plea-104/).

Rainforest Concern. 2008. "Why Are Rainforests Important?" Retrieved December 10, 2015 (http://www.rainforestconcern.org/rainforest_facts/why_are_rainforests_important/).

Raleigh, Elizabeth. 2012. "Are Same-Sex and Single Adoptive Parents More Likely to Adopt Transracially? A National Analysis of Race, Family Structure, and the Adoption Marketplace." *Sociological Perspectives*, 55(3):449–71.

Ralph, Laurence. 2014. *Renegade Dreams: Living through Injury in Gangland Chicago*. Chicago: University of Chicago Press.

Ramachandra, K., S. Narendranath, H. S. Somashekar, Navin A. Patil, S. R. Reshma. 2012. "Drug Abuse in Sports." *Journal of Pharmacy Research*, (1):593–603.

Rape Abuse and Incest National Network (RAINN). 2009. "Statistics." Retrieved August 16, 2015 (https://www.rainn.org/statistics).

———. 2015. "Sexual Assault." Retrieved August 15, 2015 (https://rainn.org/get-information/types-of-sexual-assault/sexual-assault).

Rape Crisis Center of Medina and Summit Counties (OH). 2015. "Get the Facts." Retrieved April 18, 2015 (http://www.rccmsc.org/resources/get-the-facts.aspx).

Ray, Bradley, and Cindy Brooks Dollar. 2014 (September). "Exploring Stigmatization and Stigma Management in Mental Health Court: Assessing Modified Labeling Theory in a New Context." *Sociological Forum*, 29(3):720–35.

Reaching Critical Will. 2015. "Drones." Retrieved December 29, 2015 (http://www.reachingcriticalwill.org/resources/fact-sheets/critical-issues/6737-drones).

ReachOut.com. 2015. "Self Harm and Cutting." Retrieved May 2, 2015 (http://us.reachout.com/facts/factsheet/deliberate-self-harm).

Reckless, Walter C. 1961. "A New Theory of Delinquency and Crime." *Federal Probation*, 25:42–46.

Redhage, Jill. 2006. "County Tries to Deter DUIs with Ads: Mug Shots of Offenders Will Go UP on Internet Site." *The Tribune* (Meza, AZ), December 14.

Reiss, Albert. 1951. "Delinquency as the Failure of Personal and Social Controls." *American Sociological Review*, 16:196–207.

Reuters. 2015. "Cybercrime Ring Steals up to $1 Billion from Banks: Kaspersky." February 14.

Retrieved June 22, 2015 (http://www.reuters.com/article/2015/02/15/us-cybersecurity-banks-idUSKBN0LJ02E20150215).

Reynolds, Glenn Harlan. 2015. "When Lawmakers Don't Even Know How Many Laws Exist, How Can Citizens Be Expected to Follow Them?" *USA Today*, March 29. Retrieved December 20, 2015 (http://www.usatoday.com/story/opinion/2015/03/29/crime-law-criminal-unfair-column/70630978/).

The Richest. 2015. "The 10 Biggest Ever American Riots." Retrieved April 29, 2015 (http://www.therichest.com/rich-list/nation/the-10-biggest-ever-american-riots/).

Richter, Felix. 2015. "Americans Use Electronic Media 11+ Hours a Day." *Statista*. Retrieved December 14, 2015 (http://www.statista.com/chart/1971/electronic-media-use/).

Richter, Greg. 2014. "Only 28 Percent of ALS Ice Bucket Donations Used for Research." *Newsmax*, August 31. Retrieved February 13, 2015 (http://www.newsmax.com/US/ALS-ice-bucket-challenge-charity-nonprofit/2014/08/31/id/591872/).

Richter, Marcie. 2016. "Judge Orders 'Affluenza' Texan to Spend about 2 Years in Jail." *Reuters*, April 13. Retrieved May 5, 2016 (http://www.msn.com/en-us/news/us/judge-orders-affluenza-texan-to-spend-about-two-years-in-jail/ar-BBrIb0r?form=PRHPTP&li=BBnb7Kz).

Robb, David. 2014. "SONY Hack: A Timeline." Retrieved June 23, 2015 (http://deadline.com/2014/12/sony-hack-timeline-any-pascal-the-interview-north-korea-1201325501/).

Robbins, Alexandra. 2011. *Pledged: The Secret Life of Sororities*. New York: Hachette Books.

Roberts, Kyle. 2015. "Shame, Suicide, Sadness: A Pastor Takes His Life." *Unsystematic Theology*, September 9. Retrieved December 15, 2015 (http://www.patheos.com/blogs/unsystematictheology/2015/09/shame-suicide-sadness-a-pastor-takes-his-life/).

Rocheleau, Matt. 2015. "64 Dartmouth College Students Face Discipline over Cheating." *The Boston Globe*, January 8. Retrieved January 28, 2015 (http://www.bostonglobe.com/metro/2015/01/08/dartmouth/GN8oLJcgKj7R1nOoPNiLdL/story.html).

Rogers, P. J. 1999 (Feb). "Eating Habits and Appetite Control: A Psychobiological Perspective." *The Proceedings of the Nutrition Society*, 58(1):59–67.

Rose, Mark Edmund, and Cheryl J. Cherpitel. 2011. *Alcohol: Its History, Pharmacology, and Treatment*. Center City, MN: Hazelden.

Rosenbaum, Ron. 1995. "The Great Ivy League Nude Posture Photo Scandal." *The New York Times*, January 15. Retrieved March 7, 2015 (http://www.nytimes.com/1995/01/15/magazine/the-great-ivy-league-nude-posture-photo-scandal.html).

Rosenberg, Tina. 2013. "When Deviants Do Good." *The New York Times*, February 27. Retrieved January 31, 2015 (http://opinionator.blogs.nytimes.com/2013/02/27/when-deviants-do-good/?_r=0).

Rosenbloom, Stephanie. 2011. "Love, Lies and What They Learned." *The New York Times*, November 12. Retrieved June 18, 2015 (http://www.nytimes.com/2011/11/13/fashion/online-dating-as-scientific-research.html?pagewanted=all&_r=2&).

Rosenfeld, Laura. 2015. "Will 'I Am Cait' Return for Season 2? Caitlyn Jenner Has a Lot More to Show the World." *Bustle*, September 13. Retrieved September 15, 2015 (http://www.bustle.com/articles/109572-will-i-am-cait-return-for-season-2-caitlyn-jenner-has-a-lot-more-to-show).

Ross, Jeffrey Ian. 2012. *An Introduction to Political Crime*. Portland, OR: The Policy Press.

Ross, Jenna. 2013. "Firefighters Get New Ammo in Drug Battle: Antidote for Heroin Overdose." *Star Tribune*, November 12. Retrieved June 14, 2015 (http://www.startribune.com/firefighters-get-new-ammo-in-drug-battle-antidote-for-heroin-overdose/231513901/).

Rossen, Jack. 2015. "What Pilots See When You Shine a Laser Pointer at Aircraft." *Mental Floss*. Retrieved December 29, 2015 (http://mentalfloss.com/article/65424/what-pilots-see-when-you-shine-laser-pointer-aircraft).

Rossen, Jeff, and Jovanna Billington. 2015. "Your Smartphone May Be Tracking Your Every Move." *Today*, April 28, 2015. Retrieved June 20, 2015 (http://www.today.com/money/your-smartphone-may-be-tracking-your-every-move-t17056).

Royal College of Psychiatrists. 2015. "Antipsychotics." Retrieved June 7, 2015 (http://www.rcpsych.ac.uk/healthadvice/treatmentswellbeing/antipsychoticmedication.aspx).

Rural Sociological Society. 2015. "Homepage: About Us." Retrieved November 4, 2015 (http://www.ruralsociology.org/?page_id=71).

Russian Vodka. 2015. "Russian Vodka: History of Vodka." Retrieved January 4, 2016 (http://russianvodka.com/history_of_vodka.htm).

Sahagun, Louis. 1994. "Peyote Harvesters Face Supply-Side Problem." *The Los Angeles Times*, June 13:A5. (http://www.huffingtonpost.com/2014/09/18/adrian-peterson-corporal-punishment-science_n_5831962.html).

Samakow, Jessica. 2014. "What Science Says about Using Physical Force to Punish a Child." *Huffington Post*, September 18. Retrieved May 24, 2015 (http://www.huffingtonpost.com/2014/09/18/adrian-peterson-corporal-punishment-science_n_5831962.html).

Sampson, Robert J., and Byron W. Groves. 1989. "Community Structure and Crime Testing: Testing Social Disorganization Theory." *American Journal of Sociology*, 94:774–802.

Sanburn, Josh. 2015. "More States Considering Right-to-Die Laws After Brittany Maynard." *Time*, January 23. Retrieved January 24, 2015 (http://time.com/3678199/brittany-maynard-death-with-dignity-legislation-ccalifornia/).

Sanchick, Myra. 2015. "Testimony Wraps Up in Hearing for Anissa Weier, Charged in 'Slenderman' Stabbling." Fox6News, May 27. Retrieved June 22, 2015 (http://fox6now.com/2015/05/27/hearing-resumes-for-anissa-weier-charged-in-slenderman-stabbing/).

Sanders, William B. 1994. *Gangbangers and Drive-By's: Grounded Culture and Juvenile Gang Violence*. Hawthorne, NY: Aldine DeGryter.

Sapolsky, Robert M. 2015. "150, not 149, Crash Victims." *The Los Angeles Times*, April 2:A:13.

Saul, Heather. 2015. "Species Are Going Extinct 1,000 Times Faster Than Nature Can Make New Ones—And Humans Are to Blame." *The Independent*, February 19. Retrieved November 7, 2015 (http://www.independent.co.uk/news/science/species-are-going-extinct-1000-times-faster-than-nature-can-make-new-ones-and-humans-are-to-blame-9713567.html).

Saunders, Peter. 2005. *The Poverty Wars: Reconnecting Research with Reality*. Sydney University of New South Wales Press.

Savastio, Rebecca. 2014. "Senior Citizens Spreading STDs like Wildfire." *The Guardian*, January 21. Retrieved August 13, 2015 (http://guardianlv.com/2014/01/senior-citizens-spreading-stds-like-wildfire/).

Saving Species. 2015. "Meet Our People: Scientific Board." Retrieved November 7, 2015 (http://www.savingspecies.org/about/advisory-committee/).

Schlenker, B. R., and M. R. Leary. 1982. "Social Anxiety and Self-Presentation: A Conceptualization and Model." *Psychological Bulletin*, 92:641–69.

Schmalleger, Frank. 2004. *Criminology Today, 3rd edition*. Upper Saddle River, NJ: Prentice Hall.

Schneider, Stephen. 2002. "Organized Crime—Global," pp. 1113–18 in *Encyclopedia of Crime and Punishment*, Vol. 3, edited by David Levinson. Thousand Oaks, CA: Sage.

Schofield, Matthew. 2013. "What's Most Shocking about the German Cannibal Case Is It's Not the First." *TheStar.com*, December 7. Retrieved January 9, 2015 (http://www.thestar.com/news/world/2013/12/07/whats_most_shocking_about_german_cannibal_case_is_its_not_the_first.html).

Schulz, Matt. 2014. "The Debit Card Danger You're Probably Forgetting." *U.S. News & World Report*, September 22. Retrieved March 18, 2015 (http://money.usnews.com/money/blogs/my-money/2014/09/22/the-debit-card-danger-youre-probably-forgetting).

Scientific and Technical Advisory Panel. 2011. "Marine Debris as a Global Environmental Problem: Introducing a Solutions Based Framework Focused on Plastic." Retrieved December 7, 2015 (https://www.thegef.org/gef/sites/thegef.org/files/publication/STAP%20MarineDebris%20-%20website.pdf).

Scott, Marvin B., and Stanford M. Lyman. 1968. "Accounts." *American Sociological Review*, 22 (February):46–62.

Scott, Michael S. 2002. "Street Prostitution." *Problem-Oriented Guides for Police Series*, No. 2. U.S. Department of Justice, Office of Community Oriented Policing Services. Retrieved August 22, 2015 (http://www.cops.usdoj.gov/html/cd_rom/inaction1/pubs/StreetProstitution.pdf).

Scholtus, Petz. 2009. "The US Consumes 1500 Plastic Water Bottles Every Second, a Fact by Watershed." *Treehugger*, October 15. Retrieved December 7, 2015 (http://www.treehugger.com/clean-water/the-us-consumes-1500-plastic-water-bottles-every-second-a-fact-by-watershed.html).

Schulze, Peter C. 2002. "I=PBAT." *Ecological Economics*, 40:149–50.

Search Amelia. 2015. "Land of 40,627 Laws and Regulations More." Retrieved December 20, 2015 (http://www.searchamelia.com/land-of-40627-laws-and-regulations-more/comment-page-1).

Sedgwick, Justin. 2015. "Jimmy Kimmel Wants You to Join His 'Finger of Shame' Campaign." *ABC7LA*, May 6. Retrieved December 16, 2015 (http://abc7.com/entertainment/jimmy-kimmel-launches-finger-of-shame-campaign/700124/).

Segall, Laurie. 2015. "Pastor Outed on Ashley Madison Commits Suicide." *CNN Money*, September 8. Retrieved December 15, 2015 (http://money.cnn.com/2015/09/08/technology/ashley-madison-suicide/).

Seinfeld. 1998a. "The Finale (1)." First airdate, May 14, 1998.

———. 1998b. "The Finale (2)." First airdate, May 14, 1998.

Seligman, Martin E. P. 2011. *Flourish*. New York: Free Press.

Sewell, Abby. 2015. "Gas Company Criticized for Uncontrolled Methane Leak Near Porter Ranch." *The Los Angeles Times*, November 24. Retrieved December 10, 2015 (http://www.latimes.com/local/lanow/la-me-ln-gas-company-taken-to-task-over-gas-leak-near-porter-ranch-20151124-story.html).

Sexual Assault Prevention and Awareness Center. 2015. "What Is Sexual Harassment." University of Michigan. Retrieved August 15, 2015 (http://sapac.umich.edu/article/63).

Shelden, Randall G., Sharon K. Tracy, and William B. Brown. 2001. *Youth Gangs in American Society, 2nd edition*. Belmont, CA: Wadsworth.

Sher, Julian. 2013. *Somebody's Daughter: The Hidden Story of America's Prostituted Children and the Battle to Save Them*. Chicago: Chicago Review Press.

Shibutani, Tamotsu. 1955. "Reference Groups as Perspectives." *American Journal of Sociology*, 6:562–69.

Shipman, Tim. 2006. "A Public Shaming for Child Support Dodgers." *Daily Mail*, December 11:20.

Shoales, Ian. 1994. "Infamous Toad Smoker of Calaveras County." *Las Vegas Review-Journal*, February 11:13B.

Shoemaker, Donald J. 2000. *Theories of Delinquency, 4th edition*. New York: Oxford University Press.

———. 2009. *Theories of Delinquency, 6th edition*. New York: Oxford University Press.

Showtime. 2016. *Shameless*. Retrieved July 16, 2016 (http://www.sho.com/shameless).

Siegel, Larry J., 1995. *Criminology: Theories, Patterns, and Typologies, 5th edition*. Minneapolis/St. Paul, MN: West Publishing.

Siegel, Larry J. and Brandon C. Welsh. 2014. *Juvenile Delinquency: Theory, Practice, and Law*. Stamford, CT: Cengage.

Siemaszko, Corky. 2013. "20 Years Ago: Lorena Bobbitt Cuts Off Penis of Then Husband John Wayne Bobbitt in Case That Horrified—and Fascinated—the Nation." *Daily News*, June 23. Retrieved April 11, 2015 (http://www.nydailynews.com/news/crime/20-years-today-lorena-bobbitt-cuts-husband-penis-case-horrified-fascinated-nation-article-1.1379112).

Sierra Club of Canada. 2012. "The Environmental Consequence of War." Retrieved June 1, 2013 (http://www.sierraclub.ca/national/postings/war-and-environment.html).

Simmel, Georg. 1972 [1908]. *Georg Simmel: On Individuality and Social Forms*, edited by Donald Levine. Chicago: University of Chicago Press.

Simon, David R., and Frank E. Hagan. 1999. *White-Collar Deviance*. Boston: Allyn & Bacon.

Simon, Maayan-Rahel. 2005. "On Being Queer," pp. 13–15 in *Gay, Lesbian, and Transgendered: Issues in Education*, edited by James T. Sears. New York: Harrington Park Press.

The Simpsons. 2005. "There's Something about Marrying," episode #345 (GABF04). First aired on February 20, 2005.

Singer, Patti. 2015. "URMC to Bolster Privacy Policies." *Democrat and Chronicle*, May 16. Retrieved June 13, 2015 (http://www.democratandchronicle.com/story/news/2015/05/26/urmc-taubman-hipaa-privacy-regulations/27971855/).

Skerpon, Ted. 2015. "State's Power Lines Need Upgrade." *The Post-Standard*, October 15:A-19.

Smith, Elizabeth. 2012a. "Study Finds That Many EMS Providers Are Overweight or Obese." *Journal of Emergency Medical Services*, March. Retrieved February 16, 2015 (http://www.jems.com/article/health-and-safety/study-finds-many-ems-providers-are-overw).

———. 2012b. "Deforestation & the Effects It Has on a Global Scale." *National Geographic*. Retrieved December 22, 2013 (http://green

living.nationalgeographic.com/deforestation-effects-global-scale-2214.html).

Smith, Melinda, Lawrence Robinson, and Jeanne Segal. 2015. "Alcoholism and Alcohol Abuse." *HelpGuide.org*. Retrieved May 26, 2015 (http://www.helpguide.org/articles/addiction/alcoholism-and-alcohol-abuse.htm).

Smith, Melinda, and Jeanne Segal. 2015. "Post-Traumatic Stress Disorder (PTSD)." *HelpGuide.org*. Retrieved July 30, 2015 (http://www.helpguide.org/articles/ptsd-trauma/post-traumatic-stress-disorder.htm).

Smith, Mikey, 2014. "These Thieves Are Bananas! See 5 Unusual Items Used for Bizarre 'Armed Robbery' Attempts." *Mirror*, April 19. Retrieved April 15, 2015 (http://www.mirror.co.uk/news/uk-news/bizarre-armed-robbers-see-5-3433384).

Smith, Ronald. 1988. *Sports and Freedom: The Rise of Big-Time College Athletics*. New York: Oxford University Press.

Smith, Stacie Reimer, and Antonio Villaamil. 2012. "Prostitution and Sex Work." *The Georgetown Journal of Gender and the Law*, 13:333–62.

Smith, Tyler Stoddard. 2012. *Whore Stories: A Revealing History of the World's Oldest Profession*. Avon, MA: Adams Media.

Smith-Spark, Laura and Margot Haddad. 2015. "Germanwings 'Black Box' Shows Co-pilot Andreas Lubitz Sped Up Descent." *CNN*, April 25. Retrieved July 25, 2015 (http://www.cnn.com/2015/04/03/europe/france-germanwings-plane-crash-main/).

The Society of Obstetricians and Gynaecologists of Canada (SOGC). 2012. "Sexual Orientation and Coming Out." *Sexual Health*. Retrieved August 14, 2015 (http://www.sexualityandu.ca/sexual-health/sexual-orientation-and-coming-out).

Song Facts. 2015. "Hurt." Retrieved May 2, 2015 (http://www.songfacts.com/detail.php?id=2727).

Spencer, Herbert. 2013 [1864]. *The Principles of Biology*. Stockbridge, MA: Hard Press.

Spencer, William. 1987. "Self-Work in Social Interaction: Negotiating Role-Identities." *Social Psychology Quarterly*, 50(2):131–42.

Srabstein, Jorge C., and Bennett L. Leventhal. 2010. "Prevention of Bullying-Related Morbidity and Mortality: A Call for Public Health Policies." *Bulletin of the World Health Organization*, 88(6):401–80.

Stambolis-Ruhstorfer, Michael, and Abigail C. Saguy. 2014. "How to Describe It? Why the Term *Coming Out* Means Different Things in the United States and France." *Sociological Forum*, 29(4):808–29.

Statista.com. 2013. "Total Number of Murders in the United States in 2013, by State." Retrieved April 11, 2015 (http://www.statista.com/statistics/195331/number-of-murders-in-the-us-by-state/).

Steel, Emily. 2014. "'Ice Bucket Challenge' Has Raised Millions for ALS Association." *The New York Times*, August 17. Retrieved January 28, 2015 (http://www.nytimes.com/2014/08/18/business/ice-bucket-challenge-has-raised-millions-for-als-association.html?_r=3).

Steinmetz, Katy. 2015. "These Five States Could Legalize Marijuana in 2016." *Time*, March 17. Retrieved June 11, 2015 (http://time.com/3748075/marijuana-legalization-2016/).

Stern, Victoria. 2008. "Not That I'm Thinking about Trying It, but Is Cannibalism Unhealthy?" *Science Line*, January 21. Retrieved May 9, 2015 (http://scienceline.org/2008/01/ask-stern-cannibal/).

Sternheimer, Karen. 2015. "Social Interaction and Drought Shaming." *Everyday Sociology Blog*, October 2. Retrieved December 16, 2015 (http://www.everydaysociologyblog.com/2014/10/social-interaction-and-drought-shaming.html).

Stevenson, Richard W. 1996. "G.A.O. Puts Cost of S&L Bailout at Half a Trillion Dollars." *The New York Times*, July 13. Retrieved March 19, 2015 (http://www.nytimes.com/1996/07/13/business/gao-puts-cost-of-s-l-bailout-at-half-a-trillion-dollars.html?pagewanted=print).

Stirling, Wynn C. 2014. *Theory of Conditional Games*. Cambridge: Cambridge University Press.

Stoffers, Carl. 2015. "Mark Zuckerberg Isn't Going to Give Away $4.5 Billion to Facebook Users." *Daily News*, December 29. Retrieved December 31, 2015 (http://www.nydailynews.com/news/national/mark-zuckerberg-isn-giving-money-facebook-users-article-1.2480137).

StopBullying.gov. 2015. "What Is Cyberbullying?" Retrieved June 19, 2015 (http://www.stopbullying.gov/cyberbullying/what-is-it/).

Strickler, Jeff. 2013. "Self-Style Superheroes Fight Injustice." *The Post-Standard*, October 31:A-19.

Sullivan, Barbara. 2010 (March). "When (Some) Prostitution Is Legal: The Impact of Law Reform on Sex Work in Australia." *Journal of Law and Society*, 37(1):85–104.

Sullivan, Thomas J., and Kenrick S. Thompson. 1994. *Introduction to Social Problems*. New York: Macmillan.

Surgeon General. 2006. "The Health Consequences of Involuntary Exposure to Tobacco Smoke: A Report of the Surgeon General." Retrieved June 6, 2015 (http://www.surgeongeneral.gov/library/reports/secondhandsmoke/fullreport.pdf).

The Sustainability Scale Project. 2003. "Carrying Capacity." Retrieved November 7, 2015 (http://www.sustainablescale.org/ConceptualFramework/UnderstandingScale/MeasuringScale/CarryingCapacity.aspx).

Sutherland, Edwin. 1939. *Principles of Criminology*. Philadelphia: J. B. Lippincott.

———. [1949] 1983. *White Collar Crime*. New Haven, CT: Yale University Press.

Sutherland, Edwin Hardin, and Donald Ray Cressey. 1978. *Criminology, 10th edition*. Philadelphia: Lippincott.

Sykes, Gresham M., and David Matza. 1957. "Techniques of Neutralization: A Theory of Delinquency." *American Sociological Review*, 22(6):664–70.

Szasz, Thomas S. 1961. *The Myth of Mental Illness: Foundations of a Theory of Personal Conduct*. New York: Harper & Row.

Take Justice Back. 2012. "The 10 Most Dangerous Toys of All Time." Retrieved March 19, 2015 (http://www.takejusticeback.com/news/10-most-dangerous-toys-all-time).

Takeda, Allison. 2015. "Gwyneth Paltrow: It Wasn't My Idea to Call My Divorce Announcement a 'Conscious Uncoupling.'" *US Weekly*, August 3. Retrieved August 10, 2015 (http://www.usmagazine.com/celebrity-news/news/gwyneth-paltrow-didnt-come-up-with-the-conscious-uncoupling-title-201538).

Tarantola, Andrew. 2011. "The Mojave Desert Solar Farm with More Mirrors Than a Lady Gaga Funhouse of Horrors." *Gizmodo*, June 1. Retrieved December 12, 2015 (http://gizmodo.com/5806974/the-mojave-desert-solar-farm-with-more-mirrors-than-a-lady-gaga-funhouse-of-horrors).

Tarde, Gabriel de. 1903. *The Laws of Imitation*. New York: Holt and Company.

Tech Target. 2015. "Solar Power." Retrieved December 12, 2015 (http://whatis.techtarget.com/definition/solar-power).

Teen Violence Statistics. 2009. "Sibling Abuse Statistics." Retrieved May 24, 2015 (http://www.teenviolencestatistics.com/content/sibling-abuse-statistics.html).

Temple, Jeff R., Jonathan A. Paul, Patricia van den Berg, Vi Donna Le, Amy McElhany, and Brian Temple. 2012. "Teen Sexting and Its Association with Sexual Behaviors." *JAMA Pediatrics*, 166(9):828–33.

Thiroux, Jacques P. and Keith W. Krasemann. 2011. *Ethics: Theory and Practice, 11th edition*. Upper Saddle River, NJ: Prentice Hall/Pearson.

Thomas, Cal. 2015. "Paris Talks on Climate Amount to a Lot of Hot Air." As it appeared in *The Post-Standard*, December 15:A-14.

Thomas, Katherine Woodward. 2015. *Conscious Uncoupling: 5 Steps to Living Happily Ever After*. New York: Harmony.

Thornton, William E., and Lydia Voight. 1992. *Delinquency and Justice, 3rd edition*. New York: McGraw-Hill.

Tierney, John. 2010. "Hallucinogens Have Doctors Tuning In Again." *The New York Times*, April 11. Retrieved June 7, 2015 (http://www.nytimes.com/2010/04/12/science/12psychedelics.html?_r=0).

Tipton, Jeffrey A. 2002. "Riots," pp. 1403–7 in *Encyclopedia of Crime and Punishment*, Vol. 3, edited by David Levinson. Thousand Oaks, CA: Sage.

TMZ. 2014. "Cyber Attack: SONY Pictures under Siege," December 19. Retrieved June 24, 2015 (http://www.tmz.com/2014/12/19/the-interview-sony-pictures-hackers-new-demands/).

Tompor, Susan. 2015. "Cyber-sharks Stalk the Digital World." *The Post-Standard*, September 1:B-4.

Tonzi, John. 2015. "Heroin Overdose Deaths in U.S. Have Tripled Since 2010." *Bloomberg Business*, March 4. Retrieved June 9, 2015 (http://www.bloomberg.com/news/articles/2015-03-04/drugs-heroin-overdose-deaths-in-u-s-have-tripled-since-2010).

The Topeka Capital-Journal. 2015. "Better Business Bureau: Ignoring Product Recalls Can Have Dreadful Consequences." February 15. Retrieved March 19, 2015 (http://cjonline.com/news/business/2015-02-15/better-business-bureau-ignoring-product-recalls-can-have-dreadful).

Tracy, Natasha. 2015. "What Is Self-Injury, Self-Harm, Self-Mutilation?" *Healthy Place*. Retrieved March 1, 2015 (http://www.healthyplace.com/abuse/self-injury/what-is-self-injury-self-harm-self-mutilation/).

Trojanowicz, Robert C., Merry Morash, and Pamela J. Schram. 2001. *Juvenile Delinquency, 6th edition*. Upper Saddle River, NJ: Prentice Hall.

Truman, Jennifer L. and Michael Planty. 2012. "Criminal Victimization, 2011." *U.S. Department of Justice, Bureau of Justice*

Statistics. Retrieved April 11, 2015 (http://www.bjs.gov/content/pub/pdf/cv11.pdf).

Trustworthy Cyber Infrastructure for the Power Grid (TCIPG). 2015. "The Power Grid." Retrieved November 8, 2015 (http://search.aol.com/aol/search?s_it=topsearchbox.search&s_chn=prt_main5&v_t=comsearch&q=TCIPG%2C+power+grid).

Truth about Deception. 2015. "Facts and Statistics about Infidelity." Retrieved August 10, 2015 (http://www.truthaboutdeception.com/cheating-and-infidelity/stats-about-infidelity.html).

Truth in Justice. 2015. "Arson or Accident?" Retrieved April 20, 2015 (http://www.truthinjustice.org/arson.htm).

Tsai, Tyjen and Paola Scommegna. 2015. "U.S. Has World's Highest Incarceration Rate." Population Reference Bureau. Retrieved December 20, 2015 (http://www.prb.org/Publications/Articles/2012/us-incarceration.aspx).

Turner, Jonathan H. 2007. *Human Emotions: A Sociological Theory.* New York: Routledge.

Twenge, Joan. 2006. *Generation Me.* New York: Free Press.

United Nations Environment Programme (UNEP). 2010. "Pests and Pestilence," *TUNZA Magazine* 8(2). Retrieved December 11, 2015 (http://www.unep.org/pdf/T8.2_eng_Lores.pdf).

United Nations International Children's Emergency Fund (UNICEF). 2014. "In Certain Cultures, Violence May Be Perceived as a Normal and Acceptable Way to Resolve Conflict." Retrieved February 1, 2015 (http://data.unicef.org/child-protection/attitudes).

———. 2015a. "In 19 of the 29 Countries in Africa and the Middle East Where FGM/C Is Concentrated, Most Girls and Women Think It Should End." Retrieved March 21, 2015 (http://data.unicef.org/child-protection/fgmc).

———. 2015b. "Child Trafficking." Retrieved August 22, 2015 (http://www.unicefusa.org/mission/protect/trafficking).

United Nations Office on Drugs and Crime (UNODC). 2015. "UNODC's Action Against Corruption and Economic Crime." Retrieved March 21, 2015 (http://www.unodc.org/unodc/corruption/).

University of Texas at Dallas Student Counseling Center. 2015. "Self-Help: Sexual Identity and Orientation." Retrieved August 15, 2015 (https://www.utdallas.edu/counseling/sexualidentity/).

University of Virginia the Honor Committee. 2012. "Home Page." Retrieved December 16, 2015 (http://www.virginia.edu/honor/).

Urban Dictionary. 2015. "Catfishing." Retrieved June 18, 2015 (http://www.urbandictionary.com/define.php?term=Catfishing).

USA Today. 2015. "Bryn Mawr College E-Mail Starts a 'Fat-Shaming' Controversy." February 1. Retrieved February 22, 2015 (http://college.usatoday.com/2015/02/01/bryn-mawr-college-e-mail-starts-fat-shaming-controversy/).

U.S. Census Bureau. 2015. "U.S. and World Population Clock." Retrieved December 10, 2015 (http://www.census.gov/popclock/).

U.S. Consumer Product Safety Commission (CPSC). 2012a. "Port Surveillance News: CPSC Investigators Find, Stop Nearly 650,000 Unsafe Products at the Start of the Fiscal Year 2012." Retrieved March 19, 2015 (http://www.cpsc.gov/en/Newsroom/News-Releases/2012/Port-Surveillance-News-CPSC-Investigators-Find-Stop-Nearly-650000-Unsafe-Products-at-the-Start-of-Fiscal-Year-2012/).

———. 2012b. "Consumer Product-Related Injuries and Deaths in the United States: Estimated Injuries Occurring in 2010 and Estimated Deaths Occurring in 2008." Retrieved March 19, 2015 (http://www.cpsc.gov//PageFiles/134720/2010injury.pdf).

———. 2013. "Toy Safety." Retrieved March 19, 2015 (http://www.cpsc.gov/en/Business--Manufacturing/Business-Education/Toy-Safety/).

U.S. Department of Energy. 2013. "How Fossil Fuels Were Formed." Retrieved November 8, 2015 (http://www.fe.doe.gov/education/energylessons/coal/gen_howformed.html).

———. 2015a. "How Do Wind Turbines Work?" Retrieved December 12, 2015 (http://energy.gov/eere/wind/how-do-wind-turbines-work).

U.S. Department of Health and Human Services. 2015a. "2015 Poverty Guidelines." Retrieved January 27, 2015 (http://aspe.hhs.gov/poverty/15poverty.cfm).

———. 2015b. "Definitions of Child Abuse and Neglect in Federal Law." Retrieved May 24, 2015 (https://www.childwelfare.gov/topics/can/defining/federal/).

U.S. Department of Justice (DOJ). 2010. "Crime in the United States: Offense Definitions." Retrieved April 11, 2015 (https://www2.fbi.gov/ucr/cius2009/about/offense_definitions.html).

———. 2011. "Crime in the United States: 2010 Crime Clock Statistics." Retrieved April 11, 2015 (http://www.fbi.gov/about-us/cjis/ucr/crime-in-the-u.s/2010/crime-in-the-u.s.-2010/

offenses-known-to-law-enforcement/crime-clock).

———. 2013. "Criminal Justice Information Services (CJIS) Division Uniform Crime Reporting (UCR) Program. Retrieved April 17, 2015 (http://www.dstaffordandassociates.com/wp-content/uploads/2013/06/UCRReporting-Rape2013pub5-3-13.pdf).

———. 2014. "Stalking." Retrieved August 15, 2015 (http://www.justice.gov/ovw/stalking).

———. 2015a. "What Are Identity Theft and Identity Fraud?" Retrieved June 20, 2015 (http://www.justice.gov/criminal/fraud/websites/idtheft.html).

———. 2015b. "Health Care Fraud Unit." Retrieved March 18, 2015 (http://www.justice.gov/criminal/fraud/hcf/).

———. 2015c. "Child Pornography." Retrieved June 20, 2015 (http://www.justice.gov/criminal-ceos/child-pornography).

———. 2015d. "Computer Crime and Intellectual Property Section (CCIPS)." Retrieved June 23, 2015 (http://www.justice.gov/criminal-ccips).

———. 2015e. "Sexual Assault." Retrieve August 15, 2015 (http://www.justice.gov/ovw/sexual-assault).

———. 2015f. "Citizen's Guide to U.S. Federal Law on Child Pornography." Retrieved August 21, 2015 (http://www.justice.gov/criminal-ceos/citizens-guide-us-federal-law-child-pornography).

U.S. Department of Justice Office on Violence against Women. 2012. "The Facts on the Workplace and Sexual Violence." Retrieved August 16, 2015 (http://www.workplacesrespond.org/learn/the-facts/the-costs-of-sexual-violence).

U.S. Department of Labor. 2015. "Americans in Depression and War." Retrieved January 31, 2015 (http://www.dol.gov/dol/aboutdol/history/chapter5.htm).

U.S. Department of Labor, Bureau of Labor Statistics. 2013. "A Profile of the Working Poor, 2011." Retrieved February 14, 2015 (http://www.bls.gov/cps/cpswp2011.pdf).

———. 2015a. "Databases, Tables & Calculators by Subject." Retrieved January 24, 2015 (http://data.bls.gov/timeseries/LNS14000000).

———. 2015b. "How the Government Measures Unemployment." Retrieved February 10, 2015. (http://www.bls.gov/cps/cps_htgm.htm).

———. 2015c. "Employment Situation Summary." Retrieved January 21, 2015 (http://www.bls.gov/news.release/empsit.nr0.htm).

U.S. Department of State. 2015a. "Intellectual Property Rights/Cyber Crimes." Retrieved June 23, 2015 (http://www.state.gov/j/inl/c/crime/c44641.htm).

———. 2015b. "Sexual Harassment Policy." Retrieved August 15, 2015 (http://www.state.gov/s/ocr/c14800.htm).

———. 2015c. "What is Modern Slavery?" Retrieved August 22, 2015 (http://www.state.gov/j/tip/what/index.htm).

U.S. Department of the Treasury (DOT). 2015. "TARP Programs." Retrieved March 19, 2015 (http://www.treasury.gov/initiatives/financial-stability/TARP-Programs/Pages/default.aspx#).

U.S. Energy Information Administration (EIA). 2012. "Energy Perspectives 1949–2011." Retrieved November 8, 2015 (http://www.eia.gov/totalenergy/data/annual/perspectives.cfm).

U.S. Environmental Protection Agency (EPA). 2014. "Municipal Solid Waste Generation, Recycling, and Disposal in the United States: Fact and Figures for 2012." Retrieved December 7, 2015 (http://www3.epa.gov/epawaste/nonhaz/municipal/pubs/2012_msw_fs.pdf).

———. 2015a. "Ozone." Retrieved November 8, 2015 (http://www3.epa.gov/ozone/).

———. 2015b. "Overview of Greenhouse Gases: Methane Emissions." Retrieved December 6, 2015 (http://www3.epa.gov/climatechange/ghgemissions/gases/ch4.html).

———. 2015c. "Natural Gas Extraction—Hydraulic Fracturing." Retrieved December 6, 2015 (http://www.epa.gov/hydraulicfracturing#improving).

———. 2015d. "Medical Waste Frequent Questions." Retrieved December 9, 2015 (http://www3.epa.gov/epawaste/nonhaz/industrial/medical/mwfaqs.htm).

———. 2015e. "Evaluating the Impacts of Reduced Deforestation Programs on Carbon Storage and Human Welfare in Tropical Forests." Retrieved December 10, 2015 (http://cfpub.epa.gov/ncer_abstracts/index.cfm/fuseaction/display.highlight/abstract/9415).

———. 2015f. "Overview: What Are AFOs?" Retrieved December 10, 2015 (http://www3.epa.gov/region9/animalwaste/problem.html).

U.S. Equal Employment Opportunity Commission (EEOC). 2015. "Facts about Sexual Harassment." Retrieved August 15, 2015 (http://www.eeoc.gov/eeoc/publications/fs-sex.cfm).

U.S. Food and Drug Administration (FDA). 2007. "Medicines in My Home: Caffeine and Your Body." Retrieved June 6, 2015 (http://www.fda.gov/downloads/UCM200805.pdf).

———. 2013. "Methylphenidate ADHD Medications: Drug Safety Communication—Risk of Long-Lasting Erection." Retrieved June 6, 2015 (http://www.fda.gov/Safety/MedWatch/SafetyInformation/SafetyAlertsforHumanMedicalProducts/ucm378876.htm).

———. 2014. "FDA Consumer Advice on Powdered Pure Caffeine." Retrieved June 6, 2015(http://www.fda.gov/Food/RecallsOutbreaksEmergencies/SafetyAlertsAdvisories/ucm405787.htm).

———. 2015a. "Regulatory Information: SEC. 201. [U.S.C. 321] Chapter II—Definitions 1. Retrieved June 3, 2015 (http://www.fda.gov/RegulatoryInformation/Legislation/FederalFoodDrugandCosmeticActFDCAct/FDCActChaptersIandIIShortTitleand Definitions/ucm086297.htm).

———. 2015b. "Legal Requirements for the Sale and Purchase of Drug Products Containing Pseudoephedrine, Ephedrine, and Phenylpropanolamine." Retrieved June 8, 2015 (http://www.fda.gov/Drugs/DrugSafety/InformationbyDrugClass/ucm072423.htm).

U.S. Geological Survey (USGS). 2015. "Induced Earthquakes." Retrieved December 6, 2015 (http://earthquake.usgs.gov/research/induced/).

U.S. Mission to the Organization for Economic Cooperation and Development (OECD). 2015. "U.S. Leads Anti-Corruption Efforts at the OECD." Retrieved March 21, 2015 (http://usoecd.usmission.gov/mission/combating-corruption.html).

U.S. National Library of Medicine. 2015a. "Over-the-Counter Pain Relievers." Retrieved June 7, 2015 (http://www.nlm.nih.gov/medlineplus/ency/article/002123.htm).

———. 2015b. "Pain Medications—Narcotics." Retrieved June 9, 2015 (http://www.nlm.nih.gov/medlineplus/ency/article/007489.htm).

———. 2015c. "Sexually Transmitted Diseases." Retrieved August 13, 2015 (http://www.nlm.nih.gov/medlineplus/sexuallytransmitteddiseases.html).

U.S. Securities and Exchange Commission (SEC). 2015. "Insider Trading." Retrieved March 18, 2015 (http://www.sec.gov/answers/insider.htm).

Vaksberg, Arkady. 1991. *The Soviet Mafia*, translated by John and Elizabeth Roberts. New York: St. Martin's Press.

Vandenburgh, Henry. 2004. *Deviance: The Essentials*. Upper Saddle River, NJ: Prentice Hall.

Veblen, Thorstein. 1964. *The Writings of Thorstein Veblen*, edited by Leon Ardzrooni. New York: Viking.

Velez, Natasha and Kevin Fasick. 2014. "See Spider-Man Punch a Cop in Times Square." *New York Post*, July 27. Retrieved January 27, 2015 (http://nypost.com/2014/07/27/spider-man-allegedly-punches-cop-in-times-square/).

Vold, G. B. 1958. *Theoretical Criminology, 2nd edition*. New York: Oxford University Press.

vos Savant, Marilyn. 2014. "Ask Marilyn." *Parade*, May 11:7.

Wallace, Donald H. 2002. "War Crimes," pp. 1699–1706 in *Encyclopedia of Crime and Punishment*, Vol. 4, edited by David Levinson. Thousand Oaks, CA: Sage.

Walsh, Michael. 2014. "Indiana Serial Killer Suspect's Ex-wife Shocked by Murder Spree: 'I Never Knew Him to Be Violent, Never.'" *Daily News*, October 21. Retrieved March 14, 2015 (http://www.nydailynews.com/news/crime/indiana-serial-killer-suspect-ex-wife-shocked-murder-spree-article-1.19815150).

Walters, Riley. 2014. "Cyber Attacks on U.S. Companies in 2014." *The Heritage Foundation*, October 27. Retrieved June 25, 2015 (http://www.heritage.org/research/reports/2014/10/cyber-attacks-on-us-companies-in-2014).

Walton, Alice. 2016. "Taking a Long View in Porter Ranch." *The Los Angeles Times*, July 5:B1, B6.

Wang, Wendy, and Kim Parker. 2014. "Record Share of Americans Have Never Married." *Pew Research Social and Demographic Trends*, September 24. Retrieved February 19, 2015 (http://www.pewsocialtrends.org/2014/09/24/record-share-of-americans-have-never-married/).

Ward, Brian W., James M. Dahlhamer, Adrena M. Galinsky, and Sarah S. Joestl. 2014. "Sexual Orientation and Health Among U.S. Adults: National Health Interview Survey, 2013." *CDC's National Health Statistics Reports*, 77 (July):1–12. Retrieved August 14, 2015 (http://www.cdc.gov/nchs/data/nhsr/nhsr077.pdf).

Waters, Ann. 2003. "Native Americans Use Peyote in Ancient Prayer Ceremonies." *Sierra Vista Herald*, August 5. Retrieved June 4, 2015 (http://peyote.com/peyote/native.html).

Watson, Molly. 2015. "What Is an Urban Farm?" Retrieved December 12, 2015 (http://localfoods.about.com/od/localfoodsglossary/g/What-Is-An-Urban-Farm.htm).

Webb, Jim. 2009. "Why We Must Fix Our Prisons." *Parade*, March 29:4–5.

WebMD. 2015. "Anxiety & Panic Disorders Health Center." Retrieved May 2, 2015 (http://www.webmd.com/anxiety-panic/guide/self-injuring-hurting).

The Week. 2015. "MTA Spent $76,707 on 'Manspreading' Campaign." January 16. Available: http://theweek.com/speedreads/534171/mta-spent-76707-manspreading-campaign.

Welsh, Jennifer, and Randy Astaiza. 2014. "What Marijuana Does to Your Body and Brain." *Business Insider*, April 20. Retrieved June 11, 2015 (http://www.businessinsider.com/mental-and-physical-effects-of-marijuana-2014-4?op=1).

Welsh, Jennifer, and Kevin Loria. 2014. "23 Health Benefits of Marijuana." *Business Insider*, April 20. Retrieved June 11, 2015 (http://www.businessinsider.com/health-benefits-of-medical-marijuana-2014-4?op=1).

Whitaker, Bill. 2014. "What Happens When You Swipe Your Card?" *60 Minutes*, November 30. Retrieved June 23, 2015 (http://www.cbsnews.com/news/swiping-your-credit-card-and-hacking-and-cybercrime/).

Whitehouse, Kaja. 2015. "Hackers Steal Directly from Banks in 'New Era' of Cyber Crime." *USA Today*, February 16. Retrieved June 22, 2015 (http://www.usatoday.com/story/tech/2015/02/16/bank-hesit-cybersecurity-kaspersky-report/23509937/).

The White House. 2014. "Press Release: 'FACT SHEET: The U.S. Global Anticorruption Agenda." Issued September 24, 2014. Retrieved March 21, 2015 (https://www.whitehouse.gov/the-press-office/2014/09/24/fact-sheet-us-global-anticorruption-agenda).

——. 2015. "Remarks by the President in State of the Union Address, January 20, 2015." Press Release, Office of the Press Secretary. Retrieved December 6, 2015 (https://www.whitehouse.gov/the-press-office/2015/01/20/remarks-president-state-union-address-january-20-2015).

The White House Council on Women and Girls. 2014. "Rape and Sexual Assault: A Renewed Call to Action." Retrieved April 18, 2015 (https://www.whitehouse.gov/sites/default/files/docs/sexual_assault_report_1-21-14.pdf).

Whitlock, Craig. 2015. "Rogue Drones a Growing Nuisance Across the U.S." *The Washington Post*, August 10. Retrieved December 29, 2015 (https://www.washingtonpost.com/world/national-security/how-rogue-drones-are-rapidly-becoming-a-national-nuisance/2015/08/10/9c05d63c-3f61-11e5-8d45-d815146f81fa_story.html).

Wiechelt, Shelly A., and Corey S. Shdaimah. 2011. "Trauma and Substance Abuse among Women in Prostitution: Implications for a Specialized Diversion Program." *Journal of Forensic Social Work*, 1(2):159–84.

Wilborn, Colin, Jacqueline Beckham, Bill Campbell, Travis Harvey, Melyn Galbreath, Paul La Bounty, Erika Nassar, Jennifer Wismann, and Richard Kreider. 2005. "Obesity: Prevalence, Theories, Medical Consequences, Management, and Research Directions." *Journal of the International Society of Sports Nutrition*, 2(2):4–31.

Williams, Frank P., and Marilyn McShane. 1994. *Criminological Theory*. Englewood Cliffs, NJ: Prentice Hall.

Withgott, Jay, and Scott Brennan. 2007. *Environment: The Science Behind the Stories, 2nd edition*. New York: Pearson.

Wolff, Kurt. 1950. *The Sociology of Georg Simmel*. New York: Free Press.

Worland, Justin. 2015. "Mike Huckabee Supports Denying Abortion to 10-Year-old Rape Victim." *Time*, August 16. Retrieved August 18, 2015 (http://time.com/3999799/mike-huckabee-abortion-rape/).

The World Bank. 2015. "Extractive Industries." Retrieved March 21, 2015 (http://www.worldbank.org/en/topic/extractiveindustries).

World Health Organization (WHO). 2008. "Best Practice in Workplace Violence and Bullying Interventions." Retrieved May 2, 2015 (http://www.who.int/occupational_health/publications/10_Violence%20and%20Bullying%20Interventions.pdf).

——. 2011. *Global Status Report on Alcohol and Health*. Retrieved January 31, 2015 (http://www.who.int/substance_abuse/publications/global_alcohol_report/msbgsruprofiles.pdf).

——. 2014. "Mental Disorders." Retrieved July 26, 2015 (http://www.who.int/mediacentre/factsheets/fs396/en/).

——. 2015a. "Obesity and Overweight." Retrieved February 15, 2015 (http://www.who.int/mediacentre/factsheets/fs311/en/).

——. 2015b. "Definition and Typology of Violence." Retrieved April 25, 2015 (http://www.who.int/violenceprevention/approach/definition/en/).

——. 2015c. "About the Violence Prevention Alliance." Retrieved April 25, 2015 (http://www.who.int/violenceprevention/about/en/).

——. 2015d. "Pharmaceutical Industry." Retrieved June 4, 2015 (http://www.who.int/trade/glossary/story073/en/).

——. 2015e. "Tobacco." Retrieved June 5, 2015 (http://www.who.int/mediacentre/factsheets/fs339/en/).

———. 2015f. "Pharmaceutical Industry." Retrieved June 13, 2015 (http://www.who.int/trade/glossary/story073/en/#).

———. 2015g. "Health-Care Waste." Retrieved December 9, 2015 (http://www.who.int/topics/medical_waste/en/).

World Health Organization Collaborating Centre for Drug Statistics and Methodology. (WHOCC). 2009. "Definition and General Consideration." Retrieved June 4, 2015 (http://www.whocc.no/ddd/definition_and_general_considera/).

WorldOMeters. 2015. "Population." Retrieved December 10, 2015 (http://www.worldometers.info/).

World Prison Brief. 2015. "World Prison in Brief: United States of America." Retrieved December 20, 2015 (http://www.prisonstudies.org/country/united-states-america).

Woman Within. 2015. "About Woman Within." Retrieved February 16, 2015 (http://www.womanwithin.com/Help/Help_AboutUs.aspx).

Workplace Bullying Institute (WBI). 2014a. "The WBI Definition of Workplace Bullying." Retrieved May 2, 2015 (http://www.workplacebullying.org/individuals/problem/definition/).

———. 2014b. "Here's a Bullying Thug: GOP Congressman Grimm." Retrieved May 2, 2015 (http://www.workplacebullying.org/tag/fbi/).

Wright, Colleen. 2015. "The Painted Ladies of Times Square, Drawing Looks, Tips and Critics." *The New York Times*, August 16:27.

Yang, Stephanie. 2014. "5 Years Ago Bernie Madoff Was Sentenced to 150 Years in Prison—Here's How His Scheme Worked." *Business Insider*, July 1. Retrieved March 16, 2015 (http://www.businessinsider.com/how-bernie-madoffs-ponzi-scheme-worked-2014-7).

Yerak, Becky. 2014. "FBI Seeks 'Ethical' Hackers to Be "Cyber Special Agents." *Chicago Tribune*, December 29. Retrieved July 23, 2016 (http://www.chicagotribune.com/business/ct-fbi-ethical-hackers-1229-biz-20141229-story.html).

Young, Antonia. 2000. *Women Who Become Men.* New York: Oxford.

Zambito, Thomas, and Greg B. Smith. 2008. "Feds Say Bernard Madoff's $50 Billion Ponzi Scheme Was Worst Ever." *Daily News*, December 13. Retrieved March 16, 2015 (http://www.nydailynews.com/news/crime/feds-bernard-madoff-50-billion-ponzi-scheme-worst-article-1.355459).

Zeman, Ned. 2013. "The Boy Who Cried Dead Girlfriend." *Vanity Fair*, June 2. Retrieved June 15, 2015 (http://www.vanityfair.com/culture/2013/06/manti-teo-girlfriend-nfl-draft).

Photo Credits

Index